MASTERPLOTS II

AMERICAN FICTION SERIES, REVISED EDITION

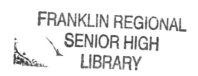
MASTERPLOTS II

AMERICAN FICTION SERIES, REVISED EDITION

1

A - Conf

Edited by

STEVEN G. KELLMAN

The University of Texas at San Antonio

SALEM PRESS

Pasadena, California   Hackensack, New Jersey

Editor in Chief: Dawn P. Dawson
Managing Editor: Christina J. Moose
Project Editor: Robert A. McClenaghan   *Research Editor:* Jeffrey Jensen
Acquisitions Editor: Mark Rehn   *Research Assistant:* Jun Ohnuki

∞ The paper used in these volumes conforms to the American National Standard for Permanence of Paper for Printed Library Materials, Z39.48-1992 (R1997).

Library of Congress Cataloging-in-Publication Data
Masterplots II. American fiction series / edited by Steven G.
Kellman.—Rev. ed.
    p.   cm.
Includes bibliographical references and index.
    ISBN 0-89356-871-6 (set) — ISBN 0-89356-872-4 (v. 1) —
ISBN 0-89356-873-2 (v. 2) — ISBN 0-89356-874-0 (v. 3) —
ISBN 0-89356-875-9 (v. 4) — ISBN 0-89356-876-7 (v. 5) —
ISBN 0-89356-877-5 (v. 6)
    1. American fiction—Stories, plots, etc. I. Title: Masterplots
2. II. Title: Masterplots two. III. Title: American fiction series.
IV. Kellman, Steven G., 1947-   .
PS373 .M37   2000
809.3′0097—dc21   99-053295

First Printing

PUBLISHER'S NOTE

The original four volumes of *Masterplots II, American Fiction Series* (1986) explored works by some of the most important writers of the Americas—North, Central, and South. A two-volume supplement published in 1994 updated and extended the original series' coverage. The six volumes of *Masterplots II: American Fiction Series, Revised Edition* incorporate 439 entries from the previous editions and add a further 128 new entries on important works by contemporary or hitherto neglected writers. (To eliminate duplication, works covered in the 1996 twelve-volume set *Masterplots, Revised Second Edition* are not included here.) The annotated bibliographies attached to each article have also been revised and updated to reflect recent scholarship.

The 567 entries in *Masterplots II: American Fiction Series, Revised Edition* thus cover a broad range of writers and works. Classics by such canonical U.S. writers as Ernest Hemingway and William Faulkner are given thorough treatment, as are the masterworks of such Latin American giants as Gabriel García Márquez and Carlos Fuentes and such Canadian notables as Robertson Davies and Margaret Atwood. The increasing prominence of ethnic voices in U.S. fiction is reflected by articles on works by such writers as Toni Morrison, Louise Erdrich, Ernest J. Gaines, and Rolando Hinojosa. Important developments in women's literature are treated in discussions of works by such authors as Barbara Kingsolver, Terry McMillan, and Amy Tan. Discussion of works by such best-selling writers as Stephen King and Scott Turow reflects the state of American popular fiction. Essays on books by such past writers as D'Arcy McNickle and John Okada help to give a more complete picture of America's literary history.

Each article begins with ready-reference information that presents the date of the author's birth (and death, if applicable); the type, time, and locale of the work's plot; and the date of the work's first publication. A brief description of the work's principal characters precedes a more extensive analysis.

This analysis begins with a summary of the work's major plot elements and continues with separate sections that explore the work in depth. "The Characters" delves into the motivations and development of the individuals portrayed; "Themes and Meanings" examines the work's larger concerns; and "Critical Context" assesses the work's place in the American literary tradition and summarizes its reception. Each entry concludes with an annotated bibliography that directs readers to recent sources for further study.

The articles in *Masterplots II: American Fiction Series, Revised Edition* are arranged alphabetically by title. Three indexes at the end of volume 6 are designed to assist the reader in selecting articles of interest. In keeping with the recent emphasis on diversity in literary studies, the Geographical and Ethnic Index, a feature new to the *Masterplots II* series, lists authors by country of origin and, where appropriate, by major ethnic group. The Author Index lists all entries for each writer surveyed, while the Title Index locates specific works.

We would like to thank the many academicians and other writers who contributed to this set. A list of their names and affiliations appears at the beginning of volume 1. Special mention must also be made of Editor Steven G. Kellman of The University of Texas at San Antonio, who applied his expert knowledge to the shaping of the set's contents, and of Kevin Bochynski and Pegge A. Bochynski, who scrutinized and updated the bibliographies of the older entries to reflect current scholarship.

CONTRIBUTING REVIEWERS

Michael Adams
Fairleigh Dickinson University

Susan S. Adams
Northern Kentucky University

Patrick Adcock
Henderson State University

A. Owen Aldridge
University of Illinois

Betty Alldredge
Angelo State University

Diane M. Almeida
University of Massachussets at Boston

Eleanor B. Amico
Independent Scholar

Terry L. Andrews
Independent Scholar

Andrew J. Angyal
Elon College

Stanley Archer
Texas A & M University

Edwin T. Arnold
Appalachian State University

Bryan Aubrey
Independent Scholar

Jim Baird
University of North Texas

Thomas Banks
Ohio Northern University

Carl L. Bankston III
University of Southwestern Louisiana

Jack Vincent Barbera
University of Mississippi

Dan Barnett
California State University, Chico

Henry J. Baron
Calvin College

David Barratt
Independent Scholar

Craig Barrow
University of Tennessee

Melissa E. Barth
Appalachian State University

Barbara G. Bartholomew
University of Houston, Downtown

Margaret Kent Bass
St. Lawrence University

Robert Bensen
Hartwick College

Richard P. Benton
Trinity College

Stephen Benz
Barry University

Mary G. Berg
Harvard University

Milton Berman
University of Rochester

Anthony Bernardo
University of Delaware

Dorothy M. Betz
Georgetown University

Margaret Boe Birns
New York University

Nicholas Birns
Western Connecticut State University

Kevin Bochynski
Salem State College

Pegge A. Bochynski
Independent Scholar

Bernadette Lynn Bosky
Independent Scholar

J. H. Bowden
Indiana University, Southeast

Harold Branam
Savannah State College

Douglas Branch
Rust College

Gerhard Brand
California State University, Los Angeles

Jean R. Brink
Arizona State University

Ludger Brinker
Macomb College

Silvester J. Brito
University of Wyoming

Wesley Britton
Harrisburg Area Community College

Mollie A. Brodsky
University of Rutgers

C. L. Brooke
Cleveland State University

Keith H. Brower
Salisbury State University

Carl Brucker
Independent Scholar

Faith Hickman Brynie
Independent Scholar

David Buehrer
Valdosta State University

Jeffrey L. Buller
Georgia Southern University

Richard Butts
University of Toronto

Charles Cameron
Independent Scholar

John Canfield
U.S. Air Force Academy

Karen Carmean
Independent Scholar

Krista Ratkowski Carmona
University of California at Los Angeles

David A. Carpenter
Eastern Illinois University

John Carpenter
University of Michigan

Caroline Carvill
Rose-Hulman Institute of Technology

Mary LeDonne Cassidy
South Carolina State University

Thomas J. Cassidy
South Carolina State College

Susanna Castillo
San Diego State University

Deborah Charlie
Antelope Valley College

Balance Chow
San Jose State University

Sandra Christenson
Eastern Washington University

Stella T. Clark
Callifornia State University, San Bernardino

David W. Cole
University of Wisconsin Center-Baraboo

James W. Coleman
Colorado College

David Conde
Metropolitan State College of Denver

John J. Conlon
University of Massachusetts, Boston

Holly Dworken Cooley
Independent Scholar

Linda Seidel Costic
Northeast Missouri State University

Cecil Costilow
California State University, Los Angeles

Joanna Courteau
Iowa State University

Michael Crane
U.S. Air Force Academy

Virginia Crane
California State University, Los Angeles

Jim Crawford
Highland Hall School

Lucia Guerra Cunningham
University of California at Irvine

Richard Damashek
Roosevelt University

James D. Daubs
Independent Scholar

Mary Virginia Davis
California State University, Sacramento

Frank Day
Clemson University

Bill Delaney
Independent Scholar

CONTRIBUTING REVIEWERS

John F. Deredita
Independent Scholar

James E. Devlin
State University of New York College at Oneonta

M. Casey Diana
University of Illinois at Urbana-Champaign

Margaret A. Dodson
Independent Scholar

Virginia A. Duck
Bloomsbury University

Joyce Duncan
East Tennessee State University

Gweneth A. Dunleavy
University of Louisville

Stefan Dziemianowicz
Independent Scholar

Bruce L. Edwards
Bowling Green State University

Clifford Edwards
Fort Hays State University

Robert P. Ellis
Worcester State College

Ernesto Encinas
Independent Scholar

Thomas L. Erskine
Salisbury State University

Clara Estow
University of Massachusetts, Harbor Campus

Thomas H. Falk
Michigan State University

James Feast
Baruch College of the City University of New York

Tom Feller
Independent Scholar

Donald M. Fiene
University of Tennessee

John W. Fiero
University of Southwestern Louisiana

Edward A. Fiorelli
St. John's University, New York

Sandra K. Fischer
State University of New York at Albany

Christopher J. Forbes
Northeast Louisiana University

Robert J. Forman
St. John's University, New York

Thomas C. Foster
University of Michigan-Flint

Teresa Chittenden Frary
California State University, Northridge

Lawrence S. Friedman
Purdue University at Fort Wayne

Jean C. Fulton
Maharishi International University

Joe B. Fulton
Dalton State College

Keith Fynaardt
Northwestern College

Robert L. Gale
University of Pittsburgh

Susan VanZanten Gallagher
Calvin College

René P. Garay
City University of New York, City College

Ann D. Garbett
Averett College

Betty G. Gawthrop
Purdue University at Calumet

Jill B. Gidmark
University of Minnesota

Marc Goldstein
University of Rochester
New York University

Flora Gonzalez
University of Chicago

Mercedes Jimenez Gonzalez
University of California at Riverside

Linda Silverstein Gordon
Worcester State College
Sandra Y. Govan
University of North Carolina at Charlotte

Hans G. Graetzer
South Dakota State University

James Grove
Mount Mercy College

Daniel L. Guillory
Millikin University

M. Martin Guiney
Kenyon College

Donna B. Haisty
Clemson University

William T. Hamilton
Metropolitan State College of Denver

Blair M. Hancock
Wilkes Community College

Joyce Ann Hancock
Jefferson Community College, Kentucky

Katherine Hanley
St. Bernard's Institute

Ronald M. Harmon
California State University at Fullerton

Natalie Harper
Simon's Rock College of Bard

Betty L. Hart
University of Southern Indiana

Terry Heller
Coe College

Diane Andrews Henningfeld
Adrian College

Rosalie Hewitt
Northern Illinois University

Emily Hicks
San Diego State University

Jane F. Hill
Independent Scholar

Robert W. Hill
Independent Scholar

Joseph W. Hinton
Portland State University

Rebecca Stingley Hinton
Indiana University, East

Arthur D. Hlavaty
Independent Scholar

Nika Hoffman
Crossroads School for Arts and Sciences

William Hoffman
Independent Scholar

Dennis Hoilman
Ball State University

W. Kenneth Holditch
University of New Orleans

Hal L. Holladay
Simon's Rock College of Bard

John R. Holmes
Franciscan University of Steubenville

Pierre L. Horn
Wright State University

Anne B. Howells
Occidental College

John B. Hughes
New York University

Mary Hurd
East Tennessee State University

Jacquelyn L. Jackson
Middle Tenn. State University

Janice A. Jaffe
Bowdoin College

Philip K. Jason
United States Naval Academy

Ronald Johnson
Northern Michigan University

Sheila Golburgh Johnson
Independent Scholar

Eunice Pedersen Johnston
North Dakota State University

Jane Anderson Jones
Manatee Community College

Anne K. Kaler
Gwynedd-Mercy College

Steven G. Kellman
The University of Texas at San Antonio

Rebecca Kelly
Southern Technical Institute

W. P. Kenney
Manhattan College

Howard A. Kerner
Polk Community College

CONTRIBUTING REVIEWERS

John Knowles
Salisbury State College

Grove Koger
Boise Public Library

Paula D. Kopacz
Eastern Kentucky University

Geeta Kothari
University of Pittsburgh

Deborah Lally
Independent Scholar

Eugene Larson
Los Angeles Pierce College

Linda Ledford-Miller
University of Scranton

Leon Lewis
Appalachian State University

Naomi Lindstrom
University of Texas at Austin

James Livingston
Northern Michigan University

Marcus "C" López
Solano Community College

Janet Lorenz
Independent Scholar

Michael Loudon
Eastern Illinois University

Bernadette Flynn Low
Dundalk Community College

William Luis
Dartmouth College

Laura Riesco Luszczynska
University of Maine

Len McCall
Clemson University

Janet McCann
Texas A&M University

Barbara McCaskill
University of Georgia

Andrew Macdonald
Loyola University of New Orleans

Gina Macdonald
Loyola University of New Orleans

Grace McEntee
Appalachian State University

Broderick McGrady
Morehouse College

John L. McLean
Shawnee State University

A.L. McLeod
Rider University

Marian B. McLeod
Trenton State College

Victoria E. McLure
South Plains College

Christopher R. McRae
The Citadel Military College of South Carolina

Jim McWilliams
Southern Illinois University at Carbondale

Mary E. Mahony
Wayne County Community College

Edward A. Malone
University of Missouri, Rolla

Barry Mann
Independent Scholar

Lois A. Marchino
University of Texas at El Paso

George Mariscal
University of California, San Diego

Peter Markus
Western Michigan University

S. Elaine Marshall
Atlantic Christian College

Patricia Masserman
Microsoft Press

William Matta
University of Guam

Charles E. May
California State University, Long Beach

Laurence W. Mazzeno
Ursuline College

D. Jan Mennell
North Carolina State University

Julia M. Meyers
Duquesne University

Walter E. Meyers
North Carolina State University

Sally Mitchell
Temple University

Leslie B. Mittleman
California State University, Long Beach

Christian H. Moe
Southern Illinois University at Carbondale

Marisa Moolick-Gutierrez
Yale University

Robert A. Morace
Daemen College

Bernard E. Morris
Independent Scholar

Gregory L. Morris
Pennsylvania State University-Erie

Katharine M. Morsberger
Independent Scholar

Robert E. Morsberger
California State Polytechnic University, Pomona

John M. Muste
Ohio State University

Marshall Myers
Kentucky Wesleyan University

Robert Niemi
St. Michael's College

Terry Nienhuis
Western Carolina University

George Thomas Novotny
University of South Florida

George O'Brien
Georgetown University

Patrick O'Donnell
West Virginia University

Rosanne Osborne
Louisiana College

Robert M. Otten
Marymount University

Lisa Paddock
Independent Scholar

Janet Taylor Palmer
Caldwell Community College

David B. Parsell
Furman University

David Peck
California State University, Long Beach

Robert W. Peckham
Sacred Heart Major Seminary

Gustavo Pellon
University of Virginia

Gustavo Perez-Firmat
Duke University

Charles A. Perrone
University of Florida

Robert C. Petersen
Middle Tennessee State University

Marion Petrillo
Bloomsburg University

Verbie Lovorn Prevost
University of Tennessee at Chattanooga

Victoria Price
Lamar University

René Prieto
Southern Methodist University

Norman Prinsky
Augusta State University

Jose Promis
University of Arizona

Jennifer L. Randisi
California State University at San Bernardino

Thomas Rankin
Independent Scholar

Ralph Reckley, Sr.
Morgan State University

Bruce D. Reeves
Independent Scholar

Rosemary M. Canfield Reisman
Charleston Southern University

Janine Rider
Mesa State College

David Rigsbee
Virginia Tech

Danny Lee Robinson
Independent Scholar

CONTRIBUTING REVIEWERS

Adriana Méndez Rodenas
Independent Scholar

Bernard F. Rodgers, Jr.
Simon's Rock College of Bard

Mary Rohrberger
University of Northern Iowa

Carl Rollyson
Baruch College of the City University of New York

Paul Rosefeldt
Delgado Community College

Joseph Rosenblum
University of North Carolina, Greensboro

Diane M. Ross
Lake Forest College

Kathleen Ross
Duke University

Robert L. Ross
University of Texas at Austin

Victor Anthony Rudowski
Clemson University

Irene Struthers Rush
Independent Scholar

J. Edmund Rush
Write Away Now

Susan Rusinko
Bloomsburg University

Elsa Saeta
University of Texas Pan American

Chaman L. Sahni
Boise State University

Roberta Schreyer
State University of New York at Potsdam

Agnes A. Shields
Chestnut Hill College

T. A. Shippey
St. Louis University

Wilma Shires
Cisco Junior College

Amy Beth Shollenberger
Miami University

R. Baird Shuman
University of Illinois at Urbana-Champaign

William L. Siemens
West Virginia University

Charles L. P. Silet
Iowa State University

Carl Singleton
Fort Hays State University

Genevieve Slomski
Independent Scholar

Nick David Smart
New York University

Gilbert G. Smith
North Carolina State University

Ira Smolensky
Monmouth College, Illinois

Katherine Snipes
Independent Scholar

A. J. Sobczak
Independent Scholar

Francisco Soto
City University of New York, College of Staten Island

George Soule
Carleton College

Susan Spagna
University of California at Riverside

August W. Staub
University of Georgia

Karen Stolley
Vassar College

Geralyn Strecker
Ball State University

Gerald H. Strauss
Bloomsburg University

James Sullivan
California State University, Los Angeles

Catherine Swanson
Independent Scholar

Roy Arthur Swanson
University of Wisconsin—Milwaukee

Judith K. Taylor
Northern Kentucky University

Teresia Langford Taylor
Hardin-Simmons University

Thomas J. Taylor
University of Akron

Betty Taylor-Thompson
Texas Southern University

Terry Theodore
University of North Carolina at Wilmington

Tiffany Elizabeth Thraves
Randolph-Macon Woman's College

Jonathan Tittler
Cornell University

Daniel Torres
Ohio University

Rebeca Torres-Rivera
Central Michigan University

Thomas Travisano
Independent Scholar

Tony Trigilio
William Rainey Harper College

Richard Tuerk
Texas A & M University-Commerce

John H. Turner
Bowdoin College

Dennis Vannatta
University of Arkansas at Little Rock

Nelson H. Vieira
Brown University

Jon S. Vincent
University of Kansas

Mary E. Virginia
Independent Scholar

Catherine Carnell Watt
University of California, Riverside

Dennis L. Weeks
University of Great Falls

Jack Welch
University of Louisville

James M. Welsh
Salisbury State University

Thomas Whissen
Wright State University

Bruce Wiebe
Independent Scholar

Barbara Wiedemann
Auburn University at Montgomery

Albert E. Wilhelm
Tennessee Technological University

Thomas Willard
University of Arizona

Shirley A. Williams
Ohio State University at Lima

Mark Royden Winchell
Clemson University

Michael Witkoski
Independent Scholar

Pat M Wong
Binghamton University

Patrick Wright
University of Texas Law School

Clifton K. Yearly
State University of New York at Buffalo

Michael Zeitlin
Independent Scholar

Weihua Zhang
State University of New York at Albany

Laura Weiss Zlogar
University of Wisconsin-River Falls

LIST OF TITLES IN VOLUME 1

MASTERPLOTS II

AMERICAN FICTION SERIES, REVISED EDITION

THE ACCIDENTAL TOURIST

Author: Anne Tyler (1941-　　)
Type of plot: Domestic realism
Time of plot: The 1980's
Locale: Baltimore, Maryland
First published: 1985

Principal characters:

MACON LEARY, the middle-aged author of a series of guidebooks for travelers who would prefer to remain at home

SARAH LEARY, Macon's estranged wife

EDWARD, Macon's dog, an undisciplined Welsh corgi

MURIEL PRITCHETT, Edward's trainer, who transforms Macon's life

ALEXANDER PRITCHETT, Muriel's son

ROSE LEARY, Macon's sister

JULIAN EDGE, Macon's publisher, who marries Rose

PORTER LEARY, Macon's brother

CHARLES LEARY, Macon's brother

The Novel

Macon Leary learns to cope with the murder of his twelve-year-old son and separation from his wife in Anne Tyler's *The Accidental Tourist*. With the assistance of Muriel, a flamboyant young dog trainer with whom he becomes romantically involved, Macon assuages his grief, learns to assume control over his life, and becomes more contented than ever before.

As the novel begins, Macon and Sarah are returning early from a vacation on the beach. Neither, it seems, "had the heart for it." Nor have they had the heart for much else since the murder of their son during a robbery the previous year. During the short car trip, the flaws of their marriage are revealed. Macon refuses to stop driving during a rainstorm, informing Sarah that he has a system for safe driving. Meantime, Sarah longs for a more spontaneous, less systematic man. When she announces that she is leaving him and abandoning their twenty-year marriage, Macon is stunned.

With Sarah gone, Macon is alone and lonely in his home in an upper-class Baltimore neighborhood. His sole companions are his son's intractable dog, Edward, and Helen, a cat. Macon seldom ventures from his house, where he writes guidebooks for Americans who must travel but long for domestic routines. While others sit in armchairs and dream of travel, "accidental tourists" travel dreaming of home.

Always a methodical man, Macon becomes obsessive when Sarah departs. Preoccupied with conserving energy, he stops using the clothes dryer, although he often has to wear damp clothes. He attaches the popcorn maker—he eschews eggs, fearing food poisoning—to his bedside clock to avoid any unessential steps while preparing breakfast. To eliminate the inconvenience of making the bed, he sleeps in "body bags," sheets that are sewn together to form a giant envelope.

As his compulsions intensify, he is overwhelmed by his systems; even his pets cannot adapt. Edward refuses to enter the basement, where his dog food awaits him after Macon dumps it in a coal chute, and Helen must use the dryer vent as a cat door to conserve litter. When Helen is inadvertently caught in the vent as the dryer is running, her howling causes Edward—who is too frightened to travel down the stairs on his own and therefore is being carried by Macon—to panic. Macon collides with his new energy-saving, wheeled laundry basket and breaks his leg. The three move into Macon's grandparents' home, where his two divorced brothers are already being cared for by Rose, their unmarried sister.

The Leary siblings are mired in routine, spending each evening playing Vaccination, a card game that they designed as children that has grown so convoluted that it proves impossible for outsiders, even spouses, to learn. They eat meticulously prepared and ritually consumed "conservative" baked potatoes nightly. They are aggressively orderly, with allspice stored next to ant poison in Rose's alphabetized kitchen pantry. Initially comforted by his siblings, Macon is before long appalled by their stasis. He descends into a mind-numbing depression.

Macon's emotional state as he returns home is mirrored by Edward, whose behavior grows alarmingly erratic and aggressive. He attacks bikers, trees visitors, and panics when family members attempt to leave the house, even biting Macon. Forced to call a trainer when his brother Charles threatens to have the dog destroyed, Macon turns to Muriel, whom he met at the Meow-Bow animal hospital.

Muriel, a thin young woman with a halo of frizzy black hair and an "unluxurious" body, aggressively pursues Macon as she simultaneously tames Edward. Macon, an accidental tourist trapped in his own life, seems unable to resist her. He gradually moves into Muriel's old row house, where he happily repairs some of the many leaks, holes, and deficiencies. Meanwhile, Muriel's strength and resiliency act as a palliative to Macon's grief. In turn, Muriel's son Alexander benefits from Macon's attentions. Disabled psychologically as well as physically by allergies and asthma, Alexander gains self-esteem as Macon and Edward draw him into their competent, male world. Macon is a passenger in Muriel's world for several months before he is forced to decide whether to remain with her or to reconcile with Sarah.

As Macon's life is being refashioned, so too are the lives of Julian, Macon's publisher, and his sister Rose as the unlikely pair move toward marriage. One of the novel's most convincing moments occurs when Julian moves into the Leary household, where he joins in the nightly ritual of Vaccination.

The Characters

To please Sarah when he was courting her, teenaged Macon adopted a cool and mysterious façade. Somehow, although he was never comfortable in the role, he became trapped by the persona he had created, unable even at his son's death to provide comfort or receive it from Sarah. Even before Ethan's death, however, Macon had difficulty finding meaning in his life, relying, therefore, on "systems" and routine to provide order and stability, if not happiness. Although he writes travel books, Macon despises travel, invariably longing for the routines of home. With Sarah and Ethan gone, however, even his routines fail to soothe him, and Macon slides into depression.

Muriel, one of Tyler's most memorable characters, is a flamboyantly dressed, unpredictable, and resourceful young woman. After a brief early marriage, she works at an assortment of unconventional jobs to support her seven-year-old son Alexander, whom she alternately coddles and ignores. When she pursues Macon, he is swept along by her strength into a world that seems both exotic and appealing. Through Muriel, Macon is drawn into a world of women: Muriel's sister, her friends, and her neighbors. As Muriel successfully trains Edward, Macon is also nurtured and strengthened. She is the catalyst through which a happier, more emotionally satisfied man emerges.

Edward is given rare depth and provides the novel with some of its best comic moments. As Macon's emotional state deteriorates, Edward, who was also traumatized by Ethan's death, is increasingly aggressive. He becomes a nuisance at best and a menace at worst. He is, however, unfailingly amusing.

The Leary siblings, Charles, Porter, Macon, and Rose, were somber and orderly as children and frequently dismayed by their widowed mother, who virtually worshipped change for its own sake. Stodgy even as children, the Learys were unnerved by their mother's enthusiasm for life. After marrying a traveling engineer, she sent her children to Baltimore to live with her parents, two "thin, severe," and "distinguished" people of whom the children immediately approved. The Leary siblings are firmly rooted in Tyler's tradition of idiosyncratic and eccentric characters. Afflicted with "geographic dyslexia," unable to avoid getting lost on the most routine trips, they dread any foray into the outside world. They are wrapped in a safe cocoon where even the ringing telephone is ignored.

Rose, unlike her divorced brothers Charles and Porter, never married. She has chosen instead to remain in the house, caring for her brothers and the many elderly neighbors who call upon her for everything from chauffeuring to plumbing. Yet Rose's fundamental dissatisfaction is evident in her nearly obsessive attention to an afternoon soap opera. While Charles and Porter remain static throughout *The Accidental Tourist*, providing a backdrop against which the others' transformations can be gauged, Rose's life changes when she meets Julian.

Although initially amused by the eccentric Macon, Julian becomes infatuated with Rose and with the hominess of the life she has created. In his mid-thirties, he is two years younger than Rose; like her, he has never married. Instead, he lives in a singles apartment, dresses nattily, frequents singles bars, and spends his leisure sailing on the Chesapeake Bay. He is the sort, according to Macon, who makes purchases without the use of *Consumer Reports*. Rose and Julian's romance provides some of the novel's most comic moments.

Themes and Meanings

The centrality of sibling relationships, a common theme in many of Tyler's novels, is the backdrop against which the events of *The Accidental Tourist* occur. It is also the litmus against which Tyler measures the degree of change occurring in her characters. In *The Accidental Tourist*, Tyler explores the effects people have on one another and the changes wrought by their interactions.

Julian, the quintessential preppy playboy, is enthralled by the homey atmosphere in the Leary house. He abandons his single life for a pedantic upper-middle-class world. Driven by his desire, Julian even manages to learn Vaccination, the only spouse to do so. For her part, Rose steps out of the groove in which she appears firmly entrenched and goes sailing on the Chesapeake.

When Sarah first leaves Macon, his grief over Ethan's death and his own sudden bachelorhood nearly overwhelm him. When he moves into the working-class neighborhood in which Muriel rents a broken-down row house, he leaves behind a persona that is at least partially an artificial construct formed during his courtship of Sarah. Muriel's flamboyance, her inner strength, and her *joie de vivre* in the face of nearly overwhelming hardship allow Macon at once to heal and to become, as Muriel calls him, soft-hearted. The original accidental tourist, Macon even finds himself extolling the virtues of San Francisco to a weary native Baltimorean who is a devotee of Macon's books.

The Accidental Tourist is, of course, a metaphor for Macon's life. He is passively swept along by events. While he is a competent and basically good-hearted man, Macon lacks Muriel's inner strength. Through her influence, he is forced finally to make decisions in his life.

With its diverse historical traditions and distinctive neighborhoods, Baltimore provides a rich background for Tyler's eccentric characters. Two sections of this multifaceted city are given clarity in *The Accidental Tourist*, Macon's upper-class Logan Park and Muriel's inner-city neighborhood of row houses. Before he meets Muriel, Macon's entire life is spent in an old neighborhood of detached houses and tree-lined streets. The houses are spacious and private compared to Muriel's domain, which consists of decrepit row houses with fake stone fronts, families sitting on front steps leading directly to the pavement, and unemployed men standing on streetcorners making small talk. Macon is a visitor in a strange world, a world in which he initially wonders how anyone can feel safe, but a world that ultimately he finds vibrant and thriving.

Social class consciousness permeates *The Accidental Tourist* as it does Baltimore. Because of their different classes, Macon's family disapproves of his relationship with Muriel. His brothers refer to her as "this Muriel person," and Sarah tells Macon that with Muriel he will be permanently on the fringe, a member of one of those couples who fit nowhere. It is a measure of Macon's growth that he rejects these class biases and makes an active decision to return to Muriel.

Critical Context

With the publication of *The Accidental Tourist*, Tyler's professional and popular reputation expanded. The third of her books to be nominated for the National Book Critics Circle Award—after *Morgan's Passing* (1980) and *Dinner at the Homesick*

Restaurant (1982)—*The Accidental Tourist* was the first to be awarded the prize. Aided by the release of a Hollywood film version of the book, Tyler's readership expanded measurably. As a result of her growing reputation, several of her earlier works that had enjoyed limited success were reprinted. In addition, her eleventh novel, *Breathing Lessons* (1988), won the Pulitzer Prize in fiction. Tyler later published a twelfth novel, *Saint Maybe* (1991). She has also written numerous book reviews and short stories.

While Tyler credits the Southern writer and master of eccentric characterizations Eudora Welty as an early and principal influence, her own writing defies classification. While there are Southern qualities in her writing, including depictions of eccentric individuals and regional speech patterns, her style is unique and immediately identifiable as her own. The setting of her latter novels is Baltimore, but her writing captures a universality of human experience. She admirably describes nuances of behavior in her characters, and she explores the depths of their natures through minutiae. Situations that would be merely banal in the hands of most other writers become profound tools for Tyler. Although her characters are often eccentric, they are nevertheless recognizably human.

Her books share common themes: relationships between siblings, between parents and children, or between husbands and wives. Families, especially brothers and sisters, are drawn together by an inexorable pull. Characters are seen reacting in unpredictable but understandable ways to the often confusing and difficult world in which they live. Because Tyler explores similar human relationships, the characters in *The Accidental Tourist* are similar to those in her other works. Yet her characterizations are sufficiently unique to hold reader interest through several books. Many characters, Muriel in this instance, are truly memorable. Edward, moreover, has become a standard by which other fictional dogs are compared.

Bibliography
Almond, Barbara R. "The Accidental Therapist: Intrapsychic Change in a Novel." *Literature and Psychology* 38 (Spring/Summer, 1992): 84-105. Discusses Macon's character development in psychological terms. Sees Muriel as functioning as Macon's therapist.
Bail, Paul. *Anne Tyler: A Critical Companion*. Westport, Conn.: Greenwood Press, 1998. Bail takes a critical look at Tyler's work. His discussions focus primarily on individual novels, including *The Accidental Tourist*. Students and general readers will appreciate the sections on plot, characters, themes, literary devices, historical setting, and point of view. Biographical information is also included.
Croft, Robert W. *An Anne Tyler Companion*. Westport, Conn.: Greenwood Press, 1998. A comprehensive and detailed guide to Tyler's works, this volume includes biographical material, as well as critical pieces on her major novels. One chapter is devoted exclusively to *The Accidental Tourist*. Also includes an extensive bibliography and appendices.
Durham, Joyce. "City Perspectives in Anne Tyler's *Morgan's Passing* and *The Acci-*

dental Tourist." *The Midwest Quarterly* 34 (Autumn, 1992): 42-56. Durham compares the characters of Morgan Gower in *Morgan's Passing* and Macon Leary in *The Accidental Tourist*, both of whom she says are urban survivors who retain hope and a sense of control despite their surroundings. She claims that their characters lend definition to the cities they inhabit and show how people can adapt to an urban environment.

Eder, Richard. "*The Accidental Tourist.*" *Los Angeles Times Book Review*, September 15, 1985, 3, 10. In a highly laudatory review, Eder discusses Tyler's techniques of characterization, including the "made-up quality" of her characters who are designed to instruct and entertain. "They are odd but utterly recognizable: mirrors set at an extravagant angle to catch what is going by," writes Eder.

Evans, Elizabeth. *Anne Tyler.* New York: Twayne, 1993. Discusses Tyler's books, including *The Accidental Tourist*, in the context of broader issues in her work. Evans sees humor as a central feature in Tyler's work and notes that the author examines women's roles in society and familial relationships in detail.

Kline, Karen E. "*The Accidental Tourist* on Page and on Screen: Interrogating Normative Theories About Film Adaptation." *Literature-Film Quarterly* 24 (January, 1996): 70-83. Comparing Tyler's book to Lawrence Kasdan's screenplay, Kline offers an assessment of how successfully a novel can be interpreted by film. She explores three approaches: the transformative, pluralist, and materialist. Her essay is an interesting commentary on the interaction of literature and film.

McMurtry, Larry. "Life Is a Foreign Country." *The New York Times Book Review* 90 (September 8, 1985). McMurtry places Macon firmly in the tradition of many of Tyler's male characters who are unusually influenced by strong women. McMurtry views Tyler's metaphor of the accidental tourist as strong, capturing the essence of most of her male characters, who live as accidental tourists in their own lives. He also discusses another common theme in her work, the magnetism of sibling relationships.

Petry, Alice Hall. *Understanding Ann Tyler.* Columbia: University of South Carolina Press, 1990. After providing context for Tyler's fiction in an overview that discusses her work in relation to other authors, Petry then devotes individual chapters to each of Tyler's books. She discusses in detail the plot of *The Accidental Tourist* and provides basic interpretations of characters and events.

Schaeffer, Pamela. "Anne Tyler: Family Novelist with a Twist." *National Catholic Reporter* 32 (May 24, 1996): 25. Schaeffer discusses four of Tyler's novels; although she finds parts of *The Accidental Tourist* "poignant and funny," she finds some characters to be "superficially drawn" and "unconvincing."

Mary E. Virginia

ACROSS THE RIVER AND INTO THE TREES

Author: Ernest Hemingway (1899-1961)
Type of plot: Realism
Time of plot: Winter, 1949
Locale: Venice, Italy, and the surrounding area
First published: 1950

Principal characters:

RICHARD CANTWELL, the protagonist, a colonel, formerly a United
States brigadier general, a professional soldier
RENATA, an Italian countess, "nearly nineteen," the colonel's mistress
JACKSON, an army sergeant, the colonel's driver
THE GRAN MAESTRO, the headwaiter at the Gritti Palace Hotel and a
member of the colonel's fictitious Order of Brusadelli

The Novel

The novel opens on a cold Sunday morning with the protagonist traveling by boat to shoot ducks along a partially frozen lagoon near Venice. He assists the boatman in poling through the ice and offers to help place decoys, becoming somewhat angry at the surly boatman's responses. Taking his place in a partially submerged barrel that serves as a blind, Colonel Richard Cantwell skillfully brings down the first two ducks that fly within range.

The narrative returns in a flashback to a physical examination that the colonel took three days earlier, when a skeptical army surgeon allowed him to pass, even though both men knew the colonel to be dying of heart disease. With Jackson, his driver, the colonel sets out from Trieste, recalling along the way sites where he fought and was wounded during World War I. Arriving in Venice, he goes by boat to the Gritti Palace Hotel and, once settled there, dines with his young mistress, Countess Renata. Afterward they make love in a gondola on the way to Renata's home.

The following morning, the colonel leaves the hotel to walk through the market in the brisk winter air, returning in time for breakfast with his mistress. In his room he begins to tell her how he lost his regiment in the Hurtgen Forest. Although she finds portions of the account confusing, she listens as if knowing that it is important for him to share the experience. Even after the countess has fallen asleep, he continues his discourse—at times through an interior dialogue, at times addressing a portrait that Renata gave him.

They go to a jewelry shop where he buys Renata a moor's head brooch that she admired; he informs her that the heirloom emeralds that she gave him have been deposited for her in the hotel safe. After martinis at Harry's Bar, they return to the hotel for lunch, where the colonel and the Gran Maestro make her an honorary member of their humorous Order of Brusadelli. At their parting Renata weeps, although she has told him that she never does, and the colonel sets off for the Barone Alvarito's estate, where he will hunt the next morning.

The narrative returns abruptly to the Sunday hunt, with the colonel in the blind re-calling stories told by other hunters the preceding evening. After modest success, he finds the chances for more kills diminished by unfavorable weather. Returning to his car, he sets out with Jackson back to Trieste but en route is wracked by a series of at-tacks which convince him that he cannot live. After repeating General Stonewall Jackson's final words, "No, no, let us cross over the river and rest in the shade of the trees," he moves to the back seat of the Buick and firmly closes the door. Jackson finds him dead shortly thereafter and reads a note that the colonel had written minutes ear-lier, ordering that the portrait and his shotguns be sent to the hotel for Renata to claim. Continuing the journey, Jackson reflects that this request will be handled through channels.

Except for the chapter narrating the physical examination, the entire plot unfolds within a period of three days. The book opens on the day of the hunt, moves backward to Friday and Saturday, and returns to the final day at the end. In the course of three days, the hero manages to tell his life's story to those he encounters, its most impor-tant stages being the two world wars. The narrow time frame beginning *in medias res* lays heavy emphasis upon his approaching death. These final three days are narrated almost exclusively from the protagonist's point of view, although one hears the authorial voice in the introduction and in the conclusion. The plot moves inexorably toward the climactic death of the protagonist.

In presenting the colonel's interaction with other characters, Hemingway achieves an economy of narrative. Rarely does the novel focus on scenes involving more than two people. At first the colonel is with the boatman on the hunt and later, he is in the car with Jackson. Much of the remaining time he is with Renata—in a hotel or dining room, walking along the street, or riding in a gondola. Other scenes involve the colo-nel and barmen, waiters, or the Gran Maestro. Often a deep emotional bond exists be-tween the hero and the other character, yet the characters serve primarily as straight men designed to facilitate the colonel's rambling discourse.

The Characters

The protagonist, Colonel Richard Cantwell, a fifty-one-year-old professional sol-dier, is dying of heart disease. A veteran of both world wars, he seeks to relive his ear-lier life among friends and former comrades in Venice. He narrates his most important experiences to Renata, whose name means "reborn." A man with strong likes and dis-likes and some regrets, he avoids laying blame. Aggressive, somewhat short-tempered, he struggles to keep control over a truculent nature. An existential hero who conquers despair and angst, he lives by his code and feels most strongly drawn to those like himself, wounded by war or life. He quotes William Shakespeare and Dante and appreciates great works of art, but he is no mere aesthete: He lives life to the full-est and dies courageously. Lacking illusions, he nevertheless holds strong personal values—physical exertion, comradeship, kindness toward the weak, chivalry toward women, toughness toward oneself.

Renata, an Italian countess nearly nineteen, genuinely loves Cantwell. A woman of beauty, sensitivity, and wisdom beyond her years, she attempts to keep the dying colonel optimistic and forward-looking, even as she hears the unfolding story of his past. Like him, she is somewhat guarded in the expression of emotion, but her depth of feeling is undeniable.

Jackson, a technical sergeant and the colonel's driver, has shared the military experience of war, having served in the Italian campaign. To a degree, he also shares the colonel's temper and sense of dignity. His name may suggest to the colonel the quotation from Stonewall Jackson that gives the novel its title.

The Gran Maestro, who has the dignity and reserve of a headwaiter, fought with the colonel in World War I. He now suffers from ulcers and a heart condition less serious than the colonel's. The two experience a kind of magical brotherhood when they are talking of their order, a magic that vanishes whenever the Gran Maestro returns to his duties. A complement of boatmen, barmen, and waiters, each making a brief appearance, remind the reader that the hero meets them on terms of easy familiarity. Sketched with brevity and economy, they exist primarily to reveal facets of Cantwell's character or past experience.

Themes and Meanings

The last three days of Cantwell's life are devoted to the values he holds dear—comradeship, intensity in romantic love, a sense of power, aggressiveness, and assertiveness. The values of living life to the full, loving passionately, killing cleanly, and dying courageously predominate in the work. Earlier Hemingway heroes often had a cause or at least a calling in life to which they were devoted. Cantwell, older and facing death, seems to have grown disillusioned with all causes. He expresses ambivalent attitudes about his profession of soldiering. A kind of existential hero, he attaches no mystical significance to life or death.

Like the later work *The Old Man and the Sea* (1952), the novel incorporates Christian symbolism. The colonel's wounded hand, for example, suggests the wounds of Christ, and there are allusions to Madonnas with reference to romantic love and love of family. The three-day plot, lasting from Friday through Sunday, may well hold symbolic significance, but the symbolism does not form any consistent allegory and at best offers only tantalizing suggestions.

The hero's almost incessant traveling in the novel—in boats, in a car, in walks with Renata—symbolically suggests a journey toward death. Cantwell undergoes a kind of Dantean journey requiring him to come to terms with his past. Recalling and to some extent reliving his war experiences, he has numerous regrets—the many dead, the loss of his regiment and his general's rank, the three failed marriages—yet he does not attempt to lay blame. Though he does not achieve a satisfactory resolution of his conflicting emotions, he comes to terms stoically with his losses even as he is upholding through living the values he affirms.

Critical Context

From the beginning, critical estimates of Hemingway's novel have been largely un-favorable, and the book continues to rank among his least successful. However fine the narrative technique and style, the novel centers so heavily on the hero that his character and expression influence readers most strongly. Cantwell closely resembles earlier Hemingway heroes such as Frederic Henry in *A Farewell to Arms* (1929) and Robert Jordan in *For Whom the Bell Tolls* (1940). Like them he is tragic, yet he carries the machismo of the traditional hero to excess. Once, while walking at night with Renata, Cantwell bridles at insults from two sailors. When they go too far, he ap-proaches and begins a fight, quickly knocking one out. After landing several devastat-ing blows against the other, he smashes him above the ear and turns rapidly away so that he will not hear the sailor's head bounce against the pavement. Then, ignoring the hurt to his previously injured hand, he tells Renata that they should walk in such a way that the backs of their legs look dangerous.

In his attitudes, Cantwell resembles Hemingway and is in fact a highly auto-biographical character. His blunt criticism of military and political leaders such as General George Patton, British Field Marshal Bernard Montgomery, President Harry S Truman, and President Dwight David Eisenhower embarrassed many readers at the time. The dialogue incorporates the mannerisms of earlier Hemingway heroes taken to excess—insider jokes, cryptic allusions to weapons and weapons sys-tems, military jargon, and slangy nicknames. Cantwell refers to a martini with fif-teen parts gin and one part vermouth as a Montgomery—the point being that British Field Marshal Montgomery wanted favorable odds of fifteen to one before attacking and even then moved with caution. The numerous references and allusions to the World War II era must inevitably pose more difficulty for readers as time passes. One must be rather well grounded in languages to recognize and understand all of the Italian, German, French, and Spanish phrases and sentences sprinkled throughout the book.

Although the novel reveals many of the qualities of Hemingway's art, it does not advance his previous achievement, either aesthetically or thematically. It remains among the minor achievements of a major novelist.

Bibliography

Benson, Jackson J., ed. *New Critical Approaches to the Short Stories of Ernest Hem-ingway.* Durham, N.C.: Duke University Press, 1990. Section 1 covers critical ap-proaches to Hemingway's most important long fiction; section 2 concentrates on story techniques and themes; section 3 focuses on critical interpretations of the most important stories; section 4 provides an overview of Hemingway criticism; section 5 contains a comprehensive checklist of Hemingway short fiction criticism from 1975 to 1989.

Bloom, Harold, ed. *Ernest Hemingway: Modern Critical Views.* New York: Chelsea House, 1985. After an introduction that considers Hemingway in relation to later criticism and to earlier American writers, includes articles by a variety of critics who treat topics such as Hemingway's style, unifying devices, and visual techniques.

Lynn, Kenneth S. *Hemingway.* New York: Simon and Schuster, 1987. A shrewd, critical look at Hemingway's life and art, relying somewhat controversially on psychological theory.

Mellow, James R. *Hemingway: A Life Without Consequences.* Boston: Houghton Mifflin, 1992. A well-informed, sensitive handling of the life and work by a seasoned biographer.

Meyers, Jeffrey. *Hemingway: A Biography.* New York: Harper & Row, 1985. Meyers is especially good at explaining the biographical sources of Hemingway's fiction.

Reynolds, Michael. *The Young Hemingway.* Oxford, England: Blackwell, 1986. The first volume of a painstaking biography devoted to the evolution of Hemingway's life and writing. Includes chronology and notes.

_____. *Hemingway: The Paris Years.* Volume 2. Oxford, England: Blackwell, 1989. Includes chronology and maps.

_____. *Hemingway: The American Homecoming.* Volume 3. Oxford, England: Blackwell, 1992. Includes chronology, maps, and notes.

_____. *Hemingway: The 1930s.* Oxford, England: Blackwell, 1997. Volume 4 of Reynolds's biography.

Stanley Archer

ADA OR ARDOR
A Family Chronicle

Author: Vladimir Nabokov (1899-1977)
Type of plot: Romance and literary parody
Time of plot: 1850 to 1965
Locale: Antiterra or Demonia
First published: 1969

> *Principal characters:*
> IVAN (VAN) VEEN, the protagonist, born in 1870
> ADELAIDA (ADA) VEEN, his cousin, born in 1872
> DEMENTIY (DEMON) VEEN, Van's father
> AQUA DURMANOV, Van's mother
> MARINA DURMANOV, Ada's mother
> LUCINDA or LUCETTE VEEN, Ada's sister

The Novel

If *Ada or Ardor* (most commonly known as *Ada*) is about people—it is subtitled "A Family Chronicle," and Nabokov supplies a detailed family tree that precedes the novel—it is also a book about literature, a parody. The difficulty for the reader is to judge correctly the proportions of the two. To what extent is it a book about people—above all about two lovers, Ada and Van—and to what extent is it a book about literary works and traditions? Clearly the novel is both. It is an interesting love story about two cousins who fall in love and consummate that love, when Van is fourteen and Ada twelve. The novel follows the vicissitudes of this love affair until the protagonists' old age. It is also a "chronicle" of the nineteenth and twentieth century novel, with almost as many literary references as James Joyce's *Ulysses* (1922). It is a love story and a *roman à clef*—or rather *aux clés*. It can be confidently predicted that graduate students and critics will want to write articles and books about *Ada*'s literary allusions well into the future. It is questionable, however, whether readers will also continue to come to *Ada* because of its love story and family chronicle. Interest in the novel will be generated by its literary complexity on the one hand, and by interest in its explicitly erotic passages on the other. Like Joyce scholars, Nabokov scholars will probably continue to say that the general reader cannot appreciate the novel without understanding its multiple literary references. *Ada* will probably have as few readers who enjoy it without reference to a literary tradition as *Ulysses*. The erotic passages will attract the curious, yet it is difficult to imagine such an audience reading the novel from beginning to end with satisfaction.

Nevertheless, reading *Ada* provides a unique kind of experience. The novel can be appreciated as a work of imagination about people, without reference to other books or literary traditions. There are obstacles to this, just as there are similar obstacles in

Ulysses, but they are not insuperable. The parody can be understood on the level of personalities and word play; above all, the major imaginative act of the novel can be clearly grasped by a Russianless reader.

Ada does not take place on the familiar Earth; it is set neither in Russia (or the literal context of Russian literature) nor in America. The novel takes place in "Antiterra," sometimes called Demonia. Terra—our Earth—is a myth, a distant world about which the characters in the book dream; it is an unattainable Utopia. This basic premise of the novel should give pause to the seekers of literary influences. Antiterra has its own laws and its own elements, which are different from those on Terra. Consequently the novel's protagonists are also different; they are not human in the normal sense, nor is the love of Ada and Van a normal human love. It is their inhuman qualities that are central to the novel. The reader's recognition of these is central to an understanding of *Ada*.

On the planet of Antiterra, not only Van and Ada but also all other people are possessed by the fury of erotic love. To the exclusion of almost everything else, the characters are obsessed with the "dementia" of ardor. The Veens are not Demonia's only libertines; nearly every minor character in the book is either inspired or victimized by passion. As the Greeks distinguished between searing Eros and Agape—the warm affection that exists in families or among friends—so Nabokov distinguishes between Antiterra and Terra. The world of *Ada* is entirely the world of Eros, with other types of love methodically excluded. No characters in the book are left unscathed by the "ardent" practices of pederasty, nympholepsy (the novel frequently harks back to *Lolita*, 1955), lesbianism, or simple promiscuity and adultery. As the critic Ellen Pifer has remarked in *Nabokov and the Novel* (1980),

> nearly everyone, from servants to stealthy heads of state, is busy fondling someone else behind a convenient tree or in a handy corner. More often than not, the object of such ardent caresses is another man's lover or spouse, a child decades younger than her (or his) adorer, or a triptych of prostitutes who have turned up for the occasion. On Antiterra, young "whorelets," beautiful and diseased, are offered to the highest bidder by their mother or older brother.

The repellent effect of these episodes is deliberate.

As the novel proceeds, the reader quickly discovers that Van, Ada, Van's father Demon, and other characters are quite unpleasant. The reader might be legitimately puzzled by this unpleasantness, and shortly after the novel appeared in 1969 several critics attributed it to Nabokov, the author. Matthew Hodgart reviewed *Ada* for *The New York Review of Books* (May 22, 1969), assuming that Van and Ada's love affair was modeled after Nabokov's own marriage. Nabokov's indignant response to the reviewer (published July 10, 1969) was this:

> I do object violently to your seeing in reunited Van and Ada (both rather horrible creatures) a picture of my married life. What the hell, Sir, do you know about my married life? I expect a prompt apology from you.

Clearly Hodgart had made a mistake. The novel is a sustained exercise in the description of "inhuman" desire that transcends or obliterates the "restraints, principles and consolations" of everyday life on the Earth. Questions of intention or consequence—of whether human life is preserved or destroyed—are irrelevant to that ecstasy; Nabokov attempts to apply this psychological principle to all the relationships in the book. It is the across-the-board premise of the fictitious world of Antiterra, which is both beautiful and cruel. The powerful and privileged practice every form of aesthetic and erotic indulgence at the expense of the weak.

What is the ultimate goal of this allegorical or fictitious world? The novel traces the passion of Van and Ada from its inception to their old age, when they are more than ninety years old. The reader is informed that when Van is eighty-seven he becomes impotent, but that does not substantially change the nature of his relationship with Ada, and Antiterra remains Antiterra. Van writes a treatise on time and space, he attempts to "caress time." As Nabokov (or rather, Van) writes, "To be eternal the Present must depend on the conscious spanning of an infinite expansure." Indeed, this conscious act is the writing of the novel *Ada* which has been composed, the reader learns, by Van himself. *Ada* is Van's "treatise on the Texture of Time, an investigation of its veily substance, with illustrative metaphors."

The novel ends with a rapid history of the world in the 1920's and 1930's, of the conquest of Rus by the Golden Horde and the rise in 1933 of "Athaulf Hindler." The narrator mentions the "L.F.T. idea," which is "leaving from Terra" in a cosmic capsule. Nabokov's "world" or allegory is consistent to the end.

Normally when irony is used in a work of art, it is signaled by a variety of devices—exaggeration, irreverent twists, understatement, or the unexpected joining of opposites. *Ada* contains an abundance of the first two devices, but there is very little of the latter two. As a result, "Antiterra" is disconcertingly a world unto itself. The parody lacks real bite, or mordancy. Is it a hypothetical world, or what the world has become? "Van" is incapable of answering this question. Nabokov declines to do so.

The Characters

The characters define Antiterra, and they are all destructive. They might be roughly divided into victimizers and victims. Demon Veen, Van's father, is a monstrous egotist and a rake. He seems to feed on live beauty with the same appetite with which he feeds on gourmet meals. Van takes after his father—he is a younger and more robust, more spontaneous and less jaded, copy. Ada has a devastating effect on the frail mortals with whom she comes in contact. From childhood on, Van's and Ada's appetites are as prodigious as their intellectual gifts—they do not have to work for their conquests, who succumb to them without the least resistance. Nor do the men work for money, or do any drudgery; they live in a world of Swiss bank accounts, of multiple villas on the most desirable spots of the globe with "staffs" of servants filling them. It would seem that there might be an element of wish-fulfilling fantasy here, of self-indulgence bordering on privatism. The "author" (technically, Van) insists that to all of his endeavors Van applies "athletic strength of will, ironization of excessive emotion, and contempt for weepy weaklings." In this black-and-white world where extremes (incestuously) meet, the victims appear little different from their victimizers; they feel no resentment or rebellion, and no doubt victims would be victimizers if only they had the means.

These values, or antivalues, are reinforced by the narration's tone. All events are seen through the prism of Van's hyperbolic disdain, his striking metaphors, constant parody, and trilingual puns. ("Demon's former valet explained to Van that the 'dor' in the name of an adored river equalled the corruption of hydro in 'dorophone.' Van often had word dreams.") The reader is never able to escape this "nasty" tone or point of view; it produces a sense of claustrophobia from which there is no respite. This is the novel's basic flaw and greatest weakness, its Achilles' heel. The narration is often sprightly, inventive—but it cloys. It desperately needs a foil, something to be set against, another voice to give relief, or proof that Van's authorial tone is not Nabokov's. None, however, is provided.

The saving grace of Antiterra is that its inhabitants long for another "more deeply moral" world to which they might escape. They dream of a paradise called Terra "on the opposite side of the cosmic lane" where cruel appetite and pride have been dispelled. Ironically, it is when the reader encounters these longings that Antiterra seems most like our own world.

Themes and Meanings

The dominant theme of *Ada* is the parody of our world by means of Nabokov's construct, Antiterra It is both Utopia and anti-Utopia combined. It has features in common with science fiction—with some of the worlds imagined by Stanisław Lem, for example—but also with books such as Aldous Huxley's *Brave New World* (1932), George Orwell's *Nineteen Eighty-Four* (1949), and Yevgeny Zamyatin's *My* (1924; *We*, 1925). Nabokov's "brave" world is, however, more elusive. It is a subtle combination of paradise and hell, without any middle ground, that is much more difficult to grasp. It is above all a parody of the world of unrestrained appetite.

The late nineteenth and twentieth centuries, Nabokov seems to say, have gradually become an Antiterra, and all that is left of Terra is our longings. The causes for this are both external and internal: the triumph of the Golden Horde and Athaulf Hindler (Joseph Stalin and Adolf Hitler) from outside, and the cruelty of our demands for gratification, for an egotistical "paradise now," from within.

Critical Context

When *Ada* first appeared it was hailed by some, strongly disliked by others. The dislike was not hard to understand—because the entire chronicle is suffused by Van's special tone of disdainful hyperbole from beginning to end, it is, in effect, "Van's book," and the reader has some excuse to think that Van is a stand-in for Nabokov. The reviewer for the *Times Literary Supplement* (October 2, 1969) thought that the novel was a form of "self-parody"—like *The Golden Bowl* (1904), *Sordello* (1840), *Pericles, Prince of Tyre* (c. 1607-1608), *The Kreutzer Sonata* (1890), and *Across the River and into the Trees* (1950).

Critics and scholars of Russian literature, however, and specialists of Nabokov's writings knew that this impression was partly misleading. Nabokov had always been a parodist, and the particular tone adopted for *Ada* was not identical to that of his other books. In an article, Simon Karlinsky sketched the literary allusions of *Ada*, opening the way to an interpretation of the book as a novel about literature. Antiterra proves to have a strong resemblance to nineteenth and twentieth century Russian literature. The novel's subtitle points to Sergey Aksakov's *Semeynaya khronika* (1856; *The Family Chronicle*, 1903), Demon Veen's ancestry goes back to Mikhail Lermontov's 1841 narrative poem *Demon* by way of Fyodor Sologub's *The Little Demon* (1916). Sologub's *The Created Legend* (1916) is partly situated in Russia during the revolution of 1905 and partly on a distant imaginary planet reminiscent of Antiterra. Karlinsky's article provided a preliminary "skeleton key" for the intellectual plot of *Ada*. Also, nineteenth century European diabolism and the Don Juan myth could be seen at the core of *Ada*—rightly so, as Ada herself acts in a mediocre film, *Don Juan's Last Fling*, and during the closing pages of the novel she and Van watch it half a dozen times with absorbed interest. Karlinsky, Alfred Appel, Jr., Carl Proffer, and others have pointed out other allusions in *Ada*; the novel begins with a parody of the opening of *Anna Karenina*, and there are numerous references to Alexander Pushkin, Anton Chekhov, Ivan Turgenev, Aleksandr Griboyedov, Miguel de Cervantes, John Milton, Lord Byron (again Don Juan), Chateaubriand, Marcel Proust, and many others, among them T. S. Eliot ("Solemn Kithar Sween, a banker who at sixty-five had become an avant-garde author; in the course of one miraculous year he had produced *The Waistline*, a satire in free verse on Anglo-American feeding habits").

There are three main purposes behind the allusions: high spirits in keeping with the multiple puns and plays on words in the novel, the extension of the "chronicle" of Antiterra deep into the past, and the criticism—by parody—of the only-too-familiar traits of Antiterra embodied in literary tradition. There is no question about it: An abundant literature about Antiterra already existed. It turned out to be right under our noses.

Bibliography

Appel, Alfred, Jr., and Charles Newman, eds. *Nabokov: Criticism, Reminiscences, Translations, Tributes*. Evanston, Ill.: Northwestern University Press, 1970. A good introduction to Nabokov's writing, including a varied sampling of material about the man, about the writer, and about his several unique works. Perhaps a hodgepodge, but an early collection that contrasts dramatically with later criticism, which suggested that Nabokov was a humanist if also a kind of verbal magician.

Bloom, Harold, ed. *Vladimir Nabokov*. New York: Chelsea House, 1987. Essays on Nabokov's handling of time, illusion and reality, and art. There are separate essays on each of his major novels, as well as an introduction, chronology, and bibliography.

Boyd, Brian. *Vladimir Nabokov: The Russian Years*. Princeton, N.J.: Princeton University Press, 1990. The first volume of the definitive biography, fully researched and written with the cooperation of Nabokov's family. Boyd has an extraordinary command of the origins of Nabokov's art. This volume includes a discussion of Nabokov's years in Europe after he left Russia.

_____. *Vladimir Nabokov: The American Years*. Princeton, N.J.: Princeton University Press, 1991. Boyd concludes his masterful biography. As with volume 1, his work is copiously illustrated with detailed notes and an invaluable index.

Field, Andrew. *Nabokov, His Life in Part*. New York: Viking Press, 1977. An intimate portrait written by an author who was often very close to Nabokov during the latter part of Nabokov's life. The book may also suggest to would-be biographers some of the difficulties of writing a biography while enjoying an intimate relationship with the subject. Follows Field's critical work, *Nabokov, His Life in Art: A Critical Narrative* (Boston: Little, Brown, 1967).

_____. *VN: The Life and Art of Vladimir Nabokov*. New York: Crown, 1986. Not as definitive as Boyd, but still a very important biographical/critical study of Nabokov. Field has been called the "father of Nabokovian studies." Includes illustrations, detailed notes, and index. The best one-volume biography of Nabokov.

Foster, John Burt. *Nabokov's Art of Memory and European Modernism*. Princeton, N.J.: Princeton University Press, 1993. Burt divides his study into three parts: Nabokov's early years in Russia, his period in Europe, and his prolonged period in America. This is a more specialized study for advanced students.

Pifer, Ellen. *Nabokov and the Novel*. Cambridge, Mass.: Harvard University Press, 1980. Uses as an epigraph Flannery O'Connor's "All novelists are fundamentally seekers and describers of the real, but the realism of each novelist will depend on his view of the ultimate reaches of reality" to develop a critical dialogue about Nabokov's technique, not surprisingly including realism. Ends in a discussion on Nabokov's humanism. Robert Alter called this book "poised and precise," and it is excellent for serious, critical readers of Nabokov.

John Carpenter

THE AGONY AND THE ECSTASY
A Novel of Michelangelo

Author: Irving Stone (1903-1989)
Type of plot: Biographical novel
Time of plot: 1487-1564
Locale: Italy, especially Florence and Rome
First published: 1961

> *Principal characters:*
> MICHELANGELO BUONARROTI, the protagonist, a sculptor, painter, architect, and poet
> LODOVICO DI LIONARDO BUONARROTI SIMONI, Michelangelo's father
> LORENZO DE' MEDICI, IL MAGNIFICO, Michelangelo's first patron and the epitome of Renaissance humanism
> CONTESSINA DE' MEDICI, Lorenzo's daughter and Michelangelo's first love
> CLARISSA SAFFI, Michelangelo's other early love
> GIROLAMO SAVONAROLA, a zealous priest bent on reforming the Church
> VITTORIA COLONNA, the object of Michelangelo's love in later life
> TOMMASO DE CAVALIERI, Michelangelo's apprentice/assistant on St. Peter's and his other "love" in later life
> LEONARDO DA VINCI, Michelangelo's rival in painting
> BERTOLDO, Michelangelo's teacher in sculpture

The Novel

The Agony and the Ecstasy, a biographical novel, spans most of Michelangelo's life: It begins with him as a twelve-year-old and concludes with his death approximately eighty years later. Although Stone covers most of Michelangelo's life, he seems most concerned with Michelangelo's apprenticeship and early work; when Michelangelo reaches sixty, approximately two-thirds of his lifetime, the novel is practically completed. Struggle appears to be more interesting than success. Because of the mass of details, many gleaned from previously untranslated letters about Michelangelo's long life, Stone had to shape his material, to provide dramatic structure to the history of a man and his time.

As Stone presents him, Michelangelo is the complete artist: painter, sculptor, poet, architect, and, ultimately, engineer. *The Agony and the Ecstasy* depicts Michelangelo's struggle to become the embodiment of Renaissance humanism. In the course of the novel Michelangelo must overcome the interference of his family, religious dogma, political intrigue, papal patronage, military campaigns, and artistic jealousy to realize his artistic ambition.

Despite his father's opposition, twelve-year-old Michelangelo becomes an apprentice, first to painter Ghirlandaio and then to Bertoldo, a sculptor, who directs a school financed by Lorenzo de' Medici, patron of Florentine art. Michelangelo quickly wins Lorenzo's esteem, meets his children (among them two future popes, Giulio and Giovanni, and Contessina, his first love), suffers the first of several attacks by jealous colleagues (his nose is broken by Torrigiani, whose later appearances always threaten Michelangelo), and through forbidden dissection learns the anatomy and physiology he needs. Eventually Savonarola, a reform priest, comes to power, and his crusading zeal threatens Lorenzo de' Medici's family and the Florentine art world.

When Savonarola gains political, as well as religious, control, Michelangelo flees Florence and travels to Bologna, where he meets the sensuous Clarissa Saffi and carves the Bambino that attracts the attention of Leo Baglioni. In Rome for the first time, Michelangelo meets Jacopo Galli, a banker, who commissions a sculpture; Giuliano Sangallo, an architect; and Bramante, another architect and an adversary. In Rome, Michelangelo carves the *Pieta*, learns about the whims of religious patrons, and becomes interested in St. Peter's—the building of the new St. Peter's will embroil him in controversy and ultimately consume his last years.

Michelangelo returns to Florence, where he carves "the Giant," a sculpture of David which becomes the symbol of Florence. There he meets Leonardo da Vinci, his principal rival, and Raphael, the painter—the three become the triumvirate of Renaissance Italian art. Jealous of Leonardo, Michelangelo competes with him as the two artists paint frescoes for the rulers of Florence. Word of Michelangelo's work reaches Pope Julius, who forces Michelangelo to work in bronze, rather than his beloved marble, and to paint the Sistine Chapel ceiling. It is Julius who resolves to build a new St. Peter's.

Julius is followed by two Medici popes who only add to Michelangelo's problems: Giovanni, by forcing him to work with marble from Pietrasanta, an almost inaccessible region, thereby making Michelangelo an engineer, and Giulio, against whose forces Michelangelo must use his engineering talents to fortify the city of Florence. The Medici popes are followed by Pope Paul III, who commissions Michelangelo to paint the Last Judgment and who, after bitter disputes about the ongoing building of St. Peter's, appoints him as architect for the cathedral. The dome, Michelangelo's last creation, is the appropriate capstone for his creative efforts. In addition to achieving artistic acclaim, he finds an assistant, Tommaso de Cavalieri, who is to complete St. Peter's, and Vittoria Colonna, the female epitome of Renaissance humanism and his last great love.

The Characters

Stone presents Michelangelo as the idealized Renaissance humanist, the artist whose commitment to his work becomes a religion and whose creative efforts are no less than godlike. In fact, his commitment to art is such that it alienates him from society, makes him a misunderstood recluse, and, in becoming the outlet for his passion, prevents him from finding love. Because art becomes religion, art cannot be commercialized; the artist is not a businessman. Overly generous to his parasitic family and deaf to the warnings of his banker/agent Galli, he lives in relative poverty, unlike Leonardo and Raphael. Also unlike them, he works alone, refusing to compromise his work by using, even in the Sistine Chapel, other painters. Leonardo da Vinci and Raphael, despite their stature, exist in Stone's novel primarily as foils, artists whose deficiencies help define Michelangelo's greatness.

Other characters serve to demonstrate the plight of the artist whose superior work is often prey to the jealousy of less talented colleagues. Torrigiani breaks Michelangelo's nose, itself part of a work of art, as Stone carefully points out in the first paragraph of the novel. Later Vincenzo, an inferior sculptor in Bologna, defaces Michelangelo's *St. Petronius* because of jealousy. Perugino's vicious attack on Michelangelo's work is motivated, according to Raphael, by envy and despair: Michelangelo has made Perugino's work obsolete. Another act of "desecration" is committed by Bandinelli, who breaks into Michelangelo's studio during the attack on Florence. These examples attest the validity of Lorenzo de' Medici's words: "The forces of destruction march on the heels of creativity."

Despite the obstacles posed by such critics, Michelangelo succeeds because of his own talent, which is shaped by his mentors: Ghirlandaio, who instructs him in painting; Bertoldo, who instructs him in sculpture; Prior Bichiellini, who instructs him in life; and, most important, Lorenzo de' Medici, Il Magnifico, whose Platonic Academy instructs him in poetry and in the blending of classical and Christian cultures that characterizes his work. Even after his death, Lorenzo's ideas and influence inform Michelangelo's art.

The women in the novel serve primarily as symbols which ultimately are related to Michelangelo's work. Contessina, Lorenzo's daughter, is inaccessible, because of her exalted position, and pure; Michelangelo is bound to her aesthetically, spiritually, and mystically. Clarissa Saffi, a fictional rather than historical character, represents the emotional and physical side of love, and she is accessible. According to Michelangelo, she is the female form "already carved" and is the incarnation of love in its "ultimate female form." During the Florentine War he thinks of both women, and when their images merge, they become one, "the figure of love itself." This blending is analogous to the blending of classical and Christian in his work.

The Agony and the Ecstasy is a lengthy, sprawling novel, a large canvas peopled with characters from all walks of life. The historical characters serve to provide a cultural and intellectual milieu, a background for Michelangelo. Many of the fictional characters are from the lower classes, which tend to be sentimentalized and contrasted with the corrupt and ambitious upper classes. Nowhere is this conflict of values more apparent than in the juxtaposition of the Topolinos, the stonecutters, and the denizens of Rome.

Themes and Meanings

In *The Agony and the Ecstasy*, Stone uses Michelangelo as a working definition of the idealized artist, a creation who is, simultaneously, a godlike creator. Early in the novel Michelangelo refers to God as the "first sculptor" and as the "supreme carver";

later, he refers to artists as the species "apart" who will speak for God. "To draw is to be like God," asserts Michelangelo, who claims elsewhere that sculpture is "my faith." As he gazes at his Sistine Chapel, Michelangelo recalls Genesis, and Stone has him, in analogous terms, see all that he has made and "find it very good."

This extraordinary analogy is extended when Michelangelo sees himself as not only God the Father, but as "God the Mother," source of a "noble breed, half man, half god"; as God the Mother, he inseminates himself with his "creative fertility." Stone thus incorporates sexuality within religiosity and provides his readers with a new metaphor involving the equation of sex with sculpture. In its coarsest terms, the relationship is described by Beppe: "What you put into the ladies at night, you can't put into the marble in the morning." In more elevated terms, the conflict between art and sexuality is akin to the traditional opposition between the body (sex) and spirit (art). Given that conflict, the sculptor expresses his relationship to marble in sexual terms; having expended himself on the marble, he has no creative energy for personal relationships. For Michelangelo, the act of creation involves the "thrust, the penetration, the beating and pulsing" toward climax. Blocks of marble are seen as "virginal"; the chisel penetrates and seeds its female form. Conversely, when he makes love to Clarissa, the sexual act is expressed in terms of sculpture: He uses a "chisel" on the "warm living marble" of Clarissa's body, which had been earlier described as being "already carved." Through the use of the analogy Stone explains Michelangelo's relative lack of sexual interest in women (Clarissa is a fictional character), but Stone avoids dealing with his subject's bisexuality.

Stone also addresses the incompatibility of art and business. During most of his life, Michelangelo is totally dependent on the patronage of the wealthy, especially the papacy, and their whims and eccentricities prevent him from expressing himself in his beloved marble. Although a creative god in theory, the artist is, as Michelangelo ruefully acknowledges, a "hireling," below a tradesman in status. Rather than financing the artist and allowing freedom of expression, the patrons exercise their vanity and force artists to work on inappropriate projects. Running throughout the novel is the notion that the artist exists only to be exploited both artistically and financially. Lodovico may not approve of his son's vocation, but he extorts money from him. Michelangelo is, in truth, his father's "quarry." Finally, he recognizes that both his Holy Fathers and his earthly one have exploited him.

It is only the committed artist who can survive, even thrive, in the midst of such materialism. Michelangelo's commitment allows no distractions and necessitates mastery of every phase of art: painting, poetry, sculpture—he masters them all. Like the amateur film director who wishes to control all phases of the filmmaking process, the sculptor wants to control the marble from the time it is cut from the quarry until the carved statue is safely installed. Therefore, readers learn that Michelangelo can cut stone, that he can build roads to the quarry, that he can protect his work from the ravages of war. According to Bertoldo, the stone "works with" a sculptor like Michelangelo.

Critical Context

The Agony and the Ecstasy, perhaps Stone's most acclaimed novel, is a worthy successor to *Lust for Life* (1934), his first venture into the artistic world, and the two novels contain many of the same themes. Stone's other novels concern, for the most part, political figures as diverse as Eugene V. Debs and Mary Todd Lincoln; he returned to the world of art in *Depths of Glory* (1985), a novel about the Impressionist painter Camille Pissarro. In his genre, the biographical novel, Stone has no American equal in quality or quantity, though Andre Maurois is a worthy foreign rival.

The lack of competition is understandable, given the demands of the genre and the lack of critical appreciation for it, despite its popular acceptance. First, the research is formidable, for the biographical novelist must know not only his subject but also his times, including history, religion, politics, science, and the arts. Second, because they believe that less imagination and creativity are required in "history," critics value fiction over fact. As Stone points out, however, a biographical novel is not simply history or biography; a biographical novelist must select and shape his material to give it dramatic structure and theme. In *The Agony and the Ecstasy*, Stone eliminates historical characters, alters them, adds fictional ones, and has them reappear so as to give unity, focus, and theme to his novel. Given the massive amount of material that was at his disposal, Stone's novel is a significant achievement.

Bibliography

Clements, Robert J. "The Artist as Hero." *Saturday Review* 64 (March 18, 1961): 18. Clements finds that Stone's Michelangelo is "an idealized version, purged not only of ambisexuality, but of the egotism, faultfinding, harsh irony, and ill temper that we know were characteristic of Michelangelo."

Current Biography 50 (October, 1989): 59. An obituary of Stone, including details of his life and career.

Golant, Susan K. "The Agony, the Ecstasy, and Irving Stone." *Writer's Digest* 61 (March, 1981): 26-29. A profile of Stone and commentary on his writings.

Stieg, Lewis, comp. *Irving Stone: A Bibliography.* Los Angeles: Friends of the Libraries, University of Southern California, 1973. A listing of Stone's novels, biographies, and other writings.

Stone, Irving. "The Biographical Novel." *The Writer* 75 (January, 1962): 9-13. Stone discusses his approaches to fictionalized biographies.

Thomas L. Erskine

ALBURQUERQUE

Author: Rudolfo A. Anaya (1937-   )
Type of plot: Magical Realism
Time of plot: 1992
Locale: Albuquerque, New Mexico
First published: 1992

> *Principal characters:*
> ABRÁN GONZÁLEZ, a twenty-one-year-old former Golden Gloves
> boxing champion who is now a first-year student at the University of
> New Mexico
> BEN CHÁVEZ, a writer and teacher of writing at the University of New
> Mexico
> FRANK DOMINIC, a wealthy attorney who is running for mayor and who
> has plans to turn Albuquerque into a city of canals and casinos
> MARISA MARTÍNEZ, the beautiful and honest mayor of Albuquerque,
> who opposes Dominic's plan
> LUCINDA CÓRDOVA, a nurse at the hospital where Abrán's mother dies
> JOSE CALABASA, a Santo Domingo Indian and Vietnam veteran who is
> Abrán's friend
> WALTER JOHNSON, a wealthy developer and candidate for mayor

The Novel

Alburquerque is Anaya's exploration of the ethnically and culturally diverse world of New Mexico in the 1990's. The book focuses on the conflict between the heritage of the past and the challenges to it posed by economic growth unscrupulously promoted by developers and politicians. In its structure, the novel parallels a young man's search for the identity of his father to the city's search for a sense of community amid divisive political and ethnic tensions. Anaya's spelling of the city's name in the title reflects the city's history; according to legend, a gringo stationmaster dropped the first "r" from the town's name "in a move," Anaya says, "that symbolized the emasculation of the Mexican way of life."

Near death from cancer, Cynthia Johnson, a highly respected New Mexico painter, sends for Abrán González, a former Golden Gloves boxing champion who is now a college student, telling him that he is the son she gave up for adoption twenty-one years ago. Intensely proud of his Mexicanness and of the culture of the Barelas barrio where he was reared by his adoptive parents, Abrán is shocked to learn that he has an Anglo mother and naturally wants to know who his father is. By the time he arrives at the hospital, however, Cynthia is too weak to speak, and she dies without revealing the identity of her lover, a secret she confided to no one, not even her parents. Abrán turns for help and companionship to Lucinda Córdova, a nurse who had been close to Cynthia during her final days and to whom he is deeply attracted. Together, they begin a search for the identity of Abrán's father.

This quest takes Abrán first to one of Cynthia's high school classmates, Frank Dominic, who is now a wealthy lawyer running for mayor on a platform of legalized gambling and commercial development. Dominic promises to use his resources to find Abrán's father, but only if Abrán agrees to return to the ring for a fight to be held as a part of an elaborate celebration Dominic has scheduled to kick off his campaign.

Drawn into the orbit of power, Abrán succumbs—but only once—to the charms of the present mayor, Marisa Martínez, a beautiful and highly capable woman whose election was in large part the result of Cynthia's support. Unaware of Abrán's intimacy with Marisa, Lucinda takes him to northern New Mexico to meet her parents in the small village where they live. Dominic, furious when he learns that Abrán has broken training, arranges for Lucinda to be told about Abrán's infidelity, causing Lucinda to break off their relationship.

Additional complication results from Dominic's attempts to convince the Indian pueblos to sell their water rights to supply enough water for the canals envisioned in his urban development plan. Abrán's friend Jose Calabasa has returned to his pueblo to try to dissuade the council from selling out, but he is unsuccessful. Discouraged and depressed, he awakens after a two-day binge to learn that it is the day of Abrán's fight. Having promised to be there, Jose rushes back to Albuquerque. After a series of wildly comic adventures, he learns that a lawyer from Santa Fe has been trying to get in touch with Abrán about one of Cynthia's paintings, which may depict Abrán's father. Jose remembers having seen the painting at the house of Ben Chávez, a writer and teacher at the university who was another of Cynthia's high school classmates. Rushing there, Jose confronts Ben, who admits to being Abrán's father. Hoping to reveal Ben's secret to Abrán and make it unnecessary for him to go through with the fight, Jose rushes to the convention center where the fight is being held. Lucinda, having talked with Marisa and forgiven Abrán, is also rushing to the convention center. She arrives to find that Jose has been badly beaten trying to get to Abrán. As he is being taken to a waiting ambulance, Jose manages to tell Lucinda that Ben Chávez is Abrán's father.

Yet the match has already started, and Abrán is taking a bad beating. It is not until the end of the ninth round that Lucinda is able to make her way to ringside, where she is joined by Ben, and together they tell Abrán the truth. Still, he decides to continue the fight although he no longer needs Dominic's help. Inspired by the discovery of his father's identity and the return of Lucinda, Abrán makes an incredible comeback, knocking out his opponent in the tenth round and giving the people of Albuquerque the hero they need. Dominic's plans to change the city collapse, and both Abrán and the city have found who they really are.

The Characters

Abrán has always been an outsider in the Mexican community in which he was reared. Because his skin was lighter, he was teased and harassed by his classmates. He began fighting, first on the playground and later in the ring, to prove that he was as good a Mexican as any of the other boys in the barrio. When he discovers that his mother is an Anglo, his sense of identity is shaken, and he is driven to find his father. Uncomfortable in the world of power, wealth, and glamour, Abrán instinctively recognizes his proper place in the mountains of northern New Mexico. He is drawn to their "pure light" and their traditional Mexican culture, and it is here that he and Lucinda plan to settle down, rear a family, and open a much-needed health clinic.

Ben Chávez, the writer and teacher, is a partly autobiographical version of the author and is the most fully realized of the novel's characters. While still in high school, Chávez was injured in a street fight and thus was hospitalized when Cynthia Johnson gave birth to his son. More comfortable with his fictional characters than with Abrán, the son he has fathered, Ben is working on a novel, which he feels compelled to write, about his love for Cynthia. He is an observer rather than a man of action, and it is largely through his consciousness that the reader understands and evaluates the other characters.

Frank Dominic, the son of a hardworking shoemaker of indefinite ethnic background, is one of the two thoroughly unsympathetic characters and the focus of the novel's pointed and often personal political satire. He is interested only in gaining power and in self-aggrandizement. An expert on image-building, Dominic has tried to link himself with the old Spanish blood in New Mexico; he married a woman who is supposed to be distantly related to the original duke of Albuquerque, and he affects a phony good-old-boy style that Ben finds offensive despite the fact that they have known each other since childhood. A person whose only loyalty is to himself, Dominic uses people ruthlessly and even bets against his own fighter, Abrán, in the big fight he has arranged. At the end of the novel, however, his empire crumbles; despite his extensive knowledge of the history of Albuquerque, he has no feel for its people or their heritage. His attempt to change the city into something it is not grows out of his own need for power and recognition, not out of the spirit and character of the people.

Walter Johnson is the other unsympathetic character. He first came to Albuquerque nearly dead from tuberculosis but was nursed back to health by Vera, whom he eventually marries. As he gains wealth and power, though, her Jewish background turns out to be a detriment to his acceptance by Albuquerque society. He buys a Spanish genealogy for Vera and gains entrance to the country-club circle to which he aspires, but he lacks an heir. Vera, in desperation, has an affair with her gynecologist, never revealing to Walter that Cynthia is not his daughter. When Cynthia becomes pregnant and Walter learns that her lover is a Mexican, he insists that she put the child up for adoption and that neither she nor Vera ever have any contact with it.

Lucinda Córdova is selfless and committed to the plain, simple, honest values of her upbringing in the remote and isolated villages of northern New Mexico. She nursed Cynthia in her last illness and feels an immediate bond with Abrán. After an idyllic week with Abrán at her parents' home in the north, she feels totally committed to him, and when she learns of Abrán's infidelity, she is shocked and profoundly hurt. Nevertheless, she overcomes her hurt and takes her place at his side when he needs her at the fight.

Marisa Martínez, the mayor of Albuquerque, is talented, beautiful, tough, and an excellent mayor. She is divorced and content to live alone; however, her powerful sexuality is roused by Abrán's physicality and youth. She refuses to pull out of the campaign when Dominic arranges for the publication of nude photographs, taken by a detective that Dominic hired, of Marisa and Abrán together.

Themes and Meanings

The novel is a complex weaving together of themes and meanings and even of literary styles. On one level, it is the love story of Abrán and Lucinda. Related closely to this theme is the conflict between urbanization, with its ethnic diversity and impetus toward continual expansion and flux, and pastoralism, which leads Abrán and Lucinda to see their future in terms of a return to the mountains, to the simplicity and cultural purity of village life, and to the spirituality that is engendered through a closer contact with nature than the city allows.

The novel also presents a critique of New Mexico politics and politicians, and many of its characters are drawn from real life. It presents an especially harsh indictment of Anglo bigotry and of unscrupulous and materialistic politicians. Contrasted with the politicians are the artists, primarily Ben and Cynthia, whose function it is to interpret the people to themselves, to show them who they are and thus to give them the sense of identity and cultural heritage of which the politicians constantly threaten to rob them. It is in this light that Anaya's use of Magical Realism can best be understood. He introduces la Llorona, the wailing woman of Mexican folklore, the trickster figure of Coyote from Indian mythology, two "fictional" characters—Juan and Al—from Ben's poem, and a figment of Ben's imagination, doña Loneliness, who suddenly becomes a flesh-and-blood whore dressed in red. These fantastic characters function side-by-side with the "real" characters to emphasize Anaya's view that the artist's creation is as much a reality as is the so-called reality it imitates. In the struggle to create the future, the artist is more important and much more to be trusted than the politician.

The man of the future that the artist has created—Cynthia as mother, Ben as father, and Anaya as author—is Abrán. He is to be the father of the people; as Anaya says, "Abrán, born of the Mexican father and the gringa mother, was the new Chicano, and he could create his own image, drawing the two worlds together, not letting them tear him apart." The future belongs not to the urban developers but to the people of mixed blood who can find a common ground for community within the diversity of ethnic heritages that threatens to tear it apart. Albuquerque, Anaya implies, is not merely a city in New Mexico; it is a microcosm of the United States—more, it is a microcosm of the planet.

Critical Context

Alburquerque brings Anaya's history of his people and of New Mexico up to the present. The history begins with the first and most famous novel, *Bless Me, Ultima* (1972), and continues in *Heart of Aztlán* (1976) and *Tortuga* (1979), between which and *Alburquerque* there is a lapse of some twenty years. It contains the elements for which Anaya has become best known—the celebration of the Mexican heritage of the Southwest, including its folklore and its deep commitment to family, to the land, and to the sense of mystery beyond the reach of science to explain. As does *Heart of Aztlán*, *Alburquerque* makes use of Old Testament typology; Clemente Chávez, the protagonist of *Heart of Aztlán*, leads the workers in a strike against the railroad, much as Moses led his people out of bondage, and Abrán, his grandson, is the Abraham who will be the founder of a new nation of chosen people, people of mixed blood.

The literary influence most apparent in this novel is that of the school of Magical Realism, an influence that places Anaya in the company of many distinguished Latin American writers. Perhaps equally important is the influence of a number of New Mexico writers who have anticipated various themes developed in *Alburquerque*. Leslie Silko, in her well-known novel *Ceremony* (1977), developed the theme of the person of mixed blood as the progenitor of a race better suited to the needs of the future than people of "pure" blood. Silko's sense that it is the storytellers who will find the answers to the problems of humankind, who will create out of the materials of the past stories to defeat the powers of the destroyers who threaten the future, represents a somewhat mystical faith in the power of art similar to that developed by Anaya in *Alburquerque*. The influence of Frank Waters can be seen in Anaya's depiction of life in the Mexican villages of the north and in his sensitivity to the spiritual as well as the physical beauties of the land. The influence of N. Scott Momaday is apparent in Anaya's treatment of the rituals and ceremonies of Indian and Mexican life as well as in the theme of the creative power of the word, a theme that is central to the story and structure of *Alburquerque*.

In this novel, Anaya takes his place in the forefront not only of Latino writers but also of all those writers who celebrate the beauty of the people and the land of the American Southwest.

Bibliography

Anaya, Rudolfo. Interview by R. S. Sharma. *Prairie Schooner* 68 (Winter, 1994): 177-187. The interview focuses on the meaning of Chicano writing and literature. Anaya specifies which cultural tradition he prefers readers associate him with, and comments on Chicanismo as a bilingual culture and the Chicano literary movement as a cultural trend. Provides useful background for any study of Anaya's work.

Augenbraum, Harold. Review of *Alburquerque*, by Rudolfo A. Anaya. *Library Journal* 117 (July, 1992): 119. Calls the novel "an archetypal quest for the father" and says that though "at times melodramatic, the work has an intense spirituality that ultimately makes it mesmerizing."

Cazemajou, Jean. "Mediators and Mediation in Rudolfo Anaya's Trilogy: *Bless Me, Ultima, Heart of Aztlán*, and *Tortuga*." In *European Perspectives on Hispanic Literature of the United States*, edited by Genvieve Fabre. Houston: Arte Público Press, 1988. This important article provides background for an understanding of the place of *Alburquerque* in the context of Anaya's earlier novels. Cazemajou sees "myth, not militancy," as Anaya's major literary tool and argues that Anaya's romanticism enables him to avoid the "pitfalls of naturalism that await most minority writers."

Clark, William. *Rudolfo Anaya: The Chicano Worldview. Publishers Weekly* 242 (June 5, 1995): 41-42. In this revealing interview, Anaya discusses his personal background, career history, and the books and novels he has written, including *Alburquerque*. Explores the groundbreaking novel Anaya has provided to a whole generation of Latino writers.

Jussawalla, Feroza. Review of *Alburquerque*, by Rudolfo Anaya. *World Literature Today* 68 (Winter, 1994): 125. Jussawalla presents a brief plot synopsis of Anaya's novel and compares it with Anaya's previous work, *Bless Me, Ultima*. Although Jessawalla believes that *Alburquerque* does not "measure up to *Ultima's* greatness," he nevertheless finds the story compelling and touching.

Publishers Weekly. Review of *Alburquerque*, by Rudolfo A. Anaya. 239 (May 25, 1992): 36-37. Sees the novel as an "explosive study of political patronage and the search for ethnic roots," a "touching love story woven into a tale of treachery," and a penetrating analysis of "the social and economic dislocations squeezing the American Southwest."

Dennis Hoilman

ALIAS GRACE

Author: Margaret Atwood (1939-   )
Type of plot: Historical
Time of plot: 1843-1873
Locale: Kingston, Ontario, Canada
First published: 1996

> *Principal characters:*
>> GRACE MARKS, a domestic servant, imprisoned for more than thirty
>> years for murder
>> SIMON JORDAN, the doctor who takes on Grace's case and resolves to
>> determine her innocence or guilt
>> THOMAS KINNEAR, a gentleman and murder victim, Grace's employer
>> NANCY MONTGOMERY, the housekeeper in the Kinnear household, a
>> murder victim
>> JAMES MCDERMOTT, the primary murderer of Kinnear and
>> Montgomery
>> JEREMIAH THE PEDDLER, alias DR. DUPONT, a jack-of-all-trades who
>> befriends Grace
>> JAMIE WALSH, a young neighbor to the Kinnear household

The Novel

    Alias Grace is a fictionalization of a historical character, Grace Marks, a notorious figure of the 1840's who was imprisoned for twenty-eight years for her part in the murder of Thomas Kinnear, her wealthy employer, and Nancy Montgomery, his mistress and housekeeper. Atwood re-creates those events and the years of Grace's incarceration. The novel itself takes place during the months that Dr. Simon Jordan spends in Kingston with Grace as his patient. An American doctor interested in the mind and desirous of opening his own lunatic asylum, he is fascinated with Grace's case and moves to Kingston to study her. Atwood uses Grace's fictional relationship with Dr. Jordan as a vehicle for retelling the story. Scenes from Grace's life during her time in prison, particularly her meetings with Dr. Jordan, frame the story of her previous life. The novel has two narrators: Grace, who tells her own story to Dr. Jordan, and a third-person narrator who gives the reader the account of Simon Jordan's life in Kingston. Grace's past unravels slowly throughout the novel. One of nine children, Grace was born in Ireland and traveled with her family to Canada in the hope of a future for her ne'er-do-well father. Her mother died during the journey. Grace was the eldest of the six children to go to Canada, and her father expected her to find work to help support the family. She did find work as a domestic, but she never returned home. As she moved around to improve her employment, she met Nancy Montgomery and ended up at Richmond Hill, the estate of Thomas Kinnear; however, she worked for Kinnear for little more than a fortnight.

Several unsettling factors made her uncomfortable at the Kinnear home. One was the presence of the hired man James McDermott, an ominous man and unsatisfactory worker whom Nancy Montgomery gave notice shortly after Grace's arrival. McDermott, vengeful, bragged to Grace that Mr. Kinnear and Nancy deserved to be "knocked on the head and thrown down into the cellar." The second factor was Grace's growing awareness that Nancy was not only Mr. Kinnear's housekeeper but his mistress as well. Grace's best friend during her previous employment, fellow maidservant Mary Whitney, had been impregnated by a son of her employers and had died from a botched abortion. Grace's reaction to Nancy Montgomery's affair was not merely a moral one; it reminded her of Mary's fate as well. Grace was also bothered by the attentions of Mr. Kinnear. He made her uncomfortable, as did Nancy as she jealously noticed his interest in Grace. Grace thus joined with McDermott when he murdered Kinnear and Montgomery. Grace's exact role in the murders is never clear to the reader. After the murders, Grace and McDermott fled across the border to the United States. They were caught quickly and returned to Kingston for trial. McDermott was hanged; Grace, considered insane, was given a life sentence.

Because she is a model prisoner, Grace is allowed to work at the governor's mansion. Here Simon visits her, questions her, and records her story. The reader watches him struggle with his own emotions as he deals with the women in his life. His real affection focuses on the one woman not available to him: Grace. When, in his misplaced ardor, he finds himself in the middle of an affair with his landlady, he flees Kingston and returns to the United States.

Grace has come to rely on Simon, as his visits provide the high point of her weeks. She is greatly saddened when he leaves, and she continues to correspond with him, never knowing if he receives her letters.

Mary Whitney once told Grace that she would marry a man whose name begins with a *J*. When Grace's pardon finally comes through twenty-eight years after her sentence, she discovers that she is to be transported to the United States to the home of a man who has arranged for her care. It is indeed a man whose name begins with a *J*: not, of course, the hanged James McDermott, not Simon Jordan, not even Jeremiah the peddler, whose life has intersected with hers through the years, but Jamie Walsh, the young man once infatuated with Grace whose testimony, provoked by jealousy, probably cinched her guilty verdict. They marry, and at the end of the novel, Grace finds herself over forty but pregnant with their child.

The Characters

Grace Marks tells her own story in Atwood's novel. She becomes a sympathetic character, even though the reader is never sure exactly what happened on the day of the Kinnear/Montgomery murders. Grace tells her tale directly to the reader and to Simon Jordan in their sessions. Grace appears as an unlucky victim of fate: born into a poor family with a worthless alcoholic father, rendered motherless at an early age, innocent friend of the ill-fated Mary Whitney, new sixteen-year-old employee at the wrong time at the Kinnear household, and prisoner who is a woman and therefore an enigma. Her demeanor in prison, with Dr. Jordan, and with the governor's wife and her guests shows a gentle, upright woman who accepts her fate without anger. She is both strong and proud. Yet Atwood never lets readers know what Grace's real part was in the murders of Kinnear and Montgomery. Was she innocent, or was she crafty? Was she affected by bouts of insanity? It is the elusiveness of her tale that keeps the reader guessing and complicates the personality of Grace.

Simon Jordan comes to Kingston a dedicated professional with only a clinical interest in the case at hand. Simon's narrative revolves around the four women in his life: his hypochondriac widowed mother, whose letters constantly beg him to come home; his lonely and impoverished landlady, Rachel Humphrey, who desires and finally gets his attentions; Miss Lydia, the governor's daughter, who also desires Simon's attentions; and Grace Marks. A conservative New Englander by upbringing, Simon surprises himself as he reacts to these women, all of whom find him the center of their lives. Jordan is an interesting study as he tries to balance his clinical interest in Grace with his emotional feelings toward her and the other women.

The other characters in the novel (Thomas Kinnear, Nancy Montgomery, and James McDermott) serve to further the action and to provoke thought and action on the part of the main characters. For example, Mary Whitney's positive effect on Grace dampens Grace's enthusiasm for Nancy Montgomery, because Grace hopes to find in Nancy another best friend. Landlady Rachel Humphrey successfully seduces Simon Jordan because his emotional guard has already been weakened by his growing feelings for Grace. Jeremiah the peddler appears at various times in various guises as he takes up mesmerism and other "professions," and his appearances seem to give Grace some hope for her own future. The surprise is Jamie Walsh, who, after making only fleeting appearances in Grace's story as a young boy with a crush on her, ends up rescuing and marrying her in the end.

Themes and Meanings

In an afterword to *Alias Grace*, Atwood notes that "the combination of sex, violence and the deplorable insubordination of the lower classes" present in the murder case gave journalists at the time of the Kinnear/Montgomery murder a heyday. She comments that the varied responses to the case and to Grace "reflected contemporary ambiguity about the nature of women." In the novel, Atwood gives readers all sides of that ambiguity. She starts her chapters with newspaper reports, letters, poems, the confessions of McDermott and Grace, and the recollections of Susanna Moodie, who recorded the story in her journal. Atwood lets readers know what others think of Grace with this "evidence" and through the events that make up the novel. Through the accounts of the murder, the trial, and the attempts to have Grace pardoned, the reader is shown how uncertain is the recording of history. What is true? Atwood says that the truth is that Mr. Kinnear and Nancy Montgomery were killed. Beyond that, no one knows. Atwood makes certain that Grace never clarifies her role in the murders.

However, the strongest voice in the novel is that of Grace herself, and it is her telling of the story that makes her a sympathetic and believable character. Yet Grace's narrative does not solve the puzzle of "Who is Grace Marks?" Instead, she appears to readers in a new ambiguity. She is not the woman whom others expect her to be, nor is she some simplification of the sex who can be easily explained. She is, like all humans, complex and unpredictable.

Grace is a woman without power, imprisoned, as it were, in all phases of her life, from her impoverished childhood to her servitude for her various employers and their demands upon her to her actual years in jail. She is dependent always on the men who surround her: her father, Mr. Kinnear, James McDermott, Simon Jordan, and even, in the end, Jamie Walsh. Yet the reader feels another kind of power in Grace; it is the power of her will, her ability to stand proud despite her situation. The narrative frees her from a stereotype and allows her to emerge whole and individual.

Each section of the book is introduced by an illustration of a quilt pattern. The image of the quilt—an undertaking demanding patience, an artifact exemplifying order—befits the life of Grace, an accomplished quilter herself, as she stitches the events of her own existence into an intricate whole.

Critical Context

Alias Grace is Atwood's ninth novel; she has also written volumes of short fiction and poetry. She is one of Canada's most prolific and respected writers. Atwood's works generally show her compelling interest in what it means to be a woman, especially a woman victimized by a society governed by men's rules and men's psyches. For example, her novel *The Handmaid's Tale* (1986) imagines a future society in which the few remaining fertile young women become the receptacles through which the ruling class of the society hopes to regenerate itself; the poem "Half-Hanged Mary" (1996) looks at the Salem witch trials through the eyes of a presumed witch whose hanging is unsuccessful. The theme is stitched through all of Atwood's work. This novel, like her other works, examines questions of power— between classes, between the sexes, between individuals.

The novel also asks the questions "What is history?" and "What is truth?" Long interested in the Grace Marks case, Atwood examined the original publicity that surrounded the murders and the trial and found it biased, theatrical, and often incorrect. *Alias Grace* questions the possibility of finding an absolute historical truth. Literary critic Terry Eagleton has postulated that, rather than being related to history, literature is another reading of it. *Alias Grace* is another interpretation of the events of 1843 and the years that followed. It is an interpretation that reflects contemporary issues of gender and power as it deconstructs some of the assumptions of the early chroniclers of the trial.

Bibliography

Atwood, Margaret. *In Search of "Alias Grace": On Writing Canadian Historical Fiction*. Ottawa: University of Ottawa Press, 1997. The transcript of a lecture given at the University of Ottawa on the researching of the Grace Marks case and the writing of the novel.

_____. *The Journals of Susanna Moodie.* New York: Oxford University Press, 1973. Atwood takes the journals of Susanna Moodie, a historical chronicler of the Grace Marks trial, and incorporates them into an epic poem.

Cooke, Nathalie. *Margaret Atwood: A Biography.* Toronto: ECW Press, 1998. A biography of Atwood, with substantial discussion of her work.

Moodie, Susanna. *Life in the Clearing Versus the Bush.* New York: DeWitt and Davenport, 1854. Moodie, an English emigrant, tells about her new life in Canada, including her reactions to the Grace Marks case.

Janine Rider

ALICE ADAMS

Author: Booth Tarkington (1869-1946)
Type of plot: Bildungsroman
Time of plot: The post-World War I era
Locale: Indiana
First published: 1921

>   *Principal characters:*
>   ALICE ADAMS, a young woman in search of a beau and an identity
>   VIRGIL ADAMS, the father, an older man in ill health
>   WALTER ADAMS, the brother with a penchant for gambling
>   MRS. ADAMS, Virgil's nagging wife, a social climber
>   MR. ARTHUR RUSSELL, a wealthy young man in search of a fiancé

The Novel

Alice Adams, the eponymous heroine of Booth Tarkington's novel, is a character very like other heroes and heroines in literature who test the American myth of success expressed best by the Horatio Alger stories. Like Alger's "Ragged Dick," Alice Adams strives to lift herself into another social realm from the one in which she was born. Yet in her desire for a marriage that would satisfy her need for a specifically economic and material freedom, she perhaps reminds readers most of F. Scott Fitzgerald's Jay Gatsby, who seeks to marry Daisy as a final acquisition marking his success in the world.

As Tarkington's novel begins, Alice's family occupies a tenuous position in the mid-level manufacturing class of post-World War I Indiana. Their position affords them a modicum of respect, but they have slowly but surely felt the pinch of declining fortune. They manage to keep a cook, for example, but they can only afford to hire the surly specimens no other, more respectable families will employ.

Intent on improving the family fortunes, Mrs. Adams browbeats her husband Virgil into leaving his position with "Lamb, & Company," where he is respected for his work ethic, honesty, and loyalty. She insists he leave the "old hole," as she calls it, to start his own manufacturing company. Virgil's ethical dilemma revolves around his knowledge of a secret glue formula, the rights to which are owned by Mr. Lamb. Because Lamb has done nothing with the formula for years, Virgil allows himself to be convinced by his wife to steal it, quit his position, and open his own glue factory.

Virgil's ethical dilemma and subsequent fall parallel his daughter's attempt to lift herself socially, also through unethical means. Alice's head is filled with romance, and she begins lying in a futile attempt to deny the grim reality of the family's declining stature. In this pursuit, she is encouraged by her mother, whose mending of old dresses so they will appear to be new is a benign example of how Alice begins by shading the truth and ends by lying outright. Tarkington masterfully illustrates the process whereby economic emulation gradually becomes pernicious dishonesty. In a famous scene, Alice meets Arthur Russell and tries to impress him by lying that she has been to the tobacconist to procure cigars for her father, who never, she assures him, smokes a pipe; this petty lie grows into a larger claim that her father occupies an almost aristocratic position of wealth and power. The lies grow as Alice and Arthur fall in love, but the lies are ultimately unable to sustain the fiction of an upper-class life she has created.

Three strands of the narrative come together when Mr. Alfred comes to dinner at the Adams home. The behavior of Alice's family clearly demarcates their social class, undercutting all the things she has said about them to her beau. Moreover, her brother Walter's embezzlement from the Lamb Company comes to light, even as the glue factory established by Virgil fails. When Arthur leaves the house, Alice knows that she will never see him again.

If the novel is a satire of class preoccupation in a supposedly "classless" country, it is also a *Bildungsroman*, or novel of growth, that charts the development of Alice's character from a romantic girl into a realistic woman. Readers see in the various scenes a growing awareness of her position, and likewise the growth of a keen understanding of the unwritten rules governing society. Her lying functions as a critique of a materialist society that judges by perceptions of character, and it also indicates her awareness of how to manipulate society, although temporarily. In the end, however, she realizes that the romantic stories she fabricated were themselves lies, and that in order to survive in post-World War I America, she must have a realistic understanding of her class and position; in short, she must go to work. The novel ends with Alice approaching Frincke's Business College, a place she had always avoided. Tarkington ends his novel with qualified optimism, and as Alice solemnly climbs the stairs, sunshine streams through an upper window, a symbolic endorsement of her more realistic attitude.

The Characters

Although the book's focus is on the title character, the other major characters in *Alice Adams* are also developed and rounded. As individual as his main characters are, Tarkington uses them all to develop his ideas about the dishonesty of a social system based upon appearances and material wealth. Through his main characters, Tarkington includes all social classes, from the lowest to the highest.

At first, Alice Adams strikes the reader as merely an appealing young woman whose main concerns are the related issues of the social life of her peers and the finding of a suitable, financially sound beau. Quickly, however, Tarkington introduces the idea that will govern his novel: the search for identity. After lying to Arthur, Alice stares at herself in her mirror and asks the question, "Who in the world are you?" The book becomes the story of her quest for identity in a society in which identity is largely a construct and extension of material wealth.

Alice's father, Virgil Adams, enjoys a naturally ethical character. His loyalty to his employer is absolute until Mrs. Adams finally breaks down his objections under the force of larger obligations to his family and its fortune. Virgil works in the "old hole," and his name suggests Dante Alighieri's Virgil, who serves as a guide to hell. The allusion refers both to the family's inexorable downward slide and to Virgil's failure or sin in ethics and judgment. Only after his fall do the family members—and the readers—realize that Virgil had been correct in his early belief that Mr. Lamb had valued him as an employee; in fact, near the end of the novel, Mr. Lamb reveals that he had retained Virgil as an employee solely because of the latter's loyalty. This revelation renders Virgil's subsequent disloyalty to Mr. Lamb all the more tragic.

Walter Adams, Alice's brother, is the black sheep of the family. Given to gambling, often with money not his own, he mortifies Alice with his low-class associations. In particular, his familiarity with African Americans in a racist society causes Alice pain; rightly or wrongly, Alice knows that the family will be judged as an entirety, not individually. It is largely through Walter's character that Tarkington extends his satire of American society to include the issue of race. Race, in the novel's society, functions as wealth does to define one's class identity.

Tarkington's depiction of Mrs. Adams is complex. On one hand, she is an unsympathetic character. She is the true cause of Virgil's downfall and is likewise the ultimate source for the character traits that cause Walter to embezzle and Alice to lie. She nags and browbeats her husband into accepting her view of American society: Material wealth is the final source of social standing and individual identity. At the same time, Tarkington depicts her negative traits as the laudable, positive extension of motherly concern for her children. Readers are ultimately conflicted in their response to Mrs. Adams. While the logic of Tarkington's novel suggests that Mrs. Adams is correct that "money's at the bottom of it all," that idea, so promoted by her, is adopted by each member of the family, to their lasting detriment.

Arthur Russell is a wealthy young man who is intrigued by Alice's character, and he might have married her in spite of her family's lower standing. Nevertheless, the chasm between the two families is so great, and so obvious at the dinner party in Alice's home, that he recoils from the entire family, including Alice. Arthur is embarrassed for her, and though he tries to tell her that he will see her again, it is apparent that even he realizes that the revelation of her lying and of her family's true station in life will put an end to their relationship.

Themes and Meanings

Alice Adams is Tarkington at his most brilliant. Selecting the coming-of-age of an adolescent girl as his ostensible subject, Tarkington establishes the novel's main theme as the much larger issue of America's coming-of-age in the years after "The Great War," World War I. The central themes are all developed around Alice's search for her own identity in a culture that seeks to impose identity based on class and economic position.

The scene in which Alice stares into the mirror and wonders who she is introduces her personal quest for identity, and it also highlights the larger issue of how society defines identity by material wealth. Alice's struggle to define herself using the material terms provided by society is expressed by her pathetic attempts to create the facade of a wealthy heiress. She cannot afford to purchase a corsage for the dance, for example, so she spends an entire afternoon picking wild violets. As might be expected, the flowers wilt, and Alice discards them. Natural worth is similarly discarded by society, Tarkington seems to say, and the symbolism surrounding the flowers illustrates Alice's inability to create her own identity separate and apart from the basic rule of measurement employed by society: money.

Alice's conflict with her brother Walter over his gambling and friends moves into a larger discussion of democracy. She responds to her brother's defense of himself based on the idea of living in a democracy by asserting, "Not quite that democratic, is it, Walter?" Indeed, Alice's awareness of the irony of her own social climbing in a democratic country is one of her most appealing traits, and yet she remains persistent in her attempts to lift herself up to a higher class position. Tarkington stresses throughout *Alice Adams* the undemocratic reality of life in an America where material wealth is the fundamental determinant of social worth. The metaphor of lying is an implicit criticism of both Alice, who lies to create her own identity, and of a culture that lives according to the democratic lie of a classless society.

Tarkington also includes some pointed jabs at romanticism as both an aesthetic movement and as a philosophical outlook. Alice has believed the romantic fictions she has been told, and she tells a few more of her own to Arthur. Only at the end does she give up her romantic illusions and become realistic in her outlook. As she approaches Frincke's Business College, Alice recalls "a French romance" she had once read and begins to grow sentimental over her own "destiny." Then, as if shaking off the idea, she mounts the stairs, turning her back on the romantic fictions that had led her astray.

Critical Context

Booth Tarkington lived to see his work hailed as brilliant and then discarded as second-rate. The apex of his career occurred in the years after the end of World War I; in 1918, he was awarded the Pulitzer Prize for his novel *The Magnificent Ambersons*. He won the honor again in 1921 for *Alice Adams*. The publication of *Alice Adams* thus marked the height of Tarkington's prestige and popularity. Indeed, the novel in some sense resuscitated a waning career, though Tarkington would never again attain either the critical or the popular success of *Alice Adams*.

Tarkington is viewed today as a minor writer of realistic fiction, as a lesser Sinclair Lewis, to whom he is often compared. If Tarkington's writing was occasionally held in overly high esteem during his lifetime—there were critics who ranked him above F. Scott Fitzgerald and Ernest Hemingway—his reputation today is artificially low. Unlike his contemporaries Fitzgerald, Hemingway, and William Faulkner, Tarkington plowed no new ground and employed no new formal literary devices. However, his achievement has often been overlooked; he perfected the forms established by the early realists William Dean Howells and Henry James, and the gemlike structure of his novels, in which all aspects of plot and characterization work together toward a common end, often appears simple on the surface. Yet like gems held to the light,

Tarkington's novels repay close study, where they flash brilliantly the larger themes he conveys through character, in the perfect blend of ethics and aesthetics.

Bibliography

Fennimore, Keith J. *Booth Tarkington*. New York: Twayne, 1974. An excellent introduction to the author's life and work.

Mayberry, Susanah. *My Amiable Uncle: Recollections About Booth Tarkington*. West Lafayette, Indiana: Purdue University Press, 1983. An important contribution to Tarkington's biography.

Sorkin, Adam J. "'She Doesn't Last, Apparently': A Reconsideration of Booth Tarkington's *Alice Adams*." *American Literature* 46 (1974): 182-199. A sympathetic and reasoned analysis of *Alice Adams*. Sorkin argues for greater critical attention to Tarkington generally and to *Alice Adams* in particular.

Woodress, James. *Booth Tarkington, Gentleman from Indiana*. Philadelphia: J. B. Lippincott, 1955. An important biography, this volume offers some analysis of the novels.

Joe B. Fulton

ALL GREEN SHALL PERISH

Author: Eduardo Mallea (1903-1983)
Type of plot: Existential psychodrama
Time of plot: The 1930's and early 1940's, prior to the rise to power of Juan Perón
Locale: Ingeniero White, Bahía Blanca, and Nicanor Cruz's *estancia* (ranch) on the southern pampa near Bahía Blanca, Argentina
First published: Todo verdor perecerá, 1941 (English translation, 1966)

> *Principal characters:*
> ÁGATA CRUZ, the protagonist, an intense and withdrawn young woman who is in search of herself
> NICANOR CRUZ, her husband, an *estanciero* (rancher)
> DOCTOR REBA, Ágata's father, a Swiss immigrant who settled in Ingeniero White
> SOTERO, a lawyer and Ágata's lover in Bahía Blanca after Nicanor's death
> EMA DE VOLPE, a self-styled courtesan and Ágata's companion in Bahía Blanca

The Novel

All Green Shall Perish is divided into two parts. Each depicts a crucial period in the life of Ágata Cruz, and virtually all the action of the novel takes place within Ágata's anguished consciousness. The theme and tone are established in the somber description of the desolate landscape of Nicanor Cruz's *estancia* at the beginning of part 1. The drought suffered by the barren land is mirrored in the barren relationship of Nicanor and Ágata Cruz, who remain childless after fifteen years of marriage and estranged from each other by their inability to communicate and by an ever growing sense of isolation and resentment. Nicanor has lost his battle with the sterile land, although he stubbornly refuses to admit the defeat which has transformed him into a withdrawn and bitter man. Ágata, more sensitive and intelligent than her husband, asks more from life than he does and would have liked to help him during the early years, but Nicanor's pride would not allow him to accept her help. Ágata is suffering from depression and resents being condemned to live out a life that she would never have chosen.

From this vantage point in time, Ágata reexperiences her past life in a series of flashbacks: first, the lonely childhood with her alienated father in the small port of Ingeniero White; then, her precipitous decision to marry Nicanor Cruz, a limited and taciturn man whom she did not love but who provided her with an escape from the stifling atmosphere of her childhood and the dreary prospect of life with her widower father, whom she loved but with whom she had never been able to communicate; finally, a series of grim and ever worsening incidents from her fifteen years with Nicanor. The cumulative effect of this introspection only deepens Ágata's depression.

In his unrelenting struggle with the land, Nicanor contracts pneumonia. While nursing him, Ágata reaches a crisis of desperation. Hoping to destroy herself and end her unhappiness, Ágata opens all the windows to let in the cold. Nicanor dies, but Ágata is found unconscious on the porch at the end of part 1.

The second part of the novel begins in the southern metropolis of Bahía Blanca, where Ágata has moved following the sale of the *estancia*. Through the intervention of Ema de Volpe, a predatory and superficial woman who insists on taking Ágata under her wing, Ágata meets the lawyer Sotero. Ágata passively allows Sotero to seduce her, and, to her own surprise, she enjoys a brief period of happiness with this charming but shallow opportunist. Sotero, however, is incapable of committing himself to anyone for long, and he coldly abandons Ágata, leaving her with a note as he departs for Buenos Aires on business. His desertion confirms Ágata's worst fears, as she is again thrown back upon herself. After her happiness with Sotero, Ágata finds solitude even more difficult to bear, and she gradually withdraws still further into her own consciousness, caring nothing for those around her or for her surroundings. In her desperate obsession to understand what is happening to her, she is drawn irresistibly back to the Ingeniero White of her childhood. Having lost all sense of time, wandering the streets of Ingeniero White like a madwoman, she is attacked by a gang of vicious children, who taunt and chase her. At the end of the novel, Ágata has lost all contact with reality except for the increasing intensity of her suffering. Her plight is poignantly captured in the last sentence of the novel: "It was very late when she got up suddenly, as if called by a scream, and, without direction or discernment, started running against the darkness."

The Characters

Mallea excels in portraying "closed" characters who are at war with themselves or somehow imprisoned within the confines of their own consciousness. The inner drama of Ágata Cruz is revealed and symbolized in her name (which translates literally as "agate cross"). What is cold and hard in Ágata is in conflict with her passion and her need for sacrifice. Ágata's passivity, her limited emotional development, her narrowness of perspective, and, above all, her awkwardness and shyness, are at war with the intensity of her need to live life to the utmost and to make life meaningful. The grim circumstances of her life and the predisposition of her own nature doom her to defeat, but Mallea succeeds in making the reader identify with Ágata's struggle and empathize with her. In spite of the melodramatic contrast between Ágata's "extraordinary beauty" and her withdrawn and pessimistic character, Mallea succeeds in making Ágata a believable heroine.

Ágata is described in terms of death, recalling the parched landscape of the beginning: "While in bed, her slender body at rest, her face white against a bedspread a thousand years old, her eyes devoid of inner scenery, her limp fingers relaxed over the material they rested on, everything in her suggested a corpse, with the exception of that knot which from the depth of her being still insisted on having hidden rights." In a conversation with Sotero, Ágata inadvertently reveals her inner awareness of futility:

"I thought the world was an enormous flight of birds and that I had only to stretch out my hand to stop the one I wanted. Then one sees that the bird is oneself, and that the world is the hand that claims one." Finally, according to Ágata, "each being is not like the water or the wind, subject to the influences and change. Each being is a single unmodified tendency. Each being is its tendency." Thus, Ágata, as do characters in other Mallea novels, condemns herself with the bias of her own perspective.

While the author's concentration on Ágata does not leave much room for the development of the other figures of the novel, these characters are clearly and believably drawn. The best realized is the taciturn but authentic Nicanor (the name means "without song") Cruz, whose stubbornness and brutish stoicism invest him with a perverse integrity. The brazen and manipulative mediocrity of Ema de Volpe is convincing, as is the blatant inauthenticity and duplicity of Sotero and the rat-like slyness of his sinister friend Romo. Doctor Reba, Ágata's pathetic father, is at best a shadowy figure, and Estaurófilo the imbecile was conceived as a symbol for the thwarted expression inherent in the human condition.

Themes and Meanings

Theme, language, tone, and mood are the controlling elements of *All Green Shall Perish*. Mallea is essentially a lyric writer, a poet, who conceives the human, novelistic material of all his works in musical terms that he controls thematically, like an essayist. In structure, the novel's division into two parts allows for greater intensity and control in each. Indeed, the two halves can be read as interrelated novellas; the only link is the tortured self-awareness of Ágata, which informs the whole. She is the sole survivor of part 1. In part 2, Ágata is given what amounts to a chance for a new life in Bahía Blanca with a new cast of characters. Unfortunately, Ágata remains the same. She cannot forget her past, which colors her present and foreshadows her future.

In *All Green Shall Perish*, character cannot be separated from theme. This is ritual narration in which the central character is offered as a sacrifice to the universe. The near consummation of part 1 is fulfilled in part 2. The rite is complete.

In *La vida blanca* (1960; the sterile life), Mallea describes what he calls the "inner war": "A sweet immanent charity illumines the lives of men; all the rest is uncertainty, pettiness and betrayal." This sentence beautifully synthesizes the theme, tone, and message of *All Green Shall Perish*. In spite of the somber conclusion, never in doubt, what draws and holds the reader's attention is the defenseless lyric affirmation of the human condition that is sensed throughout Mallea's requiem for Ágata Cruz.

Another theme, secondary in *All Green Shall Perish* but central to Mallea, is the search for authenticity in a specifically Argentine context. In *Historia de una pasión argentina* (1937; history of an Argentine passion) and other essays which probe the Argentine national character, Mallea advocates a spiritually authentic Argentina as opposed to a shadowy and successful materialism. In this context, it is clear that Ágata and, to a lesser extent, Nicanor, represent aspects of the "invisible Argentina" as opposed to the inauthentic "visible Argentina" of Sotero, Romo, and Ema de Volpe.

Yet it is in universal terms that *All Green Shall Perish* is best understood. The capacity to struggle against one's fate and to suffer is equated with authenticity and emerges as the supreme human value of Mallea's fiction.

Critical Context

All Green Shall Perish has been Mallea's most popular single work of fiction, as well as the novel that received the greatest critical acclaim. It was written at the peak of Mallea's creative powers along with the autobiographical essay *Historia de una pasión argentina* and the novels *Fiesta en noviembre* (1938; *Fiesta in November*, 1942) and *La bahía de silencio* (1940; *The Bay of Silence*, 1944).

Mallea was an extremely prolific writer who continued to publish novels, short stories, essays, and plays up to his death. He enjoyed his greatest popularity during the 1930's, 1940's, and 1950's, anticipating the "Boom" of the Latin American novel in the 1960's and 1970's. Mallea did not share the preoccupation with technical innovation of such novelists as Julio Cortázar, Carlos Fuentes, and Mario Vargas Llosa, although several of his works are innovative and experimental, most notably *La ciudad junto al río inmóvil* (1936; the city on the motionless river), *Fiesta in November*, and *All Green Shall Perish*. The themes of Mallea's fiction did not change significantly in the course of his career, and, in general, his work has fallen from fashion since the 1950's. Nevertheless, the titles cited in this article continue to enjoy a wide readership and are the subject of many critical studies.

Bibliography

Chapman, Arnold. "Terms of Spiritual Isolation in Eduardo Mallea." *Modern Language Forum* 37 (1952): 21-27. An insightful study of Mallea's use of metaphor.

Dudgeon, Patrick. *Eduardo Mallea: A Personal Study of His Work*. Buenos Aires: Agonia, 1949. Brief but useful for its discussions of *Fiesta in November* and *The Bay of Silence*.

Lewald, H. Ernest. *Eduardo Mallea*. Boston: Twayne, 1977. A sound introduction covering Mallea's formative period, his handling of passion, his cosmopolitan spirit, his national cycle, and his last fictional works. Includes chronology, notes, and annotated bibliography.

Lichtblau, Myron I., trans. Introduction to *History of an Argentine Passion*, by Eduardo Mallea. Pittsburgh, Pa.: Latin American Literary Review Press, 1983. This introduction to the first English translation of a Mallea essay provides an excellent overview of his place in Spanish American fiction. Lichtblau includes an excellent bibliography.

Polt, John H. *The Writings of Eduardo Mallea*. Berkeley: University of California Press, 1959. Polt discusses Mallea's essays and fiction through the mid-1950's. A thorough study.

Shaw, Donald L. Introduction to *Todo verdor perecerá*. Oxford, England: Pergamon Press, 1968. Cited as an outstanding interpretation.

_____. "Narrative Technique in Mallea's *La bahía de silencio*." *Symposium* 20 (1966): 50-55. One of the few studies of this kind in English.

Stabb, Martin S. *In Quest of Identity: Patterns in the Spanish American Essay of Ideas, 1890-1960*. Chapel Hill: University of North Carolina Press, 1967. Although Stabb devotes a section mainly to Mallea's essays, his comments provide helpful background for the fiction as well.

John B. Hughes

ALL THE LITTLE LIVE THINGS

Author: Wallace Stegner (1909-1993)
Type of plot: Social realism
Time of plot: The early 1960's
Locale: The San Francisco Bay Area
First published: 1967

> *Principal characters:*
> JOE ALLSTON, a retired literary agent
> MARIAN CATLIN, a neighbor, pregnant and afflicted with cancer
> JIM PECK, a beatnik
> TOM WELD, a real-estate developer
> JULIE LoPRESTI, a young girl, pregnant by one of Jim Peck's followers

The Novel

All the Little Live Things consists of seven chapters, a prologue, and an epilogue. Set in the Bay Area of California, the novel plays out some of the generational conflicts of the 1960's as a group of strong characters settle in wild, hilly country near San Francisco much like Los Altos Hills, where Wallace Stegner's family lived for many years.

Joe Allston, a retired literary agent, and his wife Ruth have built a retirement home, where they hope to live quietly, mourning the recent death of their son, who drowned in the Southern California surf, perhaps deliberately. The 1960's, as depicted in this novel, was not a good time to seek peace and quiet in this part of California. Into the neighborhood come first Jim Peck and then Marian Catlin, characters who in different ways challenge Joe Allston's convictions. Jim Peck squats on a corner of the Allstons' property and establishes a sort of commune.

Marian Catlin and her husband have come to find a sheltered place for Marian and their daughter to live while John conducts research in the North Pacific. As the Allstons soon learn, Marian is pregnant and suffering from breast cancer. Meanwhile, Tom Weld, the owner of most of the undeveloped property around the Allstons' place, is busy bulldozing the hills to build more homes.

Allston finds himself at the center of bitter quarrels with Weld and Peck about the fate of this piece of land, which he frequently compares to the Garden of Eden, and in amiable disagreement about the nature of good and evil and of life and death with Marian, who is fighting her own hopeless battle against cancer. Although he succeeds in driving Jim Peck and his followers away, he is not able to stop the relentless development of the open land around him.

The argument with Marian is inconclusive. She is an extraordinarily beautiful young woman, in love with "all the little live things." When she first meets the Allstons, Joe is firing his shotgun into a gopher hole. She fiercely criticizes Joe's violence against nature, insisting that gophers have the same right to live that she and Joe do. She misses seeing Joe in his most appalling, if accidental, act of violence against nature: when he spears a magnificent king snake with a pitchfork, man and snake in pursuit of the same gopher.

Marian's devotion to the idea that life is sacred and not to be interfered with by humankind finds its most ironic expression in her battle with cancer. She is pregnant with what could be her second child and refuses medication either to halt the cancer or to control her pain. The Allstons do everything they can to help her cope, but they find themselves pulled into a series of events as painful as the death of their son.

Marian's death provides a terrible climax to the plot of *All the Little Live Things*. When she goes into labor, Joe and Ruth Allston set out to drive her to the hospital, where she hopes her baby's life can be saved even though her own cannot. On the way, they are involved in a nightmarish accident caused in part by Joe's haste, in part by the sudden reappearance of Jim Peck and some of his followers, in part by Tom Weld's failure to keep the bridge in good repair. The last sight Marian sees is the death of Julie LoPresti's horse, clubbed to death by her husband to put it out of its pain after it breaks its leg on the damaged bridge. Julie is pregnant by someone in the commune; ironically, her baby will live and Marian's will not.

The Characters

Wallace Stegner's characters are well drawn and convincing, even though many of them represent typical attitudes of the 1960's and do not develop much in the course of the novel. The reader is invited into the mind of only one character, Joe Allston himself.

As narrator and protagonist of *All the Little Live Things*, Allston is a complex, well-rounded character who does indeed grow through the events of the novel. Although Stegner obviously wants the reader to sympathize with him, Allston is by no means perfect. Age and experience have given him considerable knowledge, a strong sense of honor and responsibility, and a sharp wit. On the other hand, he is impatient and often makes situations worse by his impulsiveness. Stegner's technique in developing this first-person narrator allows the reader to see both what Allston thinks and what he says or does, and thus to note the frequent ironic mismatch between his intentions and their consequences. While he would like to make the world safer and more orderly, he often does just the opposite. Allston's principal antagonist is Marian Catlin, in spite of their affection for each other. In some respects, she seems too good to be true, based as she is on Stegner's mother and on several friends of the Stegners who had died of breast cancer. Marian's affection for all kinds of life and her acceptance of death move Joe to both sympathy and anger. She is closely associated with the title of the novel and helps to establish the generation gap as a major theme of the novel.

Other characters dramatize the conflict between the generations that characterized so many aspects of American life in the 1960's. Joe's son has recently died, perhaps a suicide, certainly a failure in Joe's eyes. Now in his sixties and in retirement, Allston is again challenged by young people: Marian with her uncritical acceptance of things as they are; Jim Peck with his dropout's disrespect for established values; Tom Ward, who sees nothing to respect in the past, not even the shape of the landscape; and Julie LoPresti, pregnant in large part because she knows her condition will upset her mother.

Two characters, neither of them quite at the center of things, possess a more balanced view and the ability to mediate between the extremes the other characters represent. Joe's wife Ruth and Marian's husband John suffer greatly, but both are ready to go on with life after Marian's tragic death. They possess the kind of wisdom Joe gains only at the end.

Themes and Meanings

All the Little Live Things treats in fictional terms the growing tension between adult and adolescent in the 1960's. Joe Allston finds himself embroiled in a number of issues, but the reader gradually realizes that more is at stake than whether Julie LoPresti should have an abortion or what will happen to the landscape around the Allston place. The central thematic controversy goes on between Joe, the narrator, and Marian Catlin, whose losing battle with breast cancer provides the strongest plot strand in the novel.

The title points the reader toward this central theme. Joe is at war with many of the "little live things" that share his garden with him. Marian, on the other hand, values all of life; her husband has even stopped fishing to avoid giving pain to the worms he once used for bait. The conflict between Joe and Marian centers on very basic questions of life and death, made more poignant by the cancer cells, "little live things" themselves, that are killing Marian even as she struggles to live long enough to deliver her second child safely, without resorting to chemotherapy or pain medication.

On another front, Joe is embroiled with the hippie guru Jim Peck. Peck claims to be a free spirit; Joe sees him as a dangerous demagogue. Peck reminds him too much of his son; again he finds his disagreement with the young person a matter of life and death.

The struggle with Tom Weld over questions of land use also turns out to involve much weightier matters. Tom tears up the landscape, fails to keep a vital bridge in repair, and lets his dog and horses trample his neighbors' gardens and wipe out their poultry. His conduct endangers the lives, not merely the lifestyles, of others.

Joe Allston thinks in grand mythical and literary terms. He compares his estate to the Garden of Eden, and he notes how many evil forces seem to surround his little paradise, never quite coming to grips with the fact that he is as dangerous to the king snake as the serpent was to Adam. In another extended literary allusion, he sees Jim Peck as Caliban, the licentious savage of William Shakespeare's *The Tempest* (1611). In both stories, the order Joe Allston, as Adam or Prospero, tries to uphold is threatened by agents of chaos and evil. All these conflicts are brought to horrific climax in the crash scene at the end of the novel. Death is real and terrible; Joe seems quite right to refuse to love it or forgive it. The wisdom that he achieves in the epilogue is something quite different: He believes his life will be enhanced by the sorrow he feels at Marian's death.

Critical Context

All the Little Live Things was written fairly late in Wallace Stegner's distinguished career as novelist, historian, environmentalist, and teacher. The book reflects his concerns about cultural trends in the 1960's, especially what he saw as a growing rootlessness and irresponsibility in young people, including, apparently, his own students at Stanford University. He saw in the young a callous indifference to the pain of others; Marian Catlin's struggle with breast cancer connects her with Stegner's own mother and the lasting pain he felt about her death.

The novel also marks a stage in Stegner's development as an environmental writer. In essays, short stories, and historical works such as *Beyond the Hundredth Meridian* (1954), as well as in many of his novels, Stegner describes the uneasy relationship Americans, especially Westerners, have with their natural surroundings. Joe Allston is a fascinating case in point, wanting the dramatic views from his hilltop home preserved but willing to destroy any wild creature who interferes with his efforts to grow tomatoes where they never grew before.

This first-person narrative is technically brilliant; the way in which the highly literate Joe Allston relates contemporary issues to the classics—to the Old Testament, *The Tempest*, and John Milton's *Paradise Lost* (1667)—as well as to modern poetry such as Robert Frost's lets readers into the mind and personality of an extraordinarily attractive, if sometimes disturbing, consciousness. Through his eyes, and mind, natural objects attain symbolic weight without losing their realistic character; pages could be written about the redtail hawk that appears regularly over Joe Allston's retirement home or about the king snake under his brick walk. To see Allston from within is to glimpse the psychological factors that make preservation so problematic.

The issues *All the Little Live Things* raises remain significant; and this beautifully designed book is clearly the work of a major American writer, not merely a Western regionalist.

Bibliography

Arthur, Anthony, ed. *Critical Essays on Wallace Stegner.* Boston: G. K. Hall, 1982. Two of the essays, those by Barnett Singer and Lois Phillips Hudson, treat aspects of *All the Little Live Things*.

Benson, Jackson J. *Wallace Stegner: His Life and Work*. New York: Viking, 1996. A fine biography; chapters 16 and 17 treat the connection between this novel and events in Stegner's life.

Hepworth, James R. "Wallace Stegner's Practice of the Wild." In *Wallace Stegner and the Continental Vision*, edited by Curt Meine. Washington: The Island Press, 1997. Hepworth studies environmental concerns in several novels, including this one.

Robinson, Forrest G., and Margaret G. Robinson. *Wallace Stegner.* Twayne United States Authors Series. Boston: G. K. Hall, 1977. An excellent survey of Stegner's work through the mid-1970's. Chapter 5 treats this novel in some detail.

William T. Hamilton

ALMANAC OF THE DEAD

Author: Leslie Marmon Silko (1948-   )
Type of plot: Psychological realism
Time of plot: The 1990's
Locale: Tucson, Arizona
First published: 1991

>   *Principal characters:*
>   SEESE, a young white woman whose child is lost, "nurse" to Lecha
>   STERLING, a Laguna Pueblo Indian banished from his reservation
>   LECHA, a Yaqui Indian psychic who transcribes ancient notebooks
>   CALABAZAS, an Indian cocaine smuggler
>   BEAUFREY, a white cocaine smuggler
>   MAX BLUE, the head of an Italian American crime family
>   MENARDO, a Mexican mestizo who becomes wealthy dealing drugs and
>   weapons
>   CLINTON, a homeless African American Vietnam veteran
>   ROY, a homeless Vietnam veteran, chief organizer of the Army of the
>   Homeless
>   THE TWIN BROTHERS, TACHO and EL FEO, Indian brothers of prophecy

The Novel

The narrative of Leslie Marmon Silko's *Almanac of the Dead* centers on Tucson, Arizona, and the intertwining lives and events of its numerous people, among whom are "speculators, confidence men, embezzlers, lawyers, judges, police and other criminals, as well as addicts and pushers." Hauntingly, Silko's novel depicts a society of almost utter depravity, identifies as the source of this state the atrocities committed against Native Americans, and finally predicts the coming end of this cruel reign with the rise of indigenous peoples and the endurance of the sacred Earth.

Almanac of the Dead begins with a prophecy contained in the ancient tribal texts of the Americas: "Ancient prophecies foretold the arrival of Europeans in the Americas. The ancient prophecies also foretell the disappearance of all things European." Silko's story echoes that of the prophecy, depicting the downfall of the "criminals" in her novel and the commencement of indigenous people's struggle to regain stolen land. The novel consists of six sections, each divided into books and further divided into short vignettes that adopt more than thirty characters' points of view. Silko uses this structure to approximate oral tradition, thus making *Almanac of the Dead* a calendar of movement through the motion of people, events, and spirits that make up the book's present, past, and future society.

Tucson, the location to which all the characters have some tie as well as the place where the majority of the action takes place, is established as a city of witchery, presently and historically. It is peopled with whites and "breeds" whose ancestors profited from the U.S.-Apache wars and with Indians who deny their heritage. The majority of the characters, of European, Mexican, and Native American descent, participate in illegal activities: smuggling of guns, alcohol, and drugs; murdering for hire or for individual profit; and manufacturing and distributing "pornographic" films of fetus dissections, torture, and fake autopsies. The cocaine-dealing profession is not limited to the white Beaufrey and the Italian American Blue crime family but also extends to Indian descendants such as Zeta, Ferro, and Calabazas. Additionally, varying degrees of scandalous enterprises are perpetrated by the corrupt government officials, including Judge Arne, the Police Chief, and the Senator.

Mexico, as well, is mired in witchery; it is, according to history, the place of the old-world Indians who became obsessed with the power of sacrifice and bloodshed. In the beginning of the novel, cocaine smuggled across the border to the United States finances the criminals in both countries and weakens subjugated people. Indians are "disappeared," as are suspected communists. The rich white supremacist Beaufrey and his lover plan the creation of underground survival stations for when the "savages" overpopulate and dirty the aristocratic bloodlines of the world.

Silko suggests that the origins of this depravity are the horrors committed against indigenous peoples and the subsequent loss of tribal thinking; she reveals these horrors through the telling of suppressed history. The relatively recent history of Tucson during the Apache wars, when citizens profited from the deaths of their own relatives, and the long-past history of the coming of the Europeans to the Americas, when Montezuma and Hernán Cortés (kindred sorcerers who "worshiped destruction and blood" and "secretly knew one another") began the undoing of all people, are told to characters by their grandmothers and through an ancient manuscript. Suppressed history is also presented in a speech by La Escapía, the Indian wife of El Feo the Mountain Twin. Additionally, Clinton plans radio shows that will aid the rise of the people by educating them about their history and their spirits; the text of his shows describes the kinship of African spirits and Native American spirits, thus also uniting African Americans and Native Americans. The manuscript and the oral stories continually help the reader to decipher the novel as a whole.

The heyday of the current injustices is already passing, however, and the criminals begin to be destroyed. Prophetically, the wicked bring about their own destruction by the hands of their servants. The sacred Twins begin their pilgrimage north from Mexico to the U.S. border, leading hundreds of thousands of people to reclaim the land. The Giant Stone Snake proves to be a message from the spirits pointing south toward Mexico, both the original source of witchery and the source for prophecy fulfillment. The Army of the Homeless is established; a barefoot Hopi begins to organize the incarcerated across the United States; Wilson Weasel Tail preaches the need to retake the land; and Awa Gee plans to plant a virus in the computers of power stations all over the country just as the people revolt. The novel ends with Tucson in chaos but with nearby cities unaware of the turmoil.

The Characters

The sheer multitude of characters serves to emphasize the novel's focus on the interplay between characters and events. The short sections of the novel move from character to character. Sometimes the point of view changes even within the short sections. Nearly all these characters are developed fully, and they make up a wide array of bizarre, sometimes perverse individuals. The characters are clustered, and each cluster is eventually tied to other clusters of characters; this movement unravels the narrative in the novel, emphasizing each event's and person's interplay in the novel's nonstop motion.

Though no character dominates the novel, Sterling emerges as its conscience. Sterling, appearing near the beginning and at the end of the book, is unique among the characters in that he enters Tucson by accident, wandering into town with no real purpose, and then leaves it behind, taking only the awareness he has gained. His eventual gain of understanding for the endurance of the Earth and the importance of tribal spirits is the very heart of the novel. At the beginning, Sterling is immersed in the white system, and his self-delusion is rooted in his European thinking, symbolized by his obsession with crime magazines. Sterling's fascination with the white image of "Geronimo" (his favorite "criminal") illustrates his inability to understand reality in a tribal sense. Silko educates the reader about Geronimo's "true" existence, as Sterling should have been educated, through the oral stories of an Indian matriarch. The crime magazines and other trappings of white culture are abandoned once Sterling returns to his culture and begins to think in a more tribal-centered manner. Sterling leaves the corrupt world of the novel behind and returns to the Stone Snake and to his reservation. Once home, he recalls the old-time ways he was taught as a child, realizes the sacredness of the Earth, and knows that the Twin Brothers and the people will come from the south.

Seese's fate is precarious but hopeful. Her addiction to cocaine and her connection to that world of depravity are directly responsible for the loss of her child, Monte. While she searches for Monte, she begins to wean herself from her addiction; she lapses back into drug use, but her experiences while using again prove so horrifying that she apparently commits to permanent cessation. Through her dreams, she eventually realizes that Monte is dead and lost to her forever. Seese continues to survive and, at the close of the novel, remains with Lecha, who has completed the transcription of the ancient manuscript and who predicts that the unrest of the people will be followed by natural disasters and civil war. Seese's future and her beliefs regarding the prophecy are unknown, as she does nothing but cry during the final pages. Yet Silko has Lecha and Sterling rescue Seese from the crumbling Tucson, promising at least a potential future.

Silko creates the character of Lecha with many characteristics of Coyote, a Native American mythic character who is half creator, half fool and renowned for greediness and trickery. Her desertion of Ferro, her son, and her playfulness with the corrupt world—even while she translates the manuscript and believes in her grandmother Yeome's teachings—display luck, creativity, and craftiness, those attributes of Coyote that maintain vitality even in the midst of desolation. Yeome has given Lecha a gift of psychic power, which she has used to gain wealth; like many old families of Tucson, she profits from others' misfortunes, for she soon realizes that she has psychic powers only to discover the dead. Nevertheless, Lecha is the keeper of the ancient manuscript, the calendar that will predict the coming catastrophes. She holds the key to the prophecy, to the future.

Themes and Meanings

Vital to *Almanac of the Dead* is the acceptance of what Native American writer Paula Gunn Allen terms "ceremonial time," a sense of reality that transcends linear time and embraces the fluidity of past, present, and future. Silko's structural technique, which gracefully connects people and events while shifting from perspective to perspective, establishes the imperative of reading in this mindframe. The lack of an easily definable plot and protagonist is disconcerting until the accretion is recognized; then characters and occurrences become more fully understood as the multiple stories begin to unite, forming a whole instead of related parts. The reader, like Sterling, is guided toward understanding through accretion and a vision of synthesis. Only when viewed as interlocking and interrelated do the fragmented, jumbled accounts reveal a comprehensible message.

Silko insists that her narratives of the characters' lives become united, and she similarly merges specific times and places into a boundless reality. Time becomes fluid as events of the past illuminate the future, present illuminates past, and so on. Her literal movement from place to place, character to character, and time to time elucidates the novel's theme of reality as movement; she demands that characters not be conceptualized as isolated individuals and demands that time not be deciphered linearly. Only witchery enforces the notion of distinct beings in a particular place and time. Rather, the unifying elements of the novel—and, Silko suggests, of reality itself—are the connection to ritual and ceremony and the endurance of the Earth.

Almanac of the Dead shows the Feminine Power, a principal central to Silko's own Keres Pueblo, rising from forgotten history to reassert its rightful role in Native American cosmology. The passing down of the almanac itself has been matrilineal; the ancient manuscript is passed to Yeome and from her to her granddaughters. Yeome and Old Mahawala, another matriarch in the novel, both ensure the education of their children to the old ways through their written and oral tales. Once Sterling returns to his reservation and begins to compile the knowledge he has gleaned from multiple sources, he finally begins to remember these old tales from his grandmother, tales he had long ago forgotten. He knows that, regardless, the Earth will continue, for "she" will always be sacred; people only "desecrated themselves," for humanity is "too insignificant to desecrate her." The taking back of the Native Lands is itself a reclaiming of the feminine; when indigenous peoples identify themselves with the Mother Earth, they become the land, endure, and continue.

Critical Context

Like N. Scott Momaday and James Welch, two highly successful contemporary Native American writers, Silko writes within the Native American oral tradition— appropriately so, since her main agenda is the reaffirmation of tribal ways and tribal reality. She has been hailed as one of the most important writers of her time, and *Almanac of the Dead* is, to say the least, a massive undertaking. The novel, nearly eight hundred pages in length, is nothing short of Silko's personally constructed view of the apocalypse. As in her previous work, especially her novel *Ceremony* (1977), she maintains the imperative need for a return to spirituality and to traditional beliefs. *Almanac of the Dead*, however, is rampant with graphic violence and can be a disturbing, even agonizing, reading experience; Silko, no doubt, purposefully intensifies the witchery in her novel with this vivid manner of depiction in order to indelibly print the harsh realities into the minds of her readers. The novel, despite its weaknesses, is amazingly successful, inescapably haunting.

Bibliography

Allen, Paula Gunn. "Leslie Marmon Silko and Gerald Vizenor: Healing and Ritual." In *The Sacred Hoop: Recovering the Feminine in American Indian Traditions.* Boston: Beacon Press, 1986. Allen discusses the central themes of environmental integrity and pacifism in Silko's novel *Ceremony.* Comparison of *Ceremony* and *Almanac of the Dead* is interesting, especially in light of Allen's points. The book contains invaluable information on Native American culture and literature.

Birkerts, Sven. "Apocalypse Now: *Almanac of the Dead* by Leslie Silko." *The New Republic* 205 (November 4, 1991): 39-41. Birkerts describes Silko's process of stage development in the first two-thirds of the novel and sketches outlines of the events and characters. Birkerts finds fault with the last third of the novel, reasoning that Silko unwinds too quickly what she has spent such effort in originally spinning.

Evans, Charlene Taylor. "Mother-Daughter Relationships as Epistemological Structures: Leslie Marmon Silko's *Almanac of the Dead* and 'Storyteller.' " In *Women of Color: Mother-Daughter Relationships in Twentieth Century Literature.* Austin: University of Texas Press, 1996. Evans explores the effect of broken relationships between mothers and daughters on the transmission of cultural and spiritual knowledge.

Jones, Malcolm, Jr. "*Almanac of the Dead.*" *Newsweek* 118 (November 18, 1991): 84. Jones finds *Almanac of the Dead* powerful but also maddening. He claims that the novel is Silko's unfair vision of payback, peopled with "good characters and white characters." Brief and entertaining, though not very informative.

St. Clair, Janet. "Death of Love/Love of Death: Leslie Marmon Silko's *Almanac of the Dead.*" *MELUS* 21 (Summer, 1996): 141-146. St. Clair focuses on the interaction between the sexes in Silko's novel, revealing the detrimental effect that "misogynistic, arrogantly hierarchical, and egocentric traditions of Western liberal individualism" has had on Indian culture, as well as American society as a whole.

Tallent, Elizabeth. "Storytelling with a Vengeance." *The New York Times* 141 (December 22, 1991): 6. Tallent praises Silko's skill as a storyteller and offers an excellent overview of the themes of *Almanac of the Dead*, including the cruelty inherent in contemporary American culture, the unavoidable ecological catastrophe that is a result of European domination, and the dangers that the "formidable id" pose to the common good.

Tiffany Elizabeth Thraves

ALNILAM

Author: James Dickey (1923-1997)
Type of plot: Philosophical realism
Time of plot: January, 1943
Locale: Peckover and adjoining Latham Field, North Carolina
First published: 1987

> *Principal characters:*
>> FRANK CAHILL, a crusty, emotionally shallow Atlanta amusement park owner
>> JOEL CAHILL, Frank's recently disappeared and presumed-dead son
>> BOYD MCCLENDON, a Peckover hotel owner who befriends Cahill while he is staying there
>> COLONEL VERNON HOCCLEVE, the military commander of Latham Air Field, where Joel trained
>> MCCLINTOCK MCCAIG, a Latham flight instructor, Joel's friend
>> STATHIS HARBELIS, a Latham aviator cadet, Joel's friend
>> MAJOR BRUNO IANNONE, a medical doctor at Latham
>> HANNAH PELHAM, a Peckover girl who loved Joel

The Novel

Inspired, perhaps, by his own World War II flying experiences for the Army Air Corps, James Dickey's novel *Alnilam* is set in the fictional town of Peckover adjoining a military airfield near Fayetteville, North Carolina. The central character, Frank Cahill, officially notified of the accidental flying death of his son, Joel, whom he has never seen, journeys to the airbase to meet the officers and aviation cadets.

Alnilam is not divided into chapters or major parts. All the events center around Frank Cahill, recently blind from diabetes, and his quest to find out about his son and the manner of his death. Lengthy passages of the novel are set in parallel columns reflecting darkness and light, the bold left type reflecting Cahill's internal sensations and thoughts, and the right side the objective narrative of speech and events.

Alnilam opens with an interesting account of Cahill's attempt to find his way out of a boardinghouse in the middle of a winter night to relieve himself. He is accompanied by Zack, his faithful, untrained dog. This hallucinatory opening is followed by flashbacks of Cahill's life, fleshing out some biographical details and clarifying his present situation. He is the owner of Willow Plunge Amusement Park in Atlanta. Nineteen years ago, his pregnant wife, Florence, left him forever. He has never once seen or contacted his son, Joel. Cahill's blindness, the result of the sudden onset of adult diabetes, occurred less than four months ago.

The novel's events occur within a week in January, 1943. Cahill has just received a military telegram inviting him to the airbase where his son was training. The military cadets are graduating, and they want Cahill to attend the ceremonies. On a selfish whim, he decides to go and arrives with Zack in Peckover, which adjoins the base. He is enthusiastically welcomed by Colonel Vernon Hoccleve, the military commanding officer, who allows him to meet with officers, friends, and fellow cadets—anyone, in short, who knew Joel. Cahill questions all of them about his son. Cahill also meets Hannah Pelham, Joel's wild girlfriend. She reveals Joel to be somewhat sadistic. Hannah seduces a somewhat surprised Cahill.

Soon a contradictory picture of Joel emerges from the various exchanges. Joel, it turns out, was a charismatic, although secretive and mystical individual. He founded a strange cult among his fellow students named "Alnilam," which is Arabic for "string of pearls." The name comes from the middle star in the belt of the constellation Orion. Joel believed that man and flying machine were extensions of one another, and he inculcated this belief through cryptic statements that his followers have elevated to the status of gospel.

Cahill's investigative mystery deepens when he discovers that cadet-pilot Joel's plane came down because of a downdraft while he was swooping over a brush fire. He was pulled out of his plane by a farmer and taken to a farmhouse. While the farmer fought the blaze, Joel escaped back into the fire. He then made his way to a river and disappeared forever. The investigating officials were sure his body would show up soon.

Cahill does not share their confidence; neither do the Alnilam cadets, nor McClintock McCaig, Joel's flight trainer and friend. McCaig manages to get Cahill into an airplane and takes him for a flight so he can better understand Joel's love of flying. Through it all, Cahill expresses curiosity but no grief. He is neither excited nor repelled by his observations and discoveries.

Cahill's presence begins to have a negative effect at the base. Zack bites one of the cadets and attacks and kills a pack of dogs. Colonel Hoccleve orders Cahill to leave the base and not attend the ceremonies. The Alnilam group persuades Cahill to remain. They reveal to him Joel's secret philosophy and the son's prediction of his own disappearance and the appearance of his father. The cadets, allied with others at various bases, are planning a special surprise at graduation. Cahill enters the base secretly and wanders onto the airfield when chaos breaks loose. The cadets have initiated an insurrection by destroying airplanes, leading to the death of an older pilot and Zack's decapitation. The novel ends with Cahill returning home and asking Hannah to come live with him. She refuses. Cahill boards his bus, realizing he has come to terms with himself.

The Characters

Frank Cahill is a newly blind, self-sufficient, irascible individual who has been a loner all of his life. Even his marriage, recounted in flashbacks, never brought him close to his wife. She left him while pregnant, and he never tried to contact her or his child until he received the military telegram. Dickey portrays a very unsympathetic character, a cursed, blind Oedipal figure searching not for a father but for a son. He finds some measure of salvation and meaning to life in his quest to understand Joel's life and death.

Zack, Cahill's constant companion, is a large, black, wolflike dog that everybody fears, and with good reason. Untrained and newly acquired because of Cahill's sudden blindness, Zack attains mythical proportions. Afraid of nothing, the canine attacks an air cadet, kills a marauding pack of wild dogs, and is finally stopped only by whirling propellers at the novel's end. Cahill carries the dog's head in his hands in a rousing conclusion to the bloody carnage at the Latham Field graduation ceremonies.

Joel Cahill, Frank's son, is never seen but is described by most all the other characters. Dickey portrays him as a Shelley-like figure, enigmatic, brilliant, and defiant. He is also cruel, and he creates and leads a dictatorial military unit. He dies (or mysteriously disappears) and remains to the reader a creepy, sadistic character.

Boyd McClendon is the garrulous, whiskey-drinking owner of a hotel/diner in Peckover who takes a liking to Cahill. He attempts to comfort and aid him during his week-long ordeal. His presence is crucial to the newly arrived blind hero unfamiliar with Peckover.

Hannah Pelham, who loved Joel, is the wild mountain maid working in the local mill. She sees the messianic cadet clearly, particularly his sadistic impulses. Through her, Cahill attempts to express his welling emotional breakthrough by novel's end.

At Latham Air Field, Cahill meets a number of individuals. Colonel Vernon Hoccleve, a military commander, is depicted as a straightforward, no-nonsense officer who runs a tight organization. Disliked by Joel and most of the cadets, he is sympathetic to Cahill and Zack, at first, but realizes later the twosome are a disturbing presence. Sensing trouble, he attempts to bar Cahill from the ceremonies, but he is too late to stop the tragic events.

Joel's flight instructor and friend McClintock McCaig is skeptical about the pilot's reported death and disappearance. Through his investigative efforts, he discovers physical evidence that Joel may still be alive. Stathis Harbelis is also Joel's friend and a member of the secretive Alnilam conspiracy. He comes across as naïve at first, but he is a committed true believer, dedicated to carrying out Joel's cryptic commands to the very end. Finally, there is Major Bruno Iannone, the skeptical medical officer who sees Joel clearly as a dangerous demagogue and a menace to his unit and the U.S. military.

Themes and Meanings

One of Dickey's major themes in *Alnilam* is sight versus blindness. The blind father often sees more clearly than the sighted characters. Dickey repeatedly emphasizes the unreliability of the senses. He contrasts the physical power of seeing and the luminous inner sight of understanding. His use of parallel texts between the dark and the light, although clumsy, underscores his point.

Dickey is also interested in father-son relationships. He is influenced by classical mythology, particularly Sophocles' blind hero Oedipus. Cahill, like his mythical counterpart, is intrigued by his family roots. It is Cahill who comes to an understanding of himself and discovers the truth about his son and, perhaps unknowingly, a part of himself. Both Oedipus and Cahill have to contend with hubris, the classical sin of pride. Cahill listens to no one, a trait the classical hero also shares. Yet unlike Oedipus, who searches for his father, the sightless Cahill searches for his Icarus-like son, who flew too close to the flames.

Dickey is also interested in the meaning and mystery of flight. He writes highly mystical passages about the air, perhaps drawing on his own experiences as a World War II fighter pilot. The best sequences in the book occur when he is describing the mystique of flying, as, for example, when the novelist has two airmen describe their flying experiences during the war and later when Cahill takes his first flight.

Dickey is also concerned thematically about power and its abuse. Joel, the poetry-spouting cadet, pulls people toward him in a conspiratorial circle. He is a mysterious, almost mystical figure, inspiring everyone around him. Joel says he is one with the airplane while in flight. Everyone agrees, including the flight instructors; he was born to fly. Joel is someone people not only remember but also trust. He becomes a messiah figure with believers who would follow him to the grave. Dickey points out that people such as Joel are potentially destructive.

The conflict of leadership and the revolt against rational authority constitute another theme. All the Alnilam cadets, under Joel's leadership, conspire mutiny within the military system. They plan to take it over one day and, in time, to take over America and eventually the world. Cahill's arrival galvanizes them into overt action, hence the need for him to witness the destruction planned for the graduation ceremonies. Their plotting and subsequent infamy, Dickey says, serve as a reminder of the cabals that launched Adolf Hitler, Vladimir Ilich Lenin, and Benito Mussolini.

Perhaps the book's weakest thematic development revolves around the whole concept of Alnilam and its ultimate meaning. Dickey is too vague and cryptic on the subject to engage the reader's attention. Often long-winded in other areas, he never comes to grips with the topic. Also, the demonstration of Alnilam's power is awkwardly contrived and melodramatically conceived, robbing the novel's denouement of its intended impact.

Critical Context

Alnilam was Dickey's first novel since the highly acclaimed *Deliverance* (1987). Unlike his first novel, which was a straightforward, macho tale of four innocent people forced to confront their killer instincts in the wild, *Alnilam* was poetic, intricate, laced heavily with symbolism and given to visionary idealism. It was also less dramatic and less accessible to the reader. Yet *Alnilam* and *Deliverance*, while different in stylistic approach, plots, and characters, are remarkably similar in philosophy. The heroes in both novels come to an enlightened understanding of themselves through their remarkable experiences and move away from their meaningless lives.

Dickey exhibits a consistency in his writings. Years earlier, he wrote a poem stating that a man would never see until he either went blind or, like the mythical hunter Orion, became a part of the stars and light. Dickey's major character in *Alnilam*, Cahill, fulfills that earlier poetic prophecy. Cahill, recently blind, achieves his own glorious transformation by searching for the truth about his son. In his struggle with himself and the strange world he is visiting, Cahill becomes like the warrior-hunter Orion, with his faithful companion Zack symbolizing the dog Sirius.

In his work, Dickey was always intoxicated with the power of language. In *Alnilam*, he uses that power to do for air what Melville achieved with water in *Moby Dick: Or, The Whale* (1851). For Dickey, air is more fundamental to human existence than water. He examines the kind of emotional state humans achieve when flying. His aim is to show how the human body reacts to leaving the ground. His passages on flying, the importance of flight, and aerial combat are easily the best parts of the book.

Dickey attempted to break new ground in fiction with *Alnilam* but was only partially successful. Critics complained that the novel was far too long, overblown, and pretentious and was marred by slow pacing. Although the book is ostensibly a mystery, it is shaped less by plot than by poetic impulses. At his best, however, Dickey creates vivid characters, especially Southerners, and is able to create a richly detailed picture of a region.

Bibliography
Dickey, James. *Self-Interviews*. Edited by Barbara Reiss and James Reiss. Garden City, N.Y.: Doubleday, 1970. The most interesting commentary on Dickey is that of the writer himself. A collection of transcribed tapes of Dickey talking about his life and poetry. Includes an informative piece of autobiography on Dickey's life before he became a full-time writer and straightforward analyses of poems that Dickey wrote in the 1950's and 1960's.

_____. *Sorties*. Garden City, N.Y.: Doubleday, 1971. Divided into two sections. The first is a daily journal Dickey wrote in the late 1960's, which contains an interesting mix of ruminations on everything from archery to the nature of love, as well as lengthy character and plot sketching from what was to be published as *Alnilam* sixteen years later. These entries provide a firsthand glimpse into the extensive planning and rearranging that occur in the creation of a novel. The second section contains essays on other poets, including Theodore Roethke.

_____. *The Voiced Connections of James Dickey*. Edited by Ronald Baughman. Columbia: University of South Carolina Press, 1989. Baughman has selected portions of interviews with Dickey from 1965 to 1987. The range of selections includes Dickey talking about his poetry, his writing process, his fascination with sextants and celestial navigation, the work of other poets, and lengthy discussion of *Deliverance* and *Alnilam*. The image of a fascinating writer emerges, one who speaks plainly about the most sublime things.

Kirschten, Robert, ed. *Critical Essays on James Dickey*. New York: G. K. Hall, 1994. See the introduction for an overview of Dickey's career. Kirschten includes four essays on Dickey's novels; no bibliography.

_____, ed. *"Struggling for Wings": The Art of James Dickey*. Columbia: University of South Carolina Press, 1997. The introduction surveys the critical response to Dickey. There are also two essays on *Deliverance* and an extensive bibliography.

Suarez, Ernest. *James Dickey and the Politics of Canon: Assessing the Savage Ideal.* Columbia: University of Missouri Press, 1993. Contains a detailed discussion of *Alnilam* and an extensive bibliography.

Terry Theodore

AN AMERICAN DREAM

Author: Norman Mailer (1923-   )
Type of plot: Symbolic and melodramatic romance
Time of plot: 1962
Locale: New York City
First published: 1965

> *Principal characters:*
>> STEPHEN RICHARD ROJACK, the narrator and protagonist, a war hero,
>> former congressman, professor of existential psychology, television
>> personality, and murderer
>> DEBORAH, his wife, a wealthy socialite whom Rojack sees both as a
>> bitch and a witch and whom he kills in the first chapter
>> BARNEY KELLY, Deborah's politically powerful millionaire father
>> RUTA, the Rojacks' German maid
>> CHERRY, a nightclub singer with whom Rojack has an affair
>> ROBERTS, a detective who investigates Deborah's murder
>> SHAGO MARTIN, a black man with sexual prowess who has been
>> Cherry's lover and who becomes a television replacement for Rojack

The Novel

The unrealistic nature of *An American Dream* is signaled in the novel's first sentence, in which Stephen Richard Rojack, who is both the narrator and the protagonist, says that he met John F. Kennedy in 1946 and that they double-dated one night during which Rojack seduced Deborah Caughlin Mangaravidi Kelly, who later became his wife. By way of comparing his heroism with Kennedy's, Rojack then tells of a war experience during which he single-handedly wiped out a German machine-gun nest and became a hero. Although this event, narrated in the tough-guy idiom of Mailer's literary hero, Ernest Hemingway, catapults Rojack into social success—resulting in his election to Congress, his marriage to the rich socialite Deborah, and his becoming an academic and television celebrity—Rojack believes that he failed in that encounter because he did not charge the final German soldier's bayonet, for "it was gone, the clean presence of it, the grace, it had deserted me." Rojack's efforts to regain this sense of grace—a Hemingway brand of cool and simple macho identity—is what dominates the rest of the novel.

At the beginning of the present action (a nightmarish three-day period following his wife's death), Rojack contemplates suicide, although he also accepts that he has murder within him, for murder, he thinks, offers power and release; "it is never unsexual." While at a party, he flirts with suicide by walking the balustrade of a high balcony, feeling that the moon is luring him to death. It is the murderous urge, however, that dominates when he confronts his estranged wife, Deborah, whom he sees as both the great American Bitch and as a mythic, demoniac, witchlike figure. When he strangles her as a result of her taunting him with stories of her sexual escapades, the murder is described in erotic terms, and he seems to take on some of her magical power as her own life ends.

The murder/sex/power complex does not end there, but extends to Rojack's immediately following encounter with Ruta, the German maid, with whom he has both anal and vaginal sex while Deborah's body lies in the next room. Although the sexual encounter is described in graphic detail, it is transformed from a merely physical act to one with metaphysical importance in which the female vagina is described as a chapel and the anus is identified as the place of the Devil.

The remainder, and therefore the bulk, of the novel follows Rojack's journey through a mythic underground world of New York City in which he must engage in a number of threatening tasks to assure his salvation: deceive the police; fall in love with the nightclub singer Cherry; defeat her black lover, Shago Martin; and confront Deborah's powerful father, Barney Kelly. All these events are described in terms of gaining metaphysical power and thus are less realistic than they are hallucinatory—mythic adventures on the way to Rojack's becoming a true hero. Rojack's sexual encounter with Cherry takes on cosmic importance, as he is the first man to "give" her an orgasm; his defeat of Shago Martin is described as a reversal of roles, in which Shago becomes increasingly white in his value system and perception, while Rojack becomes the hipster with almost supernatural power.

Finally, Rojack's encounter with Barney Kelly is one in which Kelly is presented as a satanic figure, perhaps even the Devil himself. Kelly is a man who, like Rojack, has violated social taboos and thus has become powerful as a result. Whereas Rojack's energizing crime is murder, Kelly's has been incest with his daughter Deborah. In the meeting with Kelly, Rojack once again walks the balustrade of a high balcony, flirting with death; he defeats Kelly, who tries to push him off. Although his walk once around the balcony is sufficient to save himself, he fails to walk it a second time and thus, either from his own psychotic point of view or within the supernatural conventions of the novel, fails to save Cherry and Shago, who are beaten to death.

At the end of the novel, Rojack heads west, to Las Vegas (the ultimate corruption of the American Dream), wins a large sum of money, and then decides to go to Guatemala and the Yucatán. Like that classic American hero Huck Finn, he leaves civilization to find himself in the primitive wilderness.

The Characters

There is only one "real" character in the book—Rojack himself, and he is less a fully rounded figure than a modern-day equivalent of the mythic hero who seeks some kind of primitive or existential freedom and, thus, self-identity. The problem of responding to Rojack's character is that one can either see him as heroic figure, bravely daring to break social taboos and combat the demoniac forces of political power, coming out of it clean and pure—in other words, as the possessor of grace and power—or as a psychopath with grandiose delusions about both himself and the nature of reality. Either the book is a mythic journey into the dark night of the evil of which man is capable, or it is the dramatization of a journey into the dark night of the unconscious self. Perhaps it is both.

In Mailer's psycho-aesthetic realm of reality, the quest is always for some primitive state of elemental or medieval magic perception. Rojack is indeed a psychopath, but as the primitive state and the psychotic state are the same, the way of the psychopath is the way to salvation. Thus, in *The American Dream*, social and personal complexities are eradicated by a system of simple and elemental macho values of power, grace under pressure, and thus, finally, sex and violence. Mailer couches all of this within the seemingly conflicting idioms of, on the one hand, the pop-art world of detective fiction and spy thrillers and, on the other, the popularizing of Martin Heidegger's existential philosophy of dread. Rojack parrots many of the values that Mailer has expressed elsewhere about the need to face death in order to achieve authenticity, about the power of the orgasm, about cancer as the result of the denial of self, and about the power of a return to the world of magic. As Rojack believes, "magic, dread, and the perception of death" are the roots of motivation. Rojack is indeed a psychopath, but he is presented as a philosophic psychopath in the tradition of the murderous figures of Fyodor Dostoevski's Raskolnikov and Joseph Conrad's Kurtz.

The other characters in the novel embody the challenges that Rojack must face. Deborah is not only the bitch of Hemingway's fiction; she is also the magical witch of folklore and myth. Barney Kelly is not only the robber baron who pulls the strings of politics and power but also the satanic tempter of legend. Shago Martin is the "white Negro," the stereotypical black "stud," who sells out by exchanging values with the socially successful Rojack. Cherry is the untouched beautiful female whom the hero must make his own. They have little else to do in the novel except to perform their respective functions. In typical allegorical fashion, this modern romance presents characters only as reflectors of and foils for the dominant figure who hacks his way through the nightmare jungle to find himself.

Themes and Meanings

Unless one reads this novel as a hallucinatory allegory of the American Dream, as a philosophical parable of one man's quest for meaning and value in a corrupt social world, it is likely to strike one as completely absurd; not only do the events seem unrealistic and ridiculous, but Rojack's own perceptions, beliefs, and language often seem childish and sophomoric. This is not to say that Rojack's (and Mailer's) belief in the power of the primitive is childish, or that his understanding of the link between the mythic and the psychotic is in error. Rather, this particular novel never seems to manage to fuse these legitimate views profoundly. Moreover, Heidegger's sense of existential dread and the need to face death to achieve authenticity seem vulgar and pretentious oversimplifications coming from the mouth of the melodramatic Rojack.

Mailer has attempted to write an allegorical satire of the American Dream, as it seemingly must be played out in a fallen and corrupt world, and indeed the novel has a disquieting surreal effect, but his use of the conventions of detective fiction, the gothic novel, and the spy thriller do not transcend their sources. Thus, this novel often reads like the writing of an amateur philosopher taking himself too seriously. In its self-important reduction of everything to macho values, it equates the instinctual with the merely self-serving and brutal. Mailer laments the loss of the medieval miracle and criticizes modern society for its empiricism and anti-supernatural mode of perception; he emphasizes the need for a return to the mystical side of experience; he wishes to present Rojack as a man who yearns for a dissolution of the ego, a transformation of the self, a return to primitive wholeness. Yet either *An American Dream* is not the vehicle for such a vision, or else Mailer is simply not a sufficiently profound thinker to achieve such a synthesis.

Critical Context

When *An American Dream* was first published, it was harshly criticized by many critics who, expecting the realism of Mailer's earlier novels, lambasted it for the absurdity of its plot and the pop-art pretentiousness of its style. More recently, however, its genre has been determined to be, as one critic puts it, "romance, allegory, satire, dream vision." The problem of the novel is that it attempts to combine both the conventions of fantasy and the conventions of realism; it hovers uneasily in a realm between fantasy and fact, in which objective and subjective reality cannot be distinguished. Consequently, there are those who misread it at first as pure realism and thus dismiss it as a "dirty" book in which Rojack is only a vulgar alter ego of Mailer himself.

Critics have pointed out the autobiographical similarities between Rojack and Mailer, both in philosophical point of view and in certain events (for example, Mailer stabbed his wife but did not kill her), and thus the book has contributed strongly to the polarization of the literary community about the works of Mailer. On one hand, there are those who see him as a posturing pop-art phenomenon, combating his own insecurity with efforts to become a cultural presence and force, manufacturing books which bolster his own ego and present his own adolescent fantasies and philosophies. On the other hand, there are those who see Mailer as one of the most profound novelists of the twentieth century, a man who, like Hemingway, has an uncanny ability to cut through hypocrisy and social conventions to present a genuine vision of the plight of modern humankind. *An American Dream* is at the very center of this debate, embodying all the virtues and the vices of Mailer's art and thought.

Bibliography

Cafagna, Dianne. "Mailer's Moon over *An American Dream*." *Notes on Contemporary Literature* 22 (November, 1992): 3-4. An illuminating discussion of Mailer's use of moon imagery in the novel.

Gordon, Andrew. *An American Dreamer: A Psychoanalytic Study of the Fiction of Norman Mailer.* Rutherford, N.J.: Fairleigh Dickinson University Press, 1980. Gordon examines Mailer's novels from the perspective of psychoanalytic criticism.

Leigh, Nigel. *Radical Fictions and the Novels of Norman Mailer.* New York: St. Martin's Press, 1990. An analysis of the political and social themes in Mailer's novels.

Lennon, Michael, ed. *Conversations with Norman Mailer.* Jackson: University Press of Mississippi, 1988. A collection of interviews with Mailer in which the novelist reflects on the craft of writing and his approaches to fiction.

Mailer, Adele. *The Last Party: My Life with Norman Mailer.* New York: Barricade Books, 1997. A revealing autobiography by Mailer's former wife. Offers insights into their troubled marriage and his turbulent personality.

Merrill, Robert. *Norman Mailer Revisited.* New York: Twayne, 1992. Merrill provides a critical and interpretive study of Mailer with a close reading of his major works, a solid bibliography, and complete notes and references.

Rollyson, Carl E. *The Lives of Norman Mailer: A Biography.* New York: Paragon House, 1991. Rollyson presents a detailed overview of Mailer's life and career.

Charles E. May

AMERICAN PASTORAL

Author: Philip Roth (1933-   )
Type of plot: Realism
Time of plot: 1968-1973, 1985, and 1995
Locale: Newark, New Jersey, and environs
First published: 1997

> *Principal characters:*
>> NATHAN ZUCKERMAN, a frequent narrator of Roth's novels and a
>> writer; often described as Philip Roth's alter ego
>> SEYMOUR "SWEDE" LEVOV, a much-admired high school athlete and
>> successful businessman whose dreams are destroyed by his daughter
>> DAWN LEVOV, Catholic wife of the Jewish Swede
>> MERRY LEVOV, the Levovs' only child, who becomes a 1960's antiwar
>> terrorist
>> LOU LEVOV, Swede's father, a self-made man who is baffled by 1960's
>> culture
>> JERRY LEVOV, Swede's younger brother and Zuckerman's old high
>> school chum

The Novel

American Pastoral has three parts. Nathan Zuckerman is the first-person narrator of part 1, "Paradise Remembered," but he then fades out of direct sight as the presumed omniscient narrator of part 2 ("The Fall") and part 3 ("Paradise Lost"). In 1995, attending his forty-fifth high school reunion in Newark—a day of nostalgic recollections of youthful passions and follies, and a day of dark talk about prostates and bypasses—Zuckerman is shocked to learn from his old buddy, Jerry Levov, that Jerry's older brother, Swede Levov, a former star high school athlete whom everyone idolized, has just died of cancer. Even more distressing is the news that the Swede's only child, Merry, blew up a rural post office/grocery when she was sixteen, killing a local doctor, and then disappeared into the antiwar underground.

With this revelation, Zuckerman begins to re-create the Swede's experience with his daughter, imagining Merry at eleven flirting with her father and teasing him into a brief but passionate kiss that immediately frightens him. Unfortunately, the daughter who delights her parents suffers from a severe stutter and starts stuffing herself with cheeseburgers, milk shakes, and french fries, while at the same time beginning to rage obscenely against Lyndon Johnson and capitalist America. Terrible scenes rock the Levovs' aging stone house in Old Rimrock, New Jersey, most of them precipitated by Merry's insistence on making weekend trips to New York City—where, her father senses, she is consorting with militants. Part one ends in 1968 with the explosion that kills Dr. Fred Conlon and destroys the general store and its post office in the back.

Part 2, "The Fall," opens with a mysterious Rita Cohen approaching the Swede at his glove factory. Rita reveals that she is an emissary from Merry, who wants some of her belongings. Merry's insulting behavior in their hotel-room meeting prompts the Swede to call the police, but she disappears. Five years pass with no word of Merry, until in 1973 a letter from Rita Cohen reveals to the Swede where Merry is: working in a Newark dog and cat hospital. The Swede finds her living alone in filth and squalor. She has become a Jain, a religious believer who as part of her discipline wears a stocking over her face to protect the tiniest creatures from being inhaled. To his further dismay, the Swede learns that Merry was raped twice in her travels around the country and, worst of all, was responsible for three more deaths.

Woven into part 2 is a long account of the Swede's wife, the former Dawn Dwyer, a Catholic plumber's daughter and onetime Miss New Jersey. After their marriage—much resisted by the Swede's father, Lou Levov—the Swede bought an old stone house in the New Jersey countryside, and Dawn bought a prize bull and raised cattle. After Merry's defection from middle-class comfort, Dawn is twice hospitalized for suicidal depression. She eventually goes to Paris for an expensive facelift—which in turn lifts her spirits—and by the time the Swede tracks down Merry, Dawn is planning a new house to replace the stone pile that she now claims always to have loathed.

Most of part 3, "Paradise Lost," is devoted to a brilliant dinner party that is both comic and heartbreaking. The participants are the Swede and Dawn; the Swede's parents; Dawn's architect and near neighbor, Bill Orcutt, and his wife; an old friend of the Swede's and his obnoxious English professor wife; and a fifth couple, the Salzmans—who, the Swede has learned, had harbored Merry after the post-office bombing. During the evening's events, the Swede discovers that Dawn is having an affair with Bill Orcutt, Orcutt's alcoholic wife stabs Lou Levov in the face with a fork, and the Swede berates Sheila Salzman, his former lover, for having kept Merry in hiding. The novel ends with this tragicomic evening, offering no further news of Merry's fate, a fate about which there can be no good news.

The Characters

Nathan Zuckerman appeared first in *The Ghost Writer* (1979) and has since served as Roth's spokesman in several other novels. He appears in *American Pastoral* primarily to recall convincingly the aura that surrounded the Swede as a high school athlete. The young Zuckerman had been obsessed by a 1940 baseball novel called *The Kid from Tompkinsville*, and the Kid of this novel was matched in real life by the Swede—first baseman on the baseball team, offensive end on the football team, and center on the basketball team. Between them, the Kid and the Swede represent an idyllic past in which athletes were cleancut and wholesome, and their teen admirers wore bobby socks with their saddle shoes.

The Swede dominates the story. A Jew with blond hair, hence "Swede," he can with no trace of postmodernist irony be called a hero. His marriage to the beautiful but Irish Catholic Miss New Jersey, in which for the only time in his life he disappointed his parents, seemed to embody the American Dream: the son who continues the success story of the hardworking immigrant parents and takes his bride to live in gentrified *Town and Country* splendor in a stronghold of rural WASPs. Zuckerman's adolescent hero-worship of the Swede presents him as a model of All-American decency and honesty that remains untarnished in Zuckerman's imagination.

There is no explaining Merry's conversion to counterculture radicalism. Roth offers the diagnosis of her psychiatrist—that Merry feels burdened by her beautiful mother and perfectionist family, an explanation that Rita Cohen shares—but the diagnosis somehow seems too easy and clichéd. Is she competing with her beautiful mother for her father's love? Does she stutter to irritate her mother and gain her father's attention? Is she simply another victim of the near hysteria of her times? If Roth meant *American Pastoral* as a neoconservative fable, then Merry's story does recapitulate brilliantly the seduction of so many talented young Americans during a period when the American Dream dissolved into surrealism.

The Swede's father, Lou, and his younger brother, Jerry, dominate every scene in which they appear. Jerry is the Swede's opposite in every way: flamboyant rather than conservative, focused on his appetites regardless of what others think, and contemptuous of what he perceives as the Swede's inability to respond decisively to Merry's behavior. Jerry is crude, witty, vital, and the master of a nasty world that he understands very well. Jerry, the carnal, often-married Miami surgeon, gets his chance in the climactic scene of part 2 finally to level with the square older brother/American hero he had endured all through their youth. He is vicious in his close agreement with Merry's psychiatrist:

> Out there with Miss America, dumbing down and dulling out. Out there playing at being Wasps, a little Mick girl from the Elizabeth docks and a Jew from Weequahic High. The cows. Cow society. Colonial old America. And you thought all that facade was going to come without cost. Genteel and innocent. *But that costs, too, Seymour. I* would have thrown a bomb. *I* would become a Jain and live in Newark.

Lou Levov started from scratch to build the large glove-manufacturing company that the Swede took over. He followed all the rules, but he is baffled by Merry and much else that troubles him in post-Vietnam America. The first crack in his world came with the Swede's marriage to a Catholic, and the scene in which Lou Levov interrogates Dawn Dwyer, prospective wife to a dutiful Jewish son, strikes comic high notes as clear as any in American literature. Lou struggles at the Swede's dinner party, launching into a superb paean to the glove industry and trying to help Bob Orcutt's depressed and alcoholic wife, only to get stabbed in the face with the fork he's using to feed her apple pie.

The other characters play their roles well but have mostly bit parts. Dawn Levov's earnestness shines through. Bob Orcutt fills his role as WASP drone and adulterer, and Marcia, the acid-tongued English professor, garnishes the dinner party with her astringent contempt for the world.

Themes and Meanings

The dust jacket of *American Pastoral* features a photograph from the 1940's depicting a dozen high school youths—the tall boy in the rear wearing the white sweater must be Philip Roth—lounging around the concrete steps of a grocery-cum-post-office. The Sunoco pump, the signs for Lux and Pittsburgh paints and Coca-Cola, all proclaim Middle America in the best spirit of Norman Rockwell. This snapshot appears twice, once on the back of the jacket and again on the front, where it is positioned just beneath the title and is depicted in flames. Roth has worked this myth of pastoral nostalgia into a parable of the confused era of the Vietnam War.

Several long, nostalgic looks at the glove industry provide ballast for the historical theme and are captivating in their loving detail and exploration of a corner of American life unfamiliar to most people. Roth's narrative genius dazzles with this report from the frontier of American immigrant business sense and true grit.

The story of the Swede and Merry could be any family's tragedy, but the theme achieves an extra richness by intertwining with the story of the hardworking Jewish immigrant and his son's assimilation into the colonial heritage represented by the stone house in Old Rimrock. The Irish daughter-in-law disappoints the elder Levovs (as the Jewish son-in-law disappoints the elder Dwyers), and the younger son betrays enormous rancor about the Swede's success story. In fact, though, Lou Levov and his new Irish plumber in-law have much in common, and Jerry Levov's life story parodies the rags-to-riches myth in its awful crassness and his callous disposal of his wives. Roth so excels in creating voices that all the conflicting views are put eloquently, but surely the Swede's life is a tragedy. Summarizing the complete defeat of the Levovs, Zuckerman/Roth asks poignantly in the novel's last paragraph, "And what is wrong with their life? What on earth is less reprehensible than the life of the Levovs?"

Critical Context

American Pastoral surprised some critics with what they interpreted as a turn to the right in Roth's thinking. Not only did it affirm traditional American values, it did so by means of an admiring history of a successful Jewish family. Although Lou Levov features in some wickedly funny comic scenes, Roth here shuns the satirical treatment of American Jews that started with *Goodbye, Columbus and Five Stories* (1959), instead depicting middle-class Jews in a generally benign spirit. Moreover, the counterculture with which he had sympathized in earlier works here appears nihilistic, a negative force working against the best in American life as epitomized in the spirit of *The Kid from Tompkinsville*.

Roth has usually been praised for the care with which he constructs his novels, but *American Pastoral* has been criticized for its repetitiveness and lack of formal symmetry. Zuckerman disappears after part 1, which ends with disclosure of the Swede's death and functions as a long prologue to the story of the Swede's life. Yet despite the shaggy structure, Roth's ability to write dialogue and create scenes stands out everywhere. The verbal brawls between the stuttering Merry and the Swede completely convince, and the glimpses given in Merry and Rita Cohen of the antiwar underground of the 1960's should be familiar to anyone who lived through the period. In many ways, *American Pastoral* is a valuable supplement to the historical documents of both the antiwar years and the earlier decades when men like Lou Levov were leaving their impress on American life.

Bibliography

Halio, Jay L. *Philip Roth Revisited*. New York: Twayne, 1992. An excellent survey of Roth's life and work through 1991's *Patrimony: A True Story*. Useful bibliography.

Lee, Hermione. *Philip Roth*. New York: Methuen, 1982. Good readings of Roth's fiction.

Milbauer, Asher Z., and Donald G. Watson, eds. *Reading Philip Roth*. New York: St. Martin's Press, 1988. Stimulating essays by both American and British critics.

Podhoretz, Norman. "The Adventure of Philip Roth." *Commentary* 104 (November, 1998): 25-37. A critical survey of Roth's career, with special attention to his reception by Jewish readers.

Walden, Daniel, ed. *The Odyssey of a Writer: Rethinking Philip Roth. Studies in American Jewish Literature* 8 (Fall, 1989). A special issue devoted to Roth, including a bibliographic essay.

Frank Day

THE ANCIENT CHILD

Author: N. Scott Momaday (1934-   )
Type of plot: Psychological
Time of plot: The 1980's
Locale: San Francisco, the Oklahoma Plains, and the Navajo lands
First published: 1989

> *Principal characters:*
> LOCKE SETMAN, also called SET and LOKI, a middle-aged Native
>   American and a successful painter
> GREY, a young medicine woman of mixed Kiowa and Navajo descent
> BILLY THE KID, a legendary outlaw who figures prominently in Grey's
>   fantasies
> KOPE'MAH, Grey's grandmother, an ancient medicine woman
> LOLA BOURNE, Set's girlfriend, a beautiful and sophisticated music
>   teacher
> BENT SANDRIDGE, Set's philosophical adoptive father
> THE BEAR BOY, a figure from Kiowa myth

The Novel

This story of a Native American's search for identity alternates scenes from the lives of the two main characters, Set and Grey. Interspersed among these scenes are tales from Kiowa myths and Western legends, each with relevance to the main characters' quest for identity.

Early in the novel, Grey watches over the deathbed of her ancient grandmother, Kope'mah. She dreams of the legendary outlaw Billy the Kid, and imagines herself as his lover and companion. She is at this time also growing gradually aware of her powers as a medicine woman.

Set, in San Francisco, is at the peak of his career as a painter. Orphaned at the age of seven, Set has been reared by his adoptive father Bent with love but with little or no sense of his heritage as a Native American. Now in middle age, he enjoys a strong and mutually supportive relationship with Lola, although he and Lola remain fairly independent of one another. When a cryptic telegram summons him to Oklahoma by telling him that Grandmother Kope'mah is near death, he is intrigued. He has never heard of Grandmother Kope'mah and almost believes the telegram has been sent to him in error except for its tantalizing mention of his biological father, Cate. He goes to Oklahoma but arrives too late; the grandmother is dead. There, however, he meets Grey and is unsettled and captivated by her beauty and dignity. His other relatives convince him to attend an Indian gathering before returning to San Francisco. At the gathering, Grey asks Set to paint her face for a dance, and she presents him with a medicine bundle that contains "bear medicine" that she says belongs to him. This brief exchange creates a bond between them that Set cannot yet fathom.

Back in his own world, Set's stature as a painter continues to grow. His agent, Jason, arranges an opening for Set in Paris, and he travels there with Lola. When they learn that Bent has had a small stroke, Lola returns to San Francisco to attend him. Set has a one-night affair with the Parisienne owner of the gallery where his paintings are being shown; on returning to his hotel, he finds a frantic massage from Lola telling him that Bent's condition has worsened. He returns immediately but finds that his father has already died.

Orphaned a second time, Set is plunged into grief and depression. Lola suspects Set's infidelity, and their relationship suffers. Cut off from his only loving relationships, the lost and alienated Set experiences a kind of mental breakdown. He wanders the streets aimlessly and spends days on end in his studio, painting and drinking, often forgetting to eat or sleep. Lola and Jason eventually have Set hospitalized.

Meanwhile, on the Oklahoma plains, Grey is slowly, intuitively becoming aware both of Set's crisis and of her own role as his savior. Touched by the spirit of her grandmother, she feels her powers as a medicine woman growing. She begins writing an account of her dream life with Billy the Kid and also begins creating masks. She waits, knowing that Set will be drawn to her. One stormy day, he arrives.

With Grey's aid, Set begins to recover from his breakdown. As she leads him on a journey, both physical and spiritual, to the Navajo lands of her mother's tribe, Set and Grey begin to fall in love. Along the journey, she guides him through a spiritual metamorphosis into a bear, a necessary part of his spiritual recovery and of his discovering his identity as a Native American. At home with Grey's mother, sister, and niece in Navajo country, Set is completely healed. He and Grey are married and conceive a child. At the novel's close, Set goes alone on a "vision quest" to capture the full power of his bear medicine and to complete and solidify his identity as an American Indian.

The Kiowa myths and legends interspersed throughout the story are an important part of the novel. One myth tells of a boy who is suddenly transformed into a bear while he is playing with his sisters. Another is the story of the "lost boy," a lone child who one day appears at a Kiowa camp. The Kiowa are astonished, because the boy has appeared as if from nowhere; he speaks a strange language and amazes them by his total lack of fear. They give him food and shelter and are ready to adopt him as one of their own, but when they awake the next day he is gone. The mystery of the lost boy is so troubling to them that they find they must invent a story to explain his sudden appearance and equally sudden disappearance. Another legend that recurs throughout the novel is of the historical figure Set-Angya ("Sitting Bear"), a Kiowa chief whose courage was so great it seemed a kind of madness. The figures in these stories all provide parallels to Set's experiences.

The Characters

At the novel's opening, Grey is a self-assured, uninhibited adolescent. She develops mainly in terms of the natural maturation that comes with age. She already has a powerful sense of self, is equally at home in her two worlds (Kiowa and Navajo), and understands the sources of her strength. "Never had Grey to quest after visions,"

Momaday repeats throughout the novel; she easily creates her own. Early on, she manifests these qualities of strength and self-assurance in a fairly adolescent way— declaring herself mayor of the collection of abandoned sod-houses where she lives and daydreaming about life with Billy the Kid. Her power and freedom reach their apotheosis in her fantasies about life with Billy the Kid; in these fantasies, she is to- tally free, brave, supremely capable, and loved. As she matures, and especially after she meets Set, the same qualities she has in abundance in her dreams begin to exhibit themselves more strongly in her real life. At the age of twenty, she understands her re- sponsibility to guide and heal Set, a worldy, successful man approximately twice her age. Grey engineers Set's rites of passage and brings him into a stable and supportive Indian family. Grey's development mirrors Set's, without the turmoil and emotional and spiritual confusion. Because Grey has always been deeply connected with her na- tive culture, she knows and understands her own identity.

Set is the product of a very different environment. An orphan, he is cut off com- pletely from the Indian world. In adulthood, Set seems happy and successful but has no real connection to the community around him. His only true sense of himself is found through his art. When Bent dies and his relationship with Lola sours, Set is cast adrift. He experiences a nervous breakdown of sorts that leaves him physically and mentally weakened and vulnerable. With Grey's help, he is able to rediscover and connect with the culture of his ancestors, and thus become whole again.

Lola is a foil for Grey. She is beautiful, convivial, and talented, but she is thor- oughly Anglo-American in orientation: ambitious, cultured, and materialistic. Al- though she and Set share an emotional bond through their art, her values are con- trasted with the traditional spirituality of Grey. While she is not to play as important a role in Set's life as Grey, her love and assistance form a critical part of Set's progress toward understanding his identity.

Billy the Kid lives entirely in Grey's imagination in *The Ancient Child.* Her fantasy relationship with him serves as an important bridge, connecting Grey not only to the past of her grandmother's era and to the non-Indian world, but also to a vision of her- self as powerful, courageous, and sensuous. Billy, like many of the characters, is kind of an "ancient child"—young in years, but hardened and cynical in outlook. Despite his notoriously cold-blooded nature, Billy exhibits the charm, playfulness, and re- spectful courtesy of a child.

Kope'mah, the ancient medicine woman, is Grey's guide on her journey toward be- coming a medicine woman. In Kope'mah's memory live vivid images of her tribe's glorious past and also their deepest suffering; like Billy, she provides Grey with a powerful connection to the past. Even in death, Kope'mah remains a vital force in Grey's and Set's lives. Her funeral is the occasion of their first meeting, and her spirit continues to inform and inspire Grey as she develops as a medicine woman.

The "bear boy" connects Set to Kiowa legend and hence to his Native American heritage. Set's development parallels the ancient tale of the bear boy: He has the bear's "medicine," and one of Grey's roles is to help Set make the transformation to the po- tent bear and back to manhood again. The bear boy's connection to Set is never defined explicitly; rather, he serves as one of the novel's many "ancient children" through whom the protagonists discover themselves, as they identify with these mythic figures and interpret their lives within the framework of these powerful ancient stories.

Themes and Meanings

A major theme of *The Ancient Child* is the importance of finding one's true self and finding a home. The novel revolves around a Native American man, comfortable and successful but not quite at home in the Anglo-American world, who must discover his native culture and his own identity and role therein. Momaday's own experiences of living equally in the Anglo and Indian worlds offer him a unique and powerful insight into this question of discovering one's sense of self and one's place in the world. This, however, is not a uniquely "Indian" theme; the question of assimilating into a dominant culture while retaining one's unique cultural identity is an important part of the American experience, and the need to understand oneself and one's place in the world is universal.

Momaday believes that one of the ways for an individual to find this identity is to use stories, such as the Kiowa myths and Western legends that figure so prominently in the novel, to interpret and understand experiences. This is clearly seen in the case of Grey, who builds up a personal fantasy around the legendary character of Billy the Kid and uses the fantasy to explore and strengthen the qualities she wishes to have. Set is not an active dreamer like Grey, but Momaday shows the importance of stories to Set's life by setting up clear parallels between Set's experiences and ancient myths through the stories of the bear boy and the lost boy.

Tied to Momaday's belief in the power of stories is his theory that there is really only one essential story, told and retold in many variations. In *The Ancient Child*, he enunciates this theory through the character of Set. "Yes, he believed, there is only one story, after all, and it is about the pursuit of man by God, and it is about a man who ventures out to the edge of the world, and it is about his holy quest, and it is about his faithful or unfaithful wife, and it is about the hunting of a great beast." Part of the individual's development rests on one's ability to understand and place oneself within this story and to create one's own unique version of it.

Momaday's work exemplifies this belief; he incorporates pieces of past works and elements of his own experiences to create *The Ancient Child*. For example, Grey's writings about Billy the Kid are taken from a previously unpublished sequence of poems by Momaday entitled "The Strange and True Story of My Life with Billy the Kid." Even the book that inspires Grey to write bears a striking resemblance to Momaday's 1976 work *The Names*. In subtler ways, Momaday incorporates motifs that have occurred elsewhere in his writings: the landscape that shapes the protagonists' lifestyles, the portentous thunderstorm, the visit to the burial site of one's ancestors, and the vision quest. This is not mere recycling of previous work; rather, it is Momaday's own demonstration of how a single story (or elements of a story) can be reinterpreted to mean different things and to create different identities. By synthesizing the diverse elements of ancient myth, past writings, his own experiences, and pure fictive imagination, Momaday creates a novel that is at once a unique piece of fiction, his own story, and a universal story.

An understanding of Momaday's beliefs about telling and retelling a single story help to explain the significance of the novel's title. Ancient characters, young or old (such as the boys in the Kiowa myths), can be revived and rejuvenated by a retelling of their story. New stories (or characters) have an ancient quality because they are part of one timeless story. Grey is a kind of ancient child, a young woman undergoing a maturation process (the "story" of growing up) that is itself as old as humanity; even in youth, she has a wisdom beyond her years. ("An ancient woman inhabits the body of a girl," writes Momaday.) Set must become like a child in order to realize his full, adult identity. As the children have an ancient quality, so do the ancients have a childlike quality. Kope'mah and Worcester Meat, Grey's ancient relatives, easily conjure up and reexperience scenes from their lives through their imaginative powers. They remain simple and playful even in advanced age.

Critical Context

The Ancient Child is in many ways a natural continuation and synthesis of Momaday's earlier works. In light of Momaday's view that there is "only one story," the reader is not surprised to see themes and images repeated from such works as *The Way to Rainy Mountain* (1969) and *House Made of Dawn* (1969), chiefly the belief in the individual's power to re-create the self through the imaginative use of powerful stories.

The Ancient Child also shares with Momaday's earlier works a fascination with the power of language; Momaday has even coined the term "wordwalker" to describe his view of himself as an artist. Momaday's work displays an acute awareness of words, language, and tone—seen, for example, in Set's obsessive meditation on his own name during his mental breakdown, and in the difference between the rough frankness of Grey's (imagined) spoken dialogues with Billy the Kid and the even elegance of her writings about him. Momaday has expressed an admiration for the linguistic purity and force of the poems of Emily Dickinson and of formal Indian orations; his work shows a similar striving toward a powerful simplicity and clarity of language.

Closely linked to Momaday's feel for words is his interest in different narrative forms, a feature also found in his earlier works. In *The Ancient Child*, Momaday combines modern narrative fiction with poetry, the Western lore of the dime novel, and the oral storytelling tradition of the Kiowa people, constantly shifting time, place, and perspective. The resulting narrative is disjointed, but this is critical to the theme of the novel. The "story" of this novel synthesizes these diverse elements, just as the vision of Set's own personal "story" synthesizes the fragmented elements of his life.

Momaday, like his protagonist Grey, is of mixed Kiowa descent and spent much of his youth on Navajo reservations in the Southwest. In addition to being a writer and poet, he is, like Set, a painter. *The Ancient Child* is in many ways Momaday's own story; in it, Momaday draws heavily on his own experiences as a Native American artist balancing his life between the Indian and Anglo-American worlds.

To categorize Momaday as an "Indian" writer, however, would be to limit the scope of his work. Momaday resists being pigeonholed as a spokesman for the American Indian. *The Ancient Child*, with its thematic concerns about cultural assimilation, its emphasis on discovering individual identity, and its reliance on landscape for defining moods and developing themes, is a thoroughly American novel.

Bibliography

Meredith, Howard. "The Ancient Child." *World Literature Today* 64 (Summer, 1990): 510-511. Discusses the structure of *The Ancient Child* and its relation to the novel's themes. Notes the importance of art as "affirmation" and "resistance" for both the protagonists (Set and Grey). Focuses on the importance of the geometrical symbolism of the titles of the novel's four sections and of cultural images as the framework of the story.

Rainwater, Catherine. "Planes, Lines, Shapes, and Shadows: N. Scott Momaday's Iconological Imagination." *Texas Studies in Literature and Language* 37 (Winter, 1995): 376-393. Outlines Momaday's thoughts about art and his theory of images. Offers an iconological metadiscourse of Momaday's novels, examines the basis of Momaday's vision of self, and provides in-depth background on *The Ancient Child*.

Roemer, Kenneth M. "The Ancient Child: A Novel." *The American Indian Quarterly* 15 (Winter, 1991): 269-271. Places *The Ancient Child* in the context of Momaday's other works. Identifies recurring themes and images and discusses how Momaday's incorporation of existing material into this work typifies his aesthetic theory. Discusses the importance of structure and image in developing the novel's themes and examines Momaday's belief in the "transformative powers" of storytelling.

Schubnell, Matthias. "Locke Setman, Emil Nolde, and the Search for Expression in N. Scott Momaday's *The Ancient Child*." *The American Indian Quarterly* 18 (Fall, 1994): 468-480. Schubnell traces the connection between Set's creativity and his search for a mythic identity to a similar artistic journey undertaken by German expressionistic painter Emil Nolde. Schubnell's comparison between Set and Nolde illuminates Set's self-discovery as an artist.

Woodard, Charles L. *Ancestral Voice: Conversations with N. Scott Momaday*. Lincoln: University of Nebraska Press, 1989. A lengthy interview in which Momaday discusses the relation between his life and works, his aesthetic theories, the legend of Billy the Kid, and Indian myths. He talks about the transformative power of stories and storytelling and discusses his personal connection to the Kiowa myth of the bear boy. *The Ancient Child* is discussed as a work in progress.

Catherine Swanson

AND THE EARTH DID NOT PART

Author: Tomás Rivera (1935-1984)
Type of plot: Social realism
Time of plot: The 1970's
Locale: Southern Texas
First published: . . . *y no se lo trago la tierra,* 1971

>   *Principal characters:*
>   A BOY who fears expulsion from school
>   A BOY who tries to summon the devil
>   A BOY whose father is overcome with heat exhaustion
>   DON HILARIO and DOÑA BONAFACIO, a couple who kill a migrant
>   worker
>   RAMON, a boy who commits suicide after a failed relationship
>   DOÑA MARIA, a mother fearful of leaving her house

The Novel

And the Earth Did Not Part is made up of twelve thematically linked pieces bracketed by introductory and concluding chapters. Consisting of interior thoughts and third-person observation, the book, narrated from multiple perspectives, focuses on Mexican migrant workers in Texas as they struggle against the cruelties of Anglo bosses and the insularity brought on by their minority status.

In "The Lost Year," an unidentified character, imprisoned in a cycle, believes he is awake when he is, in fact, dreaming. "The Children Were Victims" describes one hot day when an angry boss shoots a worker's young son as the child drinks from a scarce water supply. "A Prayer" is for a man's son fighting in Vietnam. "It Is Painful" presents a dialogue between two Mexican boys, one of whom is jumped by white boys in the school bathroom but who is the only student expelled as a result. The boy fears going home, worrying what his parents will say. "His Hand in His Pocket" concerns a young boy sent by his parents to live with a Mexican couple. They murder an elderly man for his money, then force the child to help bury the body. An unnamed boy in "It Was a Silvery Night" creeps out one night and defiantly tries to summon the devil; he is victorious when the devil does not appear. In ". . . And the Earth Did Not Part," a boy, having already witnessed the tuberculosis-related deaths of his aunt and uncle, is furious at God when his father suffers sunstroke while out in the fields. When the boy's brother is struck by heat exhaustion after being denied water while working, the boy curses God. To his amazement, the earth does not swallow him. In "First Holy Communion," a man recounts his preparations for his first childhood communion. The priest entreats the children to confess all their sins prior to the ceremony. Forgetting one, he warns, constitutes a sacrilege. The night before, the boy agonizes about the possibility of having forgotten one of his sins. The morning of his communion, en route to church, the child witnesses a man and a woman making love in the back of a tailor shop. Later, he cannot bring himself to admit to the priest what he has seen, and the experience changes him profoundly. "Little Children Burned" concerns a family of five children, forbidden to accompany their mother and father to work, who die in a house fire while their parents are in the fields. Ramon, in "The Night of the Black-Out," is in love with Juanita who promises to remain faithful during a long absence. As Ramon works long days, he hears rumors of her infidelity. At a dance later, she refuses to dance with Ramon. When the town is plunged into darkness, workers find Ramon dead inside the electric plant, having committed suicide.

Doña Maria in "Christmas Eve" plans every year to buy her children presents, but she rationalizes her agoraphobia by telling herself that the family cannot afford the expense. Determined to give her children something more than nuts and oranges, she announces that she will go downtown to buy toys. Once inside the store, however, she becomes disoriented, grabbing some toys and leaving without paying for them. She is arrested, finally returning home empty-handed. If the children ask why they have no toys, Maria tells her husband, he should explain to them that there is no Santa Claus. A dishonest salesman in "The Portrait" convinces Don Mateo to pay in advance for a lifelike portrait of his son, killed in combat in Korea. When the salesman does not re-surface, children find dozens of abandoned photos of people the salesman had lied about immortalizing in portraits. Don Mateo hunts down the crook, forcing him to fin-ish the picture of his dead son from memory. In "When We Arrive," migrant workers are packed into a truck en route to a job. Inside, they speculate about the future, mull over finances, family, and opportunities. The truck overheats, killing all of its occu-pants. "Under the House" involves a man who, crouched beneath a stranger's house, thinks back to his boyhood. Voices from past stories come forward. Once discovered, the man rushes back to his own home, where he climbs a tree and imagines a person in the distance waving at him.

The Characters

The novel's characters do not fit easily into categories. Almost no one character is fully developed, nor is any so abstracted as to defy a reader's identification. The un-named man who appears in the first section, "The Lost Year," and in the final one, "Under the House," appear to be one and the same; he is the only character with whom the author seems to stay and whom he develops. After the man has initially fallen asleep, the only thing to awaken him is someone calling his name. In the same way, it is through recognition of the "other" (in the case of this novel, a migrant worker) as one with an identity that awakens the individual. Rivera accomplishes more than sim-ply using this male character as a backdrop on which to project the rest of the stories. The character functions as both a window through which readers view the Mexican workers' lives and as an increasingly more complex figure in the drama of harsh exis-tence. The first of the italicized commentaries between chapters describes a boy whose superstitious mother leaves a glass of water out for the spirits. One night, the boy drinks the water; he considers revealing this to his mother, but he decides to wait and tell her when he is grown up. So begin the subtle undertones of this boy's tender qualities. In "It Is Painful," he is deeply tied to his parents, so desperate to make them proud for his having finished school that he convinces himself he has not been expelled. Doña Bonafacio and her husband Don Hilario in "His Hand in His Pocket" are a horrible, conniving couple with whom the boy is sent to live while still in school. They openly admit to him their thievery, eventually encouraging the boy to steal. There is something particularly unsettling about Doña Bonafacio. She seduces an old man—a "wetback," as she calls him—then convinces Hilario to help her murder him for what little treasures he has. The child finds the poor man's corpse in his bed, and the couple openly laugh before forcing him to help get rid of their victim. Here, and elsewhere, is evidence of Rivera's striving not to vilify the Anglo while glorifying the Mexican and Mexican American as beyond reproach. In "It Was a Silvery Night," the boy challenges the existence of the devil by invoking his name one night while his family is sleeping. The devil does not appear, but the boy remains uncertain about its power to manifest itself nonetheless. In " . . . And the Earth Did Not Part," the boy's wrath at an unjust God who would force people to labor relentlessly is quelled only when he realizes that, contrary to local belief, the earth does not swallow him for doubting God's divine existence. Thus, readers see that the boy does not simply reject either the devil or God without a deep questioning arising directly from a justifiable sense of outrage and indignation.

Themes and Meanings

   Although the book is slim, with a deceptively simple narrative, its structure, tone, and message resonate deeply. Each of the twelve sections is prefaced by a paragraph of often elliptical introduction. Sometimes these introductions are in the third person; sometimes they include lines of dialogue. Throughout the stories, actual dialogue, the characters' interior thoughts, and changes between characters are not announced. The cumulative effect is of a random intrusion of desires, fears, hopes, and dreams as they tumble out of the migrant workers' collective psyche. What binds the stories to one another is the unidentified man in the beginning and end who tries to make sense of his childhood and adolescence as a member of a marginalized group. The other thematic consideration is that of the Chicano experience as it is affected by the devil, God, Mexican folklore, and a sense of doom. In "First Holy Communion," a boy on the brink of his initiation into a Catholic life is confronted with adult sexuality in its most primal form. Unable to erase the image of a man and woman in the throes of sexual ecstasy, he subsequently sees all adults as naked, their faces contorted. Part vignette, anecdote, short story, and memoirs, *And the Earth Did Not Part* traces a year in the lives of people whose struggle for survival in an alien land can only be tempered by communal support and a faith that things will improve. The novel also concerns itself with the coming-of-age of the unnamed boy through whose eyes readers witness acts of murder, cruelty, sex, and racism. While the unidentified Anglos are not solely responsible for the workers' troubles, the culpability for their suffering is abundantly clear.

Critical Context

As a Chicano boy growing up in Texas, Rivera continued his early education and college studies in between seasons of field work alongside his migrant parents. Originally written in Spanish and then translated into English, *And the Earth Did Not Part* won the Premio Quinto Sol, a national award for Chicano literature, in 1970, and it was adapted for the screen in 1996. A university administrator and educator, Rivera is also the author of essays such as "Into the Labyrinth: The Chicano in Literature" (1971), which helped to legitimize Chicano writing as part of a body of cultural and literary studies. A collection of his stories was published in 1989, four years after his death, as *The Harvest/la cosecha*; *The Searchers*, a collection of his poems, followed in 1990.

Rivera's book follows in the tradition of novels—including José Antonio Villa-real's *Pocho* (1959) and Richard Vasquez's *Chicano* (1970)—about Mexican migrant workers and conflicts between generations and cultures. Rivera admired American writers Sherwood Anderson and William Faulkner as well as Mexican writer Juan Rulfo. Like Anderson's *Winesburg, Ohio*, which is presented through an interconnected series of stories, the world of *And the Earth Did Not Part* advances the structural form of the short story by breaking the narrative further and allowing the voices of its characters to rise uncensored and unadorned.

Bibliography

Casañeda-Shular, Antonia, Tomás Ybarro-Frauto, and Joseph Sommers, eds. *Chicano Literature: Text and Context*. Englewood Cliffs, N.J.: Prentice-Hall, 1972. A helpful resource for information on Mexican American intellectual life, history, criticism, and literature and on Rivera's place in the Chicano literary canon.

Grajeda, Ralph F. "Tomás Rivera's Appropriation of the Chicano Past." In *Modern Chicano Writers: A Collection of Critical Essays*, edited by Joseph Sommers and Tomás Ybarra-Frausto. Englewood Cliffs, New Jersey: Prentice-Hall, 1979. Grajeda does an excellent job of analyzing and putting Rivera's novel into historical context.

Kanellos, Nicolas, ed. "Thomás Rivera." In *The Hispanic Literary Companion*. Detroit: Visible Ink, 1996. Includes criticism of Rivera's novel, a biography, and his short story "Zoo Island."

Tatum, Charles M. "Contemporary Chicano Novel." In *Chicano Literature*. Boston: Twayne, 1982. Beginning with early Chicano novels such as José Antonio Villa-real's *Pocho* (1959), this chapter places Rivera's novel at the forefront of modern Chicano literature.

Nika Hoffman

THE ANDROMEDA STRAIN

Author: Michael Crichton (1942-　　)
Type of plot: Scientific adventure
Time of plot: 1967
Locale: Flatrock, Nevada
First published: 1969

      Principal characters:
          Dr. JEREMY STONE, a bacteriologist and leader of the Wildfire Project
          Dr. PETER LEAVITT, a clinical microbiologist
          Dr. CHARLES BURTON, a pathologist
          Dr. MARK HALL, a surgeon
          MAJOR ARTHUR MANCHEK, a senior officer of the Scoop mission

The Novel

Michael Crichton's enormously popular novel *The Andromeda Strain* generated much of its appeal first by dramatizing the anxieties of its audience—playing on the "man was never meant to know" fears about space and science—and second by laying those fears to rest by demonstrating that the American doctor is equal to any emergency. The novel was one of the first to use "secret government research projects" as a villain, a device that has been used many times since. The premise of *The Andromeda Strain* is that a space satellite, the Scoop, has been sent into space by the United States to search for and to bring back to Earth samples of viruses and bacteria for study. Although scientists call for the study to protect both astronauts and the Earth from contagion by an alien bacteria, the government has quite another purpose: to bring back bacteria that might be used in germ warfare.

Under the pretense that its purpose is to discover new ways to prevent disease, the project is begun. After several failures, Scoop VII is sent into orbit in February, 1967. In the space flight, the Scoop is hit by something, a meteor perhaps, and begins to wobble. When the Scoop is brought to Earth, it lands in a small, isolated Arizona town. As the novel opens, the two men sent to recover the vehicle find all but two of the townspeople dead, and within a few seconds the soldiers themselves lie dead in their van.

The survivors, Peter Jackson, a sixty-nine-year-old drinker, and a two-month-old baby, are brought to Wildfire, a five-level underground laboratory hidden in the deserts of Nevada. A crew of scientists is hastily assembled to discover what factor has protected two so dissimilar people from the mysterious disease carried by the Scoop.

The novel is arranged in the form of a scientific report on the efforts that follow and contains numerous charts, graphs, and computer printouts. The narrator, speaking as an omniscient observer, comments on the work of the scientists during the four days of feverish activity following the disaster. The plot of the novel is arranged in strict chronological form, with background information on the characters interspersed from time to time. The book even adds a fictional bibliography including articles purportedly written by the characters.

The Characters

The brilliant but contentious Dr. Jeremy Stone, the thirty-six-year-old leader of the research project to find the source of the mysterious disease and its cure, has recently won the Nobel Prize for his work on bacteria. Stone was one of the scientists responsible for the Scoop project; he is ironically chosen to solve the problems that his brainchild originated. Stone is a tireless worker and is devoted to his team members and to the project.

Dr. Peter Leavitt is a man with a secret. Even though the scientists have to pass rigorous physical examinations before beginning work, Leavitt successfully hides his epilepsy. Finally, exhaustion and the blinking lights of the computer console bring on a seizure. Leavitt is left with the guilty knowledge that his duplicity might have caused the research project to fail. This seizure, incidentally, prevents Leavitt from noticing the one way in which the bacteria are vulnerable. The incident is only one of several unfortunate coincidences on which the plot entirely depends. Had Leavitt not gone into seizure, he would have discovered the weak spot of the bacteria and the menace would have been ended.

Just as Leavitt is wrong in trying to hide his condition, Dr. Charles Burton is careless in his scientific method. As the narrator observes, if Burton had only thought to perform an autopsy on the brains of certain research animals being exposed to the bacteria, perhaps the answer to the puzzle would have come more rapidly.

The most clearly drawn and likable character is young Dr. Mark Hall, a surgeon chosen for the project not only for his credentials but also for the fact that he is the "odd man out"—the only one of the four who is unmarried. Crichton presents a fictional psychological study supporting the very dubious premise that single men are more likely to blow themselves up when ordered to do so. Thus, only Hall is given the ability to stop the explosion of an atomic device which will detonate automatically if the security of the laboratory is breached. Perhaps the fact that Hall is the most likable and most intelligent of the group is explained by noting that Crichton is a doctor himself. Whatever the cause of Hall's talents, the success of the project depends on him. Indeed, it is Hall's research and his insight into the problem that provide the answer to the puzzle. At the climax of the story, Hall makes his heroic climb through the core of the underground laboratory to save his colleagues and the building from atomic destruction.

Of all the "characters," the reader's attention keeps returning to the microscopic bit of life that is brought back on the Scoop. It is a character without a name and with a structure unlike that of any known Earth entity. This bacterium is made of hydrogen, oxygen, carbon, and nitrogen, but lacks amino acids. It therefore contains no proteins, the building blocks of all earthly life. By all the scientists' reckonings, it cannot be alive, yet it divides, respires, and changes in form—all marks of life.

The science in the novel and the pace of the adventure must maintain the reader's interest because the characters show little individuality. For example, Stone's personality has supposedly caused four of his marriages to fail, yet in the laboratory he is even-tempered, gentle, and considerate. Despite Crichton's effort to tailor carefully each character's background, they behave much alike.

Themes and Meanings

The most obvious theme of the novel is the necessity for the human mind to use technology to solve humankind's problems. Neither the scientists with their human mistakes nor the machines with their mechanical problems are able alone to find the source of the disease; neither alone can cure it. Moreover, both parties are fallible: Human error—a misspelling—causes one prospective member of the team to be notified too late to participate; machines are not entirely dependable either—a stray piece of paper clogs a teletypewriter, preventing an important message from being received. When man and machine join together, however, the scientists are free to use their intuition while the machines shorten the hours which it takes to do the innumerable computations needed to solve the puzzle of the bacteria from space.

The novel offers a fascinating glimpse into the world of scientific research and manages to teach much about microbiology in the course of telling a fast-paced adventure. Crichton himself worked at the Salk Institute after receiving his M.D. degree from Harvard University, and his technical competence informs the novel. The reader learns about genetics, studies the treatment of infectious diseases, reads of the history of bacteriology, and discovers some of what is known about the ability of bacteria to survive and multiply in a hostile environment. In addition, the reader comes to see the world as a place filled with bacteria, ninety-seven percent of which are helpful and necessary to humankind. The most pointed example of the book is the human body, which is covered and filled with bacteria: Its complete "cleansing" is neither possible nor desirable, for to sterilize it would be to kill it.

One theme notable by its absence is any moral judgment on the action of the government in lying to the scientists about the purpose of the research on which they are engaged. The plot is not so much resolved as stopped: The bacteria magically become harmless, all the survivors recover, and the scientists return to their lives, apparently unchanged or unenlightened by the events.

Critical Context

Crichton is noted for rapid pacing and a considerable amount of scientific fact in his works. Using the pseudonym Jeffrey Hudson, Crichton wrote *A Case of Need* (1968), which won the Edgar Award from the Mystery Writers of America for the year's best mystery novel. Using the pseudonym John Lange, he wrote several novels, including *Drug of Choice* (1970) and *Binary*, which was made into a movie for television. Crichton also wrote *The Terminal Man* (1972) and *Eaters of the Dead* (1976), a retelling of the *Beowulf* story. He ventured into another creative field in 1973, writing the script for and directing the film *Westworld*. He also directed Robin Cook's *Coma* in 1978.

Bibliography

Crichton, Michael. *Travels*. New York: Alfred A. Knopf, 1988. Crichton recounts his travels throughout the world. Furnishes important insights into his personality and approaches to his fiction.

Current Biography 54 (November, 1993): 10-14. Profiles Crichton's life and career as a novelist and filmmaker. A discussion of his novels adapted to the screen is included.

Foreman, Christopher H., Jr. "Editorial Commentary: Witchcraft Science in Cinema Epidemics." *Science Communication* 17 (September, 1995): 3-5. A scientific analysis of the use of epidemics as the theme in fiction and adaptations of novels. Crichton's *The Andromeda Strain* is among the earliest to exploit the epidemic theme.

Heller, Zoe. "The Admirable Crichton." *Vanity Fair* 57 (January, 1994): 32-38. Profiles Crichton's accomplishments as a writer and director.

Kipen, David. "From Potboilers to Blockbusters in Thirty Years." *Variety* 364 (August 26, 1996): 20-21. Focuses on Crichton's transition from novelist to filmmaker.

Trembley, Elizabeth A. *Michael Crichton: A Critical Companion*. Westport, Conn.: Greenwood Press, 1996. Trembley examines Crichton's work. Her discussions focus primarily on individual novels, including *The Andromeda Strain*. Students and general readers will appreciate the sections on Crichton's life and literary heritage as well as a useful bibliography.

Winer, Rex. "Showman of the Year." *Variety* 364 (August 26, 1996): 7-10. Profiles Crichton and his career as novelist, screenwriter, and film director. Background on his career, achievements, and works as well as an analysis of his approach to storytelling are included.

Julia M. Meyers

ANNE OF GREEN GABLES

Author: Lucy Maud Montgomery (1874-1942)
Type of plot: Bildungsroman
Time of plot: The late nineteenth century
Locale: Prince Edward Island, Canada
First published: 1908

> *Principal characters:*
>> ANNE SHIRLEY, an orphan, a highly imaginative and clever young girl
>> MARILLA CUTHBERT, a spinster, the adoptive mother of Anne
>> MATTHEW CUTHBERT, a bachelor, Marilla's brother, a farmer
>> DIANA BARRY, Anne's nearest neighbor and best friend
>> GILBERT BLYTHE, Anne's rival at school and college

The Novel

  Anne of Green Gables recounts, through a series of short episodes, Anne's girl-hood, from her arrival at the village of Avonlea to the time she graduates from Teacher Training College. Based on L. M. Montgomery's own childhood memories, Anne's life is shown to be intertwined with the pastoral rhythms of this particular eastern sea-board province of Canada.

  The story begins with a middle-aged brother and sister in search of a young orphan-age boy to help around their farm, Green Gables. As the result of a misunderstanding, they get a ferociously talkative, red-haired, plain little girl. Matthew, however, takes an immediate liking to her, and Marilla is also sufficiently sorry for her not to send her back. To Anne, the farmhouse, with its little east gable room as her bedroom, is like paradise. Her imagination, already highly trained to overcome the harsh, unadorned realities of her previous existence, is kept busy as she absorbs new sights and situa-tions. Her upbringing proceeds along two domestic channels—school and home. Marilla, a spinster, has severe and old-fashioned notions of rearing a child as austerely as possible, with little encouragement or praise. Her regime, therefore, is in constant conflict with Anne's natural creativity and love of beauty. All requests for nice clothes or bedroom decoration are turned down. At times, it is a grim struggle on Marilla's part to teach traditional modes of female behavior and skills to this maverick who has no aptitude for domestic roles. Fortunately, Marilla, under her crusty exterior, is good-hearted, willing to admit to her own mistakes. Matthew keeps out of the domes-tic battleground for a while; in the end, though, he recognizes Anne's need for adorn-ment and takes her side in getting some fashionable dresses. Both brother and sister encourage Anne academically and make no attempt to tie her to the farm.

  At school, Anne is shown to be an apt pupil, soon making up for an indifferent start to her education. Her greatest rival at school is Gilbert Blythe—who, unfortunately, offends her early on by teasing her about her red hair, about which she is desperately sensitive. In a typically dramatic gesture, Anne declares undying enmity with Gilbert, and despite all of his best efforts, and even a melodramatic rescue from a sinking boat, she maintains that stance until almost the end of the book.

If her enmity runs deep, though, so does her friendship. On the next farm lives a large, prosperous family, the Barrys. Diana is about Anne's age, and their friendship ripens naturally and easily. Anne is a popular girl at school; her imagination makes life interesting. Montgomery's description of a one-teacher village school—with all its petty bickerings and rivalries, and the excitement of outings and performances— is excellent.

Anne's first teacher, Mr. Phillips, is inexperienced and at times treats Anne quite unfairly. However, her next teacher, Miss Stacy, is a "kindred spirit" who is able to nurture Anne intellectually and emotionally, providing the role model she needs (along with Mrs. Allan, the minister's young wife). In the end, Miss Stacy's efforts are rewarded, and Anne passes at the top of the entrance list for Queen's College, the island's Teacher Training College. In Mrs. Allan, Anne sees a paradigm of moral excellence, of unselfish sympathy, that counters the rigid legalism of much of church life as Anne experiences it. Gradually, Anne emerges into a more rounded adolescent; her need for a compensatory fantasy world drops away, and she is able to find the inner discipline and resources to make the most of her abilities.

The book closes with two contrasting events. First, Anne's success at Queen's College is crowned with a coveted scholarship in English to a degree-granting institution, Redmond. She can break free of the usual village school-college-village school cycle to which most of her academically gifted but poor contemporaries are consigned. At the same time, however, Matthew dies from overwork and the shock of losing his life savings in a bank failure. Anne sees it as her clear duty to support Marilla by taking over from Miss Stacy at the Avonlea school. Anne accepts this cheerfully, as she has accepted so many other vicissitudes. Her compensations are the continuing friendship of Diana and the new one of a now-acceptable Gilbert.

The Characters

The novel is densely peopled by a rural community about its everyday business. Although there is a pastoral quality to the writing, Montgomery's characterization does not idealize. Characters have faults and virtues; many have icy exteriors with softer hearts. Only Anne's two role models are idealized: They are presented as Anne would see them, on pedestals, rather than as rounded personalities. The contrasting presentations of Mr. Phillips and Miss Stacy exemplify this characterization dichotomy; however poor a teacher Phillips is, he can be imagined in real-life terms. It is difficult to do this with Miss Stacy.

The novel is dominated by Anne's strong, willful, and brilliant character, which is revealed through a series of episodes that usually fit a pattern. Anne typically experiences a situation, reconstructs its reality imaginatively, goes through a catastrophe, then experiences contrition, punishment, and insight; finally, she becomes reconciled to reality. However, several episodes depart from this pattern significantly. In one, Anne has to nurse a sick child through the night. Her bravery and initiative are shown here as constructive rather than as compensatory fantasy. The episode demonstrates both the degree to which Anne has grown up and also the community's gradual recognition of her real qualities. As she grows into mid-adolescence, Anne's successes outweigh her failures; her characterization perhaps becomes sentimentalized at times because of this.

Traditional village life is personified in Marilla and Matthew, yet both are individually characterized. Matthew's desperate shyness fights with his fondness for his orphan charge. Anne's natural and unaffected ability to communicate with him thus seems all the more poignant. By contrast, Marilla is portrayed as the one who both suffers from Anne's catastrophes and administers the traditional moral wisdom to counter them. Montgomery manages to show both the limitations of such wisdom as well as the genuine concern behind it that makes it acceptable.

By contrast, Montgomery supplies an unloving moralist in Mrs. Rachel Lynde, the village know-all and conscience. One of Anne's first outbursts of anger is directed against this moralism. The fact that Marilla sides with Anne marks an important move for her. If Mrs. Lynde represents convention, Montgomery supplies an antidote in Miss Barry, Diana's rich maiden aunt, who takes a fancy to the "Anne-child," recognizing in her the free spirit she is herself. Significantly, she lives in town.

Anne's school friends are realistically portrayed. Although none has Anne's imaginative and verbal dexterities, they are portrayed as a good-natured bunch. Only Josie Pye has the ability to make herself objectionable. The girls are most strongly characterized—Diana particularly, in her engagement with Anne's imaginative life at first and then in her domestic situations. It is she who unobtrusively gives Anne the friendship she needs to allow her to let go of her imaginary persona. Yet it is never a feminized society: Montgomery well portrays the gradual growth from preadolescent to adolescent feelings between the sexes, with its growth of consciousness of differentiation, problematized for Anne by her antipathy to Gilbert Blythe. Preadolescent enmity gradually erodes, with great difficulty, to adolescent acceptance. For contemporary readers, these adolescents have maturity thrust upon them: It is difficult to realize that at the end Anne can hardly be seventeen and yet is ready to begin her career as village schoolteacher.

Themes and Meanings

Although it is the force of Anne's personality that holds the book together and thrusts the plot forward, Montgomery explores a number of themes, giving the book an ongoing vitality and complexity that the sequels lack. The first such theme is the value of childhood. Anne's early experiences as an orphan have suggested to her that she is unwanted, fit only to be a drudge and to "earn her keep." The Cuthberts' original desire to get a boy from the orphanage to be an extra farmhand reinforces this. Anne makes an immediate challenge to it, sufficient to save her being consigned to a Mrs. Blewett as that lady's drudge. Orphans are traded around as if they have no feelings. Anne's first achievement, therefore, is to win herself enough space to prove to Marilla and Matthew that she is to be valued as a person and to be treated with respect. It takes the traumatic episodes of anger at Mrs. Lynde and a false accusation of theft from Marilla to achieve this. Marilla never really accepts the imaginative life of childhood, but she learns to tolerate it in Anne.

Marilla's treatment of Anne—harsh, discouraging, legalistic—demonstrates the dying vestiges of a Victorian discipline that sought to crush the spirit of the child in order to conform it to the moral and social confinements of a rigid and economically bound society. That society is shown to be disappearing slowly without regret. Lucy Montgomery's own life showed similar patterns. Reared by rigid grandparents after her mother's early death, she found and maintained her personal freedom via her writing ability and educational opportunities.

If this theme suggests the possibility of mobility and change, the other main theme stresses the permanence of the pastoral. Montgomery's descriptions of the landscapes, and her heroine's ability to appreciate their beauty, create a timeless world for the reader. It becomes the ideal setting to nurture Anne's spirit. The maturing process, for her, is to move her imagination away from fantasizing so that it can find its real strength in this complex of nature, community, and close personal relationships.

Critical Context

Anne of Green Gables was Montgomery's first novel. Its success was immediate (six editions in six months) and continuing; the book has been dramatized, televised, and filmed and has been translated into dozens of languages. The demand for a sequel produced a series of seven further books tracing Anne's career through marriage and motherhood. Other heroines were also created, including an Emily, who is seen to be the most autobiographical of them all. The other characters of Avonlea also feature in several volumes of short stories. All are based on Montgomery's own memories of Prince Edward Island, even though in later life she moved away. A museum in Charlottetown, the island's capital, is devoted to Montgomery's life and works. Montgomery herself never believed that she had achieved the status of a great writer, though modern critical interest has established her as a major exponent of Canadian adolescent fiction.

In a wider context, *Anne of Green Gables* belongs to the core tradition of domestic realism in North American children's literature, especially in its focus on the heroine's development from girlhood onward. Thus, Montgomery stands in a tradition stretching from Louisa May Alcott to Laura Ingalls Wilder. The novel's immediate contemporary in this tradition is Kate Wiggin's *Rebecca of Sunnybrook Farm* (1903), set just over the border in Maine. It has been suggested that Anne is a straight pastiche of Wiggin's heroine, but the germ of the idea was certainly in existence before the publication of *Rebecca*, and the novel is autobiographical enough to suggest that the material was personal, not derivative. However, the resemblances are strong.

More significant is the change in the two books away from piety and moral goodness as the major source of influence (as in the Elsie Dinsmore books) to the sheer force of personality of the heroine. A slightly later contemporary book, Eleanor Porter's *Pollyanna* (1912), reverts to moral goodness as central, though it is mediated through a vivacious and irrepressible heroine in the Anne and Rebecca mold.

The style of the book and its appeal calls into question the modern categorization of "children's literature" as something separate and linguistically and tonally different from "adult" fiction. A more useful classification of the book might be as part of a "family reading" genre, to be enjoyed by adult, adolescent, and child alike; such a grouping would be more typical of the Victorian *Bildungsroman* and adventure story tradition. The continuing popularity with such a "family" audience suggests the strength of Montgomery's writing in *Anne of Green Gables*.

Bibliography
Epperly, Elizabeth R. *The Fragrance of Sweet-Grass: L. M. Montgomery's Heroines and the Pursuit of Romance*. Toronto: University of Toronto Press, 1992. Anne is among the heroines discussed; bibliographical references and index are included.
Foster, Shirley, and Judy Simons. *What Katy Read: Feminist Re-Readings of the "Classic" Stories for Girls*. Iowa City: University of Iowa Press, 1995. Feminist readings of stories including *Anne of Green Gables*; bibliographical references and index.
Gillen, Mollie. *The Wheel of Things: A Biography of L. M. Montgomery, Author of "Anne of Green Gables."* Toronto: Fitzhenry & Whiteside, 1975.
Montgomery, L. M. *The Alpine Path: The Story of My Career*. Toronto: Fitzhenry & Whiteside, 1974. Reprinted from Montgomery's autobiographical articles written for *Everywoman's World*, a Toronto periodical, in 1917.
_____. *The Annotated "Anne of Green Gables,"* edited by Wendy E. Barry et al. New York: Oxford University Press, 1997. This edition of Montgomery's novel adds critical analyses on both the work and its author.
Rootland, Nancy. *Anne's World, Maud's World: The Sacred Sites of L. M. Montgomery*. Halifax, N.S.: Nimbus, 1996. This interesting illustrated companion to Montgomery's fiction shows literary landmarks related to the fiction of several Canadian authors including Montgomery. Includes maps and bibliographical references.
Rubio, Mary, ed. *Harvesting Thistles: The Textual Garden of L. M. Montgomery*. Contains essays on the novels and journals of Montgomery, with bibliographical references and an index.
Rubio, Mary, and Elizabeth Waterston. *Writing a Life: L. M. Montgomery*. Toronto: ECW Press, 1995. A biography of Montgomery including bibliographical references and an index.
Sorfleet, John R., ed. *L. M. Montgomery: An Assessment*. Toronto: Canadian Children's Press, 1976. A collection of critical articles seeking to reassess Montgomery's significance. Jean Little's chapter "But What About Jane?" (pages 71 to 81) is especially good.

David Barratt

ANNIE JOHN

Author: Jamaica Kincaid (Elaine Potter Richardson, 1949-   )
Type of plot: Autobiographical
Time of plot: The 1950's and the early 1960's
Locale: Antigua, the West Indies
First published: 1985

Principal characters:

ANNIE VICTORIA JOHN, the protagonist, a young West Indian girl
ANNIE JOHN, her mother, whose identity her daughter adores and against whom she rebels
ALEXANDER JOHN, the protagonist's aging father, a kind but aloof car-penter
GWEN, Annie's first childhood friend, the model of innocence
THE RED GIRL, a "wild" girl who introduces Annie to erotic love
MA CHESS, Annie's grandmother, who embraces an African worldview

The Novel

Narrated exclusively by the fifteen-year-old, first-person protagonist, *Annie John* explores the inseparable bond between mother and daughter as it provides both the illusion of security and the movement toward psychological separation. Influenced greatly by autobiographical elements, the novel traces Annie's coming of age, from her innocent adoration of her mother, who has the same name, through her rejection of her mother in the effort to establish her own individual identity, to her departure from home, the island of Antigua in the West Indies. Annie's quest is not only to emerge in adolescence with her own self-identity but also to integrate the complexity of her Caribbean heritage with its legacies of colonization, cultural differences, and pluralist ideologies. She seeks an individuality based on her separateness from all those around her.

In the opening chapters, the book's languid rhythms, sensuous imagery, and sharply honed sentences revolve around the dominant image of Annie's mother's hand. At ten, Annie learns of the death of a girl younger than herself who has died in her mother's arms. She spends her childhood completely within her mother's world. She studies her shopping in the market, talking to her friends, eating her meals, and laughing with her father. She bathes in her mother's intimacy, reveling in the scents of oils and flowers in their common bath. When Annie learns that her mother has helped to prepare a dead girl's body for burial, she recoils in horror. Her innocence broken by the reality of death foreshadows the end of her childhood and initiates the inevitable separation from her mother as Annie moves toward adulthood.

Arriving home early one day, Annie finds her mother and father in bed together, and she sees her mother's hand circling on her father's back. Having established her innocence in a world of female activities, she recognizes intuitively that her father is her chief rival for her mother's attention; she feels in danger of being shut out of her mother's world. Her ambivalence toward her mother becomes a unifying thread throughout the novel; she longs for her mother's love, yet she fears that it could suffocate her.

As Annie experiences the onset of puberty, her imminent separation from her mother is painfully felt as her mother moves further into the distance, even forbidding her to wear dresses made from the same fabric, as had been common practice when she was younger. Annie begins to move away from her mother as well. Her first close friendship is with Gwen, who is neatly dressed, always clean, and a serious student. Gwen smells like lavender, her mother's favorite scent. As Annie moves into the circle of girlfriends at school, her association with school itself becomes one of rejection. Identifying school with her mother's desires and her earlier innocence, Annie becomes a "rebel" leader, leading the girls in bawdy songs, swearing, and displaying parts of her body to the other girls.

After shifting her love for her mother to Gwen and the other schoolgirls, Annie engages in her most rebellious act yet. She explores her sexuality with the Red Girl, the opposite of all that her mother has taught her to admire in a woman. The Red Girl never bathes, never goes to church, never obeys her elders. She represents the onset of Annie's separation from her mother when she begins menstruation. With the Red Girl, Annie plays marbles, hiding them from her disapproving mother; her friendship takes on a secret, underground existence, and Annie explores her new erotic impulses. She lies with ease and pride, and she steals from her mother to buy gifts for the Red Girl.

Forced to end the friendship with the Red Girl by her mother, Annie moves further into her own world, alternately dreaming of rescuing the Red Girl and fearful of other women who have been her father's previous lovers. She fears they will use obeah, an African-based belief in power over spirits, to harm her in order to punish her father for leaving them. When a boy humiliates her, Annie's mother blames her for acting like a slut.

Annie retreats into illness, falling silent and possessed by dark, fragmented images of her early childhood. As an unusually long period of rain soaks the island, Annie becomes obsessed with cleansing her past, even washing the family's faces away from photographs. Recalling a moment of sexual arousal and fear while sitting on her father's lap, Annie retreats from her sexuality altogether and begins recasting her past and emergent maturation with the nurturing care of her maternal grandmother, Ma Chess.

As Annie recovers from her breakdown, she feels gripped by loss. Embedded in the association of images with her parents, she longs intensely to flee everything. Caught between childhood and adulthood, she wants only to escape from all that she has known. When she wins a scholarship to study in England, she has her chance. As Annie departs, however, her mother reminds her that she will always be her daughter and that Antigua will always be her home.

The Characters

Annie Victoria John, as she imagines her mother might address letters to her, is the figure of fear both of changing and not changing that is present in every adolescent. She dominates the poetic narrative through her internal monologues, her dreams, her fantasies, her distant associations, and her precise observations of all that goes on around her. Her steady pace through anxieties over origins, identity, sexuality, and maturation arrives at an uneasy anticipation of independence in England—ironically so, given that Antigua, in Kincaid's childhood, was still a British colony. Similarly, it is just as Annie leaves that she realizes the potential for a reunion with her mother's love, yet she knows too that she must leave her mother for that reunion to become real in the future.

The protagonist's mother emerges from the ambivalent images bestowed on her by her daughter's passage from childhood to adolescence. Annie's mother appears at times as tender and at others as nearly monstrous. Her compassion, however, is never far from the reader's grasp; she cares for Annie's father, modeling loving adult relationships. Yet she also knows that Annie must become herself, and her seemingly harsh responses to her daughter are only typical, caring parental warnings and discipline.

Alexander John, Annie's father, is perceived by her as distant and aloof until she moves into puberty. Actually, her father is a kind and nurturing man but is representative of West Indian male attitudes. He regards himself as free to assert his manhood in the society, yet he is particularly attentive to Annie's mother. Both Annie's initial bonds with her mother and her refuge in her father's attention as she separates from her mother are the result of his distant but dominating presence.

Gwen, Annie's first girlfriend, is the type of character that Annie must both accept and later reject if she is to reach adulthood with her own identity. She is a comfortable bridge from Annie's early security in her mother's intimacy to her first taste of independence.

The Red Girl, embraced as Annie rejects the motherlike qualities of Gwen, evokes Annie's sexual awakening. When Annie fears her father's appeal, she moves outside the home but remains in the safety of woman's bonding. The Red Girl is wild and free, signaling Annie's own yearning for defiance and personal freedom.

Ma Chess, Annie's maternal grandmother, plays a vital role in Annie's recovery from her self-induced illness. Offering both sustenance and security, she feeds her and bathes her, just as her mother had once done. Consequently, Ma Chess preserves the potential for a loving mother-daughter relationship.

Themes and Meanings

The stages of Annie's maturation and her quest for a sense of self are rooted not only in Kincaid's admitted autobiographical fashioning of her fiction but also in the context of Caribbean beliefs and customs. Annie's fear of losing her mother, which in turn spurs her independent development, begins when Annie realizes that her mother's social life and responsibilities are anchored in a community outside her own perceptions and understanding. Her mother must be available to her neighbors when sickness or death occurs, and her bathing of the dead girl's body as a gesture of social obligation raises the fear in Annie that her mother could die, leaving her alone in the world. Her father's handmade coffin for the girl further raises the possibility that she could be left with no parents at all, but Annie does not yet grasp the community's compassion for all of its children.

Up to the point where Annie reaches puberty, her mother has modeled every detail in order for her daughter to become an ideal woman. When Annie becomes a sexually potent female, however, she does not think her mother has noticed. Of course she has, but she says nothing; Kincaid suggests that modeling for this Caribbean mother stops at puberty. Annie's mother retreats into silence, paralleling her daughter's eventual illness. This failure to confront and to address sexuality directly and openly becomes a source of further fear for Annie.

Although Annie attempts to seek her father's attention when she rejects her mother, she also knows that, sexually, he belongs to her mother's world. Alexander's previous "outside children," in the Caribbean phrase, whom he does not acknowledge as his own, reflects a historical reality of Caribbean society. Hence Annie not only fears their wrath through obeah but also learns that there is silent shame inherent in sexuality. Kincaid implies that male sexuality has few consequences but that, for females, the consequence can be abandonment and a subsequent life of poverty.

Ma Chess dwells in an African world; she is an obeah woman who embraces an African sense of herself. Her beliefs are not for sale. Ma Chess helps Annie to recognize that she must choose her own values, which need not suppress or diminish any part of her complex cultural history. The security in the relationship between grandmother and granddaughter becomes the tension-free security of Annie's past. When she leaves to set her own course, she will take her own trunk, just as her mother did when she left her mother, and in it she will carry different contents in the baggage of race, class, gender, and nationality.

Critical Context

Beginning her career as a journalist for *The New Yorker*, Kincaid offered insights into American culture. She soon gained support for her own work from the magazine's editors, who began publishing her fiction in installments. *Annie John*, Kincaid's first novel, followed her collection of short stories *At the Bottom of the River* (1983) and provided a broader context for those related autobiographical stories that are told from an adult point of view. Her novel *Lucy* (1990) introduced new characters and continued the autobiographical dimension of Kincaid's observations in the United States. Between novels, she published *A Small Place* (1988), an extended essay addressed to white tourists in Antigua and reporting on the economic and social exploitation inflicted by the continuing colonial attitudes toward the island and its native residents.

Annie John is one of several novels that bear witness to the newly rising status of West Indian writing. Such established West Indian writers as poet and playwright

Derek Walcott (winner of the 1992 Nobel Prize in Literature), novelists V. S. Naipaul, Wilson Harris, Samuel Selvon, Roger Mais, and Earl Lovelace, and poets Martin Carter, Edward Kamu Braithwaite, Dennis Scott, and Merwyn Morris are commanding increasing critical attention; Kincaid thus is among a new generation of West Indians who are contributing to the formation of a distinctive literary tradition.

Bibliography
Caton, Louis F. "Romantic Struggles: The Bildungsroman and Mother-Daughter Bonding in Jamaica Kincaid's *Annie John*." *MELUS* 21 (Fall, 1996): 125-142. Caton analyzes Kincaid's use of *Bildungsroman* traditions in her novel. He explores the masculine *bildung* narrative and the narrative of female psychological growth, conflict presentation of the mother-daughter relationship, and psychological interpretations of familial alliances.
Dutton, Wendy. "Merge and Separate: Jamaica Kincaid's Fiction." *World Literature Today* 63 (Summer, 1989): 406-410. Dutton discusses the relationship between autobiographical elements in *At the Bottom of the River* and *Annie John*. She analyzes the tension between mother and daughter as not only generational in origin but also as the suppression of Ma Chess's role in curing Annie.
Ismond, Patricia. "Jamaica Kincaid: 'First They Must Be Children.'" *World Literature Written in English* 28 (Autumn, 1988): 336-341. Tracing the struggle between mother and daughter, Ismond regards their conflict as the classic confrontation between self and other. She views Annie as a kind of innate child-trickster figure whose efforts to escape her mother's influence lead them both ultimately to the need for reunion.
Kincaid, Jamaica. "A Lot of Memory." Interview by Moira Ferguson. *The Kenyon Review* 16 (Winter, 1994): 163-188. Kincaid talks about the experimental, mainstream, antibiographical anticolonialism, and radicalism in her novels. She makes clear her views about black Americans, who she says are a nationalistic minority, and black West Indians, who she believes are a contented minority. She also comments on her books *Annie John* and *Lucy*.
Murdoch, H. Adlai. "Severing the (M)other Connection: The Representation of Cultural Identity in Jamaica Kincaid's *Annie John*." *Callaloo* 13 (Spring, 1990): 325-340. Using psychoanalytic theories, Murdoch explores the Oedipal sources of Annie's rebellion, linking the girl's need for independence with the West Indian need for a distinct identity apart from that of the colonial period. In unraveling the analogies between parental-child conflicts and the colonial subject's experience of oppression, Murdoch defines several key oppositions throughout the novel.
Perry, Donna. "Initiation in Jamaica Kincaid's *Annie John*." In *Caribbean Women Writers: Essays from the First International Conference*, edited by Selwyn R. Cudjoe. Wellesley, Mass.: Calaloux Publications, 1990. Perry discusses storytelling traditions in the West Indies, seeing Annie's narrative as participatory in the matrilineal relationships that are grounded in those traditions. She also explores the role of obeah in shaping Annie's cure from her experience of dissociation.

Stanchich, Maritza. "Home Is Where the Heart Breaks: Identity Crisis in *Annie John* and *Wide Sargasso Sea.*" *Caribbean Studies* 27 (July-December, 1994): 454-458. Stanchich discusses identity crisis among women as thematic subjects in Kincaid's *Annie John* and Jean Rhys's *Wide Sargasso Sea.* She compares the similarities in the experiences of the female protagonists, analyzes the unified self within Annie in *Annie John*, and explores the fragmented self within Antoinette in *Wide Sargasso Sea.*

Timothy, Helen Pyne. "Adolescent Rebellion and Gender Relations in *At the Bottom of the River* and *Annie John.*" In *Caribbean Women Writers: Essays from the First International Conference*, edited by Selwyn R. Cudjoe. Wellesley, Mass.: Calaloux Publications, 1990. A thorough close reading of the novel. Timothy's analysis combines psychological, aesthetic, and cultural approaches in her assertion that Caribbean sexual repression elicits Annie's rebellion.

Michael Loudon

ANYWHERE BUT HERE

Author: Mona Simpson (1957-   )
Type of plot: Bildungsroman
Time of plot: Primarily the 1960's and the 1970's
Locale: Bay City, Wisconsin, and Los Angeles, California
First published: 1986

>   *Principal characters:*
>   ANN, the main narrator, the youngest of the four women whose lives
>   are the novel's focus
>   ADELE, Ann's mother, an emotionally charged person whose behavior
>   ranges from eccentric to unstable
>   CAROL, Adele's older sister, who narrates several sections of the novel
>   LILLIAN, Carol's mother, who shelters Ann when Adele cannot
>   properly care for her

The Novel

Anywhere but Here is the fictionalized saga of an American family. Three generations of women take turns narrating chapters of a personal and cultural history that
spans the years between the turn of the twentieth century and the beginning of the
1980's. The novel's nine parts do not proceed chronologically. The speakers relate events as they recall them, each adding detail and emotion to one another's
stories.

The first batch of memories is delivered by Ann, beginning with her infuriated
mother's practice of stopping the car on the roads of the family's native Wisconsin and
the highways that lead to California and forcing her daughter out of the car. After driving out of sight, Adele usually returns minutes later, often with an ice-cream cone as a
peace offering. What brings Adele and Ann to a strip of desert highway near the California border, and later to the posh Bel-Air Hotel, is a trail of men that includes Ted
Diamond, a skating instructor with whom Adele buys a house in a Wisconsin suburb.
A secret plan to flee Wisconsin for Los Angeles, where Ann can have a career in television, a dream her mother has always encouraged, is disrupted by Adele's marriage
to Ted. When life in Wisconsin finally becomes too unpleasant, Adele and twelve-
year-old Ann load up an almost-new Lincoln Continental they can ill afford and begin
the journey West.

Ann pauses, and her grandmother begins to speak. Lillian narrates the events of her
life, from girlhood in a large Catholic family to a sexual encounter with and marriage
to Art in the early years of the twentieth century. Carol is born shortly thereafter, and
Adele is born years later, at the beginning of the Great Depression. Lillian continues
to describe the family tree: Carol marries Jimmy Measey, a local Bay City man, after
she returns from World War II; they have two sons, Hal and Benny. Adele marries an
Egyptian community-college professor named Hisham; Ann is her only child.

When Ann again takes up the narration, she is recalling the difficult first days spent with her mother in California. Ann and Adele establish a tense and lonely existence, finding themselves short of friends and money. Adele works in the Los Angeles school system, and Ann attends a lower school that will lead her to the prestigious Beverly Hills High School. At this point, Ann digresses, turning to memories of her father. She sees Hisham only twice after he leaves Adele. Returning to life in California, Ann tells of Adele's fruitless affair with Lonnie Tishman, a shiftless, perhaps dangerous land developer. After breaking off with him, Adele begins seeing a dentist whose daughter is in Ann's class. She deludes herself into thinking that Dr. Spritzer will be their salvation.

Carol remembers some good times when her boys and her niece were young children. She can even recall one pleasant trip she took with Adele when the sisters were girls. Yet she also tells the story of Hal's troubled teenage years. After returning from Vietnam, Hal becomes addicted to drugs and is arrested. Lillian has her first of several strokes when she sees Hal on the news. As painful as these memories are, Carol hints, her recollections of Benny are much harder to live with.

Ann thinks back on her life in Wisconsin, particularly her attachment to Benny. She tells the story of returning to Bay City with her mother for her cousin's funeral when Carol's younger son is killed in a car crash. Ann then returns to the California years and a time when Adele's life is ruled by an obsession with her therapist, Dr. Hawthorne. Hawthorne does not share Adele's interest, and when the frustration overwhelms her, Adele attacks Ann, who decides, this time, to fight back and knocks her mother to the floor. Unable to separate from her fantasy, Adele orders a wedding gown. Left to her own devices while her mother schemes, Ann manages to land the television acting role Adele had always wanted for her. She uses the money and fame from her television career to enter Brown University; she leaves her mother and status-conscious Southern California, not expecting to return any time soon.

The women finish their stories. Carol tells of her slow recovery form Benny's death, her mother's death, Jimmy's heart attack, and her own cancer. Ann describes her college years, a time of independence and emotional fulfillment. When she finally returns to California, her mother seems more stable. Adele has the last word, articulating a developing cosmic belief in the oneness of all things and looking back with pride on her decision to leave Wisconsin and rear her daughter in California.

The Characters

Ann is a skillful storyteller. Her sensitivity to minute details and sensations is the result of a life spent watching out for Adele's volatile moods and actions. Hers is the literary voice of the novel, even though it is her mother who claims to be writing a book. Ann has a lyrical descriptive style and represents her emotions in intriguing metaphors. Her imagination has grown powerful because it is her method of escape from and defense against Adele.

Ann portrays herself as a victim of Adele's insanity. Traumatic events such as being abandoned along the roadside and having her mother threaten suicide have conditioned Ann to fear the very thing that would relieve her—separating from Adele. This love/hate relationship twists the young Ann. She exhibits signs of sexual confusion, manipulating other children into posing for nude photographs, and of moral uncertainty, growing accustomed to dishonesty, and even theft, as a survival mechanism. Ann does survive, however, and after escaping to college in the East, she begins to straighten herself out and experience personal fulfillment. She also develops an ability to appreciate her mother's unique and impressive traits and to forgive the mistreatment she suffered as a child.

Adele is capable of both compassion and cruelty. She is an unpredictable force that can suddenly change the lives of those around her. Her energy drives the novel. Although in her chaotic younger years Adele causes Ann to suffer humiliations and disappointments, the reader is given a different impression of Adele in the book's last chapter. Carol tells Ann she finally gets along with Adele, and Ann, returning from years of living on her own, is able to share a tender moment with her mother. The frightening image of an enraged, malevolent bully is replaced by the serene voice of a woman who has pacified herself with ancient as well as New Age philosophies. Adele has also repaired the self-esteem she had lacked in the days when, of she and her daughter, it was she who seemed the neediest, the most like a child.

Lillian speaks only once, and the reader comes to know her more through Ann's vision than through her own words. She provides her granddaughter with an unregulated supply of emotional and material security until Adele takes Ann to California. Ann's memory of her grandmother is idyllic. Lillian, unlike Adele, is a stoic. She is a source of calm in the novel, having endured a life of calamity without becoming warped. Her strokes mark a new period in the family history, a time when events have become so extreme that even Lillian cannot withstand their debilitating effect.

Carol is a source of compassion and tolerance even though her own life has been full of privation and tragedy. When she refuses to have a tumor in her breast treated, she is stubbornly holding onto a symbol of the pain and loss that define her. Her monologues describe her efforts to resist martyrdom and make peace with her own memories. Carol's moderate success contributes to the novel's theme of recovery.

Themes and Meanings

The lives of middle-class American women in the twentieth century is the predominant focus of *Anywhere but Here*. Recurring themes illustrate the differences and similarities between the three generations of speakers. All the women in the novel discuss their memories of food and, often in connection with food, the appearance of their bodies. Their experiences with sex and partnership illustrate a change in American values. Lillian, who comes of age in the 1920's, marries the first man with whom she is intimate and does not remarry after Art's death. Carol has many flings before returning home from the war and settling down with Jimmy. Adele marries twice during the 1960's and has a series of boyfriends in San Francisco. Whatever the social circumstances, the novel suggests, the issues of love and sex are complicated and painful ones. For Ann, sexual identity is a problem. Several upsetting episodes from childhood still trouble her as she hesitantly explores her physical desires during her high-school years. Later, after leaving California, Ann describes a rewarding romantic relationship. She is learning to experience love without the fear of destruction by which it has always been accompanied.

Ann's college years are her period of recovery from the wounds of life with her mother. Along with the turmoil each woman experiences come periods of calm and often healing. There are many physical recoveries in the novel. As a boy, Benny is in and out of hospital emergency rooms, but he never slows down until the day he dies on the road. Hal recovers from drug addiction, Jimmy from heart disease, and Carol from breast cancer. Carol and Jimmy's recovery from the loss of Benny, achieved through a lawsuit against the father of the boy who drove the car in which their son was killed, allows them to place blame and put their memory of the tragedy to rest. It also enables them to make their lives more comfortable, bringing the money for a swimming pool and other home improvements. Simpson provides a profound description of the ironic combination of physical and emotional compensation available through the legal system and the insurance industry.

Adele's recuperation is also based on both physical and spiritual well being. She is calmed by "all these various philosophies," by the New Age ambition to heal oneself. On the other hand, as Ann discovers, her stability is guaranteed by an immaculate new car, a stash of antiques, and a plentiful supply of clean, stylish clothes. Neither Adele nor Ann truly begins to revive until their poisonous relationship is all but ended by Ann's leaving home.

Anywhere but Here is an intense study of character, but the depiction of society is detailed and realistic as well. Changes in the American cultural scene and value system are carefully marked. The then-steady increase in the middle-class standard of living is comically apparent in Jimmy's anxious anticipation of a late 1950's Christmas morning. A material value system grips Adele. She often substitutes things, possessions, for emotional needs. The war in Vietnam and the social upheaval of the late 1960's is a heavy presence in the novel. Close-knit neighborhoods are sadly altered by the absence of young men who have died and by those who, as Carol's son Hal puts it, are never the same when they return. The economic hard times of the 1970's are felt by Adele and Ann, who cannot afford the social climb they are attempting. Deprived of innocence, abandoned or betrayed by those whom she had no choice but to trust, her mother and father, Ann grows up cynical and guarded. She wears the scars of the post-Vietnam era.

Critical Context

Portions of *Anywhere but Here* originally appeared in literary magazines. The novel, a bestseller, reached a wider audience. It joined a growing movement in literary and psychological writing devoted to the exploration of personality in relation to upbringing. Mona Simpson depicts what might by now be recognized as a dysfunctional family. She is also aware of the culture of healing, the self-affirmation manuals and recovery programs, to which many turn for redemption.

Domestic fiction has examined the erosion of the ideal of the nuclear family and attempted to account for the increasing number of real families headed by women living without men. In exploring such themes, *Anywhere but Here* is related to contemporary works such as Sue Miller's *The Good Mother* (1987) and Ann Tyler's *Dinner at the Homesick Restaurant* (1982). Simpson's focus on the theme of storytelling also relates to the technique of oral history, the gathering of personal narratives, which has become a prominent aspect of women's historical writing. Simpson is also the author of a second novel, *The Lost Father* (1992).

Bibliography

Beevor, Antony. "Heading West." *The Times Literary Supplement*, June 26, 1987, 698. This enthusiastic reading of the novel identifies Simpson as a member of the "hyper-realist" school of fiction. Beevor appreciates Simpson's attention to detail, finding the depiction of the paradoxes of American culture fascinating. He assures the English reader that *Anywhere but Here* is a special, not a typical, example of the great American novel.

Flower, Dean. "Anywhere but Here." *Hudson Review* 40 (Summer, 1987): 321. Flower takes the title of his review of several contemporary novels from his personal favorite. He compares Simpson's novel to, among other works, *A Summons to Memphis* (1986), by Peter Taylor.

Heller, Dana A. "Shifting Gears: Transmission and Flight in Mona Simpson's *Anywhere but Here*." *University of Hartford Studies in Literature* 21 (1989): 37-44. The theme of escape is a concern of this study. Heller also focuses on mother-daughter relationships and on the nature of desire in the novel.

Morse, Deborah Denenholz. "The Difficult Journey Home: Mona Simpson's *Anywhere but Here*." In *Mother Puzzles: Daughters and Mothers in Contemporary American Literature*, edited by Mickey Pearlman. New York: Greenwood Press, 1989. Morse's essay is an exploration of themes in the novel from a literary point of view. She discusses the mythic importance of the issue of flight and the search for home, evoking the biblical story of Eden. Morse also deals frankly with the issue of Ann's sexual development.

Schreiber, Le Anne. "In Thrall to a Lethal Mother." *The New York Times Book Review* 92 (January 11, 1987): 7. This review speculates on the reader's reactions to the novel's characters and narrative structure. Schreiber predicts a feeling of frustration in response to the psychological turmoil depicted.

Simpson, Mona. "Mona Simpson: The Return of the Prodigal Father." Interview by Jonathan Bing. *Publishers Weekly* 243 (November 4, 1996): 50-51. Simpson discusses her probing of family dynamics and her background and acknowledges that much of her work is autobiographical.

Nick David Smart

THE APPLE IN THE DARK

Author: Clarice Lispector (1925-1977)
Type of plot: Mythic quest
Time of plot: The late 1950's
Locale: A remote, desolate farming region of Brazil
First published: A maçã no Escuro, 1961 (English translation, 1967)

> *Principal characters:*
> MARTIM, the protagonist, who is on the run from the law
> VITÓRIA, the owner-manager of the farm where Martim comes to stay
> ERMELINDA, a young, widowed cousin of Vitória

The Novel

On the surface, the story in *The Apple in the Dark* could not be simpler. A man commits a crime, flees into the desolate interior of Brazil, arrives at a remote farm, is taken on as a farmhand, is reported to the authorities, and is arrested and returned to face the law. It is not the minimal action of the plot which intrigues the reader but rather the process of searching for some meaning in life, for some definition of the world and of one's place in it, that provides the interest of the novel.

Primarily, it is Martim's quest for self-awareness that forms the core of the story. The mythic nature of his quest is straightforwardly indicated by the titles of the three sections into which the book is divided: "How a Man Is Made," "The Birth of the Hero," and "The Apple in the Dark." Indeed, the author, in a stroke of brilliance, has managed to combine parallels to at least two major, complementary views of man's existence in the unfolding of Martim's symbolic journey: the biblical story of the Garden of Eden and the Darwinian theory of evolution. From the beginning of the book, the reader is alerted to these two viewpoints. Martim awakes from sleep "on a night as dark as night can get," immediately after fleeing from a crime which he will come to see as an act that frees him to start all over again in life. His flight takes him first through total darkness over unknown terrain, which permits him to focus exclusively on his sensual feelings and to ignore the burden of civilization behind him. As the sun comes up, he begins to appreciate an even closer identity with nature in its most primitive forms: stones, dirt, searing heat, silence. Bereft of language, he discovers a great joy in repeating meaningless statements to the flora and fauna around him. By the time, early in the novel, that he comes upon the farmhouse where most of the story takes place, he has duplicated a sort of climb up the evolutionary ladder. Having shed the trappings of a man, he has begun to learn what it is to be like "a creature [who] does not think and does not get involved, and is still completely there."

The farm is owned and run by Vitória, an unmarried woman in her fifties who appears to be a tower of strength and self-reliance. Staying with her is her cousin Ermelinda, a dreamy, ethereal woman recently widowed, whose rather poetic manner of approaching life is a constant source of uneasiness for Vitória. The bulk of the novel consists in observing, through the eyes of the three principal characters, the slow process of change in Martim and the effect that he has on Vitória and Ermelinda. By the novel's end, however, the reader cannot be sure that the two women have experienced any genuine enlightenment, although it is probable that the protagonist now at least realizes that he has missed gaining a firm grip on the meaning of existence. In the last paragraph of the book, Martim finally understands that "we are not so guilty after all; we are more stupid than guilty." The quest for knowledge, he learns too late, is like "reaching for an apple in the dark—and trying not to drop it."

The Characters

The principal characters differ from one another radically, but they are similar in that each has a terrible fear particular to himself or herself. For Martim, it is the fear of acting—a fear which explains why the crime that he committed, one which he cherishes as an *act*, is essential to his survival. The crime, the nature of which is revealed only toward the end of the story, represents Martim's symbolic banishment from Eden. Yet to Martim, a man who was in his former life a statistician—whose life depended on the most abstract of occupations—the crime is the impetus that sets him on the road to salvation, or so he believes. Martim is destined to be disillusioned, however, as he goes from rocks to plants to vermin to cattle to children and eventually to adults once again. Having abandoned his wife, son, job, and friends and fled into this wilderness, he nevertheless falls back into an involvement with complex human beings.

Vitória has spent much of her life caring for her dying father, and as a result, she has never had or at least has never reached for, a love of her own. She now fears love and has hardened herself against all possibility of it. The confrontation with Martim finally forces her to face her empty and near-tragic existence. At the climax of the novel, which occurs rather melodramatically during a rare and violent rainstorm, Vitória, unable to bear her dearth of love, races to the woodshed where Martim sleeps. Martim, however, has fled into the woods during the storm, like King Lear, distraught and seeking cleansing and purification in nature. It is not long after this episode that Vitória calls for the authorities to come pick up Martim.

Ermelinda has an elliptical way of talking to people. Unlike her cousin, she embraces love; in fact, she falls in love with Martim almost at first sight, and before long they have become lovers. Yet her way of expressing her feeling for him is strangely indirect. She explains that if she comes up and says to him, "Look at that fern!" she is really saying, "I love you." Indeed, Ermelinda is so frightened of death that she has retreated into a world of private symbolism.

Themes and Meanings

Clarice Lispector read her existentialists closely. One can pick up veiled allusions to novels by Jean-Paul Sartre and Albert Camus in *The Apple in the Dark*. The character of Martim contains elements of both Meursault in Camus's *The Stranger* (1942) and Roquentin in Sartre's *Nausea* (1938). Though unaware of the existentialist's dictum, "Existence precedes Essence," the protagonist has, in fact, set out in search of his own essence. What Martim fails to realize, and what will ultimately bring him up short in his quest for a new Eden, is that he has deluded himself from the beginning. It is almost as if he is telling the reader that his crime was necessary as a means of escaping from a banal and deadening existence into a chance for true, human essence. His error lies in thinking that the initial act will not color subsequent events; indeed, it will determine them.

Critical Context

Clarice Lispector achieved her first general acclaim for the collection of stories *Laços de Familia* (1960; *Family Ties*, 1972), in which many of the protagonists, like Martim, struggle—often unsuccessfully—for a sense of self and harmony with the outside world. This concern with what John Gledson has called an "intense, almost exclusive interest in the subjective world," which receives its most complex articulation in *The Apple in the Dark*, is also examined in *A Paixão Segundo G. H.* (1964; the passion according to G. H.) and *Água viva* (1973; sparkling water), and places Lispector among the Brazilian revisionists: those postwar writers whose move away from the regionalism of the 1920's and 1930's and whose focus on more universal themes has been a major force in mainstreaming Brazilian literature. Indeed, Gregory Rabassa, in the introduction to his translation of *The Apple in the Dark*, includes Lispector among those contemporary Brazilian novelists who are "in tune with . . . international currents."

Bibliography

Cixous, Helene. *Reading with Clarice Lispector.* Minneapolis: University of Minnesota Press, 1990. Chapters on *The Stream of Life*, *The Apple in the Dark*, "The Egg and the Chicken," and *The Hour of the Star.* The book includes an introduction by Verena Andermatt Conley, carefully explaining Cixous's critical approach to Lispector. Recommended for advanced students.

Coutinho, Afranio. *An Introduction to Literature in Brazil.* New York: Columbia University Press, 1960. A major Brazilian critic assesses Lispector's achievement, emphasizing her place in Brazilian literature and her powerful metaphorical and atmospheric fiction.

Fitz, Earl F. *Clarice Lispector.* Boston: Twayne, 1985. A useful introduction that includes a chapter of biography, a discussion of Lispector's place in Brazilian literature; a study of her style, structure, and point of view in her novels and short stories; and her nonfiction work. Includes chronology, detailed notes, and a well-annotated bibliography.

Lowe, Elizabeth. *The City in Brazilian Literature.* Rutherford, N.J.: Fairleigh Dickinson University Press, 1982. Discusses Lispector as an urban writer, focusing mainly on *A cidade sitiada*, *The Passion According to G. H.*, and *The Stream of Life*.

Peixoto, Marta. *Passionate Fictions: Gender, Narrative, and Violence in Clarice Lispector.* Minneapolis: University of Minnesota Press, 1994. Written with a decidedly feminist bias, *Passionate Fictions* analyzes Lispector's frequently violent subject matter, juxtaposing it with her strange and original use of language. Special attention is paid to the nexus with Helene Cixous and to the autobiographical elements of *The Stream of Life* and *A via crucis do corpo*.

Christopher R. McRae

THE APPRENTICESHIP OF DUDDY KRAVITZ

Author: Mordecai Richler (1931-   )
Type of plot: Social satire
Time of plot: The post-World War II era
Locale: Montreal and Ste. Agathe des Monts in the Laurentian mountains of Canada
First published: 1959

> *Principal characters:*
>   DUDDY KRAVITZ, a young Jewish boy determined to be a success
>   YVETTE, the French Canadian girl who loves him
>   MAX, his father, a taxi driver
>   VIRGIL, an epileptic from the United States who admires Duddy
>   SIMCHA, Duddy's grandfather
>   JERRY DINGLEMAN, the "Boy Wonder," Duddy's hero who later
>   becomes a rival

The Novel

The Apprenticeship of Duddy Kravitz is the story of an ambitious Jewish boy growing up in a poor neighborhood in Montreal. It is both a portrait of a young man who is desperately determined to be successful and of the various communities he has to deal with in his quest: working-class Jewish, Jewish establishment, French Canadian, and Anglo-Saxon. The novel opens in 1947, while Duddy is still in high school. He creates havoc throughout his neighborhood, tormenting various people who have offended or insulted him.

A series of vignettes introduces Duddy's family and neighborhood. Although Duddy loves his family, he often feels inferior to his brother, Lennie, who is struggling through medical school. His father, Max, frequently ignores Duddy's feelings in order to focus on Lennie, the successful sibling. Max's brother, Benjy, feels the same. While he sends Lennie through medical school, he shows disdain for Duddy. The one member of the family who feels real affection for Duddy is his grandfather, Simcha. He is the one who persuades Duddy that a man must have land in order to be successful.

The summer after Duddy is graduated from high school, he works as a waiter in a resort in the Laurentian mountains. The rest of the staff are college students who either mock or ignore him. One of them, Irwin Shubert, the son of a prominent attorney, continually harasses Duddy. At the summer's end, he sets Duddy up to bankroll a rigged roulette game. When Duddy loses all the money he worked so hard to make, he escapes to the beach. Followed by some worried friends, he hides, hoping they will think he drowned. He spends the rest of the night with Yvette, another worker at the hotel, who is French Canadian. When Duddy returns in the morning, Irwin is forced to return the money. Duddy has always had many money-making schemes: renting movies, making color movies of bar mitzvahs and weddings, producing feature films, establishing a newspaper. He is thrilled because now he has money to finance some of them. One day, Yvette takes him to a secluded lake near the resort. Duddy becomes obsessed with the land around it, envisioning it as a fabulous resort community. Although he and Yvette make love, he is distracted. That piece of property has become his true love, the fulfillment of his grandfather's advice.

Duddy returns home at the end of the summer, determined to succeed. He works hard and eventually sets up film-making projects. He finds an office, asks Yvette to work for him, and begins putting down payments on some of the land he so desperately wants. Because he is a minor, he is forced to put the property in Yvette's name. In his search to finance his land purchases, he turns to Max, who had frequently bragged about his friend Dingleman, the Boy Wonder, a former neighborhood resident who made his fortune in gambling. However when Max finally sets up a meeting between Duddy and Dingleman, it becomes apparent that his father has been lying about their connection. When Dingleman offers him a job as a waiter, Duddy angrily storms out. Dingleman, noticing a surprising innocent quality in Duddy, recruits him to smuggle drugs unwittingly from New York to Canada. In New York, he meets another innocent, Virgil, an American who is trying to sell ten pinball machines. Duddy promises to buy them if Virgil can somehow get them to Montreal.

Shortly after his return, Lennie disappears, and Duddy goes to Toronto to find him. He learns that Lennie has been hanging around with a crowd of rich, mostly Gentile, college students. One of them—Duddy's old nemesis, Irwin Shubert—has talked Lennie into performing an abortion. When problems arise, Lennie runs away, not wishing to face the shame. Duddy brings him back and persuades the girl's father to make sure no charges are placed against Lennie.

Virgil arrives, and Duddy hires him to drive around distributing rented movies, even though he knows that it is dangerous because Virgil is an epileptic who has begun having seizures. Although Yvette lives with Duddy, he treats her badly, never even considering marriage because she is not Jewish. As quickly as success came, things fall apart. Virgil is injured in an accident, and Yvette leaves to take care of him. Soon, Duddy is bankrupt and driving a taxi day and night to hang on to his dream of owning the land. He finally goes to visit Yvette and Virgil and begins to relax; during this visit, though, he learns that the last two owners of the property wish to sell it immediately.

He becomes desperate, trying to borrow money, even trying to blackmail Dingleman. Finally, he forges Virgil's signature to a check, stealing his insurance money from the accident. After he convinces Yvette to sign the other deeds over to his father, the land is finally his. However, when he takes his family to see it, Simcha says he is ashamed of the way Duddy got the land and wants no part of it. Duddy then goes to see Yvette, who also wants nothing more to do with him. Duddy's depression lasts until Max praises him and a waiter recognizes him as an important landowner.

The Characters

The Apprenticeship of Duddy Kravitz gives a rich portrayal of a wide range of characters who populated Montreal during the period immediately after World War II. Although it concentrates on the working-class Jewish community, Richler's work is filled with many insights into other groups as well. The novel's episodic structure and abundance of characters create an amazingly vivid portrait of a time and place. Even his minor characters stand out, presenting vivid social and satiric commentary. This rich mix of detail mirrors the complexity of real life.

Richler very dispassionately presents both the positive and negative aspects of his characters. Nowhere is this seen more clearly than in Richler's development of his protagonist. The first section of the novel presents Duddy as a rather unpleasant troublemaker. Gradually, however, he gathers the reader's sympathy when his search for his father's approval meets with dismissal and indifference. His humiliation at the hands of the upper-class waiters at the resort increases the reader's understanding. However, this scene is followed immediately by his shabby rejection of Yvette. Ironically, throughout the novel, Duddy works very hard to win the love of his family, never completely succeeding. In these relationships, he is strong and loving. However, he ignores and then brutally betrays the two people who do love him, Virgil and Yvette, in much the same dismissive manner as he is treated by his family. In a deathbed letter, his uncle Benjy sums up Duddy's two natures, the scheming bastard and the kind intelligent person. He warns Duddy that although it is possible for a boy to have many personalities, by the time he is a man, one has come to the forefront by murdering the others.

Max provides another example of a double-sided personality. He is often cheerful, a good fellow, a taxi driver who gets along well with his companions at the local cigar store. However, he is also a shallow braggart who ignores one of his sons and supplements his income as a part-time pimp. Although Duddy admires his grandfather, he picks up his value system from Max, who taught him to admire Dingleman, a poor boy who became wealthy any way that he could.

Yvette, although less fully developed than many of the less important characters in the novel, serves as a moral touchstone for Duddy. She is the first person to believe in Duddy and his dream. Although she frequently disapproves of his unscrupulous behavior, she does love him. In spite of his callous treatment of her, she supports him until his final betrayal of Virgil. Her rejection of Duddy at the novel's end, accompanied by the disappointment of his grandfather, signals the extent to which Duddy has betrayed the better aspects of his personality.

Themes and Meanings

Mordecai Richler's major theme in *The Apprenticeship of Duddy Kravitz* is the price of success. He warns that this price can be very high indeed when one seeks success at any cost. The novel explores the origins of that need in Duddy. Even as a small motherless boy, Duddy was driven to win the attention of both adults and his peers. He particularly sought the admiration of his father, equating approval with the acquisition of money. It is easy to see why he believed this. After all, the much-praised Lennie was admired because he was going to be a wealthy doctor. In fact, the entire society equates wealth with importance and worth. The pride of St. Urban Street, highly praised by everyone, is Dingleman, who made his fortune gambling and smuggling drugs. Duddy was only following in that pattern when, at twelve, he stole spare hockey sticks from the Montreal Canadiens and cheated American stamp companies. Later in the novel, the wealthy Jewish businessman Cohen tells him that every successful man has a dirty secret.

Duddy is not the typical materialist, however. He desires money because it will allow him to achieve his fantasy, to reach his grandfather's goal. Duddy is a dreamer at heart. He has convinced himself that his resort will be a haven for his family and for Virgil and Yvette as well. When he accuses Yvette of betraying him after she refuses to forgive him for the theft, he is very serious.

An underlying theme of the novel is ethnic prejudice and class consciousness as it existed during the period. Duddy's world is rigidly structured, and true friendship seldom exists between groups. The novel is filled with examples. Yvette's family rejects her for associating with Duddy. The rich Gentile Calder gets upset when Duddy tries to promote a business deal, and Duddy is convinced it is because of anti-Semitism. Even Virgil's attempt to form a union for epileptics underscores this point.

Critical Context

Mordecai Richler is one of Canada's most prominent writers. In addition to novels, he has written literary and social criticism, essays, screenplays, and some wonderfully humorous children's books. With the publication of his first novel, *The Acrobats* (1954), at age twenty-two, he was hailed as a promising new talent. *The Apprenticeship of Duddy Kravitz* was viewed as the fulfillment of that promise. While some critics find it too episodic, others consider it one of the finest Canadian novels of the twentieth century. Both a social satire and a *Bildungsroman*, it re-creates the multiethnic world of post-World War II Montreal. Many of the characters in the novel, including Duddy, reappear in a later novel, *St. Urbain's Horsemen* (1971). Both of these, like most of Richler's novels, are firmly rooted in his Jewish Canadian background. Throughout his writings, Richler gives a devastatingly accurate portrayal of that world. Although he has been accused of both anti-Semitism and anti-Canadianism, his unflinching portraits are filled with dark humor and rich characterizations. In *The Apprenticeship of Duddy Kravitz*, Richler re-creates Montreal at the middle of the twentieth century, resplendent in all its virtues and vices.

Bibliography

Craniford, Ada. *Fiction and Fact in Mordecai Richler's Novels*. Lewiston, Me.: Edwin Mellon Press, 1992. An examination of literary sources and influences on Richler. Discusses Jewish and Gentile aspects of the novel.

Darling, Michael, ed. *Perspectives on Mordecai Richler*. Toronto: ECW Press, 1986. Discusses themes and images that recur in Richler's work. Presents different critical views on the character and moral values in *The Apprenticeship of Duddy Kravitz*.

Davison, Arnold E. *Mordecai Richler*. New York: Frederick Ungar, 1983. Portrays Duddy as a shallow chaser of the American Dream. Compares his loyalty to family with his rejection of Yvette. A revealing psychological study.

Ramraj, Victor J. *Mordecai Richler.* Boston: Twayne, 1983. Discusses the ambivalent
     vision that is the core of the themes and characters in Richler's fiction. Analyzes
     use of episodic structure and humor in *The Apprenticeship of Duddy Kravitz.*
Richler, Mordecai. *The Street: A Memoir.* Toronto: Ryerson Press, 1971. Presents the
     autobiographical counterpart to many of the characters and scenes in *The Appren-
     ticeship of Duddy Kravitz,* including St. Urbain Street and Fletcher's Field High
     School. Provides helpful insights into the world of Richler's fiction.

Mary E. Mahony

AS MAX SAW IT

Author: Louis Begley (1933-   )
Type of plot: Psychological realism
Time of plot: 1974-1989
Locale: Italy, China, and the Boston area
First published: 1994

> *Principal characters:*
> MAX STRONG, the narrator and central figure, a professor of contract
>   law and legal history at Harvard University
> CHARLIE SWAN, Max's college friend, whose relationships with Max
>   and Toby become the focus of the novel
> TOBY, Max's friend and Charlie's lover, whose death from AIDS brings
>   the novel to a dramatic conclusion
> CAMILLA, Max's first wife, who has an affair with Toby, moves to
>   England after her divorce, and remarries
> LAURA, an attractive redhead whom Max meets in Italy and later
>   marries

The Novel

As Max Saw It combines introspection and observation in the narration of its princi-pal character, Max Strong, who becomes an intimate of the wealthy and famous. De-spite a failed marriage, he prospers and is drawn ever more closely into Charlie Swan's relationship with Toby, whose death from AIDS leads Charlie to choose the same fate.

At the Rumorosa, the Italian villa of Edna and Rodney Joyce on the edge of Lake Como, Max is introduced by his friend Arthur to the Joyces and their guests. As a poor, salaried academic, Max feels ill at ease, not their "sort." Among the guests is Toby, a youth so attractive that Max at first thinks he is a young woman. Max also en-counters his former Harvard classmate, Charlie Swan, now a famous architect. Large, handsome, overbearing, Charlie is angry at Max for not attending Charlie's marriage ten years earlier. The two make up, however, and their relationship continues to the end. Also at the villa is Laura, an attractive redhead with an art gallery in Milan. Their flirtation culminates in their sharing her bed that night.

Returning to Boston, Max visits Cousin Emma, an ailing widow whose chief con-cern is what to do with her considerable wealth. She decides that Max, her only re-maining relative, should receive it upon her death. A year later, Max is in Beijing to give a seminar on contract law. His attractive guide, Miss Wang, who plans to come to Harvard, takes him to the Forbidden City, where they happen upon Charlie Swan with Toby. At the hotel, Charlie explains to Max his transition from heterosexuality to ho-mosexuality.

The story then shifts ahead ten years. Max is nearing the age of fifty and enjoying both wealth and professional success. Miss Wang has come to Harvard, and their affair is pleasant and brief. Soon, he meets Camilla, marries her, and buys a house in the Berkshires near Charlie. Their active social life soon includes Roland Cartwright, Camilla's former lover now teaching at Boston University. As Max becomes absorbed in his writing, Camilla spends more time at her work in Boston and more time with Roland. Max suspects an affair, but she dodges his efforts to find the truth. His finished book is a great success, he is awarded a prestigious teaching position, but his suspicions of an affair continue. Finally, Camilla tells Max that she will move to London without him. A few months later, they divorce. Roland soon follows, but before leaving, he tells Max that Camilla was indeed having an affair—with Toby.

During the next two years, Max devotes himself to teaching and travel, and he buys a new house, again near Charlie. Toby is assigned the task of redecorating it, having discovered a talent for design and having been forgiven for his indiscretion with Camilla. Toby remains strikingly handsome, but his health has begun to deteriorate. On a return visit to the Rumorosa, Max renews his relations with Laura. Soon they marry, and she becomes pregnant, bringing him extreme happiness. Both Max and Charlie give blood to sustain Toby's life, but nothing avails, and Toby dies. Charlie arranges a magnificent funeral. Afterward, Charlie tells Max a grisly story: Toby wanted "fraternity" in death, so Charlie, in a frenzy of self-mutilation and self-sacrifice, has had sex with his dying lover, thus dooming himself to the same fate Toby faced. Max is left feeling intensely aware of the suffering and futility of life. He finally realizes that Charlie selected Giuseppe Verdi's *Requiem* for Toby's funeral not for its solemn plea for forgiveness, as he thought, but simply for its beauty.

The Characters

Begley's gift for drawing portraits lends flashes of insight to the novel, and character is often revealed not only in description but in the vocabulary and the rhythms of Begley's style, as when Camilla, speaking of Arthur, tells Max, "Don't let him come here again. He's not my kind of pansy." Begley is especially adept at painting character in brief strokes. On first seeing Toby, Max sees "Eros himself, longhaired and dimpled, his skin the color of pale amber. . . ."

Max Strong is considered an intellectual by the more worldly group with whom he socializes, but he is nevertheless liked and respected, and his inheritance gives him social authenticity. In the beginning, he is somewhat detached from others, confessing that "Relationships did not stick to me," but he is nevertheless "curious about obligations." As he prospers, his relationships deepen, and his understanding of the obligations required of human relationships matures. By the novel's end, he has become wholly attached to Charlie, Toby, and Laura. Max's transition from outsider to one who finds in human relationships a better understanding of human commitment and suffering is the book's principal subject.

Charlie Swan teaches Max much about human relationships and sacrifice. Charlie dedicates his life to the pursuit of beauty and its emotional fulfillment. This pursuit is reflected in his relationship with Toby and his profession as an architect, which has made him wealthy and famous. His development from heterosexuality to homosexuality parallels his professional and emotional development, culminating ironically in his self-destruction.

Toby, young and handsome, lacks direction and commitment. Charlie attempts to guide him, but Toby remains aimless. When he does finally discover a talent for design, he contracts AIDS and dies. His death destroys Charlie's will to live.

Camilla, Max's first wife, represents superficiality in human relations and the betrayal of loyalty. Her casual commitments are not sufficient to forge a lasting relationship with Max. After a brief affair with Toby, she goes to England and divorces Max. When told of her marriage to Roland Cartwright, Max feels only slightly hurt. He has achieved enough maturity to see that their marriage was superficial and transitory.

Laura, Max's second wife, represents the culmination of his growing maturity, but her character is more suggested than given. She implies selflessness and loyalty. The tranquillity of her marriage to Max is offset by Toby's declining health and Charlie's growing despair. When her pregnancy is threatened by a mysterious loss of blood, a dark shadow falls on their happiness. In her final scene, she is asleep as Max looks on, offering a final symbol of the peace and fulfillment that come to those who commit themselves fully and truly to a human bond, though life is fragile, the future uncertain.

Themes and Meanings

At the center of Begley's thematic focus are loyalty to those with whom one is involved and how the bonds of friendship are tested by change. Development is key to Max's understanding of the obligations that human relationships require. Max commences his story as an outsider. At the Rumorosa, when he is invited to join the others on a trip, he feels accepted "into a magical realm of cashless bounty and comfort." Symbolic of that acceptance is his sexual encounter with the attractive Laura. It is also telling that, once Cousin Emma's legacy makes him wealthy, he becomes even more at ease and more intimate with his wealthy friends. Near the end of the book, pondering his duty to care for Toby, Max asks, "Had I not assumed some sort of responsibility for how he was cared for?" He answers his own question by tending to his dying friend with compassion.

Solidarity, which is another form of loyalty, receives much of Max's attention while he is in China and afterward. Speaking with Charlie about the Chinese cultural revolution that spills over into Tiananmen Square at the very time Max is teaching at Beijing University, Max is impressed by the show of solidarity among his students. Solidarity makes strong relationships, but it brings a need to forgive. Forgiveness, born of mature understanding, is part of the nurturing of human bonds, as when Max forgives Toby for sleeping with Camilla, even joining Charlie in donating blood to prolong his life. This act makes the three of them "blood brothers," Toby says. Indeed, the transfusions symbolize the union of all humankind. Toby's nurse gives ultimate expression to this theme when she says, "We're all related like that . . . only people don't take the time to think about it."

Loyalty sometimes requires great sacrifice. Nothing in the novel makes this point more dramatically than Charlie's attempts to infect himself with the same virus that is destroying Toby. This scarifying act throws Max into great turmoil, and when he discovers that Charlie has Verdi's *Requiem* sung at Toby's funeral, Max is profoundly puzzled. In this musical work, he thinks, "the trembling soul pleads for salvation." At first Max sees the music as Charlie's mocking of God's forgiveness of human failings, specifically Charlie's and Toby's homosexuality, which "had turned the male seed into an instrument of contamination. . . ." This thought casts Max into a dark moment, and he concludes that a "lord of evil sends plagues to torment the living and infect even the unborn!" Upon reflection, he sees human suffering mitigated by the beauty that Charlie has devoted his life to pursuing and creating. The *Requiem* symbolizes Charlie's loyalty to the ideal that beauty is the ultimate bond and a defense against the suffering and futility of life.

Critical Context

As Max Saw It is Begley's third novel. His first two novels depict characters coming to terms with personal trauma. This third novel focuses on human relationships and how they give meaning to a world in which suffering is both inevitable and inexplicable. Begley's craftsmanship places him among the most respected novelists of the day, and his modern themes give his fiction even greater relevance and value.

As Max Saw It has been compared to F. Scott Fitzgerald's *The Great Gatsby* (1925) in that Max, like Nick Caraway in *Gatsby*, tells the story of a man of wealth whose romantic entanglements doom him. By naming one of his principal characters Charlie Swan, Begley suggests, too, a connection to Marcel Proust's *Remembrance of Things Past* (1922-1931), whose narrator, Charles Swann, searches for truth in retrospectives of his own life. Begley carries on the tradition of the introspective narrator in search of truth. For Max, people and events offer him insights into human nature and the human condition. The novel focuses on the way humans search for emotional fulfillment and sometimes destroy themselves in search of it. When Charlie says that Toby wants "fraternity, not equality," he defines the fundamental need of all humans and the goal toward which the principal characters of the novel unconsciously strive. In this struggle, one's humanity is revealed. Charlie implies its measure when he describes Max as "One who has power to hurt and will do none." In this novel, Begley mitigates the despair that human suffering causes and the moral dilemma in which the knowledge of evil places one. He stops short of suggesting that Toby's disease is divine retribution for his wayward life and sexuality. Nor is it a metaphor of the soul's inability to sustain itself in a fallen world. Still searching for value in human existence, Max finds a measure of it in the humanity of those who suffer, sacrifice, and, sometimes, are destroyed.

Bibliography

Alexander, Victoria N. "Louis Begley: Trying to Make Sense of It." *The Antioch Review* 55 (Summer, 1997): 292-304. Alexander traces such themes as divine retribution, justice, and good deeds in Begley's novels.

Devereaux, Elizabeth. "Louis Begley." *Publishers Weekly* 241, no. 18 (May 2, 1994): 276-278. Begley's personal life and professional writing are related to his first three novels. The last third of the article contains several helpful comments by Begley himself about *As Max Saw It* and the significance AIDS plays in the novel.

Hepburn, Allan. "Lost Time: Trauma and Belatedness in Louis Begley's *The Man Who Was Late*." *Contemporary Literature* 39, no. 3 (Fall, 1998): 380-404. The discussion of influences on Begley's second novel is useful to a reading of *As Max Saw It*. A list of works cited adds to the usefulness of this long article.

Mendelsohn, Jane. "Fiction in Review." *The Yale Review* 83, no. 1 (January, 1995): 108-120. Offers insight into characterization in Begley's first three novels and views *As Max Saw It* as the culmination of themes developed in the earlier novels.

Ribbat, Christoph. "Shiny Silk Blouses: Luxury and Memory in the Novels of Louis Begley." *Zeitschrift für Anglistik und Amerikanistik* 46, no. 3 (1998): 243-252. Ribbat highlights influences of other writers on Begley's fiction and shows how elegance and beauty contrast with disease and decay in *As Max Saw It*. A brief list of works cited is helpful.

Bernard E. Morris

THE ASIATICS

Author: Frederic Prokosch (1908-1989)
Type of plot: Picaresque romance
Time of plot: The 1920's
Locale: Asia, from Beirut to Hong Kong
First published: 1935

> *Principal characters:*
> THE NARRATOR, a nameless twenty-two-year-old American
> ANTOINE SAMAZEUILH, an unreliable French rogue and the temporary
>   companion of the narrator
> FEODOR KRUSNAYASKOV, a Communist and fellow prisoner with the
>   narrator in Turkey
> HANS DE HAHN, a Dutch adventurer
> DR. AINGER, a cynical doctor in Penang

The Novel

The Asiatics has no plot. It is a tale of an aimless vagabondage from Beirut to Hong Kong, a pilgrimage to experience made by—and told by—a nameless young American. The narrator-hero is not a rogue, but in most other respects *The Asiatics* is a picaresque romance, studded with incident and peopled by faithless opportunists and outright scoundrels. Nothing is explained of the hero's background, and the inference to be made is that he is making this long trip simply because that is what young men do. He has but little money most of the way, and he is innocent (but alert) in a way that is identified with Americans. *The Asiatics* is, in fact, partly a fable of cultural contrasts.

The hero leaves Beirut by bus, catching a ride to Damascus, where the first of his many initiation experiences occurs when he is befriended by a faintly sinister Syrian named M. Aractingi. Their journey to Turkey ends abruptly when M. Aractingi's car breaks down, and two mysterious men come along and pursue him into the fields on foot. The hero flees in another direction, finding shelter with a hospitable peasant.

Walking toward Homs the next day, the hero falls in with another vagrant, a young Frenchman named Antoine Samazeuilh. Their companionship endures for several days, strengthened by the company of a pretty girl, until Samazeuilh inexplicably disappears. The hero pushes on alone into Turkey, meeting new friends and dropping them, and in Istanbul a Mr. Suleiman petitions him to deliver a small package on his boat trip to Trebizond. He delivers the parcel—he suspects that it is opium—and soon takes up with an enigmatic Russian, Feodor Krusnayaskov, with whom he continues his travels. No sooner do they reach the city of Erzerum than they are arrested by the Turkish police and confined in a cell with twenty-eight political prisoners, thus beginning one of the more notable episodes of the novel.

The hero suffers through two wretched months in prison during the coldest months of winter, witnessing the extreme sexual corruption of his fellow inmates. During his incarceration he meets Hans de Hahn, a genial Dutchman whom he will encounter again much farther east. The necessary *deus ex machina* comes in the person of a friendly guard, and, with his help, the hero and Krusnayaskov escape and flee to Krusnayaskov's home in Tiflis. The hero, however, learns that Krusnayaskov is a dedicated Communist and flees into the night when fears of betrayal overcome him.

Soon the hero is in Persia, falling in step here and there with Nestorian priests and other patriarchs of the Asian sensibility. He takes his ease for several days in Teheran at the salon of a Mme de Chamellis, and through her agency he is able to fly to Meshed with Dr. Ainger, one of her other guests, but the plane crashes and the two walk different paths, the hero finding a short-term home in Meshed with the sophisticated Prince Ghuraguzlu. He is soon en route again, this time with a treacherous young epicene named Ahmed, who abandons him to the predations of a gang of mountain bandits.

In Peshawar, the hero reencounters his old cell-mate, the Dutchman de Hahn, who is now traveling with a lovely mistress, Ursule. They improvise a hasty *ménage à troi* until sexual infidelities break them up, leaving the hero free for his next adventure, an extended stay with the Maharajah of Badrapur. Various complications end his respite with the maharajah, and soon he arrives in Calcutta, a mere stopover on his way to Kandy, Ceylon. He soon takes a boat to Rangoon and rejoins Mme de Chamellis, his former hostess in Teheran. This new liaison is fruitful with incident: a week-long excursion up the Irrawaddy River and a joining of fortunes in Mandalay with a mercenary Mr. Maung, owner of the boat in which they go aground in a reed jungle on the upper Irrawaddy. This misadventure concludes with their kidnaping by river marauders, Mme de Chamellis's death, and the hero's release and return to Rangoon.

The hero rejoins Dr. Ainger—last seen walking away from the plane wreck in Persia—in his outpost near Panang, where he administers medical aid to the natives. The hero witnesses, in scenes that suggest Joseph Conrad's *Heart of Darkness* (1902), the degeneration of Dr. Ainger in a debilitating physical setting of heat, insect life, and disease. After Ainger's death, the hero travels via Bangkok to Pnom-Penh, where, improbably, he is reunited with the rascally Samazeuilh. They drift together to Saigon, meet (even more improbably) the lovely Ursule, former mistress of de Hahn, and proceed, the three of them, to Huë. There, in a final blaze of coincidence, de Hahn reappears. The novel ends inconclusively when de Hahn dies, Samazeuilh vanishes for a final time, and the hero goes on to Hong Kong. In the novel's last lines, the initiation ends joyously as the hero, enjoying the sunlight on his naked body after taking a cool swim, exults in the great hedonism of youth: "Yes, there was no denying it, I was feeling very happy."

The Characters

The hero-narrator at one point explains to an interrogator that he is going to Japan. "I have an uncle in Japan. He is very rich, and if I behave nicely to him I may some day have more money than I have now." This answer displeases Mostafa, the Persian bandit to whom it is addressed. He tells the hero, "Yes, you are an American. I am very disappointed in you. I thought you had a soul, but now I see that you have no soul, after all." Mostafa goes on to explain that fewer and fewer are happy. The world is too full of things to do, and people have no time to cultivate the loneliness that nurtures a soul. Mostafa originally mistakes the hero for an Asiatic like himself; that is, he thinks that he is an American Indian. "You watch and watch; no one ever knows what you think; you look strong and passionate and sly." This original sizing-up of the hero thus makes Mostafa's disappointment doubly sharp, and it underscores the differences both in culture and in temperament that distinguish the hero from the people among whom he passes.

Whatever the health of his soul, the hero benefits from his rich experiences because he keeps himself courageously open to the events that overtake him. On one occasion he is worn down by "bits of irritability, splinters of suspicion, of jealousy, of detestation, of loneliness, of wicked understanding." This condition moves him to withdraw from all people: "Don't let them toy with you, don't let them wriggle their way into that part of you that matters. Be alone. Be strong. Be proud." Yet the urge soon passes, and he decides that "to understand anything at all" he must be "fragile" and "tender" and he must humiliate himself. Only through this vulnerability can he ever know himself and remain healthy.

The hero seems to succeed in his struggle to achieve knowledge through experience. He remains in all situations a passive bystander, one who never disturbs the universe but on whom all things are registered. Yet at the end he appears as fresh a product of the New World as he was in the beginning. He is neither coarsened by his worldly initiation nor made cynical and despairing.

Most of the other characters go by in a blur. Androgynous ephebi come and go at the author's bidding, as do princes and potentates—none of any interest as a character study. Of the cynical Europeans—de Hahn, Samazeuilh, Dr. Ainger—Ainger is the most provocative for the misanthropy he expresses in his deep loathing for modern civilization. For him, all that civilization means is "making money and making things easier for those who've made it and killing the spirit in themselves as well as in everybody else." His death from plague in a rotting jungle seems an appropriate close to a life that has moved so far away from humanity.

Themes and Meanings

The Asiatics exploits one of the oldest of plot devices—the journey—and makes the appeal of geography a basic part of the story. The exotic place names roll on in an onomastic litany; Prokosch frequently has recourse to the pathetic fallacy (Damascus is "sad" and its fields are "desolate"), but his limpid poetic prose evokes climate and brings landscapes to life with great economy of description. His towns and byways are peopled with figures who blend naturally into the whole shifting panorama. In Meshed during the month of mourning, "they prostrated themselves on the dry rutted alleyways, they scratched aimlessly and absent-mindedly at their flesh until they bled and had to weep with pain and excitement." The Irrawaddy River is "dotted with houseboats full of short-legged sloe-eyed natives," and on the bank can be seen "small young priests dressed in yellow hovering on the green bank like so many dandelions."

The Asiatics is also, like that famous travel novel Samuel Johnson's *Rasselas, The Prince of Abissinia* (1759), in many respects a search for happiness. For most of the figures milling around in the exotic locales, a search for happiness means a search for some form of love. Mme de Chamellis concludes that the search is futile. In her cynical appraisal, no two lovers love each other equally strongly, and "wretchedness grows, little by little." For the hero-narrator, love is "any of a million different streams leading to some unguessed ocean, some unexplainable meeting-place." The need for love is a constant hunger. When an ugly eunuch comes to Dr. Ainger, digging at an open wound and seeking pity, the narrator's judgment is quick: "It was the only way he could get any attention. It was his way of asking for love." The search for love in *The Asiatics* is a fever, an ever-present seething in the blood that keeps humanity in motion.

The most compelling theme of the novel is suggested by its title, which draws attention to the narrator's quest for the meaning of Asia. Something of this meaning is suggested in a shocking metaphor in which a dead rat represents the Oriental: "There it lay, sloe-eyed, slim-fingered, yellow-toothed. A real Oriental with a growing look of uncontrollable evil in its posture." In another formulation, Prince Ghuraguzlu finds the essence of Asia to be in its "long and terrible ennui," its "vagueness." The prince explains that Asiatics have "woven" death straight into their lives and that "death's right there, running like a silver thread through the pattern." The Dutchman de Hahn expresses similar thoughts vividly. For him, Asia is "the land of death," and "we're all Asiatics." De Hahn envisions a dying race faced with eternal darkness, a humanity that is doomed for having replaced reason with instinct: "And do you know what instinct is?" he asks. "It's a wild lion roaming through the jungle with blood on his tongue." In de Hahn's words lies perhaps the most resonant of the meanings behind the title of *The Asiatics*.

Critical Context

The Asiatics was Prokosch's first novel, and it has always had an audience of prestigious admirers, such as Albert Camus and Thomas Mann. Prokosch's virtuoso descriptive powers, his renderings of settings and moods, account for much of the praise. Not every reader, however, could be expected to enjoy the faintly iridescent sheen of sexual corruption that clings to much of the description, especially in the novel's elicitation of androgynous youths, and there is a sameness to its dreamy descriptiveness that eventually diminishes interest in the story despite Prokosch's talent for metaphor and epithet. As a specimen of the novel of the imaginary journey, however, it deserves high rank in American literature.

Bibliography

Austen, Roger. *Playing the Game: The Homosexual Novel in America*. Indianapolis: Bobbs-Merrill, 1977. Contains a useful discussion of Prokosch, situating him in the context of twentieth century literature.

Bishop, John Peale. *The Collected Essays of John Peale Bishop*. Edited by Edmund Wilson. New York: Charles Scribner's Sons, 1948. "Final Dreading," is a favorable poetry review by Bishop of Prokosch's *The Assassins*, his first book of poems. Refers to Prokosch's extensive travels and its influence on these poems and concludes with a brief commentary on Prokosch's technique and his relationship to Oswald Spengler and Saint-John Perse.

Carpenter, Richard C. "The Novels of Frederic Prokosch." *College English* 18 (1957): 261-267. Provides much insight into the development of Prokosch's novelistic style. An appreciative essay by a sympathetic critic of Prokosch.

Marowski, Daniel G., and Roger Matuz, eds. *Contemporary Literary Criticism*. Vol. 48. Detroit: Gale Research, 1988. The entry on Prokosch presents an overview of his works, citing him as a "highly regarded novelist" who gained prominence in the 1930's. Included is a sampling of reviews, mostly favorable, of his earlier works (*The Asiatics, The Assassins, The Seven Who Fled*), as well as later works, such as *The Missolonghi Manuscript* and his memoir, *Voices*, in which he addresses his literary displacement.

Quartermain, Peter, ed. *Dictionary of Literary Biography*. Vol. 48. Detroit: Gale Research, 1986. Provides a selected checklist of Prokosch's works, giving more emphasis to his poetry, although he is better known as a novelist. Discusses his poems between 1920 and the mid-1940's. Also includes background information on Prokosch, including his numerous travels, and some brief commentary on his novels.

Squires, Radcliffe. *Frederic Prokosch*. New York: Twayne, 1964. Presents Prokosch's works in a chronological format and is useful as a critical introduction. Squires focuses on the timeless qualities of "interplay of emotion and intellect" in Prokosch's work but acknowledges that his writing was a "casualty" of World War II, which changed the values of the reading public. A selected bibliography is provided.

Frank Day

AT PLAY IN THE FIELDS OF THE LORD

Author: Peter Matthiessen (1927-   )
Type of plot: Naturalistic adventure
Time of plot: The early 1960's
Locale: Oriente State, a fictional province in an unnamed South American country
    in the Amazon jungle
First published: 1965

> *Principal characters:*
>   BORONAI, the chief of the Niaruna Indian tribe
>   LES HUBEN, a Protestant missionary from the United States who wishes
>   to convert the Niaruna
>   ANDY HUBEN, his wife
>   MARTIN QUARRIER, Huben's assistant missionary
>   HAZEL QUARRIER, his wife
>   BILLY QUARRIER, his nine-year-old son
>   COMMANDANTE GUZMÁN, the military governor of Oriente, who plans
>   to attack the Niaruna
>   LEWIS MOON, a mercenary soldier and a Cheyenne Indian
>   WOLFIE, Moon's fellow mercenary
>   PINDI, Moon's Niaruna lover
>   AEORE, a Niaruna shaman and rival of Boronai
>   UYUYU (YOYO), a Niaruna converted to Christianity

The Novel

At Play in the Fields of the Lord has the plot elements of stereotypical nineteenth century colonial novels and twentieth century Hollywood adventure films. The discovery of a savage Indian tribe, living in a remote and dangerous jungle, brings a handful of whites to a decrepit town on the edge of *terra incognita*. An ambitious and ruthless military commander competes with ne'er-do-well mercenaries and intrepid missionaries to establish first contact with the savages. All must battle the elements—oppressive heat and an unhealthy jungle—as well as resist the temptations of drink, which relieves boredom, and of forbidden passion, which eases loneliness.

The novel is not, however, a typical adventure tale. Matthiessen employs these romantic elements only to invert them. The Indians of this novel, the Niaruna, may be primitive by modern standards, but they are not savage, especially in comparison with the whites who would bring them "civilization." The outcome of the adventure will not be typical: These whites will discover, not some lost treasure, forgotten city, or secret of life, but the dark reality of their own hearts. One fortunate intruder will discover a small light amid the darkness.

Matthiessen constructs the tale around two contrasting protagonists, Martin Quarrier and Lewis Moon. Quarrier is a missionary, Moon a mercenary soldier.

Quarrier is a white Anglo-Saxon Protestant, Moon a Cheyenne Indian. Quarrier comes to Oriente to propagate the Gospel, Moon to bomb the inhabitants into submission. Though they start the novel with opposite intentions, the plot leads them to one moment of common purpose and understanding before they discover their destinies.

The first half of the novel prepares the protagonists to meet the Niaruna. When Quarrier arrives at the capital city of Madre de Dios, he is anxious to begin his missionary work. He seems well supported by his wife, Hazel, and son, Billy, as well as by his coworkers, Les and Andy Huben. From the start, however, Quarrier is uneasy. Hazel quickly grows lethargic and fearful. Les Huben's idea of conversion seems superficial. Andy Huben unwittingly arouses Quarrier's sexual interest. No one except Billy seems as anxious to learn about the Niaruna's culture and language as does Martin Quarrier.

Madre de Dios is no more hospitable to Lewis Moon. His employer, Commandante Guzmán, is imperious but stupid. His partner Wolfie attends to—and is content with—the alcohol and whores of the town. The presence of missionaries fills Moon with uneasy memories of the proselytizers who controlled the Cheyenne reservation where he spent an unhappy, degraded youth. When a Niaruna shoots an arrow at the airplane during a reconnaissance flight, Moon is awed by the Indian's bravery. That night, Moon steals away from Madre de Dios.

In the second half of the novel, Quarrier and Moon contact the Niaruna. Quarrier reopens an abandoned station along the river, and Moon parachutes into the Indian village. Quarrier intends to preach; Moon plans to help the Niaruna resist.

Quarrier's efforts are futile. The Niaruna, except for a handful of the timid and weak, avoid the missionary's enticements. Hazel becomes virtually catatonic with fear. Billy dies of a fever, but Les interprets Quarrier's loss by declaring it God's means to convert the heathen. Quarrier begins to despair: At best, he attracts "rice Christians," converts who profess Christianity to gain tools, food, and trinkets.

Moon fits in surprisingly easily with the Niaruna. He becomes Kisu-Mu, a being descended from heaven, a god-man with inexplicable links to the divine. Boronai, the Niaruna's headman, befriends Moon and teaches him the ways of the tribe, even allowing his woman Pindi to become Moon's lover. A jungle diet and strenuous activity soon harden Moon's body. Most Niaruna quickly accept Kisu-Mu as part of their world—all except Aeore, who shot the arrow at Moon's plane earlier. Aeore quietly awaits the chance to show that Kisu-Mu is not a god.

At the climax of the novel, the paths of Moon and Quarrier intersect. When Boronai dies of an influenza, Aeore persuades the Niaruna to destroy the mission, and he plans a confederation with other tribes to resist the intruders. Moon risks his life to bring a warning. Huben calls for military intervention by Guzmán, but Quarrier seeks out the Niaruna to head off violence. The Indians spare his life, but during Guzmán's attack on the village, Quarrier is murdered by Uyuyu, a converted Indian among the attackers.

Moon, now outcast from two societies, hides in Boronai's funeral canoe and escapes into an incredible isolation: "He did not know within a thousand miles where he might be, nor on what river, nor in what country."

The Characters

Just as the plot does not fulfill the romantic expectations of the adventure story, so too the characters of *At Play in the Fields of the Lord* belie the stereotypes and idealizations of romantic characters. Matthiessen's characters are naturalistic creatures whose behavior is usually determined by environment.

The environment in which the characters move, the jungle and the river towns upon its fringes, are overwhelming and hostile physical presences. This description of Madre de Dios typifies the difficult stage upon which these actors must play out their fates: It "formed a yellow scar in the green waste. With its litter of rust and rotting thatch and mud, the capital of Oriente State resembled a great trash heap, smoking sullenly in the monotony of rivers." The landscape is the antagonist of everyone in the novel; it constantly assaults the senses and the spirits of these characters. Ultimately the landscape triumphs over both the indigenous and the intruders.

The Niaruna are creatures of the rain forest who resist easy labeling. They are not noble savages inhabiting some remote and primeval Eden: The jungle is too harsh to be a garden. By hunting and cultivating, the Niaruna find enough to live on, but no surplus. The Indians are constantly alert to combat the dangers from animals, poisonous plants, and rival tribes. Their humanity is fragile: As Aeore points out to Moon, the Niaruna paint their bodies because, in the jungle, how else can human beings distinguish themselves from the animals?

On the other hand, though primitive in technology and social organization by the intruders' standards, the Niaruna are neither ignorant barbarians nor Satan worshipers. They have adapted ingeniously to the rhythm of the jungle, knowledgeably working the land in both dry season and rainy season, cunningly harvesting the river in its rising and falling stages. The Niaruna possess a stoic philosophy that enables them to accept privation, injury, and death without self-pity. Moon marvels, for example, at the quiet dignity of the Indians as Boronai, on his deathbed, receives a last respectful visit from each tribesman.

The citizens of Madre de Dios also reflect their environment. As unpleasant as the jungle, the town is at least less dangerous, but the lack of danger seems to foster inertia and decay. Freed from the necessity to wrest a daily living from the jungle, the townspeople are content to get drunk and to fornicate. Guzmán and Father Xantes, its leading citizens, possess more energy but are no less degenerate: Guzmán uses his energy to tyrannize over the townspeople; Xantes abstains from grosser pleasures, yet he abstains, too, from active pastoral care. He is content to bear silent witness to the sufferings of humanity.

The North American missionaries, who have come to transform the Niaruna, find themselves transformed by the jungle and the Indians. Utterly repelled by the constant physical realities of procreation and death, Hazel retreats into sullen passivity. Stung by resistance to his energetic pastoral work, Les hypocritically interprets misery and failure as happiness and progress: In his newsletters, he conjures unwarranted hope from the senseless death of Billy and the accidental martyrdom of Quarrier. Quarrier learns that the jungle accentuates his physical limitations (clumsiness, poor sight, low stamina) even as it challenges his assumptions about conversion. Only Andy seems little affected; she pays more attention to consoling the others as the environment's demands drain them.

Of the missionaries, only Andy Huben and Martin Quarrier engage the reader's interest. They show some capacity to learn and some humility in abandoning the prejudices with which they arrived. They alone express some sympathy with the Niaruna and antipathy for the fate they help to bring upon the Indians. Andy is an underdeveloped character, however, and Quarrier is physically unattractive; neither gains much sympathy with readers. Quarrier is something of a tragic figure, a man doomed to suffer by his own limitations as well as fate. He is an admirable man, capable of transcendence, but events overwhelm him before he can act on his insight. The reader feels a sense of loss at his death because someone valuable, someone ultimately (though not thoroughly) good has been defeated.

The soldiers of fortune, as dissolute as the missionaries are respectable, are more interesting and adaptable characters. Wolfie is unkempt, uncouth, and likable, a Falstaffian type who is admirable despite his qualities. He is at least honest about his ignoble ambitions.

Initially Moon is as unsavory as Wolfie, but he grows as the novel proceeds. Moon becomes the center of the novel because he bridges the worlds of North and South and because, like Quarrier, his encounter with the Niaruna leads him to abandon the goal which brought him to Oriente. Like Quarrier, too, Moon wins more of the reader's sympathy as he loses the sympathy of the other characters in the story. Moon moves closer to the Niaruna than any other character by becoming one of them and accepting the discipline of the jungle.

An Indian at heart, Moon alone lives well in isolation; he alone can sense the harmony which exists between man and a harsh environment. The novel ends with Moon transfigured: "Laid naked to the sun, he felt himself open like an enormous flower. Soon he slept. At dark he built an enormous fire, in celebration of the only man beneath the eye of heaven." Moon is a comic figure, in the classic sense, who defeats his antagonists and finds his place in the scheme of things.

Themes and Meanings

Many of the novel's initial reviewers noted its similarities to the works of Joseph Conrad. It seemed to echo *Nostromo* (1904) and *Heart of Darkness* (1902) in its evocation of the encounter between white Europeans and primitive societies or hostile environments. Certainly there is something Conradian about the dark atmosphere of the book, its depiction of a gloomy, sullen landscape inhabited by moral wretches. Les, Quarrier, Andy, Xantes, and Guzmán are Conradian characters whose glimpses into the dark jungle are glimpses—for the reader if not for themselves—into the dark world of their own hearts.

At Play in the Fields of the Lord goes beyond Conrad, however, in its presentation of the Niaruna and in its character of Moon. The Niaruna are presented with an anthropologist's goal of objectivity and a naturalist's instinct for appreciation more than with a novelist's eye toward symbolism. Though primitive, the Niaruna are clearly superior to the societies (the town, faraway North America) which Guzmán, the Hubens, and the Quarriers represent. The Niaruna are not ideal: Pindi, after she bears twins, buries the female so that the male will have a better chance of survival. At the same time, however, the Niaruna lack the imperialistic impulses of the Commandante as well as the equally imperialistic religious vision of the missionaries.

Though the novel could be read as an attack on the cultural egotism of missionary work, its central theme is the irreconcilable nature of the cultures which fatally interact. The worlds of the Niaruna and of the intruders are immediately separated by language (the missionaries never do learn much of Niaruna speech) and geography. More important, they are separated by ethics, theology, and morality. Most important, they look across a gulf of thinking and feeling. The oneness with nature that Moon experiences at the conclusion is not a philosophical insight but an immersion in a way of being. Symbolically Moon is alone: Even if he had sympathetic company, he could no more explain how he feels as an Indian than he could explain aerodynamics to Aeore, challenger of planes.

The thematic function of the influenza which kills Boronai and infects the tribe (with apparent fatal effects past the time of the novel) is to express this unbridgeable gap. Ironically, the influenza was carried to the tribe by Moon, the man most eager to help. He in turn caught it from Andy, the missionary who meant no one harm. Even biology seems determined to oppose intermeshing the primitive and the civilized.

Critical Context

At Play in the Fields of the Lord signaled the coming together of Matthiessen's two interests, the literary and the anthropological. Before 1965, he had published three novels on themes and in styles typical of a postwar novelist: a coming-of-age tale in *Race Rock* (1954), the making of a young revolutionary in *Partisans* (1955), and a study of human evil in *Raditzer* (1961). Beginning with *Wild Life in America* (1959), Matthiessen wrote several anthropological works on remote areas on the globe; the major ones before 1965 concern South America in *The Cloud Forest: Chronicle of the South American Wilderness* (1961) and New Guinea in *Under the Mountain Wall: A Chronicle of Two Seasons in the Stone Age* (1962).

The themes of the anthropological books echo the themes of *At Play in the Fields of the Lord*. Matthiessen chronicles the disappearance of primitive ways of life as well as primitive ways of apprehending reality and understanding experience. Civilization's thought patterns, as well as its technology and bureaucracy, threaten prior ways of enacting the natural harmony of man and nature.

The attempt to portray this conflict of ways of thinking has led Matthiessen to technical experiments in *At Play in the Fields of the Lord* and in a later book *Far Tortuga* (1975). Both books use surrealistic devices (the abandonment of traditional grammar, synesthesia, the depiction of impression rather than sequential events) to immerse readers in new patterns of perception. *Far Tortuga* is much more surrealistic; in *At*

Play in the Fields of the Lord, the experimental passages treat Moon's consciousness, the imagery of the landscapes, and the Niaruna's sense of experience.

Bibliography
Bawer, Bruce. *The Aspect of Eternity.* St. Paul, Minn.: Graywolf Press, 1993. Contains an essay called "Peter Matthiessen, Nature Boy," a generally unflattering critique of Matthiessen's novels prior to *Killing Mister Watson.* Argues that Matthiessen romanticizes the primitive and hypocritically attacks American and Western civilization. It also traces what Bawer calls an "antagonism toward fathers" in Matthiessen's work.

Bishop, Peter. "The Geography of Hope and Despair: Peter Mathiessen's *The Snow Leopard." Critique: Studies in Modern Fiction* 26, no. 4 (1984): 203-216. Places Matthiessen alongside other literary travelers such as Graham Greene, Evelyn Waugh, and D. H. Lawrence. Discusses in-depth *The Snow Leopard* and compares it to *Far Tortuga* and *At Play in the Fields of the Lord.* Sees the book's lack of conclusion as its success. A thought-provoking article which presents psychological insights into Matthiessen.

Gabriel, Trip. "The Nature of Peter Matthiessen." *The New York Times Magazine,* June 10, 1990, 30. An insightful profile, based on interviews with Matthiessen and his circle. Gabriel focuses on *Killing Mister Watson* but also provides an overview of Matthiessen's career. Neither sycophantic nor hostile, Gabriel presents a nuanced portrait of the man behind the books.

Grove, James P. "Pastoralism and Anti-Pastoralism in Peter Matthiessen's *Far Tortuga." Critique: Studies in Modern Fiction* 21, no. 2 (1979): 15-29. Discusses this highly praised novel and reflects on the influence of Zen on Matthiessen's views. An in-depth treatment of the content and intent of this novel within the theme of pastoralism.

Raglon, Rebecca. "Fact and Fiction: The Development of Ecological Form in Peter Matthiessen's *Far Tortuga." Critique: Studies in Contemporary Fiction* 35, no. 4 (1994): 245-259. Looks at Matthiessen's work, *Far Tortuga* especially, as a criticism of the dualistic view of nature and humanity. Raglon argues that Matthiessen sees no separation between nature and humanity and writes instead of their necessary interrelatedness.

Shnayerson, Michael. "Higher Matthiessen." *Vanity Fair* 54, no. 12 (1991): 114-132. Contains considerable biographical information and gives a balanced view of Matthiessen's personal strengths and weaknesses.

Robert M. Otten

AT WEDDINGS AND WAKES

Author: Alice McDermott (1953-   )
Type of plot: Psychological realism
Time of plot: The 1960's
Locale: Brooklyn and suburban Long Island, New York
First published: 1992

> *Principal characters:*
> ROBERT,
> MARGARET, and
> MARYANNE, the children, focal characters from whose memories the
> story is told
> LUCY TOWNE DAILEY, the children's mother, apparently unhappy in her
> choice of a husband and the place where she lives
> BOB DAILY, Lucy's husband, the children's father, who learns to live
> among the Towne women
> MOMMA TOWNE, Lucy's stepmother, who married her sister's husband
> and cared for her children
> MAY TOWNE, one of Lucy's three sisters, a former nun
> AGNES TOWNE, another sister, a business woman with cultivated tastes
> VERONICA TOWNE, the fourth sister, an "unfortunate" one, a
> "stayathome"
> DONALD TOWNE, Momma's son, spoiled as a child and later disowned
> by his mother because of his drinking
> FRED, a middle-aged mailman who marries May

The Novel

Momma Towne ruled the roost when she received it from her sister, who died in her fourth childbirth leaving an infant, Veronica, and three other little girls—Lucy, May, and Agnes. Perhaps Momma gathers the children closely to her because she feels guilty about taking a ready-made family from a dead sister. Perhaps she feels remorse from being angered by the killing hand of God after she waited seven years in Ireland for the chance to come to her sister in the United States. Perhaps the guilt is the result of her deliberate and successful attempt to tempt her sister's husband into marriage not by attracting him physically but by seducing him with arguments, substituting mindplay for foreplay. When she finally has a child of her own, a son, she spoils him; while he is still a young man, she dismisses him from her house and from herself so thoroughly that he appears, hat in hand, only at weddings and wakes.

Lucy is the only one of the girls who marries and leaves home, but she is so closely tied to her stepmother and her stepmother's house that she makes arduous and frequent visits home in the summer, bringing her three children. Twice a week, they make the journey from their house in Long Island, which is ten blocks from the nearest bus stop. The bus takes them past the cemetery, the churches, and out of suburbia, where they have to transfer to another bus in a crowded multiethnic neighborhood. Once there, they proceed to the subway station, where surroundings seem to the children even more bizarre. They take a train that rushes them through Queens and on to Brooklyn, then transfer to another train. The children notice their mother's confidence growing until, finally again in her old neighborhood, she settles from a hurried to a relaxed pace, sending the message that she is again at home.

Waiting for Lucy and her children are the aunts. May left a convent because she had come to realize that she loved the life of a nun too much to think of it as devotion, duty, or sacrifice. May returns to her stepmother's house and settles into the routine of caring for Momma and looking forward to the visits of Lucy's children. Veronica, the youngest of the sisters, is always at home, her face still disfigured by early skin problems, sipping cocktails that have become her nourishment. Agnes, a career woman, though able to leave the house to work as an executive secretary and to separate herself by means of her finely tuned tastes, is a stern and brittle woman.

Together, stepmother and sisters indulge in ritual complaints. Lucy is foremost in her never-ending litany of vague protests against the man she married, who dutifully drives to Brooklyn after work to fetch his family home. In the house of his mother-in-law, he performs for Momma the rites of a businessman, and he speaks politely and gently over cocktails and dinner to each of the sisters who have waited for his arrival.

Another of the ritualistic journeys that Lucy, Bob, and children take once a year is the two-week vacation, always to a similar place but never the same one. The destination is always a place with green trees, stretches of beach, and the smell of the sea, a place where Bob hopes to instill in his children a sense of wonder and beauty.

Interspersed with daily living are the weddings and the wakes, occasions that give rise to immense gatherings of family and friends in the Irish community where the Townes live. The most splendid wedding is that of May, who one day almost literally runs into Fred, the mailman, who is new to the neighborhood. Small chats become conversations, and friendly dates lead to commitments. All are happy save Momma, who insists that Fred cannot husband his resources, since the roses he sends to May in the first part of the month become daisies by the end of the month.

The children's memories of the family's joy in the wedding is allowed to overshadow, for a time, their memory of May's inexplicable death four days after her wedding; their knowledge of mortality is buried for a while as the happy event is recounted. The high point is the discovery that Fred can dance with extraordinarily nimble feet, his joy bringing life to the dance floor in song after song, couple after couple, until the dance floor is filled with a living celebration of marriage that is only later to be turned into a wake.

The Characters

In *At Weddings and Wakes*, McDermott filters what is known and discovered through the minds of the Towne-Daily children, most often through a composite consciousness that seems to mesh with the point of view of the author. Sometimes a particular child is chosen as a focal point, and readers are thus able to distinguish between the boy, for example, and his sisters. Robert, well-behaved and introverted, is an exemplary altar boy who rises in the mornings in time to attend early mass. He is a good boy, the priest says, prompt, courteous, with pressed cassock and shined shoes. When his sister Margaret decides to emulate his behavior and go to early mass herself, Robert is glad for her company and seems pleased to point out to her things that give him pleasure—pinkish clouds left in the sky, a last star, a hedge filled with sparrows in the morning dew. Try as she might, however, Margaret is unable to match her brother's generosity and selflessness. The gladioli that she finds in the cemetery and identifies as her own treasure, separate from her brother's, have to be a special gift, the child thinks, perhaps an offering to her teacher, Miss Joan. The flowers, the child thinks, would transform the teacher from ugly duckling to blushing bride gliding across a dance floor in the arms of a new husband. Margaret's joy turns to shame and humiliation, however, when Miss Joan spurns the flowers, which came from the dirt of a freshly dug grave.

Maryanne has a similar experience with a teacher, Sister Miriam Joseph, who, unlike Miss Joan, is tall, dark, and beautiful. Filled with love for Sister Miriam Joseph and trying to impress her, Maryanne tells her teacher about Aunt May, who died four days after her marriage and who had once been a nun. What happened to Aunt May becomes a sign of foreboding for Sister Miriam Joseph, and she dismisses Maryanne, relegating her back to the group, indistinguishable from the other children. In her mouth, the nun holds gum that replaces saliva caused by an illness that will, before long, kill her.

The particular point of view chosen by the author provides the magical aura that pervades the text. Entrance into the minds of the children and incidents surrounding the children not only help define their individual characters but also act to reinforce themes and images. These occur and recur until a reader becomes aware that beside every birth is a death, beside every child is an adult facing perhaps an early knowledge of death, and behind every wedding is a wake.

Since the view of every character and situation is somewhat skewed by its refraction in the consciousness of the children, every character and situation seems transformed from the usual to the unique, from the spiritless and timid to the heroic, from the commonplace to the incredible. For example, Bob Dailey, who is the subject of his wife's complaints when she is within the bosom of her family, is in the children's eyes hero and benefactor, the driver of the automobile that carries them home and to and from their annual vacations. Rather than being made angry by the constant complaints of the women of the Towne family, Bob understands that his wife's family provides for him the routine of daily life, the constant recognition that beneath all who are alive is an undercurrent of the lives of the dead.

Themes and Meanings

What is most striking about *At Weddings and Wakes* is its extraordinary tonal shadings: Every scene is a mixture of past and present, resonant of a future not yet experienced. In every present is a reverberation of other times and places; in every echo of joy or grief are re-echoes of past and future sounds and colorations of exaltation and wretchedness. Momma's joy in the birth of her own child, a beautiful boy, parallels her pleasure in hearing the sound of the baby Veronica in the belly of her sister—who would soon die at childbirth, leading to a despair similar to the one Momma experienced when she disowned her son John, grown to young manhood as an unredeemed and unrepentant alcoholic.

At no point in the novel does McDermott break point of view to explain actions or consequences. Meaning derives altogether from character and scene. A reader must be able to locate the replications, the echoes and re-echoes, the juxtapositions and parallels that find the characters all dancing on graves. The overall montage turns family lore into universal myth.

Critical Context

At Weddings and Wakes is Alice McDermott's third published novel, following *That Night* (1987) and *A Bigamist's Daughter* (1982). Though her novels have similar themes, they are startlingly different from one another. Some critics hailed *A Bigamist's Daughter* as an excellent first novel that begins as satire of authors who seek a vanity press and moves skillfully to an analysis of the protagonist herself, who is editor-in-chief of the vanity press. Gradually, the editor's cynicism turns to acceptance of women like herself who spend their time waiting for husbands and fathers to arrive. *That Night*, like *At Weddings and Wakes*, is about growing up in the 1960's, but McDermott's penchant for the evocative and ambiguous is stronger in her second novel, in which prose captures time, place, and social status in a heightened poetic style.

Bibliography

Baumann, Paul. "Imperishable Identities." *Commonweal* 119 (May 22, 1992): 15-16. Baumann describes the cluttered Towne apartment in Brooklyn as a place where many spirits, evoked by matriarch Momma and the laments of her daughters, need to be appeased. Baumann points out that Momma's litany of loss underlies even her pronouncement that mailman Fred cannot husband his resources. Momma's characterization of Fred in terms of money made and spent is echoed in the idea that May's death is the inevitable outcome of the couple's meeting, love, and marriage, since happiness must be paid for in a "currency of loss."

Cooper, Rand Richards. "Charming Alice." *Commonweal* 125 (March 27, 1998): 10-12. Cooper reviews four of McDermott's novels and calls *At Weddings and Wakes* "a nostalgic and immaculately detailed valedictory to a vanishing corner of Iish Catholicism," Cooper admires the vivid characterizations and luminous prose.

Donavin, Denise. Review of *At Weddings and Wakes*, by Alice McDermott. *Booklist* 88 (March 1, 1992): 1197. Remarks that the brightest spot in the novel is Aunt May and concludes that her death does not overshadow her life. Donavin sums up the novel as charming, pensive fiction.

Klinkenborg, Verlyn. "Grief That Lasts Forever." *The New York Times Book Review* 97 (April 12, 1992): 3. In one of the more complete reviews following the publication of *At Weddings and Wakes*, Klinkenborg characterizes the novel as the present memorialized, accomplished by a primary focus through the children, who collectively and individually underline the ambiguities and reverberations inherent in the book's themes. The continual laments of the Towne women become instant memories, extant in the past and the present and projected into the future. Klinkenborg is also one of the few reviewers who comments on McDermott's writing style, which employs formal and phrasal patterns that have a harmony of their own.

McDermott, Alice. Interview by Wendy Smith. *Publishers Weekly* 239 (March 30, 1992): 85-86. McDermott discusses her life and work, with particular reference to *At Weddings and Wakes*.

Smolowe, Jill. "Dancing on Graves." *Time* 139 (April 20, 1992): 96. Smolowe argues that McDermott's third novel secures her reputation as a storyteller of great talent. The world of *At Weddings and Wakes* is haunted, Smolowe says, conjured from the dead to the living in the same way that the vitality of the Towne-Dailey children offsets the demise of parts of the family. The children, Smolowe states, offer a "life-affirming lesson" that overcomes the family's despair.

Mary Rohrberger

AUNT JULIA AND THE SCRIPTWRITER

Author: Mario Vargas Llosa (1936-   )
Type of plot: Comic realism
Time of plot: The 1950's
Locale: Lima, Peru
First published: La tía Julia y el escribidor, 1977 (English translation, 1982)

> *Principal characters:*
> MARIO, the protagonist, partial narrator, radio journalist, and writer
> AUNT JULIA, Mario's aunt by marriage, a divorcée who is fourteen
>   years Mario's senior, and whom he finally marries
> PEDRO CAMACHO, the Bolivian scriptwriter, a "one-man industry,"
>   whose scripts form a second pattern of narration

The Novel

   Aunt Julia and the Scriptwriter is a comedic novel about the education of young Mario (called variously Marito and Varguitas) that combines numerous elements of Vargas Llosa's own life with the fictional relationship with Aunt Julia and Pedro Camacho in Lima in the 1950's to form an autobiographical fable of identity that is neither autobiography nor history but rather an artistically rendered portrait of the artist as a young man. The primary narrator of the work, Mario, recounts, from a distance of at least twelve years later, his youthful love for his aunt by marriage, their improbable courtship and hilarious attempts to circumvent the law to get married, and his own life as a law student, radio newswriter, and would-be short-story writer. Each of the novel's twenty chapters, except the last two, which conclude Mario's narrative, are arranged so that the odd-numbered ones are Mario's attempts to describe his life and fortunes and the even-numbered ones are actual scripts of soap operas by Pedro Camacho, the indefatigable and prolific Bolivian scriptwriter.

   The work begins with a semiserious Mario introducing himself as a student and news director of Radio Panamerica, the lesser of Lima's two radio stations owned by the Genaro family, with the importation of Pedro Camacho from Bolivia to write original radio serials to replace those which the Genaros brought from Cuba, and with the arrival of the newly divorced Aunt Julia, also from Bolivia. Mario's initial encounters with Camacho and Julia are equally unpromising but turn out, in true melodramatic fashion, to be important first steps in forming a professional bond between Mario and the scriptwriter and a very personal one with Aunt Julia.

   The story of the furtive courtship between Mario and Julia is the central portion of Mario's narrative, as the two fall quite hopelessly, passionately, and madly in love with each other. Their love, when it is finally discovered after their ill-starred elopement, brings down upon them a family catastrophe that competes, in all of its absurdity and odd manifestations, with elements of Camacho's soap operas, the stories which are recounted antiphonally throughout the novel. Indeed, the comedy of errors of their elopement—they dash about the countryside to find a mayor who will, for a bribe, marry the underage Mario without parental consent—has exactly enough improbability about it to make it truly resemble the vicissitudes of real life. So does life often resemble bad literature and B-pictures.

Meanwhile, Pedro Camacho's soap operas make him the toast of Lima: The stories and the fortunes of their characters are on everyone's lips when Camacho begins to evidence signs of fatigue and then madness. His villains all turn out to be Argentines or Peruvians with Argentinian proclivities. Despite official protests to Radio Panamerica by the Argentine ambassador, Camacho persists in vilifying Argentina and its people. Far more serious is the growing bewilderment among his listeners: Characters who died in one serial are resurrected in another, sometimes with different professions; other characters move in and out of several serials; still others change their names in mid-script. Public confusion and dismay grow as, one by one, the principal continuing characters are killed off in one catastrophe after another until, after a series of disasters, each worse than the one before, all of fictional Lima is destroyed cataclysmically, and Camacho is finally committed to an insane asylum.

The work's final chapter serves as a neat conclusion to all the cliff-hanger questions about Mario's narrative and explains what has happened, over a twelve-year period, to Mario, Julia, Pedro Camacho, and lesser characters such as Pascual, Javier, and Big Pablito. In so doing, it serves both to provide a neat summary of much of the novel's action and to mark a decidedly new phase in Mario's fortunes.

The Characters

Mario is, despite the title, the principal focus of interest in the novel, which covers a brief period in his life and examines the widely different effects that both Julia and the scriptwriter have upon him. This novel of the education of a young man focuses not only upon his sensations and ideas but also upon his improbable actions and their sometimes hilarious consequences for him. Although several of the minor characters, chiefly his relatives and his companions at the radio station, do, in fact, have their own existences and concerns, one sees them predominantly through Mario's eyes and in relation to his own growth, concerns, and aspirations. In his painstaking characterization of his friends and relatives and in his precise details of the urban geography of Lima, Mario the narrator consistently views his environment personally, in relation to his sense of it and its meaning for him. In this sense, he is as much "the scriptwriter" of his own life, times, and place as Pedro Camacho is the scriptwriter of dozens of domestic and civil tragedies and melodramas of his contemporary Lima. Further, both Camacho and Mario are the creations of Mario the novelist.

As the young Mario makes his way through these few weeks and months of this extraordinary period in his life, he examines his journalistic apprenticeship at Radio Panamerica and the disparate writing assignments that he undertakes to help support Julia and himself as prologues to his Stephen Dedalus-like flight to the artistic Mecca where he aspires to work: Paris.

Pedro Camacho, the celebrated Bolivian scriptwriter who soon becomes a household word in Lima, is a prime example of one who creates his art for its own sake. Steeped in a devotion to his work that would have done credit to such prodigious creators of fictional worlds as Honoré de Balzac, Émile Zola, and Charles Dickens, Camacho finds his characters moving away from him, assuming independent lives of their own, jumping from one serial to another, and finally ending in chaotic and apocalyptic episodes that evidence the deterioration and madness of their creator. Camacho is a highly comic character whose outrageous characters complement his own absurdly melodramatic view of himself and of life. It comes as an amusing but somewhat shocking revelation to Mario that Camacho begins to dress like his characters, male and female, so that he can better interpret them in his stories. It is a darker and more sober revelation that Camacho has a wife who is Argentine and who keeps food on their table through utterly unromantic prostitution.

Of great interest, at times of greater interest than Mario, is the wonderful Aunt Julia, as perfect a foil to the numerous stereotypes of Spanish American Princesses (SAP's) as can be found in Latin American fiction written by men. Independent, witty, beautiful, intelligent, resourceful, charming, arch, and eminently common-sensical, the thirty-two-year-old Julia entirely captivates the young Mario, concedes to a marriage on the condition that it will last at least five years, and shares his dreams, hardships, difficulties, and ultimately his achievement of the goal to live the life of a writer. In the wry final chapter one learns that the marriage really was a success and lasted longer than "all the parents and even she herself had feared, wished or predicted: eight years." At this point Julia fades, her function in the work now accomplished. With her fades a time of hope and joy in Mario's narrative; the remainder is the "real" world of his present in a new and ostensibly confining marriage and in a sentimental journey back to Lima and the reacquaintance with former friends and the much altered scriptwriter.

Themes and Meanings

The central theme of the work, clearly a *Bildungsroman* in nature, is the act of writing, of telling one's story and a succession of stories. The novel's epigraph, from Salvador Elizondo's *El grafógrafo* (1972), is a perfect introduction to the work and a classical statement of the metaphysical and epistemological state of contemporary literature in which writers write about writing about writing and invite readers to imagine them imagining themselves writing about writing. Surely an invitation to formalist and deconstructive critical interpretation, the epigraph reinforces the perfect Viconian circularity of the novel, in which Mario the narrator is a character of Mario the novelist and in which both are writing about being writers and about one notorious writer, the tireless but insane scriptwriter, whose creations are also those of Mario the novelist.

All other elements of the novel—the themes of romance, uproariously amusing misadventures, accidental meetings, amorous assignations, love unrequited and gloriously requited, ambition and entertainment—are subservient to the overmastering passions of Mario, Pedro, and the novelist to memorialize experience, fictionalize life, and artfully reinvent identity. The final chapter is, again, supremely important in setting several records as straight as they can be in Mario's narrative, in the supposed events and motives of Pedro Camacho's life and works, and in the ultimately enigmatic life and adventures of the ineluctable Aunt Julia.

Critical Context

Aunt Julia and the Scriptwriter has been variously hailed as a "ribald classic," a pure example of the "literature of exhaustion" that reflects upon itself, and a postmodern novel that ratifies Vargas Llosa's early preeminence in *el boom latino americano* of the 1960's and 1970's. It is likely to become an international classic and one of the basic works upon which Vargas Llosa's literary reputation will ultimately rest. Unlike most of his previous and subsequent novels (especially *La guerra del fin del mundo*, 1981; *The War of the End of the World*, 1984), it is a distinctly comic work, handled with a light touch, testimony to his versatile imagination.

Indeed, Vargas Llosa has produced a consistently first-rate series of works in the fields of criticism, journalism, fiction, and drama, explicating and elucidating the varied facets of Latin American life and culture both to fellow Latin Americans and to an increasing number of European and North American readers. While he shares, surely and clearly, the "Magical Realism" of such pioneering figures as Gabriel García Márquez and Julio Cortázar, he has transmuted this technique into a more immediately accessible form of fiction that has been widely accepted in the last half of the twentieth century.

Bibliography

Booker, M. Keith. *Vargas Llosa Among the Postmodernists*. Gainesville: University Press of Florida, 1994. A thorough examination of Vargas Llosa's works from a postmodern point of view. Includes a comparison between *Aunt Julia and the Scriptwriter* and Italo Calvino's *If on a Winter's Night a Traveler.*

Castro-Klarén, Sara. "Mario Vargas Llosa." In *Latin American Writers*, edited by Carlos A. Solé and Maria I. Abreau. Vol 3. New York: Charles Scribner's Sons, 1989. Offers a comprehensive and critical discussion of Vargas Llosa's life and works. Provides a selected bibliography for further reading.

Dipple, Elizabeth. "Outside, Looking In: Aunt Julia and Vargas Llosa." *The Review of Contemporary Fiction* 17 (Spring, 1997): 58-69. Dipple argues that Vargas Llosa's *The Storyteller* and *Aunt Julia and the Scriptwriter* are examples of the author's tendency to separate reality and fiction, revealing that the main characters are a limited version of himself. However, Vargas Llosa believes that the representation of himself in his works is distorted by his own beliefs and obsessions.

Gerdes, Dick. "Mario Vargas Llosa." In *Spanish American Authors: The Twentieth Century*, edited by Angel Flores. New York: H. W. Wilson, 1992. Profiles Vargas Llosa and includes an extensive bibliography of works by and about the author.

Kristal, Efrain. *Temptation of the Word: The Novels of Mario Vargas Llosa*. Nashville, Tenn.: Vanderbilt University Press, 1998. A collection of perceptive essays on

Vargas Llosa's novels written from the 1960's through the 1980's. A helpful bibliography for further reading is also included.

Standish, Peter. "Contemplating Your Own Novel: The Case of Mario Vargas Llosa." *Hispanic Review* 61 (Winter, 1993): 53-63. Standish explores Vargas Llosa's use of metafictional devices in *Aunt Julia and the Scriptwriter* and *The Storyteller.* He maintains that Vargas Llosa's use of metafiction is chiefly digetic rather than linguistic and reflects Vargas Llosa's preoccupation with the topic of storytelling.

John J. Conlon

AURA

Author: Carlos Fuentes (1928-   )
Type of plot: Gothic fantasy
Time of plot: The early 1960's
Locale: Mexico City
First published: 1962 (English translation, 1965)

>   *Principal characters:*
>   FELIPE MONTERO, a young historian
>   CONSUELO LLORENTE, an extremely old woman
>   AURA, her beautiful young niece

The Novel

The fantastic nature of this short novel is indicated at its very beginning when Felipe Montero, an indigent young man, reads a newspaper advertisement requesting the services of a historian. The advertisement is so suited to his own experience, needs, and skills that it seems to be addressed to him and to no one else; all that is missing is his name. This sense of Montero's being especially summoned by the advertisement is further emphasized when he arrives at an ancient mansion in the old section of town where no one lives. As he enters the door, he takes one last look to try to "retain some single image of that indifferent outside world," before entering a realm of magic and imagination.

Although the incredibly old Consuelo Llorente ostensibly wishes Montero to edit the memoirs of her dead husband for publication, one suspects that she has other, more profound plans for the young historian. Indeed, with the appearance of her beautiful young niece, Aura, who immediately exerts a hypnotic hold on Montero, the reader's suspicion that this is a sort of modern fairy tale or parable is confirmed. The mysterious, old, witchlike crone, the quietly beautiful young girl, and the summoned young man establish an archetypal fairy-tale situation.

The house itself is typically gothic and always in darkness; the old woman's room is filled with religious relics and lighted only with votive candles; in private she engages in occult rituals and makes entreaties to Gabriel to sound his trumpet. She continually caresses a pet rabbit, whose name is Saga, and the trunk which contains her dead husband's papers seems always covered with rats. Montero feels a pleasure in the house that he has never felt before, a feeling that he always knew was a part of him but that has never been set free. He decides that the old woman has some secret power over her niece, and he is obsessed with the desire not only to set her free but also to possess her himself. Consuelo's witchlike nature is further emphasized when, as Montero studies her husband's papers, he discovers that she must be at least 109 years old.

The mystery of the relationship between Consuelo and her niece deepens when Montero sees Aura skinning a young goat in the kitchen and then goes to the old woman's room to find her performing the same skinning action in mime. When he dreams of Aura, he sees the old lady's image superimposed on the image of Aura. Although Montero believes that Aura is kept in the house to preserve the illusion of youth for the old woman, the truth of the matter is even more occult and mysterious. Aura seems to age each day. One day, she appears to be a girl of twenty, the next, a woman of forty. When Montero makes love to her, the act is prefaced by Aura's rubbing a wafer against her thighs and offering him half of it to eat. He falls upon her naked arms, which are stretched out on the side of the bed like the crucifix on the wall: "Aura opens up like an altar." To complete this carnal communion, she makes him promise to love her forever, even if she grows old and dies.

As the actions of Consuelo and Aura become more and more blended, as if one is an echo of the other, Montero realizes that the "sterile conception" of their lovemaking has created another double, his own other half which he now seeks. He finally discovers the secret of the old woman's relationship to Aura on the last page of old General Llorente's papers, where he reads of Consuelo's growing herbs which will perform the magic of creating Aura as an image of her own youth. Moreover, he discovers portraits of the young couple and realizes that the old woman is Aura, and that the old general is himself. Montero fears that the hand of the past will wipe away his own features, "the cardboard features that hid your true face, your real appearance, the appearance you once had but then forgot." He rejects the human vanity of clock time and accepts what seems fated to happen to him.

In the final scene of the novel, Montero goes to Consuelo's room and calls for Aura. The voice he hears from the darkness tells him that she is gone and will not come back: "I'm exhausted. She's already exhausted. I've never been able to keep her with me for more than three days." Montero tears off Aura's robe and embraces and kisses her. As the moonlight falls on her face, he discovers it to be as brittle and yellowed as the memoirs—to be the body and face of the old Consuelo. He accepts this, however, for he has promised to love Aura even when she is old. He embraces her and waits until the cloud covers the moon, when the "memory of youth, of youth reembodied, rules the darkness." In the last line of the story, Consuelo promises that Aura will come back again: "We'll bring her back together."

The Characters

Because *Aura* is essentially a modern gothic romance, the characters of the story are not intended to be realistic, but rather representative. They are psychic archetypes in a parable of youth, love, age, and imagination. Montero is the fairy-tale protagonist who is magically summoned to fulfill old Consuelo's desire—to recapture not only her own past, but also the past of her husband and of their love. Consuelo herself is one of Fuentes's witchlike women with the magical power of imaginative creation. The headnote to the novel, from Jules Michelet, emphasizes the power of female imaginative creation embodied in the story: "*Man hunts and struggles. Woman intrigues and dreams; she is the mother of fantasy, the mother of the gods. She has second sight, the wings that enable her to fly to the infinite of desire and the imagination.*" Aura is a self-created image of Consuelo, an imaginative projection of her own youth.

Essentially there are only two characters in the story: Aura/Consuelo and Montero/ General Llorente, and neither is so much a character in the conventional sense of the term as an embodiment of an archetype—the former embodying Carl Jung's anima, or archetypal female, the latter the questing male figure who yearns to unite with, and know the secret of, the mysterious woman. Montero is drawn out of the world of external reality and into the unconscious world of the imagination and thus becomes one with the occult reality of Aura/Consuelo. This basic nature of the characters explains the mysterious blend of the occult and the erotic which dominates the story. The same character configuration and the same union of the sexual and the supernatural can be seen in the works of Henry James, Edgar Allan Poe, Alexander Pushkin, and Sir H. Rider Haggard. The basic dichotomy between the male and the female principle which *Aura* embodies is that whereas man hunts and struggles in the profane world of everyday reality, always questing for the answers to metaphysical mysteries, woman is the passive dreamer, the creator, who achieves the fulfillment of her desires by imaginative creation.

Themes and Meanings

There are several levels of meaning in the novel. On one level, it is a love story in which the desires of youth and beauty triumph over the reality of old age and death. In a basic sense, this is a story of the power of pure desire to overcome the limitations of external reality. On the unconscious level, it is an archetypal parable about the male who is seduced into the loss of the ego, which enables him to enter completely into the world of the woman, for it is indeed the imaginative reality of the female which constitutes both erotic and supernatural transcendence over the external world. Culturally, the story suggests a theme that Fuentes has explored in other works, the simultaneous existence of the old Mexico superimposed upon the new. In fact, "superimposition" is probably the key word for all of these themes, as, gradually, Aura is superimposed on Consuelo and Montero is superimposed on Consuelo's dead husband.

The novel is narrated in the second person, in the present tense, as if Montero were recounting the events as they occur. For example, as he looks into the eyes of Aura for the first time, he sees them surge and change: "You look into them and tell yourself it isn't true. . . . But you can't deceive yourself: those eyes do surge, do change, as if offering you a landscape that only you can see and desire." This unusual narrative strategy not only creates a sense of gradually engulfing mystery, much like that in a detective novel, but also effectively eradicates Montero's own personal past and creates a sense of the presentness of the past. Moreover, the second-person narrative stance emphasizes both the concrete detail of Montero's experience and his growing sense of being lost in a dream reality. As he becomes engulfed in the eerie atmosphere of the old house, the reader becomes absorbed in the eerie tone of the novel itself.

As a historian, accustomed to studying the past as it is preserved in documents—a past, that is, kept at a certain distance—Montero finds himself drawn into a past that is maintained in the present by the imaginative creation of the old Consuelo—a past that is not preserved in historical texts but which lives in the mind and the reality of the other. Although he desires to take Aura outside the occult and hermetically sealed world of the old woman, the imagination and the realm of the sacred prove more powerful than external, profane reality.

The action of the novel hovers uneasily between reality and fantasy, as both Montero and the reader search futilely for realistic explanations for the mystery of Aura and the old Consuelo. Just as Montero is caught up in an increasingly occult reality, so also is the reader, who finally must accept the magical nature of the events and the ultimate reality of the imagination. The sense that the novel has of existing somewhere in between the real world and the world of the imagination is emphasized not only by the gothic house, the occult Aura, and the old Consuelo, but also by Montero's being caught up in obsessive dreams which become so blended with the fantastic nature of his actual experience that the two realms cannot be distinguished.

Critical Context

Although many of Fuentes's novels have been concerned with political and social reality, his short stories and novellas, or short novels, have more often been mythic and symbolic. *Aura* is perhaps his best-known work in which magic, the occult, and particularly the witch archetype are of central importance. In an earlier collection of short stories, *Los días enmascarados* (1954), the same witch figure appears, as does the prevailing theme developed in *Aura* of the dominance of the past over the present.

Various sources for the story have been noted by critics. Perhaps the most commonly mentioned are Henry James's *The Aspern Papers* (1888), Pushkin's *Pikovaya dama* (1934; *The Queen of Spades*, 1896), and Haggard's *She* (1887). The single most important source, however, as Fuentes himself has noted, is Jules Michelet's *La Sorcière* (1862; *The Witch of the Middle Ages*, 1863), in which a woman is depicted as a witch who has the ability to give birth to a being identical to herself.

Aura was practically ignored by reviewers when first published because it appeared almost at the same time as Fuentes's best-known and most controversial novel, *La muerte de Artemio Cruz* (1962; *The Death of Artemio Cruz*, 1964). Now, however, *Aura* is recognized as a central text in Fuentes's continuing exploration of history, myth, and the anima archetype, as well as a particularly fine example of the genre of the fantastic.

Bibliography

Duran, Victor Manuel. *A Marxist Reading of Fuentes, Vargas Llosa, and Puig.* Lanham, Md.: University Press of America, 1994. An interesting study comparing the politics in the writings of these three important Latin American authors. Many of Fuentes's works are examined in detail.

Helmuth, Chalene. *The Postmodern Fuentes.* Lewisburg, Penn.: Bucknell University Press, 1997. A solid overview of Fuentes's work from a postmodernist point of view. Several individual works are discussed, focusing on the issues of identity, national and narrative control, and reconsiderations of the past.

Ibsen, Kristine. *Author, Text, and Reader in the Novels of Carlos Fuentes*. New York: Peter Lang, 1993. Although Ibsen does not discuss *Aura*, she offers valuable insight into the problem of communication, which remains one of the central preoccupations throughout the work of Fuentes. Her analysis focuses on the means of textualization by which Fuentes activates his reader and how this coincides with his notions of the role of literature in society.

Pollard, Scott. "Canonizing Revision: Literary History and the Postmodern Latin American Writer." *College Literature* 20 (October, 1993): 133-147. Scott analyzes the impact of Latin American narrative on Western literary history after World War II. Focusing on authors Alejo Carpentier, Carlos Fuentes, and José Lezama Lima, Scott discusses narratives of conquest and exploration, international modernism, the fashioning of cultural identity, and the primacy of European culture. Offers valuable insight into several of Fuentes's works.

Van Delden, Maarten. *Carlos Fuentes, Mexico, and Modernity*. Nashville, Tenn.: Vanderbilt University Press, 1998. Using Fuentes's writings as a springboard for his discussion, Van Delden presents a comprehensive analysis of Fuentes's intellectual development in the context of modern Mexican political and cultural life. Includes extensive notes and a helpful bibliography.

Charles E. May

THE AUTUMN OF THE PATRIARCH

Author: Gabriel García Márquez (1928-   )
Type of plot: Episodic fantasy parable
Time of plot: The late nineteenth and early twentieth centuries
Locale: An unnamed Caribbean country
First published: El otoño del patriarca, 1975 (English translation, 1975)

Principal characters:
> THE PATRIARCH, an unnamed Latin American dictator who is
> somewhere between the ages of 107 and 232
> BENDICIÓN ALVARADO, his mother, a former prostitute
> PATRICIO ARAGONÉS, his double, who is assassinated
> LETICIA NAZARENO, his wife, a former nun
> EMANUEL, their infant son
> GENERAL RODRIGO DE AGUILAR, the chief of national security
> MANUELA SÁNCHEZ, a beauty queen who vanishes during a solar
> eclipse
> JOSÉ IGNACIO SAENZ DE LA BARRA, a sadistic torturer

The Novel

The Autumn of the Patriarch, published eight years after Gabriel García Márquez's highly praised *Cien años de soledad* (1967; *One Hundred Years of Solitude*, 1970), was a novel for which both general readers and critics had waited. It was, however, a project that García Márquez had put aside earlier to write *One Hundred Years of Solitude* because, as he has commented, he was writing it at first without any clear idea of what he was doing. García Márquez has said that he got the idea for writing the work two or three days after the fall of the dictator Marcos Pérez Jiménez, when the ruling junta met. He was in the anteroom of the presidential office with other journalists when an officer in battle fatigues came out walking backward with a machine gun in his hand and mud on his boots. It was at that moment, García Márquez reveals, that he had a sudden insight into the mystery of power.

Consequently, he wanted to write a "poem on the solitude of power," in which a mythical Latin American dictator would be used as an embodiment of many such dictators, from "Papa Doc" Duvalier of Haiti to Juan Vicente Gómez of Venezuela. His first attempt at the structure of the book—a long monologue by the aged dictator as he is waiting to be executed—he abandoned for the existing polyphonic structure of a multitude of blending voices in six sections that make the book begin and end in a spiral fashion with the discovery of the patriarch's body. The result is a difficult book to read, for each of the six episodes of which it is composed is a single paragraph. There are no other breaks in the novel, and many of the sentences go on for several pages in a run-on, seemingly rambling and disconnected fashion, much like some of the novels of William Faulkner or the stream-of-consciousness works of James Joyce. The stylistic experiment of the book goes even further than Faulkner or Joyce, however, for the point of view of the work shifts constantly, sometimes even within a single line, from first-person participant to third-person author to first-person-plural choral response. García Márquez has called *The Autumn of the Patriarch* the most experimental of his novels and the one that interests him most as a poetic adventure; it is, he says, a book that he wrote like a poem, word by word, sometimes spending weeks on a few lines.

The novel begins with the discovery of the body of the aged patriarch pecked at by vultures and sprouting parasitic animals. Yet because he has not been seen by anyone in many years, and because this is the second time he has been found dead (the first time was with the death of Patricio Aragonés, his exact double), those who find him are not sure if he indeed is the dictator. Although the patriarch's entire life—from birth, to ascendancy to power, to marriage, to suspected coups, to examples of his autocratic and magical rule—is recounted in the six chapters of the work, the primary plot line (if that is possible in such a multifaceted novel as this) focuses on the twenty-four-hour period from the discovery of the body to the final celebration and jubilation at the end of the book.

There is no real sense of chronological time in the novel, for the various voices which recount the events that characterize the patriarch's life blend into a kind of grotesque tone-poem in which time becomes a mythical cycle, ranging throughout the supposed two centuries of the patriarch's mythic life and even beyond to one scene when the patriarch looks out the window and sees the ships of Columbus beside a battleship of modern-day marines. Yet this world of mythic reality, like the world of many of García Márquez's other works, is a world of violence and grotesquely brutal events. A few examples should be sufficient to indicate the nature of the details of the novel and to show the mythically mad world that the patriarch creates around him.

There is, for example, the execution of General Rodrigo de Aguilar after he is suspected of instigating an attempt on the patriarch's life. On the night when he is to be the honored guest at a banquet for the palace guards, he makes his entrance on a silver platter decorated with cauliflower and laurel branches, marinated in spices, browned in the oven, then carved and served up with the order to eat heartily. There is the death of Bendicion Alvarado, the patriarch's mother, who rots away of some mysterious disease but whose body is preserved and displayed throughout the country, revived and, according to some, still alive as the patriarch attempts to have her canonized as a saint. There is the death of Leticia Nazareno, the patriarch's wife, and his small son, Emanuel, devoured piece by piece by a pack of trained dogs.

After this murder, José Ignacio Saenz de la Barra, who is hired to find the killers, sends the patriarch numerous bags of what appear to be coconuts but which really contain the heads of some of his enemies, until, finally, 918 heads are delivered, many of which decay in a filing cabinet. There are the two thousand children who have been used by the patriarch as a way to cheat on the national lottery and who, because of their innocent complicity, must all be killed—an atrocity that is achieved by placing them in a ship filled with concrete which is then exploded. The list of absurd and grotesque events goes on and on—countless horrors that become so numerous that the reader can no longer take them completely seriously but must allow them to blend together in a kind of lyrically maintained mythical world of madness and extremity.

The Characters

The central character, the figure for whom the entire novel exists, is the patriarch himself. Yet he is less a unified character than a pastiche of the idea of the dictator: one who has ultimate power to create his own world and to manipulate other human beings as though they were dispensable pieces in an elaborate, self-indulgent game. If the patriarch were to be taken as a real person, he could be dismissed simply as mad. Since, however, he is an embodiment of the horrors of ultimate power that corrupts absolutely, he suggests the madness of power itself, which is a much more horrifying concept.

He is given all the attributes of the magical personage—one who can change the weather, who is invulnerable to bullets, who fathers hundreds of children, who is destined to live forever, who rules so absolutely that when he asks what time it is, the answer is whatever time he wishes it to be. At the same time, however, he is also seen as weak, fearful of assassination, often sexually impotent, at the mercy of those around him, and generally in a state of aging decay. His gigantic herniated testicle, which he must carry about in a leather case, is a central symbol of this double image: Even as it suggests the magnitude of his sexual organs and thus his power, it also is like a hump on his back, a burden that limits him. Moreover, his seemingly unrestrained power is made ridiculous by the various ruses that his followers must employ to maintain the illusion of power; for example, the young virginal schoolgirls whom he sexually accosts on their way home are really prostitutes hired by his men, and the soap operas he watches are created for his eyes only, because he insists on happy endings.

The other named characters in the novel (there are hundreds who are not named) are similarly extreme and grotesque images rather than real people. The patriarch's mother insists on living in the servants' quarters and paints birds to make them more colorful for sale, seemingly unaware of her great wealth. At one point, during an official parade, she hands a basket of empty bottles in the window of her son's car and asks him to drop them off at the store. Leticia Nazareno, the patriarch's wife, continually goes to the marketplace and buys numerous useless items with the order to "send the bill to the government"—bills which never get paid. During the wedding itself, when she is seven months pregnant, she squats in the "steamy puddle of her own water" and brings "out from among the tangle of muslin the premature infant."

Themes and Meanings

Certainly *The Autumn of the Patriarch* is a political novel concerning the nature of the paradigmatic Latin American dictator. Yet it is less a novel that focuses on particular political realities than it is about the most universal truth that underlies the nature of all political reality: the truth of absolute power. Moreover, it is about the need of the people to create a supernatural leader, a kind of demigod who, although his decisions are often arbitrary, still represents a sense of destiny and a source of control or responsibility for all the seemingly unpredictable absurdities that dominate life. It is a book about power and the ultimate solitude of power: He is ultimately alone, less in control than controlled by the demands and expectations of those who created him to fulfill their own needs.

Although there are indeed social themes in this novel—where petty corruption is magnified to the gigantic, where there are dark hints at the threat of American imperialism, and where the fundamental unjustness of the rigid economic and class distinctions in Latin America are revealed— *The Autumn of the Patriarch* is ultimately not a political novel. Rather, it is a grotesque lyric poem, a richly metaphoric and mythical experience that overpowers the reader who has the fortitude and the dedication required to read it and become lost in its comic absurdity and its horrific reality. Reading the book is like being caught up in an obsession of the invisible presence that has created it, for the reader who allows the rhythm of the poetic prose of the work to engulf him becomes carried away by the continuous and unrelenting assault on his sense of reality. *The Autumn of the Patriarch* is a book so richly and completely imaginative that it seems to be a palpable embodiment of the mind of García Márquez; indeed, the author has called it an autobiography in code, a confession, "the only book I always wanted to write and never could."

Critical Context

García Márquez has admitted that his primary literary debts are to the lyric, stream-of-consciousness style of William Faulkner, the restrained and stylized realism of Ernest Hemingway, and the nightmarishly concrete world of Franz Kafka. After the publication of *One Hundred Years of Solitude*, a work which astonished the critics and the reading public with its fantastically realized world of myth and magic, many wondered how García Márquez could go beyond the experimental narrative style of that work. *The Autumn of the Patriarch* did not disappoint them, although many found it much less readable than his earlier works. As might be expected, professional critics have had a field day with the book, for it is surely ripe for explication. Indeed, they have itemized the obsessively repeated symbolic motifs of the novel, have suggested historical sources for the patriarch himself, and have generally delighted in demonstrating their ability to "read" and then to clarify what seems to be an extremely demanding book. Although the book has been generally praised, it has also been criticized for being too long, often too self-indulgent, and too stylistically idiosyncratic to be widely read.

Still, although it is a book more often referred to than actually read, it reaffirms García Márquez's place as the most famous and respected figure of the Latin American literary renaissance—an elite group that includes Julio Cortázar, Carlos Fuentes, and José Donoso, all of whom share García Márquez's narrative worldview of a reality that is much more fictional and absurd than our common sense and our sense of common decency will allow us to accept.

Bibliography
Bloom, Harold, ed. *Márquez*. New York: Chelsea House, 1989. A collection of eighteen essays by various authors on different aspects of Márquez's works. Covers the whole range of literary criticism and offers in-depth analysis of several of Márquez's novels.

Dolan, Sean. *Hispanics of Achievement*. New York: Chelsea House, 1994. A solid introduction to Márquez's work, featuring photographs and quotations. Discusses Márquez's family background, literary influences, and personal politics and how these shaped his writing.

McMurray, George R. "Gabriel García Márquez." In *Latin American Writers*, edited by Carlos A. Solé and Maria I. Abreau. Vol 3. New York: Charles Scribner's Sons, 1989. Offers a comprehensive and critical discussion of Márquez's life and works. Provides a selected bibliography for further reading.

Márquez, Gabriel García. Interview. *UNESCO Courier* 49 (February, 1996): 4-7. Márquez offers his views on the teaching and protection of culture. He also discusses his daily writing discipline and how it has influenced and enhanced his work. An informative and interesting interview.

Styron, Rose. "Gabriel García Márquez, Carlos Fuentes, and Kenzaburo Oe: From the Rose Styron Conversations." *New Perspectives Quarterly* 14 (Fall, 1997): 56-62. A revealing interview with three renowned authors. They share their views on topics such as women and power, first and lost love, journalism as literature, spirit and faith, and multiculturalism.

Charles E. May

AVALOVARA

Author: Osman Lins (1924-1978)
Type of plot: Existential quest
Time of plot: 200 B.C.E., 1908-1940, and 1938-1970
Locale: Pompeii, France, Holland, Italy, Germany, England, São Paulo, Recife, and
  Rio Grande do Sul, Brazil
First published: 1973 (English translation, 1980)

> *Principal characters:*
> ABEL, the protagonist, a Brazilian writer in his early thirties
> ANNELIESE ROOS, his German lover
> CECILIA, his Brazilian lover in Recife
> Ⓞ, his Brazilian lover in São Paulo
> PUBLIUS UBONIUS, a Pompeiian businessman
> LOREIUS, a slave of Publius Ubonius
> JULIUS HECKETHORN, a German clockmaker
> OLAVO HAYANO, the husband of Ⓞ

The Novel

The structure of Osman Lins's *Avalovara* is at once astonishingly complex and altogether transparent. The sequence of events is predetermined by a geometric design which appears before the first page of text, consisting of a Latin palindrome of five five-letter words with a spiral superimposed on it. To visualize this palindrome here, draw a large square subdivided into twenty-five smaller squares—five across and five down. In the first row of squares place the letters S-A-T-O-R; in the second, A-R-E-P-O; in the third, T-E-N-E-T; in the fourth, O-P-E-R-A; and in the fifth, R-O-T-A-S. The entire square is centered over a fourteen-ring spiral.

Each letter of the palindrome represents one plot line, and when the spiral touches a letter, a passage of that plot line appears. Since some letters are more frequent than others, plot segments vary in number of episodes from twenty-four (letter "O") to two (letter "N," which is in the center of the design). In addition, episodes increase in length each time that particular plot line reappears—most are ten lines long in the first episode, twenty lines long in the second, and so on. Exceptions are the themes corresponding to the letters "P" and "T," whose first episodes are twelve and twenty lines long, respectively.

Such a contrived structure would make *Avalovara*'s plot seem to be an extremely easy one to recount, but in fact the reading experience is nearly impossible to describe, because the reader is simultaneously witnessing a dazzling display of literary legerdemain and being led in and out of eight very different but interrelated plot lines. Plots of such visible artifice often turn out to be admirable failures, but Lins never sacrifices his fiction to the contrivances that order its unfolding, and the novel betrays none of the self-centeredness many cleverly concocted novels have.

Though there are eight plot divisions, six of them involve the protagonist Abel directly, two dealing with his love affairs with Roos (largely set in Europe) and Cecilia (largely set in Recife). The other four are all in some way concerned with the enigmatic $\circlearrowleft$, with whom Abel lives a consuming passion and in whose arms he dies, at the hands of Olavo Hayano. One of the other remaining plot lines deals with the Pompeiian Publius Ubonius, who offers to free his slave Loreius if the slave can construct a magic sentence which reflects the mobility of the universe and the immutability of the divine. The sentence Loreius invents is "Sator arepo tenet opera rotas" ("The farmer carefully maintains his plow in the furrows"); the square in which it lies is space; the spiral superimposed on it is time. The final subplot is the story of the obsessed clockmaker Julius Heckethorn, who early in the twentieth century attempts to devise a clock unencumbered by the bothersome ticks of ordinary clocks. He abandons the scheme but does design a clock with a complex triple sound system which will some day play Domenico Scarlatti's Sonata in F Minor.

As the reader approaches the end of the book, the spiral approaches the center of the square, and the various narratives, separated in time and space, draw together as Abel approaches something like an erotic transcendence in the arms of his mysterious and oddly polymorphous lover. The moment of this epiphany coincides with the beginning of a solar eclipse, which is precisely the second that the intricate clock, now in the same room with Abel, begins the sonata.

The Characters

Each of the characters in *Avalovara* is identified with a particular notion, either abstract or concrete, which contributes to an understanding of the character in the context of the whole. Abel's German lover Roos, for example, is identified with cities, and part of her function appears to be to suggest the mobility, even random movement, of people and objects in the space of the cosmos. Cecilia, his first Brazilian lover, is identified with a series of animals but has as a salient characteristic not some animal trait but a complex of non-traits, which contribute to her ambiguity—she is neither woman nor animal, woman nor man, and she is surrounded by characters who similarly have interchangeable or indeterminate names. Abel himself is most clearly identified with water, a traditional symbol of some richness, but he is the seeker of truth, not an embodiment of it. Undoubtedly the most interesting, and the most difficult, character is $\circlearrowleft$, a woman "twice-born" whose behavior makes her seem more mythic than human but who is at the same time the object of Abel's almost hallucinatory erotic obsession. Even Olavo Hayano, who is important in the action only at the climax and who remains a sketchy figure throughout, is likely to be associated in the reader's mind with the "Yolyp," an imaginary creature of great destructive power.

Avalovara is not really a character here, but it is most closely associated with $\circlearrowleft$, and many of its attributes are hers. The name derives from the Buddhist *Avalokitesvara*, a male Bodhisattva, one who has attained enlightenment but who postpones Nirvana in order to help others attain enlightenment. $\circlearrowleft$ is not only magical but also double, because there is within her another set of eyes, another life, another self.

One of the most interesting characterization devices in *Avalovara* is found in the use of names. Novelists have long used suggestive names to hint at the configuration of soul of a character, but Lins seems to have been determined to force readers into a more active role in determining a character's goodness or badness. Most of the principal characters here have no last name—one of the two principals has no name at all, but rather a symbol.

Themes and Meanings

Avalovara is clearly a very ambitious work. Two themes—time and space—are suggested by the geometric design at the front of the text, and the entire structure of the novel is determined by the relationship of the physical space of the squares and the progression of the spiral of time over that space. Julius Heckethorn's clock is a variation on the theme, since he decides to set the device in motion at the exact second that will cause its musical culmination to coincide with Abel's moment of fruition. That moment of fruition is a contrary one, since in the process of attaining paradise (Nirvana, knowledge, awareness) he must die, a conceit which is only partially in harmony with any orthodoxy, at least any Western orthodoxy. The title itself suggests that the philosophical framework for Abel's quest is rooted in a mysticism more encompassing than can be found in Roman Catholicism, though there are also allusions to Western notions of transcendence, which might indicate that the substructure of the inquiry is not exclusively Buddhist but eclectic.

The interrelationship of time and space is, then, the overriding conceit in *Avalovara*, but numerous other kinds of questions are included in this central quest. Each major theme is elaborated contrapuntally by secondary ones: The cities embodied in Roos are part of the search for Absolute City; the names and non-names of the characters suggest a search for *the* name, the Word; the spiral reappears in the shape of a unicorn's horn and in the spiraling descent of a vulture; time is viewed both as the linear progression marked by the ticks of a clock and as a (spiral) flow toward fruition. The geometric design itself suggests two different views of the cosmos, one rooted in symmetry and cosmic order, the other based on the unforeseen and unforeseeable chance meeting of the spiral on one of the squares.

Yet time and space are really only the setting for the central theme, which is contained in the metaphor of a fish which leaps from the water and is devoured—at the moment of its plenitude. Abel's route to plenitude is through the sexual act, and his fruition is a cosmic orgasm and the moment of death and knowing, counterpointed by the eclipse and the chiming of the clock.

Finally, it is useful to note that one-to-one relationships are not easily established in a work of such scope. The palindrome itself is ambiguous, and the structure of the novel is based on two opposing numerical systems, one based on the magical number three, the other based on the symmetrical ordering number ten.

Critical Context

Osman Lins published his first novel, *O visitante*, in 1955, and his second, *O fiel e a pedra*, in 1961. His first novel won for him several literary prizes, and two of his books of short stories, *Os gestos* (1957) and *Nove, novena* (1966), contributed substantially to his reputation as a serious and very talented writer. His works also enjoyed notable success abroad, especially the French translation of *Nove, novena*. *Avalovara* itself was ready for publication in Italian, French, and German before the Brazilian edition appeared.

Lins has not been a "popular" writer in Brazil because his works are all, like *Avalovara*, intellectually and philosophically challenging. He does, however, have a solid reputation as one of Brazil's most accomplished, as well as one of its most difficult, authors. *Avalovara* is legitimately regarded as the culmination of a brilliant writer's career. Though he published one more novel before his death in 1978, *Avalovara* had obviously been germinating in its author's mind for some time, since some tentative suggestions of it appeared in earlier works, notably the short stories. Brazilian critics have consistently admired his works, though there have been reservations expressed about some of his technical innovations, occasionally so complex as to produce not much more than perplexity in his readers.

Consistent with such perplexities, *Avalovara* can be seen as belonging to two important but apparently contradictory literary traditions: apocalyptic fiction and Utopian fiction. It is in some ways comparable to such apocalyptic works as Thomas Pynchon's *Gravity's Rainbow* (1973)—there is even a symbolically suggestive Nike rocket launch in *Avalovara*, reminiscent of Pynchon's symbolic V-2's—but it also fits into the more established Utopian tradition. What is unusual about *Avalovara* is that it presents the apocalypse as the means of achieving the utopian state.

Avalovara is also a distinguished example of yet another literary fashion, one which has had particular importance in the twentieth century: the self-referential novel. In fact, it is so intensely self-referential that some are reluctant to call it a novel at all, preferring to see it more as a tour de force of fiction about writing fiction than as a story about characters. There is some validity to this point, since few novels obey such a rigid and elaborate predetermined structure, but the only episodes which belabor this premeditation are the sections of the geometric design itself (the ten episodes corresponding to the letter "S"), and the rest of the stories are so densely evocative and so symbolically suggestive that readers become so involved as to overlook the artifice. Even those who do not are likely to remember *Avalovara* as an incomparable reading experience.

Bibliography

Frizzi, Adria. "Osman Lins: An Introduction." *The Review of Contemporary Fiction* 15 (Fall, 1995): 155-160. An excellent presentation of Lins and his work. Frizzi notes that Lins was the "epitome of an outsider" and that although his experiments in narration and textual time and space sometimes make his works difficult to understand, they are not inaccessible.

Ladiera, Julieta Goloy. "Osman Lins: Crossing Frontiers." *The Review of Contemporary Fiction* 15 (Fall, 1995): 186-195. Ladiera discusses the power of literature to cross, even transcend, borders. She examines Lins's fiction from this perspective, showing how his work surmounts cultural and social boundaries by means of ideas.

Scliar, Moacyr. "Living on Literature or for Literature?" *The Review of Contemporary Fiction* 15 (Fall, 1995): 196-197. Offers insight into Lins's career and his struggle to succeed as a writer in spite of the political, economic, and cultural crisis in his native Brazil. Although living conditions were at times harsh, the greater challenge for Lins was to develop his craft.

Simas, Rosa. *Circularity and Visions of the New World in William Faulkner, Gabriel García Márquez, and Osman Lins*. Lewiston, Maine: Edwin Mellen Press, 1993. A perceptive series of essays, exploring the common themes and visions of three great writers. Includes an essay devoted to *Avalovara*.

West, Paul. "Osman Lins's *Avalovara*." *The Review of Contemporary Fiction* 15 (Fall, 1995): 208-210. West analyzes the style of Lins's novel, noting that the text is dense, uses the structure of a palindrome, and incorporates visual signifiers. West also addresses the symbolism of the characters, particularly Abel's mistress.

Jon S. Vincent

BABEL-17

Author: Samuel R. Delany (1942-   )
Type of plot: Science fiction
Time of plot: The distant future
Locale: Aboard various spaceships and on several planets of the Alliance
First published: 1966

> *Principal characters:*
> RYDRA WONG, a renowned poet, cryptographer, and linguist
> THE BUTCHER, a linguistically handicapped crew member and a figure
> of mystery
> JEBEL, the pirate captain of the spaceship *Jebel Tarik*
> DR. MARKUS (MOCKY) T'MWARBA, a psychologist, teacher, and patron
> of Rydra
> MOLLYA,
> CALLI, and
> RON, crew members of Rydra's spaceship *Rimbaud*
> DANIL D. APPLEBY, a customs official who helps Rydra assemble the
> *Rimbaud* crew

The Novel

Babel-17 is much more a spy story set centuries in the future than a space adventure of the Flash Gordon kind. The novel takes its name from the central mystery of the plot: A group of planets—the Alliance—is under attack by forces called the Invaders. The Alliance is hampered in the struggle by sabotage attempts on their defense installations, and the only clue is that each attack has been preceded by a radio transmission in an unknown language, a language that the Alliance has called "Babel-17." Alliance general Forester consults Rydra Wong, a famous poet and a superlative student of language, and asks for her help in breaking the code.

Rydra agrees to help, and to pursue the saboteurs she immediately begins enlisting a crew for her spaceship. Much of Delany's inventiveness is shown in the recruiting scenes of the story. The demands of galactic navigation make it impossible for normal humans to carry out some necessary tasks, so these duties are handled by "discorporates," beings who are essentially ghosts. Rydra finds one such, Mollya, to add to her crew.

During the voyage of her spaceship *Rimbaud*, Rydra suspects one of her crew of being an Invader agent. She survives one sabotage attempt and, after a landing at a defense installation, returns to the ship only to have it blast off under someone else's control. When she regains her senses after blacking out, she finds herself imprisoned in a web, on a strange ship. At this point, she makes her first use of the fragments of Babel-17 that she has managed to learn. She has intuited that the structure of words in Babel-17 models the structure of the things the words name. When she thinks of the word for "web" in Babel-17, she understands the structure of the web that holds her and is able to release herself and her crew from it.

The group is rescued by the arrival of the *Jebel Tarik*, a privateer whose captain is sympathetic to the Alliance. Aboard the ship, Rydra meets an intriguing character, called only the Butcher, who has no memory. The Butcher, whose affection for Rydra lends romance to the story, suffers from a strange affliction: He has no concept of self, the reader is told, because he has no first-person pronouns in his speech. Rydra succeeds in teaching him the words "I," "me," "mine," and their definitions.

After entering the Butcher's mind, Rydra proceeds from solution to solution: first, that the Butcher, originally an Alliance agent, was captured, brainwashed, and trained as a saboteur by the Invaders; then, that the messages in Babel-17 held both the instructions for the sabotage and the programming that directed the saboteurs. With this knowledge, Rydra is able to foresee both a quick end to the war and the development of yet another language, Babel-18: one that will contain both the information about reality that Babel-17 offers and the personal pronouns that allow a sense of identity and therefore responsibility.

The Characters

Rydra Wong, supremely competent as a linguist, as a poet, as a polyglot, and as a spaceship captain, seems almost overburdened with talent. If she has a flaw as a character, it is that she never seems seriously threatened: In any situation, she will think of something. She must also be one of the most loved and respected characters in the genre: General Forester is in love with her, as is the Butcher; her mentor, Dr. Markus T'Mwarba, has a deep affection for her; even her poetry is universally admired.

The Butcher is much more interesting as a character because of his vulnerability. At some time in his past, he has been inhumanly treated and left with his strange defect. Rydra succeeds in giving the Butcher a sense of self in one of the most touching (and affectionate) scenes in science fiction.

The minor characters serve well to supply the novel with the sense of strangeness, of the exotic, that science fiction must have. These touches of the unusual are illustrated in realms ranging from unconventional sexual groupings (a common theme in Delany's work) to the altering of the human form. In that future time, bodies may be surgically changed, both for practical purposes, such as the adding of extra limbs, and for the cosmetic whim of the patient—perhaps the addition of retractable claws and a mane.

Themes and Meanings

Throughout his career, Delany has been intensely interested in problems of communication and theories about it. He is obviously a man of both wide and deep reading, much of which shows up in his fiction. In *Babel-17*, one finds the speculations about language of several linguists, all of whom share a common theme. Alfred Korzybski, a Polish aristocrat and émigré, published *Science and Sanity: An Introduction to Non-Aristotelian Systems and General Semantics* in 1933. This turgid and cranky book attracted many admirers both in and out of science fiction by its thesis that if one clearly distinguished words from the things that they represent, one could free oneself from many misunderstandings and follies.

Korzybski's principal advocate in the United States was S. I. Hayakawa, who promoted the ideas of general semantics in a much more readable form. Some of Korzybski's ideas resembled those of Benjamin Lee Whorf, a noted American linguist of the 1930's, after whom the Whorfian hypothesis was named—the idea that the language one speaks controls the way one experiences reality. According to the Whorf hypothesis, to control someone's language is to control his behavior.

This notion had been explored in science fiction before *Babel-17*, most notably in Jack Vance's *The Languages of Pao* (1957), but Vance's work dealt with the action of language on the mass of people, while Delany's is concerned with the control of language over the individual. One of Delany's characters specifically argues that if one does not know the word, one cannot know the idea for which the word stands. This is precisely the control used to manipulate the Butcher (and the Invader saboteurs) in *Babel-17*: Since the Butcher has no word for "I," he does not understand the concept, and only superb teaching by Rydra remedies that lack.

Linguistics is the science in the science fiction of *Babel-17*, but one must not forget that the generic label also includes the word "fiction." Delany uses the Whorfian hypothesis in the novel because of his general interest in communication, much as he was later to use other theories from the realm of semantics and linguistic philosophy.

For that reason, one should not read *Babel-17* as a textbook on linguistics—it is not—but one who reads the novel with the general theme of communication in mind cannot help but be impressed with the degree to which we are all creatures of our speech, an idea copiously illustrated by comments that show Delany's wide range of interest in language.

Critical Context

Babel-17 was one of nine novels that Delany published in a burst of creativity at the beginning of his career between 1962 and 1968. It was chronologically the seventh, after *The Jewels of Aptor* (1962), *Captives of the Flame* (1963), *The Towers of Toron* (1964), *City of a Thousand Suns* (1965), *The Ballad of Beta-2* (1965), and *Empire Star* (1968), this last written after *Babel-17* but published earlier in the same year. *Babel-17*, though, was the work that clinched Delany's reputation in the science-fiction community: It was his first work to win a Nebula Award by ballot of the Science Fiction Writers of America.

His writing up to that time, although often showing as high a quality as his later works, and the same interest in communication, had not reached as wide a readership as it would later. *The Ballad of Beta-2*, for example, was published by Ace as half of a paperback "double-novel," one novel piggybacked with another, each having its own cover, each upside down with respect to the other. *Empire Star* and *Babel-17* had been written with that sort of publication in mind, a lowly form, subject to the ephemeral life of a genre paperback, on the shelf for a few months and then never seen again. After *Babel-17*, however, Delany began to gather critical attention and praise with almost every novel, and his later works especially became longer and much more philosophically ambitious.

Finally, no study of Delany's fiction should overlook his own criticism, especially his collection of essays on writing science fiction, *The Jewel-Hinged Jaw* (1977), in order to understand and appreciate one of the most thoughtful and articulate of today's authors.

Bibliography

Delany, Samuel R. *Silent Interviews: On Language, Race, Sex, Science Fiction, and Some Comics: A Collection of Written Interviews*. Hanover, N.H.: University Press of New England, 1994. An enlightening series of interviews that offer solid insight into Delany's background, writing career, and themes found in his novels. Includes bibliographic references for further reading and an index.

Malmagren, Carl. "The Languages of Science Fiction: Samuel Delany's *Babel-17*." *Extrapolation* 34 (Spring, 1993): 5-17. Malmagren explores the way language is used to create reality in Delany's novel. He notes that Delany resolves conflicts by shifting from one language paradigm into another, thus allowing for the creation of new ways of thinking.

Sallis, James, ed. *Ash of Stars: On the Writing of Samuel R. Delany*. Jackson: University Press of Mississippi, 1996. An interesting collection of critical essays by various scholars that address specific aspects of Delany's fiction. Includes an essay on *Babel-17* as well as a selected bibliography.

_____. "Samuel R. Delany: An Introduction." *The Review of Contemporary Fiction* 16 (Fall, 1996): 90-96. Offers brief background information on Delany's life and career. Discusses Delany's reputation as a major critical voice in science fiction, as well as the unifying factors in his work, including central characters as storytellers, revolutions with real consequences, and sexual concerns. A good overall view of Delany's work.

Samuelson, David N. "Necessary Constraints: Samuel R. Delany on Science Fiction." *The Review of Contemporary Fiction* 16 (Fall, 1996): 165-169. Argues that Delany's criticism reflects his position as a marginalized figure. His unique critical stance by necessity transcends current literary conventions and offers a mixture of detachment and presence, storytelling and analysis. Although this essay does not address *Babel-17*, it provides valuable insight into the point of view from which Delany writes.

Walter E. Meyers

BANANA BOTTOM

Author: Claude McKay (1889-1948)
Type of plot: Regional romance
Time of plot: The early 1900's
Locale: The country town of Jubilee and the village of Banana Bottom in Jamaica
First published: 1933

> *Principal characters:*
> TABITHA (BITA) PLANT, the protagonist, a Jamaican girl adopted by the
> Craigs and educated abroad, age twenty-two
> MALCOLM CRAIG, an ordained Calvinist minister of a mission church in
> Jubilee
> PRISCILLA CRAIG, an ordained Calvinist minister, the wife of Malcolm
> and the mother of a deformed child, Patou
> CRAZY BOW ADAIR, the descendant of a Scots settler and landowner,
> Bita's first lover
> HOPPING DICK, a wild, sensual, fine-strutting dandy who is interested in
> Bita
> HERALD NEWTON DAY, a black trainee minister intended by the Craigs
> as Bita's future husband
> SQUIRE GENSIR, a freethinking British aristocratic settler who studies
> black culture and promotes black self-esteem
> JUBBAN, a black laborer whom Bita later marries

The Novel

In a series of flashbacks the reader learns that Bita Plant was "seduced" by Crazy Bow Adair (actually, it was a willing sexual union, but the social niceties of Banana Bottom required that a twelve-year-old had to be an unwilling victim); that she was adopted by the Reverends Malcolm and Priscilla Craig, who wanted to demonstrate their ability to transform a wayward black girl into a cultured Christian; that she was educated in England and had visited Europe before returning to Jubilee seven years later.

The Craigs have planned that Bita marry a local black theological student, Herald Newton Day, who is egotistical, ashamed of his blackness, and a perfect example of the transformation that the Craigs would like to effect in all the villagers; Bita immediately discovers that she has little in common with him, although she agrees to an engagement. Soon after her return, she meets Hopping Dick at a local market and is attracted by his undisguised sensuality and even by his reputation for being "wild." She discovers his skill in dancing and romancing, and she learns that he is the antithesis of the Craigs' ideal, Herald. Squire Gensir accompanies Bita to a "teameeting" at which the locals enjoy themselves with dancing, singing, and merriment; she dances enthusiastically and recognizes her affinity with the village folk. When Mrs. Craig learns of

Bita's behavior from Sister Phibby Patroll (the local midwife and gossip), she is apprehensive about "saving" the atavistic Bita.

Bita escapes from Jubilee and visits her own village, Banana Bottom, for a weekend. Here she notices Jubban, her father's drayman, who is a stalwart, self-confident, and absolutely admirable black laborer of fine physique and natural dignity: Their mutual attraction is obvious. Bita visits the swimming hole where, as a child, she had many delightful moments: In the Edenic situation her sexuality is aroused (and described in truly poetic prose). In this situation she realizes that her roots lie in the rural countryside with the folk rather than with the Westernized and Christian converts.

On her return to Jubilee and at a harvest festival, Bita introduces Herald and Hopping Dick; Herald's pomposity repels her and his superficiality impresses Squire Gensir. (Discovered in an act of bestiality, Herald is dispatched to Panama.) Yet when Bita decides to marry Hopping Dick, he backs out and converts to Christianity, forsaking his unrestrained folkways.

Bita attends a revival meeting with Squire Gensir, but when it becomes a non-Christian religious orgy, she succumbs, dancing wildly and surrendering to masochistic flagellation. She is rescued by Jubban—who also subsequently rescues her from the sexual advances of Arthur Glengley, a wealthy near-white, and later marries her.

During a hurricane and flood, Malcolm Craig and Jordan Plant, Bita's father, are drowned returning from a church meeting. Mrs. Craig dies shortly after, "worried to death by disappointment": Her speechless adult son is dead, Herald has disgraced both the Craigs and their whole little world, and Bita has forsaken the values and lifestyle of the white community.

Squire Gensir returns to England, dies, and leaves his Jamaican property and house to Bita, who is rearing her son, Jordan, in an environment that represents an amalgam of the best of West Indian rural values modified by some of those of European society. Thus, the reader sees the significance of Bita's full name, Tabitha, which is also the name of a free-spirited gazelle, a coarse-woven silk (taffeta), and (in the form "tabby") a cat of variegated color.

The Characters

Bita Plant is without doubt McKay's most skillfully drawn character, and she embodies all those traits that McKay admired: freedom from the hypocrisy that all too frequently accompanies religiosity, unrestrained enthusiasm for the arts and entertainments of the folk, pride in black institutions and heritage, independence in thought and behavior, and discernment in the choice of competing ideologies. Whether the choice is between Christianity and God or Obeah and the Devil, between village society or rural isolation, between cantatas or digging *jammas* (songs), Bita is seldom persuaded by others' opinions: She exercises her independent judgment, which had been developed during her European schooling. In some ways she exhibits the characteristics of the Pankhursts, the British liberals with whom McKay worked in his early years while contributing to the *Workers' Dreadnought*: They were liberal, independent, indefatigable—though not given to the free expression of sexuality that characterizes Bita's life.

The Craigs, determined Christians and well-intentioned as they are, are nevertheless unforgiving, confining, and sexually repressed; their generosity in adopting and educating Bita is negated by their inability to grant her freedom to develop in her own way; their goal is conversion to middle-class Christian ways and the expunging of natural, instinctive, emotional behavior—especially as it is manifest in physical attraction and consummation. Theirs is a battle against sin that is equated with the folkways of their black congregation and neighbors, and their ideal—before his fall—is the convert Herald.

Herald Newton Day and Hopping Dick are carefully balanced as foils: One is the sanctimonious missionary trainee intent upon succeeding to the leadership of the local church, yet unable to repress his base sexuality; the other is the profligate ne'er-do-well and womanizer who is unable to accept the responsibility that is part of mature interpersonal relationships, including marriage, and escapes from the consequences of his enticements by retreating into a convenient conversion to Christianity. To both of them, Jubban is an ideal contrast: He is thoughtful, not overly intellectual, hardworking, and an emotional, responsive, and responsible lover.

Most of the characters in *Banana Bottom* have names that are meaningful if not necessarily symbolic or emblematic; in a novel that is clearly intended to portray the sexual emancipation of the central character, many have sexual overtones. The Plants, as the name implies, are rooted in the soil, and Bita is growing into full womanhood; Herald Newton Day is the herald of the new town and new day for which the Craigs work; Sister Phibby Patroll is a sister (in both the British sense of nurse and the black sense), a "fibber" (or storyteller, or liar), and a patrol member, constantly on the watch for others' misdeeds; Hopping Dick and Yoni Legge (a sexually unrepressed village girl) have names that indicate their predispositions.

Themes and Meanings

In this more than in his other fiction, Claude McKay concurrently develops a number of themes: Principal among them are the merging of intellect and instinct (or emotion and reason, the physical and the mental) in the younger members of an agricultural, colonial community to the end that a characteristic, natural, local personality will develop; also that in the maturation of the "natural" self, one has to choose between hypocrisy and instinct. Bita's discarding her clothes to have a swim in her favorite mountain pool is symbolic of her casting off the veneer of acquired tastes and values: She displays her body and admires those of the bathing boys nearby without embarrassment or shame; likewise, she is not ashamed to display her inner self, her natural instincts.

In addition, McKay shows the debilitating effects of traditional Christian morality: The Craigs' denial of sexuality has resulted in an only child who is unable to speak (and is therefore named Patou, dialect for "screech-owl"), and who dies of "knot-guts" just when he reaches adulthood; they try to hide any sign of their intimacy from their housekeeper; they denigrate affection and reproduction. By way of contrast, McKay imbues the rural folk with a sense of joy, sharing, and wholesomeness that is admirable. Ultimately, these themes coalesce into praise for the distinctive, unrepressed behavior of the Jamaican (and hence Third World) peasants and disdain for the paternalistic and dampening influence of Western, Eurocentric civilization. Primitive positiveness survives, though it benefits from training, cultivation, and hybridization, no matter where it is planted.

Critical Context

While McKay's first novels, *Home to Harlem* (1928) and *Banjo* (1929), depict the world of men (mainly Caribbean) in distant urban centers (New York and Marseilles), *Banana Bottom* presents a Jamaican woman returning to her native land after having been introduced to urban life in England and Europe and attempting to find a middle way between the spontaneous expression of natural emotion that McKay always presents as the norm in Caribbean rural communities and the carefully measured (and often hypocritical), socially acceptable behavior that he sees as typical of urban life. Bita's reading Blaise Pascal's *Pensées* while enjoying the property that she inherited from Squire Gensir suggests that she has, in fact, managed to bridge the two cultures. Her husband, Jubban, has provided her with a child who constantly affirms her blackness; her benefactor has provided her with a home and culture that is a continual reminder of the white culture that she has absorbed and valued. Her characteristic openness, honesty, and independence of judgment reveal her to be an admirable person. She is perhaps the best-drawn character in McKay's fiction: Though she never expounds a philosophy in the propagandistic fashion of Jake and Ray in the earlier novels, she nevertheless represents a way of life that is inescapably the one that McKay would have his readers accept. She is also dynamic: She returns from England a "made-over" islander, a brown-skinned Briton, as it were; she quickly evaluates the life-style of her own people and that represented by the Craigs and sees that neither is ideal, that each can contribute to the creation of something better than each alone. She is McKay's best symbol of his philosophy of cultural dualism—even pluralism. At times extravagant with her emotions and sympathies, she is also, from time to time, pensive, articulate, intellectual, and considerate. She is never mean-spirited, cruel, niggardly, or wanton.

Perhaps because he was writing about the leisurely life in the West Indies, McKay's prose in *Banana Bottom* is much less agitated and frenetic than that of *Home to Harlem* and *Banjo*: There are fewer short, simple declarative sentences and sentence fragments; there are many long, descriptive sentences, frequently marked by parenthetical elements and polysyllables. There are also a dozen or more songs and poems that help to impart a general air of tranquillity to the novel even when it carries a message of less than tranquil content. This adaptation of style to content is especially effective: Had McKay continued the Hemingwayesque, reportorial prose of the urban, man's-world novels, *Banana Bottom* would not have succeeded as it does.

It is not unreasonable to suggest—as some critics have done—that *Banana Bottom* is the first truly mature novel by a West Indian writing in English: The occasional dialect is no impediment to comprehension (and is mastered with the use of the glossary that the author provided) and provides a measure of authenticity; the characters comprise almost the entire range of those encountered in a colonial environment (black and white, religious and secular, master and servant, illiterate and savant); the exotic and erotic, both true-to-life, are never overdone.

The explanation of McKay's success in this novel is not easily located, but it may be that (as with his poetry) his best writing was usually evinced by his reminiscing about his homeland, about his green hills of Clarendon in Jamaica. Twenty years after having left Jamaica, he returned symbolically in the character of Bita Plant, a fine representation of his ideal woman, his ideal Caribbean.

Bibliography
Cooper, Wayne F. *Claude McKay: Rebel Sojourner in the Harlem Renaissance: A Biography.* Baton Rouge: Louisiana State University Press, 1987. Traces McKay's life from his birth in Jamaica through his years in America and England and his journey to Russia, as well as his eventual conversion to Catholicism. A chapter is devoted to the period in which he wrote *Banana Bottom.*
Draper, James P., ed. *Black Literature Criticism.* 3 vols. Detroit: Gale Research, 1992. Includes an extensive biographical profile of McKay and excerpts from criticism on his works.
Giles, James R. *Claude McKay.* Boston: Twayne, 1976. Giles provides a critical and interpretive study of McKay with a close reading of his major works, a solid bibliography, and complete notes and references.
Tillery, Tyrone. *Claude McKay: A Black Poet's Struggle for Identity.* Amherst: University of Massachusetts Press, 1992. Tillery's biography is a well-documented and fascinating study of McKay's life. Focuses on McKay's turbulent life and personality and examines his various associations with black radicalism, socialism, and communism and his ultimate rejection of them for the refuge of the Catholic church.

Marian B. McLeod

BANG THE DRUM SLOWLY

Author: Mark Harris (Mark Harris Finkelstein; 1922-   )
Type of plot: Tragicomedy
Time of plot: 1955
Locale: Perkinsville, New York; Rochester, Minnesota; Bainbridge, Georgia; and
   New York City
First published: 1956

> *Principal characters:*
>> HENRY W. WIGGEN, the unlettered narrator, a pitcher for the New York
>>   Mammoths
>> BRUCE PEARSON, the third-string catcher for the Mammoths and
>>   Henry's roommate
>> HOLLY WEBSTER WIGGEN, Henry's wife
>> KATIE, an expensive prostitute with whom Bruce is in love
>> DUTCH SCHNELL, the team manager, whose principal aim is to win
>>   baseball games
>> RED TRAPHAGEN, the first-string catcher and a college professor
>> GOOSE, an aging catcher, who rags Bruce
>> LESTER T. MOORS, JR., the wealthy owner of the Mammoths
>> PATRICIA MOORS, his daughter
>> PINEY WOODS, a catcher for the Mammoths and a motorcycle enthusiast

The Novel

   Bang the Drum Slowly is not a sequel to *The Southpaw* (1953), even though many
of the characters in Mark Harris's earlier novel reappear in this second novel narrated
by Henry W. Wiggen (the full title is *Bang the Drum Slowly by Henry W. Wiggen:
Certain of His Enthusiasms Restrained by Mark Harris*). When references are made
to *The Southpaw*, those passages are reprinted in *Bang the Drum Slowly*. Henry
Wiggen, who tells the story, is a star pitcher for the New York Mammoths. Bruce
Pearson, his roommate and the third-string catcher for the Mammoths, is dying of
Hodgkin's disease. The novel begins as Bruce calls Henry from the Mayo Clinic in
Rochester, Minnesota, to tell him that he must come to see him, and it ends with a win-
ning season for the Mammoths and Bruce's death.

   After Bruce checks out of the hospital, Henry and Bruce drive to Bruce's hometown of Bainbridge, Georgia. The principal activities in Bainbridge are waiting for the
mail and swatting flies on the front porch. The high point of the visit for Bruce is
learning to play Tegwar, a game in which the rules change all the time and the object is
to keep a straight face.

   Bruce wants to continue to play ball as long as he can. Realizing that Lester T.
Moors, Jr., the owner, and Dutch Schnell, the manager, would release Bruce if they
knew of his illness, Henry and Bruce decide to keep it a secret. When Henry negoti-

ates his contract for the year, he includes a clause stating that he and Bruce must be treated as a package: "[I]f he is traded I must be traded the same place. Wherever he goes I must go." Humor is introduced in this very poignant scene, when Henry is asked if Bruce Pearson owes him money. When he says no, Dutch considers, but then discards the idea that the two men are "fairies."

Long after most of the team knows about Bruce's illness, the management finds out but has to keep Pearson with the team because of the clause in Henry Wiggen's contract. The knowledge of Bruce's illness draws the team together. As Henry puts it, "It was a club, like it should of been all year but never was but all of a sudden become." Bruce stays with the team and dresses for every game. He leaves after the Mammoths are assured of winning the World Series. Henry is one of the pallbearers at Bruce's funeral, but no one else from the Mammoths attends.

The Characters

Mark Harris's characterization of Bruce Pearson is brilliantly successful. Bruce is not a charming, intelligent, valuable player whose fellow players love him. Bruce is a third-string catcher who laughs at his teammates' jokes in order to belong. When he sends postcards to his family, he manages to write only three words on the card: Pearson, Mill, Georgia; the rest is left blank. Bruce is a natural athlete, but not very bright. He sits at the window of the room that he shares with Henry, spitting and watching to see if the spit curves in or out.

The team players amuse themselves by taunting and ridiculing Bruce. Henry tries to protect Bruce from their ragging without revealing his roommate's approaching death. After Henry tries to stop the ridicule of Bruce, Perry, who was the first black man on the Mammoths, alludes to Bruce's Southern background and sneers, "Pearson would not give me the time of day if I was dying." Henry replies: "He does not know it himself half the time."

Harris juxtaposes the cocky, talented, and successful Henry Wiggen, who writes books and sells insurance, with the simpleminded Bruce Pearson. Henry is nicknamed "Author" by his teammates, and Bruce thinks that they are saying "Arthur," which becomes his name for Henry. Bruce gets drunk once a year every spring before training begins because he is a third-string catcher and has little to do other than assist pitchers in warming up.

After Henry becomes Bruce's roommate, the two men become friends, although they have little in common other than their friendship. Henry comments, "We hit it off pretty good once I got used to the stink of shaving lotion and this filthy chewing tobacco called Days O Work and spitting incurves and outcurves out the window and urinating in the sink and calling me 'Arthur.'" When Henry and Holly are given a place in which to live, Bruce spends all of his time with them, but Henry cannot tell him to stay away because Bruce is always so happy to see them.

Bruce falls in love with Katie, a successful prostitute who is fond of dining at expensive restaurants. Katie agrees to marry him, after she learns that he is dying, if he makes her the beneficiary of his insurance. Henry, who sold Bruce his insurance policy, stalls about changing the beneficiary until Katie finally attempts unsuccessfully to bribe him. Katie's affection for money is handled lightly; she is not censored for her greed.

Even minor characters in *Bang the Drum Slowly* are carefully drawn. Goose, the aging catcher who has not saved for his old age and who abuses his wife, comes alive when Henry confides to him the truth about Bruce. Goose is an excellent catcher, but he is not in the same class as Red Traphagen. His position on the team affects his sense of self and his marriage: "But there was Traphagen and all, and finally the only person that loved me I bashed her in the eye now and then to keep up my spirit." Harris views ragging teammates and bashing loved ones as needless cruelty. On the other hand, he very sensitively describes why Goose, the aging second-string catcher with debts, or Perry, the black player who has had to withstand verbal abuse from fans, want to rag Bruce in order to make themselves feel better. It is human nature to take out anger and frustration on those weaker than oneself.

Piney Woods, a brash young catcher who adores his motorcycle, remarks when he is being sent back to the minor leagues, "Well, maybe somebody will drop dead soon and open up a slot for me." Bruce will die by the end of the novel, necessitating Piney's return to the Mammoths. Harris consistently uses the cliches and slang with which the characters habitually express themselves to generate ironic wit. The dialogue is amusing, even comic, but its implications are serious.

Themes and Meanings

The title of *Bang the Drum Slowly* is adapted from a line in "The Streets of Laredo," a song about a cowboy who dies young. That the novel is not about baseball is suggested by the epigram taken from Wright Morris's *The Huge Season* (1954) that "a book can have Chicago in it, and not be about Chicago. It can have a tennis player in it without being about a tennis player." *Bang the Drum Slowly* is not about baseball, nor is it really about the friendship which develops between Henry Wiggen and Bruce Pearson. Red Traphagen, the catcher and college professor, reads part of *Bang the Drum Slowly* in manuscript and comments that few people will read the book and that "even the people that read it will think it is about baseball or some such stupidity as that, for baseball is stupid, Author, and I hope you put it in your book, a game rigged by rich idiots to keep poor idiots from wising up to how poor they are." Red tells Henry to "stick to death and Pearson." Ironically, Mark Harris has done precisely that. Whatever Henry Wiggen sees or says, the knowledge of Bruce Pearson's death is ingrained in his consciousness. Every chance reference to death, from the lyrics of a cowboy song to the jeer of a cab driver, resounds in Henry's mind and reminds the reader of human mortality.

When Bruce becomes ill and Henry sends Goose for the doctor, Bruce accuses Henry of having told Goose that he is dying. He realizes that people are likely to be nice to a dying person. Reassuringly, Henry says, "Everybody knows everybody is dying. . . . That is why people are nice. You all die soon enough, so why not be nice to each other." What Henry has said is not true, but the reader wishes that it were.

Bang the Drum Slowly was made into a touching film which some critics have described as sentimental; the novel is not sentimental. Harris concludes the story of Bruce Pearson's death by having Henry forget to send him the scorecard from the World Series: "Wouldn't it been simple instead of writing a page on my book to shoved it in the mail? How long would it of took? Could I not afford the stamps?"

Henry acts as Bruce's pallbearer; flowers are sent, but "no *person*" comes from the Mammoths. The novel concludes with his epitaph for Bruce and the moral he draws from it: "He was not a bad fellow, no worse than most and probably better than some, and not a bad ballplayer neither when they give him a chance, when they laid off him long enough. From here on in I rag nobody." Henry intends to remember that everyone is dying.

Critical Context

Bang the Drum Slowly is a deceptively simple book, which, like *The Southpaw*, has suffered from being assessed as a "baseball book." Even in the clichés and slang of the ballplayers, the word "death" is repeated with telling irony. The reader shares Henry Wiggen's sensitivity to the word and gradually comes to realize that Bruce's death foreshadows that of everyone. The understatement of the dialogue accentuates the impact of *Bang the Drum Slowly*. The characters are inarticulate, most of all Bruce, but their very lack of sophistication is skillfully used by Harris to engage the reader's emotions.

Bang the Drum Slowly merits comparison with some of Ernest Hemingway's best short stories. As a work of art, it is better written than Hemingway's story of Colonel Cantwell's death in *Across the River and into the Trees* (1950).

At the end of the novel, when Henry forgets to send Bruce a copy of the winning scorecard, Harris resists the temptation to sentimentalize the relationship of Henry and Bruce. Henry Wiggen quite nobly works out his contract so that Bruce will remain with the Mammoths throughout the season, but he forgets to send the scorecard. Ironically, too, Harris makes a point of the fact that Henry Wiggen has been writing the book about Bruce's death while Bruce is dying. At one point, Henry even wonders if the book will have an audience if Bruce lives. Though Harris resists any hint of sentimentality, he resists the pressure on contemporary artists to depict the world as valueless and empty. The owners and manager would sever Bruce's relationship with the Mammoths if they knew of his illness, but the men on the team are united and inspired by the fact of his approaching death.

Few novels with such a serious theme manage to be so amusing. *The Southpaw* had great energy and charm; *Bang the Drum Slowly* ought to be regarded as a minor classic. Perhaps because it has baseball as its setting, this important novel has not received the careful scrutiny that it deserves.

Bibliography

Fimrite, Ron. "Fiction in a Diamond Setting: Mark Harris's Novels Sparkle with Hard-Edged Realism." *Sports Illustrated* 73 (October 15, 1990): 117-122. A biographical and critical profile of Mark Harris. The models for some of the characters in *Bang the Drum Slowly* are discussed. Fimrite details the evolution of serious literature on baseball and asserts that until the publication of Harris's *The Southpaw*, baseball literature consisted of mostly "fairy tale" boy's books written by fabulists. Fimrite also notes the influence of Ring Lardner and Mark Twain on Harris's baseball books.

Harris, Mark. *Best Father Ever Invented: The Autobiography of Mark Harris*. New York: Dial Press, 1976. In his autobiography, written during the 1960's and published in 1976, Harris portrays himself as depressed over his work, categorizing his earlier baseball novel, *The Southpaw*, as "facile realism in a facile style." A fascinating early self-portrait of a writer who has since come to terms with himself and his writing.

_____. *Diamond: Baseball Writings of Mark Harris*. New York: Donald I. Fine, 1995. A collection of baseball writings by Harris spanning 1946 through 1993. Provides an illuminating view into Harris's devotion to the game and the evolution of his thinking on numerous topics. Also included is Harris's screenplay of the movie version of *Bang the Drum Slowly*.

Lavers, Norman. *Mark Harris*. Boston: Twayne, 1978. Lavers provides a critical and interpretive study of Harris, with a close reading of his major works, a solid bibliography, and complete notes and references.

Jean R. Brink

BANJO
A Story Without a Plot

Author: Claude McKay (1889-1948)
Type of plot: Social criticism
Time of plot: The early 1920's
Locale: Marseilles
First published: 1929

> *Principal characters:*
> LINCOLN AGRIPPA DAILY (BANJO), a vagabond from the South
> RAY, a West Indian would-be writer and a beachboy
> LATNAH, a woman of mixed blood who befriends Banjo
> BUGSY, small, wiry, aggressive boy who is antiwhite
> TALOUFA, a young Nigerian who has been in Wales and the United
> States and supports the Back-to-Africa cause
> GOOSEY, a flute-playing mulatto and an exponent of the uplift
> philosophy of the Harlem Renaissance intellectuals
> BUCHANAN MALT AVIS (MALTY), a West Indian drummer and
> beachboy
> GINGER, a long-term beachboy, former seaman, and ex-convict
> DENGEL, a Senegalese

The Novel

  Banjo is subtitled "A Story Without a Plot," but it is not a novel in the manner of Virginia Woolf—although it is conversational and at times even dialectical. Rather, it is an episodic narrative involving a small group of relatively permanent residents of the Vieux Port section of Marseilles and a larger cast of incidental characters who are encountered briefly in the varied but fundamentally routine activities of unemployed black seamen trying to maintain a sense of camaraderie and well-being. It is, therefore, basically a picaresque fiction that offers a measure of social criticism (sometimes at considerable length, at other times with considerable force); this social message, however, is extraneous to the novel and is a structural weakness.

  Except for occasional excursions to Aix-en-Provence and other nearby locations in the Midi for seasonal employment or diversion, the characters spend their time frequenting the bars, nightclubs, and restaurants of the Ditch, Boody Lane, and Bum Square—names that they have given to the Quartier Réservé, rue de la Bouterie, and Place Victor Gelu in Marseilles.

  Some chapters introduce Arabs, Orientals, and Europeans, who are shown less favorably than the motley assortment of blacks who constitute McKay's principal concern; other chapters present hospitals, rooming-houses, bordellos, gambling rooms, and pornographic movie houses. Both people and places sample the exotic as well as the erotic, and Marseilles becomes an overseas replica of the New York City of *Home to Harlem* (1928).

   The book is divided into three sections. The first introduces Lincoln Agrippa Daily (Banjo), strolling along the breakwater and encountering Malty, Ginger, Dengel, and Bugsy, who have arrived in the boxcars of a train. All are seeking "the joy stuff of life" and believe that they can find it by playing as a black band in the cafés and "love spots." In the second part, Ray (who has left Harlem to become a seaman) appears and joins Banjo's little group, becoming a somewhat sobering influence through his incessant philosophizing, though participating in the life of the Monkey Bar, the Anglo-American Bar, and similar establishments. Yet times are changing: White crews are replacing black ones on ships, and work is scarce; foreigners are being subjected to irritations. The beachboys are broke and scatter: Banjo accompanies a group of Europeans to Nice and Monte Carlo; Ray and Malty (in company with Latnah) go to the vineyards; Goosey and Bugsy are sent by a municipal agency to an up-country factory; only Ginger and Dengel remain, taking their chances on the docks of Marseilles: "Now that Banjo was gone and the group dispersed, the spell was broken."

   The third section of the novel opens with Ray, Malty, and Latnah (enjoying a beer on the waterfront after their return from bringing in the vintage) spotting Banjo working as a coal handler. He has been tricked out of his banjo and has undergone a complete metamorphosis: "Even the wine he drank afforded him little pleasure," and Ray finds him "exasperatingly melancholy." To Ray, the life of the Ditch has become "gray," and he decides to move on. Banjo dreams of reuniting his musicians (instrumentless and without rehearsals) in a band. Bugsy dies; Banjo is hospitalized and then cared for by Latnah; the boys are beaten by the police, sign on as crew for a voyage to the West Indies, and foresee a new lifestyle. Banjo, however, influenced by Ray's outlook and arguments, takes his advance of a month's pay and skips ship before sailing, in order to continue the vagabond existence. The novel concludes with Banjo addressing Ray: "Come on, pardner. Wese got enough between us to beat it a long ways from here." Though the goal of a band has disappeared, Banjo clearly has a new goal: conjunction (the word he uses in referring to women, particularly Latnah) of the physical and the intellectual.

The Characters

   As in any eponymous work, the author's principal focus is on Banjo, whose name receives special notice from McKay: "The banjo dominates the other instruments. . . . And Banjo's face shows that he feels that his instrument is first . . . the banjo is preeminently the musical instrument of the American Negro." Yet Goosey, the "yellow" exponent of the philosophy of uplift, a thoughtful and at times philosophic character who can be thought of as a representative of the W. E. B. DuBois-Alain Locke school of thought, counters that the banjo is a symbol of Dixie, of bondage, of slavery; and he advocates blacks' playing the violin, the piano. He and Taloufa refuse to play "any of that black-face coon stuff," he says, to which Banjo replies that he likes the instrument and sees "saxophone-jazzing" as "the money stuff today." His liking for the banjo is clearly the effect of his being a "child of the Cotton Belt." His enthusiasm for the ukulele and mandolin likewise reveals an attachment to the old days and ways of the

South, but wherever he goes in Marseilles he finds that though people are amused by the banjo, they are more often entertained by the piano. The beachboys are therefore clearly identified with a musical tradition and technology that have been superseded, and when Banjo and Ray set off together at the end of the story, they do so as itinerant workers rather than as poets or troubadours, regardless of their spiritual state of mind and predilections. Ray is an unsuccessful writer; Banjo is an unsuccessful musician; the arts are merely accompaniments to their lives.

The beachboys of the Ditch are a polyglot group: They represent the broad spectrum of blacks: West Indian, African, and American. Yet they have a cohesion that is admirable, and overall Banjo represents the hegemony of blackness: He deprecates both racial inferiority and "passing."

Yet none of the black characters is an exclusivist: They all share a common sympathy toward and appreciation of Latnah, who is olive-toned, of mixed race, and "not young and far from old, with an amorous charm." She suggests an Earth Mother who comprises every admirable trait: sensuality, practicality, compassion, energy, and adaptability among them. She is, however, unique in the novel: The other women are prostitutes, minor criminals, European ruins, and jaded drifters. It is instructive when Ray laments that it would have been good if he and Banjo had been able to take Latnah with them as they left Marseilles. "Don't get soft ovah any one wimmens, pardner" is Banjo's response. One wonders just how they will fare without her love and care.

The remainder of the central group of characters are not well limned, yet they do develop sufficient individuality to become discernible. Bugsy is consistently anti-white; his complexion is described as dull black, but this might as well have been used to describe his mental type; he is fittingly small, wiry, and aggressive. Taloufa, the Nigerian who was born in the bush, is young, well-traveled (he has been in Wales, the United States, and Europe), and an advocate of Marcus Garvey's Back-to-Africa movement. When he landed in England, the authorities wanted to deport him to West Africa, but "Taloufa did not want to go there. Christian missionaries had educated him out of his native life." When he returned to Marseilles (with his guitar), he was "broke, but unbroken." In many ways he is an interesting and absorbing—though minor—character, since he represents the great mass of present-day Africans who are cut off from traditional village life and not integrated into contemporary urban and industrial society. Malty, the West Indian drummer and guitarist, is ebullient and indefatigable: He is reminiscent of the type of person whom McKay admired and remembered from his Jamaican days. Each of these (and the score of minor characters such as the Arab taxi-driver-cum-tout and Chère Blanche, the prostitute) is memorably drawn in colorful vignettes.

Themes and Meanings

By placing the story in Marseilles, McKay is able to draw together a variety of blacks, just as he had done in *Home to Harlem*. Yet because all of the blacks in Marseilles are expatriates, mere temporary residents, and beachboys, there is a smaller and less interesting range with which to work. Nevertheless, the novel reiterates

McKay's constant themes: that the folk rather than the black intelligentsia represent the best in the race; that blacks should have a high regard for their heritage and hence a racial self-esteem; that the ideal life is one of vagabondage, of natural gusto and emotional response, allowing one to "laugh and love and jazz and fight." The breakup of the beachboys at the end of parts 2 and 3 suggests that cohesiveness is less powerful among McKay's favorite people than individualism—the very characteristic of the materialistic, commercial class that Ray inveighs against in his numerous diatribes and asides. Ironically, it is this assertion of individuality (which is, however, always punctuated by examples of group concern for others in distress) that plays into the arms of those classes and attitudes that Ray sees as inimical to racial betterment.

Ray is the mouthpiece for an unrelenting indictment of white civilization. In his eyes, its chief shortcomings are crass commercialism (one shipping line is called the Dollar Line); an unwarranted sense of racial superiority; hypocrisy (white Europeans assert that they make the best pornographic films, yet they condemn the uninhibited—even justifiable—sexuality of the blacks); nauseous patriotism, rather than internationalism; standardization; and Calvinist attitudes toward sex, alcohol, music, and entertainment.

Yet the behavior of Banjo and the other denizens of the Ditch is far from admirable—if one excepts Ray, who is moderate, literate, and emotional. When he arrives in port, Banjo has 12,525 francs—a considerable sum—but he quickly spends it on a girl who leaves him as soon as he is broke. He is wholly improvident and far from admirable: "He was a type that was never sober, even when he was not drinking." Accordingly, it is difficult to maintain any sympathy for him and to feel that he is anything more than a wastrel, a womanizer, a loafer, and an impractical dreamer. His word is seldom binding. When he leaves with Ray, it is with the advance in wages that he has received from the shipping line: He breaks a contract to pursue a drifter's dream in the company of a husband and father who has apparently turned his back on his social responsibilities.

Yet if McKay means *Banjo* to be a paean to the free life, the life of the spirit and the emotions untrammeled by responsibilites, he seems to be suggesting that his motley sybarites are enviable models. They most certainly are not: They are irresponsible and without any admirable ambition. Their parallels are the Europeans who attend the "blue" cinema, who are rootless, affected, and suffering from ennui. (Their Satanism and sexual aberrations have cut them off from their cultural bearings.) It is hard to understand how any reader could come away from the novel believing that the beachboys—and Banjo in particular—are to be admired for their instinctive, spontaneous, sensual behavior. Moreover, at the end most of them express their dissatisfaction with pointless drifting, with unemployment, with poverty, and with temporary liaisons dependent on money alone. It is little wonder, then, that *Banjo* has been subjected to criticism on the basis of its not having a clearly defined and defensible theme. Similarly, one can see a weakness in Banjo's saying that his instrument is his "buddy," that it is more than a "gal, moh than a pal; it's mahself." The Jazz Age had not ended, but the banjo was a symbol of a past era, and its owner, who places a thing above persons, seems to be disoriented. Banjo has become an anachronism.

Critical Context

In essence, *Banjo* is a continuation of *Home to Harlem*: The location has been shifted from the United States to France, but the *dramatis personae* are remarkably similar, and their exploits differ only insofar as Harlem and Marseilles differ. Naturally, the problem then became what to do with a third novel. The answer was to shift from the urban world of men to the rural world of men and women, families and children, teachers and preachers in Jamaica, and remarkably, *Banana Bottom* (1933), with its balance of sense and sensuality, showed that McKay could combine emotional and social realism, propaganda and polemics, characterization and plot. It seems that he recognized the limitations of *Banjo* and that it did not enhance his growing reputation as poet and fiction writer.

One of the most frequently cited weaknesses in *Banjo* is the tendency for Ray's comments to overwhelm the story and change the balance from fiction to propagandist tract, and when Goosey adds his philosophical—and at times sophomoric—musings, the novel is endangered. Yet the inclusion of discussion on major matters of the day (such as race, capitalism, socialism, and xenophobia) should not be condemned per se: The unemployed and discriminated against are often voluble critics of social policy and not infrequently have some well-informed, first-class exponents of their causes as spokesmen.

While advocating the cause of the black masses, McKay leaves the reader confused at times about his social policy. Latnah, the quintessential black mother-figure, is deserted by Banjo for Chère Blanche, the "pink sow"; and after loving and nursing, feeding and housing him, she is unceremoniously left in the Ditch while he and Ray head off on their continuing odyssey. In his fiction, as in his personal life, McKay was unable (until *Banana Bottom*) to develop a lasting black married relationship. Ironically, it is Latnah who criticizes Banjo for his lack of race pride—the one thing that he thought that he exemplified.

In his unpublished "Romance in Marseilles" and "Harlem Glory" (both written some time after 1935, when he was already in declining health, fortune, and reputation as a Harlem Renaissance writer), McKay tried to recapture the spirit of the two cities and their black communities, but he was too far from his sources in time and geography, and the novellas lack the qualities of the earlier works. One short story, "Dinner at Douarnenez," which was first published in 1985, conveys McKay's deep attachment to France and his belief that blacks have generally been more welcome there than in other countries. Most of the social and political topics that Ray addresses are the subjects of articles in *The Liberator* and *Amsterdam News*, for which McKay worked as a journalist; many of them were treated also in *The Negroes in America* (1979), which McKay wrote when he visited the Soviet Union in 1922-1923 but which remained unpublished until its discovery decades later among some materials in the New York Public Library.

Bibliography

Cooper, Wayne F. *Claude McKay: Rebel Sojourner in the Harlem Renaissance: A Biography.* Baton Rouge: Louisiana State University Press, 1987. Traces McKay's life from his birth in Jamaica through his years in America and England and his journey to Russia as well as his eventual conversion to Catholicism. A chapter is devoted to the period in which he wrote *Banjo.*

Draper, James P., ed. *Black Literature Criticism.* 3 vols. Detroit: Gale Research, 1992. Includes an extensive biographical profile of McKay and excerpts from criticism on his works.

Giles, James R. *Claude McKay.* Boston: Twayne, 1976. Giles provides a critical and interpretive study of McKay, with a close reading of his major works, a solid bibliography, and complete notes and references.

Tillery, Tyrone. *Claude McKay: A Black Poet's Struggle for Identity.* Amherst: University of Massachusetts Press, 1992. Tillery's biography is a well-documented and fascinating study of McKay's life. Focuses on McKay's turbulent life and personality and examines his various associations with black radicalism, socialism, and communism and his ultimate rejection of them for the refuge of the Catholic church.

A. L. McLeod

THE BARRACKS THIEF

Author: Tobias Wolff (1945-   )
Type of plot: Moral
Time of plot: The mid-1960's to the mid-1970's
Locale: Seattle, Washington, and Fort Bragg, North Carolina
First published: 1984

> *Principal characters:*
> PHILIP BISHOP, a young paratrooper from Seattle
> KEITH BISHOP, his younger brother
> GUY BISHOP, their father
> LEWIS, a paratrooper from Kentucky
> HUBBARD, another paratrooper

The Novel

Tobias Wolff's novella-length *The Barracks Thief* reads more like a long short story than a novel. Consisting of seven brief chapters, it seems at first to be a simple and unassuming story with little or no thematic significance; however, as is often the case with novellas, the more one thinks about the work, the more psychologically and morally complex becomes this exploration of the motivations of three inarticulate young men caught up in the demands of masculinity.

Although the story begins with the teenage brothers Keith and Philip Bishop's reactions to their father's desertion of the family for another woman—Keith runs off to be a hippie, while Philip joins the Army—the central focus is on Philip's relationship with Lewis and Hubbard, two other young and inexperienced paratroopers who are waiting at Fort Bragg, North Carolina, to be shipped to Vietnam. Because the book is in some ways Lewis's story as well as Philip's, Wolff shifts the point of view a number of times. The first chapter describes the father's desertion, Keith's running away from home, and Philip's joining the Army from a third-person-omniscient point of view. In the next three chapters, however, the point of view abruptly shifts to Philip himself, who tells of his initial experiences in the Army.

This second section presents a central episode in the story. Philip, Lewis, and Hubbard—outsiders to the other, older men, most of whom have already served together in Vietnam—are assigned to guard an ammunition dump on the Fourth of July. Lewis plays the stereotyped role of the Kentucky redneck, and he brags about his prowess with women; Hubbard complains about Army life and longs to be back home with his friends; Philip remains, as he does throughout the book, uncommitted and noncommittal. It is a long, boring day until a deputy sheriff shows up and asks the soldiers to leave the ammo dump because of a brush fire heading their way. Lewis, acting out of either braggadocio or a simplistic sense of duty, refuses to go and threatens to shoot the deputy if he tries to force them to desert their post. When the wind changes and the danger is eliminated, the three soldiers, bound together in a masculine sense of camaraderie, feel that they have proven themselves to be real men.

In chapter 5, the focus of the novel shifts to Lewis; however, because he is less articulate than Philip, his story is told by the omniscient narrator in the present tense. Lewis's experiences focus on abortive sexual encounters. While hitchhiking into town, he is picked up by a male schoolteacher who puts calamine lotion on his injured hand. The homosexual suggestions of the scene are made quite clear by the omniscient narrator, but Lewis seems to have only an inchoate awareness of the significance of the event. When he gets to town, he awkwardly picks up a prostitute, but when he does not have enough money to pay for her services, she forces him to leave at the point of a knife.

The next day, Lewis steals wallets from other men in the barracks and returns to the prostitute. Following a violent sexual encounter, Lewis tells the girl that he loves her; thinking that he is mocking her, she drives him out with the knife again. After stealing another wallet and breaking the owner's nose when he is almost caught, Lewis finds a letter in the wallet that identifies the owner as Hubbard. When Lewis is discovered to be the "barracks thief," the point of view of the novel shifts back to Philip, who tells of a "blanket party" in which the men beat up Lewis. Hubbard will have nothing to do with the beating; Philip watches but does nothing to prevent it.

The final four-page chapter of the novel, told from the point of view of Philip after the war, ties up the loose ends: Lewis gets a dishonorable discharge, Hubbard deserts and goes to Canada, and Philip's brother Keith returns home and gets a job as a security guard. Philip himself goes to Vietnam and then returns home to become what he calls a "conscientious, careful, responsible" man, "addicted to comfort, with an eye for the safe course." He sometimes wishes that the fire had set off the ammunition dump and that he, Hubbard, and Lewis had been blown up in a blast that made the earth shake. He thinks, "It would have been something."

The Characters

The Barracks Thief is radically split in its character focus. On one hand, it is Philip's novel, for it both begins and ends with his situation, and much of it is told from his point of view. On the other hand, Lewis is the barracks thief of the title, and it is his inner conflict about his image as a man that constitutes the central conflict of the novel. Because both Philip and Lewis seem more acted upon than acting, however, the reader does not learn much about either of them. Because the novel has something to do with Philip's experience of male bonding and betrayal, his personality frames the novel. The story begins with Philip's father breaking up the family and his brother running away, and it ends with Philip becoming a "good man"—a role he both accepts and chafes against.

Lewis is a more "interesting" character, although he seems almost incapable of complex thought. His motivations are central to the novel: He is the one who refuses to leave his post at the ammunition dump (an episode that establishes the theme of male bonding in the novel), and he is the barracks thief of the title (which destroys that bonding). On the one hand, Lewis is a simple stereotype, a dumb redneck who boasts

and tries to prove himself as a man but who only ends up looking foolish and ineffectual. On the other hand, there is something centrally compelling about his problematical experiences with his comrades at the ammunition dump, with the teacher who rubs
lotion on his swollen hand, and with the prostitute whom he says he loves. He cannot
easily be dismissed as either simply stupid or simply mentally disturbed, for he seems
to embody some of the problems surrounding the novel's central theme—men trying to
be men in a world governed by stereotyped masculine roles.

Themes and Meanings

The Barracks Thief is an elusive novel, a rare work that seems so simple as to be in-
consequential, yet so suggestive as to be profound. First of all, it is a man's story; the
only woman in the novel is the prostitute—the classic object of desire, good for nothing else but the sexual pleasure of the male, but at the same time a menacing figure, refusing to be loved and threatening the male with the emasculating knife. Wolff's novel
is about the kinds of things that concern men when they are together as men. Because
Philip, Lewis, and Hubbard are treated as if they were sissies or children by the more
experienced soldiers, they need something to prove themselves to be men—which in
this context means confronting danger, facing down opponents, being sexually powerful. Thus, the ironic heart of the novel is that when the three men actually face danger at the ammunition dump, it is no danger at all. As Philip says, "Nothing happens."
Moreover, the very sense of camaraderie created by the confrontation is violated by
Lewis's need to satisfy the prostitute in the only way he can—with money that he
steals from his barracks buddies.

Male bonding, which is at the very center of this novel, is a subject so easily open to
ridicule that it is a tribute to Wolff's skill as a writer that he can successfully explore
the many complexities of being a male in a male world with such subtlety. As is typical of examples of the short-story or novella forms, every event in the story is motivated by its central theme. The opening episodes focus on the loss of Philip's father as
a role model and his rejection of his own role as his brother's keeper. Particularly symbolic is a scene in which the father tries to give Philip a folding bicycle as a graduation
present, telling him that with it he will never be without transportation. When the father pitches over the handlebars and lies tangled up with the bike, he calls to his son, "I
can't move. Give me a hand." Philip, however, turns away, and he joins the Army the
next morning.

The theme of male bonding crystalizes with the ammunition dump scene; like everything else in this novel, however, the event is problematical and inconclusive.
Lewis feels that he must explicitly follow his orders to shoot anyone who dares to put
a hand on the fence surrounding the dump, but it is a foolish, quixotic act that defies
reason and common sense. The fact that the three men feel mysteriously bonded because they have faced danger together thus is made to appear childish and trivial.

The scene with Lewis and the male schoolteacher suggests the inherent homosexual nature of any male bonding. As the teacher rubs cooling lotion on Lewis's painful
hands, both Lewis and the teacher close their eyes and lose themselves in the experi-

ence, forgetting their sense of "being absolutely alone"; the image of both their hands joined with fingers interlaced is a central one of inchoate male longing for union. Thus, when Lewis clumsily tries to pick up the prostitute, and she angrily asks him what he wants, the answer is not simply that he wants sex. In addition to wanting to prove himself as a man, Lewis desires something from the woman similar to what he felt with the teacher. This is not to say that Lewis is a latent homosexual, but rather that he wants what all men want—to be at one with someone else. Wolff seems to suggest here that although that sometimes may be easier with another man than with a woman, it is never easy with anyone.

Lewis's theft of a wallet that turns out to be Hubbard's further emphasizes the difficulty of male bonding in any genuine way, especially in light of the demands of women. When the rest of the men join together to beat Lewis up, a false kind of macho bonding based on violence completely disrupts any hope of genuine male union based on love and trust. As the men wait for Lewis, they "goof around," do a bump and grind, tell dirty jokes, and talk about torture. Just before they put the blanket over Lewis's head, Philip sees his face full of humiliation and fear. He says it is the face he saw on Vietnamese he interrogated later during the war and the face that has become his brother's face through all of his troubles.

This is the climactic moment and thematic center of a complex work that deals with the difficulty of being a man in a man's world, with the problematical nature of male bonding, and with the basic human desire to unite with someone, whether it be a brother or an enemy. The novel ends with Philip looking back over the events with a sense of helplessness about what has happened to Lewis, Hubbard, and himself. He says that Hubbard never set out to be a deserter any more than Lewis set out to become a barracks thief, and he puzzles over what could have been the cause of these actions. He says that he did not set out to be what he has become, a conscientious, responsible man who mows his lawn and is good to his wife. Although he is grateful for what he has become, he has moments when he remembers what it was like to be a reckless man with reckless friends. Imagining the ammunition dump exploding, destroying all three of them, he thinks, "It would have been something." This final statement provides closure to the central theme of the novel: whether being a man means being brave and living life dangerously or whether it means being responsible and living life comfortably. To say that the former would have been "something" is not the same as saying the latter is "nothing." In *The Barracks Thief*, however, Wolff has created a compelling novel that explores the basic complexity of this choice.

Critical Context

The Barracks Thief is Tobias Wolff's first novel. Its brevity and highly unified thematic focus are reminders that he is first and foremost a master of the short story. His first book, the collection of stories *In the Garden of the North American Martyrs* (1981), was one of the most highly acclaimed short-story collections of the 1980's. After *The Barracks Thief* was published, his third book was another collection of stories, *Back in the World* (1985). *The Barracks Thief* initially received little attention from critics. When the book won the PEN/Faulkner Award for the most distinguished work of American fiction, however, critics began to take the book more seriously as a complex work of fiction.

Bibliography
Allen, Bruce. "Name Book Year's Best." *The Christian Science Monitor* 77 (June 7, 1985): B7. Calls the work a powerful treatment of antagonisms and apprehensions of youth, intensified by war. Compares Wolff with Ernest Hemingway in his creation of abbreviated and understated scenes. Suggests that so many longings and fears are packed into such a short book that readers will finish it hardly believing that they and its characters have been through so much.
Campbell, Don. "The Barracks Thief." *Los Angeles Times Book Review* 8 (July 29, 1984). Emphasizes the brush with danger in the ammunition dump scene in the novel, arguing that it marks the three men forever. Praises the book for its sharp focus on fears, uncertainties, tangled loyalties, and instincts for betrayal of the three central characters.
Dubus, Andre. "The Barracks Thief." *America* 151 (September 1, 1984): 109. An enthusiastic review. Points out that the story focuses primarily on the complex motivations and desires of the three central characters. Compares the book to Joseph Conrad's *The Nigger of the "Narcissus"* (1897) in its dramatization of the isolation of men joined together by male work.
Hannah, James. *Tobias Wolff: A Study of the Short Fiction*. New York: Twayne, 1996. Features biographical information on Wolff as well as criticism of his short stories. Although *The Barracks Thief* is not discussed, this reference provides solid insight into themes that appear in most of Wolff's fiction. Includes a helpful bibliography for further reading.
Kendrick, Walter. "Men with Rifles." *The New York Times Book Review* 90 (June 2, 1985): 42. Says the story presents a bleak world short on joy and long on suffering. Notes that Wolff does not editorialize in the novel but leaves the reader to decide whether it is better to die spectacularly or to live out a life in safe conventionality. What dignity the characters have is based on their telling their own story without apology or complaint.
Lyons, Bonnie, and Bill Oliver, eds. *Passion and Craft: Conversations with Notable Writers*. Urbana: University of Illinois Press, 1998. A collection of informative interviews with several well-known American authors, including Tobias Wolff.
Simpson, Mona. "The Morality of Everyday Life." *The New Republic* 193 (December 9, 1985): 37-38. Calls the novel a small-scale yet intense moral drama typical of Wolff's earlier short stories. Notes the identification between Lewis and Philip, who somehow feels guilty for Lewis's acts. Points out the irony of the story's being told by a "good man" who is neither victim nor perpetrator and the only one of the three main characters who goes to Vietnam.

Charles E. May

BARREN LIVES

Author: Graciliano Ramos (1892-1953)
Type of plot: Social realism
Time of plot: The 1930's
Locale: Northeastern Brazil
First published: Vidas Sêcas, 1938 (English translation, 1965)

>   *Principal characters:*
>   FABIANO, a poor herdsman
>   VITÓRIA, his wife
>   THE OLDER BOY, never named
>   THE YOUNGER BOY, likewise anonymous
>   THE DOG, also nameless

The Novel

Barren Lives is an episodic novel divided into thirteen chapters, each with its own title. Set in the northeast of Brazil, the novel follows the lives of Fabiano and his family as they struggle for survival in a region known for its drought cycle, with periods of severe drought killing cattle and making agriculture impossible, eventually followed by torrential rains and life-threatening floods. Though the novel is told by a third-person-omniscient narrator, the point of view shifts from character to character.

The story opens with Fabiano, Vitória, the two boys, their dog, and their parrot on the road during the drought season, in search of a new home. Exhausted, thirsty, and starving, with no food in sight, Vitória kills the family bird out of necessity. As an occasional cloud begins to appear in the sky—signaling possible rain—they come upon a deserted ranch house. Fabiano contracts work with the landowner, herding his cattle. The landowner pays him in cattle and goats, but since Fabiano raises no feed, he must sell his earnings to his boss at bargain prices. He is thus never able to get ahead and is always in debt to the landowner. He goes to the market in town to stock up on staples such as flour and salt. He wanders from store to store, certain that he will be cheated by the town folk, who understand sums better than he does. When a policeman invites him to a game of cards, he accepts, primarily because the policeman is a figure of authority. Both he and the policeman lose all their money at cards. The policeman then provokes Fabiano, who finally responds by insulting the man's mother. Fabiano quickly finds himself in jail for the night, though he has committed no crime, and his fear of authority is again confirmed. He later runs into the same policeman in the country; he nearly kills him, but his respect for authority prevents him from acting.

The younger boy admires his father greatly. Watching Fabiano break a horse, dressed in the typical leather clothing of the herdsman—chaps, chest protector, jacket, and hat with a chin strap—he decides to imitate him. Unfortunately, the goat he chooses to tame is uncooperative, and the boy lands on his stomach in the dirt with his shirt torn.

The older boy overhears a neighbor mention the word "hell," and he asks his mother what it means. Vitória, like the rest of the family, is illiterate and inarticulate; in frustration at her inability to answer her son's question, she slaps him in the head.

The entire family goes to town for their yearly attendance at church. Fabiano and the boys have new suits; Vitória has a new dress. The boys walk comfortably in sandals, while Fabiano and Vitória struggle in their town shoes, finally taking off their fancy shoes and stockings until they come to the edge of town, where they bathe their feet and again put on their shoes. Fabiano's fear of townspeople returns. He considers them evil cheaters who look down upon country folk like him. He makes the same mistake he made the last time he was in town: He buys a drink of rum. The rum makes him bold, and he considers gambling again, but Vitória casts a disapproving glance. He refrains from gambling but treats himself to another shot of rum, more than he can handle. The dog becomes ill. She is thin, with patchy hair and sores on her mouth. Though she has been a loyal member of the family, Fabiano decides he must kill her in order to protect the children. While Vitória huddles in their dark bedroom with the two boys, trying to cover their ears, Fabiano gets his gun and tries to kill the dog. He misses, hitting her in the hindquarters. She drags her bleeding body along, trying to reach her favorite tree. She dies dreaming of happy times with the family and plentiful food.

The drought comes again, and the family abandons the ranch to search for survival. This time, they plan to leave the northeast and look for a new way of life, perhaps even in the city.

The Characters

The characters in *Barren Lives* are individuals who also portray typical types of the backlands in which the novel takes place. The adults have no surname and the children have no given names, suggesting their function as archetypes. Like the backlanders they represent, Ramos's characters are uneducated and illiterate, superstitious and fearful, and barely capable of using language to express themselves. Yet Ramos creates sympathetic characters through his use of shifting perspective. Vitória, the younger boy, the older boy, and even the dog each seem to tell the story from their own perspectives in the chapters that bear their names. Fabiano likewise narrates the "Fabiano" chapter, but his point of view dominates four other chapters and is represented in three others. Such use of point of view reveals the inner thoughts and feelings of each character, even though that character is unable to articulate those thoughts and feelings to the other characters.

Fabiano is a typical backlander herdsman, at once the lord of his family and the victim of the landowners for whom he works, simultaneously highly skilled at his job and frightened by his superiors. He plods through life with little imagination. What small dreams he does have are beyond his reach.

Vitória is the smart one in the family, able to figure sums by using seeds of different kinds and sizes. Her one dream is to have a real bed, a bed made of leather stretched across a frame, instead of the bed of tree branches on which she and Fabiano sleep.

Such a bed represents a luxury beyond the means of a couple whose children play naked and whose belongings must be easily portable in the event of a drought. More creative than Fabiano, she imagines a new and different life, and she sets her family on a new course, toward the city, away from the destructive and inevitable drought cycle that controls their lives.

The older boy longs to understand more than his parents can explain. He communicates best with the dog, each of them communicating by gesture and sound rather than language.

The younger boy unsuccessfully attempts to imitate his father's actions. Like his father and his brother, he is most comfortable in the company of animals.

The dog, though nameless in the English translation, is named Bailee in the original Portuguese. She is as much a member of the family as the two unnamed boys. The chapter told from her point of view is the one in which Fabiano tries to kill her, wounding her instead. In the most emotional chapter of the novel, she passes through the stages of fright, pain, paralysis, and finally death.

Themes and Meanings

Barren Lives is both a portrait of a place and its people and a critique of a system. The place is the backlands, or the northeastern interior of Brazil; the people are the backlanders, rugged, hardworking, simple folk who struggle against all odds for survival. The system is that of landowners and their hired hands. The backlands are known for their cruel cycles of drought and flood. The backlanders are known variously as simple or stupid, ignorant or innocent, superstitious or devout, as likely to die from lack of water and food as by drowning. They are tenants on the land of others, working for landowners who provide them with housing and supplies in exchange for labor, paying them for that labor in cattle that they cannot afford to keep. The laborer must sell his profits to the landowner at unfairly low prices. The backlander is subject to the cycle of drought and flood and the cycle of debt peonage, always working and always owing, never able to move forward. Told from the perspective of each of the characters and especially from Fabiano's point of view, the novel portrays a social determinism from which the characters cannot escape, and a fatalism with which they view the events of their lives.

Critical Context

Barren Lives was Graciliano Ramos's fourth and last full-length work of fiction. Later works were principally autobiographical, though he did publish some children's stories. Unlike his other novels, which are narrated in the first person, this novel has an omniscient third-person narrator; however, the clever shifting of point of view nearly erases the presence of the narrator.

Like all Ramos's novels, *Barren Lives* originated as a short story. Ramos first told the story of the death of an unusually intelligent female dog, then added pieces about her owners. When asked by his publisher for a new work of fiction, he added some chapters to the pieces already published separately, which may account for the episodic structure of the narrative. With the exception of the first and last chapters, the individual chapters seem much like self-contained short stories; the order could be changed without damage to the work itself, yet together they form a unity of vision. Nevertheless, the novel has sometimes been criticized for its episodic nature.

Ramos portrays elementary characters such as Fabiano and his family by revealing their psychology and simplifying textual language to approach the linguistic level of his characters. Even the dog is an empathetic character.

Ramos was an exemplary regionalist writer, locating all of his works in northeastern Brazil. Indeed, the landscape is a constant, if harsh, presence in *Barren Lives*, often in contrast to the corruption of town life. Ramos remains one of the most important authors of the modernist period in Brazil, and *Barren Lives* remains essential reading for students of South American literature.

Bibliography
De Oliveira, Celso Lemos. *Understanding Graciliano Ramos*. Columbia: University of South Carolina Press, 1988. Provides an overview of the author's life and work and a bibliography. Chapter 5 examines *Barren Lives*.
Dimmick, Ralph Edward. "Introduction." In *Barren Lives*, by Graciliano Ramos; translated by Ralph E. Dimmick. Austin: University of Texas Press, 1965. A general introduction to the author, along with an analysis of the novel.
Ellison, Fred. *Brazil's New Novel: Four Northeastern Masters*. Reprint. Berkeley: University of California Press, 1979. An introduction to the novel of the Northeast and four of its principal authors. Chapter 4 is dedicated to Ramos.
Martins, Wilson. *The Modernist Idea*, translated by Jack E. Tomlins. New York: New York University Press, 1970. An overview of Brazilian modernism, with a chapter on Ramos as one of modernism's exemplary authors.
Mazzara, Richard A. *Graciliano Ramos*. New York: Twayne, 1974. An excellent introduction to Ramos and his work, with a chronology and a bibliography. *Barren Lives* is discussed in several of the thematically arranged chapters.
Willem, Linda M. "Narrative Voice, Point of View, and Characterization in Graciliano Ramos's *Vidas Sêcas*." *Mester* 16, no. 1 (Spring, 1987): 18-26. A thorough discussion of Ramos's use of a narrative strategy that seems to present the novel through the thoughts of illiterate, nearly inarticulate characters.

Linda Ledford-Miller

BASTARD OUT OF CAROLINA

Author: Dorothy Allison (1949-   )
Type of plot: Domestic realism
Time of plot: The 1950's and 1960's
Locale: Greenville County, South Carolina
First published: 1992

> *Principal characters:*
> RUTH ANNE (BONE) BOATWRIGHT, the narrator, a strong-minded little
>   girl, the "bastard" of the title
> ANNEY BOATWRIGHT PARSONS WADDELL, her mother, a waitress
> REESE PARSONS, Bone's younger sister, Anney's child by her first
>   husband
> GLEN WADDELL, Anney's second husband, a troubled, insecure, and
>   violent man
> GRANNY BOATWRIGHT, Anney's mother, the matriarch of a large family
> RAYLENE BOATWRIGHT, Anney's unmarried sister, who becomes
>   Bone's protector
> EARLE (BLACK EARLE) BOATWRIGHT, Anney's favorite uncle

The Novel

   Bastard Out of Carolina is the story of a young South Carolina girl's childhood, which, though blighted by illegitimacy, poverty, and her stepfather's abuse, is made bearable by the love of her extended family and even by the love of the mother who seemed to have abandoned her.

   The novel is organized chronologically, taking the narrator, Ruth Anne Boatwright, or "Bone," from birth to her thirteenth year. While her own experiences provide the narrative thread for *Bastard Out of Carolina*, much of the book's thematic content can be found in incidents that Bone does not witness but that are related to her by other characters such as her grandmother, the intrepid Granny Boatwright. These stories, many of them from the past, most of them about the members of her own family, become very important to Bone. She absorbs them and reflects on them, making them as much a part of her own world as the events in which she is personally involved.

   From the beginning, Bone has problems with identity. She is born while her mother, Anney Boatwright, is still unconscious after being in an automobile accident. Since the relatives do not list a father on the birth certificate, Bone is officially classified as "illegitimate."

   Despite this unfortunate beginning, for a time Bone's life goes smoothly. Anney marries a sweet-tempered man, Lyle Parsons, and soon Bone has a little sister, Reese Parsons. Then Lyle is killed in an accident, leaving Anney, at nineteen, a widow with two children to support.

   While she is working as a waitress, Anney meets Glen Waddell. Even though her family warns her that Glen has a nasty temper, Anney is lonely, and she marries him. From the first, Glen seems to dislike Bone. While he and the two children are sitting in a hospital parking lot waiting for Anney to have his baby, Glen puts Bone on his lap and molests her. From that time on, she fears and distrusts him.

After their baby dies at birth and Glen learns that Anney can have no more children, he seems to become even more violent than before. Because of his hot temper, he loses one job after another. Unable to pay their rent, the family is constantly moving, and the children are often hungry. The only bright spot in Bone's life is her visits to the Boatwrights. Despite the fact that Glen sneers at them as "poor white trash," it is from them, especially from her favorite uncle, Earle Boatwright, that Anney gets the affection and the approval that she lacks at home.

When Bone is ten, Glen starts finding excuses for beating her. Because she does not want her mother to be hurt, Bone pretends that nothing is wrong. When a medical examination reveals the extent of Bone's past injuries, however, Anney realizes that she must either leave Glen or somehow keep Bone away from him. Since Anney still loves Glen and feels peculiarly protective toward him, she starts finding other places for Bone to stay.

Bone's first refuge is the home of one of her mother's sisters who is dying of cancer. Despite the circumstances, her months here are among the happiest of her childhood. As she listens to the stories told by her aunt and by her Uncle Earle, Bone realizes what it is to be a Boatwright woman. As Uncle Earle explains, the women in his family are so strong and so stubborn that they can conquer any man they meet.

When Bone is no longer needed by her aunt, she finds another consolation. After experiencing a religious conversion at a revival, she starts traveling to gospel music performances with a classmate, Shannon Pearl, and her parents, who are in the business. Once Bone realizes that the performers are more interested in liquor and lechery than in religion, however, she decides that Jesus and country music will not solve the problems in her life.

Because she bears her abuse so stoically and even lies when her relatives ask questions about "Daddy Glen," Bone is almost thirteen before the Boatwrights finally learn the truth. When they do, her three uncles beat Glen so badly that he ends up in the hospital. Glen, however, is still not finished with Bone. Finding her alone, he beats her until she is almost insensible and then rapes her. Just then, Anney walks in. At first she is furious, and she attacks Glen; then, typically, when he begins to whine and sob, she takes him in her arms to comfort him.

After she gets out of the hospital, Bone goes to live with her unmarried aunt Raylene Boatwright, a wise and kind woman who tries to explain Anney's kind of love by telling about an experience of her own. By the time Anney turns up to tell Bone that she must stand by Glen, her daughter is able to forgive her. Bone knows that this is goodbye; Anney is going to join Glen in some distant place where her brothers cannot find him. Oddly, Bone feels a certain pride in her mother; in her strength, she has shown herself a true Boatwright woman, like Raylene and, in fact, like Bone herself.

The Characters

As the narrator of the novel as well as the protagonist, Bone is recalling past events. The fact that she can see humor in the peculiar circumstances of her birth, her raid on Woolworth's, and her venture into religion indicates that by the time she tells her story, Bone has recovered her zest for life. Yet it is clear that at the time it occurred, Glen's abuse warped her personality. Not only was she forced to detach her mind from her body so that she could endure the beatings, but in guarding her secret, she also had to withdraw from the people who loved her. Bone describes how through all of this she clung to her sense of identity, so that, once freed from Glen and from her own rage, she could once again love life.

Anney is a pretty, tender-hearted woman whose flaws are generally perceived as virtues. It is her irrational optimism that first propels her into marriage to Glen and then keeps her believing that he and his luck will change. It is her tenderness toward the weak that makes it impossible for her to turn Glen away. Ironically, though Anney lacks clearsightedness, she does, like all the other Boatwright women, have strength.

Glen, the villain of the story, is incapable of love and rules his life by his own needs. Because he has been rejected by his own family, he needs Anney's love; because he sees Bone as a rival for her mother's affection, he needs to destroy her. Although Allison makes his motivations clear, by the time one sees Glen covered with Bone's blood and whining to Anney, it is difficult not to wish Bone's uncles good luck.

Granny Boatwright, the matriarch of the Boatwright family, has many admirable qualities: toughness, resiliency, and affection for her offspring. By excusing the irresponsibility of men, however, Granny helps to perpetuate a social system that suppresses even the strongest of women.

Raylene Boatwright, a loving and perceptive woman, finally provides Bone with the maternal affection and protection she needs. Raylene is also important in the healing process, which is just beginning as the book ends. Having seen the woman she loved forced to choose between her child and her lover, Raylene can help Bone to understand her mother's conflicts and thus to forgive her.

Earle is the most fully developed of Anney's three brothers. Called "Black Earle" because of his black, curly hair and his devilish charm, he attracts women effortlessly. Like his brothers, Earle is the stereotypical good old boy, with all the vices of the type, but he can also be kind and gentle. Although his good qualities were not enough to hold his wife, they do make him Bone's favorite uncle.

Themes and Meanings

On the most obvious level, *Bastard Out of Carolina* is a story of child abuse, movingly told from the point of view of the victim. More profoundly, it is an examination of gender roles among lower-class Southern whites of the 1950's and 1960's.

The Boatwrights define masculinity in terms of certain activities and attitudes. When a real man is not fixing a car, driving his truck, or going hunting, he will be getting drunk, whoring, and fighting. Admittedly, because of his mechanical skills, he is a valued worker, and because he has a sense of honor, he is loyal to a fault, especially to the members of his own family.

Trouble arises only when a man like Glen, who is already considered a loser by the standards of his own prosperous family, also fails as a good old boy in the Boatwright tradition, or when a woman in this culture rebels against her role as an attractive, baby-bearing work animal. Glen's insecurity turns into anger; his outlet is an action that any Boatwright would reject, the abuse of a child. With women, it is a matter of rejecting a role. Refusing to accept the excuse for infidelity, that "a man has his needs," Earle's wife leaves him, taking his children, and Alma Boatwright Yarnell eventually goes crazy and destroys everything in her house. While she is growing up, Bone feels ambivalent about gender roles; on one hand, she admires and imitates her boy cousins, even dressing like them; on the other hand, she also enjoys being with the women of the family, especially when they describe triumphs over their men. At the end of the novel, she identifies with the strong Boatwright women, specifically Raylene and Anney; however, after Bone's experience with Glen, it is difficult to imagine her ever again permitting any man to wield power over her.

Critical Context

Although *Bastard Out of Carolina* is Dorothy Allison's first novel, it was preceded by a book of short stories, *Trash* (1988). Both that collection and this novel contain somewhat fictionalized versions of the author's own life story. Yet as Allison has noted, real life is "meaner" than fiction. She herself was not as strong as Bone, Allison has commented, nor did she have Bone's chance to escape.

It is not Allison's treatment of child abuse, however, that has most interested critics. While they find the account of Bone's response to her ordeal both psychologically valid and deeply moving, Allison's most impressive achievement, they agree, is her accurate and sympathetic description of a social class that has generally been described in unflattering terms, as "crackers," "rednecks," or "white trash."

With *The Hamlet* (1940), William Faulkner began his trilogy about a family of poor whites named Snopes, whose dominant characteristics are dishonesty, disloyalty, bigotry, and the total lack of an ethical or moral code. Because they are so aggressive and so numerous, Faulkner shows them steadily rising to political and economic power in the South. In Harper Lee's Pulitzer Prize-winning novel *To Kill a Mockingbird* (1960), the antagonist of the idealistic lawyer Atticus Finch is the unsavory Bob Ewell, who constructs a set of lies that get an innocent black man killed rather than admit that his love-starved daughter has made sexual advances to a black.

Both Lee, with her poor but upright Cunningham family, and Faulkner, in *As I Lay Dying* (1930), did point out that there is a difference between merely being poor and being "trashy." Until recently, however, Southern fiction writers tended to concentrate their interest on the gentry, upwardly mobile business owners, and blacks, while they reserved the poor whites for their lynch mobs. It is, of course, purely coincidental that Bobbie Ann Mason's acclaimed novel *Spence and Lila* (1988) and Dorothy Allison's collection *Trash* were published in the same year; however, the date does indicate how short a time has passed since Southern writers began to substitute a realistic picture of the Southern working poor for the contemptuous stereotypes that had prevailed for so long. Because of its insights and its high literary quality, *Bastard Out of Carolina* is an extremely important novel.

Bibliography

Allen, Kimberly G. Review of *Bastard Out of Carolina*, by Dorothy Allison. *Library Journal* 117 (March 1, 1992): 116. Sees the focus of the story as the Boatwrights, "a proud and closeknit clan." Praises Allison for her "rich sense of family." Allen also mentions the author's accuracy and sensitivity in revealing the feelings of a sexually abused child.

Boyd, Blanche McCrary. "Dorothy Allison, Crossover Blues." *The Nation* 257 (July 5, 1993): 20-21. Allison discusses her work, particularly *Bastard Out of Carolina*, a novel that has been categorized as a "crossover" book, or one that was written by a lesbian author and has been well-received by the mainstream public.

Donlon, Jocelyn Hazelwood. "'Born on the Wrong Side of the Porch': Violating Traditions in *Bastard Out of Carolina*." *Southern Folklore* 55 (Fall, 1998): 133-144. Donlon explores the symbolism of the porch in Allison's book, perceiving it as a space that defines cultural traditions and norms. She discusses the various porches where Bone experiences significant events in her life.

Garrett, George. "No Wonder People Got Crazy as They Grew Up." *The New York Times Book Review*, July 5, 1992, 3. A highly favorable review by a critic who is himself a much-admired Southern writer. Points to the skill with which Allison incorporates so many details, episodes, and stories into a unified whole. She avoids the dangers of "cuteness" inherent in a Southern setting as well as the sentimentalizing or sociologizing that often tempt those writing about the poor. Perhaps her most impressive achievement is in the use of language, which rings true and yet is as lyrical as a gospel song.

Harris, Gale. "Ashamed and Glorified." *Belles Lettres* 8 (Spring, 1993): 4-6. Assesses the novel as an "American classic." One of the major themes of the work is pride, which in excess, as often with the Boatwright men, can be destructive, but which sometimes, as in the case of Bone, is all that enables one to endure. Another theme is human vulnerability, as seen in the universal need for love. Praises Allison's descriptive prose, her "emotional intensity and honesty," and her "complex and compassionate" characterization.

Hawthorne, Mary. "Born of Ignorance." *The Times Literary Supplement*, August 14, 1992, 18. Sees the main subjects of the novel as the "complexity of cruelty," the product of poverty, "social inequity," and "the psychosis of the family." The defects of *Bastard Out of Carolina* include a lack of unity, excessive "wisecracking bonhomie" on the part of the Boatwrights, and sometimes, particularly in the case of Glen, unconvincing characterization. Finds the book, however, vivid, compelling, and emotionally honest.

Horvitz, Deborah. "'Sadism Demands a Story': Oedipus, Feminism, and Sexuality in

Gayl Jones's *Corregidora* and Dorothy Allison's *Bastard Out of Carolina.*" *Contemporary Literature* 39 (Summer, 1998): 238-261. Horvitz draws parallels between Jones's and Allison's novels, focusing on the trauma enacted on the female body in both books, and emphasizing the need to move into the future without repressing the memory of the sadism of the past.

Irving, Katrina. "'Writing It Down So That It Would Be Real': Narrative Strategies in Dorothy Allison's *Bastard Out of Carolina.*" *College Literature* 25 (Spring, 1998): 94-107. Discusses Allison's strategy of disavowal in her portrayal of poor Southern characters in her novel. Irving maintains that such a strategy is in keeping with Allison's self-designation as an iconoclast, influenced by her desire to assert her true sexuality.

McDonald, Kathlene. "Talking Trash, Talking Back: Resistance to Stereotypes in Dorothy Allison's *Bastard Out of Carolina.*" *Women's Studies Quarterly* 26 (Spring-Summer, 1998): 15. McDonald sees Allison's novel as a presentation of "an insider's perception of so-called white trash experiences which help those on the outside understand the reality and diversity of those experiences." McDonald evaluates Allison's work from a pedagogical point of view.

Young, Elizabeth. "Trash Tales." *New Statesman* 234 (January 8, 1993): 41-42. Allison's aim is to portray accurately a social class "that has been neglected and misunderstood by other novelists." Because of her "force and accuracy," she is more successful than such notable writers as Bobbie Ann Mason and Carolyn Chute. Young also admires her clean style, which, though avoiding dialect, has captured the "rhythms of Southern speech."

Rosemary M. Canfield Reisman

THE BEAN TREES

Author: Barbara Kingsolver (1955-   )
Type of plot: Bildungsroman
Time of plot: The 1980's
Locale: Principally Tucson, Arizona
First published: 1988

Principal characters:

> TAYLOR GREER, a young woman who heads west to "get away" and
> ends up accepting the responsibility of rearing a child
> TURTLE, a two-year-old Indian girl
> LOU ANN RUIZ, a woman with whom Taylor and Turtle make a home
> MATTIE, the proprietor of a used-tire shop
> ESTEVAN, a Central American refugee
> ESPERANZA, Estevan's wife, also a refugee

The Novel

The Bean Trees is the story of a spirited young woman who leaves her rural Kentucky home to head west and ends up forming a nontraditional family. Her new family works largely because of the simple goodwill of those involved and because of their mutual need to survive through difficult personal times. Shortly after Marietta Greer (who changes her name to Taylor once she gets on the road) sets out from Kentucky, she acquires an abused child, whom she takes in at first almost begrudgingly, but with increasing warmth and good humor. She settles in Tucson, Arizona, where she develops a friendship and creates a home with another single mother and her son, learning cooperation and responsibility in the process.

When Taylor leaves her mother and her rural Kentucky home, she is seeking only adventure. Taylor has lived a rather uneventful life. She grew up without a father, and there were few opportunities for her. Her mother worked as a cleaning lady in rich people's homes. During high school, Taylor got a job as a lab assistant at the local hospital, but several years after high school, that, too, seemed to be a dead end. When she managed to save up enough money to buy a car, she bought a 1955 Volkswagen and headed west in an open, adventuresome mood.

Having never been out of Kentucky before, she has no real destination and determines to travel until her car gives out. She is not, however, prepared for what lies in store. Stopping at a small roadside restaurant in Oklahoma for something to eat, Taylor is surprised when a woman insistently pushes a baby through the open window of her car, then gets into a truck. Only when Taylor unwraps the baby at a motel many miles later does she learn anything at all about the child. The baby is a girl, and Taylor sees evidence that the baby has been abused. Even though in her work at the hospital she had seen a corpse and a woman with a gunshot wound, Taylor is so astonished by the bruises on the baby that she doubles up in pain on the bathroom floor.

The Indian child appears to Taylor to be slightly more than a year old. She does not speak, nor does she walk. What she does do is cling to Taylor or to anything she can get her hands on. For this reason, Taylor calls her Turtle, like the mud turtle she had studied in her high-school science class.

After working through the Christmas holidays at the motel, Taylor is ready to continue on. By the time she arrives in Tucson, Arizona, she has two flat tires and not enough money for new ones. She likes Tucson, however, so the city seems to Taylor like a good place to settle down until she can earn a little money. By chance, Taylor gets her car into a small tire-repair establishment called Jesus Is Christ Used Tires. A widow named Mattie befriends Taylor and ultimately offers Taylor a job.

To find a place to live, Taylor answers an advertisement in the newspaper. Lou Ann Ruiz, who has advertised for a housemate, is also from Kentucky, and the two young women strike up an immediate friendship. Lou Ann is looking for someone to share expenses because her husband had left her while she was pregnant with their first child. She has a little money from his disability insurance, and occasionally he sends her a check. She and Taylor work out fairly good living arrangements: Lou Ann stays home with her baby, Dwayne Ray, and Turtle, and Taylor works for the tire business nearby.

Much of the interest of *The Bean Trees* involves the growing relationship between Lou Ann and Taylor. Although they are very different in personality and outlook and are thrown together by circumstances and need, they discover strength in each other; they are complementary personalities. Slowly and unconsciously, the group becomes a family, committed to one another and compassionate about one another's weaknesses.

Taylor's relationship with Mattie also develops into a friendship that opens the door to a wider world. Mattie is involved in the sanctuary movement, helping Central American refugees flee their native lands. Through Mattie, Taylor meets Estevan and Esperanza, and gradually she learns of hardship and sacrifice that go beyond anything she had ever seen in Kentucky.

After a trip to a local physician, Taylor learns that Turtle's abuse was even worse than she had surmised; the child has suffered many broken bones. X-rays also show that Turtle is probably about three years old, considerably older than she acts or appears. The physician diagnoses Turtle's condition as failure to thrive, although it is clear that Turtle is developing in the home environment Taylor has provided for her.

When the state becomes aware that Taylor has no legal claim to Turtle, Taylor begins to think she has to do something to keep Turtle. She decides to make a return visit to Oklahoma to try to find Turtle's relatives and get them to appoint her Turtle's legal guardian. She also volunteers to transport Estevan and Esperanza to a church in Oklahoma, because their situation is becoming precarious in Tucson.

In a trip that is both scary and funny, the Guatemalans and Taylor and Turtle succeed in accomplishing a legal adoption for Turtle and finding another safe haven for Estevan and Esperanza. They also learn about love, loss, respect, and the true meaning of "family."

The Characters

Taylor Greer, the main character, enlists the warm wishes of the reader immediately through her open, honest narration. She quickly lets the reader into her middle-American background. With her rural Kentucky regionalisms and dialect, she is open and sincere. She has a good sense of humor and can laugh at herself as well as at others and at the comedy of human life. As both the narrator and the main character, she carries the story of growing into responsibility and love. She learns her own ignorance and political naïveté, and while her goodheartedness and compassion for others cannot protect her from pain, they reinforce her moral fiber, which gives her the courage to do right. She did not seek the responsibility of a child, but she accepts what fate seems to throw in her path.

Turtle, the child, is seen gradually to emerge from the cocoon of silence and withdrawal with which she surrounds herself, presumably as a result of the abuse she has suffered. She is the catalyst for Taylor's discovery of responsibility, commitment, and love.

Lou Ann Ruiz is at first only Taylor's housemate, but gradually the two develop a relationship that is strong, supportive, and mutually beneficial. Lou Ann constantly belittles herself—about her appearance, her capabilities, and her potential. Yet despite desertion by her husband, she slowly gains some self-confidence and is able to take a job in a salsa factory. Obsessed with the safety of her baby, Dwayne Ray, she nevertheless understands that even the best of mothers cannot protect her child from all the world's sources of harm, a fact she points out to Taylor when Turtle is accosted by a stranger. Lou Ann helps Taylor to understand her responsibility for Turtle, encouraging her to take steps to avoid Turtle's being taken as a ward of the State of Arizona. Like Taylor, she speaks in a Kentucky dialect that is wholesome, warm, and rich. Although Lou Ann notices that similarity almost immediately, it takes both Lou Ann and Taylor some time to acknowledge the even deeper sources of compatibility between them.

Estevan, a Central American who has come into the United States illegally, is a well-educated, sensitive man whose life accidentally intersects with Taylor's. Through Estevan, Taylor learns about political atrocities elsewhere and about physical and emotional torture that might cause one to flee one's country. Estevan recognizes Taylor's naïveté and only gradually, over time, tells her of his past. Despite his loneliness, he remains faithful to his wife, even though he must perceive that Taylor has fallen in love with him.

Esperanza, Estevan's wife, is much more withdrawn than her husband. In the hope of getting Estevan and Esperanza's cooperation in naming the members of their teacher's union, political enemies kidnapped their only child, Ismene. Esperanza has difficulty coping with this loss, and at one point takes aspirin in a suicide attempt. During the trip to Oklahoma, she becomes very attached to Turtle, and Turtle to her. Only when she voluntarily poses as Turtle's real mother and signs legal papers giving up custody to Taylor does she seem finally to work through her grief over the loss of Ismene.

Themes and Meanings

The novel is about the struggles of American life for the vast number of people for whom the rags-to-riches dream is never realized. This is the real America, the America of unskilled labor, low levels of education, and limited access to the perks of American society. Yet in Kingsolver's novel there is no bitterness, no petty jealousy or envy, no crime, merely an easy acceptance of the way things are and an appreciation of life's good parts.

The novel is also about growing up. While the device of the journey has often been used to focus such a theme, Taylor's growing up comes not so much as a result of her experiences traveling as a result of her attempts to deal with the new and unexpected responsibility of a needy child. Taylor must learn how to be a mother—how to provide for Turtle's physical needs and, even more important, how to provide for Turtle's emotional needs. Slowly, she becomes committed to satisfying those needs, to being a real parent for Turtle.

Another theme of the novel is women's strength. All the major characters are women, and they form a community of support for one another. They accept one another's weaknesses, helping one another to change what can be changed and to work around what cannot. This is a story of women who are not empowered in any way but who nevertheless have the will, the spirit, and the commitment to find the resources within themselves to do right individually.

Critical Context

The Bean Trees, Barbara Kingsolver's first novel, was greeted with critical acclaim. Following a chronological structure, with past episodes related only as memories, the story moves swiftly along by virtue of the charm and spirit of its main character. Structure and style reinforce the pedestrian atmosphere of the novel, where no miracles happen except those that happen every day—finding the strength of love, discovering commitment, and feeling that one belongs somewhere. The comedy of humanity plays itself out with a warmth and reverence that are a pleasure to read.

Kingsolver's favorite themes of family and relationships also appear in her other work. *Homeland and Other Stories* (1989) was published in the year following *The Bean Trees* and carried on the earlier book's fresh and hopeful outlook. *Animal Dreams* (1990) expressed Kingsolver's concerns for humanity and the environment. *Pigs in Heaven*, published in 1993, was a sequel to *The Bean Trees*. *Holding the Line: Women in the Great Arizona Mine Strike of 1983* (1989), a work of nonfiction, revealed Kingsolver's continuing interest in human rights and women's issues. Many critics have praised Kingsolver's fiction as "poetic"; not surprisingly, she has published poetry in a number of magazines and in a collection.

Bibliography

Butler, Jack. "She Hung the Moon and Plugged in All the Stars." *The New York Times Book Review*, April 10, 1988, 15. A good essay that praises Kingsolver's style, pointing out her success in both dialogue and description. Butler also notes that language is one of the subthemes of the novel, linking Lou Ann and Taylor through their Kentucky dialect, Estevan through his work as an English teacher, and Turtle as a child learning to speak. Butler points out, however, that the novel seems to lose "immediacy" near its end, with the characters becoming almost too good and the plot perhaps overly contrived.

FitzGerald, Karen. "A Major New Talent." *Ms.* 17 (April, 1988): 28. In this appreciative review, FitzGerald puts Kingsolver in the context of contemporary feminists writing about friendship. In Kingsolver's fiction, however, as opposed to the nonfiction of other feminists, a reader comes to feel the power of women's relationships and their ability to provide a haven in which the women can blossom.

Lyall, Sarah. "Termites Are Interesting but Books Sell Better." *The New York Times*, September 1, 1993, C1. A lengthy, informal profile of Kingsolver.

Schwarzbaum, Lisa. "Bound for (More) Glory." *Entertainment Weekly* (May 1, 1998): 58. A highly favorable tenth anniversary review that praises Kingsolver's novel for its memorable characters and recommends it be taught in high schools.

See, Lisa. "Barbara Kingsolver." *Publishers Weekly* 237 (August 31, 1990): 46-47. This biographical account talks about Kingsolver's major and recurring themes—the environment, Native Americans, U.S. involvement in Central America, parental relationships, and women's control of their own lives. Notes that Kingsolver is committed to examining political issues but that her main goal as a writer is to entertain the reader; perhaps as a second goal, she clings to the belief that her writing can change the world.

Paula D. Kopacz

BEARHEART
The Heirship Chronicles

Author: Gerald Vizenor (1934-   )
Type of plot: Apocalyptic satire
Time of plot: The end of the world
Locale: The central United States
First published: Darkness in Saint Louis Bearheart, 1978; 2d edition titled *Bearheart: The Heirship Chronicles*, 1990

> *Principal characters:*
> PROUDE CEDARFAIR, the last leader of the cedar nation, he is forced into exile with his wife, Rosina
> BIGFOOT (also known as BENOIT SAINT PLUMERO and DOUBLE SAINT), a trickster with great sexual appetites
> BELLADONNA, a mixed-blood obsessed with her Indianness
> BISHOP OMAX PARASIMO, a cleric who has been providing shelter for tribal mixed-bloods
> SIR CECIL STAPLES (the Evil Gambler), the "monarch of unleaded gasoline"

The Novel

Bearheart: The Heirship Chronicles is an unorthodox narrative. A work of mixed genres, the book incorporates materials from the indigenous and mainstream literary traditions. The novel follows the traditional framework of the emergence myth, which involves the cyclical destruction and creation of the world; an integral part of the myth is the survival and renewal of the tribe through migration. Because of its experimental techniques and language, however, *Bearheart* has also been associated with post-modernism.

The novel opens with a preface, entitled "Letter to the Reader," by Saint Louis Bearheart, a bear-spirit who hovers above the cabinets of files of tribal histories in a government building. Invaded by a sense of darkness (hence the title of the first edition), he turns into the fictional author of "The Heirship Chronicles: Proude Cedarfair and the Cultural Word Wars," a futuristic narrative about the flight of Proude and his wife from the cedar nation, his adventures with a group of followers, and the achievement of his vision quest. The "pilgrimage" represents a migration from "the third world" to the fourth, and hence alludes to American Indian myths of emergence and the end of the world. The narrative is replete with hyperbolic and incredible events and details (including cannibalism and graphic acts of sex and violence) that are simultaneously shocking and amusing.

"The Heirship Chronicles" begins with the encroachment of whites upon the "cedar circus" around Migis Sandridge, a sacred site. Proude Cedarfair, the last in a line of tribal leaders, resists white exploitation of the remaining trees during an energy crisis. His cabin is burned down; he and his wife Rosina, together with seven clown crows, go into exile.

At the Scapehouse on Callus Road, they visit a commune of thirteen women poets. Bigfoot (Benoit Saint Plumero), a trickster who resides there, is the object of these women's desire. With Bigfoot, Proude and Rosina continue with their journey in a rare silver cabriolet that the women have given them. Along the way, they pick up Belladonna, but soon their car is ripped apart by racist killers of drunk Indians. Walking along the abandoned interstate, the pilgrims chance upon various characters who join them or harass them. Among the new recruits are Bishop Omax Parasimo and the people he has been sheltering; these include Inawa Biwide, an orphan, and Lilith Mae Farrier, a former teacher who is in love with two boxers.

A major challege confronts the pilgrims at What Cheer in the middle of Iowa, where Sir Cecil Staples, the "monarch of unleaded gasoline," reigns. Victimized as an abducted child before becoming the Evil Gambler, he relishes killing his adversaries. He challenges the circus pilgrims to play word games; he defeats Lilith Mae, but he loses to Proude and is tortured to death.

The pilgrims come to Dumfries, which is populated by disfigured victims who are crippled or suffering from skin cancer. Out of goodwill, one pilgrim does a striptease for them. They masturbate as they watch and, lusting after her body, eventually dismember her. In another episode, at the Witch Hunt Restaurant, where meals made from body parts of ordinary humans and "witches" are served, one pilgrim attempts to rescue a woman who is a victim of the witch hunt. While the pilgrim (dressed as a woman) starts copulating with her, he is killed by the "food fascist." His head is chopped off and propped up on a stick, which the pilgrims retrieve and bury.

Belladonna also runs into trouble. As a mixed-blood conceived during the standoff at Wounded Knee, she takes pride in being a Native American. Yet she is also undone by her narcissism when she gives a clichéd speech at a community the residents of which are opposed to fixed ideas. After she has rejected their challenges of her Native American identity, they stop asking questions, applaud her speech, and reward her with a poisoned cookie for her "terminal creed." As she dies, Proude cuts open her womb (her pregnancy is a result of her rape by whites), takes out the fetuses of twins, and buries the three ceremonially.

As the pilgrims enter Oklahoma, they obtain the help of the Luminous Augur to cross the Canadian River. To climb over the hills without being hit by thunder, they also seek the help of the Master Stranger, who charges food for his service. Bishop Parasimo, who has replaced the tribute of food with bark, is struck dead by lightning. The other pilgrims then arrive at New Liberty, where they catch a freedom train headed for Santa Fe. The train, operated by a regime of five veterans known as the "pentarchical pensioners," turns out to be a prison. The pilgrims are branded and given an inquisition; during the ordeal, the pensioners put out Inawa Biwide's eyes.

It is not clear whether what happens next is a vision or a continuation of the journey, but the pilgrims reach a pueblo near the Jemez River, where they meet two sacred clowns waving wooden penises. Aroused by their ritual, Bigfoot grabs Rosina and makes her perform oral sex on him. Out of nowhere, one of the women poets appears and strangles him. Leaving Rosina behind, Proude and Inawa Biwide move on into the barren mountains toward Wanaki Pueblo Bonito, the ancient place of vision bears. Around the time of the winter solstice, the two have a vision of a giant bear, which tells them to enter the fourth world as bears.

The Characters

As a mixed-genre narrative, *Bearheart* contains an assortment of characters who are given different levels of aesthetic treatment. While some characters are portrayed more elaborately than others, none is truly rounded in the realistic sense. Many embody certain traits exemplifying ideas with mythical, allegorical, allusive, or satirical significance.

The most prominent character, Proude Cedarfair, is portrayed not only as a medicine man and a shaman, but also as a repository and transmitter of tribal wisdom and values. Ultimately, he attains the stature of a culture hero in his quest to become a bear, a motif common in Native American mythology and literature. His gamble with Sir Cecil Staples is reminiscent of cosmic struggles in Anishinabe myths. Apart from cultural and mythical heroism, Proude is also endowed with a strong sense of humanism—which can be seen, for example, when he tries to save Lilith Mae, or when he cuts open Belladonna's womb in order to give her and her twins a proper burial.

At the other end of the spectrum, Sir Cecil Staples stands out as an archetype of evil. Even so, such a character exhibits certain complexities. For all of his Satanism, he also serves as an agent of social satire; his tremendous power to annihilate is derived from his ability to hoard unleaded gasoline, which he then uses as a lure to his victims, who in fact gamble with him with the full knowledge of the consequences. Furthermore, a psychological basis for his deeds is also provided in the novel. As one of thirteen abducted children raised in a big-rig trailer constantly on the road, and having developed deformities after being subjected to repeated dousings of pesticides, he is a victim turned victimizer, a person poisoned by a pathological and dysfunctional society.

Artistically and thematically, Bigfoot is the most interesting character. An embodiment of the sacred and the profane, he is both a buffoon and a hero whose carnivalistic and disruptive playfulness nevertheless contributes to the general cause of his band. Amusing and scandalous, he is particularly significant as a character because of the comic vision he brings to bear on the pilgrims' quest for tribal survival and renewal. His sexual dalliance (or assault, depending on the perspective) with Cedarfair's wife, though perplexing, suggests that one of his major functions is to interact with the reader—as, for example, by challenging any sense of complacency that might have developed in the reading process.

A mixture of the tribal hero, the antisocial, and the trickster is manifest in many of the other characters or character groups; such a mixture often turns out to be a formula for a certain kind of wisdom essential to the survival and renewal of the pilgrims. Belladonna, who takes tremendous pride in her Indian heritage because she is the off-spring of a militant Indian and a sympathetic white woman, serves as an illustration of Vizenor's argument against the invention of the "Indian." Hence, according to the overall schema of the quest, the Breeders and Hunters at the Great Wall of Orion, who applaud Belladonna's hackneyed speech but poison her for her "terminal creed," are also purveyors of truths rather than merely the adversaries of the pilgrims. In fact, the rivalry between the pilgrims and their persecutors can be seen in terms of such a play, or dialogue, involving a spectrum of characters and character traits.

Themes and Meanings

The titles of the novel's two editions suggest that its major thematic concerns are the "darkness" in Saint Louis Bearheart and Bearheart's "heirship chronicles"; the preface, which sets up a metafictional frame, also serves as an exposition of the titles. The novel can be understood as a historian's statement, in the form of an imaginative narrative derived from tribal archives ("chronicles"), about the predicament of American Indians ("darkness"), the sources of their problems, and the solutions. "Darkness," understood psychologically, also stresses the sense of destiny, with hints of a radical response (which Vizenor implies in his use of the term "word war"). "Heirship," though not necessarily without ironic implications, also refers to predicament and destiny, but the term's emphasis appears to be on survival and renewal. The name of the fictional narrator, "Bearheart" or "St. Louis Bearheart," who claims that the bear is in his heart, alludes to the tribal myth of bear-becoming.

According to the novel's sociomythical framework, the bear-becoming of Cedarfair is a response to the historical disaster that has annihilated American Indians, their original habitats, their meager reservations ("circus"), their culture, and their identity. The ongoing oppression is further aggravated by the ecological and energy crises that Western civilization has brought upon whites and Native Americans alike. The grim, apocalyptic reality of impoverished existence and general extinction causes the characters to refer to the book's setting—the central United States—as the "third world." The quest of the pilgrims, which begins at the point where the "third world" is being destroyed, comes to a conclusion around the winter solstice, when the rebirth of the year and the creation of the fourth world coincide. The bear-becoming of Cedarfair and Inawa Biwide is an integral part of this regenerative process, an index of which is the state of powerful balance achieved in the identification of the human and the animal.

Vizenor's professed views about American Indians, Amerian culture, and aesthetics often shed light on specific themes such as the "invention" of Indians, the problem of "terminal creeds," and the comic vision of trickster figures. Critical of the term "Indian" as a label applied by whites, Vizenor often warns against the label's perpetuation of identity problems for Native Americans. Fixations on certain ideas, known as "terminal creeds" in his terminology, are akin to terminal diseases in the sense that they are stifling rather than productive. In dealing with these issues, the tribal trickster is the most effective in upsetting stereotypes about American Indians as noble savages

with values readily exploitable and consumable by whites, and in introducing elements of play and chance to disrupt the complacency associated with fixed ideas. As a
"word-war" narrative, *Bearheart* in general is a dramatization of these positions.

Critical Context

As a mixed-blood Anishinabe who grew up in Minnesota off the reservation,
Vizenor had a traumatic childhood (the murder of his father is unsolved) and acquired
a varied education before beginning his writing career. Biographical information
about the author shows that *Bearheart* is more than a fantasy; rather, it is a piece of
fiction that reverberates with the totality of the author's personal, professional,
academic, tribal, and American experiences. Vizenor's use of the trickster as a privileged figure within a narrative text employing techniques and devices suggestive of
"trickstery" is closely tied to beliefs derived from those experiences.

Bearheart, like many of Vizenor's other works, challenges assumptions about Native Americans and their literature. At the most radical level, it refutes the notion of
"Indians" and seeks to undermine the structure of thinking that sets up the
"Indianness" of tribal people as the containable Other of Western civilization. Because such a challenge also applies to Indians who pride themselves on their
Indianness, the book stands out as an unorthodox text with a special message for Native American readers and authors. Nevertheless, *Bearheart* is paradigmatically Native American in its efforts to confront the internal colonialism of America and to affirm the vital spirit of tribal traditions at a higher level of consciousness. On this
higher level, the Indian ends where the tribal mixed-blood begins.

Because *Bearheart* draws its inspiration from tribal myths, it can be associated
with the body of work created by authors such as James Welch, N. Scott Momaday,
Leslie Marmon Silko, and Louise Erdrich. In addition, however, the novel is also full
of allusions to such canonical works of the Western tradition as the poems of Geoffrey
Chaucer. Furthermore, Vizenor's academic and scholarly expertise has contributed to
the book's distinctly philosophical, postmodern, and poststructuralist outlook.
Thanks to his balancing—though not necessarily reconciling—of insights from Native American, European, and possibly Asian sources, Vizenor has created a fluid text
with abundant possibilities for interpretation.

Bibliography

Armstrong, Meg. "'Buried in Fine White Ash': Violence and the Reimagination of
    Ceremonial Bodies in *Winter in the Blood* and *Bearheart*." *The American Indian
    Quarterly* 21 (Spring, 1997): 265-298. Armstrong explores the themes of power,
    transformation, and identity. She argues that the texts must be read with the under-
    standing of ceremony and the body.
Blair, Elizabeth. "Text as Trickster: Postmodern Language Games in Gerald
    Vizenor's *Bearheart*." *MELUS* 20 (Winter, 1995): 75-90. Blair focuses on
    Vizenor's use of the trickster text in *Bearheart* to link the written word with the
    mythic aspects of the story. She demonstrates that the trickster is part of the satirical

language in storytelling that tribal people use to understand themselves, as well as the truth.

Bruchac, Joseph. *Survival This Way: Interviews with American Indian Poets*. Tucson: University of Arizona Press, 1987. Contains "Follow the Trickroutes: An Interview with Gerald Vizenor," in which the author discusses his career and his use of history in his writing.

Hochbruck, Wolfgang. "Breaking Away: The Novels of Gerald Vizenor." *World Literature Today* 66, no. 2 (Spring, 1992): 274-278. An overview of Vizenor's fiction, focusing on its unorthodox and disruptive elements.

Martin, Calvin, ed. *The American Indian and the Problem of History*. New York: Oxford University Press, 1987. Discusses historical revisionism and its central place in Native American literature. Views Vizenor as a skilled practitioner of revisionism.

Pasquaretta, Paul. "Sacred Chance: Gambling and the Contemporary Native American Indian Novel." *MELUS* 21 (Summer, 1996): 21-33. Pasquaretta discusses the gambling motif in works by Louise Erdrich, Leslie Marmon Silko, and Vizenor. He views the scenario of good gamblers pitted against evil ones as a metaphor representing the relationship between European Americans and Native Americans.

Ruoff, A. LaVonne Brown. "Woodland Word Warrior: An Introduction to the Works of Gerald Vizenor." *MELUS* 13, no. 1-2 (Spring/Summer, 1986): 13-43. Comprehensive review of major works by Vizenor, with a useful bibliography.

Velie, Alan R. "Gerald Vizenor's Indian Gothic." *MELUS* 17 (Spring, 1991): 75-85. Explores Vizenor's futuristic novel *Darkness in Saint Louis Bearheart* as a tale that reverses the traditional Western genre format, showing Indians terrorized as they venture into the savage wilderness of white civilization in decline. Discusses the mythic roles of Proude in the role of Trickster and Sir Cecil Staples as the Evil Gambler.

Vizenor, Gerald, ed. *Narrative Chance: Postmodern Discourse on Native American Indian Literature*. Albuquerque: University of New Mexico Press, 1989. Contains several relevant essays, including "'Ecstatic Strategies': Gerald Vizenor's *Darkness in Saint Louis Bearheart*," by Louis Owen, "The Trickster Novel," by Alan Velie, and "Trickster Discourse: Comic Holotropes and Language Games," by Vizenor.

Balance Chow

THE BEAUTIFUL AND DAMNED

Author: F. Scott Fitzgerald (1896-1940)
Type of plot: Romantic satire
Time of plot: 1913-1921
Locale: New York City and environs, and the vicinity of a military training camp in
   South Carolina
First published: 1922

   Principal characters:
      ANTHONY PATCH, the protagonist, a young man with great expectations
         of wealth
      GLORIA GILBERT PATCH, a beautiful young woman from the Midwest
         who marries Anthony
      ADAM PATCH, an aging millionaire and philanthropist, Anthony's
         grandfather
      RICHARD CARAMEL, Gloria's cousin and Anthony's best friend, a
         successful novelist
      MAURY NOBLE, Anthony's friend
      DOROTHY RAYCROFT, Anthony's mistress during World War I

The Novel

   Originally called "The Flight of the Rocket," *The Beautiful and Damned* is the
story of Anthony Patch's life between his twenty-fifth and thirty-third years. The
novel follows the progression of his intense love for the dazzlingly beautiful Gloria
Gilbert. It traces their attachment through their courtship and marriage, through their
apparently endless round of parties and gaiety, to their eventual financial difficulties,
and finally to their triumphant achievement of Anthony's "great expectations." The
victory comes too late, however, and the conclusion is more bitter than sweet.

   As the novel opens, Anthony Patch, handsome, intelligent, and moderately well educated, wants only to live a life of luxury. When he inherits his grandfather's many
millions, he will be able to do exactly that. Until then, he has enough money to continue to live comfortably although without any particular goal. Someday, he tells his
family and friends, he may write, but in actuality he lacks both the discipline and the
ambition of his friend Richard Caramel.

   When Anthony meets the incredibly beautiful Gloria Gilbert, his life changes. He
pursues her, eventually marries her, and believes that he has everything that he needs
to be happy—except his grandfather's money. The years that follow, however, gradually take Anthony and Gloria from blissful romantic happiness to alcoholic boredom.
The novel becomes the story of how a lack of purpose and discipline can undermine
everything else in life.

   Fitzgerald saw *The Beautiful and Damned* as the story of a man with the tastes and
weaknesses of an artist, but with no creative inspiration. While this outline suggests

that Fitzgerald himself had a rather romantic idea of what makes an artist, the pertinence of the novel's diagnosis is not confined to the artist manque. Anthony's weaknesses are those of a rootless generation writ large. He has no focus to his life beyond Gloria's beauty and his grandfather's millions. Similarly, Gloria sees herself as a beautiful flower that needs only to be displayed to full advantage. The void at the center of their lives is soon filled with liquor.

Anthony and Gloria buy a car, rent a summer home, give endless parties, all the while living beyond Anthony's income. Soon, they are dipping into their capital in order to pay their bills. As they become more desperate financially, they quarrel more and more frequently. When Adam Patch surprises them during a wild party at their summer home, he disinherits Anthony. When the old man dies, he leaves his millions to his secretary. To recover the fortune, Anthony begins a suit that drags on for years.

The world of illusion in which both Gloria and Anthony have been living is emphasized when Anthony is drafted in World War I and is sent to the South for training. Gloria has always been told that she is beautiful enough for a career in films, but now, when she finally tries to do it to earn a little money, she discovers that—at twenty-nine—she is too old. With despair, she realizes that her beauty is fading.

Anthony's friends, Richard Caramel and Maury Noble, have made successes in literature and business, but when Anthony returns to New York after the war, he discovers that his financial situation is worse than he thought. He and Gloria barely have enough to survive, and that money is running out. They become desperate to win the lawsuit. Finally, they do win, but it is too late. Anthony has been broken, both mentally and physically.

The Characters

Anthony Patch was intended by Fitzgerald to be a tragic character, but Anthony does not have enough substance for his fate to be tragic. At times, Fitzgerald treats Anthony satirically, as if Anthony is not to be taken seriously. Yet the moments of poignancy—especially in the love affair of Anthony and Gloria—undermine any satirical intent. At the end, the reader has confused feelings about Anthony, pitying him but believing that, after all, he brought about his own destruction.

Gloria Gilbert Patch is, in some ways, more sympathetic than Anthony. Gloria believes above all in the rights and privileges of her beauty. She believes in this with a passion that is lacking in Anthony's supposed belief in his own undemonstrated intellectual and moral superiority. When she is forced, brutally, to recognize that her beauty is fading, she accepts it with a dignity of sorts. She is not crushed, as Anthony finally is.

Richard Caramel, who enjoys the kind of early literary success that Fitzgerald himself experienced, is too heedless to realize that he is compromising his talent as he churns out one popular book after another. He is incapable of recognizing that the success which he has achieved through compromise is not worth having. The character is, in some ways, a warning from Fitzgerald to himself, of what he feared he might become.

Maury Noble, supposedly based on the contemporary wit George Jean Nathan, is cynical enough to compromise with full awareness of what he is doing, although he knows the worthlessness of what he thereby achieves. His wit and philosophy are shallow, and Fitzgerald devotes all too much space to his orations. Yet his success, along with that of Caramel, forms a counterpoint to Anthony's decline and fall.

Dorothy Raycroft, the nineteen-year-old South Carolina girl whom Anthony makes his mistress while he is stationed at the army camp, is sharply distinct from the other characters. Warmhearted, realistic, and sensible, she accepts her life with the ingrained stoicism of those who have no illusions. It is easy to see how Anthony becomes involved with her, although she possesses none of Gloria's beauty or glamour.

Themes and Meanings

On the surface a study in failure, *The Beautiful and Damned* might more accurately be said to be a study of the atmosphere of failure. Through chapter after chapter, one finds Anthony and Gloria overwhelmed by nothing more substantial than the depressing, claustrophobic ambience of the world in which they find themselves. They are constantly fleeing places—their apartment, their summer house, parties—trying to escape their own emotions and sense of frustration. Similarly, they escape into alcohol, fleeing the sense of desperation and failure that surrounds them like an ever-growing shroud.

The thrust of the novel is blunted by Fitzgerald's ambivalence. At times, Anthony is portrayed as an admonitory example of the man without purpose, a representative figure of his generation. At other times, he is more sympathetically portrayed as a man who will not compromise with a brutal and meretricious world. The focus of Fitzgerald's criticism shifts correspondingly. In the end, the reader is moved by Anthony and Gloria's pathos rather than by their tragedy, and the moral message of the novel is shortchanged by the frailty of its underlying sentiment.

Critical Context

Coming only two years after Fitzgerald's first novel, *This Side of Paradise* (1920), *The Beautiful and Damned* was a much more literary and thought-out book. Yet although it was in most respects a superior and more controlled performance, it was far short of the advance in craftsmanship and in maturity of perception that Fitzgerald would demonstrate only three years later in *The Great Gatsby* (1925). Although *The Beautiful and Damned* was not as popular with the readers or with the critics as was Fitzgerald's first novel, the novelty of its subject matter helped its sales and consolidated his position as the spokesman of the Jazz Age.

Bibliography

Bloom, Harold, ed. *F. Scott Fitzgerald.* New York: Chelsea House, 1985. A short but important collection of critical essays, this book provides an introductory overview of Fitzgerald scholarship, plus readings from a variety of perspectives on his fiction.

Bruccoli, Matthew J., ed. *New Essays on "The Great Gatsby."* Cambridge, England: Cambridge University Press, 1985. This short but important collection includes an introductory overview of scholarship, plus interpretive essays on Fitzgerald's best-known novel.

_____. *Some Sort of Epic Grandeur.* New York: Harcourt Brace Jovanovich, 1981. In this outstanding biography, a major Fitzgerald scholar argues that Fitzgerald's divided spirit, not his lifestyle, distracted him from writing. Claims that Fitzgerald both loved and hated the privileged class that was the subject of his fiction.

Eble, Kenneth. *F. Scott Fitzgerald.* New York: Twayne, 1963. A clearly written critical biography, this book traces Fitzgerald's development from youth through a "Final Assessment," which surveys scholarship on his texts.

Kuehl, John. *F. Scott Fitzgerald: A Study of the Short Fiction.* Boston: Twayne, 1991. Part 1 discusses Fitzgerald's major stories and story collections; part 2 studies his critical opinions; part 3 includes selections from Fitzgerald critics. Includes chronology and bibliography.

Lee, A. Robert, ed. *Scott Fitzgerald: The Promises of Life.* New York: St. Martin's Press, 1989. Includes essays on Fitzgerald's major novels, his *Saturday Evening Post* stories, his treatment of women characters, and his understanding of ethics and history.

Bruce D. Reeves

BEAUTIFUL LOSERS

Author: Leonard Cohen (1934-   )
Type of plot: Stream of consciousness
Time of plot: The mid-1960's
Locale: Montreal, Canada
First published: 1966

> *Principal characters:*
> THE NARRATOR, an unnamed folklorist, a student of his own suffering
> F., a politico, a manipulative lifelong friend of the narrator
> EDITH, the deceased wife of the narrator
> CATHERINE TEKAKWITHA, a seventeenth century saint, the focus of the narrator's study

The Novel

Beautiful Losers is divided into three books. In book 1, the narrator speaks. In book 2, F. writes to the narrator. Book 3 is "An Epilogue in the Third Person." Book 2 fills in gaps (though only for the reader) in the narrator's story; the epilogue shows the speakers of books 2 and 3 as old men. Cohen once remarked of the writing of this novel that he had to "write or die"; the book is a fictional portrait of one very dark time of the author's soul.

The constipated, oversexed narrator of book 1 speaks from the vantage point of a man who has lost his wife to a freak accident resulting from a possible suicide attempt and who has lost his best friend to a political suicide. The narrator is a folklorist who is studying a tribe of Indians, the A_____s, which is nearly extinct.

Edith, the most recently deceased of the A_____s, had felt neglected by her husband because of his devotion to his study. She consequently secreted herself at the base of the elevator shaft outside their basement apartment. She might have been safe in her hiding place, as few visited the basement, and she might have won the attention of her scholar-husband had a delivery boy not descended upon her.

Catherine Tekakwitha is the seventeenth century A_____ upon whom the narrator focuses his study. Her death, like Edith's, was hastened by her own acts and by an outside power. A convert to Christianity, Catherine rejected her physical nature in spite of the efforts of tribal associates to find her a suitable spouse. As she grew more disassociated from her physical self and more closely wed to the spiritual, she became more and more abusive of her physical body. Toward the end of her life, her self-inflicted torture was so great that others of her tribe forced her to agree to set limits on her homage to her Savior. Catherine did not, however, stop fasting, and she did not stop punishing her outer body; it was found, too late, that she slept each night wrapped in a blanket of thorns. (The end of Catherine's story is provided by F. in book 2.) The narrator, who continues to seek communion with Edith, Catherine, and F., all of whom he believes to have predeceased him, is lured to F.'s treehouse by a message he finds from F. in the bottom of a bag of fireworks.

F., like Catherine Tekakwitha, is thought by the narrator to have sacrificed himself to his beliefs. F. had last left the narrator's side telling him that he was going to blow himself up during Queen Elizabeth's visit in protest of Canada's affiliation with Great Britain. The letter reveals that F. lost only a thumb and not his life to the explosion. F. admits in his letter that he has never been perfectly honest with the narrator. Book 1 shows the narrator's feeling of being the lesser partner in the friendship. Book 2 shows that F. had nurtured the feelings of humility in the narrator because he considered humility a strength, and he thought the narrator the potentially stronger man of the two.

As he had directed the narrator to his study of Catherine and her tribe, F. reveals to his "darling" (the narrator) that he had created the Edith whom the narrator found so beautiful. F., always associated in the narrator's mind with soap and the perfect body, had, with his medicated products and direction, made Edith the beautiful woman whose face and body the narrator adored. In his tutelage of the narrator, F. now admits, he had held back information because he wanted the narrator, through his pain (the narrator suffers tortures of body and soul), to become the good man that F. feared that he himself could never be.

F. writes his letter from a hospital for the criminally insane. Much of the letter is written with one hand while the other does the physical bidding of nurse Mary Voolnd. Once satisfied, Mary tells F. that it is time for their escape. Mary dies in the attempted escape, but F. appears, free, as the second old man of the epilogue.

In the epilogue, a bearded old man descends from his treehouse. He is still constipated but no longer hopeful that this problem will be resolved. He is still, however, in search of sexual gratification; he is shown in pursuit of young boys. Another bearded old man missing a thumb is likewise shown in pursuit of sexual gratification, also with young boys. (The narrator and F. had begun their physical and spiritual relationship as young boys in a Catholic orphanage.)

The Characters

Leonard Cohen's novel is a study of four characters, the "beautiful losers." Their questionable beauty and their status as losers provide the substance of the novel. In their intensive quests for physical and spiritual beauty, they are representative of all human aspiration.

It is the narrator's tortured mind, spirit, and body that are revealed in the unraveling and the raveling of the plot in book 1. While first-person narrative is by its nature limited, it is the limitations themselves that are the subject of the narrative. The narrator is all too aware of his shortcomings, and book 2 confirms and adds to the idea of these. He is physically and intellectually inhibited: He is constipated, and, though he does not know it, he has been in all ways manipulated by his closest friend. His spiritual longings and his ability to ejaculate, however, are unlimited. (He, literally, and his pages, figuratively, are covered in semen.)

The narrator's anonymity and his refusal to name the tribe he studies in order to save them the humiliation of association with him are evidence of the narrator's self-deprecation. While his frequent discussions of the condition of his bowels is in keeping with his self-deprecatory manner, his constant discussion of his sexuality remains more ambiguous.

Longing is the essence of the narrator's being. He longs for physical and spiritual union with F., his friend and physical mate from boyhood. He longs for physical and spiritual union with Edith and with the sainted Catherine. Blaming his scholarship for the death of his wife, the narrator blames himself as well for not having the courage of his convictions, as F. had in sacrificing himself for his beliefs. F.'s letter shows that, in fact, the narrator had been the more truly dedicated of the two. While F. created his physical self in the image of an Adonis advertised in the pages of a comic book and Edith as his physical counterpart, and while he directed the narrator's studies, he shows himself to believe himself the spiritual inferior of the narrator. The epilogue, in keeping with the dark tone of the novel, shows the two men as equals in look and in action—the only difference being that one old man is missing a thumb.

The female characters are presented as physically flawed: Edith had not always been beautiful, and in her final appearance she had been damaged beyond recognition by an elevator; Catherine Tekakwitha had smallpox as a child and was wasted and tortured to death by her wish to deny the flesh in the elevation of her spirit. Spiritually, Edith's longings are satisfied by her union with the narrator and with F. and by drugs; Catherine's are consecrated in her sanctification by the Catholic Church and by the narrator.

Themes and Meanings

The yearnings of humankind in general and toward a higher humanity, and the merging of human beings with one another and with the spiritual, are the themes of *Beautiful Losers*. The dark tone of the novel and the antiheroic stature of its protagonist and his admired friend make the themes all the more poignant. Human beings who see themselves and who are seen as good men and women struggling to be better may see themselves and be seen by others as partially victorious in their struggles. Cohen's protagonist, in particular, does not see himself as a good man. He is suffering, struggling with constipation and unfulfilled longings. Even his spiritual longings are couched in base physical terms. His is the exaggerated baseness of every man and woman, and his are the highest aspirations of every man and woman. Mired as he is in his physical pains and desires, mired as he is in his own past sins and in those of his fellow Americans (in terms of their destruction of Native Americans), and confined as he is for so many years in his basement apartment, he continues, seemingly, to atone for his sins and the sins of humankind in his study of Catherine Tekakwitha and her almost-extinct tribe and in the study of his own mortified and mortifying flesh.

Self-mortification in one or another sense is common to each of the four characters of the novel. While Catherine's self-denial and self-mortification are thought to be excessive by her associates, each of the two characters allowed to speak in his own person humiliates himself in his self-revelation. Edith dies in a humiliating manner for love of her husband, and Catherine humbles herself to the point of death for love of

Christ. The narrator and F. mature from boyhood lovers and seekers of the ideal to dirty old men hankering after young boys.

Cohen shows that human beings are beautiful losers. Their path is a long and a humiliating one. Only Catherine's life is, finally, blessed—and even she, in the narrator's account, is shown as unbeautiful in appearance and as soiled by his sordid twentieth century narrative.

It may be said, finally, that if the physical ills and foibles of most human beings are not so extreme as the narrator's, neither are their mental and spiritual pursuits so constant. If most human beings are not so full of their own excrement or so covered with semen as Cohen's narrator, neither are most of them continually studying their own sins or the sins of their peoples' pasts, or the virtues of or their oneness with the sanctified.

Critical Context

Beautiful Losers, Cohen's second novel, was hailed upon its publication as demonstration of the continued existence of James Joyce. It combines the ridiculous and the sublime, the moral and the immoral, the sexual and the spiritual, the serious and the comic.

Cohen, a student of literature, calls to mind Dante Alighieri's *La divina commedia* (c. 1320; *The Divine Comedy*, 1802) as his novel probes the depths of hell and the journey toward heaven. Cohen's scruffy pilgrims are reminiscent of Geoffrey Chaucer's Canterbury pilgrims as they so imperfectly travel toward a spiritual shrine. His is surely the Slough of Despond of John Bunyan's *The Pilgrim's Progress from This World to That Which Is to Come* (1678); his characters are secular descendants of John Milton's *Paradise Lost* (1667). His tortuous humor recalls the apocalyptic humor of William Blake: As the heaven of Blake's major prophecies makes readers laugh and, immediately, cry at their monstrous stupidities and aspirations, so does Cohen's hell in Montreal make readers almost laugh and almost cry as it causes them to marvel at their monstrous journey.

The novel has obvious associations with Fyodor Dostoevski's *Zapiski iz podpolya* (1864; *Letters from the Underworld*, 1913; also known as *Notes from the Underground*) as the two narrators write literally from underground and from the cavernous depths of their despair. The narrator of Jean-Paul Sartre's *La Nausée* (1938; *Nausea*, 1949) seems a spiritual brother to Cohen's narrator. American Saul Bellow has with great good humor explored the ridiculous and the sublime in the low-keyed heroes of his novels, though Bellow's heroes are much more appealingly presented than Cohen's. Cohen's contemporaries John Updike and Philip Roth have had their fictional characters wallow and revel in their sexuality as Cohen's narrators wallow and revel in theirs.

Though the novel was not initially successful, by 1998 some 800,000 copies of *Beautiful Losers*, Cohen's second and last novel, had been sold. Its success has doubtless been spurred by the popularity of its author as a poet and, especially, as a singer and songwriter.

Bibliography
Devlin, Jim. *Leonard Cohen: In Every Style of Passion*. New York: Omnibus Press, 1996. A biography that is also a guide to Cohen's work.
Hutcheon, Linda. *Leonard Cohen and His Works*. Toronto: ECW Press, 1989. A deep analysis of Cohen's life and works.
Morley, Patricia A. *The Immoral Moralists: Hugh MacLennan and Leonard Cohen*. Toronto: Clarke, Irwin, 1972. Addresses the obvious problem of Cohen's novels and writing. The study includes a bibliography and an index.
Nadel, Ira Bruce. *Various Positions: A Life of Leonard Cohen*. New York: Pantheon Books, 1996. An in-depth study of the man and the artist.
Ondaatje, Michael. *Leonard Cohen*. Montreal: McClelland and Stewart, 1970. Traces Cohen's early career as an artist.

Judith K. Taylor

BECAUSE IT IS BITTER,
AND BECAUSE IT IS MY HEART

Author: Joyce Carol Oates (1938-   )
Type of plot: Psychological realism
Time of plot: The 1950's and the early 1960's
Locale: A small town in western New York State
First published: 1990

Principal characters:
> LITTLE RED GARLOCK, a poor white delinquent
> IRIS COURTNEY, a bright, lower-middle-class teenage white girl
> PERSIA COURTNEY, Iris's alcoholic mother
> DUKE COURTNEY, Iris's gambler father
> JINX FAIRCHILD, an African American teenager and star of the
>   high-school basketball team
> MR. and MRS. SAVAGE, a wealthy and cultured college professor and his
>   wife
> ALAN SAVAGE, their son

The Novel

Because It Is Bitter, and Because It Is My Heart is divided into three parts and an epilogue. With the exception of the omniscient perspective of part 1, the narrative is presented from the third-person point of view, allowing Oates to explore the perspectives of many different characters.

Because It Is Bitter, and Because It Is My Heart explores the impact of race and class on the formation of identity in America. Oates uses four families to illustrate this: the poor white Garlocks, the struggling black Fairchilds, the ambitious working-class Courtneys, and the upper-class Savages. All the individual characters are placed within the larger context of their families and social class.

The novel begins in 1956 with the discovery of the corpse of Little Red Garlock, the demented son of a poor white family. After this discovery, the novel begins its large second section, moving back three years in time to 1953. This crucial section concerns the relationship between Iris Courtney, a white working-class teenager, and Jinx Fairchild, a black teenager and star basketball player. It is Jinx who accidentally murders Little Red. In defending Iris against this repulsive sexual bully, Jinx finds himself committing a violent act that forges a secretive and powerful bond with Iris.

Iris Courtney is the central consciousness of the novel. Ambitious and bright, Iris is seeking to overcome the obstacles presented to her by her social class and by her alcoholic mother, Persia, and her gambler father, Duke. After the murder, Iris develops an erotic attachment to Jinx; she continues her obsession with him even after he breaks off their relationship. This is a side of herself that she keeps hidden from the outside world.

It is Jinx who carries the lion's share of guilt. The overheated quarrel that ends with the murder of Little Red has a serious effect on Jinx. Although he is never caught, the crime destroys his hopes and dreams. He cannot trust the white community of Hammond to give him a fair trial, because he knows that as a black man he has no presumption of innocence. Jinx begins to keep up his guard, to feel alienated from the white world that once seemed to promise him great opportunities. His guilt feelings lead to a breakdown of his personality, and he develops a troubled and self-destructive side. This leads to an "accident" on the basketball court that ruins his career as an athlete; readers understand that this accident is an unconscious self-punishment. After the accident, Jinx must quit school and basketball and give up the dream of a college scholarship that was to be his bridge to the successful white world. He marries, works at a low-level job, and eventually is sent to Vietnam, where he will die, both self-defeated and defeated by the rigidities of the racist Hammond community.

The third section of the novel begins in 1962. Iris is in radically altered circumstances. Gone is the tragic world of Hammond, along with her guilty attachment to Jinx and her ties to her dissolute mother and her distant and feckless father. Iris has reinvented herself. This third section introduces its final representative American family, the Savages. They are not part of the grubby world of Hammond but belong to the upper crust of Syracuse, where Iris is attending the university. Using her strength, her intellect, and a single-minded ruthlessness, Iris has moved up the social and economic ladder into success and well-being. This section demonstrates the distance Iris has traveled from her origins. She is to marry Alan Savage, the patrician son of the cultivated, wealthy Savages, and she is determined to forget the past, which she keeps largely hidden from her new family. At the end of the novel, Iris models her bridal gown in front of the mirror and smirks, "Do you think I'll look the part?" These final lines tell readers that Iris has constructed a persona that does not reflect her true self and that this duplicity has made her bitter and cynical. Her cool façade belies the secrets of her troubled past. Although she, unlike Jinx, has successfully crossed over into the affluent white America, Iris does not find fulfillment.

The Characters

Little Red Garlock, a violent and possibly retarded young man, is the product of Hammond's underclass. He has been badly brought up by his racist mother, whose life is one of squalor and mental instability.

Duke Courtney has an addictive personality over which he has little control. Duke's name suggests his identity as a "sporting gent" and inveterate gambler. This identity eventually takes precedence over his responsibilities as a husband and father.

Persia Courtney, the wife of Duke, was once a "golden girl" but has fallen on hard times. Persia is a free spirit whose name evokes the Orient, which in the Western imagination also links her to the irrational and the unconscious. She carries an aura of the erotic and the exotic, but she is often intoxicated, and she eventually succumbs to insanity and alcohol. Oates uses Persia to comment on Iris's identity—there is a "Persia" side to her character. Mother and daughter both become involved with a black man; both are drawn toward forbidden love and out-of-bounds behavior.

Iris Courtney is the daughter of Duke and Persia. There are two sides to her personality. On the surface, she is a high achiever and a good girl; underneath is an overheated world of fear and desire. She papers over this side of herself with an agreeable persona. As a result, she becomes increasingly false and duplicitous; her outer being does not bear any resemblance to her inner self. Her name is deployed ironically; she is not the fragile flower she appears to be. Her name also suggests that she is the eye or "I" of the novel, and may indicate an autobiographical core.

Jinx Fairchild is a black teenager who has a chance to make it in the respectable white world. His name is a basketball nickname, but it is also a metaphor for his unlucky life. Like Iris, Jinx undergoes a fragmentation of his identity, developing a secret side filled with turbulent and inchoate feelings. Trusting and idealistic as a youth, he becomes increasingly bitter and cynical.

Mr. Savage, a cultured, intellectual college professor, exudes social confidence and an elite liberalism that does little to mitigate the social and economic inequalities of the country.

Mrs. Savage, his wife, is a kind and handsome woman who presides over a beautiful home and fine family. She virtually adopts Iris and becomes like a second mother to her. For all of the family's civility, however, the name Savage suggests that underneath their beautiful home and high-minded values is a social dominance that wages class war on the less privileged members of American society. The name suggests that this family represents the "savage inequalities" in American life.

Alan Savage, the weak but agreeable son of the Savages, is a secretive young man who may be homosexual. It is clear that Alan has denied his desires in order to assume an image in line with his family's wishes. One might say that his instincts and desires have been "savagely" repressed; like Iris, he has a hidden side of his nature that he attempts to repudiate.

Themes and Meanings

Oates's main purpose is to depict the impact of race and class in America. The tragedy of Jinx Fairchild suggests that while the black man can use the narrow venue of sports as a way to achieve the American Dream, he is still largely disenfranchised. Race and class have also formed the character of Iris Courtney. Her increasingly erotic relationship with Jinx must be kept secret; in addition, the status of Jinx as a forbidden love seems to intensify her feelings. Iris cannot have a relationship with Jinx that is not premised on the racism of her society.

While Iris does not have the barriers of race to prevent her from rising in the world, her success is a betrayal of her class and of herself. The idyllic life of the Savages contrasts in an almost grotesque way with the novel's previous scenes of turmoil and tragedy. For all their charm, the Savages preside over an America of injustice and inequality. By making sure the Savages do not appear until the final section of the novel, Oates demonstrates their separation from the rest of America. It is Iris who has the eyes to see that America is "two nations." Although she looks as if she is one of the elite, her roots are in the working-class town of Hammond, home of the "other" America. Yet the sense of liberation and security Iris enjoys has come at a cost. The Savages, like a test case from Sigmund Freud's analysis of civilization and its discontents, in which desire is renounced in exchange for social and economic security.

Eroticism is another strong theme in *Because It Is Bitter, and Because It Is My Heart*, depicted as the forbidden sexual spark between Iris and Jinx. This transgressive sexuality also establishes a sense of fear and danger. Iris's most genuine sexual feelings—those for Jinx—have been thwarted and denied, so that her erotic desires are contained within a roiling inner life. The socialization of women in America, Oates suggests, requires the development of a sexual identity of either the "good girl" or the "bad girl." Iris must suppress her sexual feelings if she is to maintain her respectability. The character of Iris illustrates the theme of sexuality, repression, and gender in contemporary American life.

Violence pervades Oates's vision of race, class, and gender in America. The inequities of race and class in Hammond inevitably lead to conflict and aggression. In addition to examining the social causes of violence, Oates also suggests that an unstable streak in the American character marks all but the most educated and secure classes.

Finally, Oates looks at the meaning of success and failure in American life. Jinx dies a bitter man because he has been cheated out of the American Dream; Iris, conversely, is bitter because her success is purchased at the price of her real identity. Whether a success or a failure, no character in the novel is not thwarted and diminished by the social and psychological forces that shape American society.

Critical Context

Because It Is Bitter, and Because It Is My Heart continues Oates's return to the psychological realism of her earlier fiction. After a series of historical novels that deployed the techniques of the Magical Realists, Oates returned to the familiar contemporary terrain of upstate New York and to her usual explorations of the social and psychological issues that confront postwar America. This novel is of a piece with the two novels closely preceding it, *Marya* (1986) and *You Must Remember This* (1987). All three concern the psychological development of a gifted young woman who overcomes a troubled small-town 1950's youth.

Because It Is Bitter, and Because It Is My Heart, like the highly acclaimed *You Must Remember This*, explores the world of sports in contemporary America, especially the way in which the sports world is a gateway to success for the underprivileged male. Both novels also deal with forbidden love and offer a revisionist reading of the 1950's as a decade that was not so much a celebration of the American Dream as a realization of its worst nightmares. As with all of Oates's work, the human personality is depicted as a seething cauldron of excitations; these surges of emotion create an atmosphere of intensity and passion that comments on the intemperate side of the American character. The typical "Oatesian" personality is overwhelmed by fears and wishes only partially understood. One can detect the influences of William Faulkner, Flannery

O'Connor, and D. H. Lawrence in this presentation of the self.

A popular and prolific writer, Oates has been publishing novels, essays, stories, poems, and plays continuously since 1963. The two most-discussed aspects of her work are its quantity and its propensity for violence. Oates attributes these concerns about excess to a wish to limit her creative potential as a woman. Although her recent work suggests elements of autobiography, moreover, Oates maintains that her writing is not confessional but rather representative of the social and psychological issues that make up the American experience. In this regard, Oates is a good example of what she has called the "visionary" novelist, who writes not for herself or out of her own experience but as a medium for the lives of those around her.

Bibliography

Bomberger, Ann M. "'If I Was Colored . . . I'd Know Who I Was': Yearning White Women, Guilt, and the Past." *Women's Studies* 27 (November, 1998): 581-612. Explores the concept of white racial identity in *Because It Is Bitter, and Because It Is My Heart*. "Whiteness" is perceived to affect the idea of gender, especially for women. Bomberger also discusses the novel's characters, who have hidden their past so well that they do not acknowledge who they really are.

Creighton, Joanne V. *Joyce Carol Oates: Novels of the Middle Years*. New York: Twayne, 1992. A discussion of fifteen Oates novels written between 1977 and 1990. Of *American Appetites* (1989) and *Because It Is Bitter, and Because It Is My Heart*, Creighton comments, "The American dream is fractured by an unintentional killing; in both, violence is an upwelling of tension, breaking through the civil games of society and the conscious control of character; in both, appetites remain unfulfilled."

Gates, Henry Louis. "Murder, She Wrote." *The Nation* 251 (July 2, 1990): 27. While he singles out Oates's rendering of racial resentment, Gates maintains that "the real spine of the book may be in its brilliant depiction of downward mobility, the painful fragility of the Courtneys' standing in the world."

Johnson, Greg. *Invisible Writer: A Biography of Joyce Carol Oates*. New York: Dutton, 1998. Furnishing a candid portrait of Oates, Johnson explores Oates's private and public life. He pays considerable attention to her later, largely ignored novels, and suggests that future critics will be more appreciative of her insightful commentary on American life.

_____. *Understanding Joyce Carol Oates*. Columbia: University of South Carolina Press, 1987. Johnson sees Oates as a writer with a broad and sweeping vision of contemporary America. Discusses her deployment of gothic strategies and her ability to explore intense psychological states.

Storace, Patricia. "A Home Is Not a Fist." *The New York Review of Books* 37 (August 16, 1990): 22. Praises Oates's ability to interlace the various lives and families in her novel, but complains that she is not able to "rouse her interest in a character unless the character is in crisis." Approves of her description of social life and her sense of "history refracted through fiction."

Wesley, Marilyn C. *Refusal and Transgression in Joyce Carol Oates' Fiction.* West-
    port, Conn.: Greenwood Press, 1993. A feminist appreciation of Oates that empha-
    sizes the "gendered psychological experience" of Oates's heroines. Using the ideas
    of Fredric Jameson, Wesley explores Oates's picture of the family as a patriarchal
    system of power. She also adds some useful remarks about Jinx Fairchild as
    "transgressive other."

Margaret Boe Birns

THE BEET QUEEN

Author: Louise Erdrich (1954-   )
Type of plot: Family
Time of plot: 1932-1972
Locale: The small town of Argus, North Dakota
First published: 1986

>   *Principal characters:*
>   MARY ADARE, the protagonist, who possesses magical powers,
>   interprets signs, and tells fortunes
>   KARL ADARE, Mary's brother, a weak and wandering soul
>   SITA KOZKA, Mary's cousin, the daughter of Mary's Aunt Fritzie and
>   Uncle Peter
>   CELESTINE JAMES, Sita Kozka's best friend, who becomes Mary's best
>   friend and employee
>   DOT ADARE, the Beet Queen of the title, the daughter of Karl Adare
>   and Celestine James
>   WALLACE PFEF, a prominent citizen who becomes Karl Adare's lover
>   and Dot Adare's "uncle"

The Novel

The Beet Queen narrates the adventures of several characters of mixed Native American and European background from Louise Erdrich's first novel, *Love Medicine* (1985), as they interact with Mary and Karl Adare. The novel illuminates the lives of these characters over a forty-year period.

The Beet Queen's sixteen chapters fall into four parts. Most are recounted by a single character; some are told by several characters. The chapters include short scenes sketched by an omniscient narrator who seems more detached than the characters. Each chapter is dated to give the reader some sense of time, but the chapters are not chronological in the traditional sense. Told and retold by different characters, the events repeat, circle, overlap, and digress.

Erdrich centers her novel on the adventures of Mary Adare, whose father is dead and whose mother abandons her and her two brothers at a fair by flying off with a stunt aviator. After the baby brother is snatched by a recently bereaved father, eleven-year-old Mary and her older brother, Karl, take a freight train to see their Aunt Fritzie and her husband, Uncle Pete, who are butchers in Argus, North Dakota. On arrival, Karl is mysteriously drawn to a flowering tree, where he is attacked by a dog; he escapes by running back to the train and leaving town. Mary plods on to the butcher shop and is taken in by her aunt and uncle, although their daughter, Sita, resents her presence.

Mary shares Sita's room, wears her clothes, steals Sita's best friend, Celestine, and performs a miracle at their school. Sita, a pretty, vain, self-centered girl, longs to have her own apartment in the big city and become a model. When Fritzie develops lung trouble and she and Pete move to Arizona, Sita moves to Fargo to seek her fortune. Mary, who has been working at the butcher shop all along, hires Celestine to help her and continues to run it successfully.

Karl Adare, a traveling salesman of various sleazy products, comes to Argus to visit Mary and perhaps Wallace Pfef, with whom he has had a homosexual encounter at a crop and livestock convention in Minneapolis. He arrives at the butcher shop when Mary is out and meets Celestine, ripe for her first romantic adventure. Overcome with lust, they entangle in a brief coupling that astonishes them both. Karl then sells Celestine a knife from his sample case and vanishes, but he turns up two weeks later at Celestine's house. Still filled with ideas of popular romance, Celestine leads him upstairs to her bedroom. This time, Karl stays. After two months, Celestine asks him to leave because of Mary's disapproval and her own independent spirit. Unwillingly, he goes, but as a parting shot, he informs Celestine that she is pregnant with his baby.

Karl next visits his cousin, Sita, who has divorced her first husband and is now married to Louis, a county health inspector. Because of the divorce, Sita has lapsed from the Catholic church that was a mainstay of her life and is in precarious mental health. When Karl gives her a Bible that has Celestine's name in it, the unbalanced Sita calls the police before breaking down completely.

Celestine sets out for the hospital in a blizzard one night when she is about to have her baby, and she crashes her Buick into Wallace Pfef's fence. He takes her in and delivers the healthy baby according to Celestine's instructions. In gratitude, she names the girl Wallacette Darlene, but Mary nicknames the child "Dot," which sticks. Celestine brings the baby with her to the butcher shop every day, and Mary becomes attached to the child. Over the years, Mary constantly meddles in her niece's life, causing tension between Mary and Celestine. They squabble constantly.

Dot grows up a sturdy, strong-willed young woman, feisty, fearless, and angry. As Wallace Pfef says, "They loved Dot too much, and for that sin she made them miserable." Yet Wallace loves her almost as much and acts as foolishly. He arranges an eighteenth birthday party for Dot that turns into a comic fiasco, but his crowning folly is to arrange a beet festival and rig the votes so that "Wallacette" is elected Beet Queen.

In a stunning finale, Dot discovers what Wallace has done. Before she can be crowned queen, she runs from the royal platform to an adjoining field, where a plane awaits the moment to take off and write "Queen Wallacette" across the sky. After a terrifying flight, the pilot returns Dot to the field, where she finds the grandstand deserted but for her mother, awaiting her and brimming with love.

The Characters

Mary's odd nature defies her ordinary appearance. As a child, she performs a miracle, falling on the school playground ice and leaving a "manifestation" that is interpreted by the nuns as the face of Jesus. Mary sees only Karl's face in the imprint, while Celestine sees nothing at all. Mary's power to tell fortunes and foresee the future arouses fear in some of the other characters. Sita's mental illness and Dot's bad temper are blamed on her. Even the clothes she wears, tasselled turbans and wild prints, contribute to her oddness. Like other characters in the book, Mary does not develop over time but becomes more deeply what she is.

Karl would seem to be a weak, irresponsible man by his actions. He abandons Mary when they are children, he moves in and out of Wallace's house according to whim, and he changes jobs frequently. It is Celestine who asks him to leave when she is pregnant, however, and he agrees to the formality of a marriage after the baby is born. The way he is presented depends upon which character is speaking at any given time. He is frequently associated with Christian images, and sometimes with Satanic ones. When he visits Sita, she sees him sinking into the soft grass beneath her garden chairs until he is swallowed up by earth. Karl refers to himself as a "poor fool," and he may represent the fool of the tarot cards that Mary reads. He is the most ambiguous figure in the novel.

Celestine, who is half Chippewa, is a wonderful creation whose large size influences the way she sees the world and the way the world sees her. Orphaned early and reared by an older sister, Celestine develops a strong, independent spirit that stands her in good stead in dealing with the powerful Adares. She is Mary's only friend.

Dot Adare, the child of Celestine and Karl, inadvertently unites the major characters. She is an aggressive child, "as big as most children twice her age, strong and spoiled" when she enters first grade, and she grows into a wild, spiteful teenager. Still, she brings love and joy into the lives of Celestine, Mary, and "uncle" Wallace. Even Karl, her absentee father, returns to Argus for the crowning of the Beet Queen because of a sweet memory associated with his daughter.

Wallace Pfef discovers he is homosexual in his first sexual encounter with Karl Adare, and he is smitten for life. Karl sums him up: "He'd do anything to please me, but didn't have the nerve to please himself." Wallace brings this same fawning devotion to his relationship with Dot, who treats him as disdainfully as she treats everyone. Yet there is a very different side to Wallace. He is active in the Argus Chamber of Commerce, the Sugar Beet Promoters, the Optimists, the Knights of Columbus, and other civic organizations. A major force in bringing the dependable cash crop, beets, to the area, he is thoroughly sensible in all things but love.

Themes and Meanings

The Beet Queen deals primarily with marginal people who live socially and culturally displaced lives. This marginality is a source of both strength and grief for Erdrich's characters. Wallace Pfef, an outstanding civic leader, is marginal as a homosexual in a small, Midwestern town and in his role as substitute father to Dot Adare. Yet it is precisely his love for Karl and Dot that provides his greatest joy and pain. In addition to being socially marginal, Erdrich's characters are culturally marginal; they live under codes of both Christianity and archetypal myths.

The families in *The Beet Queen* are also marginal. Although the novel might be seen as a family saga portraying three generations, the plot suggests that there are many nonbiological ties that link people. Mary grows up with her Aunt Fritzie, who prefers Mary to her own daughter, Sita. Celestine, who is Karl's wife, spends much more time with Wallace, who often plays the role of husband. Celestine's relationship with Mary is also ambiguous. While the two women are close friends by choice, it is not until Celestine bears Mary's niece that confrontations arise. These complex, mixed roles produce gaps in the clear line of relationships that inform traditional family sagas and are suggestive of tribal kinship systems.

Erdrich's method of characterization emphasizes this conflict between nuclear family and tribal codes. Mary, Karl, Celestine, and Dot are not defined by traditional European family roles. There are no "main" characters. Only in his or her own narration is each character central; otherwise, the character exists on the margin of someone else's life. Some critics have suggested that these sometimes conflicting narrations reflect an American Indian concept of individuality independent of personal psychology. Characters are sometimes associated with the natural elements, air, water, earth, and fire. The Adare family is clearly related to the element air when Karl and Mary's mother abandons them and her new baby by flying away with a stunt pilot. Years later, the one postcard Mary ever sends her mother depicts an aerial view of Argus, as if she is still circling overhead. The mother's flight is mirrored at the end of the novel when Dot flies off with a skywriter to escape the humiliation of her arranged victory as Beet Queen. Karl also escapes his early humiliation with a transient by leaping straight out of a moving boxcar into the night air.

Although these blended voices never produce an individual hero, a sense of the whole community seems to replace it. The structure of the narrative is formal and the voices are complementary, so that the major characters together create the protagonist. In the last scene, when Dot has descended to Earth after her precipitous flight and has returned home with her mother, she and Celestine lie in bed in their separate rooms. Each feels the rush of wind and hears the first drops of rain that will break the drought Argus has suffered for months. With that fresh breath of air, the reader rejoices not only for Dot and Celestine but for the entire community as well.

Critical Context

Louise Erdrich, of German American and Chippewa descent, was already a highly acclaimed writer when *The Beet Queen* appeared. Her 1984 collection of poetry *Jacklight* had won high praise. In that same year, her first noel, *Love Medicine*, received the National Book Critics Circle best fiction award, the Sue Kaufman Prize for best first novel, and many other awards. The second volume of her planned quartet of novels, *The Beet Queen*, came out two years later; it was followed by a third, *Tracks*, in 1988.

Erdrich's novels are all circular rather than linear, and several of the characters reappear, although new ones are also introduced. Each book stands alone as a novel but each gains from a reading of the others, since a reader familiar with the series is better able to trace the tangled relationships of the characters. In a broad sense, the novels chronicle the struggles of Native Americans to survive and maintain their fragmented and mixed culture.

Erdrich's work can be seen as part of a flowering of Native American literature that goes back to 1969, when N. Scott Momaday won the Pulitzer Prize for *A House Made of Dawn*. Erdrich herself attributes this new literature to the generally improved conditions among Native Americans, and she describes herself as one who has benefited from Bureau of Indian Affairs money and education. Majoring in English and creative writing at Dartmouth, she later received her master's degree from the writing program at The Johns Hopkins University. Although she mentions William Faulkner as an influence, the whole literary canon has left its traces on her work. One important connection with Faulkner is her strong sense of place, which for her is the plains area of North Dakota—a region that is as much a presence in her novels as are her characters.

Bibliography
Banks, Russell. "Border Country." *The Nation* 243 (November 1, 1986): 460-462. Banks reviews *The Beet Queen* and finds it an almost perfect example of classical comedy. Mary Adare is described as "one of the most memorable women in recent American fiction." The novel is compared favorably with recent books of similar style.
Castillo, Susan Perez. "Postmodernism, Native American Literature, and the Real: The Silko-Erdrich Controversy." *Massachusetts Review* 32 (Summer, 1991). Castillo compares the tone and approach of Erdrich's novels *The Beet Queen* and *Tracks* to Leslie Marmon Silko's works. She concludes that although these writers differ in many respects, they have much in common. It is this commonality that offers the reader an instructive glimpse into Native American oral tradition.
Rainwater, Catherine. "Reading Between Worlds: Narrativity in the Fiction of Louise Erdrich." *American Literature* 62 (September, 1990): 405-422. Rainwater examines the various conflicting messages in Erdrich's first three novels, with emphasis on the structure of time. The article concludes that a guiding concept in Erdrich's work is that "the world takes on the shape of the stories we tell."
Storhoff, Gary. "Family Systems in Louise Erdrich's *The Beet Queen*." *Critique* 39 (Summer, 1998): 341-352. The power of the self over and against that of the family is a common theme in Erdrich's novels. Focusing on the influence of the family to shape or determine the choices an individual makes, Storhoff examines how different family backgrounds, experiences, and expectations effect the personal identities of members of the Adare and Kozka families.
Wickenden, Dorothy. "Off the Reservation." *The New Republic* 195 (October 6, 1986): 46-48. Praises *The Beet Queen* for Erdrich's prose style, her "poetic turns," and her "observant eye." Yet Wickenden points out the problems that arise when a novel is told in a series of extraordinary scenes rather than an evolving plot, and she finds the climactic scene at the Beet Festival contrived.

Sheila Golburgh Johnson

BEETLECREEK

Author: William Demby (1922-   )
Type of plot: Existential realism
Time of plot: The American Depression era
Locale: Beetlecreek, West Virginia
First published: 1950

    Principal characters:
        BILL TRAPP, a white recluse who lives close to the black community
        JOHNNY JOHNSON, a teenage black boy from Pittsburgh, Pennsylvania,
            who develops an acquaintanceship with Bill
        DAVID DIGGS, Johnny's uncle, a black man who develops an
            acquaintanceship with Bill
        MARY DIGGS, David's wife
        EDITH JOHNSON, a former resident of Beetlecreek who returns to the
            town and renews an old relationship with David

The Novel

The plot of *Beetlecreek* develops chronologically, in four parts focusing on three different sets of human circumstances, actions, and events that converge at the end. Part 1 introduces four of the five main characters. In chapter 1, Bill Trapp, a white hermit feared by a large number of the black people who live nearby, chases four young black boys from under a fruit tree in his yard and discovers that there is one young black boy up in the tree. Bill, whose reputation is unjustified, invites young Johnny Johnson to come down out of the tree and into his house. After Johnny and Bill talk and drink cider together, Johnny's uncle, David Diggs, arrives looking for him, the other boys having reported that the strange white man has caught Johnny up in the tree. Trapp also invites David to have some wine, and the two men become acquainted and later go to Telrico's Bar and get drunk together. The budding relationship carries a sense of heightened expectancy for Johnny and David, because they are stepping across racial lines, violating black and white community conventions by associating with the ostracized white recluse. For Bill, the potential relationship is exciting because it represents his coming out of seclusion, the end of his isolation from both blacks and whites.

The last chapter of part 1 focuses on David's wife, Mary Diggs, as she immerses herself in the trivial social activities and church events that define her life. Throughout the novel, Mary's actions and activities remain on the level of the petty. The events of Mary's life are one of the three sets of events that are important in the novel; her actions suggest all the negative possibilities in life.

Part 2 centers on the attempts of Bill and Johnny to develop the sense of rich possibility which they had when they first met. Bill comes out of seclusion, associates with both black and white people, and actively tries to win community favor by doing kind deeds. Johnny, who is visiting Beetlecreek from Pittsburgh, Pennsylvania, struggles to reconcile his friendship with Bill with his need, as a newcomer to the community, to prove himself to the local black youth gang. The gang attempts to force Johnny into behavior that is callous and insensitive and that interferes with his deepest responses to Bill. The connection between Bill and Johnny is the catalyst for a second group of events, which allow Demby to examine the possibility that two people can interact with each other on a spontaneous, human level that is above societal insensitivity.

In part 3, Bill, with the intention of continuing his pursuit of a meaningful life through significant human interaction, has a picnic that brings together young black and white girls. His good intentions, however, have negative consequences: The black girls feel intimidated by the white girls, and more important, one of the white girls steals a picture of a naked human body from Bill's anatomy book and takes it to her parents, who start the rumor that Bill has molested the girls. The community rejects Bill even more strongly than before and with great pleasure spreads and magnifies rumors of what happened at the picnic. Although Johnny knows what really happened, he allows peer pressure from the gang to stop him from revealing the truth and also renounces Bill. Johnny decides that he wants to be a member of the gang more than anything else.

Edith Johnson enters the novel in part 3 and renews an old romance with David. After his encounter with Bill, which has awakened his desire to escape what he calls the "death grip" of the average human life, David is ready to leave his wife, Beetlecreek, and their pettiness. He agrees to go away with Edith to Detroit, hoping to draw from her the strength to live as a self-determined, independent person, free of society's death grip. The situation in which Demby places David by means of this relationship provides the impetus for the third major set of circumstances in the novel, circumstances that hold forth the possibility of true freedom and fresh, authentic living.

In part 4, as part of his initiation into the gang, Johnny agrees to burn down Bill's shack to punish him for molesting the girls, but when he starts the fire and is confronted by Bill, he hits Bill over the head with the gasoline can. The blow apparently seriously injures Bill or kills him, and Johnny runs away. David leaves for Detroit on the bus with Edith: The tone and atmosphere of the last chapter are suggestive of his negative future. To the tragic end of the relationship between Bill and Johnny, Demby adds the strong implication that David, too, will fail to escape the meaningless death trap that life is for most people.

The Characters

It is through the three major male characters—Bill, Johnny, and David—that Demby conveys his concern in *Beetlecreek*: the pursuit of a significant life experience. These three characters and the relationships between them form three perspectives from which to view this concern.

Bill, an orphan, has always had to struggle against his sense of being alone and outside the human community. Before coming to Beetlecreek, he tried to live a meaningful life among other people, but he became frustrated and eventually retired to the seclusion of a farm in Beetlecreek. At the time of the novel, he has lived there for fifteen years. Now an old man, his encounter with Johnny at the beginning of the novel rekindles in him a desire to pursue a significant life through relationships with others. Bill's character incorporates a broad range of qualities with which readers can identify: When inspired, he can be almost heroic, devoting energy, patience, and tolerance to others in an attempt to get them to see him for the compassionate human being that he is; on the other hand, he can be small, weak, pathetic, and ineffectual as he gropes for his identity in seclusion.

Johnny, a teenager adrift in the world, is trying to find the most significant pattern for the life ahead of him. He is perceptive enough to know that it is important to respond spontaneously and humanely to Bill; moreover, his soul instinctively revolts when he sees acts of wanton cruelty, such as those practiced by the gang members in an attempt to prove their manhood as dictated by society. Despite this revulsion, however, Johnny, like many teenagers, is highly vulnerable to peer pressure, and his desire to be accepted by the gang—to become what he calls the "new Johnny"—is so strong that he is willing to burn down Bill's shack to gain that acceptance. Johnny is adrift, with no landmarks but his own emotions. His precarious position shows how easy it is to slip from achieving true personhood, which is based on spontaneous human emotion as demonstrated in his warm response to Bill, to "achieving" a shallow, insensitive version of manhood as touted by the gang.

David, at thirty-two, knows that it is "necessary for himself to act for himself"— that is, to move beyond what other individuals or society in general prescribes for him—but this nevertheless frightens him. He has spent much time in pursuit of pleasure, as well as in the mundane activities of his life with Mary—all socially sanctioned behaviors—despite his knowledge of the importance of independence. David believes that when he first married Mary, he was, for a time—before he settled into Beetlecreek's superficial community patterns—actually beyond the clutches of life's death grip. He has the opportunity to live beyond that death grip again with Edith, yet he suspects (indeed, knows) that the same thing will happen in his relationship with Edith that happened with Mary. His challenge is to renew his struggle for meaning constantly, without falling into negative patterns. The reader can identify with David because his crisis—the crisis of maintaining meaning and relevance in one's life—is one that many people face.

Mary and Edith are less well developed than are the male characters of *Beetlecreek*; rather, they serve symbolic functions. Mary is a totally one-dimensional character. Although the narrative is related from her point of view several times in the novel, Demby never shows her as having a thought that is not selfish or narrow. Her stereotyped characterization therefore serves as a mundane standard against which the reader can judge the strivings of Bill, Johnny, and David.

Edith is somewhat less easily defined. Since Demby never narrates the novel from her point of view, as he does for the other major characters, it is difficult to tell exactly what he intends to achieve through her. At times, Edith seems to be the character who has attained the individual freedom for which David is searching; she appears to do whatever she wants and to answer to no one. On the other hand, she is limited by her lack of compassion—for the woman who adopted and reared her, for poor people, and for people in general. It is clear that she is seductive and alluring and will probably place David in another death grip after he has been with her for a while. From one perspective, she represents the extreme of the carefree life of sensual pleasure, the opposite of Mary's overly structured life. Yet, from another perspective, Edith, like Mary, represents a conventional approach to life that David needs to avoid. Her characterization, then, is almost as one-dimensional as that of Mary.

Themes and Meanings

The novel focuses on the idea that there is the ever-present challenge to make something of one's life, no matter what stage of life in which one may be—Bill's, Johnny's, or David's. This quest for meaning is one that transcends race—racial concerns and mores being factors that aid in keeping people locked in superficial interactions—and it also transcends the routine religious activities, in which Mary and the Beetlecreek community are very much involved.

Finding human connection briefly, as the three main male characters do, is important, but being trapped in a meaningless existence is inevitable, Demby suggests. One can accept the challenge to escape, as these characters do, and that attempt to escape can be courageous, humane, and heartwarming, but it is ultimately doomed to failure. The most that man can do is accept the terrible responsibility of acting for himself, although he will certainly fail. Thus, in this context, the human experience is tragic, and the tragedy is not diminished by the fact that the novel suggests an unachievable, ideal life. That ideal is an existence that is fresh, humane, independent, sensitive, spontaneous, and free—somewhere between the structured but mindless triviality of Mary and the careless, insensitive abandon of Edith.

Critical Context

Perhaps, the best way to see *Beetlecreek* is in the context of the literary "mainstreaming" which was popular among some black writers and scholars during the time that Demby wrote the novel. Black literary mainstreamers believed, in part at least, that black writing would mature when it lost its distinctive identity, as manifested in a focus on concerns that were specifically black, and merged thematically with the general body of American and world literature. In *Beetlecreek*, some readers may find that Demby is too easily and too summarily rising above racial concerns in his attempt to produce the mainstream, universal novel that depicts broadly the problems of human existence. Perhaps Ralph Ellison's *Invisible Man* (1952), another work by a black author that aims to enter the mainstream, is more successful in the manner in which it works through to the universal by concerning itself first with specifically racial themes. Yet one must remember that *Beetlecreek* preceded *Invisible Man* by two years and, at least in the context of literary history, achieved very early something that a number of black writers and intellectuals were trying to achieve.

It is also important to note that Demby's approach to his existential theme (the idea that man is cast alone into a meaningless universe in which he has to determine his own meaning) is more like the approach of Ellison, who followed him, and less like that of the French existentialist Albert Camus, for example. Camus not only assumed that man's search for meaning was doomed to failure, but he also failed to stress that the values of sensitivity and humanity were important in the search. For Demby and Ellison, the values of humanity and sensitivity are important in this quest. Demby's fiction is thus an example of one important direction that literary existentialism took in the mid-twentieth century.

Bibliography
Berry, Jay R. "The Achievement of William Demby." *College Language Association Journal* 26 (June, 1983): 434-451. Berry analyzes themes in Demby's novels.
Christensen, Peter G. "William Demby." In *Contemporary African American Novelists: A Bio-Bibliographical Critical Sourcebook*, edited by Emmanuel S. Nelson. Westport, Conn.: Greenwood Press, 1999. Christensen provides a biographical and critical assessment of Demby's works as well as a primary and secondary bibliography for further study.
Draper, James P., ed. *Black Literature Criticism*. 3 vols. Detroit: Gale Research, 1992. Includes an extensive biographical profile of Demby and excerpts from criticism on his works.
Perry, Margaret. "William Demby." In *Afro-American Fiction Writers After 1955*. Vol. 33. *Dictionary of Literary Biography*, edited by Thadious M. Davis and Trudier Harris. Chapel Hill: University of North Carolina Press, 1984. Basic biographical information, with an overview of Demby's work and a survey of criticism of his writings.

James W. Coleman

THE BELLAROSA CONNECTION

Author: Saul Bellow (1915-   )
Type of plot: Psychological realism
Time of plot: 1959 to the 1980's
Locale: Principally Jerusalem
First published: 1989

> *Principal characters:*
> SORELLA FONSTEIN, an imposing woman who is the center of the action
> HARRY FONSTEIN, Sorella's husband, the man whose life story is the source of both plot and theme
> BILLY ROSE, an impresario whom Sorella seeks out
> THE NARRATOR, the storyteller whose memories shape the meaning of the novel

The Novel

One of Saul Bellow's shorter works, *The Bellarosa Connection* tells the story of a wife's persistence in gaining an interview with impresario Billy Rose, who was responsible—through his anonymous underground railroad—for saving from the Nazis a number of Jews, Harry Fonstein among them, by bringing them to America. The narrator, a distant relative of the Fonsteins, remembers being told Harry's history.

Harry Fonstein has made his way to Italy in fleeing the Nazis, but in Rome, he is arrested and faces deportation to a concentration camp. A representative from the American impresario Billy Rose—whom the Italians called "Bellarosa"—arranges for Harry's prison door to be left open and for him to be met by a car, given false papers, and put on a ship bound for America.

In New York, Harry learns English and studies refrigeration and heating. He sails to Havana and is employed as a "legman" tracking down other Jews whose surviving relatives are looking for them. A few years later, he meets Sorella, an American girl from New Jersey. Back in America, married to Sorella, Harry works hard, studies diligently, and becomes rich.

Harry harbors a desire to meet Billy Rose, his benefactor. For years, Harry had sent Billy numerous letters, but Rose had never acknowledged them. Harry had been turned aside at Billy's office and had been snubbed by Rose in New York's famous Sardi's restaurant. Harry, though, had never given up his desire simply to thank his savior.

All this the narrator has recounted as prelude to his personal involvement with the Fonsteins. Himself now prosperous and on the eve of his retirement as head of the Philadelphia-based Mnemosyne Institute, which he has directed for forty years, the narrator meets the Fonsteins in Jerusalem, where they are vacationing. He is particularly impressed with Sorella, whom he had remembered as a huge woman whose bulk of body was matched only by her tenacity of will and the solidity of her convictions.

Over tea on the terrace of the King David Hotel, Sorella continues the story of the "Bellarosa connection."

She had decided personally to take up Harry's cause, to force Billy at least to meet the man whom he had refused even to acknowledge. To this end, she explains, she had tracked down the agent whom Billy Rose had sent to meet Harry on Ellis Island. The agent, a Mrs. Hamet, had been a frustrated actress and had probably loved Billy. She was living miserably when Sorella found her and the two struck up a kind of bond, each sympathetic to the other's needs. Old and dying, Hamet tells Sorella of a journal she has been keeping, a record of Billy's "comings and goings" and of his scandalous behavior. The journal is now in Sorella's possession, and the narrator is convinced that Sorella intends to use it in some way.

A few days later, Billy Rose arrives in Jerusalem to donate a sculpture garden. The narrator now realizes that Sorella intends to confront Billy and to blackmail him with the journal. This confrontation, the central scene in the book, takes place in Billy's suite in the hotel. In spite of Billy's crudeness and his attempts to disavow any relationship with Harry, Sorella successfully intimidates him into believing that she will expose Billy's excesses to the press unless he acknowledges Harry. Billy becomes irate, mean, insulting, and dehumanizing. At this point, Sorella flings the journal at Rose and leaves.

The narrator does not see the Fonsteins again. Thirty years later, alone in his Philadelphia mansion, beset by loneliness and bad dreams, he receives a telephone request from a rabbi seeking information about the Fonsteins for a man claiming to be a relative. The narrator makes a phone call or two and learns that the Fonsteins' only son has become a failed gambler in Las Vegas. The Fonsteins themselves are dead, killed in an automobile accident. He has recorded their story as a kind of memorial.

The Characters

Sorella Fonstein, the central figure in the novel, is a woman of great intelligence. Her bulk and her plainness serve, to the narrator, as physical emblems of her inner strength and dignity. Unlike some other women portrayed in Bellow's novels, Sorella is a "tiger wife" of admirable force and humanity. She does not subdue Harry with the force of her character but acts as his liberator, one who understands his need for respect beyond the middle-class values of success. She has impressed the narrator with her persistence and her wit. She takes on the role of the Furies to Billy Rose's conscience, forcing him to acknowledge what his personal crudity and selfishness seek to conceal. Like the Furies of ancient Greek myth, Sorella is unbending, inexorable. There is nothing of self-consciousness, nothing of personal vanity in her campaign. It is deliberate, direct, and natural, like a life force.

Though his is the story that forms the central focus of the book, Harry Fonstein is, ironically, not the central character nor even a minor one. Though his rags-to-riches narrative is summarized early in the novel, Harry himself is a pointedly shadowy figure, existing on the periphery of the action. He has little dialogue, no movement, no real physical presence. Harry is, in fact, an abiding presence as a concept, a point of reference from which Sorella and the narrator develop their own courses of action.

Billy Rose, the half-real, half-fictional "villain" of the piece, is the most puzzling of the group. His crudity, selfishness, and hypocrisy, his blatant egotism, and his human cruelty are highlighted all the more by his one seemingly genuine act of altruism, the underground railroad. Billy seems threatened by his connection with Harry. He shows no pity, no admiration, no feelings of any kind. As a showman, Rose is more concerned with his public image than his private life; his disavowal of his "connection" is his way of sealing the crack in his public image, a crack through which his emotional, moral life might reveal itself.

After Sorella, the narrator is the most compelling character. A case may be made, in fact, that he is the central figure, since the events and their meaning are filtered through his observations and his memory. The narrator is both historian and judge. As he recalls the story, he admires Sorella and damns Billy Rose as he fully understands the real meaning of the connection. Additionally, he understands his own connection: He is the means through which the Fonstein-Rose story lives on, and the meaning of the story reverberates through his memory to the world at large.

Themes and Meanings

For the narrator, as for the reader, the meaning of the Fonstein-Billy Rose story—the real "Bellarosa connection"—is not just the need for the recognition of one man's responsibility to another but the human need to recognize the value, the importance, the overarching supremacy of moral kinship. What, indeed, Sorella is seeking, what Billy Rose attempts to conceal, what the narrator ultimately comprehends, is that all the participants in life's drama are connected by chains forged of the spirit and the mind. Billy's act of secret generosity has liberated Harry from physical death but has, ironically, snared Billy himself in a kind of spiritual bondage by which Billy has become connected to Harry the Jew and Harry the human being. The private Billy Rose has come into conflict with the public persona. Billy has become his brother's keeper and must recognize his kinship and his responsibility.

The narrative structure is more supple than it first appears. Though the action is related second-hand, as it were, events and conversations spanning thirty years are seen through the narrator's memory and clarified by his insights. The narrator's own working motto is "memory is life"; his position as president of a memory institute in Philadelphia (the city of brotherly love) gives him credibility as a judge and validates his observations that "God doesn't forget" and that human beings must not forget their vital connections with one another.

Finally, a lesser theme emerges near the conclusion, when the narrator learns that the Fonsteins' son has become a Las Vegas gambler. Whereas the Fonstein-Rose story gained significance in the holy city of Jerusalem, the direct descendent of the Fonsteins, son Gilbert (not a "Jewish" name) has taken his place in America's most secular city. Las Vegas has become the new Jerusalem. The question implied by the narrator is whether the new generation of Jews, American-bred, will survive with its values intact or if it will go the way of Gilbert Fonstein—or, perhaps, of Billy Rose.

Critical Context

The Bellarosa Connection can serve as a good introduction to Bellow's works. Despite its brevity, the book treats major themes of human compassion and kinship that have engaged Bellow during his long career as a writer. The characters, though not as fully drawn as in earlier, more ambitious novels, are suggestive of the fine portrayals of heroes and villains that fill Bellow's books. Billy Rose, for example, is a kind of antithesis to Tommy Wilhelm in *Seize the Day* (1956), fleeing the demands of humanity that Tommy is seeking to validate. He is also in the tradition of such Bellovian villains as Dr. Adler in *Seize the Day* and the fast-talking con-man Einhorn in *The Adventures of Augie March* (1953), unfeeling men who never come into contact with their humanity.

Bibliography

Bach, Gerald, ed. *The Critical Responses to Saul Bellow.* Westport, Conn.: Greenwood Press, 1995. A collection of critical essays on Bellow's career from the 1940's to the 1990's. Includes essays on *The Bellarosa Connection*, a chronology of Bellow's life, and a bibliography.

Braham, Jeanne. *A Sort of Columbus.* Athens: University of Georgia Press, 1984. Examines Bellow's novels as centering on the theme of discovery. The central characters seek to understand their spiritual conflict within an American context. Bellow's works thus sit squarely in the American literary tradition; his heroes pursue a personal vision tempered by, yet transcending, the American experience.

Clayton, John J. *Saul Bellow: In Defense of Man.* 2d ed. Bloomington: Indiana University Press, 1979. Traces the affirmation implicit in Bellow's work. Examines Bellow's characters as alienated and paranoid, yet acting in such a way as to reject alienation and to affirm the brotherhood of man. Clayton insists that Bellow is a psychological novelist first and a moral spokesman second.

Cronin, Gloria, and Ben Seigel, eds. *Conversations with Saul Bellow.* Jackson: University of Mississippi Press, 1994. A collection of interviews with Bellow from 1953 to 1992 in which the novelist reflects on the craft of writing, his approaches to fiction, and his times.

Newman, Judie. *Saul Bellow and History.* New York: St. Martin's Press, 1984. An interesting study, concentrating on the five "major" novels from *The Adventures of Augie March* (1953) to *Humboldt's Gift* (1975). Provides an introduction summarizing critical opinions on Bellow's religious and psychological views of life. Newman's thesis is that Bellow is a novelist concerned with the effect of history and specific time on the actions of the protagonist.

Pifer, Ellen. *Saul Bellow Against the Grain.* Philadelphia: University of Pennsylvania Press, 1990. Argues that each of Bellow's heroes is in conflict with himself. The conflict between reason and religion ends with the hero's affirmation of a metaphysical or intuitive truth. Bellow's novels thus "go against the grain" of traditional realism and are radical in their "questioning of accepted notions of reality."

Trachtenberg, Stanley, comp. *Critical Essays on Saul Bellow.* Boston: G. K. Hall,

1979. A compendium of the most significant critical essays about Bellow and his work. Beginning with the novels of the 1940's and 1950's, the reviews and articles discuss Bellow's heroes as seekers and doubters and treat some of the author's main themes. The article on Herzog as a latter-day Odysseus is particularly insightful.

Wasserman, Harriet. *Handsome Is: Adventures with Saul Bellow—A Memoir.* New York: Fromm, 1997. An illuminating memoir by Bellow's former literary agent. Wasserman gives insights into Bellow's personal and literary life and his approaches to writing.

Edward A. Fiorelli

BEND SINISTER

Author: Vladimir Nabokov (1899-1977)
Type of plot: Surrealistic tragicomedy
Time of plot: Sometime during the first half of the twentieth century
Locale: An unnamed European country where the people speak a language that
  blends Slavic and Germanic elements
First published: 1947

> *Principal characters:*
>> ADAM KRUG, the protagonist, an internationally known philosopher
>> DAVID KRUG, his young son
>> PADUK, the leader of the Party of the Average Man, which is in control
>>   of the government

The Novel

Bend Sinister is the story of a philosopher who tries to keep himself remote from the politics of his country by reasoning that he is too well-known a figure to be hurt. He watches his friends disappear and seems to have little concern for what happens to them. Finally, government forces remove Krug and his son from their apartment and separate father and son. Only now does Krug realize that he will do or say anything to save his son. Unfortunately, the son is mistakenly, pointlessly killed, and Krug takes refuge in madness to remove himself from a world become absurd.

A simple summary of the plot of the novel, however, misses most of its thematic and structural complexities and its creation of a surreal, fictional realm where cosmic tragedy and comedy mesh (Vladimir Nabokov once said that the trouble with the "cosmic" was that it was always threatening to lose its "s") and where protagonist and narrator/author are reflections of each other in a drama in which the terror of dreams intertwines with nightmarish reality.

The novel begins and ends with images reflected in a rain puddle situated in the middle of an asphalt road. Krug sees the puddle first at the beginning of the novel as he looks into the street from the window of a hospital, where his wife has just died unexpectedly. The narrator/author sees the same puddle at the end of the novel as he wonders whether people leave an imprint in the texture of space similar to the imprint made by the depression in the ground that is filled with rainwater. Nabokov himself, in a 1963 introduction to the novel, points out how the puddle reappears in various guises throughout the book. The puddle becomes an ink blot in chapter 4, an ink stain in chapter 5, spilled milk in chapter 11, a ciliated thought in chapter 12, and a footprint in chapter 18.

Such recurring images are representative of the many rhetorical devices that Nabokov uses in the course of the novel to provide the intricate patterning and stylistic play with words that are the basis of his style and the essence of his perennial theme—that it is not reality that matters but what one makes of it. The emphasis on artifice with its concomitant factors—imagination and memory—provides the rationale for Nabokov's characteristic use of point of view, which allows an omniscient author to show himself through certain tears in the narrative fabric in ways peculiar to Nabokov's fiction.

In *Bend Sinister*, an omniscient narrator begins to reveal his presence in the first chapter, where a reader must wonder about the identity of the "I" who reports what is seen and felt. Soon the "I" becomes a character whose wife has died, changing brightly dappled surfaces into dull, liquid-white traversed by dead-black and then becoming inky black. In chapter 2, the first person changes to the third person, and the "I" becomes Krug, but a Krug with a shadow-double—the throbbing one and the one who looked on, "the last stronghold of the dualism he abhorred," Krug thinks. "The square root of I is I." In every mask that he tries on, Krug believes, there are slits for his shadow's eyes. In chapter 5, an omniscient narrator separates himself from Krug again and appears as "a nameless, mysterious genius," author of a "dream-code" which permeates the entire novel.

The dreamlike experience on the bridge, where Krug finds himself doomed, he believes, to walk back and forth with neither bank attainable, is a microcosm encapsulating every event of the novel, each of which is a replay of the first. References to stage plays and motion pictures intertwine with Krug's dreams to provide a network of images at the interstices of which creator and created are revealed as one. Thus it comes as no surprise to a reader when the author/narrator emerges at last in his own person to remove Krug from the action the instant before he is to be killed; thus, the artist dismantles the props that he has created.

The Characters

Adam Krug is a supreme individualist. The name "Adam" suggests the archetypal individuation that occurred in the Garden of Eden with the naming of the first humans. "Krug" is Russian for "circle," suggesting a whole, a unity that circles back upon itself. Yet with Krug's wife, Olga, dead, the Garden is under attack; evil has entered and must be confronted. This Krug refuses to do, believing that he cannot be hurt by anyone in government, feeling arrogantly secure in his international reputation. The nether side of Krug, his mirror image ("bend sinister" is a term from heraldry, denoting a diagonal band that divides a shield from upper left to lower right), is Gurk, "Krug" spelled backward. Gurk is an Ekwilist soldier who wants his share of the brutalizing fun. Yet Gurk and all the soldiers, like all the citizens of Padukgrad, are, Nabokov says, merely anagrams of everybody else. Thus, the leader Paduk is simply a slightly brighter Gurk and, at the same time, the inverse side of Krug, the brutalizing side, the selfish side. In their youth, Krug had tormented Paduk. "I was something of a bully," Krug says, "and I used to trip him up and sit upon his face . . . every blessed day for about five school years."

As a philosopher, Krug works with words, attempting to come to rational conclusions about the nature of the universe, but, although he has been successful in demolishing the theories of other philosophers, he has not posited one of his own. In the end, he is unable to comprehend the stupidly excessive and senselessly brutal behavior of the Ekwilists. Madness is an appropriate response to the all too literal nightmare of history. Madness allows escape from the prison of space and time.

Paduk, known to Krug as "Toad," is pictured, like all of Nabokov's tyrants, as stupid, coarse, brutal, unhealthy, sadistic, grotesque, and mechanical. Within the Party of the Average Man, all Ekwilists, as replicas of one another, are the lowest common denominator of human potential. The concluding scenes, in which Ekwilists foolishly kill the wrong child and then show Krug motion pictures of what happens to captured children, are an absurd foreshadowing of the grotesque "shoot 'em up" conclusion, which seems a nightmarish replay of the obligatory showdown in Westerns and crime and spy films, raised to preposterous and bizarre proportions.

Krug's son David plays a small role in the novel. He is an object of love, as his mother was, and he is a throwaway in the society, the tick of a clock already moved ahead, as Olga is, present only in memory, and then only as long as Krug is rational and lives (or *Bend Sinister* stays in print).

Themes and Meanings

Nabokov's basic theme in everything that he writes is human imprisonment in space and time where there is infinite foretime before birth and infinite aftertime, one would assume, after death. Krug cannot make up his mind with regard to death. Intelligence will not "accept the transformation of physical discontinuity into the permanent continuity of a nonphysical element . . . nor can it accept the inanity of accumulating treasures of thought" and sensation to lose them all at once in black "nausea followed by infinite nothingness."

John Shade, the poet in Nabokov's novel *Pale Fire* (1962), makes precisely the same point:

> And I'll turn down eternity unless
> The melancholy and the tenderness
> Of mortal life; the passion and the pain;
>
> Are formed in Heaven by the newly dead.

The only redemption from the horror of mortal existence is the metaphoric, thematic, and structural harmony of art. Art is a repository of the joy of existence expressed by Nabokov in his loving presentation of minute detail, his passionate concern for pattern, and his delight in style. Thus, at the end of *Bend Sinister*, the author/narrator removes Krug from the action, commenting that his death is "but a question of style."

Critical Context

Bend Sinister was Nabokov's second novel written in English, the first being *The Real Life of Sebastian Knight* (1941). Before publishing books in the English language, Nabokov published ten others in his native Russian. It was not until the publication of his best-selling *Lolita* (1955), however, that Nabokov began to receive worldwide attention and acclaim as one of the most important literary figures of the century. Major novels following *Lolita* are *Pnin* (1957), *Pale Fire*, and *Ada or Ardor: A Family Chronicle* (1969). Besides novels, Nabokov published short stories, poems, essays, memoirs, and critical works.

Often called the last of the great modernists, the peer of such masters as Marcel Proust, James Joyce, and William Faulkner, Nabokov has just as often been hailed as one of the pioneers of metafiction, the father of such postmodernists as John Fowles, Robert Coover, Donald Barthelme, and Gabriel García Márquez. Nabokov's work has been the subject of numerous books and articles, which have been increasing in number steadily since his death.

Bibliography

Appel, Alfred, Jr., and Charles Newman, eds. *Nabokov: Criticism, Reminiscences, Translations, Tributes*. Evanston, Ill.: Northwestern University Press, 1970. A good introduction to Nabokov's writing, including a varied sampling of material about the man, about the writer, and about his several unique works. Perhaps a hodgepodge, but an early collection that contrasts dramatically with later criticism, which suggested that Nabokov was a humanist if also a kind of verbal magician.

Bloom, Harold, ed. *Vladimir Nabokov*. New York: Chelsea House, 1987. Essays on Nabokov's handling of time, illusion and reality, and art. There are separate essays on each of his major novels, as well as an introduction, chronology, and bibliography.

Boyd, Brian. *Vladimir Nabokov: The Russian Years*. Princeton, N.J.: Princeton University Press, 1990. The first volume of the definitive biography, fully researched and written with the cooperation of Nabokov's family. Boyd has an extraordinary command of the origins of Nabokov's art. This volume includes a discussion of Nabokov's years in Europe after he left Russia.

_____. *Vladimir Nabokov: The American Years*. Princeton, N.J.: Princeton University Press, 1991. Boyd concludes his masterful biography. As with volume 1, his work is copiously illustrated with detailed notes and an invaluable index.

Field, Andrew. *Nabokov, His Life in Part*. New York: Viking Press, 1977. An intimate portrait written by an author who was often very close to Nabokov during the latter part of Nabokov's life. The book may also suggest to would-be biographers some of the difficulties of writing a biography while enjoying an intimate relationship with the subject. Follows Field's critical work, *Nabokov, His Life in Art: A Critical Narrative* (Boston: Little, Brown, 1967).

_____. *VN: The Life and Art of Vladimir Nabokov*. New York: Crown, 1986. Not as definitive as Boyd, but still a very important biographical/critical study of Nabokov. Field has been called the "father of Nabokovian studies." Includes illustrations, detailed notes, and index. The best one-volume biography of Nabokov.

Foster, John Burt. *Nabokov's Art of Memory and European Modernism*. Princeton, N.J.: Princeton University Press, 1993. Burt divides his study into three parts:

Nabokov's early years in Russia, his period in Europe, and his prolonged period in America. This is a more specialized study for advanced students.

Pifer, Ellen. *Nabokov and the Novel*. Cambridge, Mass.: Harvard University Press, 1980. Uses as an epigraph Flannery O'Connor's "All novelists are fundamentally seekers and describers of the real, but the realism of each novelist will depend on his view of the ultimate reaches of reality" to develop a critical dialogue about Nabokov's technique, not surprisingly including realism. Ends in a discussion on Nabokov's humanism. Robert Alter called this book "poised and precise," and it is excellent for serious, critical readers of Nabokov.

Mary Rohrberger

BETRAYED BY RITA HAYWORTH

Author: Manuel Puig (1932-1990)
Type of plot: Bildungsroman
Time of plot: 1933-1948
Locale: Vallejos, a provincial town in Argentina
First published: La traición de Rita Hayworth, 1968 (English translation, 1971)

Principal characters:
> JOSÉ (TOTO) CASALS, the central character of the novel, which follows
>   him from infancy to adolescence
> MITA, his mother, educated as a pharmacist but devoting her life
>   primarily to her family
> BERTO, his father, a businessman
> HÉCTOR, Berto's nephew, several years older than Toto; he lives with
>   his uncle's family
> PAQUITA, a promiscuous young girl of Vallejos
> COBITO, a schoolmate of Toto, rough and vulgar
> ESTHER, a schoolmate of Toto, infatuated with Héctor

The Novel

Although *Betrayed by Rita Hayworth* does not resemble a traditional novel in form, its subject matter is highly conventional: the maturation and education of a sensitive young man. Because this is Puig's first novel, and because he shares the birth date of his protagonist, most readers suspect that *Betrayed by Rita Hayworth* is autobiographical to some degree. The novel reveals the world of young José Casals, nicknamed Toto, by exploring not only his fantasies and daydreams but also those of his parents, aunts, cousins, schoolmates, and teachers. Through this sometimes indirect method, the reader absorbs the multitude of influences that shape Toto's life. At the same time, Puig delineates the spectrum of provincial life in Argentina, providing insight into such facets of that culture as the meaning of machismo, the importance attached to education, and the pervasive influence of romantic fiction and Hollywood films.

Most of the novel's sixteen chapters are internal monologues of the major and minor characters. A few chapters are made up of dialogues (consisting mostly of revealing gossip) between female characters; the novel also includes excerpts from diaries, two letters, and a school essay by Toto on the topic, "The Movie I Liked Best."

A minimal plot emerges from this collage of material, although it may be difficult to discern on a first reading. Toto's mother, Mita, marries Berto even though he has less education than she, because he resembles a film star. As a consequence of the marriage, she leaves her large family in a busy town and moves to sleepy Vallejos. During the early years of her marriage she works, to Berto's discomfort, but increasingly becomes absorbed in her children and in going to films. Instead of bedtime stories, she recites to Toto the plots of films such as *Romeo and Juliet* and *The Great*

Ziegfield. As soon as he is old enough, Toto also becomes a cinema buff, especially enjoying those with beautiful female stars such as Rita Hayworth. The first half of the novel revolves around the female characters who make up Mita and Toto's world.

As Toto gets older, he naturally grows curious about sex and is given many opportunities to hear about its mysteries from his older playmates and cousins. A neighborhood girl, Paquita, teases him with salacious stories. One of his teachers, helping him to draw a model of the digestive and reproductive systems, explains the biological processes to the confused nine-year-old. Even at this early stage of his life, Toto is perceived by others as small for his age and effeminate. He prefers to play with girls, does not like sports, and spends much time with his mother. Eventually, Toto is sent away to school where, as revealed by the sexually knowledgeable Héctor and the rough Cobito, he becomes the target of sadistic older boys. The savage voices of Héctor and Cobito provide a marked contrast to the predominantly female voices of the earlier chapters.

When the novel ends, Toto is still only fifteen years old, and thus no final word can be said about his development either sexually or socially. He remains immersed in the world of books, film, and music, and like a typical sensitive adolescent has begun to be scornful of the lowbrow tastes of others and of the pieties of religion. Almost the last word, however, is given to Toto's music teacher, who writes in her commonplace book that "Toto reminds me more and more of that unfriendly homosexual."

The final chapter of the novel consists of a letter written by Berto to his brother shortly after Toto's birth. This is the only chapter that is not placed in chronological sequence, and it poignantly reveals an unexpectedly tender side of Berto. Particularly emphasized is his love for his son, and his hope to educate him to a proud place in society. Berto, like many of the other characters, has been in some fashion betrayed, not by Rita Hayworth, as the novel's title suggests, but by the gap between his dreams and reality. He had hoped to get a good education; instead, he left school at fifteen to work for his brother.

Berto's disillusionment, as revealed in his letter, is typical of the loss of innocence exhibited in many of the chapters in the second half of the book. In this generally depressing litany, the one note of romantic hope is suggested by Toto's essay on "The Movie I Liked Best." Toto's favorite film appears to be a version of *The Great Waltz*, the life of Johann Strauss. Toto's retelling emphasizes not only Strauss's musical genius, but also his passionate love affair with a brilliant soprano. Although the love affair ends sadly, the film goes on to detail Strauss's ultimate triumph as an artist, ending in a scene in which the emperor leads him onto a balcony before the cheering crowds of Vienna. Near death now, Strauss has a vision of his lost beloved, and he is torn between the agony of dying without real knowledge of love's meaning and the ecstasy of remembering his beloved's beauty. Thus ends Toto's version of the film. In its extreme romanticism and emphasis on exquisite variations of feeling, Toto's favorite film provides a strong counterpoint to the brutality and discouragement glimpsed elsewhere in the novel.

The Characters

The process of characterization is central to *Betrayed by Rita Hayworth*. Each of the main characters (and some of the minor ones) is allotted his or her own chapter (Toto is given three, counting his essay on the films) and also is more fully presented through the eyes of the others. For example, Héctor is mentioned frequently by Mita, Toto, and others, creating an image for the reader which then must be tested against Héctor's own monologue in the ninth chapter. His rampant sexuality is later ironically contrasted to Esther's perception of him in chapter 12. Esther, a scholarship student at the school Héctor and Toto attend, writes her diary in a style imitated from romantic magazines and imagines Héctor to be the kind of "gentlemanly" date she has long desired. Interestingly, it is Toto who perceives Esther's danger and calls off the rendezvous he had been helping to arrange. Esther resigns herself to her loss and goes back to dreams of helping humankind through a career in medicine.

In the stories of most of the characters certain emphases recur; in particular, each character meditates on sexuality, and most of them reveal, directly or indirectly, how their education has affected their lives. These traits are equally true in men and women, although Puig certainly presents men, particularly Héctor and Cobito, as more voracious, predatory, and impulsive with regard to sex. Even Paquita, presented earlier in the novel as promiscuous, is revealed in her monologue in chapter 10 as surprisingly cultured, reading, for example, Victor Hugo's *Les Misérables*. By the end of the novel, the reader learns that she is about to marry a good man and receive her certification as a teacher.

Although men and women in this novel can be seen to share the same concerns, there can be no doubt that Puig perceives a great deal of difference in the way the two sexes react to cultural pressures about education and sexuality. The women, more inclined to romantic fantasies, nevertheless consistently finish school and have a chance at careers with intellectual aspirations. The men, more caught up by economic concerns, find themselves out of school at an early age, perhaps, like Berto, looking back regretfully at lost opportunities. In this regard it appears that Toto is, again, more like a woman, holding on to romantic ideals and yet continuing to develop intellectually.

Themes and Meanings

In *Betrayed by Rita Hayworth*, the method is part of the meaning. By presenting each of his characters from such a variety of perspectives, Puig underscores the complexity of human personality, both in its development and in the effort to understand any individual. Part of this complexity, he asserts, is the struggle between the raw impulses and factors which bring man down and those which can uplift. Puig shows suffering in the form of illness, death of loved ones, economic hardship, and spiritual poverty and suggests redemption through art, intellectual sensitivity, and meaningful work. The triumph of good over evil is by no means clear as the novel ends, however, even for Toto, who still has many years to develop before his fate will be certain.

Critical Context

Puig's first novel, *Betrayed by Rita Hayworth*, established themes that would be evident in later works including *Boquitas pintadas* (1969; *Heartbreak Tango: A Serial*, 1973) and *El beso de la mujer araña* (1976; *Kiss of the Spider Woman*, 1979): the rough-and-tumble world of political and economic survival versus the sensuous dream of art, often symbolized in lushly filmed Hollywood motion pictures. In his exploration of these themes, as well as his experimentation with the form of the novel, Puig is working in concert with other important Latin American writers such as Gabriel García Márquez, Julio Cortázar, and Mario Vargas Llosa. Puig also repeatedly explores the traditional social understanding of sexuality, with a particular interest in the development of the homosexual personality. In *Betrayed by Rita Hayworth*, he indirectly explores this theme through the composite portrait of the somewhat effeminate Toto. In *Kiss of the Spider Woman* the subject of homosexuality is directly addressed through a series of scholarly footnotes.

Betrayed by Rita Hayworth also shows the beginnings of Puig's characteristic experimentation with the use of dialogue as a replacement for conventional narration. The opening chapter consists of a conversation between a group of women at Mita's parents' house; another chapter consists entirely of the conversation of two maids; still another shows the reader one side of a telephone call. Always the speaker must be determined from context; no explicit attributions are given. Puig's use of this stylistic device increases in his later fiction and indicates his desire to reduce authorial intrusion: in other words, to permit the characters to speak for themselves, and to make the reader work to reconstruct the world of the characters.

Bibliography

Bacarisse, Pamela. *The Necessary Dream: A Study of the Novels of Manuel Puig.* Totowa, N.J.: Barnes & Noble, 1988. Chapters on the major novels. The introduction provides a useful overview of Puig's career and themes. Includes notes and bibliography.

Kerr, Lucille. *Suspended Fictions: Reading Novels by Manuel Puig.* Urbana: University of Illinois Press, 1987. Chapters on each of Puig's major novels, exploring the themes of tradition, romance, popular culture, crime, sex, and the design of Puig's career. Contains detailed notes but no bibliography.

Lavers, Norman. *Pop Culture into Art: The Novels of Manuel Puig.* Columbia: University of Missouri Press, 1988. Lavers finds a close relationship between Puig's life and his literary themes. Biography, in this case, helps to explain the author's methods and themes.

Magnarelli, Sharon. *The Lost Rib: Female Characters in the Spanish-American Novel.* Toronto: Associate University Presses, 1985. In "Betrayed by the Cross-Stitch," Magnarelli provides a close reading and feminist analysis of *Betrayed by Rita Hayworth*.

Tittler, Jonathan. *Manuel Puig.* New York: Twayne, 1993. The best introduction to Puig. In addition to providing useful survey of Puig's career in his introduction,

Tittler devotes separate chapters to the novels. Chapter seven discusses Puig's theatrical scripts, screenplays, and short stories. Includes detailed notes and an annotated bibliography.

Wheaton, Kathleen. "The Art of Fiction: Manuel Puig." *The Paris Review* 31 (Winter, 1989): 129-147. An intensive exploration of Puig's themes and techniques.

Diane M. Ross

THE BEULAH QUINTET

Author: Mary Lee Settle (1918-   )

Type of plot: Historical realism

Time of plot: Prisons, 1634-1649; *O Beulah Land,* 1754-1774; *Know Nothing,* 1837-1861; *The Scapegoat,* June 7, 1912; *The Killing Ground,* 1978-1980

Locale: England, Virginia, and the western frontier of Virginia, later the state of West Virginia

First published: Prisons, 1973; *O Beulah Land,* 1956; *Know Nothing,* 1960; *The Scapegoat,* 1980; *The Killing Ground,* 1982

Principal characters:

Prisons

JONATHAN CHURCH, the protagonist, a young volunteer in the Parliament army

THANKFUL PERKINS, a friend and fellow soldier of Jonathan

GIDEON MacKARKLE, an old soldier and a friend of Jonathan

NELL COCKBURN LACY, the aunt of Jonathan and wife of Sir Valentine Lacy

OLIVER CROMWELL, the shrewd, ambitious leader of the Parliament forces

O Beulah Land

HANNAH BRIDEWELL, a transported felon and escaped Indian captive

JEREMIAH CATLETT, a solitary squatter in western Virginia

"SQUIRE" JOSIAH DEVOTION RAGLAN, Hannah's fellow prisoner in England, who is transported and bought by a young dandy, Peregrine Cockburn

JONATHAN LACEY, a Provincial captain and planter

SALLY LACEY, his young and frivolous wife

JARCEY PENTACOST, a Virginia printer

EZEKIEL CATLETT, the son of Hannah and Jeremiah Catlett

SARA LACEY, the strong-willed daughter of Jonathan and Sally Lacey

Know Nothing

JOHNNY CATLETT, the protagonist, the son of Peregrine Lacey Catlett and Leah Catlett

PEREGRINE LACEY CATLETT, a wealthy slave owner

LEAH CATLETT, Peregrine's Methodist-reared wife

LEWIS CATLETT, Johnny's cruel, obsessive brother

MELINDA LACEY, Johnny's penniless orphan cousin

BRANDON LACEY, a wealthy cousin of the Catletts, who finds himself land-poor and desperate for cash

SALLY LACEY, Brandon Lacey's "frail" wife

SARA LACEY, the pampered but tenderhearted daughter of Brandon and
    Sally Lacey

ANNIE BRANDON, the cousin of Peregrine Lacey Catlett who lives with
    the Catletts, embittered because she had hoped to marry Peregrine

BIG DAN O'NEILL, a "Black Irish" laborer

The Scapegoat

LILY ELLEN LACEY, the protagonist, an idealistic college student, the
    daughter of Beverley and Ann Eldridge Lacey

BEVERLEY LACEY, a well-meaning but weak mine owner

ANN ELDRIDGE LACEY, the wife of Beverley Lacey

MARY ROSE LACEY, Lily's youngest sister

ANN ALTHEA LACEY, Lily's boy-crazy sister

JAKE CATLETT, the head of a union local but also a friend of Beverley
    Lacey

CAPTAIN DANIEL CHESTER NEILL, a mine detective who loves violence

ANNUNZIATA PAGANO, an Italian matriarch

EDUARDO (EDDIE) PAGANO, the son of Annunziata and a friend of Lily

CARLO MICHELE, a new immigrant, the "scapegoat" of the title

NEVILLE ROUNDTREE, an English employee of the mine owners

The Killing Ground

HANNAH MCKARKLE, the protagonist, a middle-aged writer

JOHNNY MCKARKLE, the brother of Hannah, who was killed in jail

KITTY PUSS BASEHEART, formerly a mistress of Johnny McKarkle

CHARLIE BLAND, a womanizer and model for Johnny

THELMA LEFTWICH, a spinster devoted to Johnny McKarkle

ANN ALTHEA LACEY NIELL, Hannah McKarkle's aunt and the widow
    of Daniel Chester Neill of *The Scapegoat*

JAKE CATLETT, Johnny's killer, the youngest son of Jake Catlett of *The
    Scapegoat*

The Beulah Quintet has had a complicated genesis. At first, Mary Lee Settle projected a trilogy set in what is now West Virginia. She published the eighteenth century
story *O Beulah Land* in 1956, followed in 1960 by a novel taking descendants of the
characters in the earlier work up to the Civil War. After *Know Nothing* came a contemporary novel entitled *Fight Night on a Sweet Saturday* (1964). Settle was not happy
with the published version of the third novel, however, and furthermore, she wished to
take her story back another century in time, as well as across the Atlantic to England,
in order to set up the themes that pervaded the trilogy already written. The result was
Prisons (1973), whose very title emphasizes the dichotomy between freedom and
captivity, which had been important throughout the Beulah novels written earlier. In

1980, Settle published *The Scapegoat*, which is set immediately before World War I and which, because it involves the battle between landless workers and the owners of land which is being mined, nicely bridges the gap between the three earlier works, with their emphasis on land as a source of wealth, and *Fight Night on a Sweet Saturday*, a contemporary novel of business and industrial wealth, rewritten and published in 1982 with a new title, *The Killing Ground*. With this final novel, the Beulah Quintet was complete. The four later books in the series are all set in the same area, and all five of the novels shared the same family and Christian names, in varying conjunctions; the same character traits, appearing in men and in women; the same conflicts; and the same themes, embodied in the changing face of history.

The Novels

The first novel of the quintet, *Prisons*, is set in mid-seventeenth century England. From babyhood, Jonathan Church has been torn between his loyalty to his mother's dour Puritanism and the appealing warmth of his young aunt, Nell Cockburn Lacy, who presides over a Royalist festival atmosphere at Lacy House. Jonathan's mother has married a self-made man who has no love for the aristocracy; her younger sister, Jonathan's aunt, married Sir Valentine Lacy, who does not question the right of his kind to govern an unchanging England. When Jonathan is sixteen, he discovers that his father can be heartless. He self-righteously judges and defies his father and leaves his home. Taking refuge at Lacy House, he encounters Nell, who is weeping over her elderly, dying husband. Her grief for Sir Valentine, her pity for young Jonathan, and the love she and her nephew have always felt for each other combine in some unforgettable hours, which result in Jonathan's only descendant, a supposed son of Sir Valentine.

The narrative begins as a confession at the point of death by Jonathan, now twenty, and the main story line traces his disillusionment as he learns that the Parliament forces, ostensibly fighting for freedom, are themselves as repressive as the Royalists and that the ambitious men who rule them are not only as tyrannical as the king's men but hypocritical as well, mouthing prayers as they use and discard, sacrifice and execute the ordinary men who follow them in fear or in hope. To break the democratic spirit which the ordinary soldiers have developed, Oliver Cromwell, the leader of the Parliament forces, and his subordinates resolve to execute a number of ringleaders, Jonathan among them. Because of Jonathan's youth and his substantial family, however, Cromwell is willing to spare the boy if he will agree to influence the troops as the leaders wish. Jonathan cannot desert his friends or his principles. He and his friend Thankful Perkins are among the young men with dreams who are murdered by the old men who have only ambitions.

Like *Prisons*, *O Beulah Land* places its characters in the midst of violent conflict—in this case, the French and Indian War and the continuing Indian resistance against the settlers. In the prologue, Hannah Bridewell, a transported thief and prostitute, survives capture by the Indians and a long period in the wilderness, to appear at last at the cabin of the squatter Jeremiah Catlett, who saves her life and eventually marries her in the informal manner of a frontier to which the law and the church have not yet come.

Moving backward in time, the novel follows Hannah and "Squire" Josiah Devotion Raglan from crime and prison in England to what amounts to sale in Virginia, a colony ruled by wealthy planters such as Jonathan Lacey, who leaves his young wife, Sally, to march toward Fort Duquesne with his own Provincial forces and with the British regulars. Hannah and Squire Raglan accompany their new masters on this venture, and the Squire's theft of a tomahawk, along with the arrogant bad manners of the English commander, so anger the Indians that an ambush and a massacre result. After her captivity, Hannah escapes, as the prologue revealed. The Squire's final act of rascality, some years later, results in his quite justifiable murder by Jeremiah Catlett.

Jonathan Lacey and his spoiled young wife Sally venture west, along with Jarcey Pentacost, a printer whose passion for freedom has cost him his shop. Sally refuses to adjust to frontier life, treating her neighbors with contempt, and Jonathan begins to regard her as a stranger instead of the friend and wife for whom he had wished. Finally, a rough frontier prank at the wedding of the gently reared daughter of Jonathan and Sally, Sara Lacey, results in Sally's madness. At the end of the novel, however, Sara evidences not only great love for her husband, Ezekiel, the son of the lower-class Catletts, but also great courage. Unlike her mother, she is worthy of Beulah Land.

Like *O Beulah Land*, *Know Nothing* traces the social and financial histories of various family units in a society still in flux—in this case, torn by differences on the issue of slavery as well as by differences between the values of the frontier in western Virginia and the values of the settled East. To prosperous Peregrine Lacey Catlett come Brandon and Sally Lacey, who are rich in land and slaves but unable to meet their obligations. When Brandon takes the gentleman's way out, Sally becomes a permanent fixture, glorying in her heredity. Other women who need the social status only a man can provide must compromise. Bitter Annie Brandon sleeps with Big Dan O'Neill, becomes pregnant, marries him, and spends years attempting to civilize him. Melinda Lacey, rejected as a wife for Peregrine's son, Johnny Catlett, by Johnny's mother, Leah Catlett, marries a wealthy man but finds life without Johnny so unhappy that she wills her own death. Without her, Johnny takes a slave girl and unwittingly causes the death of the girl's husband, Johnny's devoted servant.

As aristocrats and new immigrants, rich and poor, become involved in this mating dance, the differences on the issue of slavery split existing families. Peregrine Lacey Catlett comes to despise his son Lewis, an abolitionist like his mother Leah. In her pity for him, Sara Lacey marries Lewis, who stifles her sweet and happy personality with his grim preoccupations. Returning from his escape to the West, Johnny takes up his father's duties as farmer, slave owner, and protector of women and in the final pages of the book joins the Confederate army to fight in a war that he knows will be lost, hoping only that he will not have to kill his unionist brother Lewis.

The next novel in the quintet, *The Scapegoat*, traces the defeat of friendship and decency in the conflict between mine operators and workers. In the middle of the conflict are Beverley and Ann Eldridge Lacey, decent people who hope that their mine can avoid the violence being urged by the operators of British-owned mines and their hired detectives and thugs on one hand and union agitators on the other. The presence of their daughters Lily Ellen Lacey, Mary Rose Lacey, and Ann Althea Lacey prevents an attack on their home, and for a time it seems that Beverley's friendship with Jake Catlett, on whose property the strikers are living, will prevent the threatened violence. Yet those who hunger for a confrontation take advantage of the idealism of Lily, whose friendship with Eduardo Pagano, a young Italian striker, is deliberately misinterpreted by the war lover Captain Daniel Chester Neill and made the excuse for an attack on the strikers' camp, to the delight of the union agitator, who will use the event for her own purposes. To protect her son Eddie, Annunziata Pagano permits the new immigrant Carlo Michele to be killed in Eddie's place. Even the conspiracy between the well-intentioned Neville Roundtree, Lily, and Beverley to rescue Eddie is tainted by the fact that a human scapegoat makes Eddie's escape possible.

The Killing Ground, the final novel in the quintet, brings the middle-aged writer Hannah McKarkle to her home, Canona, West Virginia, so that she can at last understand the life and death of her brother Johnny McKarkle. (At the beginning of the book, set eighteen years after Johnny's death, Hannah has returned to Canona for a lecture.) There is no mystery about the facts; in 1960, Hannah had been called home by Johnny and had learned immediately after his death that it was the result of a brawl in a jail cell where he had been thrown with other drunks. That Jake Catlett knocked him down Hannah has known ever since the event; that the death resulted from Johnny's hitting his head against a bench in the fall makes it clear that there was no premeditation. The central section of the book details these events.

In the first section, set in 1978, Hannah is seeking more complex answers to much deeper questions. As she talks to clubwomen such as Kitty Puss Baseheart, as she gossips about meaningless lives such as that of the womanizer Charlie Bland, as she sees dried-up Thelma Leftwich, a "good" woman who found no happiness in her hopeless love for Johnny, and as she visits the old family home with her aunt, Ann Althea Lacey Neill, the widow of the war-lover Captain Neill of *The Scapegoat*, Hannah tries to find a pattern in human history. Because Hannah McKarkle is Mary Settle's alter ego (Hannah is referred to in the novel as the author of the four previous books of The Beulah Quintet), it is logical that in the two years after her 1978 visit to Canona she would visit all the places of quintet significance, including the churchyard where Jonathan Church was shot in 1649. Her conclusions come in the epilogue, set in 1980.

The Characters

At the end of *The Killing Ground*, Settle suggests that there are repetitions of character-types throughout history. In that human motivations are certainly limited in number, though unlimited in particular combinations, this point seems logical. One strain which she sees throughout history is that of rebellion against the status quo. In *Prisons*, Jonathan Church left his home rather than submit to his father, then died rather than submit to Cromwell and his henchmen. In *The Killing Ground*, Jake Catlett struck out at Johnny McKarkle because Johnny represented rule by wealth and social position. At the end of *The Killing Ground*, Settle includes among these restless spirits Hannah Bridewell of *O Beulah Land*, the Provincial captain Jonathan Lacey, troubled Johnny Catlett of *Know Nothing*, the Italian scapegoat Carlo Michele and intelligent Eddie Pagano from *The Scapegoat*, and idealistic Lily from the same book. At the end of *The Killing Ground*, Hannah McKarkle realizes that she is like those characters in her independent spirit and in her need for freedom. Throughout the novels, such characters are contrasted with other types—the unprincipled, such as Cromwell and Charlie Bland; the cruel, such as Lewis Catlett and Captain Daniel Chester Neill; the pampered and petty, such as Sally Lacey in *O Beulah Land*, Sally Lacey in *Know Nothing*, and the clubwomen in the final novel; and the weak, such as Beverley Lacey in *The Scapegoat* and Brandon Lacey in *Know Nothing*. Although none of her characters is exactly like another, Settle's repetition of types suggests that human qualities, as well as human choices, are repeated again and again in history.

Settle reveals the inner lives of her characters by skillful shifts in point of view. Even in *Prisons* and *The Killing Ground*, the two works which are primarily written in the first person and concentrate on the perceptions of a single character, there are sections that move to other characters. *The Scapegoat* begins with Mary Rose Lacey, speaking in the first person with childish candor. Just as the reader has begun to accept Mary Rose's vision of reality as certainly more accurate than that of the adults around her, however, Settle switches to limited omniscience, moving from one character to another, and later once again has a first-person account, this time from Mary Rose's sister Ann Althea Lacey, who says that Mary Rose never tells the truth but invents and believes her own reality. The complex handling of point of view is a characteristic of Settle's fiction. It is a tribute to her craftsmanship that the reader is not confused as to whose mind is being exposed, whether in the first or in the third person, and the changes of perspective, like the repetition of character-types, produce a richness of texture like that of a Gobelin tapestry.

Themes and Meanings

The fact that the most important characters of the Beulah Quintet are the rebels points to the dominant theme of the novels: that throughout history freedom must be won again and again from varying kinds of enslavement. There is, first, enslavement by authority. In *Prisons*, Gideon MacKarkle is pressed into military service first by one side, then by the other, and Robbie Lokyar, who joined the Parliament forces to fight for freedom, is executed because he agitated for freedom of speech, which was more freedom than Cromwell and his subordinates wished to permit. In *O Beulah Land*, the transported criminals are sold as servants, and Jeremiah Catlett kills a blackmailer who threatens to put him and his wife Hannah once more into that bondage from which they have escaped. In *Know Nothing*, the emphasis is on the slavery of the blacks, and there, as throughout the other novels, those who have power over others are oblivious to the resentment which that power engenders. Because of the lack of knowledge which seems to accompany power, those in authority are vulnerable to the loss of their power.

A second kind of enslavement arises from an accepted social hierarchy. Although often the men and women of the upper classes are well-intentioned, like Sir Valentine Lacy in *Prisons* or slave-owning Johnny Catlett in *Know Nothing*, those of lesser rank harbor a bitterness, spawned by injustice and nourished by pride, which often erupts in violence. Sometimes the upper classes realize the menace of those for whom they have contempt; thus, the Catletts in *Know Nothing* retreat from the anger of "Black Irish" Big Dan O'Neill. Often, however, the anger is unrecognized. Yet in *The Killing Ground*, Jake Catlett, member of a family now low in the social scale, strikes out at Johnny McKarkle because Johnny has been acting superior all of his life. On the frontier, the less-educated, the unpolished, strike out at the educated and the polished; yet as the frontier recedes and established society moves westward, the hierarchical system follows, and the inevitable anger of those who are treated as inferiors is suppressed until an explosion occurs. The biblical epigraph to *Know Nothing* suggests that the powerful are themselves victims of their power.

Sometimes enslavement is rooted in the social and economic system. In *Know Nothing*, Brandon Lacey, who is wealthy in land and slaves, is ruined financially because he cannot find cash to pay his obligations. In the same novel, Melinda Lacey and Johnny Catlett cannot marry because she is penniless, and Johnny's mother expects him to marry money. Women must marry or live as subordinates in other women's households; if they err, there is no way out. In *Know Nothing*, Brandon's wife, Sally, is doomed to dependency by her husband's ruin; their daughter will be destroyed by her marriage to the cruel, intolerant Lewis Catlett, and Annie Brandon, pushed by passion into marriage with Big Dan O'Neill, will never be able to make him into a gentleman.

Finally, enslavement may come from an obsession, which blinds one to reality. For Lily in *The Scapegoat*, the obsession is her college-learned idealism; because she does not think before she acts, she endangers the very people whom she intends to help. In *Know Nothing*, Lewis Catlett is so obsessed by abolitionism and religious fanaticism that he strikes out at everyone and everything around him—his father, his brother, his wife, even an affectionate kitten, whom he kills with a kick. Lewis's family comments on the fact that Lewis, who defies his father and his community for his cause, has never done a kindness to a black. It is clear that the obsession is rooted in Lewis's love of his mother and hatred of his father, not in pity or in principle.

Whatever the source of enslavement, it is battled by Settle's most sympathetic characters, and the external struggle finally becomes less important than the internal struggle. A real triumph is generally achieved through knowledge, both of the real situation and of the self. Jonathan Church's final defiance of Cromwell is far more significant than his defiance of his father. In the first case, Jonathan did not understand the degree to which his father was shaped by his past and by his society, and Jonathan's refusal to accept his father's authority was based on his own feelings of religious superiority, his own stiff-necked pride. At the end of *Prisons*, however, Jonathan has come to understand that there is no freedom on either side in the English Civil War and that he himself is imperfect. Knowing that his death will be futile, he nevertheless speaks and dies for freedom. In *Know Nothing*, Johnny Catlett goes off to war as a loyal son, knowing that the South will not win, knowing that without evil intention he has participated in the evil inherent in the institution of slavery. His triumph is in his compassion, his self-knowledge, and his courage. Similarly, in *The Scapegoat*, Lily Ellen Lacey must come to realize that her well-meaning idealism has worsened the struggle between mine owners and workers. Her death in World War I is an expiation for the lack of knowledge which, like Johnny Catlett's, was rooted in a kind of upper-class innocence; like Johnny, however, in her attainment of knowledge and her acceptance of duty, Lily triumphs. In the final book of the quintet, Hannah McKarkle says that unlike the clubwomen, who hide themselves from themselves, she must reject her training as a "know-nothing" woman. Like Antigone, she must bury a brother who was not admirable, and she must seek the full knowledge of what he was so that the burial will be complete. Those characters in Mary Lee Settle's novels who quest, who wander, and who question all desire the internal triumph which comes with freedom through knowledge.

Critical Context

It is surprising that Mary Lee Settle is not better known. In 1978, when she received the National Book Award for Fiction for *Blood Tie* (1977), there were many critics who questioned the decision. Even since the completion of The Beulah Quintet, critical articles about her have been few. Yet her longtime admirer, George Garrett, himself an outstanding historical novelist, continues to point out Settle's scope, the depth of her vision, the proficiency of her technique. In even one historical novel, to handle varied points of view and a multitude of characters so deftly and so clearly is a notable achievement. To juggle families, characters, themes, motifs, and historical details in five related novels without departures from a high level of craftsmanship and the consistent search for truth, clearly expressed, is a task at which few other contemporary writers could succeed.

As a Southern writer, Settle is typically conscious of the burden of the past, of the anti-intellectualism and jubilant boorishness which are the inheritance from the frontier, of the stagnant smugness which accompanied the elevation in a new social hierarchy of those who had been inferior in an older hierarchy. Without family, wonders a lady in *Know Nothing*, what could the Yankee women at Egeria Springs find to talk about? Settle's use of eastern Virginia-western Virginia setting is particularly useful in illustrating the social changes which accompanied the movement of established traditions into the resistant frontier. Yet with all of her regional and historical accuracy, Settle transcends mere local color and, like the best writers of the continuing Southern Renaissance, achieves universality in characterization and in theme.

Bibliography

Galligan, Edward L. "The Novels of Mary Lee Settle." *The Sewanee Review* 104 (Summer, 1996): 413-412. Galligan details several of Settle's novels, including

The Beulah Quintet. The theme of mortality in Settle's work is explored as well as her ability to examine the subconsciousness of her characters.

Garret, George P. *Understanding Mary Lee Settle*. Columbia: University of South Carolina Press, 1988. A critical interpretation of Settle's major works is included in Garret's extensive survey of Settle's fiction and influences. A fine examination of the writer that explores the major themes and settings that unify her writings.

Rosenberg, Brian. *Mary Lee Settle's Beulah Quintet: The Price of Freedom*. Baton Rouge: Louisiana State University Press, 1991. Rosenberg presents a thematic study of the novels and places The Beulah Quintet in the context of English and European historical fiction. Rosenberg includes an interview with Settle in the book's appendix in which the author comments on her novel's complex origins.

Stephens, Mariflo. "Mary Lee Settle: The Lioness in Winter." *The Virginia Quarterly Review* 72 (Fall, 1996): 581-588. Stephens profiles Settle and discusses how her works draw readers into the story, making them privileged eavesdroppers. Stephens also discusses Settle's reputation for passion and explosive behavior in the literary world.

Rosemary M. Canfield Reisman

BEYOND THE BEDROOM WALL
A Family Album

Author: Larry Woiwode (1941-   )
Type of plot: Domestic chronicle
Time of plot: From 1935 to the mid-1960's
Locale: North Dakota, Illinois, and New York City
First published: 1975

> *Principal characters:*
> CHARLES NEUMILLER, a carpenter and the nominal head of the
>   Neumiller family
> MARTIN, the protagonist, Charles's son, a teacher, plumber, insurance
>   salesman, and, above all, father
> ALPHA JONES, Martin's first wife
> CHARLES, an actor, the eldest son of Martin and Alpha
> JEROME, a student doctor, the second son of Martin and Alpha
> TIM, a teacher, the third son of Martin and Alpha
> MARIE, the eldest daughter of Martin and Alpha
> SUSAN, the second daughter of Martin and Alpha
> LAURA, Martin's second wife

The Novel

A sprawling, episodic family history, *Beyond the Bedroom Wall* conveys with extraordinary fidelity and an enlightening sense of wonder the lives of ordinary people. It focuses on the Neumiller family, originally of North Dakota, but ranges over their extended families, their antecedents, and their communities. In doing so, the novel succeeds at times, without particularly attempting to, in surpassing the conventions of its genre. It attains an idiosyncratic, though nevertheless authentic, eminence as an anthropology of the affections.

The protagonist is Martin Neumiller, a sensitive, awkward, God-fearing son of the Midwest. Such story as the novel contains derives from him, his achievements, and his disappointments. The latter outnumber the former. Virtually all of his significant experiences take place within the rigid frame of the here and now. His failures and attainments, therefore, are no greater and no less than those of any ordinary man.

Martin has, however, one important, distinguishing feature: his Catholicism. His faith creates some problems as he attempts to establish his teaching career—predictably, given that he lives in North Dakota. Yet again, these difficulties are not given a decisive dramatic influence in the novel's development. They are, like everything else in Martin's world, part of the varied tapestry of which his life consists. Moreover, as though to compensate for professional frustration, Martin is able to marry Alpha, although she is not a Catholic and her family objects.

Martin is a firm believer in hard work, and in addition to his work at school, he takes on extra employment, restlessly attempting to satisfy himself by pursuing a dream of material adequacy for his growing family. As his family expands, and Martin is seen through the eyes of some of its members, it becomes clear that his restlessness is more illustrative of his nature than is his capacity for satisfaction. As though to confirm this view, Martin decides to move to Illinois—ostensibly to be near his father—just when circumstances seem to be about as good as they are going to get in North Dakota.

Life in Illinois begins disastrously and only slowly improves. By this time, however, it is Martin's children—Charles, Jerome, and Tim, particularly—who command attention. In a strictly unsentimental manner, the novel succeeds in conveying all the moodiness, irrationality, and idiosyncrasy of childhood. Collisions between the different children's private worlds are as lovingly recalled as are bouts of extemporaneous harmony. By keeping the small world of childish concerns to the fore here, the author is able to increase the shock value of adult problems when they intrude. Intrude they do: Alpha dies of uremia, Martin's father dies, floods almost destroy everything, Martin remarries.

Eventually, the Neumiller children begin to go their different ways. Charles goes first and goes farthest—from the University of Illinois to New York City and, at length, a modest acting career. Much of Charles's history away from the family deals with his sojourn in Greenwich Village and his encounters with various Bohemian types there. Charles's experiences here are portrayed in the exhaustive detail characteristic of the novel. Yet whereas this approach brings the unfamiliar American heartland authentically to life, it succeeds merely in depicting the sterility of the metropolis. Charles himself recognizes this sterility only when he and his wife return to Illinois for the funeral of Martin's second wife, Laura.

With this funeral, the novel ends. The family is both wounded and reunited. The novel has also come full circle, for its opening and most powerful sequence depicts Martin's father, also named Charles, making a coffin and burying his father. Those two deaths are, in effect, the dark covers of the document referred to in the novel's subtitle, "A Family Album." Such a subtitle is an appropriately but unnecessarily modest indication of the celebration of the everyday enacted in *Beyond the Bedroom Wall*.

The Characters

Since *Beyond the Bedroom Wall* is a novel of condition rather than a novel of character, it contains very little sense of character development. In addition, Woiwode treats doing as a form of being. Therefore, the novel contains little investigation of motive, not very much introspection, and seems, in general, to be resistant to the concept of the psychological man. As though to make the resistance explicit, a feature of Charles's alienated life as a newlywed in New York is that he is "deep in analysis."

On the other hand, Woiwode also resists the depiction of his characters as stereotyped pillars of society. The characters' personalities are too quirky and require too many outlets of expression to be pigeonholed: Variety and idiosyncrasy are their middle names, and it is one of the author's most impressive achievements that the novel is too densely populated with clearly visible, diverting, and widely differing characters.

The Neumillers are the predominant representatives of character conceived as erratic, copious, and different. Martin is the model upon which his wife and family are based. In his longings, his impatience, his kindness, and his energy, he embodies a wonderful zest for life, without in any sense being presented as a superman or even as a conventional hero. Martin is all the more impressive because he has little awareness of, or interest in, his own uniqueness. Moreover, his distinctiveness is most readily appreciated by observing what he does, and how he responds, rather than what he thinks.

A paradoxical feature of Martin's character is that it never amounts to anything definitive. Despite his energy and capacity for involvement and thoroughness, the world seems to resist his best efforts. His authenticity is measured most accurately in terms of his failures. His stature is most clearly visible in his ability to sustain loss. It may be that, as Martin remarks, "A man should be grateful for what he gets and not expect to get one thing more." Yet his appeal lies in the fact that his experience, in effect, restates that sentiment as a question rather than as an assertion.

Martin is a dominant influence on the novel's sense of character, but the author allows Alpha and Tim as well to make their own distinctive contributions to the narrative: Alpha's takes the form of a diary covering her courtship and the early years of her marriage, while Tim documents his childhood in a first-person narrative. Both of these resources, however, are used intermittently and arbitrarily.

In addition, Martin disappears at times while the author constructs a community in which the family can live. The community is constructed by means of a series of thumbnail sketches of its citizens, a procedure which, because of repetition, comes to have a weary air of obligation about it. For all the fascinating peripheral characters which the novel contains, notably the members of Alpha's family, Martin looms over all, an archetype of adequacy.

Themes and Meanings

Superficially, it seems that *Beyond the Bedroom Wall* serves no greater ambition than to live up to its subtitle. Its formal preoccupations deal fundamentally with chronicling, documenting, and remembering. Its central meaning seems contained in a need to keep faith with real life, reality in this case being synonymous with family intimacy and small towns.

Yet Woiwode resists the temptation to create a mere inventory of the past. The dream with which the novel opens places the narrator in the position of seeing again and seeing afresh, and throughout the novel there are numerous reminders that the activity of seeing is as important as the thing seen.

As though to confirm the significance of sight, moments in the novel are sometimes graced by light. The night that the family arrives in Illinois and finds itself unwelcome, Martin catches sight of "the celestial geometry of the children around Alpha's waiting face." Yet such moments do not occur predictably and do not provide a dependable means of perceiving the world. Rather, they are part of the total reality which the human experiences of the characters embrace.

Martin confirms that the family album of the novel's subtitle is the most fitting. He says, "My life is like a book. . . . There is one chapter, there is one story after another." A book does seem to be the most suitable means of embodying the character of experience as described in the novel's epigraph. The epigraph is a statement by Erik H. Erikson: "'Reality,' of course, is man's most powerful illusion; but while he attends to this world, it must outbalance the total enigma of being in it at all."

This novel's objective is to denote the quality of the illusion, to keep faith with the warmth and familiarity within the bedroom wall, as well as with the mystery and difficulty of life beyond the bedroom wall.

Critical Context

Although *Beyond the Bedroom Wall* uses some modernist technical devices, largely in varying point of view, it is essentially an old-fashioned family history. In fact, it might seem to owe its artistic lineage to more primitive sources such as the saga, or as the quotations at the beginning from an early traveler's account of the Dakotas suggest, the voyage-narrative. As such, it suffers from some artistic limitations. The author overindulges his powers of recall. Apart from death and threatened death, the novel lacks dramatic incident. It is too diffuse.

Nevertheless, it is the best of the author's three novels. Nominated for a National Book Award and a National Book Critics Circle Award in 1976, it enjoyed both a critical and commercial success. Moreover, it is a significant landmark in an important struggle which continues to characterize a recent important trend in American fiction.

This struggle is between the city and the soil, between metropolitan styles and rural values, between individual freedom and family obligations. *Beyond the Bedroom Wall* not only reflects such cultural tensions but also attempts to articulate their sources and their human urgency. Despite its technical deficiencies, therefore, this novel goes beyond being an admirable act of homage to everyday life. It is also an important chapter in the sociology of the contemporary American novel and a meditation on the culture of Middle America in mid-century.

Bibliography

Nelson, Shirley. "Stewards of the Imagination: Ron Hansen, Larry Woiwode, and Sue Miller." *Christian Century* 112 (January 25, 1995): 82-85. Nelson interviews Hansen, Woiwode, and Miller, focusing on the role of religion in their works and on readers' reactions to their novels.

Scheick, William J. "Memory in Larry Woiwode's Novels." *North Dakota Quarterly* 53, no. 3 (1985): 29-40. Scheick discusses the importance of memory in three of Woiwode's novels, *What I'm Going to Do, I Think* (1969), *Beyond the Bedroom Wall*, and *Poppa John* (1981). He identifies two types of memories, those that make a character feel guilt and long for death and those that develop a sense of connection to one's family. The ability to order these allows Woiwode's characters to achieve a balance between them.

Woiwode, Larry. "Homeplace, Heaven, or Hell." *Renascence* 44 (1991): 3-16. Woiwode discusses the problem of being considered merely a regional writer because he writes about the Midwest. He says that all writers must write about some place and that only geographical chauvinism makes one place better than another. The author also asserts that the main duty of a Christian writer is to write the truth, which means to write about a place in precise detail.

_____. "Where the Buffalo Roam: An Interview with Larry Woiwode." Interview by Rick Watson. *North Dakota Quarterly* 63 (Fall, 1996): 154-166. A revealing interview about Woidwode's homecoming and the effect it has had on his writing.

George O'Brien

THE BIG CLOCK

Author: Kenneth Fearing (1902-1961)
Type of plot: Suspense
Time of plot: The 1940's
Locale: New York City
First published: 1946

> *Principal characters:*
> GEORGE STROUD, *Crimeways* magazine executive editor
> EARL JANOTH, Janoth Enterprises publisher
> STEVE HAGEN, Janoth's second in command
> LOUISE PATTERSON, a painter whose work is admired and collected by
> Stroud
> PAULINE DELOS, Janoth's girlfriend

The Novel

The Big Clock is a psychological suspense novel that achieves its effect primarily through irony. The major character, George Stroud, is assigned the task of finding a missing person, a phantom witness both he and the reader know is actually George Stroud himself. As the novel builds, his position becomes ever more precarious, and the suspense is enhanced by the seeming inevitability of his being found out. He is racing, literally, against the clock, because time is playing with his life, and the suspense of the net closing around him keeps the narrative alive.

The story begins when Stroud meets Pauline Delos, the girlfriend of his employer, at one of Janoth's fabled big parties. Events coincide, and he has an affair with the woman. As he is dropping her off at her apartment on their return from a weekend together, Stroud sees Janoth meet her at the door of the building. In turn, Janoth sees only the shadowy image of a man. Up in her apartment, Janoth asks her about the man with whom she has been and accuses her of harboring lesbian tendencies. Janoth becomes so enraged when she implies he has a similar relationship with Steve Hagen that he strikes her. The next day, Stroud discovers that Delos has been murdered. Immediately, Janoth's second in command, Steve Hagen, has Stroud set up an investigation to find the man his boss had glimpsed on the street. Hagen spins a tale of a business conspiracy in which the man is involved, but Stroud knows that Janoth intends to pin the murder on him in order to deflect suspicion from himself.

Stroud's team of investigators follow up details of the weekend that Delos had told to Janoth before she died, details that will surely bring the investigators straight to Stroud. The searchers know the pair had visited Gil's Bar and Grill, a Third Avenue antique shop where the man had bought a painting by Louise Patterson (by outbidding another woman, who coincidentally turns out to have been Patterson herself), and the cocktail lounge of the Van Barth. In the finale, witnesses from these establishments all gather at the Janoth building to identify the phantom, whom one of them has seen enter the building. With the building about to be subjected to a floor-by-floor search and his discovery made increasingly inevitable, Stroud makes a last dash for Janoth's penthouse office. There, he discovers that the company is being taken over by another publishing conglomerate. With the search called off, Stroud is safe. Later, Janoth is pushed or pushes himself out a window in his thirty-second-floor office.

The Big Clock is presented through seven different viewpoints, each of which occupies at least one chapter. The use of multiple first-person narratives is a feature of Fearing's genre mystery writing, and it is most effective in the novel. As the focus of the plot, George Stroud's point of view is given in eleven chapters and thus influences the reader more than the rest. Interestingly, the woman who dies is not represented by her own words and remains a shadowy character, rather in keeping with much *noir* fiction. Stroud's wife, however, is given a chapter in which she contributes to the unflattering portrait of her husband. The other characters with chapters include Earl Janoth, with three chapters, Steve Hagen with one, Georgette Stroud with one, Louise Patterson with one, and Janoth Enterprises employees Edward Orlin and Emory Mafferson each with one, a total of nineteen chapters. These viewpoints serve to round out the characters, provide extra information, and move the narrative forward, especially as details of the mysterious witness begin to emerge.

An interesting play on the name "George" echoes throughout the novel, from George Stroud to his wife Georgette to his daughter Georgia. Curiously, within the family, all are called "George," as though interchangeable, which gives rise to some amusing dialogue. Delos gives the name of the man with whom she has spent time as yet another George, George Chester.

Two film versions of the novel have been produced: *The Big Clock* (1948), with Ray Milland as Stroud and Charles Laughton as Janoth, and *No Way Out* (1987), with Kevin Costner and Gene Hackman in the lead roles. In the latter film, which deviated from the novel more than the first, the setting was changed from a behemoth magazine publishing house to a branch of the U.S. military.

The Characters

The characters of Fearing's novel range from fairly stock figures of hard-boiled fiction, such as Steve Hagen and Pauline Delos, to the unclassifiable raucous individuality of Louise Patterson, the artist. None of the characters seems to achieve any self-knowledge that ultimately matters. Although the characters philosophize to some extent, they are caught in webs of varying degrees of cynicism and self-delusion.

George Stroud, like many hard-boiled characters, is not particularly likable; however, the reader empathizes with the terrible irony of his position. Stroud's cynicism and apparent dissatisfaction with modern life are evinced by his constant job changes and continual desire for more money. He assumes that he will move to a bigger house in a better neighborhood, and he spends his time figuring out how to ask for more money. He expresses no regret at the death of the woman with whom he has been sleeping; his only concern is for himself. His moral position is questionable on all counts, yet the reader sympathizes with his plight. If the reader does not cheer when

George gets out of his predicament, it is only because he is, in truth, rather despicable. Although he did not commit murder, he seems capable of it, even if Janoth sees him as all intellect. His most interesting characteristic is his ability, although those around him are blind, to see into and through the painting of Louise Patterson to its truth.

Earl Janoth is a business mogul on a losing streak. He is competitive and manipulative. He overestimates himself and his powers, and he tends to underestimate others.

Steve Hagen is a stock character, the man who will do anything for his boss, the practical underling who will clean up whatever mess he is presented. His is a realistic use of power; he furthers himself by furthering Janoth.

Louise Patterson is a delight, a woman who cannot control her own reactions and blurts out whatever she feels. Untamed by society, she is ruled by raw emotion, has had four love children, and is not constrained in the least by the rules of the business world within which the others live. As a result of Janoth Enterprises publicity related to the painting bought by the missing witness, Patterson's work skyrockets in value. Fearing thus implies that the media manipulates the public's taste in art as well as everything else. Clearly, both Patterson and her art are beyond most people's understanding.

Georgette Stroud is the long-suffering wife who cannot understand her husband. With her fairly nondescript voice, she is the foil against which George Stroud seems somehow too sharp.

Pauline Delos is hardly delineated except as the novel's sexual interest. She is there to romance and to be romanced and, specifically, to lead Stroud astray. Fittingly, she is described in age-old siren fashion, as the blonde who will only bring trouble. Her murder sets the rest of the novel in motion.

Themes and Meanings

The Big Clock's title is indicative of the symbolic level on which the novel operates. The "big clock" is time or fate, which dictates human lives. Early in the novel, Stroud wonders how one circumnavigates through the big clock's maze of traps and baits to find the truth. After the murder, the clock is ticking away George Stroud's life and chances at happiness, and he is desperate to get them back. Throughout the novel, unconcealed references to the big clock appear. Stroud's cynicism about the gigantic watch turns to fear as he discusses it after his life is in danger. At the outset, the big clock is ticking for everyone or no one, but during the search for the mysterious witness, the clock appears to be ticking only for him. At the end of the novel, the big clock is looking, in its blind and impersonal way, for someone else.

As the big clock is a machine, so is Janoth Enterprises a similar kind of machine that quashes the individual. Fearing has presented a less than sympathetic character in George Stroud, but at least he sees the crippling power of the corporate machine, as relentless in its own way as fate itself. The nonconformist Louise Patterson and her art might represent the other end of the spectrum, the only means of arriving at truth. Louise Patterson's paintings themselves are symbolic, particularly in their titles. A painting of hands that Delos names "Judas" (she is betraying her boyfriend, he is betraying his boss) is called "Study in Fundamentals" by the artist. "The Study in Fury" hangs on Stroud's wall at Janoth Enterprises, and it is Janoth's blind fury that leads to his girlfriend's death.

Corporate conspiracy, the ongoing conspiracy of the media in particular, is the backdrop to the novel. Janoth's feelings of paranoia that his operation has been targeted for takeover counters Stroud's practical way of seeking ways to avoid being found. Stroud accepts his fate in a way that Janoth cannot, because, as Stroud implies, his insight lets him know the big clock is there. Just as he sees the truth in Patterson's paintings, Stroud has an uncanny ability to see beyond the manipulation of the truth by the media to the real truth. Janoth tries to manipulate, to work against the big clock, but in Hardyesque fashion, his efforts are minuscule against inexorable fate. Because he knows that fate, not people, dictates what will happen, Stroud aims to set the big clock ticking for someone else, preferably the murderer himself. Further, the facelessness of the corporate machinery is echoed by the facelessness of the phantom witness, who manages to outwit all two thousand employees of Janoth Enterprises looking for him.

Critical Context

The multifaceted Janoth Enterprises, manufacturing truth tailor-made for the masses, is based in part on Kenneth Fearing's experiences in the years he worked as a staff writer at *Time* magazine. Through his jaded discussion of Janoth Enterprises magazines providing decisions, reasoning, and judgments for the masses, Fearing creates a scathing commentary on modern journalism. At magazines such as *Crimeways*, the staff manipulates the truth, creates the standard logic, and influences the public with a frightening power. By looking behind the doors of a fictional media empire, Fearing gives the reader an inside look at who is determining the generally accepted truth, and the picture is by no means an attractive one.

Thriller writing was essentially a sideline for Fearing, who wrote mysteries and journalism to subsidize his poetry. Nevertheless, *The Big Clock* is a classic of suspense writing that rises above the standards of the genre. Its use of symbolism is impressive, and it is burdened with neither the clichéd characters nor the stereotypical plot lines of most *noir* fiction. The speed of its narrative, the intriguing technique of multiple viewpoints in chapter format, the tight dialogue, and the steady inexorable movement toward doom—these are all the elements of superior fiction. The novel is also a compelling documentary of the corporate world of 1940's New York City—a lifestyle of cigarettes, alcohol, and apparently easy living masking roiling tensions. The sharpness and cynicism of modern life are etched by Fearing as if with a razor.

Bibliography
Anderson, Andrew R. *Fear Ruled Them All: Kenneth Fearing's Literature of Corporate Conspiracy.* New York: Peter Lang, 1996. An overview of Fearing's commentaries on corporate culture.

Barnard, Rita. *The Great Depression and the Culture of Abundance: Kenneth Fearing, Nathanael West, and Mass Culture in the 1930's*. Cambridge, England: Cambridge University Press, 1995. Discusses Fearing's response as a leftist writer to mass culture and consumerism.

Evans, T. Jeff. "Narratology in Kenneth Fearing's *The Big Clock*." *Journal of Narrative Technique* 23, no. 3 (Fall, 1993). Explores the novel's narrative strategies, including the use of multiple viewpoints.

Kunitz, Stanley. "More than a Thriller: *The Big Clock*" *Armchair Detective* 16, no. 4 (Winter, 1983). Examines the novel in terms of the conventions of the mystery genre.

_____. "Private Eye." *Saturday Review* XC (June 29, 1957). An interesting contemporary look at Fearing's work.

Holly Dworken Cooley

BILLY BATHGATE

Author: E. L. Doctorow (1931-   )
Type of plot: Adventure
Time of plot: The 1930's
Locale: New York City and upstate New York
First published: 1989

> *Principal characters:*
> BILLY BATHGATE, the novel's hero
> DUTCH SCHULTZ, Billy's gangster employer
> BO WEINBERG, a Schultz gang member murdered by Schultz
> ABBADABBA BERMAN, Schultz's accountant
> DREW PRESTON, Weinberg's girl, who becomes Schultz's and Billy's
>   lover

The Novel

   Billy Bathgate centers on the career of the notorious gangster Dutch Schultz as told through the sympathetic voice of his fifteen-year-old acolyte, Billy Bathgate. Schultz represents to Billy a way of getting out of the slums, of distinguishing himself as an important figure by joining a powerful and much-feared organization. Indeed, the novel begins with a breathless rendition of a punishment favored by gangsters: the disposal of a rival by encasing his feet in cement and drowning him. The victim is Bo Weinberg, once a trusted Schultz associate, now a man condemned for betraying his boss.

   Billy vividly portrays both the cruelty and the courage of these men. Bo is defiant to the last, refusing to abase himself or show any fear. Schultz is ruthless but respectful, conceding Bo's talents, and even admitting that Bo can get the best of him in their arguments. Bo has always had a way with words, Schultz wryly admits.

   Although Schultz's violence is repugnant—he physically smashes a man into a pulp—his very irrationality makes him appealing; that is, he is not a calculating, evil man but rather an impulsive, poorly educated one who has learned how to dominate a brutally competitive world. He has his code of honor, and he demands loyalty, which, except for Bo, he commands. This is also why he can win over Drew Preston, Bo's girl. She is not awed by the gangsters, but she is stimulated by him, because he is such a contrast to her society husband and to the world of wealth that masks its evil behind good manners. Schultz may be abrupt, crude, and awkward, but he is also direct and plainspoken. Like his expressions of violence, his expressions of love are unfettered and robust, so that there is a thrilling quality to his masculinity.

   Schultz, though, is in trouble, because the government has brought a case against him for tax evasion. His solution is to cultivate the upstate New York community where the trial will be held. Exhibiting himself as a public benefactor, Schultz and his lawyers craft a persona that predisposes the jury to look favorably on him as an individual abused by a government vendetta.

While Schultz busies himself with his defense, he assigns to Billy the task of escorting Drew Preston in public. Billy quickly falls in love with her, and she reciprocates his tender feelings, though both are aware that they court discovery by Schultz, which would mean their murder. Billy's affair with Preston is part of his maturation, of his becoming his own man, although he never forsakes his loyalty to the gang, which has become his second family.

Schultz's great strength is also his great weakness. By making all of his business revolve around him, he fails to see how crime is becoming organized and corporate. His way of doing business is almost feudal—depending almost entirely on violence and on the loyalty of subordinates—and he has no grasp of how to put together an organization that can compete with the combinations of power being amassed by the government and by his rival, Lucky Luciano. Schultz wants to personalize everything, so that it all evolves out of his own ego. That ego is unstable, however; on impulse, he kills an uncooperative colleague in an Onondaga hotel.

Members of Schultz's gang—particularly his accountant, Abbadabba Berman—sense that the old ways of doing things are nearly finished. Weinberg's defection is only the beginning of events that put Schultz on the defensive and that culminate in his gangland murder near the end of the novel. Berman tries to convince Schultz to do business in the new way, to recognize that he is part of a larger crime network, but Schultz can think only in terms of his own ambitions and calls off plans to amalgamate with Lucky Luciano and other gangsters. In compensation, perhaps, for Schultz's inability to adapt to new times, Berman turns to Billy, making him an apprentice and lavishing attention on the boy. Berman plies Billy with advice and gives him assignments that build his confidence and extend his knowledge of the business.

Through Berman and Preston, Billy gains perspective on Schultz. Preston, Billy finds, has her own sort of power and sense of ease. When she tires of Schultz, she simply leaves him, conveying to Billy the impression that Schultz's charisma has its limits. Billy never dares to think of actually leaving the gang, but he keeps his own counsel and is prepared to take care of himself when Schultz is murdered. At the death scene, in which Schultz, Berman, and Irving have been shot, Billy learns from Berman the combination of the safe where Schultz has stashed much of his loot. Evasive about his subsequent career, Billy intimates at the end of the novel that he has indeed amassed the Dutchman's fortune, but he does not vouchsafe what he will do with it.

The Characters

Dutch Schultz is a remarkable fictional achievement, largely because his spare dialogue so accurately reflects his view of the world. He uses words bluntly to say exactly what he means and what he wants. His style is to have no style, so to speak, no barrier of words that coat or deflect his true intentions. His aim is to amass power, and power is an all-encompassing reality for him, making possible not only his reputation as a gangster but his success as a lover. He would seem less impressive were it not for Billy's faithful recording of his words without editorializing. Schultz would probably appear to an adult as merely a thug, as someone not quite grown up who cannot control his impulses. For the adolescent Billy, however, the gangster appeals for precisely such reasons: Schultz has not trimmed his character to fit the normal world; he has not shaped up to suit society's dictates.

Billy is equally well realized as a character. He is a fascinating mixture of Tom Sawyer and Huckleberry Finn. On the one hand, he has Huck's outlaw mentality; Billy will be educated by his adventures, by pursuing the raffish world outside the classroom and the home. He has a mother, but he is—practically speaking—an orphan, and must acquire an identity by adopting the ways of Schultz's world. He does not share his boss's appetite for violence, but he does not flinch at it either, accepting it as part of the bargain for his apprenticeship in crime. On the other hand, Billy has some of Tom's romanticism, of his desire to act like a noble knight in the service of a lady. He is attracted to rules and codes in a way that Huck is not, though Billy has none of Tom's insufferable smugness about what he knows from reading books. Billy's feelings are always fresh and firsthand.

Abbadabba Berman, Schultz's accountant, senses that Billy is both a loyal member of the gang and possessed of a personality that stands apart from it as well. That is why he confides to Billy that the old days of gangstering are about finished and that the methods of crime will have to match the subtle methods of legitimate business. Billy is the future, Berman realizes, and he tries to speed Billy's realization of that fact.

Drew Preston is not as complicated as Billy. She is essentially passive—a bored, beautiful woman, fascinated with the gangster's energy and touched by Billy's tenderness. She has little within herself on which to rely, and she depends on others to provide the excitement that makes her otherwise useless life meaningful. She is there also to woo Billy away from his exclusive devotion to Schultz, making Billy think of his own needs and desires.

Although Bo Weinberg disappears after the first pages of the novel, his presence is felt throughout the narrative, for in killing Bo, Schultz ensures his own destruction. Bo tells Schultz home truths that Schultz cannot bear to hear or to confront. Bo, in fact, is a smarter, more handsome version of Schultz. He tells Schultz, for example, that the more he has done for him, the less Schultz has counted on him, even though Bo has looked upon Schultz as a brother. This implication that Schultz's execution of Bo is fratricidal suggests that Schultz is dooming his own organization by eliminating his best partner.

Themes and Meanings

As the title suggests, the main focus of the novel is the education of Billy Bathgate. In this fast-paced adventure novel, which takes quick tours of the Bronx, upstate New York, Saratoga, and the docks of Manhattan, Doctorow supplies the color and the feel of the 1930's. As Billy prospers and gets to know these different worlds, he finds it impossible to return as he was to his old neighborhood. He is immediately perceived as a different person. He dresses differently, carries himself differently, and has a consciousness of a world that extends far beyond the Bathgate Avenue from which he derives his assumed name. Billy becomes, in other words, a self-invented figure, tran-

scending his origins not only in the actions he narrates but in his very language, which
is at once colloquial and formal, a blend of popular and sophisticated vocabulary that
precisely captures the boy and the man who has become the narrator of this novel. In
this quintessential American story, Doctorow has managed yet another stunning version of the hero's quest for identity and success.

For Billy survives the wreck of Schultz's gang and, like Herman Melville's
Ishmael, lives to tell the tale. Billy hides Schultz's fortune, goes back to school, graduates from an Ivy League college, and becomes an Army officer in World War II and
later a business entrepreneur—an inconceivable career in Dutch Schultz's world.

Billy is also like Melville's Ishmael in that he tells his story from the point of view
of an outcast peculiarly attuned to the conventions of society that exclude him. In De-
pression-era America, it is very difficult for a poor boy from the Bronx to make a career for himself, and the novel makes clear that Billy is the product of certain social
conditions—particularly of an economy that has no place for him unless he makes one
for himself in the underworld. What is extraordinary, of course, is that his early life of
crime prepares him for a position in society that is perfectly legal and respectable.
Doctorow thus seems to be suggesting that the attributes that make Billy successful
among criminals are not so different from the qualities needed for achievement in a
law-abiding society.

In presenting Schultz and Billy in such a complex light, Doctorow seems to call
into question hard and fast distinctions between right and wrong. At the very least, his
novel's study of human character situates morality in an ambiguous realm, informed
not merely by the personalities of his characters but by how they interact with their environment and, more specifically, with a capitalistic culture in which individuals, except for those in the privileged classes, must fight hard to earn and to maintain their
status.

Critical Context

E. L. Doctorow is a political novelist concerned with those stories, myths, public
figures, and literary and historical forms that have shaped public consciousness. Even
when his subject is not overtly political—as in his first novel, *Welcome to Hard Times*
(1960)—he chooses the genre of the Western to comment upon the American sense of
crime and justice. Knowing that the Western has often been the vehicle for the celebration of American individualism and morality, Doctorow purposely writes a fable-
like novel in which he questions the American faith in fairness and democracy. He
accomplishes the same purpose by turning to the genre of the gangster novel in
Billy Bathgate. The reality of American history has been much grimmer than its literature or its popular entertainment has acknowledged, and Doctorow's fiction shows
again and again an America whose myths do not square with its history.

In most of Doctorow's work there is a tension between a naïve, childlike point of
view and an older, ironic, detached perspective. In *Ragtime* (1975), the narrator seems
simultaneously to be a little boy and his older self, both witnessing and remembering
the past. *World's Fair* (1986) and *Billy Bathgate* seem more conventional than these

earlier novels, for they are told from the standpoint of mature men reviewing their youth. Yet both novels unfold with such immediacy that they appear to be taking place as their narrators reminisce.

E. L. Doctorow has shown himself to be a master stylist, a shrewd commentator on popular genres and political themes who maintains a strong sense of narrative and storytelling. Indeed, his work should be viewed as a major evocation and critique of the American mythos and a brilliant creation of new American fables. His experiments with point of view and with the relationship between history and fiction have marked him as a major innovator in contemporary fiction.

Bibliography
Baba, Minako. "The Young Gangster as Mythic American Hero: E. L. Doctorow's *Billy Bathgate.*" *MELUS* 18 (Summer, 1993): 33-46. Baba explores the blending of fiction and history in Doctorow's novel, which results in a mythic representation of the American gangster. She praises the book as a "gripping historical fantasy of a young American's perilous journey."

Clerc, Charles. "Dutch Schultz's Last Words Revisted." *Journal of Modern Literature* 18 (Spring, 1994): 463-465. Clerc focuses on the final chapter of *Billy Bathgate*, specifically on the last words of the real-life gangster, Dutch Schultz. Clerc demonstrates how Doctorow adapted the text to fit the characters in the novel by emphasizing Schultz's violent life and death and by providing links between fact and his character, Billy.

Harter, Carol C., and James R. Thompson. *E. L. Doctorow*. Boston: Twayne, 1990. A study of Doctorow's major fiction up to *World's Fair*. Contains a chronology, a chapter of biography, separate chapters on the novels, notes and references, and a selected bibliography. A succinct introductory study.

Henry, Matthew A. "Problemized Narratives: History as Fiction in E. L. Doctorow's *Billy Bathgate.*" *Studies in Contemporary Fiction* 39 (Fall, 1997): 32-38. Henry argues that Doctorow rearranges historical accuracy to fit his fictional constructs in *Billy Bathgate*, a common attribute of postmodern historical narratives. Henry explores the differences between traditional historical fiction, which begins in history and fills in the gaps with imagination, and postmodern books that rewrite the past.

Isaacs, Neil D. "Bathgate in the Time of Coppola: A Reverie." *Literature-Film Quarterly* 24 (January, 1996): 109-110. Isaacs compares Doctorow's *Billy Bathgate* to Francis Ford Coppola's 1984 film *The Cotton Club*. In both works, Dutch Schultz's recognition of the protagonist's talent allows Billy or Dixie Davis to go on to success. Both works also realize the dark side of success in the underground world.

Levine, Paul. *E. L. Doctorow*. New York: Methuen, 1985. The first full-length study of the novelist's career. Levine provides sound and often insightful readings of individual novels as well as substantial discussions of the recurring themes in the fiction: politics, the nature of fiction and history, and Doctorow's critique of the American Dream. A useful bibliography and a discussion of film adaptations of Doctorow's work make this a comprehensive study.

Parks, John G. *E. L. Doctorow*. New York: Continuum, 1991. Includes an excellent chapter on *Billy Bathgate*, situating the novel in the context of Doctorow's career. A remarkable introductory study that includes discussion of Doctorow's major and minor work, a chronology, notes, bibliography, and a chapter on his biography.

Strout, Cushing. "Historizing Fiction and Fictionalizing History: The Case of E. L. Doctorow." *Prospects* 5 (1980): 423-437. A detailed analysis of the strengths and limitations of Doctorow's handling of fiction and history. Should be read in conjunction with Barbara Foley's article "From U.S.A. to *Ragtime*: Notes on the Forms of Historical Consciousness in Modern Fiction," included in Richard Trenner's *E. L. Doctorow: Essays and Conversations* (1983).

Trenner, Richard, ed. *E. L. Doctorow: Essays and Conversations*. Princeton, N.J.: Ontario Review Press, 1983. Yields valuable biographical and critical insights into the novelist's work. Includes several of his important essays as well as articles by others about his fiction, which are well chosen to reflect the range of critical opinion on Doctorow, the variety of his themes and techniques, and the historical background required to read his novels.

Vieira, Nelson H. "'Evil Be Thou My Good': Postmodern Heroics and Ethics in *Billy Bathgate* and *Bufo and Spallanzani*." *Comparative Literature Studies* 28 (Fall, 1991): 356-378. Vieira argues that both Doctorow's *Billy Bathgate* and Brazilian author Rubem Fonseca's *Bufo and Spallanzani* challenge conventional beliefs about goodness and beauty. Both books are characterized by incorporation of "high" and "low" aesthetics and a dislocation of ethical standards.

Weber, Bruce. "E. L. Doctorow: Myth Maker." *The New York Times Magazine*, October 20, 1985, 25-26, 42-43, 74-77. Primarily useful as an overview of the novelist's life and career, with special emphasis on *World's Fair* and on the growth of his reputation. This profile emphasizes Doctorow's growing importance in contemporary fiction.

Carl Rollyson

BLACK WATER

Author: Joyce Carol Oates (1938-   )
Type of plot: Psychological realism
Time of plot: The afternoon and early evening of July 4, 1991
Locale: Grayling Island, Maine
First published: 1992

> *Principal characters:*
> KELLY (ELIZABETH ANNE) KELLEHER, a sexually insecure
>   twenty-six-year-old magazine writer living in Boston
> THE SENATOR, a powerful, fiftyish Massachusetts politician who meets
>   Kelly at a Fourth of July party
> BUFFY ST. JOHN, Kelly's closest friend, who is giving the party
> RAY ANNICK, Buffy's lover, a friend of The Senator

The Novel

Black Water is a fictional tragedy that refuses to abandon its origins in American political history. "The Senator," the powerful fifty-something politician whose name is never given beyond his title, arrives at a Fourth of July party hosted by Buffy St. John at her parents' home on Grayling Island, a twenty-minute ferry ride from Boothbay Harbor, Maine. During the course of this afternoon, which he spends talking, drinking, and playing tennis with the younger people gathered at the party, he captivates Kelly Kelleher, and the two of them leave late that evening to catch the last ferry off the island, to have dinner in Boothbay Harbor, and, presumably, to spend the night at the motel where The Senator is staying.

Yet something goes terribly wrong. The drunken senator misses the ferry road and ends up on a narrow and abandoned track. Kelly says, "I think we're lost, Senator," but it is finally Kelly who is lost. In the rush to catch the ferry, the rented car skids off the road and plunges into the deceptively deep Indian Creek. The car overturns in the water; The Senator escapes by scrambling over Kelly, who, pinned in the car with broken bones, slowly drowns. The Senator stumbles several miles to call his friend Ray Annick back at the party for help; the accident, he yells into the phone, was the girl's fault.

The events follow closely the July, 1969, incident at Chappaquiddick, Massachusetts, when thirty-seven-year-old Senator Ted Kennedy left the scene of a similar accident and Mary Jo Kopechne was drowned. The major difference is time; while the model occurred decades earlier, Joyce Carol Oates brings this incident up to the present. Still, readers are witnessing a fictional version of recent political, but very personal, history.

Although Kennedy is never named, many other political players are; The Senator, for example, is described as "eleven years younger than George Bush." Oates uses undigested political history, discussing the 1988 presidential campaign and its attendant controversies in detail, and she has The Senator tell the younger people around him that "the Gulf War has given your generation a tragic idea of war and of diplomacy: the delusion that war is relatively easy, and diplomacy *is* war, the most expedient of options."

The short, 154-page novel is broken into two parts and thirty-two chapters. Part 1 opens with a chapter that gives the core action of the book:

> The rented Toyota, driven with such impatient exuberance by The Senator, was speeding along the unpaved unnamed road, taking the turns in giddy skidding slides, and then, with no warning, somehow the car had gone off the road and had overturned in black rushing water, listing to its passenger's side, rapidly sinking.
> *Am I going to die?—like this?*

The following chapters alternate between descriptions of the accident, The Senator's escape, Kelly's slow drowning, earlier incidents in the day (a tennis match, their first kiss, his suggestion that she join his staff) and in her young life (snippets of scenes with her parents, with Buffy at Brown University, with her earlier lover). Much of the action is described from somewhere within Kelly's fractured head; increasingly in part 2, readers get her fantasies of escape and rescue; the first sentence of part 2, for example, reads: "He was gone but would come back to save her." Almost as a refrain in the novel, Oates repeats that the water is rising: "As the black water filled her lungs, and she died." This prose has an intense, poetic quality characteristic of Oates at her best; the entire chapter 10, for example, consists of one two-page sentence that provides both momentum to the story and tension to the writing. Metaphors of loss of sight and direction, moreover, reverberate through the short novel.

It is a tribute to the power of this writing that, though the outcome of this story is certain, Oates makes it exciting. In fact, like Ambrose Bierce's famous short story "An Occurrence at Owl Creek Bridge"—in which readers watch a convicted Confederate spy escape only to realize that it was all a dream in the seconds before he was hung—Oates builds the hope that in this version of history, at least, the innocent young woman may in the end escape.

The Characters

The model of the Kennedy character is only thinly disguised. While he does not have brothers, The Senator is otherwise easy to recognize: Described as separated from his wife of thirty years, he is a man with a "diminutive first name" and "an old-style liberal Democrat out of the 1960s, a Great Society man with a stubborn and zealous dedication to social reform" who "had been among the three leading candidates for the Democratic presidential nomination in 1988."

The center of the novel, however, is less the powerful senator and contemporary political history than Kelly Kelleher, a naïve young woman who is the innocent but willing victim of The Senator's political and sexual power. Ironically, Kelly wrote her senior honors thesis at Brown on The Senator, and her collegiate idealism still thrives: She not only writes articles now on such issues as capital punishment for the liberal *Citizens' Inquiry* but she also teaches two nights a week in a literacy program in inner-city Boston. Kelly is a young woman with a history of acne but not much else; she will not talk about her one lover ("G_____"), and she has regularly starved herself as self-punishment for her imagined failures. The child of a rich suburban New York City family, she ends up at the bottom of a creek with a fractured skull and broken kneecap, trapped in a slowly sinking car and abandoned by the man to whom she has been so powerfully drawn. The real tragedy in *Black Water* is hers. She is another in a long string of familiar Oates characters: single women who lack confidence in themselves and security in their sexuality and who are thus easy prey for more powerful males. Kelly even thinks that "the black water was her fault." Oates implies that one source of Kelly's problem is the Kelleher family in Westchester, which gave her all the material things she needed, but few of the emotional. A clue in the novel is the refrain, "You know you're somebody's little girl don't you?" The implication is that the adult woman has never been able to grow satisfactorily beyond that unhealthy childhood line.

Themes and Meanings

Black Water is really a novella; it is only three times as long as "Where Are You Going, Where Have You Been?," for example, one of Oates's many well-known short stories. Like that story, or her longer *Because It Is Bitter, and Because It Is My Heart* (1990), *Black Water* explores the theme of what could be called "Death and the Maiden" (the original title for "Where Are You Going, Where Have You Been?"). In work after work, Oates has probed this situation of the naïve young woman seduced by some powerful, almost demonic male figure. In "How I Contemplated the World from the Detroit House of Corrections and Began My Life Over Again," another regularly anthologized Oates story, the villain is a seductive young drug addict. In "Where Are You Going, Where Have You Been?," it is Arnold Friend (or "an old fiend," a thinly veiled representation of the Devil) who lures Connie to her death.

In *Black Water*, the antagonist is much more lifelike and fleshy—but just as evil. Selfish and greedy, The Senator thinks of nothing but trying to save himself. In the end, he has, but another Oates heroine has drowned in the waters of male power and selfishness. Again and again, Kelly thinks of The Senator's charisma, "his manly power," as she is drawn to his presence that afternoon, and when he moves closer to her, she is lost.

This is not, however, merely another story of an older man misusing a younger woman. In one short paragraph, Oates defines two central concerns of her book: "Politics, the negotiating of power. Eros, the negotiating of power." Readers witness both kinds of negotiation here; they are, she implies, two parts of the same violent American culture, and The Senator, in his charm and power, abuses both.

Critical Context

Increasingly in American writing in the last decades of the twentieth century, the line between fiction and nonfiction has been harder and harder to find. Nonfiction writers such as Hunter S. Thompson and Gay Talese have invaded the territory of the fictionists and appropriated most of their weapons. Conversely, novelists such as E. L. Doctorow and Kurt Vonnegut, Jr., have felt perfectly justified in placing their fictional characters in real worlds peopled by historical figures. As Doctorow has remarked, there are no longer separate categories of fiction and nonfiction today, only narrative.

In *Black Water*, Joyce Carol Oates enters this tradition. There is no denying that the basis for the action in her novella is recent political history, specifically the events at Chappaquiddick. What Oates has accomplished is to make that history taut with terror in the retelling. Yet in dredging up this tragedy, Oates has made little attempt to disguise its origins, and the reader can only feel a kind of vague discomfort; the history is too recent, the players all too alive—or dead. Doctorow's *Ragtime* (1975), in contrast, uses historical personages at the turn of the century to flesh out the tale; Susan Sontag's more recent *The Volcano Lover* (1992) is a historical romance set in the late eighteenth century. For the first time, Oates is using living people as the foundation for her fiction, and it is unsettling.

Oates has always posed questions with uneasy answers, however, and it is thus relatively simple to place *Black Water* in the context of her literary career. Like many earlier novels and short stories, *Black Water* delineates American culture not only from its violent outside but from the troubled inside as well. Reviewing *Because It Is Bitter, and Because It Is My Heart*, critic Henry Louis Gates, Jr., commented that "a future archeologist equipped only with her *oeuvre* could easily piece together the whole of postwar America." That description applies to *Black Water* as well—not merely the actual American social history, the misuse of political power, but also the psychological truths. *Black Water* continues the excavation Oates has been doing for thirty years, at a different site, and perhaps with different tools, but bringing up the same truthful artifacts of American life. Few novelists have done as much.

Bibliography
Bausch, Richard. "Her Thoughts While Drowning." Review of *Black Water*, by Joyce Carol Oates. *The New York Times Book Review*, May 10, 1992, 1, 29. Praises *Black Water* as "taut, powerfully imagined and beautifully written." Compares the novel to ancient Greek tragedies in its use of a chorus and its pervasive irony.
Bradley, Jacqueline. "Oates's *Black Water.*" *Explicator* 56 (Fall, 1997): 50-52. Bradley discusses the depiction of women in Oates's novel. She explores the problem of value and significance in the act of naming and the relationship between naming and power. Her analysis of Kelly's character is particularly pertinent.
Creighton, Joanne V. *Joyce Carol Oates: Novels of the Middle Years*. New York: Twayne, 1992. A discussion of fifteen Oates novels written between 1977 and 1990. Of *American Appetites* (1989) and *Because It Is Bitter, and Because It Is My Heart*, Creighton comments, "The American dream is fractured by an unintentional killing; in both, violence is an upwelling of tension, breaking through the civil games of society and the conscious control of character; in both, appetites remain unfulfilled."

Driscoll, F. Paul. "Going to the Opera with Joyce Carol Oates." *Opera News* 62 (January 3, 1998): 26-29. Driscoll's conversation with Oates focuses on the libretto she wrote for the opera "Black Water," which is based on her fictional accou. * of the Chappaquiddick incident involving Senator Edward Kennedy. After viewing the performance, Oates critiques the composer, the librettist, and the production.

Robinson, Sally. "Heat and Cold: Recent Fiction by Joyce Carol Oates." *Michigan Quarterly Review* 31 (Summer, 1992): 400-414. Robinson observes that Oates has always "specialized in a narrative technique that intrudes upon the private pains and pleasures—but mostly pains—of Others. Her narratives often explore the dynamics of a voyeurism in which subject and object confront one another across a gulf of social difference."

Seaman, Donna. Review of *Black Water*, by Joyce Carol Oates. *Booklist* 88 (February 15, 1992): 1066. Comments that the novel displays Oates's "penchant for morbidity and command of suspense" and shows her "at her most facile and provocative."

David Peck

THE BLACKER THE BERRY
A Novel of Negro Life

Author: Wallace Thurman (1902-1934)
Type of plot: Satiric realism
Time of plot: The 1920's, during the Harlem Renaissance
Locale: Boise, Idaho; Los Angeles; and Harlem
First published: 1929

> *Principal characters:*
> EMMA LOU MORGAN, the protagonist, a college student, maid, and teacher
> ALVA, Emma Lou's lover in Harlem
> GERALDINE, Alva's wife and mother of his son
> MARIA LIGHTFOOT, Emma Lou's grandmother, leader of Boise's blue veins
> JANE LIGHTFOOT MORGAN, Emma Lou's mother
> GWENDOLYN JOHNSON, a close friend of Emma Lou in Harlem

The Novel

The main action of *The Blacker the Berry: A Novel of Negro Life* focuses upon the protagonist's struggle to be accepted by light-skinned blacks. In the opening scene of the book, Emma Lou is sitting with members of her high school graduating class, waiting to receive her diploma. Emma Lou, who is a very dark-skinned girl, is also the only black student in her class. She feels self-conscious about her appearance onstage, dressed in white, surrounded by her white classmates. As the ceremony draws to a close, Emma Lou ponders the value of a high school diploma and decides that it will mean nothing to her. She would gladly trade her diploma for an "effective bleaching agent, a magic cream that would remove this unwelcome black mask from her face and make her more like her fellow men." From her mother's family of color-conscious mulattoes, she has learned to despise her dark skin and to expect few opportunities for success and happiness.

After Emma Lou is graduated from high school, her mother persuades her to enroll at the University of Southern California in a teacher education program, as no one in her family thinks she will find a husband. Encouraged by a sympathetic uncle's assurance that color-prejudice is largely confined to small towns such as Boise, Emma Lou looks forward to her studies at the University of Southern California and to the possibility of making friends with her mulatto schoolmates, for mulattoes and light-brown-skinned blacks are, in her view, "the people who really mattered." Shortly after her arrival on the USC campus, Emma Lou sets out to meet people with whom she would like to associate socially. Yet, despite sincere attempts to gain admission to the exclusive mulatto circles, Emma Lou finds these students aloof, polite, but steadfastly unwilling to accept her. During her two years at USC, she tries to ignore the indications of color-prejudice. When she finds herself repeatedly excluded from activities sponsored by the mulattoes, however, Emma Lou, discouraged and depressed, abandons her studies and moves to Harlem, seeking a job and, most important for her, a congenial mulatto community.

In Harlem, Emma Lou quickly discovers that color-prejudice plays a major role in the lives of blacks. This becomes evident to her when landlords in mulatto neighborhoods refuse to rent her a room. Although she is qualified to fill clerical positions, black businessmen will not hire her because they prefer light-complexioned female employees. She finds work as a maid, however, and subsequently becomes romantically involved with a mulatto who exploits her sexually and financially. Her relationship with Alva, the hustler, ultimately forces her to reexamine the myth of mulatto superiority which has shaped her sense of self and opens the door to a crucial confrontation with her negative self-image.

In the novel's conclusion, Emma Lou summons the courage to leave Alva, even though she still loves him. As she reorders her priorities, she determines that "what she needed to do now was to accept her black skin as being real and unchangeable. . . ." With this new awareness, Emma Lou moves toward a positive self-image and achieves a victory over the terrible interracial color-prejudice that has dominated her life and undermined her self-esteem, causing her tremendous emotional pain and suffering.

The Characters

Emma Lou Morgan is one of the most skillfully drawn characters in African American fiction. Born in Boise, Idaho, to a mulatto mother and a dark-skinned father, Emma Lou inherits her father's dark color, broad nose, and thick lips, much to the chagrin of her mother's color-conscious family. Rebuffed by his in-laws because of his color, Emma Lou's father soon deserts his wife and baby daughter, never to be heard from again. Consequently, Emma Lou grows up under the influence of a family whose motto is "whiter and whiter every generation." Maria Lightfoot, Emma Lou's maternal grandmother and the leader of Boise's exclusive mulatto society, abhors dark-skinned blacks, her granddaughter included. Even Emma Lou's mother loathes dark-skinned people, terming her marriage to Emma Lou's father a silly mistake. Not surprisingly, Emma Lou develops an intense color-prejudice herself; she, too, detests dark skin and African features. She, therefore, decides to choose her friends among mulattoes and light-brown-skinned blacks. She underestimates the depth of the mulattoes' commitment to maintaining the status quo, however, to holding themselves above and apart from their darker brothers. She suffers great emotional distress when she fails to gain admission to the closed circles of mulattoes and light-complexioned blacks in Los Angeles and in Harlem. Despite her obvious flaws, color-prejudice, and self-hatred, Emma Lou displays a sincere, compassionate heart, a remarkable capacity for love and forgiveness. These qualities are particularly evident in her relationship with Alva and his sick baby. Like all well-conceived, multidimensional characters, Emma Lou is a complex mixture of good and bad traits. During the course of her struggles, the reader learns to understand her faults and to admire her strengths.

While staying at the YWCA in Harlem, Emma Lou meets Gwendolyn Johnson, an amiable, light-brown-skinned girl whose mother has taught her to value relationships with dark-skinned blacks and to avoid contacts with light-complexioned blacks. In short, Gwendolyn is Emma Lou in reverse. As one would expect, these two color-conscious women are immediately attracted to each other and become friends. Given their color preferences, theirs would seem to be an ideal friendship. Yet Gwendolyn's unceasing condemnation of light-skinned blacks does nothing but make Emma Lou more sensitive about her dark skin. Indeed, Gwendolyn's glorification of dark skin intensifies Emma Lou's desire to be transformed into a pretty, light-brown-skinned woman. Gwendolyn dates only dark-skinned men and tries to persuade Emma Lou to follow her example. Therefore, she is extremely irritated when Emma Lou decides to resume her relationship with Alva, her mulatto lover. In her angry response to Emma Lou's decision, Gwendolyn reveals her suppressed color-prejudice. She tells Emma Lou: "There's probably something in this stuff about black people being different and more low than other colored people. You're just a common ordinary nigger." Gwendolyn's unintentional revelation casts a new light upon her alleged preference for dark-skinned blacks.

Of the several male characters in the novel, Alva (who is given no surname) is the most fully developed. The son of an American mulatto and her Filipino husband, Alva possesses the physical attributes that Emma Lou finds attractive—skin color between yellow and brown, finely textured hair. Seeing Emma Lou in a Harlem cabaret with her white employer, Alva notices that no one has asked her to dance, so he takes pity on her and asks her to dance. She is flattered and pursues him, hoping to establish a serious romantic relationship with him. As an experienced hustler, Alva quickly recognizes the potential advantages of a discreet affair with a lonely, employed woman, and so he encourages Emma Lou's advances. Through the force of his charm and tact, he manipulates her into sharing her income with him. His scheme is so clever that Emma Lou, his naïve victim, "never realized just how she had first begun giving him money." Although he is ashamed to take Emma Lou among his light-skinned friends, he is nevertheless polite and attentive when they are together. Ironically, he breaks off the relationship when he can no longer tolerate her complaints that he intentionally subjects her to situations in which her color is ridiculed. Alva denies the charges and allows Geraldine, his mulatto girlfriend, to move in with him.

Geraldine gives birth to a sickly, retarded baby boy. The baby's handicap has a profound effect upon Alva. He loses interest in Geraldine, and "he hated that silent, staring idiot infant of his. . . ." Seeking an escape from his unhappy home life, Alva turns to alcohol for solace. His heavy drinking, despite his doctor's warnings against it, undermines his health, activating a self-destructive impulse. Fearful that Alva will succeed in drinking himself to death, leaving her alone to care for the baby, Geraldine deserts him and the baby. Determined to reestablish her relationship with Alva, Emma Lou returns to his room, nurses him back to health, and introduces Alva Junior to love and affection. While her rescue of Alva seems, for a time, to be successful, he resumes his excessive drinking and treats Emma Lou with contempt and disrespect. Alva is not only conceited and hypocritical, he also lacks moral courage; with Emma Lou's help, he could have developed strategies for coping with his son's disability, but he chose to be consumed by despair.

Themes and Meanings

The novel's major themes concern self-hatred and the dynamics of color-prejudice among black Americans. The novel's title, taken from the familiar black folk saying, "the blacker the berry, the sweeter the juice," is bitterly ironic, for although many blacks have traditionally embraced the notion that dark-skinned women are attractive and desirable, a significant segment of the black community has treated dark skin and other African physical features with disdain, while venerating Caucasian physical features. With this preference for white skin and values comes a clash or conflict of identities. Thurman comments on this shift of identity in his portrayal of Arline Strange, the white actress who plays the part of a mulatto in a melodrama of black life in Harlem. With make-up, the actress effects a superficial, temporary shift in identity, but unlike the mulattoes who confuse their imaginary or assumed identity with their true self, the actress shifts easily between her fictional and real identity, never losing sight of who she is.

The ultimate goal of mulattoes such as Emma Lou's mother and grandmother, however, is to achieve a complete and permanent shift of identity by eradicating all physical traces of their African ancestry through selective marriage and by assimilating the attitudes and values of the white society. Total assimilation into the white society, many color-conscious mulattoes reasoned, would free them from the limitations of interracial prejudice. Yet the inevitable result of this denial of the authentic self was a deep-seated self-hatred, as well as alienation from those blacks whose dark skin was viewed as an emblem of dishonor and inferiority. Emma Lou is the brilliant embodiment of both these penalities associated with denial of the self. She experiences self-hatred and alienation from other blacks. Thus, the novel traces Emma Lou's painful journey toward self-acceptance. As the novel closes, the end of her journey is near. Emma Lou wisely realizes that she must "begin life anew, always fighting, not so much for acceptance by other people, but for acceptance of herself by herself."

Critical Context

When *The Blacker the Berry* was published in 1929, the Harlem Renaissance was nearing its end. Extending from the 1920's to the early 1930's, the Harlem Renaissance was a period of previously unparalleled literary productivity among black writers. Readers, both black and white, exhibited an almost insatiable appetite for books written by and about blacks. Publishers anxious to profit from this fascination with black life and culture sought out promising black writers. Wallace Thurman was one of those talented young artists. In his first novel, he set out to expose and condemn what he perceived as a disturbing contradiction in black life; he noticed blacks enthusiastically proclaiming the value and uniqueness of their African heritage, while displaying a decided preference for light skin and Caucasian features.

Moreover, many blacks routinely attacked interracial prejudice, but they remained silent on the equally reprehensible practice of intraracial prejudice. This was a sensitive topic that many of Thurman's image-conscious black readers did not care to confront in their literature. Claude McKay had touched on the issue in his controversial novel, *Home to Harlem* (1928), but Thurman was the first black writer to make the color-prejudice directed against black women by other blacks the main subject of a novel. Not surprisingly, the novel aroused a flood of criticism from black readers, many of whom denounced it as being overly harsh in its treatment of the topic. Other blacks complained that the novel did a disservice to those blacks trying to upgrade their image in the larger American society. Nevertheless, *The Blacker the Berry* became one of the most widely read and most frequently discussed novels of the Harlem Renaissance.

Thurman's novel is significant because it focused much needed attention upon the undue emphasis that many blacks of the 1920's and 1930's placed on skin color, and it encouraged other black writers to explore the issue. For example, George Samuel Schuyler, one of Thurman's contemporaries, published *Black No More* (1931), an alternately satiric and humorous novel that describes what happens in America when a black scientist discovers a way to transform black people into white people. Thurman published two other novels during his brief career, *Infants of the Spring* (1932) and *The Interne* (1932), which he wrote in collaboration with a white author, Abraham L. Furman, but his first novel, *The Blacker the Berry*, remains his most important contribution to African American literature.

Bibliography

Draper, James P., ed. *Black Literature Criticism*. 3 vols. Detroit: Gale Research, 1992. Includes a biographical profile of Wallace Thurman and excerpts from criticism on his works.

Gaither, Renoir W. "The Moment of Revision: A Reappraisal of Wallace Thurman's Aesthetics in *The Blacker the Berry* and *Infants of the Spring*. *CLA Journal* 37 (September, 1993): 81-93. Gaither asserts that Thurman used satire and social realism to explore "New Negro" identity in his novels. He states that Thurman challenged the assumptions of the Harlem Renaissance and saw the need to establish honest portrayals of black people.

Notten, Eleonore Van. *Wallace Thurman's Harlem Renaissance*. Atlanta: Rodolphi, 1994. Notten analyzes Thurman's role in creating and defining the Harlem Renaissance. The author details Thurman's view of the New Negro movement as failing to live up to its promise and being overly concerned with race, self-consciousness, and faddism. Notten describes Thurman's complex and brief life during the Jazz Age.

Andrew J. Angyal

BLESS THE BEASTS AND CHILDREN

Author: Glendon Swarthout (1918-1992)
Type of plot: Adventure
Time of plot: The late 1960's
Locale: Arizona
First published: 1970

> *Principal characters:*
> COTTON, the fifteen-year-old leader of a group of "misfits" who have
> been deposited at Box Canyon Boys Camp
> GOODENOW, a bed wetter and crybaby who threatens suicide until
> Cotton accepts him
> LALLY 2, the youngest of the group, who can find solace at home only
> in the company of imaginary creatures he calls Ooms
> LALLY 1, the older brother of Lally 2, violently jealous and given to
> screaming temper tantrums
> TEFT, a boy who hates all authority and the patriarchal world in which
> he lives
> SHECKER, the son of a loud and tasteless but famous comic

The Novel

Bless the Beasts and Children is one of Glendon Swarthout's most successful novels, though it is often thought of as a book for adolescents as well as about adolescents. The novel tells the story of a group of boys who turn from sniveling, cowardly behavior to heroic action in order to rescue a herd of buffalo. Terribly troubled, the boys have been "made strange" or "paranoid" by their parents, who are representative of an American culture that shapes its citizens according to cultural ideals of wealth and power for men and beauty for women, ideals that conflict with society's professed values.

As the novel opens, Cotton and his group have obviously suffered major traumas that have thrown them into regressive patterns of behavior. Even Cotton, the most nearly normal of the group, is disturbed by a terrible nightmare. He dreams that he and his group are animals penned together and released, only to face the gunfire of a line of humans who stand in front of a line of vehicles. As the shots reach their targets, several of the boys, imaged in the dream as animals, fall heavily and yield brilliant red blood. Cotton, snorting and battering object after object, is maddened by his frustration and fear. At the climax of the dream, Cotton recognizes the face of the human firing at him, and the boy's heart is shattered because the face is that of his mother. The imagined death pulls Cotton from the nightmare, and he finds himself bathed in sweat and recalling an episode in which the boys' counselor had forced them to witness the slaughter of a herd of buffalo. The boys, who had identified with the animals, were horrified by the event. When Cotton discovers that one of his group, Lally 2, has disappeared, he wakes the others, and they all know where Lally 2 went. Moreover, they know they have to join him, to somehow find their way back to the scene of the "crime" that had so outraged and frightened them. The rest of the novel follows the boys on a fantastic mission to save a group of animals and themselves from destruction.

As the story progresses, exposition about the boys and their past behaviors accompanies the action, thus making credible the growth to manhood achieved by each member of the group and manifested in their present actions. Cotton recognizes this growth when he insists, at the beginning of their pilgrimage, that he will not assume authority and that what they will do will be decided by the vote of the whole group.

Though he does not impose his will on the others, he does lead, as a sergeant would the men in his battalion on a guerrilla operation. Cotton leads by doing, by showing himself as strong as his oppressors, by refusing to give up even in what appear to be impossible circumstances. In this behavior, Cotton is the tragic hero, strong enough to fight the gods but doomed to personal failure.

Overall, however, this novel is no tragedy. Cotton leads the boys to victory. In the face of setback after setback, they regroup, change plans, and set their hearts on eventually accomplishing their objective: Symbolically, to return the chamber pot (the symbol of the lowest group of boys at the camp) and gain the buffalo head with horns and beard (the symbol of the skill and power of the beast).

Unable to take a truck from the camp grounds—starting the motor would wake the other campers, and they cannot push the heavy truck up a sandy incline—they abandon the truck and concoct another plan. They saddle horses and ride into town, where they find another vehicle to "borrow" and later return. As they face and surmount each succeeding obstacle, the boys more and more identify with the heroes of every American adventure story, which they summarize as "some men with guns going somewhere, to do something dangerous" for the good of the land and the people.

Sometimes, in moments of danger, when they come to the point of disintegration, they form a circle, get into a huddle, and hug one another, heads touching. In this bonding exercise, they confirm their being. In each episode that gets them closer to their destination, each of the boys says or does something to keep the group going or to save them from obvious mistakes.

Their destination is a corral holding thirty buffalo that are destined to be shot in an annual three-day "hunt" staged by the Arizona Fish and Game Department. The purpose of the hunt is to thin the herd to maintain the proper ratio of the animals to their habitat. The people who come to the animal slaughter are not called "hunters" but "shooters," because there is no sport or need involved. Before long, the event takes on all the characteristics of a blood orgy; it is, moreover, metaphoric of Americans killing their own totem animals, mythic creatures encapsulating much past history.

Already, sixty buffalo have been killed, but the boys have come to free the animals, and free them they do. Though Cotton is killed in the effort, the buffalo run free. The rest of the boys respond; they feel songs in their toes, poetry in their hearts, and tingling in their fingertips, because they know they have made a significant step toward liberating themselves also.

The Characters

Characterization is achieved in *Bless the Beasts and Children* by several means. Flashbacks, set in italics, are relevant to one boy at a time, giving each boy's history and providing a picture of a sick psyche brought on by neglect of basic human needs. In each case, the boys are castoffs, children of parents too busy with their own affairs to really care about the well-being of their own sons. Stephen and Billy Lally, for example, are shown in one flashback competing for the affection of their parents, who bribe each of the boys with a gift and then fly off to winter in Morocco. Another example shows Laurence Teft III trying to get the attention of his parents by stealing money from his mother and driving off in his father's big car, only to collide with two other cars. Instead of speaking to his son, the father locks his cars away, and Teft simply steals a neighbor's car.

The author also illustrates the boys' characteristic behavior in interactions with others, as when Cotton decides that, since he is the oldest and most normal of the group, he needs to take control. Cotton thus hunts about in his footlocker and finds some army tags that jingle when he puts them on; he pulls out an electric razor and runs it over his face, though he has no need to shave; and, finally, he pulls out four tiny bottles of whiskey, takes a drink, and then lights a cigar—actions enough to mark him as the leader he sets out to be.

Lastly, Swarthout sometimes delineates his characters through direct exposition by the commenting narrator or by entry into the mind of a character or an animal. The careful identification of the boys with the animals helps to cast the boys' mission in a heroic mode and gives the plight of the animals considerable urgency, an urgency reflected in the death of Cotton at the end of the novel.

Themes and Meanings

In *Bless the Beasts and Children*, Glendon Swarthout laments the passing of a time when ideals were clear and morality unambiguous; when men were men, and boys became men by imitating their fathers; when buffalo were allowed to roam the plains and were killed only when there was a need for food; and when these magnificent animals represented for the citizens of the United States a primal innocence and a noble and praiseworthy past. The six boys, as much misfits in their society as buffalo are in the last half of the twentieth century, act out of a sense of unambiguous morality and clear ideals. The boys thus become representative of what humans can still aspire to if they can see their selfish behavior for what it is, recognize their lust for power and possessions, and once again bond together in a common course for the greater good.

Cotton's death places him into the archetypal role of tragic hero. He battles forces bigger than he is, and though he is doomed to defeat, his death is cathartic, freeing his followers from their bondage. In this action, Cotton becomes also a kind of savior of his people: "They made a splendid thunder. It pulled down temples. It smote the ears of gnats and governments. It caused an impious planet to slip a cog. It must have been heard in heaven." In the end, the misfits triumph. Though they are frightened and all in tears, they are able to jeer at their elders: "Yah! Yah! Yah!"

Critical Context

Glendon Swarthout won several awards, including the National Society of Arts and Letters Gold Medal. *Bless the Beasts and Children* is generally considered to be his best work. A prolific novelist, short-story writer, and dramatist, Swarthout also had several of his novels, including *Bless the Beasts and Children*, made into films. Perhaps the best known of these is the 1976 film *The Shootist* (starring John Wayne).

Most of Swarthout's fiction can be said to be social commentary on what he identified to be the ills of American society. In his first novel, *Willow Run* (1943), he tackled the subject of the manufacture of bombers; in *Loveland* (1968), a young man struggles against depression. *They Came to Cordura* (1958) is about bravery and cowardice and how people behave under great stress. *Where the Boys Are* (1960) is a comic novel set in Fort Lauderdale at the time when thousands of teenagers descend into Florida during spring break.

Criticism on the body of Swarthout's work is about equally divided. Some critics argue that the linearity of his plots and his frequent appeals to sentiment, sometimes approaching the maudlin, greatly mar his novels. Others, however, have found Swarthout's appeal to absolute values and past ideals to be a welcome relief from much modern fiction.

Bibliography

Bridgers, Sue-Ellen. "*Bless the Beasts and Children* by Glendon Swarthout." In *Censored Books: Critical Viewpoints*, edited by Nicholas J. Karolides, Lee Burress, and John M. Kean. Metuchen, N.J.: Scarecrow, 1993. An informative essay devoted to the reasons why Swarthout's book has been censored.

Conner, John W. Review of *Bless the Beasts and Children*, by Glendon Swarthout. *English Journal* 61 (January, 1972): 139. The reviewer points to the book's use of archetypal patterns and situations as well as exuberance and wit. Praises Swarthout for retaining a hold on the general populace and not relying on the avant-garde.

Garfield, Brian. Review of *Bless the Beasts and Children*, by Glendon Swarthout. *Harper's Magazine* 240 (April, 1970): 107. Garfield calls *Bless the Beasts and Children* a compassionate and compelling drama about six adolescents who start out on a quest for "redemption, pride and justice." The novel, Garfield says, is one superb example of what happens "when a writer's craft is equal to the grandeur of his theme."

Schickel, Richard. Review of *Bless the Beasts and Children*, by Glendon Swarthout. *Saturday Review* 53 (May 2, 1970): 29. Although Schickel calls the novel an exciting adventure story, he is careful to make the point that the novel uses adolescents as major characters but is not for adolescents. The death of Cotton, Schickel believes, is necessary, because the author needed an event of such magnitude to underline the proportions of the change in the characters.

Mary Rohrberger

BLOOD MERIDIAN
Or, The Evening Redness in the West

Author: Cormac McCarthy (1933-   )
Type of plot: Western
Time of plot: The mid-1800's
Locale: The Southwestern United States and Northern Mexico
First published: 1985

>   *Principal characters:*
>   THE KID, the unnamed protagonist, who joins a band of professional
>   scalp hunters
>   CAPTAIN JOHN JOEL GLANTON, the leader of the band
>   JUDGE HOLDEN, his mysterious, almost supernatural
>   second-in-command
>   TOBIN, the kid's closest companion, a former priest who has become a
>   scalper
>   ANGEL TRIAS, the governor of the Mexican state of Chihuahua, who
>   hires the scalpers
>   TOADVINE, DAVID BROWN, BATHCAT, GRANNYRAT, and BLACK JOHN
>   JACKSON, members of the band

The Novel

   Based on historical events and actual personages, *Blood Meridian: Or, The Evening Redness in the West* recounts the exploits of a brutal band of professional scalp hunters who, employed by local governments in the American Southwest and in Mexico, murder Indians for bounty. The novel emphasizes the violent manner in which "civilization" is imposed on a savage land and thus challenges accepted notions concerning Manifest Destiny and the settling of the West.

   McCarthy's protagonist is "the kid," an unnamed boy who runs away from home in Tennessee and heads west, arriving in Nacogdoches, Texas, in 1849. Although only sixteen years old, the kid is an experienced fighter, a survivor in a vicious world. Moving on to Bexar, Texas, he is offered a position with a Captain White, who is leading an expedition into Sonora, Mexico. White argues that the Mexicans are a degenerate race, deserving of conquest, and that the land is godless and needful of salvation. White proves to be mad, but the kid accompanies the group. After days in the desert, they are attacked and slaughtered by a Comanche war party; the kid is among the few survivors of the exceedingly brutal massacre. Finally reaching a town, he is arrested by the local authorities and sent with other remnants of the group to Chihuahua City, where they are put to work cleaning filth from gutters in the street.

   Into Chihuahua City rides a party of professional scalp hunters, led by Captain John Joel Glanton, with the monstrous, mysterious Judge Holden as second-in-command. Holden arranges freedom for those prisoners who wish to join the scalpers, and the kid takes the offer. Glanton has been hired by Angel Trias, governor of the state of Chihuahua, to eradicate Indians in the vicinity; the fee set is one hundred dollars for each scalp brought in. Thus, the small gang of men sets out into the Mexican territory, searching for prey. Roving through the wild land, the scalp hunters find and slaughter stray groups of Apaches—men, women, and children—in addition to occasional Mexicans whose scalps might pass for Indian. A war party then catches their trail and pursues them in a series of skirmishes back to Chihuahua City, where they collect their money and proceed to take over the town in drunken riot. From that point, they ride from city to city, bringing violence, death, and horror with them wherever they go.

In Jesus Maria, Mexico, the citizens of the town turn against the rampaging gang, kill several of them, and force them to flee. They are soon hired by the governor of Sonora and again set out on their bloody business, murdering almost without distinction whatever unlucky wayfarer they encounter. Glanton's gang is then attacked and chased by Mexican soldiers under the command of General Elias; several of the band are killed, and the survivors are forced to draw arrows to determine who will have horses to ride through the desert. The kid is one of those who escape, and after a torturous journey arrives in the town of Santa Cruz, where he again joins Glanton.

The gang goes on to Tucson, losing more men on the way, and then heads for California, taking with them new recruits, including an idiot boy kept in a cage. Reaching the Colorado River, they take over a ferry crossing, killing a number of Yuma Indians in the process and enslaving others to work for them. Finally the Yumas rebel, attack the scalp hunters, and massacre most of them, including Glanton himself. The kid, although wounded in the leg, again escapes and later meets other survivors in the desert. There he is encouraged by Tobin, a former priest, to kill Judge Holden—who, Tobin insists, will kill them if the kid does not. The kid, however, is unwilling to ambush the judge. He and Tobin are later rescued from certain death in the desert by a wandering band of Dieguenos Indians and find their way to San Diego, where they are imprisoned. It is now 1850; the kid has been with Glanton's gang for less than a year.

The last chapters of the book jump forward twenty-eight years, during which time the kid—now known as "the man"—has wandered, an outcast, through the West. He has tried to renounce killing, though he is sometimes forced into it. In 1878, he enters Fort Griffin, Texas, once the main supply point for buffalo hides but now a veritable boneyard, on the brink of extinction. There he once again meets the judge, unchanged over the years, and there he is apparently killed by the judge in an outhouse behind the saloon, his death horrible enough to frighten even the most hardened witnesses of violence in that dark and brutal land. The book ends with the judge dancing in a celebration of death.

The Characters

The kid is the novel's primary protagonist, although, like Ishmael in *Moby Dick: Or, The Whale* (Herman Melville's 1851 classic, echoed throughout *Blood Meridian*), he disappears for considerable periods in the narrative. Although he is almost instinctively capable of violence and appears to be undisturbed by the brutality of the life he pursues, McCarthy sets him apart from the other men of Glanton's gang. The reader is never given insight into the kid's thoughts; he must be judged solely by his actions and occasional statements. Nevertheless, the book does dramatize its concept of moral struggle through the kid. Judge Holden chooses him as disciple or victim from the first time he sees him, and their final encounter, though delayed for almost thirty years, is, according to the judge, predetermined. In the judge's words, only the kid, of all the group, holds back from giving himself fully to the act of bloodletting. Throughout, the kid performs acts of minor mercy, which the other members of the group refuse to do. Yet he is never able to confront the judge. After the massacre at Yuma Crossing, the kid seems increasingly haunted, finally sated with murder and gore. Still, when the judge approaches him in the Fort Griffin saloon, the kid, now the man, continues to hold back, refusing either to join the judge or stand against him. His subsequent death seems a consequence of his failure to make a choice.

Judge Holden is the most intriguing, fascinating, and horrifying of this appalling band of killers. Based on a historical figure, he is well over six feet tall, monstrous in build, and completely hairless. Yet the judge seems almost supernatural, invested with marvelous powers and knowledge, which makes his numerous acts of carnage all the more terrible. Indeed, McCarthy strongly suggests that Judge Holden embodies a greater evil than the other men of the band, that he is, in fact, demonic, a "sootysouled rascal" who waits to snare the lives and hearts of those who, like the kid, live ambivalent lives. The judge is aptly titled, for he does render verdicts and enacts punishments. Larger than life, he espouses a philosophy of the world that reduces existence to war and exacts violence and death, but he himself seems beyond death, an eternal figure in a desolate and bloody land.

John Joel Glanton comes from historical record, his exploits as a scalp hunter and outlaw profiteer found in dozens of accounts of the Old West. McCarthy's version of Glanton accords in detail with these accounts. Glanton is, in McCarthy's telling, a mad captain pursuing the Indian as Ahab does the white whale. Glanton's madness, though, is different from that of Captain White, the leader of the expedition into Mexico described in the early parts of the novel. Glanton is shrewd, a tough and hardbitten soldier. His murderous chase of the Indian has metaphysical overtones, as if he, like Ahab, is demanding that God reveal itself. Although the judge is second in command to him, Glanton seems at times manipulated by Holden; in his times of raving, only the judge can calm and quiet him. Glanton faces his death without fear, spitting in the presence of his killer and challenging, "Hack away you mean red nigger."

Of the other members of the gang, several stand out. Tobin, the former priest, is a paradoxical figure who speaks of the presence of God but participates in the most awful atrocities. He acts as moral adviser to the kid, warning him from the judge and advising him in the matter of survival. Toadvine, a horse thief whose ears have been cropped and forehead branded in punishment, is one of the first men the kid meets in Texas; they engage in a brutal fight in the mud outside a saloon but later become companions in Glanton's gang. Although Toadvine survives the Yuma Crossing massacre, he is later hanged in San Diego along with David Brown, another scalper. John Jackson is the one identified black member of the gang. Shortly after the kid joins Glanton's gang, this Jackson kills a white member, also named John Jackson, for his racial slurs; the black Jackson is the first to die in the Yuma Crossing massacre. Although most of the scalp hunters are identified by name and personality, they are largely secondary, although distinctly drawn, characters in the novel.

Themes and Meanings

Blood Meridian can be read on a number of levels. Although far too graphic and relentless to be considered an adventure novel, it is nevertheless a compelling narrative, full of fights, escapes, mysteries, and astonishments. McCarthy is masterful at creating a believable picture of the Old West in his expert physical description of landscape, his full and detailed knowledge of place and people, and his ability to reveal character through dialogue. The novel is also fascinating for its historical re-creation of a time and way of life generally romanticized or glossed over. Indeed, *Blood Meridian* may be read as revisionist history, a much truer picture of what the settling of the West was all about. McCarthy's research into the time is everywhere evident; his authority gives the story a sense of authenticity that compels belief. There are no heroes in McCarthy's tale, nor does he glorify or excuse or even explain either whites or Indians. Each acts according to needs and desires that seem almost atavistic, and the constant violence is presented as a necessity in such a rough and barbaric world.

The novel, however, is primarily a philosophical exploration of the nature of evil and the significance of moral choice. While most of the characters, including the kid, are not introspective, two figures stand in debate with one another. Judge Holden is the primary exponent of the violence of life. There is no mystery in the world, the judge argues; all things simply are. War, then, is the only "holy" act, the only true game, for only in combat, in the taking of another life, does man prove his existence. If a higher will exists, combat becomes proof of that will, for in battle one must survive and one die, and the battle itself forces a decision to be made by the greater power. Holden argues that all things are preordained and that there is no ultimate escaping from destiny. Thus, he faults the kid for failing to give himself totally to his destiny, to the act of blood, and he accuses him of having a "flawed place" in his soul that retains "some corner of clemency for the heathen."

Tobin, the former priest, speaks for the other side. He argues for the existence of a knowing God, for individual free will and choice. He warns the kid away from the judge early in the novel, and near the end he urges the kid to face the judge, to kill him and the evil he embodies before Holden kills them. The kid has three chances to do so, but each time he refuses. Although he then wanders for twenty-eight years, the kid cannot escape the judge's decree. "Was it always your idea . . . that if you did not speak you would not be recognized?" the judge asks him shortly before he takes his life. It apparently is the kid's failure to take a stand that brings him to his terrible end.

Critical Context

In 1980, McCarthy moved from his home state of Tennessee to El Paso, Texas, where he wrote *Blood Meridian*. It was his fifth novel and the first set outside Tennessee. The first four (*The Orchard Keeper*, 1965; *Outer Dark*, 1968; *Child of God*, 1974; and *Suttree*, 1979) do, nevertheless, anticipate the themes, characters, and moral concerns found in *Blood Meridian*. McCarthy now appears to have taken the Southwest as his primary setting. His *All the Pretty Horses* (1992) also takes place in Texas and Mexico, although it is set a hundred years later than *Blood Meridian*. Its protagonist, John Grady Cole, is another sixteen-year-old boy setting out to make his way in a violent world, but John Grady is a stronger, more principled character than the kid, and his choices give the reader hope for his future.

Blood Meridian was not a commercially successful novel at the time of publication, although it did receive a number of very appreciative reviews. It is, however, now ranked by many as McCarthy's masterpiece. After many years of writing in obscurity, McCarthy achieved both popular and critical success with *All the Pretty Horses*, which won the National Book Award and the National Critics' Circle Award for fiction and was a finalist for the Pulitzer Prize. *All the Pretty Horses* is the first volume in a proposed "Border Trilogy," and it seems certain that McCarthy's reputation will continue to grow with each new work.

Bibliography

Bell, Vereen M. *The Achievement of Cormac McCarthy.* Baton Rouge: Louisiana State University Press, 1988. The first book-length study of McCarthy's work through *Blood Meridian*. "The Metaphysics of Violence: *Blood Meridian*" is the last chapter in the book and compares the novel to Herman Melville's *Moby Dick: Or, The Whale* (1851) and Joseph Conrad's *Heart of Darkness* (1899) as a study of evil. Bell views McCarthy as primarily a nihilist.

Campbell, Neil. "'Beyond Reckoning': Cormac McCarthy's Version of the West in *Blood Meridian or the Evening Redness in the West.*" *CRITIQUE: Studies in Contemporary Fiction* 39 (Fall, 1997): 55-64. Campbell discusses McCarthy's portrayal of the West as a symbolic landscape combining the power of life and death in *Blood Meridian*. He explores McCarthy's pursuit of the West in American mythology as McCarthy seeks to make the myth contain the certainty of its own failure, a movement toward death.

Daugherty, Leo. "Gravers False and True: *Blood Meridian* as Gnostic Tragedy." *Southern Quarterly* 30 (Summer, 1992): 122-133. Argues that gnostic thought is central to McCarthy's work, especially *Blood Meridian*. There is a good god somewhere in the universe, but he is separated from the world, which is ruled by "archons" who establish their own form of justice and rule. Judge Holden, Daugherty maintains, is such an archon.

Donoghue, Denis. "Reading *Blood Meridian*." *The Sewanee Review* 105 (Summer, 1997): 401-418. Donoghue offers a critique of McCarthy's novel. He recommends it for use in a graduate literature course in the teaching of aesthetics and aesthetic ideology because of its narrative style, which discourages ethical judgments.

James, Caryn. "Is Everybody Dead Around Here?" *The New York Times Book Review*, April 28, 1985, 31. A mixed review of *Blood Meridian* that praises McCarthy's originality but decries the novel's "stylistically dazzling but facile conclusion."

Masters, Joshua J. "'Witness to the Uttermost Edge of the World': Judge Holden's Textual Enterprise in Cormac McCarthy's *Blood Meridian*." *CRITIQUE: Studies in Contemporary Fiction* 40 (Fall, 1998): 25-37. Masters analyzes the character of Judge Holden in *Blood Meridian* and sees him as a "Mephistophelean figure who seduces a nomadic horde of scalp hunters into a terrible covenant." The judge is a metaphor of amoral colonial expansion, symbolic of "the discursive and political practices that defined and created the Frontier."

Phillips, Dana. "History and the Ugly Facts of Cormac McCarthy's *Blood Meridian*." *American Literature* 68 (June, 1996): 433-460. Phillips finds that categorizing McCarthy's novel in terms of period and genre is difficult because it fails to fit into the character of a historical novel as defined by Georg Lukacs in his essay "Narrate or Describe?" Phillips explores McCarthy's calm treatment of violence and death, which McCarthy believes are the ultimate truths of human experience.

Sepich, John Emil. *Notes on "Blood Meridian."* Louisville, Ky.: Bellarmine College Press, 1993. An expanded and revised version of Sepich's master's thesis. An exhaustive study of possible historical and literary sources for *Blood Meridian*.

Shaviro, Steven. "'The Very Life of the Darkness': A Reading of *Blood Meridian*." *The Southern Quarterly* 30 (Summer, 1992): 119-129. Shaviro maintains that although *Blood Meridian* is primarily about death, dying, and destruction, there is nevertheless a vitality and even a joy and comedy in the presentation. He considers McCarthy "our greatest living author."

Shaw, Patrick W. "The Kid's Fate, the Judge's Guilt: Ramifications of Closure in Cormac McCarthy's *Blood Meridian*." *The Southern Literary Journal* 30 (Fall, 1997): 102-119. Shaw believes that most critics misinterpret the Griffin Jakes scene that appears at the end of *Blood Meridian*. The prevailing opinion is that Judge Holden murders the boy. Shaw argues that simple murder did not satisfy the Judge. Instead, he claims, the ultimate encounter with Jakes is sexual.

Edwin T. Arnold

THE BLOOD OF THE LAMB

Author: Peter De Vries (1910-1993)
Type of plot: Comic realism
Time of plot: 1920's-1950's
Locale: Chicago and New York City
First published: 1962

> *Principal characters:*
> > DON WANDERHOPE, the narrator, the son of a Dutch immigrant in
> > > Chicago; he becomes an advertising executive in New York
> > BEN WANDERHOPE, his father, an immigrant garbage collector
> > LOUIE WANDERHOPE, his brother, a medical student who dies of
> > > pneumonia
> > GRETA WIGBALDY, Don's girlfriend, later his wife; she eventually
> > > commits suicide
> > CAROL, their daughter, who contracts leukemia
> > RENA BAKER, the tubercular girl with whom Don falls in love in the
> > > sanatorium

The Novel

Peter De Vries's *The Blood of the Lamb* is a deeply religious novel, although the religious sensibility is often expressed in unconventional ways: through the comic, the grotesque, the mundane, and the tragic. The novel's protagonist, Don Wanderhope, whose name suggests a religious quest, grows up in a strict Dutch Calvinist immigrant family in Chicago and later tries to escape from the confines of his immigrant background and become more fully Americanized. Yet he finds his aspirations to the good life thwarted by a series of unhappy circumstances as baffling in their own way as the Calvinistic God whom he has eschewed. The novel is written as Wanderhope's autobiography, with the first section presenting the rather conventional, albeit comic story of an ambitious young man, but the last part of the book, the heart of the novel, deals with the religious crisis brought on by Wanderhope's discovery that his daughter Carol has leukemia. "What people believe is a measure of what they suffer," Wanderhope remarks early in the novel, and his daughter's illness tests his faith and spiritual resources.

The novel opens in the Wanderhope apartment in Chicago with Don's father, Ben, his uncle, and other relatives arguing over the infallibility of the Bible and trying to coax Ben back to orthodoxy, while his son Louie interjects wisecracks as he dresses for a date. Understandably, Don and Louie are more interested in the secular world of Chicago than in Calvinistic Dutch Reformed theology. Don idolizes his older brother for his freethinking and worldliness, but Louie, the golden-haired, healthy boy, dies of pneumonia at the age of nineteen. After his death, Louie remains a model for his younger brother, who strives to escape from the provincialism of his Dutch immigrant background.

Eventually Don meets a Dutch Reformed girl, Greta Wigbaldy, the daughter of a successful builder, who encourages him in his worldly quest. She obtains a key to one of her father's model homes, which they use for their rendezvous until they are caught while making love one evening when her parents arrive with buyers. Don soon finds himself committed to marry Greta.

Around this time, he contracts a slight case of tuberculosis, which requires him to go to a sanatorium near Denver for rest and recuperation. His marriage postponed indefinitely, Don finds himself bedridden and bored. He becomes a member of a small Thursday night literary group which gathers at the home of Dr. and Mrs. Simpson, but his reprieve comes when he meets Rena Baker, a lovely, demure girl who has just been moved from the infirmary to the ambulatory section. The two fall in love, although Rena is still quite ill and does not survive the winter. The pathos of Rena's death foreshadows that of Don's daughter Carol later, as does Dr. Simpson's confession that he had a son, Stevie, who died of leukemia. Rena's death further erodes Don's faith, as he reflects, "Perfect love did not quite cast out fear, but rage did grief, or nearly so."

Don returns to Chicago to find both his father and Greta Wigbaldy hospitalized in the same psychiatric institution, his father for depressive symptoms, and Greta for brooding over a child she had conceived out of wedlock with a married man at her office. When Greta's parents discover that Don is back, they railroad him into marrying their daughter. Unfortunately, Greta's emotional instability only worsens after they move to New York with Don's advertising firm. Alcoholic binges and an extramarital affair mark the progress of her self-destructive behavior, which culminates in a suicide attempt that sends her to the hospital for six months. In the meantime, their daughter Carol has become a child of extraordinary grace and charm, and her father shifts his love and affection to her as Greta succeeds in her second suicide attempt.

The heart of the novel presents Don Wanderhope's intense love and affection for his daughter, as he learns to cherish the joy of the ordinary, which, rather than suffering, best nourishes the soul. Having suffered so much already, Don is determined to enjoy every moment with his daughter, especially after a puzzling extended illness sends her to the hospital for a series of diagnostic tests. The novel deepens in religious significance as Wanderhope confronts the meaning of human suffering and death. He becomes a kind of modern, secular Job, buffeted by sorrow and loss, culminating in the last and greatest test of his faith, the discovery that his daughter has leukemia.

Through the final year that he spends with Carol, Wanderhope alternates between hope and despair as his daughter's condition temporarily improves or worsens. The spectacle of other parents living through the agony of their children's illness is enough to test anyone's faith, as the novel confronts the theological issue of why the innocent suffer. Another parent, Stein, is driven to cynicism and bitterness by the tacit assumption among the hospital staff that "everything was fine." Stein's daughter, Rachel, and Carol become fast friends as he and Wanderhope share a fellowship of parental misery. They often commiserate during their long weekends on the children's ward.

Carol becomes more thoughtful and mature as her disease worsens, actually helping to comfort her father. Birthday parties and weekend outings become great events during her temporary remissions, but the "beast" always returns. Wanderhope contemplates a statue of Christ near the hospital, which comes to represent for him the suffering servant. He prays to St. Jude, the patron saint of hopeless cases, to give them but one more year, but as Carol's leukemia slips into remission, a drug reaction destroys her immune system and leaves her vulnerable to staph infection, which runs throughout the children's ward. The blood of the lamb is sacrificed, meaninglessly, to the foul disease, which has come back to strike in disguised form. In his dignity as a suffering parent, Wanderhope achieves a kind of holiness akin to that of his brave child, who slips away as he watches over her one afternoon. He takes her unused birthday cake and flings it at the statue of the suffering Christ, the comedian who takes a pie in the face for all human suffering.

The Characters

Though De Vries is skilled at creating comic caricatures, Don Wanderhope is clearly at the center of the novel. An immigrant's son from a poor and unpromising Dutch family, his principal motivation is to become successful enough to enjoy some of the benefits of the good life. Yet he is thwarted by a series of personal and family calamities. Wanderhope, as his name suggests, is born to wander (away from his childhood religion, in search of other consolations) and to hope (for some respite from the suffering meted out to himself and those he loves). A secular pilgrim, he chooses the comfortable path of an advertising career, but he is still beset by heartaches in his private life—Louie's and Rena Baker's deaths, his wife's suicide, and finally, Carol's death from leukemia.

A modern Job, he faces many temptations to his faith, and like Job, he is too honest to accept the easy answers of orthodoxy; but unlike Job, suffering does not deepen but diminishes his faith. For as Wanderhope comments at one point, "there seems to be little support in reality for the popular view that we are mellowed by suffering. Happiness mellows us, not troubles; pleasure, perhaps, even more than happiness."

Carol Wanderhope, his daughter, is depicted as a graceful, charming, and vibrant girl, with blue eyes and straight blonde hair, an impish grin, and remarkable courage and fortitude. She is no doubt modeled after De Vries's own daughter Emily, who also died of leukemia. Carol becomes the center of her father's life after Greta's suicide, and he lavishes such intense love upon her that one almost senses a foreboding of loss. She also becomes the focal point of her father's faith and belief. Once her disease is diagnosed, she courageously endures the long and painful treatment for leukemia, and when her death finally comes, it is a shock, though not unexpected. Carol shows a wisdom beyond her years in her understanding of her father, especially in the tape-recorded message that she leaves for him after her death, and in her ability to bring joy and happiness to others despite her affliction. De Vries captures all the charm of her girlish mannerisms with great affection and care in making her an unforgettable character.

Greta Wanderhope, Don's wife, on the other hand, is in many ways an unsatisfactory character. One is never given any credible motivation for her depression, alcoholism, or affairs, especially after her daughter's birth, nor for her suicide. She seems to function primarily as a plot convenience, to be discarded when no longer needed. Rena Baker, though briefly presented, is a far more appealing character than Greta.

Some of De Vries's minor characters are unforgettable comic types, such as Ben Wanderhope, Don's immigrant Dutch father, with his insomnia and religious doubts; the quack Doc Berkenbosch; the organ-grinder, Mr. Italia; his voluptuous daughter Maria; the cynical Dr. Simpson at the sanatorium; the bitter unbeliever, Stein, whose daughter Rachel also has leukemia; and Mrs. Brodhag, Wanderhope's sturdy New England housekeeper.

Themes and Meanings

The thematic significance of De Vries's novel may best be expressed in a credo that Don Wanderhope drafts for his college newspaper in response to their request. In it, he writes,

> I believe that man must learn to live without those consolations called religious, which his own intelligence must by now have told him belong to the childhood of the race. Philosophy can give us nothing permanent to believe either; it is too rich in answers, each canceling out the rest. The quest for Meaning is foredoomed. Human life "means" nothing. What does a Debussy *Arabesque* "mean," or a rainbow, or a rose? A man delights in all of these, knowing himself to be no more—a wisp of music and a haze of dreams dissolving against the sun. Man has only his own two feet to stand on, his own human trinity to see him through: Reason, Courage, and Grace. And the first plus the second equals the third.

This may seem like too easy a denial of God, and too evasive a response to the problem of gratuitous pain and suffering, but what Don is actually denying is the Calvinistic concept of a Deity who is directly responsible for human suffering, who metes out punishment to those who deserve it. Wanderhope rejects this God of his childhood and accepts instead a humanistic ethic that values love and intimacy and cherishes these moments in his relationship with his daughter. Life becomes meaningful through shared intimacy with others, not through any transcendent beliefs. After Carol's death, Don finds through his recollections of their shared life together the courage to continue, even if, as he remarks, "time heals nothing."

Critical Context

Many critics regard *The Blood of the Lamb*, published midway in De Vries's career, as his finest as well as his most serious novel. Basically a comic novelist, De Vries has often dealt with religious issues in a circumspect manner, but here he allows his seriousness of purpose to become more apparent. He employs a confessional format as a way of placing his narrator in a grotesque, bewildering world in which his characters have little control over events. His response to that world has been comic, as if to say that our only defense is to laugh at the tragic absurdity or grotesqueness of life. This tragicomic note is best illustrated by the birthday party in the hospital for the children suffering from leukemia. There is nothing more pathetic than the death of a child, and De Vries registers that pathos in the cynicism of Stein and the impulsive anger of

Wanderhope, who flings his daughter's birthday cake at the statue of Christ.

In *The Blood of the Lamb*, De Vries employs his comic genius to serious purpose in confronting the contemporary meaning of suffering. If the tone of the novel seems mixed, that is intentional, since the grotesque is "a blend of the tragic and the comic." De Vries does not escape into nihilism in his rejection of traditional religious views but affirms, in his narrator's credo, a clear set of humanistic values. In refusing to hold God responsible for the death of his daughter, Wanderhope dignifies himself in his suffering and affirms a compassionate Deity, worthy of worship, who shares the burden of human sorrow.

Bibliography
Bowden, Edwin T. *Peter De Vries*. Boston: Twayne, 1983. A concise critical biography that provides a useful overview of De Vries's life and works. After an introductory biographical chapter, Bowden discusses each of De Vries's major novels. The text is supplemented by a chronology, notes, and a selected bibliography of primary and secondary works.

Campion, Dan. *Peter De Vries and Surrealism*. Lewisburg, Pa.: Bucknell University Press, 1995. Provides chapters on De Vries's literary life, his encounter with surrealism in the 1930's, his novel *But Who Wakes the Bugler*, and his use of humor. Includes very detailed notes and bibliography.

David, Douglas M. "An Interview with Peter De Vries." *College English* 28 (April, 1967): 524-530. A lively interview in which the author raises some interesting questions about De Vries's style of humor. De Vries discusses his use of suburban settings, his character types, and his humorous attitude toward sexuality.

Higgins, William R. "Peter De Vries." In *American Novelists Since World War II*. Vol. 6 in *Dictionary of Literary Biography*. Detroit, Mich.: Gale, 1980. A standard author entry that provides a useful profile of De Vries's life and works. It includes a list of primary and secondary sources.

Jellema, Roderick. *Peter De Vries: A Critical Essay*. Grand Rapids, Mich.: William B. Eerdmans, 1966. This monograph in the Contemporary Writers in Christian Perspective series includes a critical study of De Vries's first eight novels. This study points to the religious issues that are often overlooked in discussions of De Vries as a humorist.

Sale, Richard B. "An Interview in New York with Peter De Vries." *Studies in the Novel* 1 (1969): 364-369. This interview touches on De Vries's writing habits and includes questions about the type of humor in his novels and his view of the world. De Vries discusses the question of whether he is a black humorist.

Yagoda, Ben. "Being Seriously Funny." *The New York Times Magazine*, June 12, 1983, 42-44. A feature article that presents a portrait of De Vries and an overview of his literary career. Yagoda's article offers a good introduction to the writer and his work.

Andrew J. Angyal

A BLOODSMOOR ROMANCE

Author: Joyce Carol Oates (1938-   )
Type of plot: Historical romance fantasy
Time of plot: 1879-1900
Locale: Bloodsmoor, a valley in Eastern Pennsylvania
First published: 1982

> *Principal characters:*
> JOHN QUINCEY ZINN, a gentleman-inventor and the father of a large
> family
> PRUDENCE KIDDEMASTER ZINN, his wife, mother of the Zinn daughters
> CONSTANCE PHILIPPA, their oldest daughter who later becomes a son
> MALVINIA, another daughter, later a famous actress
> OCTAVIA, another daughter, later a wife and mother
> SAMANTHA, another daughter who serves as her father's laboratory
> assistant
> DEIRDRE, an adopted daughter and spiritualist

The Novel

Joyce Carol Oates's book *A Bloodsmoor Romance* is not a kind of fiction that is easily named, although it is not hard to recognize. The work combines both realism and fantasy in a display of authorial skill: Oates uses several techniques to achieve this effect. First, she sets her romance in a past that closely resembles the historical past; in that setting one finds both fictional characters and characters who bear the names of figures from history. In addition, the characters of the work are interested in many of the things that interested the real nineteenth century: spiritualism, the theater, the westward movement, experimental science, abnormal psychology, female sexuality, and the nature of marriage.

It is Oates's second technique that sets the work apart from historical romances per se: She freely manipulates the order of historical events and even adds events that could not possibly occur. John Quincey Zinn demonstrates both of these intrusions of fantasy: He invents the ballpoint pen and solar heating but dismisses them as useless. He invents an operating time machine, but he destroys it after he uses it to misplace one of his pupils. Similarly, Zinn's daughter Constance combines fantasy with history. Reared for marriage, Constance spends her early life accumulating household linens, but when the wedding night comes, she panics, and placing in her groom's bed the dress form used to fit her trousseau, she runs away. Disguising herself as a man, she heads west and tries her hand at being a cowboy, an outlaw, a deputy sheriff, and a gambler. During her masquerade, she turns physically into a man as well, and when she returns to the family home at Bloodsmoor, she poses as Philippe Fox, Constance's agent. Eventually, "he" apparently elopes with a childhood girlfriend.

The plot of the book unfolds by following the lives of the daughters as they grow up. In their adventures, the reader meets several characters drawn from history. For example, Deirdre, the Zinns' adopted daughter, is kidnapped by a mysterious stranger in a black balloon who deposits her on the lawn of a character named Madame Elena Blavatsky. This Madame Blavatsky shares the quirks of the historical Madame Blavatsky, cofounder of the American Theosophical Society. Recognizing Deirdre's talents, Oates's Blavatsky teaches Deirdre to become a medium, contacting spirits beyond the grave, and takes her on a world tour. The reader meets other fictional characters with real counterparts as well: Mark Twain, for one.

As may be inferred from the events recounted above, *A Bloodsmoor Romance* is an often hilariously comic work, yet one that at the same time attempts to capture some of the boundless enthusiasm of the late nineteenth century, an enthusiasm that was often as undiscriminating as it was energetic.

The Characters

Each of the characters seems specially chosen to exemplify many of the attitudes and interests—both common and bizarre—of the nineteenth century.

Deirdre, as has been seen, illustrates the fascination of the time with the occult, but the century had an equal passion for the stage. This love is shown through Malvinia, who runs away as a girl to join a troupe of actors. She becomes a star, attracts her leading man, and, in the first turning point of her life, discovers a horrible secret: She likes sex. Malvinia, like many people of the nineteenth century, thinks that women are too fine and high-minded to possess sexual feelings. Thus she is caught in the ironic situation in which she delights in her sexuality while despising herself for having zest for what she calls "the beast." Although she regards her lustiness as unwomanly, she is unable, as she puts it, to "control herself." Only later, when she reforms and marries a clergyman, is she freed from her "burden." She then becomes the kind of obedient and pure wife celebrated in nineteenth century domestic literature.

Her sister Octavia, on the other hand, from her earliest age wants only to be a wife and mother and through her story shows the century's commitment to a stern duty and an almost equally stern religion. The taboos of the time prevent frank instruction in reproduction, and she searches unsuccessfully for the facts of life in books. Even her mother is worse than useless: Mrs. Zinn, clearly uncomfortable at the question, scolds Octavia and tells her simply to do whatever her husband wants. This advice has unforeseen consequences when an older man, a jaded deviant, becomes Octavia's husband. He ties her up; he puts a bag over her head; he does strange things to her. Octavia, however, is rewarded: She bears two babies, whom she cherishes. When they and her husband die, she is then freed for what she calls a "higher calling," giving herself over to prayer, good works, and the care of her aged parents.

Two of the family members show the optimism of the age, an enthusiastic conquest of nature through both exploration and understanding. In Constance Philippa and her adoption of the advice to go west, the reader sees the work of the nation in consolidating its continent-wide borders and its taming of a wild environment. In her father, the reader sees the gentleman-scientist, the chief actor in the drama of scientific discovery in the time before Thomas Edison established the research laboratory. Even here, though, one finds the tendency of the age to be lured from its path by golden yet quirky goals. Despite inventing myriad useful devices, Zinn quests for one grail only—the perpetual motion machine (and only his daughter Samantha believes that he can do it).

One last character deserves description—Oates's narrator. She is the filter through which the reader sees the story, an elderly and sheltered virgin, self-effacing and inno-cent. She happily absorbs every piece of received wisdom of the time: For example, she is never happier than when describing Octavia or the converted Malvinia in their roles of traditional wife and mother. If the Zinn daughters try to escape from the roles society has decreed for them, they find little sympathy from the narrator. Indeed, she is so much of a type that the reader never even learns her name.

Themes and Meanings

Some of the themes of the book are clear and straightforward: In her history of a family with five daughters, Oates has ample opportunity to explore the beginnings of feminism as those daughters react against the strictures of their times. There is a clear picture of the century's attitudes toward female sexuality, for example, in the lives of Octavia and Malvinia. Neither seems to illustrate either a desirable or natural re-sponse to natural stimuli. The awkwardness of the time in explaining sex—an awk-wardness that produced actual books such as Katherine Lee Bates's euphemistic *The Wedding Day Book* (1882)—hampers rather than helps Octavia. Without guidance she has no standard of comparison.

Malvinia, on the other hand, cannot simply enjoy her sensual nature, even in mar-riage. She despises herself for being what she is, regarding her sexual enjoyment as a perversion rather than a reward. A character as physically satisfied in marriage as, say, Geoffrey Chaucer's Wife of Bath would be incomprehensible to either Octavia or Malvinia. Few of the daughters seem to find an accommodation with sex. It is the thought of what must occur on her wedding night, after all, that sends Constance flee-ing to the West. Only with Samantha is there no suggestion of neurotic sexuality. In her role as scientist and later as a woman who freely chooses her own husband, Samantha portrays the new woman that the new century would call into being. The most modern-seeming of the sisters, Samantha is also the most satisfied. Perhaps in the pictures of these sisters is there the strongest condemnation of the century's treat-ment of women.

Closely connected with the theme of sexuality is that of religion. Many of the char-acters seem to regard spirituality as a medicine for sexuality. Even those who, like Octavia or Malvinia, find genuine fulfillment in charitable work seem to be in retreat from the urgings of their flesh. Religion makes Malvinia meek and compliant, a change made more, rather than less, dramatic because it is a change that she desires. The less pleasant underside of religion is illustrated by Deirdre. The spiritism that she practices is worse than a hoax. Under the control of the spirits, the unwitting Deirdre sometimes says vicious things. The spirits themselves become stronger through their association with her, strong enough to kill a team of doubters attempting to test the reality of Deirdre's powers.

Another theme of dark destruction is displayed in the work of the father. Nineteenth century science is naturally the foundation of twentieth century science, and the bending of scientific means to perverted ends is explored in the story of John Quincey Zinn. The quiet of the Zinn household ends when Zinn is interviewed by a reporter from the *Atlantic*. As a result of the notoriety that follows the publication of the article, Zinn's talents come to the attention of Congress. In a parody of congressional appropriation of contemporary times, the government funds Zinn's research on the condition that he direct his efforts toward finding a new method of execution. The ever-creative inventor then builds the first electric chair. Until this point, Samantha has been her father's faithful assistant and disciple, but she regards his latest work as a prostitution of his talent. She can no longer stay, but ironically when she runs away, it is with another younger inventor.

Critical Context

A Bloodsmoor Romance attempts to re-create a period novel form that no longer exists. Contemporary fiction is generally either realistic or fantastic. In the nineteenth century, however, fantasy and reality could mix freely in what was known as the romance. Contemporary novelists who try to insert fantasy in reality are often misunderstood or scolded by critics for mixing their genres. When British novelist Nevil Shute added some fantasy to one of his novels, the critics advised him to stick to the type of realism that his readers had come to expect in his works.

Joyce Carol Oates, by calling her novel a romance, is clearly signaling her readers that there will be certain elements of fantasy in addition to the real-seeming story that she is trying to tell. Some of the fantasy includes the mysterious balloonist who kidnaps Deirdre Zinn, the time machine invented and destroyed by Mr. Zinn, and the mysterious change by which Constance Philippa becomes a man in body as she becomes more masculine and assertive in character.

The realistic story line includes the poor but loving family, the real inventions of an age of inventiveness, as well as the enthusiasm with which the nation moved from the innocence of a primarily agrarian culture into the somewhat jaded technological realities of the twentieth century.

Of all the writers who might try to create a romance, Oates is one of the ablest. She is a prolific writer of more than thirteen novels, including *them* (1969), the winner of the National Book Award. In addition, she has published volumes of short stories, poems, and essays, as well as several plays.

Besides being a writer, Oates is a teacher, too, with credentials in literature. She has written much criticism in which she often takes male writers to task for their limited views on women's potential, both intellectual and sexual. She portrays in her own intellectual life the sorts of honors that gifted women can accomplish. Oates is the winner of awards from the Guggenheim Foundation, the National Institute of Arts and Letters, and the Lotos Club.

Bibliography

Creighton, Joanne V. *Joyce Carol Oates: Novels of the Middle Years*. New York: Twayne, 1992. Creighton presents the first critical study of the novels Oates published between 1977 and 1990, including the mystery novels published under the name of Rosamund Smith. Includes analysis of *A Bloodsmoor Romance*.

Daly, Brenda. *Lavish Self-Divisions: The Novels of Joyce Carol Oates*. Jackson: University of Mississippi Press, 1996. An excellent study that argues that the "father-identified daughters in her early novels have become, in the novels of the 1980s, self-authoring women who seek alliances with their culturally devalued mothers." Offers a perceptive reading of the evolution of feminist elements in Oates's work and includes critical analysis of *A Bloodsmoor Romance*.

Johnson, Greg. *Invisible Writer: A Biography of Joyce Carol Oates*. New York: Dutton, 1998. An illuminating look at the novelist once dubbed "the dark lady of American letters." Drawing on Oates's private letters and journals, as well as interviews with family, friends, and colleagues, Johnson offers a definitive study of one of America's most gifted novelists.

Wesley, Marilyn C. *Refusal and Transgression in Joyce Carol Oates' Fiction*. Westport, Conn.: Greenwood Press, 1993. An interesting study spanning the spectrum of Oates's work. Includes a helpful bibliography and index.

Walter E. Meyers

THE BLUEST EYE

Author: Toni Morrison (1931-   )
Type of plot: Psychological realism
Time of plot: 1940-1941
Locale: Lorain, Ohio
First published: 1970

> *Principal characters:*
> CLAUDIA MACTEER, the narrator, a nine-year-old black girl
> PECOLA BREEDLOVE, the protagonist, Claudia's eleven-year-old friend
> PAULINE (POLLY) BREEDLOVE, her mother, a maid
> CHOLLY BREEDLOVE, her father and the father of her baby
> FRIEDA MACTEER, Claudia's ten-year-old sister
> MICAH ELIHUE WHITCOMB (SOAPHEAD CHURCH), a West Indian and a
>   self-proclaimed psychic and spiritual adviser

The Novel

The events in *The Bluest Eye* are seen from the point of view of Claudia MacTeer. As the novel begins, Claudia is looking back at the year when she was nine and when her friend Pecola Breedlove, then eleven, became pregnant, having been raped by her own father, Cholly Breedlove. In the summer of 1941, Claudia and her sister, Frieda, planted marigold seeds in the childish belief that if the marigolds survived, so would Pecola's baby. Even as the novel opens, however, the reader knows that the seeds never germinated and that the baby died. Years later, it is still impossible for Claudia to explain why the events of that year happened, so the novel becomes instead her account of how they happened.

The Bluest Eye has two structuring devices. One is the four seasons, which provide the four major divisions of the book. Claudia begins her account with the fall of 1940, when Pecola is placed temporarily in the MacTeer home because her father has tried to burn down the storefront apartment that serves as the Breedloves' home. In the spring, Pecola is raped by her father, and by summer, her increasingly obvious pregnancy is the subject of gossip all over town, and Pecola herself has retreated into madness, kept company in the fantasy world of her own mind by an imaginary friend.

Also giving structure to the novel is a passage that imitates the Dick-and-Jane readers once so popular in elementary schools. The picture that the passage presents of the perfect white family—Mother and Father, Dick and Jane, the dog and the cat, all living happily in their pretty green and white house—contrasts sharply with the world of the Breedloves and the MacTeers, the world of poor blacks. To show the contrast, Morrison repeats the passage three times: first, as it would normally appear on the printed page; then, with all punctuation removed; and finally, with even the spaces between words removed. The Dick-and-Jane story degenerates on the page into a jumble of letters; lines from the storybook-perfect account of its characters' lives are interspersed throughout the Breedloves' story to emphasize the contrasting ugliness and disorder of theirs. A few run-together sentences describe Dick and Jane's pretty house. The Breedloves' home is a converted store with beaverboard panels providing the only inner walls. The mother from the world of Dick and Jane is laughing and playful. Pecola's mother, Pauline Breedlove, has seen all of her dreams fade into nothingness. She finds escape from the ugliness of the storefront and her life there as a maid in a white family's home as clean and orderly as the world in which Dick and Jane live. Her own family is an intrusion into that orderly world, and she returns from that world each day to fight with her husband and to beat her children into respectability. The father, too, unlike the smiling father of Dick and Jane, has seen his dreams shattered and has suffered the humiliation associated with growing up black in a white-dominated world. He has responded to the mistreatment he has received with violence. Ironically, even the love that he wants to express to his daughter takes a violent form when he returns home drunk one afternoon and rapes her.

Early in the novel, Pecola lies in bed listening to her parents go through the mechanical but painful ritual that their fights with each other have become. She longs to make herself disappear, and in her mind she does make her whole body cease to exist, except for her eyes. She can never make her eyes go away. Eyes become the center of Pecola's life and of her constant search for love. She believes that if only she had beautiful blue eyes, the world would look prettier—that even her parents would be hesitant to fight in front of such pretty blue eyes.

After the rape and the resulting pregnancy and suspension from school, Pecola goes to Lorain's "Spiritual and Psychic Reader," Soaphead Church, to ask him to give her blue eyes. Fraud that he is, he does in a sense grant her wish. Soaphead knows that from that day on, Pecola will have blue eyes, but only in her own mind. Before she leaves the house, Soaphead uses Pecola to rid himself of a nuisance: a mangy old dog that spends its days on his doorstep. He gives Pecola poisoned meat to feed the dog, telling her that the dog's response will be a sign to her whether she will get her wish. Pecola watches in horror as the dog stumbles around the yard and dies. This episode, combined with the earlier rape as well as a second assault on her by her father, drives Pecola over the edge into insanity. In her madness, Pecola does have blue eyes, although no one sees them except for her and the imaginary friend that she invents to reassure her constantly that her eyes are indeed the bluest in the world.

The Characters

Although the eleven-year-old Pecola is the most obvious victim in the novel, most of the black characters are presented as victims of white society. In her childish innocence, Pecola really believes that the world would be better if viewed through the blue eyes so highly valued according to the white standard of beauty. Pecola has been made to feel ugly because she is black. Her quest for blue eyes is symbolic of her quest for the attention and love that she has missed during her bleak childhood.

Claudia feels loved by her family, yet she also feels rejected by society in general because of her blackness. By having Claudia narrate the events of the novel, Morrison (who herself was born in Lorain, Ohio, in 1931) presents them with some of the naïveté of the child but also with the clarity of vision that prejudiced adults have lost. Claudia is too young to accept without question what everyone else seems to assume: that little black girls are somehow lesser beings because of their blackness. She hates white baby dolls and the little white girls (including Shirley Temple) on whom they are modeled. She would like to tear both apart to find their secret: What is it that makes all adults, black and white, prize little white girls so much and little black girls so little? Claudia and her sister, Frieda, seem to be the only people who believe that Pecola's baby deserves to live and be loved. The older Claudia who tells the story, however, knows that she has lost her innocence and her idealism. By the time she looks back on 1941 from the perspective of later years, she has transformed her hatred for the Shirley Temples of the world into a type of fraudulent love.

While the young Claudia can still look upon the inequities of life as the injustices that they are, her parents have long since accepted the roles in which society has cast them. If the white world has declared them ugly, then ugly they will be. Early in the Breedloves' marriage, Cholly makes Pauline, with her one lame foot, feel beautiful for a time, but she later comes to believe the films and billboards which tell her constantly that white is beautiful and black is ugly: She accepts the mantle of her own ugliness. Cholly shows his ugliness through his actions. As a boy, he was surprised in the middle of his first sexual encounter by three white hunters and forced to conclude the act under the glow of their lights and their laughter. Too young and small to strike out at his tormentors then, he has been striking out ever since. Ironically, he makes his own daughter's first sexual experience as painful as his own.

Soaphead Church, the fraudulent spiritualist, provides another perspective on the issue of race. For generations, his family has tried to marry "up" and nurture its white blood. Marriage between relatives, however, has also weakened the faculties of certain family members, including Soaphead. He occupies himself by promising his clients the impossible and molesting little girls. He is wise enough in his own mad way, though, to recognize the pathos of Pecola's situation. He writes a letter to God chastising Him for failing to answer Pecola's prayer and thus forcing Soaphead to do God's work for Him.

Themes and Meanings

The principal themes of the novel are summed up in the spring section, when the narrator speaks of the ideas of physical beauty and romantic love as "probably the most destructive ideas in the history of human thought." In this novel with no single major white character, white ideas about beauty still exert their power upon the lives of blacks, creating within the black community a strict caste system based on shades of blackness. Black adults and children alike, with the exception of Frieda and Claudia it seems, admire the "high-yellow dream child" Maureen Peal. The minor character Geraldine teaches her light-skinned son that there is a line between colored people and niggers, a line that must be carefully guarded against attempts to erode it. At the opposite extreme from Maureen Peal is Pecola, whose own mother knew from the moment of Pecola's birth that her very black baby was ugly. At both the beginning and the end of the novel, Pecola is identified with a certain type of seed that the soil will not nurture. Pecola is described at the beginning as the plot of black dirt into which her father had dropped his seed. By the end, Cholly, Pecola, and their baby are all dead, and Claudia tries to explain why:

> This soil is bad for certain kinds of flowers. Certain seeds it will not nurture, certain fruit it will not bear, and when the land kills of its own volition, we acquiesce and say the victim had no right to live. We are wrong, of course, but it doesn't matter. It's too late.

If ideas of physical beauty are destructive, so are ideas of romantic love. Once Pecola starts to menstruate, she knows that physically she is ready to have a child, but Frieda tells her that first she must get someone to love her. Pecola's tragedy is that she does not know how to do that. She is aware of the choking sounds and silence of her parents' lovemaking and the commercial sex of the three prostitutes—China, Poland, and Marie—who live upstairs, but her father's attempt to show his love for her gives her a painful initiation into sex as devastating as his own was. In trying to express his love for her, Cholly destroys her: "He, at any rate, was the one who loved her enough to touch her, envelop her, give something of himself to her. But his touch was fatal, and the something he gave her filled the matrix of her agony with death. Love is never any better than the lover."

Critical Context

The Bluest Eye is significant as the first novel of a writer whose succeeding works have built upon the strength and the promise of the first to establish Morrison as one of the most respected of contemporary black novelists. In the three novels that closely followed *The Bluest Eye*—*Sula* (1973), *Song of Solomon* (1977), and *Tar Baby* (1981)—Morrison expanded her fictional world beyond the limited black community of Lorain, Ohio, where she herself grew up, to encompass other American cities and towns and, in *Tar Baby*, the Caribbean. She also expanded her range of characters, focusing in *Sula* on the black female both as child and as adult, in *Song of Solomon* on the young black male, and in *Tar Baby* on the young black woman who has achieved success even by white standards.

The publication of *Song of Solomon* brought Morrison immediate and immense popular success. Even as early as *The Bluest Eye*, however, she was acclaimed for her poetic language, the mythic scope of her vision, and the fresh perspective from which she presented the black community and the relationships among its members. In presenting the separate but unequal world of blacks from the point of view of a child and in focusing on the child as victim, she gave the literary world a new look at a world of injustice and oppression that in itself was hardly new.

Bibliography

Alexander, Allen. "The Fourth Face: The Image of God in Toni Morrison's *The Bluest Eye*." *African American Review* 32 (Summer, 1998): 293-303. Alexander discusses the concept of the fourth face of God as portrayed in Morrison's novel. He argues that while the image of the fourth face is viewed as a source of evil, it can also be seen as an attempt by Morrison to humanize God and draw a picture of a God who has more in common with the deities of traditional African religion than the Western notions. Alexander also looks at Morrison's attempt to address the question of how a supposedly omnipotent and loving God can allow evil to exist in the world.

Dahill-Baue, William. "Insignificant Monkeys: Preaching Black English in Faulkner's *The Sound and the Fury* and Morrison's *The Bluest Eye* and *Beloved*." *The Mississippi Quarterly* 49 (Summer, 1996): 457-473. Dahill-Baue compares the ways William Faulkner and Morrison challenge the boundaries that separate black and white. While Faulkner merely challenges blacks' position as stereotyped members of a racist society, Morrison goes one step further and portrays blacks as breaking down most racial stereotypes.

Garabedian, Deanna M. "Toni Morrison and the Language of Music." *CLA Journal* 41 (March, 1998): 303-318. Garabedian explores Morrison's use of the language of music in *The Bluest Eye*, *Sula*, and *Song of Solomon*. She contends that the discourse of music in each of Morrison's novels highlights characters, shapes their value systems, and reveals how their values affect their identity as blacks in a sexist and racially oppressive society.

Thomas, Leester. "When Home Fails to Nurture the Self: Tragedy of Being Homeless at Home." *The Western Journal of Black Studies* 21 (Spring, 1997): 51-58. Thomas explores the concept of home in relation to identity in Morrison's novel. He draws parallels between the disruption of identity when an individual is rejected by society and family and the self-rejection African Americans have suffered. An insightful deconstruction of African Americans' feelings about their cultural identity.

Wren, James A. "Morrison's *The Bluest Eye*." *The Explicator* 55 (Spring, 1997): 172-175. Wren focuses on the character of M'Dear and her nontraditional methods of healing. Wren asserts that M'Dear's deductive methodology was based on factual observations and verifications, in contrast to the superstitious beliefs of that period, and that her advanced medical knowledge allows her to pin down a correct diagnosis.

Donna B. Haisty

BONE

Author: Fae Myenne Ng (1956-   )
Type of plot: Family
Time of plot: The 1960's to the 1990's
Locale: San Francisco, California
First published: 1993

> *Principal characters:*
>> LEILA LEONG, the narrator of the story, the oldest of three Chinese American sisters
>> ONA LEONG, the second sister, who has committed suicide before the present action of the novel
>> NINA LEONG, the third sister, who works for a travel agency in New York
>> MAH LEONG, the girls' mother, the owner of a children's shop
>> LEON LEONG, the father to the three girls, second husband to Mah, and biological father of Ona and Nina
>> MASON LOUIE, Leila's lover and, later, husband
>> TOMMIE HORN, the owner of a sweatshop, who becomes Mah's lover during her marriage to Leon

The Novel

Fae Ng's novel *Bone* chronicles the fictional history of a family of Chinese immigrants living in San Francisco's Chinatown from the 1960's to the 1990's. The main characters are three sisters, American by birth and environment, struggling to make their ways to peace as persons, women, and Chinese Americans. The central event of the story is the death of the second daughter, Ona, who has recently killed herself by jumping from the thirteenth floor of a building while on drugs.

The novel itself is divided into fourteen chapters, all simply but beautifully written and all narrated by the older sister Leila, to whom the story belongs most. It is she who tells and retells, from different though not contradictory perspectives, the story of her family and of her sister's suicide. Most of the action is in the present, yet Leila's memory frequently wanders to past events that are recounted in detail.

The book begins at some point after the recent death of Ona. Leila has just returned from New York, where she has married Mason Louie, another Chinese American from San Francisco, without her parents' permission or foreknowledge. She is seeking Leon Leong, her stepfather, to inform him of the marriage; oddly, it is not her mother whom she wishes to tell.

Events of the family's history are not given in chronological order. Particular events are referred to in conversation or are recorded in the narrator's mind as she revisits those parts of the family's struggles in America that are important to her. Leila provides various interpretations and gives the perspectives of others in the family.

Leila's best and most meaningful relationship is with her stepfather, who somehow comes to represent America itself. Leila, who is employed by the local school system as a "community relations expert," does succeed in coming to terms with herself, her family, her Chinese ancestry, and her American identity.

As Leila reports her marriage to other family members, the events of their respective lives are told in turn. This organizational method provides the structure of the novel.

Leon's story is given first. He is a collector of junk, a repairman who is always undertaking projects that are never finished. Moreover, he signs on to ships as a crew employee and disappears for weeks and months at a time with little or no explanation. When he learns that his wife has been unfaithful to him, he removes himself from the house for some indefinite but extended period until the three daughters somehow succeed in getting him to return. Leon is guilt-ridden for having promised to return the bones of his father to China for burial—a promise he has never been able to keep, because of financial difficulties and the lack of direction in his life.

Mah is in many respects a good mother. On the other hand, she is always too busy at work to be a perfect mother, and she is seemingly handicapped by language and her Chinese way of thinking. Victimized by Leila's father, her first husband, who had deserted her with the child, Mah makes a second marriage with Leon and becomes unfaithful to him. When Ona kills herself, she blames her own adultery for the death.

Ona's story is one of disillusion. She has been in love with Osvaldo, whose father enters a business venture with Leon that fails. Consequently, the two men fall out as friends, and Leon forbids Ona to marry her young lover. After an abortion that she keeps secret from everyone except Leila, Ona kills herself while on drugs.

Only Nina seems to have some degree of happiness and security, perhaps because she has moved herself to New York, where she lives independent of her family. As such, she remains something of an outsider to the family, and she does not wish to return to Chinatown for her sister's funeral.

In the middle of the novel, the family visits the Chinese cemetery where Grandfather Leong (Leon's father) is buried. Unable to locate his grave and irritated by a caretaker who denies them access because it is not visiting hours, the family does succeed in learning what has happened to Grandfather Leong's bones. They have been cremated without the knowledge or permission of the family, and they can now never be recovered or returned to China.

Following this event, Leila relates the immediate responses of friends and others after Ona's death. All members of the family want to be left alone in their grief, so that they can alternately blame themselves and then other family members for the suicide. There is plenty of guilt to go around: Leon blames himself for forbidding her marriage to Osvaldo; Mah blames herself for her adultery; Leila blames herself for not trying to talk to her sister; and Nina blames herself for being absent and in New York.

The characters are never truly reconciled to their own feelings of guilt, nor do they really come to find peace within themselves. The novel concludes, however, with Leila's realization that the family's problems and, in particular, Ona's suicide, are not because the family members are transplanted Chinese. Leon's assertion that "The heart never travels" concludes the novel and is doubtless its most meaningful theme and occurrence. Yet Ng's point is that the heart never travels from home (now America, not China).

The Characters

Leila Leong is the central character of the novel and the person whose story is being told. She has problems in coming to terms with her identity because of her Chinese heritage, yet she lives and succeeds as a third-generation American who can speak little or no Chinese and who has no real or functional identity with her heritage. Ng develops this main character primarily by revealing Leila's thoughts; indeed, most of her actions are of little consequence. Leila's story is one of self-discovery, a matter of growing up as a person and growing into an awareness of the American she has been since birth.

Readers learn of Ona Leong only from the recollections of others. Ng relates on the first page of the novel that this middle sister has killed herself. Slowly, through hints, memories, and half-memories of other characters, the reasons for her actions are revealed, if not explained. Ona kills herself because she is the daughter most assimilated into American culture; she is the one who has the fewest problems as an American and, therefore, the most problems as a Chinese American. Her abortion and forbidden affair with Osvaldo, like her drug use, are only symptomatic of what is wrong with her character.

The youngest sister, Nina, tries to escape all the family's problems by changing her geography. A job and apartment in New York accomplish this, and as a tour guide for a travel agency, she actually leads tours to China. There, she feels as out of place as the other American tourists, though she can speak enough Chinese to succeed at her employment. Nina, like the other sisters, has no problems with such things as preferring American to Chinese foods, but she cannot live in Chinatown, or even close to it, as the other family members choose to do.

The mother, Mah, experiences more real problems with cultural assimilation than the other characters. She agonizes both for and over the past; she claims it and its customs and traditions when it is to her advantage, but readily denies or ignores these on choice. Her reaction to Leila's marriage to Mason demonstrates the point. She disapproves of the marriage and therefore uses Chinese language and traditions to make Leila feel guilty.

Leon, as stepfather to Leila, serves to symbolize America, the "stepfather" of the three girls. As such, he often embodies characteristics that are not good. He can never hold down a good job; he perpetually has trouble with his business schemes; he disappears for long periods of time without explanation; he is not a good husband to his wife; and he is not a good representative of the old China. He has been unable to return his father's bones home for burial.

Mason Louie, the young mechanic with whom Leila lives, then loves, then marries, is already Americanized: He repairs foreign cars, occasionally uses drugs, and is generally at peace with himself as a man, mechanic, and husband. He helps Leon to get out of trouble on several occasions, and he will have a typical relationship with his mother-in-law in the American fashion.

Tommie Horn, as owner of a sweatshop in which Mah works, had been a candidate to marry Mah, but Leon asked her first. Tommie embodies the worst of all that was true about life in China. He is a ruthless slave-driver who at once takes care of Mah and her daughters and uses them whenever he needs to get his business orders filled hurriedly.

Themes and Meanings

Most centrally, the novel is a story of ethnic assimilation; the realization of the main character is that the transformation has already occurred. Leila learns that she is and has always been an American. The extent to which this Americanism is defined by her Chinese heritage is the real question.

Basically, the problems that confront the Leong family are not, at least in the present, caused by their ethnicity or race. For the three girls, at least, their problems are those of most young women. They are concerned with life, love, happiness, perhaps marriage if it is convenient, and careers. The social problems around them, issues such as drugs and abortion, are not unique to them, and they experience and cope with such matters as do Americans of other ethnic descent.

It is Leon, rather than Leila, who voices Ng's themes. At the beginning of the novel he asserts that "it's time that makes a family, not just blood." His comment applies generally to the Leong family and specifically to his relationship to Leila. Through the years, these two characters come to love each other more than they do those to whom they are related by blood. Ng's point is that enough time in America will assuredly make the bonds stronger to this country than the blood ties to those of China. As the novel progresses, characters accept or reject this idea, both in terms of the family and homeland, to their own benefit or detriment.

The central symbol of the novel is indicated by its title. What is the "bone" of contention here? And whose "bone" is it, anyway? Are the family's problems rooted in Chinese ancestry, heritage, and tradition, or in their perhaps misplaced and displaced lives as Americans? Regardless, the question is rendered irrelevant in the central scene in the cemetery. Grandfather Leong's bones are unidentifiable and will never be located. The past is lost to eternity. There is no bone, though there once was.

Critical Context

Bone is Fae Ng's first novel. Published in 1993, it is a poignant statement about cultural assimilation of ethnic groups, particularly Asian Americans, into the American way of life. The characters and events in the novel demonstrate that the process in the 1990's is not what it has been for various immigrant groups, particularly Asians, in the past. Barriers caused by language and education are not what they were even as recently as the 1960's and 1970's. As the characters recollect their lives in America, it is undeniable that the problems of Grandfather Leong, and even of Leon himself, are not those of the three girls.

It is important that this work of fiction reads as biography. The novelist writes in this manner so as to give more credibility to her experiences and themes, which have appeared in her previously published short stories.

In its social context, *Bone* realizes that "becoming American," too, has been accelerated in today's world just as other aspects of American life. Time itself becomes the cure for all the Leong family's problems, even the death of Ona.

Bibliography

Cheng, Lucie, et al. *Linking Our Lives: Chinese American Women of Los Angeles*. Los Angeles: Chinese Historical Society of Southern California, 1984. The authors discuss problems of Chinese women as they become Americanized in Southern California. The women of the Leong family, including the mother and three daughters, confront these obstacles.

Hunnewell, Susannah. "When the Old Begin to Die." *The New York Times Book Review* (February 7, 1993): 9. This article describes the sweatshops where Ng grew up in Chinatown, San Francisco, California, and where many older people worked hard to give their grandchildren a better life. Ng's novel pays tribute to the dedication of her grandparents' generation.

Kim, Elaine H., with Janice Otani. *With Silk Wings: Asian American Women at Work*. San Francisco: Asian Women United of California, 1983. Kim lists problems of Chinese and other Asian American women on the job market. Particularly relevant to Ng's novel are the depictions of women in a sweatshop such as the one in which Mah Leong works.

Knoll, Tricia. *Becoming Americans: Asian Sojourners, Immigrants, and Refugees in the Western United States*. Portland, Oreg.: Coast to Coast Books, 1982. Knoll describes the problems and circumstances of numerous Asian immigrant groups throughout the Western United States, including the Chinese in San Francisco.

Stephenson, Heather. "Out of the Kitchen and Travelling On: New Fiction by Asian Women." *New England Review* 16 (Winter, 1994): 169-176. Stephenson reviews novels by Banana Yoshimoto and Doug Thu Huong as well as *Bone*. Her comparisons are revealing.

Suh, Mary. "Fae Myenne Ng: Sparse Words, Rich Images." Review of *Bone*, by Fae Myenne Ng. *Ms.* 3 (June, 1993): 75. Suh's review of Ng's novel focuses on the insider's account of life in Chinatown, the family life of Chinese immigrants, and the immigrant's story. Provides an excellent perspective of the cultural background of Ng's book.

Tsai, Shih-shan Henry. *The Chinese Experience in America*. Bloomington: Indiana University Press, 1986. Tsai gives a broad outline, replete with numerous details, about problems of cultural assimilation of the Chinese in America. The book is recent enough to take up problems of present-day first- and second-generation Chinese immigrants.

Carl Singleton

THE BONFIRE OF THE VANITIES

Author: Tom Wolfe (Thomas Kennerly Wolfe, Jr., 1930-   )
Type of plot: Social realism
Time of plot: The 1980's
Locale: New York City
First published: 1987

> *Principal characters:*
> SHERMAN McCOY, a bond salesman who considers himself a "Master of the Universe" but who is going broke on an annual income of a million dollars
> JUDY McCOY, Sherman's fading wife, who loves to spend her husband's money and fancies herself an interior decorator
> MARIA RUSKIN, Sherman's Southern-born mistress, the unfaithful wife of an elderly multimillionaire
> PETER FALLOW, an alcoholic English reporter for a New York scandal sheet
> LAWRENCE KRAMER, the ambitious assistant district attorney in Sherman's first trial for reckless endangerment
> THOMAS KILLIAN, Sherman's streetwise defense attorney
> JUDGE MYRON KOVITSKY, a feisty judge who presides over Sherman's first trial
> REVEREND REGINALD BACON, a black minister with dubious credentials who exploits black unrest for profit

The Novel

In *The Bonfire of the Vanities*, an upper-middle-class white Wall Street investment banker who thinks he is on top of the world discovers that his fragile world is in imminent danger of destruction from within. At age thirty-eight, Sherman McCoy is near the peak of his career. He is married and has one young daughter whom he loves but rarely sees because of his hectic double life. In addition to being absorbed in business, he maintains an adulterous relationship with a sexy blonde who is having fun while waiting for her elderly multimillionaire husband to die.

One night while driving his mistress, Maria Ruskin, home, Sherman accidentally takes a wrong turn off the expressway and finds himself in one of the poorest and most dangerous slums of the Bronx. After finding his way back to the expressway, he discovers that the on-ramp is blocked with rubbish, and when he gets out to clear a path, he sees two black youths approaching with obviously sinister intentions. Maria, in panic, slides behind the wheel and calls for him to jump in. Backing up to get around the barricade, she bumps one of the youths and then speeds off without looking back.

They read in the next day's newspaper that a teenager named Harold Lamb was felled by a hit-and-run driver at that location and is hospitalized in a coma. Lamb eventually provides a description and partial license number of the car that struck him. An alcoholic journalist named Peter Fallow publicizes the incident in his tabloid because of its dramatic potential—a rich white man in a Mercedes-Benz knocking down a poor black youth and driving off without stopping. To further dramatize the contrast, Lamb is falsely described as a model youth and an honor student.

The police are forced to investigate because of the publicity and the public outcry fueled by the Reverend Reginald Bacon, an opportunist who blackmails wealthy liberals with threats of mob violence. When the police get around to Sherman, he breaks down and admits his involvement but does not implicate Maria.

During the rest of the novel, Sherman is processed through a cynical legal system in which he stands out conspicuously as the "Great White Defendant." The prosecution wishes to make political capital out of convicting him; the defense wishes to milk Sherman for as much money as possible. Ironically, no one really cares about the truth but only about capitalizing on the situation.

Sherman is thrown into cells with hardened criminals, most of whom are ignorant members of the underclass. Having been educated in the best schools and sheltered from the cruel realities of life, Sherman is horrified by the conditions he sees. The experience toughens him and teaches him the need to fight for himself in a ruthless, dog-eat-dog world.

Sherman quickly loses his job, because his company is afraid of adverse publicity. Without his big paychecks, he is driven to the brink of bankruptcy. He is forced to sell his expensive cooperative Park Avenue apartment, but the proceeds are tied up in a civil suit by Lamb's mother and a real-estate broker. Maria Ruskin refuses to corroborate Sherman's account of the hit-and-run incident or to admit she was driving on the night in question.

His first trial on a charge of reckless endangerment is thrown out of court by Judge Kovitsky, an old-time jurist who still believes in due process and refuses to bow to mob or media pressure. Sherman's second trial ends with a hung jury. In the meantime, Lamb dies, and Sherman is indicted for manslaughter; he faces a possible sentence of up to twenty-five years. At the end of the novel, Sherman has been reduced to poverty and has become a sort of urban guerrilla, fighting the justice system and the ignorant masses who have been whipped into frenzy by a demagogue and a corrupt newspaper.

The Characters

Characterization is Wolfe's Achilles' heel, and his weakness in this aspect of fiction writing might explain why he had never tried to write a novel before. He has been criticized for creating characters who are stereotypes or caricatures. Throughout his career, Wolfe has been known as a social satirist, and this venture into fiction writing did not represent a radical change in technique. His previous writings, which were all important contributions to the school of the "New Journalism," focused on human foibles. In this novel, he was more anxious to point out the foibles of social classes than to attempt to invent three-dimensional characters.

Sherman represents the upwardly mobile, well-educated upper-middle-class capitalists who bring billions of dollars flowing into New York City and thereby attract hordes of "have-nots." His wife represents all the spoiled, selfish women who are married to the Sherman McCoys. Judy is sexually frustrated because her husband has turned his affections to a younger woman, and she consequently expends her energies on extravagant purchases that keep them chronically in debt.

Maria Ruskin has been criticized for being nothing more than a stereotypical "dumb blonde." She has been given a thick Southern accent to make her stand out as a character. She is just as selfish, spoiled, and bitchy as Sherman's wife, but she is quite a few years younger.

Peter Fallow is lazy and incompetent, an alcoholic and a freeloader, but he has good manners and valuable social connections. He has no conscience about what he writes for his trashy tabloid, and his editor will accept anything that can be printed without getting the paper sued for libel.

The Reverend Reginald Bacon is a self-appointed African American "leader" who stirs up trouble for what amounts to nothing more than blackmail. White liberals donate money to his various causes to keep him and his followers pacified, and much of the money finds its way into Bacon's own pockets.

The only character in the novel who develops is Sherman McCoy himself. His character change, however, is a little too radical to be plausible. He changes from a spoiled, elitist Yale University graduate into an urban guerrilla fighting a lone battle against hopeless odds.

Wolfe's forte is not characterization but rather his penetrating social intelligence, which typically finds expression in satire. The other characters in the novel can be read as New York types, and it has often been suggested that *The Bonfire of the Vanities* is a *roman à clef*, with such characters as Fallow and Bacon representing people known to insiders if not to the general reader.

Thomas Killian and Lawrence Kramer are stereotypical New York lawyers. The police officials are also stereotypes who could have come out of any police television drama. *The Bonfire of the Vanities* is strongly reminiscent of Theodore Dreiser's *An American Tragedy* (1925), a masterpiece in the realist genre that Wolfe admires. Like the men involved in apprehending, prosecuting, and defending Clyde Griffiths in Dreiser's novel, Wolfe's representatives of law and order care nothing about morality or truth; all they care about is how they might benefit from a publicity bonanza.

There is not a single admirable character in the book. Wolfe portrays all humans as greedy, selfish, narrow-minded, and often sadistic. He treats the lower classes with utter contempt, but he has little regard for the upper classes either.

Themes and Meanings

Tom Wolfe received a Ph.D. from elite Yale University in American Studies, demonstrating his erudition as well as his focus of interest. The ideas that form the foundation of his novel can be traced to many sources.

In his 1989 essay "Stalking the Billion-Footed Beast: A Literary Manifesto for the New Social Novel," Wolfe stated that his "immediate model was Thackeray's *Vanity Fair*" (1847-1848). William Thackeray's novel is a satirical portrait of the greedy, selfish, unscrupulous inhabitants of nineteenth century London. In the essay, Wolfe observed that his main objective was to paint a comparable picture of modern New York City, in all of its grandeur and squalor and with all of its ethnic diversity:

> New York and practically every other large city in the United States are undergoing a profound change. The fourth great wave of immigrants—this one from Asia, North Africa, Latin America, and the Caribbean—is now pouring in. Within ten years political power in most major American cities will have passed to the nonwhite majorities.

Wolfe's novel is essentially a story about how the white power structure is losing out to this new, nonwhite social force. Whites are losing the privileged position they have always taken for granted and will have to learn, like Sherman McCoy, to compete vigorously for their share of the good life that America has to offer.

Wolfe, like Thackeray, professes to be amused by the spectacle he presents; however, Wolfe's mocking tone conceals an underlying concern about the future of the city he knows and loves. Like many ultraconservative thinkers, he believes that welfare payments in their various forms are insidious because they condition recipients to develop a "welfare mentality." The handouts also attract more and more needy applicants from inside and outside the country, so that affluent cities such as New York become overrun with indigent people who have nothing to contribute to a high-tech society. According to this view, liberals who advocate government and private charity are motivated not by feelings of compassion but by fear of the growing masses of discontented poor, who can use voting power or violence to confiscate property. Some leaders, like Wolfe's Reverend Bacon, orchestrate such violence for their own political and financial benefit.

There is a fatalistic thread running throughout Wolfe's novel. He believes that the white ruling class in America is doomed to be engulfed by a rising tide of have-nots who do not sympathize with the ideals upon which the country was founded. His novel echoes such pessimistic books as José Ortega y Gasset's *La rebelión de las masas* (1930; *The Revolt of the Masses*, 1931), in which the brilliant Spanish philosopher stated that Western civilization was threatened by a "vertical invasion of the barbarians."

Critical Context

Wolfe paints a picture of America's biggest, richest city in the late twentieth century. Like all the major cities of America, New York is suffering form unprecedented social unrest. The white upper classes who have run things since before the American Revolution are retreating into enclaves as the cities become flooded with poor, nonwhite immigrants from other countries and from American farmlands, where mechanization is making their labor superfluous. Many of these newcomers remain unemployed because they have no marketable skills. They become a drain on the welfare system, and government subsidies are one of the attractions that draw more and more such people to the big cities.

In many American cities, the white majority is turning into a white minority. Political power is passing from whites to nonwhites because the one thing the nonwhites possess is their voting power. Some charismatic leaders in the minority communities take advantage of unrest to obtain power and profit.

Human greed and selfishness are not monopolized by any single race. Affluent whites are so obsessed with enriching themselves that they are content to buy time with government handouts while surrounding themselves with barred windows, watchdogs, electronic protection devices, and private armies of security guards. The underprivileged nonwhites are conditioned to develop a passive-aggressive attitude—the so-called welfare mentality—demanding more and more bribes in the form of welfare payments, food stamps, subsidized housing, and other benefits as the price for not engaging in open revolution. Wolfe has been accused of exaggerating the situation and deliberately falsifying the facts to make his case more dramatic. Whether readers agree with him or not is likely to depend on their political perspectives.

Bibliography

Black, George. "The Far-Right Stuff." *The New Statesman* 115 (February 12, 1988): 31. An extremely negative review of *The Bonfire of the Vanities*. Black accuses Wolfe of distorting the truth about the underprivileged residents of the Bronx. He calls the book "a set piece for cartoon characters."

Shomette, Doug, ed. *The Critical Response to Tom Wolfe*. Westport, Conn.: Greenwood Press, 1992. A collection of essays, both positive and negative, on books published by Wolfe up to 1990. This excellent reference source contains incisive essays on *The Bonfire of the Vanities*. Also contains a chronology of important events in Wolfe's life and a generous bibliography.

Thompson, James. "The Phoenix and the 'Bonfire': The Death and Transformation of Sherman McCoy." *World and I* 8 (January, 1993): 526-539. Thompson explores the relationship between religion and morality in the life of Sherman McCoy. Although Thompson is careful to point out that Sherman's experiences should not be viewed as a mirror of Wolfe's, he does draw parallels between Sherman's Anglican affiliation and Wolfe's childhood exposure to the Episcopal Church.

Vigilante, Richard. "The Truth About Tom Wolfe." *The National Review* 39 (December 18, 1987): 46-48. An enthusiastic review of *The Bonfire of the Vanities* reflecting ultraconservative views. Vigilante calls Wolfe the most important writer of his generation. He predicts that because of Wolfe's example, the "social-realist novel will soon re-emerge as an accepted and perhaps dominant force on the serious fiction scene."

Wolfe, Tom. "Stalking the Billion-Footed Beast: A Literary Manifesto for the New Social Novel." *Harper's Magazine* 279 (November, 1989): 45-56. In this landmark essay written shortly after publication of *The Bonfire of the Vanities*, Wolfe proposes that American writers return to the tradition of realism. He describes the characteristics of realism and criticizes contemporary fiction writers for neglecting the panorama of modern life in favor of cryptic subjectivism and frivolous experimentalism. As he gleefully anticipated, his essay provoked a storm of controversy.

Bill Delaney

BOOK OF BEBB

Author: Frederick Buechner (1926-　　)
Type of plot: Religious satire
Time of plot: The early 1970's
Locale: Florida, Houston, South Carolina, New York, New Jersey, Connecticut, and other New England locales
First published: 1979: *Lion Country,* 1971; *Open Heart,* 1972; *Love Feast,* 1974; *Treasure Hunt,* 1977

> *Principal characters:*
> ANTONIO PARR, Bebb's son-in-law and the narrator of the story
> LEO BEBB, the protagonist, the shady evangelist of the Church of Holy Love and Gospel Faith College
> SHARON BEBB, Bebb's adopted daughter, who eventually marries Antonio Parr
> LUCILLE BEBB, Bebb's wife
> BABE BEBB, Bebb's twin brother
> BROWNIE, Bebb's assistant, whom he resurrected

The Novel

In the 1970's, Frederick Buechner published four novels centered on his most animated and most fully realized character, Leo Bebb: *Lion Country* (1971), *Open Heart* (1972), *Love Feast* (1974), and *Treasure Hunt* (1977). These four novels form the tetralogy which was reissued as one volume entitled *The Book of Bebb* (1979). Buechner took advantage of this reissuing to make some slight revisions, none of which materially altered the structure, characterization, or tone of his raucously comic creation.

Though the incorporation of these four novels in one volume results in some repetition, in reading *The Book of Bebb*, one has the sense of following a single continuous narrative. This is a remarkable achievement by Buechner, considering the fact that the four novels were written over a six-year period without an initial design for a tetralogy. Buechner accounts for the unity of the four works by reference to the ease with which the characters came to him. In regard to its eventual expansion into a tetralogy, Buechner explains that when he wrote the last sentence of *Lion Country,* his first Bebb novel, "I thought I had finished with them all for good but soon found that they were not finished with me."

The Book of Bebb is not easy to summarize without making its characters and plot sound pretentiously eccentric and quirky. Its multileveled plot, however, basically chronicles the bawdy, hilarious life of Leo Bebb, "rogue preacher," founder of Gospel Faith College, and pastor of the Church of Holy Love. His story is told by Antonio Parr, a listless man in search of a cause to which he can dedicate himself. Parr originally visits Bebb in order to expose him as a religious fraud, a charlatan who operates a shameless diploma mill. Parr becomes instead Bebb's follower—and son-in-law—

fascinated by Bebb's eccentric "parish" of outcasts and nobodies. Parr is not, however, easily won to Bebb's outlandish, decidedly anachronistic gospel of miracles and prophecy.

Parr's encounter with Bebb and the trail of sorrows, joys, paradoxes, and incongruities that follow them illustrate the winding path a believer's life may take, fraught with peril and adventure at every turn. In these four comic novels of great religious fervor, Buechner underscores the fact that faith in God is always difficult—"Hard as hell," in Bebb's words—but ultimately the only foundation on which to stand in a secularized world.

The first entry in the revised tetralogy, *Lion Country*, introduces the reader to all the main characters in Bebb's entourage: his adopted daughter, Sharon; his alcoholic wife, Lucille; Brownie, a Christian whom Bebb has apparently resurrected from the dead; and Parr, the narrator and Bebb's reluctant convert. *Lion Country* is a broad satire of religion, church life, and clergy, but rooted in a serious examination of what it means to believe in God in an age where He has been ruled out of court.

Ordained by mail, Parr journeys to Armadillo, Florida, to expose Bebb's Gospel Faith College for the diploma mill it is. He finds, however, that Bebb is a sincere, down-to-earth believer with no illusions about himself or the world. Parr soon finds himself caught up in a new web of relationships that liberates him from the pretensions of modern life into the freedom of faith.

Open Heart, the second novel in the tetralogy, continues the Bebb chronicle two years later, employing Parr again as narrator, now married to Bebb's adopted daughter Sharon and teaching at a Connecticut high school. *Open Heart* introduces a new assortment of eccentric characters, including Gertrude Conover, a rich Princeton Theosophist whose beliefs in reincarnation preview events to occur in the last volume of the tetralogy. The story opens with Bebb in Houston and concerns the outlandish events surrounding the death of Herman Redpath, an Indian millionaire whom Bebb had healed of impotence. Redpath leaves a small fortune for Bebb; with this new bounty, Bebb moves northward (where "the Great Whore is . . . holding a golden cup in her hand full of the abominations and filthiness of her fornications"). Now in New York City, he tries another of his peculiar adventures in evangelism, attempting to establish his new Open Heart Church. Attendance, however, is poor at his revival meetings, and he decides to turn aside to the "Pepsi Generation" to lead them to "Beulah Land." The disappearance of his wife and the discovery of her suicide, the emergence of the mysterious Mr. Golden out of his past, and the imperiled marriage of Sharon and Antonio all militate against the success and buoyancy of Bebb's endeavors, and *Open Heart* ends ambiguously enough to permit a sequel.

The third novel in the series, *Love Feast*, picks up the narrative where *Open Heart* ends, retelling several episodes from the previous volumes, including Parr's crumbling marriage, Lucille Bebb's death, and Bebb's encounters with his circle of patrons: his paramour, Gertrude Conover, his former cellmate Clarence Golden, and a number of oil-rich Indians. Bebb attempts to recover his ministry despite having no church and having lost his companion by evangelizing the Pepsi Generation on the campus of Princeton University. His "Love Feast movement" is poised "to set up the Supper of the Lamb in groves of Academe."

Bebb and his clan are eventually prohibited by the authorities from saving souls on campus, and in a last act of defiance, Princeton becomes the scene of a "sacramental orgy." The rest of *Love Feast* is anticlimactic except for the death and funeral of Bebb, who apparently dies in a fiery plane crash while buzzing through the skies of Princeton with streamers advertising "Here's to Jesus . . . here's to you!" Leo Bebb, dying in a blaze of balloons and glory, is memorialized in a potato field north of Princeton, and the Bebb saga presumably has ended.

The final novel in the volume, *Treasure Hunt*, ties up remaining loose ends of the narrative, revealing essential biographical facts about Bebb and his twin brother, Babe. As Antonio and Sharon pick up the pieces of their marriage, Sharon discovers that Leo Bebb and Babe's wife, Bert, had been adulterous lovers and that she is the offspring of Leo and Bert. Leo Bebb, as far as anyone knows, went up in flames at the end of *Love Feast*.

The setting is now Poinsett, South Carolina, where a cassette recording of Bebb explains that he has left a home to his daughter Sharon, suggesting that she and Antonio "do something nice with that old place . . . for Jesus." The reader quickly gets a strong suspicion that Bebb has been reincarnated—and in, of all places, the body of a blind, one-year-old son of food-stamp parents in Poinsett. *Treasure Hunt* contains the kind of grotesquerie and carnival humor found in the three previous works, but finally settles into a serious contemplation of the demands of true faith on the believer. Bebb's legacy, ultimately, is an uncompromising determination to live life fully, through to its end, refusing to concede anything to the darkness and hatred of memory or past failure. The God of Bebb, and of Buechner as well, is a God of redemption and forgiveness, and a God of limitless beginnings.

The Characters

Buechner's narrative techniques place most of the weight of his novels on plot and theme; characterization is designed to exemplify those basic themes of grace and faith that Buechner sees as the fundamental principles by which mankind can work its way through the world. In *The Book of Bebb*, Buechner has thus given the reader a gallery of eccentric characters, all of whom must confront the basic issues of faith and despair, physical life and spiritual death. Their various reactions to this challenge confirm Buechner's belief that life is indeed a matter of choices among the mundane affairs of life and not in hearing voices or seeing miracles. In most cases, Buechner's characters are shrewdly drawn caricatures who appear onstage in fleeting moments, dramatizing those choices. Buechner creates Leo Bebb as the supreme example of grace operating through the least likely channel; Bebb is profane, earthy, sometimes blasphemous in the way he "preaches the gospel." Nevertheless, he is but one more reminder that all men have feet of clay, that God loves His creatures in spite of their shortcomings, and that the evidence of God's grace is all around for all to see.

Bebb is the fulcrum on which the tetralogy balances—even after his death, one is not quite done with Bebb, since he is reincarnated as Jinny Bob in the fourth and final volume in the tetralogy, *Treasure Hunt*. In many ways, however, the tetralogy is really the "Book of Parr," the private journey of Antonio Parr, the tracing of one man's sacred journey. It is through the eyes of Antonio Parr that the reader "sees"; all is filtered through the consciousness of one whose original mission was to strip away the religious veneer of fraud and who becomes instead a witting accomplice in his "victim's" exploits.

The female characters, principally Lucille Bebb and Sharon Bebb, serve as foils to the central male characters, Bebb and Parr, establishing their fallibility, which is to say their humanness. Lucille withdraws into herself, unable to reach contentment or hope, retreating behind dark glasses and drinking herself into a stupor, until one day she summons up enough strength to do away with herself. With the loss of Lucille, Bebb is unable to retain the joy of his ministry and is revived only by his later fleshly indulgence. Sharon, Bebb's illegitimate daughter, is compelled by her husband's absence and general neglect to seek warmth and affection in the arms of her nephew, Tony. Parr's complicity in the adultery is thus magnified, and his realization comes nearly too late to save the relationship.

Each Buechner character is neither saint nor sinner, but a hybrid of both; the man or woman of God is not free from temptation or doubt. The triumph of faith is achieved by working through worldly lusts to restore balance and hope, not by denying their existence and retreating into false piety.

Themes and Meanings

The Bebb novels well illustrate the wry comment of one critic, who suggested that Buechner's art is too religious for the secular reader and too secular for the religious reader. Secular readers, in the end, find the religion of Bebb and Parr preposterous; religious readers, in the end, find the bawdy and profane lifestyle of Bebb and his followers equally reprehensible. In *The Book of Bebb*, Buechner thus portrays the paradox of "holiness"; Bebb is every would-be religious person: part hypocrite, part devotee, part human, part divine. The novelist's task is thus to hold these seeming dichotomies in tension, demonstrating how each can be true in a single person.

Buechner's view of narrative is evangelistic; he believes that storytelling reveals the form of human life, its direction and its meaning. Each human life contains a hidden agenda, a pattern of events that bears close attention. As most people are blind to it, it is up to the storyteller to reveal that agenda. *The Book of Bebb* is intended by Buechner to offer such a revelation, a "love letter" to that "beloved stranger," his reader, who might, for a moment, entertain the reality of the author's colorful cast of characters and recognize in their oddness and in their ordinariness that life's meaning is mediated and God's presence is confirmed. The principal themes of *The Book of Bebb* are those which undergird most of Buechner's fiction as well as his theological works: the religious nature of all human endeavor, the ability of God to speak to humankind in the ordinary, mundane affairs of human existence, and the necessity of faith and vision against the despair of the modern world.

Critical Context

Buechner's best-selling first novel, *A Long Day's Dying* (1950), a rarefied and intellectual treatment of the ethical malaise of modern life, was highly praised as an impressive debut for a new "modernist storyteller." Buechner's subsequent work, from 1952 to 1969, while attracting a dedicated and enthusiastic audience, failed to achieve the acclaim evoked by his first novel.*The Book of Bebb*, however, comprising as it does his four most successful works of fiction in one volume, has returned Buechner to critical favor. *The Book of Bebb* is a pivotal work in his career, representing the maturity of a comic narrative style which began to evolve in Buechner's first explicitly religious novel, *The Final Beast* (1965). In *The Final Beast*, Buechner had made a sharp break from the baroque, Jamesian narrative technique of his earlier novels, moving from mannered "drawing room" characters and brooding narrators to more ordinary people speaking in direct and unpretentious dialogue.

Suddenly, it seemed, Buechner had developed a sense of humor, and he had. Both the style and substance of his fiction became much lighter and more joyful, celebrating the inexplicable meaningfulness of human life discovered in the most mundane of circumstances.

An ordained Presbyterian minister, Buechner remains the most skillful contemporary chronicler of mankind's search for faith in a secular age. Impressive in his control of diverse fictional and nonfictional modes of discourse, he is at once a leading Christian apologist, writer of meditations, novelist, and memoirist. The common strain through all of Buechner's works is his conviction that life is, in the end, a story: a story to be celebrated, a story to be endured, but above all, a story to be told. No one who reads Buechner's prose can come away from it knowing less of himself; his readers become, finally, the parish of this minister without a church, a minister turned master storyteller.

Bibliography

Anderson, Chris. "The Very Style of Faith: Frederick Buechner as Homilist and Essayist." *Christianity and Literature* 38 (Winter, 1989): 7-21. Focuses on Buechner's nonfiction, but with many insights that make the full purpose and interest of his fiction more accessible.

Brown, W. Dale. "A Faith to Live and Die With." *Sojourners* 27 (May/June, 1998): 52-55. Brown surveys some of Buechner's works, showing how they reflect the position of faith in modern life. He also shows how Buechner has reaffirmed the value of Christianity by constantly questioning its relevance.

Davies, Marie-Helene. *Laughter in a Genevan Gown: The Works of Frederick Buechner, 1970-1980*. Grand Rapids, Mich.: Eerdmans, 1983. The most comprehensive introduction to the life and work of Frederick Buechner, locating both author and works in the context of their religious background. A useful orientation for a reading of *The Book of Bebb*.

Nelson, Rudolph L. "'The Doors of Perception': Mystical Experience in Buechner's Fiction." *Southwest Review* 68 (Summer, 1983): 266-273. Stresses the visionary element in Buechner's work and how it assists in the articulation of his fiction's overall point of view. A sense of the position of *The Book of Bebb* in the development of Buechner's imaginative output may be inferred.

Yancey, Philip. "Crazy, Holy Grace." *Christianity Today* 41 (June 16, 1997): 33. Yancey recounts Buechner's conversion at the age of twenty-seven, when a sermon by George Buttrick changed his life. Buechner's view of God as a humorous, friendly presence whose grace appears in unexpected ways is reflected throughout his writing.

Bruce L. Edwards

THE BOOK OF LIGHTS

Author: Chaim Potok (1929-   )
Type of plot: Psychological realism
Time of plot: 1950-1957
Locale: Brooklyn, Manhattan, Boston, Philadelphia, Korea, Japan, and Jerusalem
First published: 1981

> *Principal characters:*
> GERSHON LORAN, the protagonist, a Jewish chaplain in Korea
> ARTHUR LEIDEN, his roommate in seminary
> JACOB KETER, a professor of Jewish mysticism

The Novel

The Book of Lights is divided into three sections. The first details the seminary days of Gershon Loran and Arthur Leiden at Riverside Hebrew Institute in Manhattan. The second section follows Gershon in his year of chaplaincy duty in Korea right after the war. The third is a moving account of the visit to Kyoto and Hiroshima by Gershon and Arthur who are now reunited.

After his parents were killed in terrorist cross fire in Palestine in 1937, Gershon was taken in by his aunt and uncle. His aging uncle, afflicted with emphysema, attempts to run the decaying apartment house in which they live. The surrounding Brooklyn neighborhood is itself decaying, and there are frequent fires. Gershon is reared in pious Judaism but chooses to attend the nonorthodox Riverside Hebrew Institute. There he is introduced to the academic study of Jewish mysticism by one of his professors, Jacob Keter. Gershon's plodding, unorganized ways as a student give way to a fervency in his exploration of what Keter called the feeling side of Judaism.

Arthur Leiden becomes Gershon's roommate at the institute. Arthur, a Harvard graduate, had fled his studies in physics for the rabbinate. He is disorganized, taciturn, with something strange inside waiting to explode. Arthur comes to depend on "dear Gershon" for help in his studies.

Gershon comes to the institute at the outbreak of the Korean war; even after the war has ended, there remains a great need for chaplains for American military personnel stationed in Korea and elsewhere. Indeed, as a condition of graduation, those in the institute are required to make themselves available to the chaplaincy corps. Gershon, without understanding why, volunteers to serve in the army. Nevertheless, his entrance into the service is delayed a year because the institute awards him the first Leiden prize.

The award is named after Arthur's brother, who was killed during World War II. Gershon learns that Arthur's father, Charles Leiden, had worked closely with Albert Einstein and other scientists in the development and testing of the first atomic bomb. In retrospect, Gershon realizes that during their seminary days together, Arthur had been haunted by the destructive death light which his father had helped unleash. Arthur had recommended to his parents that Gershon be the first recipient of the Leiden prize.

The award provides a year's deferment from the service, and Gershon spends the time in study of the Jewish cabala with Jacob Keter. Central to that collection of mystical writings is the Zohar, a series of books describing God and his creation in terms of emanations, the pure radiance of God.

Gershon, after his year of study with Keter, becomes the only Jewish chaplain in Korea, for a time assigned to a medical unit north of Seoul. The debilitating snow and intense heat of Korea provide stark contrast to the sheltered environment of the institute, but for Gershon the experience is a transforming one. Though he continues to study cabala and frequently visits with Keter in visions, his chaplaincy is an active one. He becomes sensitive to his men and is well liked. His management skills and frequent trips to serve other units result in front page write-ups in *Stars and Stripes*, a boost in the morale of the medical unit, and Gershon's eventual transfer to division headquarters. There, he learns that chaplain Arthur Leiden has arrived in Korea.

Arthur is desperate to get to Japan, to visit Kyoto and Hiroshima. When the navy refused to provide Arthur with a security clearance (he had signed some left-wing petitions in college), he managed to get accepted by the army. Arthur prevails upon Gershon, and early in 1957 they travel together to Hong Kong and Japan. Arthur is struck by the beauty of Kyoto, its temples and gardens, yet he is filled with darkness when the two enter Hiroshima and stand before the saddle-like monument to those killed in the blast. Arthur searches for words, something to say to atone for the destruction which his father's work helped bring about. One morning, Arthur stands before the monument and reads from the Psalms, reading of forsakenness and pleading for God's restoration.

Events move rapidly. Both men return to Korea, but soon Arthur is on board another plane bound for Japan. The plane crashes on takeoff, and Arthur is killed. Later, as Gershon ends his tour of duty in Korea, he visits Arthur's parents in Boston. They are thankful for Gershon's friendship with Arthur, and seem themselves to be haunted by the death light. It is here that Gershon learns the secret of Arthur's love of Kyoto: His mother, an art historian, had indirectly persuaded the government to spare Kyoto, the first intended target of the atomic bomb.

Soon Gershon finds himself in another garden, this time in Jerusalem. He has flown to the home of Jacob Keter, there to study with one of the giants, there to encounter the God of lights.

The Characters

The Book of Lights is the story of two young men and their navigation through an evil and crumbling world. Indeed, when author Chaim Potok brings Albert Einstein onstage to honor the first recipient of the (fictitious) Leiden award, Einstein observes that "loran" has something to do with navigation (it is an acronym for Long Range Navigation) and that in his studies Gershon Loran has set an example for others to follow.

Gershon has long sought the Light that could somehow encompass the death light. At sixteen, he witnesses a dog giving birth on the roof of the family's old apartment building. Such fecundity triggers an ecstatic vision: Gershon feels for a moment as if he could touch the sky, the very stars. The promise of this moment is fulfilled when he begins to study cabala in seminary; his mystical visions are given legitimacy within the Jewish tradition.

Korea changes him further. His feelings of abandonment, of the randomness of events, are no less strong, but he returns from the service with a new strength. He has learned and suffered much in Korea, but he has survived. His studies in the Zohar, he realizes, provided a curious refuge for gathering the resources within himself needed for facing a demanding chaplaincy. Inwardly, he had done battle with the voices from the other side, the voices that called for him to give up hope and dreams in a broken century.

Gershon finally understands that those voices are not foreign to the Jewish mystical tradition; somehow the voices of despair and the voices of hope are all intertwined. This realization does not explain away evil, yet it means that in the midst of conflict and contradiction, God's radiance still shines. Personal choices can still be significant.

Jacob Keter, a widower, one of the giants of Jewish mysticism, is Gershon's mentor. Keter, over six feet tall, mostly bald, incisive, humorless (like Gershon), is a secular Zionist. He explains to Gershon that while the Talmud shows Jews how to act, it is the cabala that tells how Judaism feels, how the world is to be perceived. In one of Gershon's visions, Keter talks with a Talmud teacher, explaining that cabala was full of poetry and contradiction, giving Judaism its drive and creative genius. It is significant that in the Zohar there are ten emanations of God; the first is called "Keter," the Crown, from which all other emanations flow.

Arthur Leiden is consumed by his past. He abandons a brilliant career in physics because he is afraid that any advances he might make would only lead to more destruction. His Boston accent, his suaveness and handsomeness, all belie the struggle in Arthur to atone for that in which his parents participated. Mysticism is not for him; cabala is nothing but magic charms and numerology. He seeks a solution in political activism—from signing petitions to trying to organize Korean students to protest the militarization of their country. Yet Arthur is stalked by a vision of his own: the vision of the death light when the bomb was tested at Alamogordo, New Mexico. Arthur calls himself the offspring of killers. He insists that those who died are owed something by those who produced the bomb, but he can discover nothing in himself to bequeath. Arthur's death merely quiets his frantic voice; it does not atone for the evil.

Themes and Meanings

There is light everywhere. In reportorial style, Potok writes of sunlight, fire, the death light, and the emanations of God. Gershon frequently studies the Zohar, the compendium of Jewish mysticism from the fifteenth century. It is a book of radiance, of enlightenment, and details the ten emanations of God through which the mystic must ascend to encounter his Creator. *The Book of Lights* contains ten chapters, each reminiscent of the corresponding emanation (or *sefirah*).

The novel is an attempt to come to terms with evil through means of the Jewish mystical tradition. Gershon is the navigator who sees "creation as a vast error; the world broken and dense with evil; everything a bewildering puzzle; . . . I especially like the ambiguities. . . . You can't pin most of it down the way you can a passage of Talmud. I live with ambiguity, I think, better than I can with certainty. Doubt is all that's left to us. . . . Doubt and desperate deeds." This is not only Potok's legacy for contemporary Jews, but also his gift to the modern world as well: We must navigate by our deepest visions, with fear and trembling, understanding that God encompasses the evil as well as the good; God himself is found in the very feeling of abandonment, of in-betweenness, of being a stranger in the land.

Critical Context

The Book of Lights grew out of Potok's experiences as an army chaplain in Korea in the late 1950's. Though the author originally intended to trace the boyhood of his protagonist in flashbacks, other books intervened to tell the stories: *The Chosen* (1967), *The Promise* (1969), and *In the Beginning* (1975). Earlier themes developed in those novels appear in *The Book of Lights*, such as anti-Semitism, textual criticism and Jewish tradition, and narrow fundamentalism's inability to come to grips with the modern world. Yet here Potok goes beyond controversies within various Jewish traditions to confront the death light that has been let loose upon the world. Real world events no longer filter into the story from newscasts in the background; now the players themselves are brought onstage. Albert Einstein and former president Harry S Truman visit Riverside Hebrew Institute. If this device is not entirely successful (the two men appear larger than life in a kind of television walk-on), nevertheless Potok has avoided a simple formula piece. His descriptions of life as a Korean chaplain are sympathetic and detailed, as are his pictures of academic and Asian cultures.

Potok has written a moving story of the way of practical mysticism. It might perhaps be noted that the author's father was a Polish émigré, and that Potok's previous novels have dealt with the conflict of Orthodox Hasidic Judaism and modern Jewish scholarship. According to a noted cabala scholar, in eighteenth century Poland one man provided a link between the development of the Hasidic tradition and that of the cabala: one Abraham Gershon. Gershon Loran is perhaps the fruit of that marriage.

Bibliography

Hock, Zarina Manawwar. "Authority and Multiculturalism: Reflections by Chaim Potok." *Language Arts* 72 (April, 1995): 4. Hock discusses Potok's use of multicultural themes to expose attitudes toward current social issues. She demonstrates how his fiction reflects the battle between traditional and new sources of conduct.

Potok, Chaim. "The Invisible Map of Meaning: A Writer's Confrontations." *TriQuarterly* 84 (Spring, 1992): 17-45. Potok discusses the major theme that runs throughout his works, that of cultural conflict and the influence this conflict has on the direction of an individual life. Potok describes his first encounter with main-stream Western literature and shows how this experience shaped his subsequent writing.

_____. *Wanderings: Chaim Potok's History of the Jews*. New York: Fawcett Books, 1990. Potok's compelling history of the Jews re-creates historical events and explores the many facets of Jewish life through the ages. Although this work does not address Potok's fiction, it does provide insight into Potok's ethnic heritage, which has a direct bearing on his writing.

Walden, Daniel, ed. *The World of Chaim Potok*. Albany: State University of New York Press, 1985. This rich resource on the writing of Chaim Potok features critical essays, as well as reviews and a bibliographic essay. It provides valuable insight into Potok's fiction that can be extended to the entire body of his work. Includes an essay on *The Book of Lights*.

Dan Barnett

THE BORDER TRILOGY

Author: Cormac McCarthy (1933-   )
Type of plot: Adventure
Time of plot: 1939 to 1952
Locale: Texas, New Mexico, and Mexico
First published: 1999: *All the Pretty Horses*, 1992; *The Crossing*, 1994; *Cities of the Plain*, 1998

Principal characters:

> JOHN GRADY COLE, a sensitive and intelligent young man looking for continuity in a changing world
>
> LACEY RAWLINS, Cole's sidekick, who rides with him to Mexico
>
> JIMMY BLEVINS, a spunky and comical young runaway who emerges as an unlikely hero
>
> ALEJANDRA, a young girl loved by Cole
>
> BILLY PARHAM, an outlaw who works with Cole in New Mexico
>
> BOYD PARHAM, Billy's younger brother
>
> MAGDALENA, a teenage Mexican prostitute and the object of Cole's desires

The Novel

The Border Trilogy is a fictionalized portrayal of two boys' pilgrimage from youth to manhood during the years immediately before, during, and following World War II. John Grady Cole and Billy Parham are the central figures in a sweeping story depicting the decline of the cowboy way of life in the American Southwest.

All the Pretty Horses opens in 1949 with sixteen-year-old John Grady Cole, the last in a long line of Grady ranchers, facing an uncertain future. His grandfather has just died, and his father has returned from the war disillusioned and sick, prompting his mother to sell the ranch and leave Texas. With his horse Redbo and his best friend Lacey Rawlins, Cole decides to head south across the Pecos River into Mexico. At the border crossing, the two pick up young runaway Jimmy Blevins. When Blevins's horse is spooked during a lightning storm, Rawlins and Cole are reluctantly drawn into a plan to retrieve it. During the attempt, bedlam breaks out, and Blevins is separated from Rawlins and Cole. Subsequently, he is caught by the Mexican police and later executed. Cole and Rawlins eventually wind up being hired to break horses on a large hacienda, where Cole engages in forbidden love with the owner's beautiful daughter, Alejandra. This leads to a succession of disasters, from the boys' arrest and incarceration to Cole's involvement in a prison killing. Once they are released from jail, Rawlins decides to return to Texas.

The Crossing begins in 1939, when brothers Billy and Boyd Parham are living near Cloverdale, New Mexico. Billy is obsessed with trapping a renegade she-wolf that has crossed the border from Mexico to raid his father's cattle ranch. Once he has trapped the wolf, Billy becomes attached to her and decides he must restore the animal to her home in the mountains. Upon his return, Billy discovers that his parents have been murdered by horse thieves. He takes his younger brother Boyd and heads to Mexico to find the men who killed their parents and to reclaim what is rightfully theirs, a crucial decision that ultimately determines their individual fates. As World War II heats up, the boys fight their own battles with bandits, desperadoes, and gypsies. In Becerac, they find their father's horse in the possession of a German doctor who claims to have bought the horse from a Mexican. The boys steal the horse back, knowing that it will not really be theirs until they are able to return to New Mexico. They are branded as horse thieves, and their lives take a more dangerous turn when Boyd one night becomes infatuated with a young girl walking on a lonely road; eventually, Boyd rides away with the girl without Billy's knowledge. When Billy is unable to locate his brother, he returns to New Mexico, where he attempts to join the Army but is rejected. Restless, he decides to go back and find his brother. He later learns that Boyd has killed two men and, in turn, has been gunned down by the brother of one of his victims. In San Lorenzo, he claims his brother's body and crosses the border one last time to bury him in American soil.

In *Cities of the Plain*, John Grady Cole and Billy Parham come together, working side by side on a cattle ranch in New Mexico in 1952. Cole at age nineteen is the "kid" but has earned the reputation of having a way with horses that impresses the owner of the ranch as well as the other cowhands. Parham, now twenty-eight and happily settled on the ranch, is still a bit of an outlaw. Cole and Parham become inseparable friends bound by horses, cattle, and life on the range. Soon, Cole falls in love with an epileptic teenage prostitute from Juarez named Magdalena. He is desperate to rescue her from an abusive pimp, Eduardo, and Parham reluctantly agrees to help him. After they make elaborate plans for her escape, however, Magdalena is found with her throat slashed. Enraged, John seeks out Eduardo and a violent confrontation ensues, ending with the deaths of both Eduardo and Cole. The epilogue reveals that a military installation near Alamogordo is fast encroaching on the range. Parham decides to move on; he wanders for almost fifty years and finally ends up back in New Mexico at age seventy-eight.

The Characters

Cormac McCarthy is known for instilling wildness in his characters. They are often depicted as outcasts, homeless or living in hovels, usually just scraping by, whether in an adobe hut or sleeping on the ground in a desert. In *The Border Trilogy*, the characters do not change or grow over the course of the story. Rather, they are intricately blended into the rough landscape.

John Grady Cole commands the reader's attention from the beginning of *All the Pretty Horses* with his quiet countenance, firm values, common sense, and maturity beyond his years. Not one to take the easy way out, Cole must endure the consequences of his noble approach to life, from surviving a Mexican prison after helping Jimmy Blevins retrieve his horse from thieves, to losing his life in an effort to save a prostitute from her nefarious pimp. He never loses sight of his dreams, but he never sees them fulfilled either.

Jimmy Blevins captures the reader's sympathy as the pathetic, hapless, atypical hero who would risk death to get back what is his. Blevins is a multidimensional character who surprises others at every turn. Lacey Rawlins says of Blevins: "The little son of a bitch wouldn't stand still for nobody high-jackin his horse."

Although Billy Parham is more of a realist than Cole, he is a cowboy to the core as he chases a disappearing culture. In *The Crossing*, he endures the mournful loss of everything he cares about, starting with the lone she-wolf and including his parents, his brother, and even his dog. He finds kinship in *Cities of the Plain* when he meets Cole and the other ranch hands, who have all suffered losses, individually (daughters, siblings, wives) and collectively (a shared lifestyle and Old West philosophy). He is an outlaw at heart, never afraid to walk on the wrong side if it is for a good cause.

McCarthy typically uses old men to convey wisdom and guidance to his younger characters, and he does so in each volume of *The Border Trilogy*. He also introduces a number of lesser characters, including a band of gypsies, *vaqueros*, and a blind musician to add to the regional flavor.

Themes and Meanings

Throughout *The Border Trilogy*, there runs the notion that the dreams of youth are often more enduring than the realities of adulthood. Friendships fade, passions die, and a way of life becomes threatened. With a blend of historical fact and fictional characterization, McCarthy gives the reader a panoramic view of a society teeming with unrest and violence. The Southwest is changing quickly, and with industrialization comes the decline of the cowboy's existence and the deterioration of the free range. The events of the trilogy transpire during a time when America is at war and boys everywhere are yearning to join up, while Mexico, still volatile and raw, is cleaning up following its own revolution. It is a straightforward story with complex issues. In one sense, it is a classic coming-of-age tale. In *All the Pretty Horses*, John Grady Cole leaves home at sixteen without direction, and he spends his adolescence discovering a society seething in depravity and corruption, where a man is judged only by his readiness to defend himself to the death. In *The Crossing*, certain symbolic elements underscore the theme, from the crossing of languages, to the crossing of a border, to the crossing of a stage of life. Thus the meaning of the title becomes more than geographical. The focus on the two young men's initiation into manhood serves as the vehicle to carry McCarthy's story through its course. With *All the Pretty Horses*, the reader is lured into a false sense of well-being when both of the central characters emerge alive, although somewhat disillusioned by their adventures. In comparison, *Cities of the Plain* is the end of the trail for John Grady Cole, as morbid reality manifests itself when death appears suddenly in the form of Magdalena's mutilated body.

Critical Context

Cormac McCarthy is a prolific writer of novels, all of which reflect his ability to capture realistic local color and a dramatic sense of place, whether it is the Appalachia area of Tennessee as in *The Orchard Keeper* (1965), or the desert plains of the Southwest in *Cities of the Plain*. His style is characterized by sparse use of punctuation. By omitting quotation marks and avoiding the use of commas, colons, and apostrophes, he develops long run-on sentences that demand the reader's full attention, a style that intensifies the energy and exactness of his words. English and Spanish are interwoven in patchwork fashion, providing a dual perspective for his prose style. His characters' slow, laconic speech and monosyllabic exchanges are evocative of the time and place. With vivid acuity, McCarthy describes the eerie desolation of the plains and the august beauty of the mountains that surround them. He paints a glorious landscape and spatters it with bleeding horses, packs of wild dogs, blind musicians, traveling gypsies, corrupt politicians, and tragic love. It is a style of narrative discourse that has led him to be compared to William Faulkner.

Cormac McCarthy has been awarded grants from the American Academy of Arts and Letters, the William Faulkner Foundation, and the Rockefeller Foundation, and he received a MacArthur Fellowship in 1981. *All the Pretty Horses* won the National Book Award and the National Book Critics Circle Award and was named one of the best books of 1992 by *Library Journal*.

Bibliography

Aldridge, John W. "Cormac McCarthy's Bizarre Genius." *Atlantic Monthly* 274 (August, 1994): 89-97. Aldridge portrays McCarthy's earlier novels as plotless narratives that contrast sharply with the clearly defined story line in *All the Pretty Horses*. Nevertheless, the protagonists throughout McCarthy's fiction are seen as sharing a similar circumstance, that of an individual adrift from society who struggles to find a place insulated from the encroachments of modern civilization.

Bell, Vereen M. *The Achievements of Cormac McCarthy*. Baton Rouge: Louisiana State University Press, 1988. Bell's study of the early works of McCarthy, including *The Orchard Keeper* (1965), *Outer Dark* (1968), *Child of God* (1973), *Suttree* (1979), and *Blood Meridian* (1985), reveals the gothic elements of his fiction and the innovative techniques that eventually came to full bloom in his later works.

Jarrett, Robert. *Cormac McCarthy*. London: Twayne, 1997. According to Jarrett, there are three distinctive features to McCarthy's fiction: an original narrative discourse, a core theme of the quest, and a systematic integration of parable into text and conversation. Altogether, they reflect a blend of individualism, historical setting, and cultural cross-currents that is unique in contemporary literature.

Jaynes, Gregory. "The Knock at the Door." *Time*, June 6, 1994, pp. 62-64. Jaynes views McCarthy's personal odyssey that led him from the Appalachian South to the American Southwest as a road map for his characters. It is there they discover not only a landscape to inspire them but also a diverse collection of locals with tales to captivate them.

Woodward, Richard B. "Cormac McCarthy's Venomous Fiction." *The New York Times Magazine*, April 19, 1992, pp. 28-31. In a rare interview, McCarthy relates his views on evil and the human appetite for violence. He opines that the effort to achieve harmony in society is a futile one as long as individuals cling to the more noble goal of preserving their independent nature.

William Hoffman

BORN BROTHERS

Author: Larry Woiwode (1941-   )
Type of plot: Psychological realism
Time of plot: The 1940's through the 1980's
Locale: North Dakota, Illinois, and New York City
First published: 1988

> *Principal characters:*
> CHARLES NEUMILLER, one of two brothers
> JEROME NEUMILLER, the other brother, a year older than Charles
> MARTIN NEUMILLER, their father, a teacher
> ALPHA NEUMILLER, their mother
> KATHERINE NEUMILLER, Charles's wife

The Novel

Based on Larry Woiwode's own life, *Born Brothers* reveals the inside of Charles Neumiller's mind as he remembers, rearranges, and finds meaning in events from his past. These memories appear as short, poetic fragments told in the first person and in present tense, with often-abrupt shifts in place and time. Letters, journals, poems, and scripts provide some information; they also serve as prompts that stimulate the thinking of a much older Charles who thinks about making ready for death.

Born Brothers is divided into seven sections. The main story line, mostly in chronological order, follows Charles from his earliest childhood memories to a suicide attempt when he is in his mid-thirties. Interspersed throughout the book are memories of the time when Charles, then in his early twenties, lived in a hotel called the Chesro in New York. He describes this as a "pilgrimage" and a "retreat." Occasionally, an older Charles, one who has survived the suicide attempt, appears. This Charles no longer drinks, is a caring husband and father, and has become a devout Christian who says that religious principles have turned his life around.

The book opens with a letter written in 1964 by Jerome, then a medical student in Chicago, to Charles, who is trying to break into acting in New York. Jerome announces that he is planning to visit Charles. An older Charles says that the sight of this letter triggers memories of that time. A brief image of his suicide attempt surfaces, and then his memories go back to his early childhood in Hyatt, North Dakota, where his father is a teacher.

Early childhood is the happiest time for Charles. Jerome is only a year older; they look like twins, are dressed like twins, and do everything together. Although they have a growing number of siblings, they pay little attention to them. Their father is a devout Catholic, and the boys attend St. Mary Margaret Elementary School and serve as altar boys. Charles's heroes are Dr. Rex Morgan and Joe Louis. He imagines he would like to be a doctor, but he also discovers his talent for acting, an activity that his mother, whom he loves dearly, encourages.

Childhood holds some painful memories also. His mother, afraid he will turn out badly, punishes him severely and often. The older Charles, who has a four-year-old son, comments that children spend much of their time grieving. Charles also develops an early awareness of death when he almost dies from pneumonia.

The summer after Charles completes the third grade, the Neumiller family moves to Illinois, where Martin has been promised a teaching job. After they move, everything goes wrong. The teaching job falls through, the family cannot find a place to live and must stay with Martin's parents in their partially finished house, and Alpha is pregnant again with her sixth child. Martin goes to work for his brother's construction company, and the family moves into a converted gas station. Alpha loses the child, then succumbs to a kidney disorder and dies.

Their mother dead and their father lost in his own grief, Jerome and Charles are adrift. When a classmate taunts Charles because he has no mother, Charles challenges him to a boxing match with Jerome to be the referee. Although the fight ends in a standoff, Jerome, trying to be fair, declares the other boy to be the winner. Charles, betrayed and devastated, attacks Jerome. Charles shoplifts candy from the local store and eventually involves Jerome in the misdeed. They eat too much, read a lot, and try various hobbies. As a young adolescent, Charles becomes interested in a girl named Dewey. She encourages his attentions for a time but then rejects him for another boy.

Eventually, Martin obtains a teaching job, and the boys become interested in high-school activities such as basketball and speech. Martin develops acute appendicitis and almost dies, and Jerome and Charles drive to the nearby town to visit him. On the way home, Jerome, suddenly possessed by the need to speed, loses control of the car, and it crashes into a marker in the cemetery. Both of Charles's legs are badly broken; they do not heal easily or quickly. Charles becomes involved with a girl, Bobbie, and Jerome becomes attached to her friend. The boys are increasingly obsessed with sexual exploration, and they find it increasingly difficult to reconcile these feelings with the admonitions of the priest. Bobbie pushes Charles into having intercourse, but Charles fails even to have an orgasm. Disappointment, guilt, and a fear of being trapped cause him to break off the relationship.

In high school, Jerome participates in speech and drama, but after taking care of Charles and his father, he considers going into medicine. Charles, who has always wanted to be a doctor, becomes interested in speech and drama. After his first year of college, Jerome does switch his major to premedical studies, while Charles enrolls in speech and theater. Although they are roommates again, Charles feels that their paths have crossed and that they are moving away from each other. Charles stops going to church altogether when he hears that the campus priest buys a new Cadillac every year while ignoring all the problems in the world.

Charles meets Rick Purkeet, an upperclassman who is also involved in theater and who also lost his mother at an early age. Rick makes homosexual advances toward Charles. Charles feels some attraction to Rick, who seems to be a kindred spirit, but he resists Rick's advances. One night, after getting drunk on Rick's liquor, Charles threatens to kill himself.

Charles meets Jill through the college theater. They consummate their relationship, and Charles assumes that she will want to marry him. Jill, however, breaks off with him when she gets involved with a fraternity man. At one point, with no money, no girlfriend, and no hope, Charles contemplates suicide again. At a graduation party for Jerome, Charles discovers Jill kissing Jerome; he loses control, hits Jill, becomes hysterical, and decides to leave for California. Jerome assures him that he and others do care about him, and Charles decides to stay.

Jerome goes on to medical school, while Charles, still in college, meets a fair-haired, blue-eyed woman named Katherine and falls in love. Her father hopes to break them up, so he sends Katherine to school elsewhere. Charles decides to go to New York to try his luck at acting; it is during this time that he stays at the Chesro.

After this, the main narrative line moves ahead rapidly. Charles and Katherine are married, and Jerome marries Julie, a black woman who teaches English. There are references to Charles's new show, which is doing well. Both marriages are having problems. Charles and Katherine have a daughter, Becky. Jerome tells Charles that their father has cancer, and two years later, Jerome tells Charles that the cancer has reappeared. In the fall of 1975, Martin goes to New Mexico, where Jerome is living, and Charles, separated from Katherine, goes to help take care of him. This Charles tries not to drink and reads the Bible.

Martin dies in March of 1976. At the funeral, Katherine and Charles try living together again, but Charles must go to North Dakota to take part in a bicentennial celebration. Unable to handle the stress, he starts drinking. Most of the trip is a drunken blur, and he apparently sleeps with Jerome's childhood friend. Back in Illinois, he immediately confesses to Katherine. Feeling that he has failed both personally and professionally, increasingly obsessed with thoughts of guilt and death, Charles slashes his wrists and is carried away in an ambulance. He gives a signal to start a recording. The last thing to appear is a poem in which Charles tells his brother to remember their life in North Dakota and their experience there, because the bond between them is formed by their memories of each other.

Themes and Meanings

The importance of memory is the main theme of *Born Brothers*. Events themselves are less important than what Charles remembers about them and what connections he makes among them. Through this process, he discerns a pattern, an emotional framework that enables him to function and gives him the will to go on living.

Some memories evoke feelings of grief, loss, or guilt; others create a sense of being connected to family members who care. Often, the two types are juxtaposed. Immediately after Charles remembers his mother's funeral, there is a radio script in which he tells about the birth of his son. The last section, called "Last Light," ends with his suicide attempt, but it begins with Charles walking over the farm in North Dakota to which he and his family have moved, thinking about the ways in which he has changed, changes that will allow him to survive.

At the worst of times, Charles seeks death as a release from his painful memories.

Once, when remembering his suicide attempt, Charles says that the death of his mother left him so unattached to life that he could sever that cord. The memories of his family forge ties, however; Charles, through this process of remembering, maintains and reinforces those ties.

The relationship between Jerome and Charles is the most important one. They are like yin and yang, two parts of a whole. Charles wants to be a doctor but ends up in speech and theater. Jerome wants to study speech and theater but studies medicine. Charles marries Katherine, a woman who reminds him of Jerome, fair-haired with the same blue eyes; Jerome marries Julie, a woman like Charles, dark and skillful with words.

No one can comfort Charles as Jerome does. The book opens with Charles remembering his anticipation of Jerome's visit to New York, a visit that has a healing effect on him. Fragments about this visit appear throughout the book. At the end of the book, when Charles is overcome with feelings of guilt and failure, he remembers frantically trying to get to the place where he was to meet Jerome. No one can hurt him as Jerome can, either. Charles is devastated when Jerome sides with the boy who had been taunting him. Jerome is driving the car when Charles is badly injured. These incidents seem almost self-destructive.

Although the relationship between Charles and Jerome is most important, the pattern existed before they were born, and it changes as they grow older. Jerome, named for their mother's favorite brother, who died young, is more like their mother. Charles, named for his father's father, is more like their father. When Charles looks at Jerome, he sees his mother's eyes and her concern. When he looks in the mirror, he sees his father. As the years pass, they go in opposite directions, and Jerome cannot help Charles through the crisis that leads to his suicide attempt. Charles realizes that only Katherine, who reminds him of Jerome, can help him through to the "other side."

The older Charles who has survived the suicide attempt has put his life together. His religious belief based on the study of Scripture has formed a new connection with God and other believers. He has moved back to North Dakota, to the land he associates with his mother, thus reestablishing that connection. He has a son who reminds him so much of Jerome that he sometimes thinks of him as a brother rather than as a son. The process of remembering helps him to understand the pattern of his past life and the new pattern that has been woven, one that allows him to survive.

Critical Context

Born Brothers is Larry Woiwode's fourth novel, the second to deal with the Neumiller family. The first, *Beyond the Bedroom Wall: A Family Album* (1970), was nominated for both the National Book Award and the National Book Critics Circle Award. It includes many of the same characters and covers many of the same events, but it is told from different perspectives by several members of the family. Memory is an important theme in this book also; as its subtitle suggests, it is like a series of snapshots. It stops before Charles experiences the crisis that leads to his suicide attempt, however, and readers do not see how his life has changed. Because the older and wiser character of Charles appears in *Born Brothers*, the overall impression is much different.

Several parts of *Beyond the Bedroom Wall* were originally published as short stories, many of which appeared in *The New Yorker*. Several of these, plus three more written between 1982 and 1989, have been published in their original form in a book called *The Neumiller Stories* (1989).

Bibliography

Chappell, F. "American Gothic." *National Review* (March 24, 1989): 45-46. A favorable review of Woiwode's novel that explores the book's American roots.

Field, Michele. "Larry Woiwode." *Publishers Weekly* 234 (August 5, 1988); 67-68. Includes biographical information relevant to stories about the Neumiller family and discusses the background of the writing of *Born Brothers*.

Freise, Kathy. "Home Again on the Prairie." *North Dakota Horizons* 23 (Summer, 1993): 19-23. Details Woiwode's connections with the state and its role in his books dealing with the Neumiller family.

Nelson, Shirley. "Stewards of the Imagination: Ron Hansen, Larry Woiwode, and Sue Miller." *Christian Century* 112 (January 25, 1995): 82-85. Nelson interviews Hansen, Woiwode, and Miller, focusing on the role of religion in their works and on readers' reactions to their novels.

Scheick, William J. "Memory in Larry Woiwode's Novels." *North Dakota Quarterly* 53, no. 3 (1985): 29-40. Scheick discusses the importance of memory in three of Woiwode's novels, *What I'm Going to Do, I Think* (1969), *Beyond the Bedroom Wall*, and *Poppa John* (1981). He identifies two types of memories, those that make a character feel guilt and long for death and those that develop a sense of connection to one's family. The ability to order these allows Woiwode's characters to achieve a balance between them.

Woiwode, Larry. "Homeplace, Heaven, or Hell." *Renascence* 44 (1991): 3-16. Woiwode discusses the problem of being considered merely a regional writer because he writes about the Midwest. He says that all writers must write about some place and that only geographical chauvinism makes one place better than another. The author also asserts that the main duty of a Christian writer is to write the truth, which means to write about a place in precise detail.

_____. Interview by Ed Block, Jr. *Renascence* 44, no. 1 (1991): 17-30. Woiwode explains his views on the lack of genuine emotion and standards in much modern fiction. He explains his spiritual conversion and his reasons for moving back to North Dakota. The fragmentation and discontinuity in the structure of *Born Brothers* are used, Woiwode says, because he wants readers to experience the inside of the central character's mind and his struggle.

_____. "Where the Buffalo Roam: An Interview with Larry Woiwode." Interview by Rick Watson. *North Dakota Quarterly* 63 (Fall, 1996): 154-166. A revealing interview about Woidwode's homecoming and the effect it has had on his writing.

Eunice Pedersen Johnston

BREAD GIVERS

Author: Anzia Yezierska (1885-1970)
Type of plot: Cultural realism
Time of plot: The early twentieth century
Locale: New York City's Lower East Side
First published: 1925

> *Principal characters:*
> SARA SMOLINSKY, a Polish-born Jewish immigrant
> MR. SMOLINSKY, Sara's Old World father
> BESSIE SMOLINSKY, Sara's oldest sister who supports the family
> MASHA SMOLINSKY, Sara's beautiful sister, who is ruined by an
>   arranged marriage
> FANIA SMOLINSKY, Sara's sister who is forced to wed a gambler
> HUGO SEELIG, Sara's American, educated fiancé

The Novel

Hester Street, heart of Jewish immigrant life on New York's Lower East Side in the early twentieth century, with its blend of poverty, dirt, and religious fervor, is the colorful milieu of Sara Smolinsky, *Bread Givers'* main character. The youngest of four daughters born to a Polish Judaic scholar and his wife, Sara personifies the clash between the demands of tradition and the beckoning opportunities of a new land—America.

Sara's first-person narration recollects those incidents of her childhood and young adult life which shape her ambition. Sara's journey to independence is obstructed by the conditions of poverty and the traditional expectations of Jewish women, yet she fights the often bitter battle to, as she says, "make myself for a person," with determination. At age ten, she earns money by peddling herring in the street. Along with the sweatshop earnings of her three older sisters and her mother, who takes in boarders, Sara shares the burden of her father's household. The contrast between the apparent luxury of Mr. Smolinsky's time, spent in prayer, spiritual contemplation, and religious study, and the unending toil which falls to the women, is decreed by the holy law of the Torah. As Mr. Smolinsky is quick to remind his family, "women get into heaven because they were the wives and daughters of men. Women had no brains for the study of God's Torah, but they could be the servants of men who studied the Torah."

As she sees her sisters bargained away into arranged marriages which make Mr. Smolinsky's reputation as a professional matchmaker, Sara's will hardens against him and the law that he represents. Although the three older daughters all have suitors of their own, Mr. Smolinsky forbids these relationships, preferring to exercise his absolute control by forcing the girls into loveless unions with men he chooses. When Masha's "great catch" turns out to be an unemployed salesman, and not the diamond dealer her father believed him to be, Mr. Smolinsky blames the situation on his daughter's ill luck.

Sara, refusing to be cowed like her sisters, rebels against her father. After a bitter confrontation with him, Sara runs away, choosing to live for herself instead of under his domination. Living in squalor, always hungry, Sara sustains herself with night-school lessons and dreams of college and a teaching career. Suspect for living alone instead of with her family and working to help support them, she is ostracized by the other sweatshop girls with whom she works. The grim reality of her sisters' lives, coupled with dreams of the future, supports her choice.

Sara manages to complete night school and attend college in New England. An outcast among the people on Hester Street, she is truly an outsider in the middle-class college community. Realizing her dream of becoming an educated woman eases the pain of not belonging, and returning to the Lower East Side as a teacher helps heal the wounds of Sara's displacement and ease her guilt over shirking family responsibility. Still, she does not win her father's approval, for which she yearns, although she knows that it would require the self-sacrifice that she refuses to make—her compliance with the idea of innate female inferiority.

Mr. Smolinsky's remarriage almost immediately after the death of Sara's mother reinforces her determination not to succumb to his self-centered will. Yet, ultimately, she cannot refuse his needs, and, encouraged by her fiancé, Hugo Seelig, she agrees to help support him and his new wife. Hugo, also a teacher and the child of immigrants, tries to uphold the continuity of tradition by learning Hebrew from Mr. Smolinsky. Sara, still unsure of how to negotiate between her own and her father's needs, is finally able to accept that inextricable part of her nature which can only be fulfilled through the culture that Mr. Smolinsky represents: "It wasn't just my father, but the generations who made my father whose weight was still upon me."

The Characters

The characters in *Bread Givers*, from coarse pushcart clothing to their speech peppered with Yiddish expressions, are faithfully modeled upon the real immigrants of Yezierska's own acquaintance. Some, such as Zalmon the fish peddler, are literary memorials to the people whom Yezierska cherished for their inspiration. Other characters, such as Sara and Mr. Smolinsky, replicate the struggle that Yezierska herself experienced between the demands of traditional culture and the opportunities of contemporary American society. The Smolinsky family illustrates the gender arrangements which constrained Yezierska, even as she celebrated the culture which created them.

Many of the details of Yezierska's life coincide with those of her character, Sara Smolinsky (both are children of poor, Jewish immigrants, both helped support their families while still children, and both sacrificed much to earn an education). Yet as a literary character, Sara is able to act out conflicts in a manner both dramatic and satisfying. Sara is a model of resourcefulness at fighting the hostile influences of family and culture. As a child, Sara's character is largely formed by reacting to the example set by her three older sisters—Bessie, Masha, and Fania.

Like their mother, the three older girls do not question female submission. Mrs.

Smolinsky, once the petted daughter of well-to-do parents in a Polish *shtetl*, considers herself blessed by the honor of marriage to Mr. Smolinsky, a highly esteemed scholar. In Poland, Mr. Smolinsky's devotion to study is a sign of the inherited wealth which supports it. Even when financial reverses force them to emigrate and face great changes, Mrs. Smolinsky still believes in her husband's godliness and her responsibility to enable him to study. She wavers only when Mr. Smolinsky, taking matters into his own hands, makes their financial situation worse. Even though he gives much of the women's earning away to charity and is swindled out of the small savings which might have made them comfortable, Mrs. Smolinsky never fails to see the light of God shining in her husband's eyes.

Mrs. Smolinsky's acceptance of her husband's spiritual, and hence essential, superiority, is solidly reinforced in the minds of the three older daughters. Bessie, the oldest, is famous for being the burden-bearer of her father's house. Working long hours in a sweatshop and bringing home piecework makes her more valuable to him. Her father turns the one suitor she has out of the house because he refuses to pay a dowry. She knows that she has been broken to her father's will, and the loss of her lover increases her despair. True to her self-sacrificing nature, she marries a widower who willingly pays Mr. Smolinsky's price, rationalizing her lot by concern for the man's wild, unkempt children. Like their sister Bessie, Masha and Fania are unable to overcome the injunction of submissiveness to the father's will. Masha and Fania watch helplessly as their father bans the men they love from the house as well for what he calls their godlessness and inability to support his daughters adequately. When Mr. Smolinsky arranges marriages for the two girls with truly unsuitable men, they are forced to accept their situations. Believing that the unhappiness and poverty which marriage has brought them is the norm, and unable to see beyond the cultural pattern which determines their lives, they even encourage Sara to marry a man, selected by her father, whom she dislikes.

Supported by tradition, Mr. Smolinsky assumes the right to make a profit from his daughters. Sara, demanding the right to live her own life, confronts her father, who is ensconced among the holy books that the women are not allowed to touch. Backed up by the law of patriarchy that has blinded him to the rights and worldly needs of his wife and children, he justifies her duty to him: "Now, when I begin to have a little use from you, you want to run away and live for yourself?" Fueled by years of internalized anger at her father's absolute control, Sara saves herself from a life of submission.

Starving herself to save money for school, Sara's desire to realize the American Dream is marked by ambivalence. The childhood nickname "blood and iron," bestowed on her by her father, signifies her opposition as well as likeness to him. Hating his tyranny, yet yearning to express their shared love of study and knowledge, Sara finds in secular education a spiritual bridge to the Jewish tradition of learning which shuts out women. Disdaining arranged marriage, she still wants her father's approval of the man she chooses for herself. Sara's attempt to reconcile her heritage with American culture, she realizes, places her "between two worlds," but she accepts that uncomfortable position as the only possible one.

Themes and Meanings

Yezierska does not romanticize the poverty of Hester Street, but she does make apparent the wisdom of the ages used to make conditions there tolerable. As Mr. Smolinsky says, "The God that feeds the worms under the stone, and the fishes in the sea, will he not feed us?" In trying to express both the beauty of Jewish culture and its incompatibility with early twentieth century urban life, Yezierska shows that Sara's success in meeting modern challenges is founded upon her realism.

While following the traditions of ritual law, Mr. Smolinsky's opportunism illustrates the inherent hypocrisy of having one foot in the Old World and the other in the New: "I want to get into some quick money-making thing that will not take up too many hours a day, so I could get most of my time for learning." Not wanting to disown the cultural identity which venerates scholarship but also realizing that, as a woman, she is excluded from that tradition, Sara's ambivalence is the result of being caught between contradictory ideals. The promise of America—individual success—can turn the subordination of women under patriarchal Judaism on its ear. Essential as such self-definition is for survival, however, the loss of cultural place creates a lack which cannot be denied.

Overcoming that lack by synthesizing personal need and cultural identity is the message of *Bread Givers*. Sara returns to the Lower East Side as a schoolteacher, believing that she has a debt to pay to the past she once thought had no claims on her. "Once I had been elated at the thought that a man wanted me. How much more thrilling to feel that I had made my work wanted!" The rewards of love may come second to career, but it is no less important. Securely independent prior to romantic involvement, Sara uses marriage to affirm culture, instead of being destroyed by it. Sara's engagement to a man of like background and ambition helps close the gap between herself and her culture. As her fiancé recognizes, "You and I, we are of one blood." Together they give life to Yezierska's hope of preserving culture without sacrificing either independence or romantic desire.

Critical Context

By the time she wrote *Bread Givers*, Yezierska had undergone the pivotal experience of her literary career. The success of *Hungry Hearts* (1920), her collected short stories, brought her fame and a contract as a Hollywood scriptwriter. Away from the ghetto which was both the setting and inspiration for her creative efforts, Yezierska suffered from writer's block and a painful sense of dissociation. The experience confirmed Yezierska's cultural identity, and her resolve to return to Hester Street was marked by the awareness that with financial success, "I could buy everything I wanted except the driving force I had to inspire my work."

Faithfully reproducing the battle Yezierska waged against poverty and cultural taboo, the romantic plot which gives Bread Givers a conventional sense of closure solves another dilemma that Yezierska faced: How can one establish independence without giving up the notion of romantic happiness? Variation on the themes of her own life was deliberately cathartic; as she wrote, "I thought by writing out what I don't know and can't understand it will stop hurting me."

The clear poignancy of her literary style does not belie the hardships Yezierska endured to learn English from a janitor's daughter, but instead transports the reader into her world without pretense or self-effacement. As one contemporary critic noted of her writing, "One does not seem to read, one is too completely inside."

Approaching middle age, Yezierska stopped writing novels and stories, and her popularity waned. In *Red Ribbon on a White Horse* (1950), her autobiography, she voices the belief that sacrificing cultural roots was too high a price for the recognition she had once craved. The mid-1970's republication of *Bread Givers* and other out-of-print books by Yezierska has fortunately made her work widely available. The returning popularity of her work testifies to the universal emotional appeal and unique voice which first established her literary reputation.

Bibliography
Crocco, Margaret S. "Women's History of the 1920's: A Look at Anzia Yezierska and Charlotte Perkins Gilman." *Social Education* 59 (January, 1995): 29-30. Crocco compares Yezierska's *Bread Givers* with works by Charlotte Perkins Gilman. Both authors express the dilemmas women face when having to choose between a home life and a career.
Dearborn, Mary V. *Love in the Promised Land: The Story of Anzia Yezierska and John Dewey.* New York: Free Press, 1988. Details the relationship between Yezierska and philosopher John Dewey. Dearborn provides insights into Yezierska's private life as well as her career as a writer.
Ferraro, Thomas J. "'Working Ourselves Up' in America: Anzia Yezierska's *Bread Givers.*" *South Atlantic Quarterly* 89 (Summer, 1990): 547-581. Ferraro profiles Yezierska and offers an extended discussion of *Bread Givers*, her other novels, her short fiction, and her sketches.
Henriksen, Louise L. *Anzia Yezierska: A Writer's Life.* New Brunswick, N.J.: Rutgers University Press, 1982. A biography of Yezierska, with an analysis of her writings and overview of her career.
Rhoades, Chip. "Education as Liberation: The Case of Anzia Yezierska's *Bread Givers.*" *Science and Society* 57 (Fall, 1993): 294-312. Rhoades asserts that *Bread Givers* can best be understood as a reflection of Yezierska's own acceptance of progressive educational philosophy as espoused by John Dewey, with whom she had a love affair. Rhoades maintains that the theme of a woman's attempt to escape from an oppressive power structure of Jewish immigrant society is evident in Yezierska's own escape to freedom.
Schoen, Carol. *Anzia Yezierska.* Boston: Twayne, 1982. Schoen provides a critical and interpretive study of Yezierska with a close reading of her major works, a solid bibliography, and complete notes and references.
Shapiro, Ann R. "The Ultimate Shaygets and the Fiction of Anzia Yezierska." *MELUS* 21 (Summer, 1996): 79-88. Shapiro explores the theme of a Jewish woman

seeking acceptance from a Gentile man. Shapiro points out that the story in *Bread Givers* is believed to be based on Yezierska's affair with John Dewey.

Wilentz, Gay. "Cultural Mediation and the Immigrant's Daughter: Anzia Yezierska's *Bread Givers.*" *MELUS* 17 (Fall, 1991): 33-41. Wilentz asserts that *The Bread Givers* illustrates a clash of cultural forces for Jewish immigrant women in the United States in the 1920's. The conflict between traditional ways and Americanization and independence is a major theme in the novel. Sara laments that something is lost in order to succeed in America. A balance must be maintained between her Jewish roots and her new American identity.

Zierler, Wendy. "The Rebirth of Anzia Yezierska." *Judaism: A Quarterly Journal of Jewish Life and Thought* 42 (Fall, 1993): 414-422. Zierler profiles Yezierska and offers an analysis of why she achieved popularity in the 1920's, was forgotten, and was rediscovered after her death in 1970 by Jewish feminists. Zierler maintains that Yezierska is regarded as the foremother of Jewish feminism because of her portrayal of young Jewish women characters in her novels.

Mollie A. Brodsky

BREATH, EYES, MEMORY

Author: Edwidge Danticat (1969-   )
Type of plot: Social realism
Time of plot: The 1970's to the 1990's
Locale: Haiti and New York City
First published: 1994

> *Principal characters:*
> SOPHIE CACO, a young girl
> MARTINE CACO, Sophie's mother
> TANTE ATIE, Sophie's aunt, who raises her in Haiti before her mother
>   sends for her
> GRANDMA IFE, Martine's mother

The Novel

Breath, Eyes, Memory tells the story of Sophie Caco from her younger years in Haiti to her mother's death. Over the course of the novel, Sophie must come to terms with her family, her family's past, her childhood, and her own identity.

The third-person narrator begins with Sophie in Haiti, living with her Tante Atie, who had moved from her mother's home to town to assure Sophie's education. The early part of the novel (part 1) shows the details of Sophie's world: the close neighborhood, the political turmoil, the struggles of Tante Atie as a single woman in this society, and Sophie's struggles to understand Atie's sorrow. During this section, Sophie learns that her mother, Martine, has sent for her to come to America and live.

Sophie's ambiguous feelings about her identity are apparent when she tries to give Atie a Mother's Day card, which Atie insists she give to her mother instead—the mother who is only a voice on the tape recordings she sends regularly. When Sophie arrives in New York, she learns that her mother works two jobs to support herself and send money home to Haiti. Sophie also learns that her birth was the result of a rape by a man who kept his face covered; her mother dreams nightly of this horror and the faceless man.

In part 2, Sophie has started college. She and her mother have moved to a larger house; her mother continues to work two jobs, and Sophie continues to struggle with the attitudes of those around her regarding her Haitian heritage. During this time, Sophie meets Joseph, an older musician who lives next door. Martine feels strongly about what she has been taught about a mother's duty to protect her daughter's chastity and reputation. When Martine discovers that Sophie is involved with a man, she insists on carrying out a "test" of her virginity—a humiliating ordeal that Martine and Atie also suffered through with Grandma Ife. To escape this ordeal, Sophie bodily injures herself to ensure that she will fail the test. She asks Joseph to marry her and take her with him to Providence; the prospect of living in a town named after the Creator encourages Sophie.

Part 3 begins with Sophie's return to Haiti with her daughter, Brigitte, to visit Atie and Grandma Ife, a trip she has undertaken without telling her husband. Atie again lives with her mother. Sophie quickly sees the strained relationship between her aunt and grandmother, as Atie has learned to read, drinks rum, and disappears for hours at night. Martine arrives also, having been called by Joseph to report that Sophie has disappeared and having been told by her mother that Sophie had arrived in Haiti. Sophie asks her mother about the test—as she had asked her grandmother—and receives the same reply: They did it because their mothers had done it. While tenuous, a reconciliation does take place between the mother and daughter. In this section, readers learn that Sophie experiences sexual difficulty with her husband and struggles to overcome and understand her past, an attempt that has brought her to her grandmother's. The interactions among the four generations of women reveal the complex dynamics of the family.

In part 4, Martine and Sophie return to New York, where Sophie spends the night with her mother. Their conversation reveals that Sophie suffers from bulimia and that Martine is pregnant. The child's father is a long-term partner whom Martine has refused to marry. Her pregnancy surprises her—cancer has resulted in two mastectomies—and brings back many painful memories of the circumstances of her first pregnancy. Sophie reunites with her husband, who finally meets Martine a week later. Sophie belongs to a support group for women who have suffered sexual abuse; she receives counseling, and she struggles with her marriage. Sophie is distraught when her mother's lover calls to tell her that Martine has committed suicide to end her pregnancy. All of them return to Haiti for the burial, according to her mother's wishes, and the novel ends with the four generations of Caco women again reunited by the tragic event.

The Characters

Sophie Caco grows from a young girl to an adult woman with her own child. She is the emotional, as well as the narrative, heart of the novel. The third-person limited narration gives Sophie's often bewildered view of a world over which she feels she has no control. She cannot stop herself from being shipped off to America; she cannot stop her mother's nightmares and the tests; she cannot understand the circumstances of her own reactions to the events around her. She fights back the only way she knows how: by marrying Joseph and leaving her mother's house. By the end, she comes closer to understanding her own behavior and the behavior of her family members, but the cost has been great—estrangement from her mother, problems with her husband, and anger at her family. Her relationship with her mother—who moves from a voice on a tape recording to a living presence to a tormentor to a role model—shapes her world in ways she only begins to understand by the end of the novel.

Tante Atie spent years of sacrifice to rear Sophie, only to have her returned to her mother. While she insists that Sophie belongs with her mother, the loss of Sophie greatly affects Atie's life for the worse. Readers learn that Atie as a young woman planned to marry but that the man left her for someone else. Atie and Sophie live across the street from this man and his wife; Atie watches them at night and cries. When Sophie leaves, Atie returns to care for her mother—the duty of the elder, unmarried daughter. Sophie sees her suffering, but for many years cannot understand it.

Martine Caco also lives her life according to her duties. She works long hours to support herself, to send money to her mother, sister, and daughter, and to enable her to send for Sophie. She has endured many hardships, from the rape that resulted in Sophie's birth to cancer to nightly terrors in her sleep. Martine desperately wants a better life for her daughter than the one she has lived.

Grandma Ife takes her role as matriarch seriously, never hesitating to instruct, correct, bully, and lead her family. Sophie comes to understand her wisdom, her ability to hear things others cannot, and her fear for the future of her family, but she holds her responsible as well for some of the indignities of her life, such as the "test."

Sophie's husband Joseph and Martine's lover Marc also fit into the story, but both are presented as relatively flat, static characters. Both support the women in their lives and care deeply about them.

Themes and Meanings

Breath, Eyes, Memory presents readers with many painful, difficult realities about human suffering and society, yet it does so with lyrical beauty and insight into the courage and fortitude of its characters. While the novel deals with the political turmoil and deprivation of Haiti and the difficulties of racism, prejudice, and identity in America, the main focus remains on the four women central to the novel. The theme of mothers and daughters weaves itself throughout all four parts. Sophie sees herself as "my mother's daughter and Tante Atie's child." Much of the power of the novel stems from the slow attainment of understanding about her family.

The women created, both the major and minor characters, inhabit a world controlled, and sometimes invaded, by men. From the rapist who attacked Martine to the soldiers in Haiti to husbands and lovers and jilters, the novel portrays a world that revolves around men. While there are positive male characters presented, the effects of repression, stereotypes, and tradition take center stage. Sexual behavior is a case in point: Because this world prizes chastity in women, mothers submit their daughters to the "test" in order to preserve them. Sophie learns that her mother administered the test because her mother did; Grandma Ife, in turn, did the same because her mother did.

To focus only on the pain in the novel, however, misses much of the power and lyricism of Danticat's work. Along with negative traditions and difficulties, she shows the strength, indomitability, and endurance of these lives. Sophie finally sees the courage and gifts in their lives, including that her mother was "brave as the stars at dawn." For all the other turmoil in the novel—political, sexual, societal, generational—one question remains the central theme: Can Sophie free herself to see the complexity, the sacrifice, the good and the evil of these relationships central to her life?

Critical Context

Breath, Eyes, Memory achieved both critical and popular success. The characters, the lyrical prose, and the interweaving of myth, tradition, experience, and knowledge all combine to create a powerful novel.

Danticat draws on her Haitian American heritage; she, too, stayed behind when her parents went to New York City for work, living with relatives until the age of twelve, when she also moved. The Duvalier dictatorship in Haiti during her childhood provides the novel's political backdrop, evoked by the fear of the citizens, the brutality of the soldiers, and by Sophie's encounter with a boy who has lost his father to the violence. Danticat has said that part of her attraction to writing stemmed from her wish to break the silence imposed on Haiti; she was also drawn by the inherent danger of such an activity.

Sophie's quest requires her to come to terms with her own history, the strength in her own family, and the beauty, as well as the hardships, of Haitian society. She must also balance her two identities, American and Haitian. She faces prejudice from Americans and questioning by the Haitians when she returns. A small but intriguing example of this occurs when she goes jogging on her last visit to her grandmother, as the people working in the fields wonder, "Is this what happens to our girls when they leave this place? They become such frightened creatures that they run like the wind, from nothing at all."

Danticat's themes of political repression, feminism, and cultural identity all coalesce in the attention to storytelling. Readers hear the stories passed down from mother to child for generations, both to delight and to terrify. After her mother's funeral, Sophie hears the following from Grandma Ife: "There is always a place where, if you listen closely in the night, you will hear your mother telling a story and at the end of the tale, she will ask you this question: 'Ou libere?' Are you free, my daughter?" For Sophie, Martine, Atie, Grandma Ife, Haiti, and America, the question echoes throughout Danticat's novel.

Bibliography

Campbell, Elaine. *The Whistling Bird: Women Writers of the Caribbean.* Boulder, Colo.: Lynne Rienner, 1998. Includes a useful discussion of Danticat.

Charters, Mallay. "Edwidge Danticat: A Bitter Legacy Revisited." *Publishers Weekly* 245, no. 33 (August 17, 1998): 42-43. A profile of the novelist. Discusses the experiences that led to the writing of *Breath, Eyes, Memory* and her other novels.

Shea, Renee H. "The Dangerous Job of Edwidge Danticat." *Callaloo* 19, no. 2 (Spring, 1996): 382-390. Includes an interview with Danticat in which she discusses her feelings toward Haiti, her preoccupation with mothers and daughters, and the translation of *Breath, Eyes, Memory* into French.

_____. "Traveling Worlds with Edwidge Danticat." *Poets and Writers Magazine* 25, no. 1 (January-February, 1997): 42-51. An overview of Danticat's life and writings.

"Three Young Voices." Interview with Edwidge Danticat, Veronica Chambers, and Sheneska Jackson. *Essence*, May, 1996. Danticat discusses her childhood and her life as a writer.

Caroline Carvill

BRENDAN

Author: Frederick Buechner (1926-   )
Type of plot: Historical
Time of plot: The sixth century
Locale: Ireland, Wales, and the North Atlantic Ocean
First published: 1987

> *Principal characters:*
> BRENDAN, the book's protagonist, an Irish cleric and voyager, the
>   alleged discoverer of the New World
> FINN, the book's narrator, Brendan's faithful companion
> ERC, the bishop responsible for Brendan's education and upbringing
> CROSAN, one of Brendan's crew members
> COLMAN, a powerful poet who converts to Christianity and takes up the
>   monastic life
> ITA, an abbess, Brendan's educator
> BRIGID, a saint, Brendan's inspiration

The Novel

Although it is set in the sixth century and features many of the historical personages who gave significant impetus to the learning, building, and evangelizing that distinguished the onset of Christianity in Ireland, *Brendan* is less a historical novel than a meditation on the profound simplicities of the religious faith. It takes as its focus the remarkable career of Saint Brendan and through it represents the spirit of the age. The period is depicted as one in which the human mind was more liable to be overwhelmed by the proximity of God's presence in the world and when the world of creation impressed itself more immediately and strikingly on the senses of those who lived in it.

As the historical note at the end of the novel makes clear, the protagonist Brendan is noteworthy for a number of different reasons. The fact that he was a saint is one obvious reason for his significance. He was also an important churchman, and he founded the monastic settlement of Clonfert, a name that survives in contemporary Ireland as that of a Catholic diocese. Yet these achievements, relevant as they are to an appreciation of the reality of the protagonist's context, pale in comparison to Brendan's legendary status. From at least the tenth century onward, Brendan's name has been synonymous with voyages of discovery.

Two of these voyages are recounted in the novel, the first by Brendan himself in what is in effect a ship's log. Nothing more than extremely localized geographical locations and climatic conditions are provided in this clearly incomplete narrative of the journey. Internal evidence suggests that the coast of Iceland is sighted. Of much greater importance is the second voyage, an account of which is provided by the novel's narrator, Finn. The second voyage locates the other world of pre-Christian

Irish mythology, Tír-na-Nog, a name that means "the land of eternal youth." This landfall is not only Brendan's apotheosis as a navigator but is also the basis of his historical status as a legendary figure among whose exploits is said to be the discovery of America.

Exciting as these journeys are, however, the author carefully insinuates that these are simply a means to an end. They are simply spectacular and risky phases in a career that is replete with restlessness and dedication, and the novel itself is conceived as a biography of Brendan by his lifelong companion, Finn. For that reason, the voyages are not seen as the climax of Brendan's career; rather, they vie for significance with other episodes that have an explicit historical dimension. These episodes include the establishment of Brendan's monastic settlement at Clonfert and his trip to Wales in later life. The visit to Wales culminates with Brendan's involvement with the internal politics of Camelot and features a cameo appearance from King Artor, as he is called.

Yet while the historical element of Brendan's career is unavoidable, *Brendan* does not dwell on it. The background to the protagonist's life is economically sketched, but no effort is made to provide a comprehensive picture of the emergence and consolidation of Christianity in Ireland, of the religion's relationship with the religions it supplanted, or of the complex territorial and juridical issues that formed a constant undercurrent of turbulence in the politics of clan life in ancient Ireland. Such omissions make all the more plausible the intimate view of Brendan's career that Finn's narrative provides. The overall effect of the omissions is to emphasize the novelty and interest of Brendan, so that the view of him that ultimately emerges is of a personage who is representative of more elusive and awe-inspiring facets of humanity than those that typify a given historical period.

The novel's concentration on these facets is clearly indebted to the author's theological training and influenced by his well-known theological writings. The end that Brendan's life is understood to serve is that of maintaining a sense of spiritual wonder, an almost palpable awareness of the greatness of God's creation. Such an emphasis is maintained primarily by the impressive spiritedness and color of the novel's style. At times, the style is virtually a pastiche of the simplicity, sensoriness, and delight in detail that may be found in both the lyric poetry of early Christian Ireland and in the ornamented gospels such as the Book of Kells. A judicious sprinkling of Magical Realism also contributes to the establishment of the novel's remote and poorly documented environment. This perspective does not merely assist in underlining the element of wonder that runs throughout *Brendan*; it also makes acceptable the various miraculous events with which Brendan is involved that provide him with the basic credentials for sainthood. These events heighten and crystalize the undogmatic faith in, and commitment to, the divine dimension to the mortal lot by means of which the world of *Brendan* maintains an even keel.

The Characters

In *Brendan*, the protagonist's nautical attainments constituting the heart of the story are not presented as great feats of heroism in Brendan's mind. He does not see them as a means of spreading the gospel, nor—unlike in other stories about his contemporaries who leave Ireland—are they a punishment. Instead, they are presented as expressions of Brendan's naïve, foolhardy, God-seeking personality. Despite his education, Brendan remains essentially simple. His clerical eminence, established by his monastic foundation at Clonfert, is not synonymous with the secular power that abbots and other high-ranking members of the hierarchy possessed in those times. On the contrary, Brendan makes his way in ignorance and in poverty, with a humble, unassuming, and rather doubt-laden cast of mind.

Although Brendan is equipped with the power to work miracles and is able to apply that power opportunely in moments of danger, it is his humility that attracts adherents. Finn, in particular, provides a clear perspective on the combination of uncertainty and devotion that are continually at odds within Brendan. Unlike Brendan, Finn is not a cleric. He is more worldly, as his marriage and paternity suggest, and though he is touched by the wonder of the Christian message, he is less driven to experience the glory of it than is Brendan. Finn is clearly conceived as a foil to the protagonist, and his greater steadiness and narrower psychological range show Brendan in bolder relief than would be possible under more conventional narrative circumstances. The fact that Finn survives Brendan acts as a reminder that Finn embodies the less spectacular, more down-to-earth fate of the common man.

Most of the other characters may be thought of in terms of the contrast between Finn and Brendan, particularly when that contrast is seen as a complement rather than as a polarity. The combination of the mundane and the spiritual is located in the two conversion episodes in which Brendan is involved. Crosan, the court jester at the court of the High Kings at Cashel, is attracted to Brendan because of his mundanity. On the other hand, the bard Mac Lennin joins his fortunes to Brendan's on the basis of the latter's spiritual appeal. Not surprisingly, Mac Lennin eventually establishes his own monastic settlement. Even the most notable of the clerics whom Brendan encounters, such as Ita and Brigid, possess an earthiness through which their spiritual passions are articulated. This is particularly true of the vivid and volatile Brigid, with whose zeal and vigor Brendan's adventures make a stimulating comparison.

The characters' sexuality is one of the most consistent ways in which their earthiness is expressed, and their lack of prudery about sexual and other natural functions is one of the basic means by which they are revealed to be at home with themselves in the natural world. It is that sense of home, expressed in terms of self-possession, which is brought into critical focus through Brendan's character. He is the one who goes to extreme lengths in order to prove his worthiness to feel at home. By doing so, he demonstrates the relevance of the issues that his searching commitment represents.

Themes and Meanings

It is in the light of Brendan as at once the least assured and most courageous of the novel's characters that his voyages are to be perceived. They are presented not as remarkable feats of navigation but as practical manifestations of the mystery of faith. On his first voyage, Brendan deems it as reasonable to be guided by the seabirds as to take commonsensical navigational decisions. His second voyage in search of the Other World is even more obviously a test of faith. More important, however, it is a provocative resolution of the test, offering a sense of reward that it is impossible to translate back into the struggle of the mortal lot.

The spectacular validation of Brendan's commitment that the discovery of Tír-na-Nog provides comes in forms that parody the solemnity that matters of holiness usually generate. Brendan reaches an eschatological epiphany—only to find it to be a combination of a zoo, a circus, and a paradise along the lines depicted by Paul Gauguin in his paintings of Tahiti. This discovery is not something Brendan can understand. The reader sees what Brendan himself finds difficult: that it is the journey and not the arrival that matters. The extent to which Brendan remains blind to this truism suggests that part of the author's intention is to portray his protagonist as a version of that traditional archetype of unworldliness, the Holy Fool.

Brendan's lack of conceptual awareness of the questing spirit within him is offset by his physical embodiment of it. There is nothing he can do to allay the promptings of his ardent and restless nature, and by accepting this fact of his life, he too finds his way in the world. The emphasis throughout *Brendan* of the physical as a manifestation of the spiritual is a persuasive means of integrating the characters with their environment. By showing how the characters themselves find such an integration natural, the novel reveals humanity's appreciation and awareness of creation. The sense of duality and alienation that modern humankind has been alleged to feel, and the so-called death of God that is frequently held to be responsible for this feeling, are counteracted here by the strength of faith that the characters are capable of generating.

The dangers of sentimentalizing the human condition of the remote and colorful characters who make plausible the world of *Brendan* are obvious. A work dealing with the issues addressed in *Brendan* could easily take the form of a simple-minded sermon on the spiritual purity of early Christian Ireland, viewing its inhabitants as people living in a land flowing with milk and honey whose lives consist of a paean of praise to everything that lives. For this reason, the harshness of life, the menace of the weather, the physical difficulties even of travel by land are vividly portrayed. The effect is that the novel, rather than being a homily, is something of a hymn to the possibilities of spiritual enlightenment and to the struggle that must necessarily attend the pursuit of anything so complex.

Critical Context

It is possible to see *Brendan* in a number of literary, cultural, and religious contexts. One of these is the literary tradition to which the life of Saint Brendan the navigator has given rise. The founding work of this tradition, the Latin work *Navigatio Sancti Brendani* (c. 900; the voyage of Saint Brendan), became one of the most popular legends of an age that saw the appearance of many such works and was widely known in various languages throughout Europe. Widespread awareness of this work is a reflection of the missionary presence of Irish clerics in Europe during the early medieval period. This historical fact is glanced at in *Brendan* by the inclusion among the protagonist's intimates of a character named Malo, whose name is commemorated in the noted French resort of St. Malo.

In addition, *Navigatio Sancti Brendani* belongs to the medieval Irish genre known as the *imrann*, or tales of journeys to other worlds. The genre still has imaginative appeal. The modern Irish poet Paul Muldoon has written poems within the loosely defined specifications of the *imrann*, and Seamus Heaney, the best-known Irish poet of the postwar period, has included a poem, "The Disappearing Island," inspired by an incident in Brendan's voyages in his collection *The Haw Lantern* (1987).

Frederick Buechner's reputation as a novelist who addresses important theological issues has been highly regarded since his first novel, *A Long Day's Dying* (1950). In his early work, he located his concerns in contemporary settings. A more imaginatively free treatment of these concerns is what distinguishes novels such as *Brendan* and *Godric* (1980), the life of a twelfth century saint. In addition, his work has gained from his theological writings, which not only seek to disseminate the Christian vision, as in *Telling the Truth: The Gospel as Tragedy, Comedy, and Fairy Tale* (1977), but also meditate on its wonder, relevance, and appeal. The confluence of the various traditions in *Brendan* suggests the continuing fascination of the sense of disturbing renewal that is such a dramatic component of the Christian message.

Bibliography

Anderson, Chris. "The Very Style of Faith: Frederick Buechner as Homilist and Essayist." *Christianity and Literature* 38 (Winter, 1989): 7-21. Focuses on Buechner's nonfiction, but with many insights that make the full purpose and interest of his fiction more accessible.

Davies, Marie-Helene. *Laughter in a Genevan Gown: The Works of Frederick Buechner, 1970-1980.* Grand Rapids, Mich.: Eerdmans, 1983. The most comprehensive introduction to the life and work of Frederick Buechner, locating both author and works in the context of their religious background. A useful orientation for a reading of *Brendan.*

Nelson, Rudolph L. "'The Doors of Perception': Mystical Experience in Buechner's Fiction." *Southwest Review* 68 (Summer, 1983): 266-273. Stresses the visionary element in Buechner's work and how it assists in the articulation of his fiction's overall point of view. A sense of the position of *Brendan* in the development of Buechner's imaginative output may be inferred.

O'Faolain, Julia. "St. Patrick Monkeys Around." *The New York Times Book Review* 92 (August 9, 1987): 15. A sympathetic review, informative and appreciative of the novel's excursion into the world of Celtic Christianity.

Severin, Timothy. *The Brendan Voyage.* New York: McGraw-Hill, 1978. An account of a detailed reconstruction of Saint Brendan's alleged voyage to America, using the same kind of vessel and the same apparent route.

George O'Brien

THE BRICK PEOPLE

Author: Alejandro Morales (1944-   )
Type of plot: Historical realism
Time of plot: The 1890's to the 1940's
Locale: Southern California
First published: 1988

> *Principal characters:*
> OCTAVIO REVUELTAS, a worker in the Simons brickyard
> NANA DE LEÓN REVUELTAS, a strong worker, mother, and wife
> WALTER SIMONS, the son of the brick company's founder
> MALAQUIAS DE LEÓN, one of the first workers to arrive at the newly
>   built brickyard
> ROSENDO GUERRERO, the worker who lays out the plan of the original
>   brickyard
> ARTURO REVUELTAS, the eldest son of Octavio and Nana

The Novel

Based in part on the actual experiences of the author's parents (to whom the book is dedicated), *The Brick People* is the story of several generations of Anglo and Chicano/Mexicano families and their interactions in Southern California in the first half of the twentieth century. The principal clans are the Simons and the Revueltas families, representing the capitalist and working classes respectively.

The novel begins in 1892, with Rosendo Guerrero laying out the ground plan for the original Simons brickyard in Pasadena, California. The coordinates of the plan are based on an Aztec mandala, suggesting that the legacy of the indigenous cultures of the region lie buried under the ground. This idea is reinforced by the figure of Doña Eulalia, who identifies with an ancient oak tree and who turns into millions of brown insects upon her death.

Joseph Simons, the eldest son of Reuben Simons, the brick-making dynasty's founder, makes every attempt to keep his workers complacent. One of his greatest concerns is the worldwide increase in radical unionism. When a mass grave of Chinese workers is found on the brickyard grounds, Joseph notifies the authorities and orders that the bodies be burned so as to preclude any labor unrest. Joseph's relationship with his younger brother Walter is strained at best; he finds Walter to be arrogant and at odds with his own political views. A third brother, Orin Elmer, is a physical and intellectual weakling who is unable to participate in the family business.

Walter Simons is an "enlightened capitalist" who seeks to understand Mexican culture in order to make better use of his workers. On the suggestion of Rosendo Guerrero, Walter undertakes a fact-finding trip to Mexico, where he experiences firsthand the daily workings of U.S. imperialism under the dictator Porfirio Díaz. In the state of Chihuahua, he confers with William Randolph Hearst and other California businesspeople and witnesses the abuses of the hacienda system, including a massacre of peasants by government forces.

Upon Walter's return, the Simons company begins construction on a new brickyard in the Los Angeles suburb of Montebello. In the wake of the San Francisco earthquake of 1906, demands for building materials increase dramatically; the Simons business expands at an incredible rate. Rosendo decides to promote one of his workers, Gonzalo Pedroza, to the status of foreman. Gonzalo will become one of the most powerful and hated figures at the brickyard. The arrival of Malaquias de León and his family marks a significant moment in the history of the brickyard, for it coincides with the Mexican Revolution of 1910, the tremendous rise in immigration to the United States, and the dissemination of socialist and communist ideology throughout the Southwest. Orin Elmer's death (and the consumption of his body by brown insects) marks an end to the initial stage of the narrative.

The tension between the Simons brothers, Joseph and Walter, is aggravated when the two compete for economic control of the family assets. Walter's decision to build a home in Los Angeles essentially makes him an absentee owner at the Montebello brickyard, where recently arrived workers from Mexico are becoming more politicized. The departure of Malaquias de León coincides with the increased importance of Octavio Revueltas, who marries Malaquias's daughter, Nana, in 1926. The stock-market crash of 1929 and the resulting Depression worsen economic conditions for the entire country. Some of the Simons workers (with Octavio as their leader) establish contact with various union organizers, despite harassment from the Simons family and the foreman Gonzalo Pedroza. The Long Beach earthquake of 1933 marks the symbolic end of the boom in the brick industry, since newer and more reliable building materials have been invented.

The Simons workers finally walk out, but the strike is broken with use of poor African American workers. The Simons workers break ranks, some of them return to work, other are reduced to desperation and cynicism. The events of World War II overshadow whatever problems had existed previously: Mexican Americans serve proudly in the U.S. military, Japanese Americans are interned, the Zoot Suit riots (in which Anglo sailors attacked Chicanos) break out in Los Angeles, and Simons workers leave the brickyard to take jobs in wartime industries. Once outside the walls of the yard, Mexican families experience racial discrimination with regard to housing and bank loans. The Revueltas family is forced to move back to the home of Octavio's parents. News arrives of Walter Simons's death by choking on brown insects.

The final chapter consists of Octavio's memories of his family's original journey north from Mexico. The novel ends on an optimistic note: The Revueltas family is building a new home and moving ever so tentatively into the middle class.

The Characters

Octavio is a complex character who gambles compulsively and who is often absent from his family, yet he commands the respect of most readers for his sense of social justice and his dedication to his children. He functions as the radicalized worker who decides to fight the exploitation to which he has been subjected, and he provides an opportunity for the reader to learn something about the multiethnic unions that existed in Southern California throughout the 1920's and 1930's. Octavio is the first-generation immigrant whose children will live better than he did thanks in large part to their parents' hard work.

As a child, Nana de León Revueltas experiences discrimination because of her family's poverty; at one point, she meets and identifies with an African American baseball player. Once married to Octavio, she provides a solid base for her family even as she struggles to better their living conditions by making contacts outside the closed circle of Simons workers. In many ways, she is a proto-feminist character who insists upon equal status with her husband, though always within the limits of traditional Mexican values.

Walter Simons inherits a family business from wealthy parents. Unlike his brother Joseph, Walter attempts to understand Mexican culture, not because he is socially progressive but because he wants to know how to better manage his workers. He believes that if the brickyard satisfies the basic needs of the workers and their families, the threat of unionism and strikes will not arise. As a representative of "benign capitalism," Walter is the ideological foil to Octavio Revueltas and the union movement.

Malaquias de León is a precursor to Octavio's radicalism in that he is the first character who challenges the arrangement at the brickyard and decides to leave its confines in order to seek economic independence.

Rosendo Guerrero functions as a vehicle for the indigenous elements of Chicano/Mexicano culture. He is in touch with the ancient traditions and myths that periodically assert themselves over and against the rationalization of society by capitalism and Anglo puritanism.

Arturo Revueltas represents the younger generation in the novel, already anglicized to a certain extent and less familiar with Mexican traditions. His difficulty with language learning typifies the problems of all children of non-English-speaking immigrants, yet the novel presents bilingualism itself as a gift.

Themes and Meanings

The novel is a fictional treatment of Chicano/Mexicano history, specifically the periods immediately before, during, and after the Mexican Revolution. *The Brick People* represents for the reader Chicano involvement in a series of key historical events, ranging from the Díaz dictatorship in Mexico, to the Mexican Revolution, to the Great Depression, to successful and unsuccessful strikes organized by Mexican, Japanese, and Filipino farm workers in the 1930's, to World War II. The novel's historical sweep is grounded in the everyday lives of engaging and lifelike characters.

The text is structured upon the relationship between the Simons and Revueltas families. If the Simons family represents (on a small scale) the powerful U.S. industrialist class and, by extension, capital itself, the Revueltas family (the name means "uprisings" in Spanish) symbolizes the Chicano/Mexicano working class whose interests are necessarily opposed to those of their bosses. In addition to this political subtext, the novel incorporates images of nature (insects, earthquakes, serpents) and American Indian societies (Aztec deities, the mandala) that suggest that there are more powerful forces at work than the dominant Anglo culture may be equipped to recognize. The recurring image of the brown insects may be linked to the Chicano people in general (as it has in other works of Chicano literature)—the despised yet persistent "cockroach people" who survive against all odds.

In the character of Nana, the novel constructs a model for Chicanas that incorporates specific values of traditional Mexican society even as it breaks with certain limitations placed on women. The entire question of gender is an important undercurrent throughout the text.

By linking the important issues of class, gender, and ethnicity within the frame of a historical novel, *The Brick People* provides readers with a fascinating account of a particularly rich episode of Chicano history.

Critical Context

The Brick People, Alejandro Morales's fourth novel, is undoubtedly his most personal in that it is a fictionalized account of his parents' life. Unlike his earlier texts, which often have a fragmented structure, *The Brick People* is organized as a relatively straightforward historical novel; it follows the chronology of the early twentieth century with references to key events such as the Great Depression and World War II. The combination of historical fact and elements of fantasy places the novel in the Magical Realist tradition of contemporary Latin American literature associated with Alejo Carpentier, Gabriel García Márquez, and others.

Morales was one of the first Chicano novelists at a time (the late 1970's) when Chicano literature was not yet accepted as an important area of American studies. Chicano texts were not included in the curriculum of major universities; Chicano writers and scholars in many English and Spanish departments were greeted with outright hostility. In a real sense, Morales's role in the U.S. academy was to be one of the founders of an emergent discipline. By the time *The Brick People* appeared (written entirely in English), Chicano literature enjoyed an international readership and academic respectability, and Morales was counted among the most influential Chicano critics and writers of fiction.

Bibliography

Gutierrez-Jones, Carl. "Resisting Cultural Dependency: The Manipulation of Surveillance and Paranoia in Alejandro Morales's *The Brick People*." *The Americas Review* 22 (Spring-Summer, 1994): 230-243. Gutierrez-Jones discusses *The Brick People* in terms of the fear experienced by many U.S. citizens in the aftermath of the signing of pan-American trade agreements. His commentary focuses on the Mexican workers living in a small town and their interactions with factory workers.
Hernández, Roberto E. "*The Brick People*." *Vista Magazine* (November 27, 1988): 14. Short summary of the novel, with special attention paid to the characters Nana and Octavio Revueltas. Hernández is troubled by Morales's "fascination with the gro-

tesque." Nevertheless, he recommends: "*The Brick People* should be read by Americans of all walks of life, but it will strike a familiar note in those of us who came to North America in the hope of finding more than one alternative to life."

_____. Interview by Yves Charles Grandjeat and Alfonso Rodríguez. *Confluencia* 7 (Fall, 1991): 109-114. Morales talks about his interest in history, the construction of Chicano identity, and the social responsibility of the writer. His remarks on *The Brick People* are especially interesting.

Marquez, Antonio. "The Use and Abuse of History in Alejandro Morales's *The Brick People* and *The Rag Doll Plagues*." *Bilingual Review* 20 (September, 1995): 76-85. Marquez declares that the focus of his study "is on Morales's post-modernist tack" and the relationship between history and literature. *The Brick People* and *The Rag Doll Plagues* are historical narratives which blend myth and history in order to tell "a larger story."

Morales, Alejandro. Interview by José Antonio Gurpegui. *Bilingual Review* 20 (September, 1995): 5-13. Morales discusses his views on Chicano literature, the ethnic influence of Chicano literature on the whole body of American literature, and his reason for the shift from Spanish to English works.

George Mariscal

A BRIEF LIFE

Author: Juan Carlos Onetti (1909-1994)
Type of plot: Psychological novel
Time of plot: The twentieth century
Locale: Buenos Aires and Santa María
First published: La vida breve, 1950 (English translation, 1976)

Principal characters:

JUAN MARÍA BRAUSEN, the protagonist, a publicist
JUAN MARÍA ARCE, his other self
DR. DÍAZ GREY, a creation of Brausen's imagination
GERTRUDIS, Brausen's wife
QUECA, Arce's lover, a prostitute
ELENA SALAS, Díaz Grey's patient and love

The Novel

A Brief Life presents the inner conflict of a man who, after suffering a traumatizing experience, feels lost and seeks an identity. He splits into two selves, and, at the same time, he finds refuge in his own fantasy.

Juan María Brausen is about to be fired from his job. His wife, Gertrudis, has undergone surgery on her left breast, and her scarred body is so repulsive to him that it has become an obsession. He begins to realize that he is not the same person he thought he was and suffers a crisis of identity: "I understood that I had been aware for weeks that I, Juan María Brausen and my life were nothing but empty molds, pure representations of an old meaning kept out of indolence, of a being dragging himself among the people, the streets, and the time of the city, routine acts."

Through the wall of his apartment, Brausen can listen to the incidents that take place in the world of Queca, a prostitute. He decides to enter this adjacent world as an alternative to his tortured existence. In his imagination, Brausen becomes Juan María Arce, a new man who will exist simultaneously but apart from Brausen. Arce will live "a brief life in which time could not be enough to engage him, to make him repent, or grow older."

The agency for which Brausen works has ordered him to write a screenplay. For that purpose, he has invented the imaginary world of Santa María at the shores of the Río de la Plata. There, an imaginary alter ego, the mediocre forty-year-old Dr. Díaz Grey, spends his life selling morphine to Elena Salas, the woman with whom he is in love. Brausen repeatedly escapes to this world and projects himself into the doctor.

These "brief lives" exist primarily in Brausen's consciousness, rather than in the real world. The conclusion of the novel completes the image of failure presented at the beginning: Brausen has been fired from his job and has been abandoned by his wife. Queca has been killed, and Elena Salas also has died. The novel ends with Brausen walking along the streets of Santa María, integrated into his own fantasy.

The Characters

Onetti presents in *A Brief Life* an interesting, three-dimensional protagonist. By splitting the character's personality, the author is able to make a more profound study of human identity.

Onetti concentrates on Brausen's psychological problems, fears, and fantasies, rather than on a narrative description of his life. For this reason, Brausen's internal life, depicted through his reflections and through passages of stream of consciousness, predominates over action in the book.

Juan María Brausen, like many of Onetti's protagonists, is an imaginative man who refuses to develop the practical qualities that his world demands of him. Brausen is an alienated, existentially tortured man, an outsider. He knows that the world in which he lives is full of falsehood, but he does not fight it. He adopts a skeptical and resigned attitude. He invents new lies, new identities. Brausen creates other selves through which he evades his anxiety, taking refuge in his fantasy as a self-defense mechanism, but he does not undergo change in the course of the novel. His life has changed with his wife's surgery and the consequent trauma, but Brausen has the same wandering attitude from the beginning to the end. He is consistently a failure.

The noises and voices to which Brausen listens through the wall of his room invite him to enter the world of sex, a world from which his wife's scars have separated him. Brausen transformed into Arce will visit Queca, the prostitute, to overcome the impotence that he feels with his wife. Arce can live with Queca a life that is "without memories and without foreknowledge." Arce becomes Brausen's strongest persona.

In his attempt at salvation, Brausen has also invented Dr. Díaz Grey. This fictitious doctor is based on Brausen's monotonous life and on the revulsion that his wife's scarred body provokes in him.

Brausen projects himself into Arce and Díaz Grey, all three sharing a life of failure and lies. They incarnate the fatalism in which Onetti seems to believe. They accept their colorless lives without attempting to change them. Indeed, they seem unwilling to attempt external change.

The protagonist's sense of alienation is underlined by the fact that most of the secondary characters belong to a marginal world—the world inhabited by prostitutes and pimps. Onetti does not even place his hero (or antihero) in a historical context, or in a clearly defined place. Brausen lives in some obscure part of Buenos Aires that contaminates him with its dullness and mediocrity.

The other characters are presented through Brausen's eyes and are totally dependent on Brausen-Arce-Díaz Grey. Gertrudis, a character who rarely speaks, represents Brausen's past. Queca passively accepts Arce's love and Arce's beatings. It seems that she has been created to be abused by others; this is her role, she knows, and she merely plays it. Elena Salas is a projection of Gertrudis. These three women, the foundation of Brausen-Arce-Díaz Grey's life, will have to disappear before Brausen can find his real identity.

Themes and Meanings

A Brief Life, with its complex narrative structure, suggests that man is one and many, a multiple being made of a series of distinct and alienated selves. As the title of the book indicates, a man can live many short lives.

Fatalism and failure govern Brausen's world. It is a world in which man is surrounded by deception which makes futile any fight against the natural obstacles of life. (The book begins and ends symbolically during carnival; life is a masquerade.) There is no way to succeed. The only possibility of salvation is in oneiric inventions, in fantasy: "I had in my hands the paper, the blotter, and the fountain pen necessary for my salvation. . . . I would be saved if I began to write the plot. . . . If I wrote only one phrase." Salvation through the act of imagination is a recurring theme in Onetti's work.

Critical Context

Onetti belongs to a group of writers, born in Uruguay and Argentina, who reached maturity during the politically tumultuous 1930's and who became known as "the lost generation." They share a nihilist vision of the world, expressed through the solitary, alienated characters they create. These writers practice a kind of existentialism; their conflict with society is reflected in the deliberately fragmentary quality of their fiction. A good example of such fragmentation can be seen in Onetti's *A Brief Life*.

A Brief Life is considered to be a pivotal work in Onetti's career. His previous works—*El pozo* (1939), *Tierra de nadie* (1941), and *Para esta noche* (1943)—sketch the psychological conflicts that are fully developed in *A Brief Life*. Many of the works that follow—*Los adioses* (1954), *Para una tumba sin nombre* (1959), *Juntacádaveres* (1964), and *La muerte y la niña* (1973)—base their plots on the inventions created in Juan María Brausen's mind.

Indeed, the world of Santa María, first introduced in *A Brief Life*, appears as a constant in Onetti's following works. Santa María, like Macondo in Gabriel García Márquez's books, becomes a mythical place. Onetti succeeds in transporting the reader to his character's fantasy world, because, although nonexistent, it seems perfectly real.

A Brief Life explores man's search for an answer to his existence. "People believe they are condemned to one life until death. But they are only condemned to one soul, to one identity. One can live many times, many lives, shorter or longer." By creating an imaginary world, and imaginary selves, Brausen can enjoy several lives, although he remains the same person, the same soul.

Bibliography

Adams, Michael I. *Three Authors of Alienation: Bombal, Onetti, Carpentier.* Austin: University of Texas Press, 1975. Adams presents a sociopsychological critical interpretation of three Latin American authors whose works share similar themes. Includes a chapter focusing on Onetti's view of spiritual disillusionment as inevitable in the urban setting.

Ainsa, Fernando. "Juan Carlos Onetti (1909-1994): An Existential Allegory of Contemporary Man." *World Literature Today* 68 (Summer, 1994): 501-504. A tribute to and biographic profile of Onetti as well as an analysis and evaluation of his work.

Kadir, Djelal. *Juan Carlos Onetti.* Boston: Twayne, 1977. Kadir provides a critical and interpretive study of Onetti with a close reading of his major works, a solid bibliography, and complete notes and references.

Lewis, Bart L. "Realizing the Textual Space: Metonymic Metafiction in Juan Carlos Onetti." *Hispanic Review* 64 (Autumn, 1996): 491-506. Lewis compares Onetti's style to that of Boris Pasternak. Lewis asserts that through his works, Onetti reveals that there are many openings to be filled in the fictional scheme because fictional characters live in a web of words.

Verani, Hugo J. "Juan Carlos Onetti." In *Latin American Writers*, edited by Carlos A. Solé and Maria I. Abreau. Vol. 3. New York: Charles Scribner's Sons, 1989. An essay on the life and career of Onetti. Includes analysis of his works and a bibliography.

Mercedes Jimenez Gonzalez

BROWN GIRL, BROWNSTONES

Author: Paule Marshall (1929-   )
Type of plot: Bildungsroman
Time of plot: 1939 to the late 1940's
Locale: Brooklyn, New York
First published: 1959

Principal characters:

SELINA BOYCE, the protagonist, the bright and talented daughter of
    immigrants from Barbados
SILLA BOYCE, Selina's mother, a hard-edged immigrant woman
    determined to get ahead
DEIGHTON BOYCE, Selina's father and Silla's husband, a dreamer who
    drifts from one would-be profession to another
INA BOYCE, Selina's sister, who is browbeaten by Silla into submission
BERYL CHALLENOR, Selina's best friend when she is young
CLIVE SPRINGER, a Barbadian World War II veteran with whom Selina
    has an affair
RACHEL FINE, a dancer who encourages Selina to dance in a public
    recital

The Novel

Written as an attempt by Paule Marshall to reflect on her own life, *Brown Girl, Brownstones* is an autobiographically based novel about a young black woman growing up among the Barbadian immigrant community of Brooklyn in the 1940's. From the beginning, *Brown Girl, Brownstones* is a novel about the conflicting set of values represented by Deighton and Silla Boyce, with Selina, their daughter and the novel's main character, caught in the middle. On one side is Deighton Boyce, idle because he lacks the drive and discipline to embrace a culture and its materialistic values that he knows devalue him. Deighton studies to become an accountant, but never becomes one; he studies to learn to play the trumpet, but never performs. Opposing him is Silla Boyce, who embraces a hard-edged, penny-conscious immigrant ethic. Silla is determined to do what it takes to own land and get ahead materially. Though Selina identifies explicitly with her father throughout much of the novel, she slowly comes to realize that her deeper affinities are to her mother.

At the novel's start, Selina is ten, but she is described by the narrator as possessing a manner seemingly wise beyond her years, with eyes "too old . . . in their centers." When her father unexpectedly inherits a two-acre plot of land, he begins dreaming of moving back to Barbados. Silla, who has no intention of returning to her homeland and who resents her husband's dreaming as much as his idleness, plots to have the land sold.

The first two short sections of *Brown Girl, Brownstones*, "A Long Day and a Long

Night" and "Pastorale," establish the close relationship between Selina and her father, the emerging similarities between Selina and her mother, and the frequently unstated attraction and respect between Silla and Deighton that underlies their fighting. The third section, "The War," covers the years of World War II, years when the conflict between Silla and Deighton erupts into a domestic war.

After Deighton is notified that he has inherited land, Silla plans to have the land sold behind his back. She succeeds, but because the check is issued in Deighton's name, she cannot stop him from getting access to the "nine hundred odd dollars" payment for the land, all of which he spends on gifts for himself and his family in a single extravagant shopping binge. For a short time, he gets a job working at a factory, but an accident sends him to the hospital, where he finds newspapers printed by a religious sect led by a man called Father Peace. Quickly accepting the gospel of this organization, he becomes a devoted follower, and when he is released from the hospital, he spends most of his time praying to Father Peace or attending meetings. Eventually, he moves out to live and work in a coffee shop run by the Father Peace group. In retaliation, Silla has him arrested for desertion, and he is deported back to Barbados on a ship. On the day World War II ends, however, a message arrives saying that Deighton jumped or fell overboard in sight of land and drowned.

In the fourth section, "Selina," Selina's own personal growth and conflicts become the agents of change and chaos in her family. Now on the verge of entering college, she begins this part of the novel in an extended state of grief over her father's death. Blaming Silla for Deighton's death and unwilling to accept her mother's values, Selina nevertheless goes with her mother to attend a meeting of the Barbadian Association, a group devoted to upward social mobility for Barbadian immigrants. Selina, though, storms out of the meeting condemning the association as "narrow-minded," "selfish," and "pitiful." She is followed out of the meeting by Clive Springer, a Barbadian former soldier and would-be artist. After a night of wandering together, the two make love on a park bench.

Clive and Selina continue to have a clandestine relationship, and Selina plots to get back into the good graces of the Barbadian Association. She hopes to win a scholarship the group is offering, but she wants to use the money to live with Clive. Fooling the members of the association proves to be easy, and she does indeed win the scholarship. Before the check is actually awarded, however, Selina and Clive argue over Clive's relationship with his mother. Selina realizes that Clive would never leave his mother, and she is also forced to reexamine her own values. Coming to the conclusion that she has no right to behave with such contempt toward the members of the association, she publicly declines to accept the scholarship money, and she admits that she had been trying to manipulate the association for reasons she no longer respects. She also realizes that although she has always wanted to identify with her father, she has always been much more like her mother in spirit. At the end, though the mother and daughter fight once more over Selina's plans to go to Barbados for at least a little while, Silla implicitly gives her daughter her approval and her blessing by accepting Selina as a woman every bit as strong as Silla herself is.

The Characters

Selina Boyce is very much the central character of *Brown Girl, Brownstones*. Even though the novel also offers glimpses into the lives of many members of the Barbadian community and details the struggle between Silla and Deighton Boyce over power and values, these other people are seen from Selina's perspective. The novel's central consideration is the influence of various people and forces on Selina's development. Additionally, although Selina is occasionally described from a third-person-omniscient point of view, the majority of the novel is told from a third-person-limited point of view that describes what Selina perceives and how she reacts.

At the novel's beginning, Selina is still an adolescent girl, but she is respected by her parents not only for being headstrong but also for being in many respects the emotional center of her family. As the conflict between her parents develops, Selina explicitly tries to identify with her father; however, she is in fact more similar to her mother. Both love Deighton Boyce and seek his love in return, but neither knows how to deal with his unhappiness or seeming aimlessness. After her father's death, she falls in love with Clive Springer, a man who, like Deighton, is an idle dreamer. Selina's plans to leave with Clive and save him from his family and his own withdrawal make her relationship to Clive seem remarkably like Silla's relationship to Deighton. Clive, like Deighton, is willing to be controlled by a woman of stronger will but is not willing or able to change. Selina finally recognizes that she cannot control Clive, and she abandons her hopes for the two of them, planning instead to travel to Barbados alone.

Silla and Deighton represent opposing viewpoints of the immigrant's plight in America. Silla focuses primarily on the possibilities of land ownership and wealth her adopted society offers; Deighton sees primarily the cost of living in America as a West Indian immigrant and treats the benefits contemptuously. Though their positions are squarely opposed to one another, and they battle openly, they are each also aware of the extent to which they need the other. Deighton needs Silla for material, daily survival, and Silla needs Deighton for his sense of life and wonder.

Clive is, like Deighton, a dreamer and a would-be artist. Though Clive is more intellectual by nature than Deighton, he is no more effective, and he is just as dependent on strong-willed women—his mother and Selina—as Deighton was before his death.

Selina's friend and classmate, Rachel Fine, is one of the few developed white characters in the novel, and to a large extent, she represents the community of art and artists to Selina. Her friendship and encouragement of Selina's dancing provide Selina with exactly the type of encouragement Selina could not find in the Barbadian Association. When another white woman blithely insults Selina's skin color and accent after a dance recital, however, Selina begins to realize that she cannot simply replace her Barbadian community with an artistic community. This understanding supports Selina's decision to travel to Barbados to search for values.

Themes and Meanings

It is typical for a *Bildungsroman* to focus on the growth and education of a young person. In depicting a protagonist's maturation and acceptance or rejection of social values, the novelist can hold those values themselves up to inspection. This is certainly true of *Brown Girl, Brownstones*.

Selina, like her father and like Clive, intuitively rejects the impulse to get ahead at any cost, an impulse best represented by her mother and by the Barbadian Association. What she cannot simply reject, however, is the strength and direction of character that allows Silla to work long hours at menial wages to support and improve the lot of her family. Despite Silla's flaws, Selina respects her as a strong woman.

So long as Deighton is besieged daily by Silla and is struggling to find a sense of self-respect not founded upon the assimilationist and materialist values of Silla and the Barbadian Association, Selina can use his lonely anguish as the focus of her own anger and uncertainty. Thus, Selina supports her father throughout much of the novel because he so clearly needs her emotional support, whereas Silla does not seem to.

After Deighton's death, Selina faces the task of resolving for herself the conflict of values that was always embodied by the struggle between Silla and Deighton. It is in the spirit of resolving these issues that she attends her first meeting of the Barbadian Association. Yet because of her anger toward Silla and the members of the association for their treatment of Deighton, and because of her continued rejection of the association's values, she storms out of the first meeting. Clive, who intercepts her as she leaves, proves to share her reservations about the values of the association.

When Selina begins her affair with Clive, she does not appreciate how closely she is reenacting the attitudes and roles of her mother. Like Silla, Selina manipulates those around her, especially her mother, the association, and Clive. Her mother and the association—both of whom recognize Selina as a potential leader and want her to succeed—prove to be remarkably easy to manipulate. Clive, who is weaker willed than either Silla or Selina, proves to be as difficult for Selina to manipulate as Deighton was for Silla.

When Selina, after a successful dance recital, is humiliated by a white woman (who compares Selina to a housekeeper she once hired and asks Selina to say something in her charming West Indian accent), Selina begins to see the members of the association in a new light. Recognizing not only that they have had to struggle throughout their working lives in America with such racial discrimination, but also that they have been strong enough to protect her generation from some of the most searing aspects of racism, Selina realizes that she cannot simply reject the members of the association. Because she still cannot accept their values, she decides that she must travel back to Barbados, searching for values that might be predicated on more than a desire for, or a rejection of, assimilation into the culture of mainstream America.

Critical Context

The critic Barbara Christian has pointed out that before the publication of *Brown Girl, Brownstones*, there were very few novels written by black women focusing on the interior life of a black woman. The two most notable precedents to *Brown Girl, Brownstones* are Zora Neale Hurston's *Their Eyes Were Watching God* (1937) and Gwendolyn Brooks's *Maud Martha* (1953), neither of which was widely known when

Marshall was writing her first novel. Against such a context of silence about black women's inner lives, Paule Marshall's coming-of-age story can be read as a demand that the voices of black female writers be recognized as culturally significant.

Yet because it appeared in the midst of the civil rights era and immediately prior to the 1960's, Marshall's inquiry into social values by a young person can also be read as a prelude to and an affirmation of a social upheaval that was then forming. Like many of the college activists of the 1960's, Selina is a young person challenging her community over its values and simultaneously searching for her own values.

Although it was favorably reviewed when it first appeared, *Brown Girl, Brownstones* was widely neglected for many years. Even as the works of Toni Morrison and Alice Walker during the 1970's created a widespread interest in the works of black women writers, interest in Marshall's first novel remained relatively sparse. The appearance of Barbara Christian's landmark study: *Black Women Writers: The Development of a Tradition, 1892-1976* in 1980 and the republication of *Brown Girl, Brownstones* by the Feminist Press in 1981 helped to rekindle interest in the book. With the publication of two well-received novels, *Praisesong for the Widow* (1983) and *Daughters* (1991), Marshall's reputation continued to grow. With the growth of her literary reputation has come the critical recognition of her first novel, not only as a worthy coming-of-age tale but also as a pivotal text in the development of twentieth century African American literature.

Bibliography

Christian, Barbara. *Black Women Novelists: The Development of a Tradition, 1892-1976.* Westport, Conn.: Greenwood Press, 1980. In a landmark critical study of black women writers, Christian praises Marshall as a consummate sculptor of character. Christian particularly praises Marshall's ability to dispense with stereotypes and present multidimensional characters who have a complex relationship to history and culture.

Christol, Hélène. "Paule Marshall's Bajan Women in *Brown Girl, Brownstones.*" In *Women and War: The Changing Status of American Women from the 1930's to the 1950's,* edited by Maria Diedrich and Dorothea Fischer-Hornung. Providence, R.I.: Berg, 1990. An excellent essay that focuses especially on the mother-daughter relationship between Selina and Silla. Notes that despite the frequent fighting, theirs is the most constructive relationship in the book.

Evans, Mari, ed. *Black Women Writers (1950-1980): A Critical Evaluation.* Garden City, N.Y.: Anchor Press/Doubleday, 1983. This extensive collection of essays about black women writers contains two essays about Marshall's works. Eugenia Collier's article focuses on the tendency for characters in Marshall's novels to develop from divided selves into fully integrated whole selves. John McCluskey's essay explores the interplay of social and personal forces in Marshall's fiction.

Japtok, Martin. "Paule Marshall's *Brown Girl, Brownstones*: Recalling Ethnicity and Individualism." *African American Review* 32 (Summer, 1998): 305-315. Japtok addresses the "potential of coercion behind the notion of ethnic solidarity" in Marshall's novel. He explores the novel's dualities, such as the opposition of the protagonist to a communally prescribed ethnic identity, as well as the ethnic hybridity the protagonist experiences as she tries to adapt to two different cultures.

Jones, Gavin. "'The Sea Ain't Got No Back Door': The Problems of Black Consciousness in Paule Marshall's *Brown Girl, Brownstones*." *African American Review* 32 (Winter, 1998): 597. Jones explores Marshall's characterization of black identity in *Brown Girl, Brownstones*. He discusses the book's "prism-like perspective of selfhood" associated with issues related to gender, sexuality, nativity, ethnicity, urban experience, and immigration.

LeSeur, Geta. "The Monster-Machine and the White Mausoleum: Paule Marshall's Metaphors for Western Materialism." *CLA Journal* 39 (September, 1995): 49-61. LeSeur discusses Marshall's belief that surrendering one's ethnic identity to Western materialism is unwise. The dangers of technology are seen as "monsters, deities of technology" that may subjugate and destroy blacks and those from Third World countries.

Marshall, Paule. Interview by Joyce Pettis. *MELUS* 17 (Winter, 1991): 117-129. Marshall discusses her concern for the need for cultural continuity in Caribbean culture. She shares her own experiences with West Indies culture and talks about her novels, including *Brown Girl, Brownstones*.

"Paule Marshall: A Bibliography." Compiled by Harihar Kulkarni. *Callaloo* 16 (Winter, 1993): 243-267. This bibliography includes listings of Marshall's novels, collections, and essays; interviews; bio-bibliographies; and criticism, interpretations, and reviews. A good overall source of information concerning Marshall's work.

Washington, Mary Helen. Afterword to *Brown Girl, Brownstones*, by Paule Marshall. 1959. Reprint. Old Westbury, N.Y.: Feminist Press, 1981. A brief but thoughtful exploration of the themes embodied in *Brown Girl, Brownstones*. Provides a helpful glimpse of the social context in which Marshall's novel was produced and the effects of this context on the novel itself.

Thomas J. Cassidy

THE BURDEN OF PROOF

Author: Scott Turow (1949-   )
Type of plot: Suspense
Time of plot: The 1980's
Locale: Kindle County, a fictitious Midwestern American locale
First published: 1990

> *Principal characters:*
> ALEJANDRO "SANDY" STERN, a brilliant trial attorney originally from
> Argentina
> CLARA STERN, Stern's constant, reticent wife of thirty-one years, who
> commits suicide
> DIXON HARTNELL, a financial speculator who is Stern's client and his
> brother-in-law
> SONIA "SONNY" KLONSKY, the federal prosecutor investigating the
> government's case against Hartnell

The Novel

Based in part on the experience Scott Turow gained while working as a white-collar criminal defense counsel in Chicago, Illinois, *The Burden of Proof* employs a plot involving suicide and insider trading to explore the psyche of its protagonist, Sandy Stern. Narrated in the third person, *The Burden of Proof* consists of fifty chapters and is divided into three parts. Throughout the book, the reader shares Stern's point of view. Although Turow uses flashbacks to illuminate Stern's relationship with his wife, on the whole the plot advances in a linear fashion.

The Burden of Proof opens in a somewhat unorthodox fashion for a mystery, however, revealing in its first chapter that the pivotal event of the book, Clara Stern's suicide, has already taken place before the action commences. As the book opens, Stern, who has just returned from a business trip, discovers his wife's body slumped in the driver's seat of her Cadillac in the garage, dead of asphyxiation. Stern, like his children and everyone else, has difficulty coming to terms with the apparent suicide of his upright, reserved, seemingly content wife. That Clara's death was not accidental is confirmed when Stern finds a note in her handwriting that says, "Can you forgive me?" This enigmatic clue as to the reasons for her suicide is quickly followed by other equally ambiguous discoveries: Shortly before she killed herself, Clara wrote a check to an unknown payee that reduced almost to nothing Stern's prospective share of her estate, and prior to her death, she had been taking medication for a venereal disease.

The scant evidence Clara leaves behind strongly suggests a desire to punish her husband. As the understated Stern tells a police officer investigating the suicide, "Lieutenant, it should be evident that I failed to observe something I should have." In order to unravel the mystery of Clara's death, Stern must look to his own interior landscape.

The outside world quickly intrudes, however, when Stern's brother-in-law (his beloved sister's husband), Dixon Hartnell, the owner of a commodities brokerage house and apparently Stern's most significant client, is charged with illegal trading. The normally proactive, manipulative, and unprincipled Hartnell seems uncharacteristically disinterested in defending himself against the extremely serious federal charges he faces. Because the case against Hartnell implicates Stern's son-in-law, John, an employee of Hartnell's firm, Stern is forced to take an unusually active role in ferreting out the recalcitrant facts that will explain the extent of Hartnell's involvement in criminal activity.

Owing, perhaps, to his preoccupation with Clara's death, Stern fails to observe until late in the book that there is a connection between his wife's suicide and the troubles at Hartnell's firm, Maison Dixon. Hartnell's unwillingness to be forthcoming with his attorney about the former results from his involvement with the latter; gradually, Stern realizes that although his brother-in-law is innocent of charges of insider trading, he is the one who gave Clara an incurable, if comparatively innocuous, case of herpes. It is Stern's ambitious but injudicious son-in-law who carried out the illegal trades. Clara had attempted to save him, and her daughter, by drawing on money earmarked for Stern and by extracting a promise from Hartnell that he would take the blame for John's actions. In the wake of Clara's suicide—occasioned, at least in part, by her belief that the recurring nature of her disease would force her to reveal her infidelity to her husband—the typically unscrupulous Hartnell displays his own brand of honor by keeping his word to her.

While pursuing the dual mysteries that confront him, Stern must also struggle with his own part in Clara's death. He is forced to come to terms with his failures as a husband and a father—failures that stem in large measure from his commitment to his demanding legal practice. Along the way, he finds a kind of salvation in a touching, although unconsummated, love affair with the pregnant, married, former cancer patient Sonny Klonsky, who is prosecuting the government's case against Hartnell. He does not end up with Sonny, but it is largely through her agency that he comes to forgive Clara and himself, ending his story as it began some five hundred pages earlier, where it is first revealed that "full of resolve and a measure of hope, he would marry again."

The Characters

Alejandro Stern is very much an outsider, a reserved, formal man, an Argentinean immigrant and a Jew, on whom the nickname "Sandy" sits not a little uncomfortably. Turow further distances the reader from his main character by using a third-person narrator who, although sharing Stern's point of view, frequently refers to Stern as "Mr. Alejandro Stern." Such techniques go some way toward explaining Stern's predicament in *The Burden of Proof*, his alienation from his family, his incomprehension in the face of his wife's suicide. Unfortunately, these techniques sometimes also make Stern incomprehensible to the reader, so that the mystery at the heart of the novel—why did Clara kill herself?—is never entirely resolved. Clara Stern committed suicide because of the consequences of her anger at her husband. Because the novel's focus on him is not always sharp, the causes of his wife's destructive behavior are themselves blurred.

In contrast, the portrait of Stern's antagonist, Dixon Hartnell, is vividly drawn. Here, as in John Milton's epic *Paradise Lost* (1667), the hero's opposite number is more energetic and attractive than those on the side of the angels. Indeed, Hartnell is portrayed in terms that make him out to be the devil in disguise. Toward the end of the novel, when his sins have been revealed, Hartnell tells his brother-in-law, "I've always wanted to do what other people wouldn't," to which Stern replies, "I believe that is called evil, Dixon." Although Hartnell bears the most conspicuous responsibility for Clara's death and almost manages to destroy the rest of Stern's family, he is hard to damn entirely. Stern's attitude toward Hartnell is finally disapproving but indulgent: Hartnell may be corrupt and manipulative, but he is charming and daring and—perhaps most important—uxorious. He is clearly everything that Stern is not.

The two main female characters in *The Burden of Proof* are a similar study in contrasts. Clara, like her husband, remains elusive, a kind of vacant center around which the plot revolves. This sense of absence results in part from the fact that she is dead before the novel begins. Even after Turow attempts to bring her back to life in flashbacks, however, she remains more an embodiment of principle than a human being. As Hartnell says when searching for an explanation of why he seduced her, "She was a woman to admire."

Sonny Klonsky, on the other hand, is only too mortal. A fortyish victim of breast cancer, she is also, when Stern becomes involved with her, unhappily married and pregnant with her first child. Yet Sonny is remarkably self-aware and self-possessed, and although she has far more excuses for instability than the genteel, monied Clara, she is the survivor. Doubtless it is these qualities that make her so attractive for Stern, who loves not so much the look of this younger woman as the wisdom she incorporates.

Themes and Meanings

Sandy Stern first made his appearance as the protagonist's defense counsel in Turow's best-selling novel *Presumed Innocent* in 1987. As Turow has described the genesis of *The Burden of Proof*, it seems to have grown almost entirely out of his meditations on Stern's character:

> I had carried around with me for years this image of a guy in his mid-fifties who was getting married again. . . . Then one afternoon . . . I realized that character is Stern. I had felt bad about letting go of Stern after *Presumed Innocent*, because you don't see much inside of him in that book. I was interested in what really goes on inside this man with his exotic background and his reserved, formal exterior.

Indeed, *The Burden of Proof* is largely devoted to explorations of Stern's and other characters' psyches. While the book clearly qualifies as a mystery, it is a mystery with a difference: Not only is the victim dead from the outset, but the reasons for her death are not the obvious ones. Certainly there is enough of the usual greed and lust to propel the plot forward—the clues to Clara's death are an uncashed check for $850,000 and a prescription for medication used to combat venereal disease—but in order to discover their connection to his wife's suicide, Stern must investigate his own soul and the untold ways in which he had failed in his marriage.

The Burden of Proof, with its opening emphasis on Stern's marriages, is all about family, which Turow calls the "magic circle where the law ends." Clara Mittler, with her inherited wealth and good manners and her successful lawyer father, had been Stern's ticket to acceptance and success in America. In pursuing his career as a trial attorney, however, Stern seems to have lost, if not his soul, certainly his ties to his wife and children. When her youngest child left for college, Clara, seemingly desperate for human contact, finally surrendered to Hartnell's blandishments after years of putting him off. Stern did not take notice of his wife's despair, then or later. Neither did he seem to make time to develop relationships with his three children.

Stern's one strong bond is to his sister Silvia, on whom he lavishes all the courtly protectiveness and affection he possesses. Their relationship seems as ineffaceable as the Latin accent that marks Stern's speech even after decades of exile from Argentina. By such means, Turow manages to suggest at once Stern's singularity and his potential for redemption and reintegration. Finally, Stern is able to make his peace with his first wife's death and—after another death in the family, that of his old nemesis, Hartnell—marry again, thus closing the magic circle.

Critical Context

The Burden of Proof is Scott Turow's third book and second novel. After teaching creative writing at Stanford University and receiving his master's degree there in 1974, and before beginning law school at Harvard University in 1975, Turow obtained a contract for a nonfiction account of his first year of legal studies. *One L*, published in 1977, just before Turow began his final year of law school, proved to be both a critical and popular success.

After receiving his law degree, Turow worked for eight years in the U.S. Attorney's Office in Chicago, during which time he wrote his first novel. *Presumed Innocent*, published in 1987, made headlines before it appeared, largely because of the record sums of money connected with it. Turow received an advance of two hundred thousand dollars from Farrar, Straus & Giroux, the largest the publisher had ever paid for a first novel. Warner Bros. paid three million dollars for paperback rights, the highest price ever paid for reprint rights to a first novel, and film rights were sold to director Sydney Pollack for one million dollars. The hardback version stayed on best-seller lists for forty-four weeks, the paperback edition for twenty-nine weeks.

Before the publication of *Presumed Innocent*, Turow had accepted a position at a major Chicago law firm, where he worked half-time while writing *The Burden of Proof*. Like its predecessor, Turow's second novel quickly became a best-seller. A third novel, *Pleading Guilty*, appeared in 1993.

Although all of Turow's works, even *One L*, are fraught with mystery, his heroes' respective moral dilemmas make his books memorable. It is the philosophical quandaries his lawyer-heroes face—those forcing them to choose between their obligation as officers of the court to uphold the "truth" and their responsibilities toward their families—that lend Turow's novels resonance.

Turow's storybook success as a writer revived the genre of the legal thriller, which has grown to accommodate lawyer-novelists such as John Grisham, whose 1991 novel *The Firm* dominated best-seller lists much as *Presumed Innocent* had done a few years earlier. Still, *Presumed Innocent* remains the standard against which the products of these other writers—and those of Turow himself—are judged. Reviews of *The Burden of Proof* were not as uniformly favorable as they had been for its predecessor. The strength of both books, however, is that they are told from the vantage point of a lawyer obsessed not so much with solving a mystery as with discovering the truth of his own involvement in an ambiguous death. The insight into the equivocal nature of morality, which seems to grow out of Turow's dual existence as a lawyer and a writer, is clearly the greatest strength of his books, helping them to rise above the conventions of their genre.

Bibliography

Dalton, Katherine. "Power of Attorney." *Harper's Bazaar* 123 (June, 1990): 38-39. Briefly reviews the novel, comparing it with *Presumed Innocent*. Chiefly rehearses Turow's biography, emphasizing the phenomenal success of Turow's first novel.

Diggs, Terry K. "Through a Glass Darkly: John Grisham and Scott Turow Lay Down the Law for Millions of Americans. Just What Is It They're Trying to Tell Us?" *ABA Journal* 82 (October, 1996): 72-75. Diggs argues that Grisham and Turow's distinctive portrayals of versions of the law stem from different historical perspectives. He compares Grisham's novels, which harken back to the Great Depression, and Turow's works, which recall the film noir that emerged at the end of World War II. An interesting analysis of the works of two contemporary authors.

Feeney, Joseph J. "Recent Fiction: The Burden of Proof." *America* 163 (October 13, 1990): 250. A highly respectful review, finding in Turow's novel an exploration of the conventions of Greek tragedy. Feeney does a good job of analyzing Turow's style.

Gray, Paul. "Burden of Success." *Time* 135 (June 11, 1990): 68-72. Cover story on Turow, including excerpts from interviews with the author, emphasizing his biography. Reviews both *The Burden of Proof* and the film version of *Presumed Innocent*. Turow's second novel is praised for its substantial themes as well as its entertainment value.

Grisham, John. "The Rise of the Legal Thriller: Why Lawyers Are Throwing the Book at Us." *The New York Times Book Review*, October 18, 1992, 33. Locates the revival of the genre in *Presumed Innocent*, the success of which has prompted other lawyers to write about their exploits. Evaluates other contributions to the genre.

Maas, Peter. "And Scott Turow's New Mystery." *The New York Times Book Review*, June 3, 1990, 1. Compares Turow's second novel unfavorably with his first. Maas finds the pace slow, Stern poorly developed, and the book's themes overblown.

Lisa Paddock

BURR

Author: Gore Vidal (1925-   )
Type of plot: Historical chronicle
Time of plot: 1776-1840
Locale: New York, Washington, D.C., and the western states and territories
First published: 1973

> *Principal characters:*
> AARON BURR, Vice President of the United States under Thomas
>   Jefferson, killer of Alexander Hamilton in a duel (July 11, 1804),
>   tried for treason (March 30, 1807)
> ELIZA BOWEN JUMEL, Burr's second wife
> CHARLES SCHUYLER, Burr's biographer and a journalist and law
>   student
> HELEN JEWETT, Schuyler's mistress
> WILLIAM CULLEN BRYANT, editor of the New York *Evening Post*
> WILLIAM LEGGETT, Schuyler's editor at the *Evening Post*
> WASHINGTON IRVING, a famous American writer, diplomat, and adviser
>   to Schuyler
> GEORGE WASHINGTON, Burr's commanding officer during the
>   American Revolution
> ALEXANDER HAMILTON, Washington's aide, later Secretary of the
>   Treasury and Burr's political foe
> ANDREW JACKSON, friendly to Burr, hostile to the Jeffersonians
> JAMES MADISON, Jefferson's protégé and part of what Burr calls the
>   "Virginia junto"
> JOHN MARSHALL, Supreme Court Justice, disaffected cousin to
>   Jefferson, who presided over Burr's treason trial
> JOHN RANDOLPH, a Virginia politician who is cool to Jefferson and a
>   significant factor in Burr's acquittal
> JAMES WILKINSON, at first Burr's ally in an effort to conquer Mexico,
>   then Jefferson's tool in the treason trial

The Novel

Burr begins on July 1, 1833, with a special dispatch from the New York *Evening Post* announcing the marriage of "Colonel Aaron Burr, aged seventy-seven" to "Eliza Jumel, born Bowen fifty-eight years ago (more likely sixty-five but remember: she is prone to litigation!)." The author of the dispatch, and narrator of the novel, is Charles Schuyler, who is studying law under Burr, an attorney still active in the affairs of love and politics. Schuyler's narrative intended to resolve some of the confusion and the conflicting claims that mark historical accounts of Burr's controversial career, while not pretending to offer the ultimate truth about the man. As Burr himself will suggest, the printed history of his affairs has been unreliable; the point of Schuyler's dispatch is that even at this late stage in his subject's life, accurate information is difficult to obtain and to publish on a figure who refers to the legend of himself as "the hellish Aaron Burr [who] meant single-handedly to disband the United States."

Vidal has wisely chosen not to present Burr's life in strict chronological order. The most fascinating and historically significant period of the protagonist's life is over by his fiftieth year, and while Burr's personality remains intriguing, his last thirty years are of minor importance and are telescoped into a few pages of Schuyler's speculations about how Burr has coped with his infamous past.

Like many historical novels, *Burr* puts one historical period inside of another, so that one acts as a frame for the other, and the reader's sense of history, of how one period develops into the next, is superbly enriched. The novel's past covers the years of the Revolution and the first three presidential administrations by presenting Burr's point of view in twenty-one autobiographical installments that Schuyler edits and that are inserted into the ongoing narrative.

The novel's present, 1833-1836, is the era of the second administration of Andrew Jackson, in which political maneuvering has already begun to ensure that Vice President Martin Van Buren will succeed to the nation's highest office. Schuyler is employed by William Leggett (bent on discrediting Van Buren) to write about Burr in the hope of proving that Van Buren is Burr's illegitimate son. Yet Schuyler finds Burr admirable because he is free of the usual cant and hypocrisy associated with politicians and generously admits his errors. Schuyler proves to be the perfect narrator, since he is forced to explore all sides of Burr and is unaware, until the last page of the novel, of his true relation to his subject. In other words, Schuyler is the classic hero of historical fiction as it was first developed by Sir Walter Scott. He is part of the action but also removed from it; he is connected to a losing cause (the Burrites who still think their chief was correct in trying to liberate Mexico and the West), but he is also very much a man of the present, somewhat aloof from politics but nevertheless drawn into political intrigue.

By giving his novel a double time frame, Vidal is able to demonstrate that Burr's forthright opportunism is hardly what makes him a unique figure in American history. On the contrary, Burr and the other founding fathers set up a factionalized political system that was responsible for the scheming that Schuyler cannot avoid. Burr was not extraordinary for his faults but was necessary as a scapegoat for Thomas Jefferson and others who wanted to mask their own motivations in building an American empire.

The Characters

The character studies in *Burr* are extraordinarily vivid and often amusing. George Washington is portrayed as an inept military commander but an astute politician who realized at an early age that he would have to play the aloof, austere, American "god." Thomas Jefferson is a canting hypocrite of the highest order, who nevertheless earns Burr's accolade as the greatest politician and empire builder of his age. James Madison, aware of Jefferson's duplicity, is treated as a complex figure doggedly loyal to his mentor and most impressive in his subtle construction of constitutional principles. John Marshall appears as a titanic figure in support of the Constitution, yet he is not immune to fears of his cousin Jefferson's efforts to undermine the chief justice and the United States Supreme Court. Alexander Hamilton, fiercely ambitious and contentious, finally goes too far (perhaps sensing his political failure in New York, which leads to Burr's leadership of the Federalists) in accusing Burr, not of political impropriety, but of incest with his beloved daughter Theodosia.

In *Burr*, politics and personalities are finely fused, so that it is not certain whether Hamilton and Burr fight over personal or political insults. Both men, it is clear, are deeply disappointed when they do not achieve their highest ambitions. While the novel is dominated by Burr's obviously partisan view of his opponents, it is clear from the dialogue between Burr and other political figures and from the questions that Schuyler asks him that Burr's central failing has been his inability to articulate his understanding of the Constitution and of his country's future. What puts Jefferson ahead of Burr is not simply his superior maneuvering for power; rather, Jefferson enunciates, however ambiguously, a national purpose that transcends his own person. Burr, on the other hand, has depended throughout his life on the personal loyalty of his followers. In his own words, Burr has been too frank in admitting that he is "equivocal" on the Constitution.

Themes and Meanings

The theme of *Burr* centers on the meaning of the Constitution. Is it a document that will endure, or is it subject to changes brought about by the exploration of a vast continent composed of many different peoples who may seek many different forms of government which the Constitution cannot absorb? Vidal shrewdly shows that with the exception of Madison and Washington, most of the founding fathers, at one time or another, undermined the authority of the Constitution. Jefferson, when it was convenient for his politics, argued for nullification, the right of any state to reject a federal law deemed injurious to its interests. Hamilton favored a government closer in structure to the British parliamentary system. John Adams suppressed dissent and took, in some respects, a far more authoritarian view of his powers than the Constitution permitted.

Burr, in line with many other young men of his day, entertained the idea of a separate country west of the Mississippi and dreamed as well of liberating Mexico. Whether in this atmosphere his views were treasonous has never been clear in spite of Jefferson's best efforts to demonstrate that Burr's Western expedition was for the purpose of seizing territory and declaring a new nation.

What is clear is that Burr is the perfect tool for Vidal's debunking of several of America's revered national figures. The novelist does not deny their greatness, but he shows that it was of a different kind from that commonly celebrated. It is political craft, not political principle, that Vidal lauds and criticizes. Figures such as William Cullen Bryant and Washington Irving, discreet upholders of pious maxims and diplomatic versions of American history, would like to remove Schuyler from the fluid political realities that enmeshed Burr and Jefferson and in which politicians today, Vidal implies, are still trapped.

Critical Context

Burr is one of a series of novels by Vidal providing a lively and incisive history of the American republic. Considered by many critics to be the finest of his historical fictions, *Burr* was followed by *1876* (1976) and *Lincoln* (1984). An earlier novel, *Washington, D.C.* (1967), centers on politics in the era of Franklin D. Roosevelt and Harry Truman. Of these novels, *Burr* has the most complex narrative structure and the smoothest integration of fictional and historical characters.

Charles Schuyler is fictional, and his own story, involving an intricate balancing of private and political life, is the Burr story in a minor key. Historical novelists often have difficulty making their passive heroes, who are usually devoted to domestic life and unwillingly involved in historical epochs, sufficiently interesting, but Schuyler is like a more modest Burr in his adventuring, in his sad affair with Helen Jewett, a prostitute whom he tries to live with and marry. Schuyler has almost betrayed Burr, as did James Wilkinson, who turned into Jefferson's stooge, and Schuyler almost becomes William Leggett's lackey in the plot to bring down Van Buren, who is Burr's protégé.

For the most part, Vidal has stuck to the facts and to the chronology of history, since it is his purpose not only to entertain but also to advance provocative notions concerning the motivations of historical figures, notions of a kind that historians, relying only on data and guarding their professional reputation, are reluctant to venture. Extrapolating from the known personalities of historical figures, he creates dialogue and description that capture history in the making.

Bibliography

Baker, Susan, and Curtis S. Gibson. *Gore Vidal: A Critical Companion*. Westport, Conn.: Greenwood Press, 1997. A biographical sketch precedes a general discussion of Vidal's early writings, followed by critical discussions of individual novels. The discussions include sections on plot and character development, thematic issues, narrative style, and critical approaches. Includes an essay on *Burr*.

Goodman, Walter. "History as Fiction." *The New Leader* 71 (May 16, 1988): 11-12. Vidal defends himself against critics who charge that his books are "unhistorical or antihistorical exercises." Although Goodman believes that the harsh criticism is unwarranted, he argues that Vidal's novels should "best be taken for what they are, which is something different from history."

Parini, Jay, ed. *Gore Vidal: Writer Against the Grain*. New York: Columbia University Press, 1992. A collection of essays by various critics that covers the important works of Vidal's career. An interesting overview that places Vidal's historical fiction within the context of the entire body of his work.

Vidal, Gore. "The Importance of Being Gore." Interview by Andrew Kopkind. *The Nation* 257 (July 5, 1993): 16-19. Vidal discusses the influence of his same-sex orientation on his work. Although he does not specifically discuss *Burr*, he does give examples from history where the sexual preference of certain important figures could have been a factor in determining the course of events.

_____. Interview by Jay Parini. *The New England Review* 14 (Fall 1991): 93-101. Vidal talks about his career as a novelist and television scriptwriter. He cites writers who have influenced him, including Jonathan Swift and William Golding. He also shares his views on contemporary literary criticism. A revealing interview that offers valuable insight into Vidal's artistic motivations.

Carl Rollyson

BY LOVE POSSESSED

Author: James Gould Cozzens (1903-1978)
Type of plot: Social realism
Time of plot: Around 1950
Locale: The New England town of Brocton
First published: 1957

> *Principal characters:*
>> ARTHUR WINNER, JR., the protagonist, a lawyer who struggles with a
>> moral dilemma
>> NOAH TUTTLE, also a lawyer, accused of misappropriation of funds
>> JULIUS PENROSE, the husband of Winner's lover and the third partner in
>> the law firm
>> HELEN DETWEILER, the secretary to Tuttle, Winner, and Penrose

The Novel

Set in a small Northeastern community, *By Love Possessed* chronicles forty-nine hours in the life of Arthur Winner, Jr., a respected lawyer and citizen of Brocton. The title refers to the different types of love—sexual love, parental love, friendship, love for community and church—which play a part in Winner's life as a man and as a lawyer. The novel opens as Winner contemplates the clock in his mother's house with the inscription *omnia vincit amor.* Winner has patterned himself after his deceased father, the "Man of Reason," and the conflict between love or passion and reason dominates the action.

As the defense attorney in a rape case against eighteen-year-old Ralph Detweiler, the much younger brother of Helen Detweiler, a legal secretary in the firm of Winner, Tuttle, and Penrose, Winner attempts to apply reason and logic to the emotionally charged situation. The case is complicated by the fact that, although Ralph admits having had intimate relations with Veronica Kovacs, a young woman with a tarnished reputation, he also admits being involved with Joan Moore, whom he has gotten pregnant. Winner assures Ralph that the charge of rape will almost certainly be dropped, but the immature, spoiled Ralph panics at the thought of facing a trial and a pregnant girlfriend. He jumps bail and in the process steals money from one of the boarders in Helen's rooming house. Helen, having reared Ralph since their parents' death in a tragic boating accident, sees all of her plans for Ralph's future collapse, and she commits suicide. Winner's reasoned approach is thwarted by people tangled in passions, and he is unable to prevent tragedy.

After Helen Detweiler's death, Winner visits the law office to obtain her will and accidentally uncovers evidence that sets another conflict in motion. Noah Tuttle, the eighty-year-old senior partner of the law firm and a man of unquestioned integrity, has been misappropriating funds over a number of years to protect local investors from financial ruin as a result of the collapse of the Brocton Rapid Transit Company, which he had recommended as an investment. When Winner presents Julius Penrose with this discovery, he learns that Penrose has been aware of the situation for more than ten years and has chosen to keep silent and give Tuttle the chance to replace the money. The Orcutt trust, a fund designated for use by the Episcopal Church of Brocton (where Winner is a prominent layman), is also involved.

Winner knows that his father, the "Man of Reason," would have immediately done the "right thing" and turned Noah over to the authorities, thus destroying all the members of the firm professionally as well as financially. Penrose persuades Winner that Noah has acted out of love: "He would betray himself, sacrifice himself, before he let down, sacrificed, those who had put faith in him." During this tense discussion, Winner makes another discovery. Although he prides himself on his ability to act on reason, shortly after the death of his first wife he succumbed to passion during a brief, but intense, affair with Penrose's wife, Marjorie, and—Winner now realizes—Penrose has been aware of this affair since its inception.

Winner's simplistic moral code is challenged by Penrose's deeper understanding of moral complexity; Penrose persuades him that the strict honesty which would demand revealing Tuttle's deeds is not the best policy but only the easiest one. Their duty, like Tuttle's, lies in doing what is necessary to protect their community. Winner learns that what seems a clear choice, with freedom to act, is often no choice at all but merely the acceptance of a fate that has been predetermined. He recognizes the truth in his brother-in-law Fred Dealey's words: "Freedom is the knowledge of necessity." Winner's faith in reason has been tempered by the effects of passion, and he now asserts that "Victory is not in reaching certainties or solving mysteries; victory is in making do with uncertainties, in supporting mysteries."

The Characters

Arthur Winner, Jr., a middle-class, middle-aged, dispassionate man, has tried to live his life in the light of reason, patterned after his father—"the nearly unique individual; the Man, if not perfectly, at least predominantly, of Reason." Ruled by a strong sense of duty and responsibility, he serves his community, law practice, church, and family. In the space of an afternoon, he deals with the problems of his distressed secretary, Helen, her brother Ralph's rape case and bail jumping, court opinion imputing ineptness by his law partner Noah Tuttle, a cherished tree struck by lightning, a lesbian Catholic proselytizer, the discovery that his love affair with his partner Julius Penrose's wife is no secret, and a disgruntled choir director. Winner's brother-in-law Fred Dealey remarks: "You're really a kind of universal fall guy, Arthur! They all come to you! Philosophy and religion assure me that 'fall guy' is the righteous man's other name." Winner is proud of his ability to order other people's lives and problems, and his sense of security and complacency in his power in his personal life is an extension of his professional life. He is a product of his profession. Only through deep contemplation of his failure as a father with his son Warren and his weakness in participating in a passionate affair does his sense of complacency become shaken. He is further humbled by his inability to prevent Helen Detweiler's suicide and his realization of Noah Tuttle's unethical professional activities. The Arthur Winner at the end of the novel is no longer secure in his power to rule by reason.

Noah Tuttle has reached the age of senility, and his brilliant law career is coming to a sad end with his secretary and partners covering for his lapses of memory—at least that is what Arthur Winner thinks until he discovers the misappropriation of funds that was prompted by Tuttle's magnanimous concern for the investors whom he had advised. Until this discovery, Winner has been unaware of Noah's "occasional propensity to act emotionally, of Noah's sometimes sentimental sensibilities," and therefore his assessment of Tuttle's possible range of actions has been faulty.

Julius Penrose is not blinded by reason, and his powers of perception and understanding are the catalysts for Winner's revelation. As a young man, Penrose was a powerfully built, handsome athlete, but he was crippled by polio at age forty, and now his shriveled, useless legs are encased in heavy braces. Possibly as a result of this incongruous tragedy, being struck by a childhood disease in the prime of his life, Penrose has developed great insights into the human condition. Penrose's compassion for his wife's infidelity with Winner, and his deeper understanding of the implications of Noah Tuttle's indiscretions, cause Winner to reevaluate his philosophy. Penrose, however, is not ruled by passion or feeling. He decries the overt sentimentality he sees around him. "Yes; the spirit of the age! We're in an age pre-eminently of capital F feeling—a century of the gulp, the lump in the throat, the good cry. . . . We've made sentimentality of the respected essence. . . . The grave and learned are no whit behind the cheap and stupid in their love of it." Penrose is wise enough to recognize the motivating power of passion in people's lives and to make decisions in the light of both reason and feeling. When Winner gives in to feelings of guilt about Helen Detweiler's suicide, Penrose admonishes him: "Regrets of that kind are unreasonable, unrealistic. *It might have been*—not so much the saddest as the silliest words of tongue or pen. Let us face it. What happens to people is simply what was always going to happen to them. To think otherwise is vain visioning." Penrose shakes Winner out of his inclination to "play God" by his pragmatic assessment. Winner is forced to face the fact that he is not as omnipotent or omniscient as he had once thought.

Helen Detweiler, the conscientious, responsible, nervous secretary of the Tuttle, Winner, Penrose law firm, has been robbed of her youth by willingly assuming the duty of rearing her younger brother Ralph. She has felt too strongly her responsibility for him, has loved him too dearly, acting on the basis of feeling rather than reason. Overindulged by Helen in her admirable attempts to compensate for the loss of their parents, Ralph is "rather spiritless and spineless." Julius Penrose's harsh judgment of Helen's suicide appears to be Cozzens's own, finding in Helen's final act "a want of principle, which is to say, too much feeling." Penrose's conclusion is that she was "possessed by love."

Themes and Meanings

Cozzens often places at the center of his novels a mature professional man whose success demands that he accept responsibility for his community. These men have considerable authority and power over others, and the exercise of this power and their duty to wield it justly prompt most of the action. His characters are molded by their professions, and the world is presented through their eyes. Cozzens is a social realist in that he presents things as they are and does not prescribe simple resolutions for his conflicts. Moral dilemmas are explored in all their complexity: There are choices where no alternative is ideal. Indeed, Cozzens often suggests that the power to choose is an illusion, that men are the victims of fate. This Calvinist sense of predestination places Cozzens squarely in the tradition of such "dark" American novelists as Nathaniel Hawthorne and William Faulkner.

Many conflicts develop out of the conflicts between love and reason. Cozzens manifests a great respect for the traditions and established social order of the middle classes, whose virtues of rationality, self-discipline, and stability are contrasted with the irrational, undisciplined, impassioned actions of other members of the community, usually of a lower social class. Man is seen as a product of his past and as consciously influenced by it: Events from the past continually force themselves into present moments. The implication is that although time passes, man never really changes, and there is no natural progression toward perfectibility.

Critical Context

By Love Possessed, an enormously successful best-seller, provoked *Time* magazine, in which he expressed unfashionable opinions with aristocratic disdain. The consequences of this affair were long-lasting, but since the late 1970's there has been a renewal of critical appreciation of his work.

Cozzens's style is often elaborate, filled with allusions and choked with subordination often to the point of obscurity. His habit of referring to his characters by their full names is indicative of his self-consciously formal style, one that distances him from his characters and, to a certain extent, from his readers. Independent of the literary mainstream, Cozzens successfully introduced a substance and a style counter to contemporary fashions.

Bibliography

Bracher, Frederick. *The Novels of James Gould Cozzens*. New York: Harcourt, Brace, 1959. Of the eight novels by Cozzens published between 1931 and 1959, Bracher argues that at least four of them are of "major importance by any set of standards." Defends Cozzens from attacks by critics for his lack of personal commitment, showing him to be a novelist of intellect whose strength is storytelling. A thorough commentary on Cozzens's literary career.

Bruccoli, Matthew J. *James Gould Cozzens: A Life Apart*. New York: Harcourt Brace Jovanovich, 1983. This book-length story of Cozzens is essentially a biography with useful information on his upbringing and his development as a novelist. Includes a chapter each on *Guard of Honor* and *By Love Possessed* and an appendix containing excerpts from his notebooks. A must for any serious scholar of Cozzens.

Hicks, Granville. *James Gould Cozzens*. Minneapolis: University of Minnesota, 1966. An accessible introduction to Cozzens with some criticism of his novels from *Confusion* to *Guard of Honor* and *By Love Possessed*. Argues that the pretentiousness in Cozzens's early work was transformed in later novels to "competent, straightforward prose."

Mooney, John Harry, Jr. *James Gould Cozzens: Novelist of Intellect*. Pittsburgh, Pa.: University of Pittsburgh Press, 1963. A straightforward, useful study. Each chapter focuses on a different novel, from *S.S. San Pedro* to *Castaway*, and the final chapter covers the critical material available on Cozzens.

Pfaff, Lucie. *The American and German Entrepreneur: Economic and Literary Interplay*. New York: Peter Lang, 1989. Contains a chapter on Cozzens and the business world, with subsections on "The Business Activities of Henry Dodd Worthington," "Small Business," and "Recurring Themes." Pfaff is particularly interested in Cozzens's entrepreneurs.

Sterne, Richard Clark. *Dark Mirror: The Sense of Injustice in Modern European and American Literature*. New York: Fordham University Press, 1994. Contains a detailed discussion of *The Just and the Unjust*.

Len McCall

THE CALL

Author: John Hersey (1914-1993)
Type of plot: Historical chronicle
Time of plot: 1878-1981
Locale: Upstate New York and northeast China
First published: 1985

>   *Principal characters:*
>   DAVID TREADUP (T'AO TU HSIEN-SHENG), an American missionary in
>   China
>   EMILY TREADUP, his wife
>   JAMES B. TODD, the charismatic leader of the Student Volunteer
>   Movement for Foreign Missions

The Novel

The Call follows the dedicated life of David Treadup, who leaves rural New York as a young man of twenty-seven and devotes his life to the welfare of the Chinese people. In the background of Treadup's career are the tumultuous events that have changed Chinese life drastically in the twentieth century, and *The Call* is thus also an impressionistic history of modern China through the Communist Revolution. John Hersey divides his seven-hundred-page narrative into ten sections, each focusing on an important phase of Treadup's life. Sketches of Treadup's pioneer forebears give the story additional historical sweep, as does the account of the futile efforts of Treadup's oldest son, Philip, to get his father's ashes buried in Shanghai in 1981.

David Treadup is born in 1878 in Salt Branch, New York, in Onondagan country, and after an erratic beginning, he is graduated from Syracuse University. The call to missionary work comes to him in his last year in college, and in 1905—after courting Emily Kean, who will join him in China a year later as his wife—he arrives in Tientsin as a YMCA missionary under the sponsorship of Syracuse University. Through 1910, Treadup teaches and develops his literati campaign, a program to introduce modern science to China's educated elite with the expectation that knowledge will then trickle down the cultural scale. His favorite teaching aid is a gyroscope he has had shipped to him, and with its properties he fascinates and charms large audiences.

Treadup's lecture program gets new strength in 1911, when his New York boss, the eloquent James B. Todd, visits China and the two give a series of talks together, Treadup expounding science and Todd preaching the Gospel. This two-pronged approach becomes the standard format for Treadup's endeavors to educate and convert the Chinese, but his work is interrupted during World War I by his duties in France as an overseer of Chinese coolies sent to Europe as manual laborers. Treadup is pleased by efforts to teach the homesick coolies simple reading and writing while they are in France, and he returns to China in 1921 with serious doubts about his theory that education should be directed toward the elite. He then undertakes his own literacy campaign in the Chinese villages west of Tientsin.

Civil war shakes China in the 1920's, and the Japanese invasion of Manchuria in 1931 intensifies the country's distress. By 1937, China is in chaos and the missionary organization is retrenching with a much-diminished budget. Treadup is himself recalled by his New York office, but he vows to stay in China on his own since he has made a commitment to a life's work. In 1937, Paoting, his home, is captured by the Japanese; in 1940, Emily returns to New York (their three sons are already in the United States), and Treadup "lives Chinese" under Japanese occupation. When Pearl Harbor is bombed, Treadup is interned but finds the closest friend of his life in Dr. Phinneas Cunningham. Camp life humiliates Treadup and leads to his loss of faith in God.

Treadup returns to New York in 1943 to find Emily much aged and infirm. Their oldest son, Philip, is successful and dull; the second son, Absolom, lives in eccentric estrangement in Maine; and the third son, Paul, has become an entrepreneur in a double-breasted pinstripe suit. When Emily dies in 1945, never having learned of Treadup's apostasy, he returns to China as part of the postwar reconstruction effort. The corruption he finds dismays him, the Red Chinese mortify him in a public castigation aimed at him as an abstract symbol of Western capitalist exploitation, and he returns to New York in 1950 and dies shortly afterward.

The Characters

As a child growing up in rural New York, David Treadup reveals no special abilities, but when he is seventeen he falls severely ill with osteomyelitis, and with nothing to do but read books, he experiences a new insight into the life of the intellect. He is guided in this revelation by a perceptive, kind teacher, Maud Chase. Thus he is enthusiastic when a year later he is allowed to attend the Enderby Institute, where he studies under Absolom Carter, an inspired teacher who is ultimately the greatest influence on his life. As a role model of the "all-around thinker-athlete," Carter is to Treadup a paradigm of what the naïve youth knows he wants to become. Carter tutors Treadup in Benjamin Franklin, Plato, Xenophon, and Plutarch, treating him to a secular education that forms his thinking for good. So "the agnostic Carter's instinct in giving David this extracurricular course in ethics was to bear fruit: Something skeptical, temporal, and sophisticated would stay with David all his life—and would give him difficulties as a missionary."

Treadup's conversion to Christianity comes when he is a twenty-five-year-old sophomore at Syracuse and provides him with great relief. He is freed from the terrible aimlessness that has bedeviled him and is given moral support in his struggle with carnal desire. His new purpose in life so enriches his spirit that his vague hypochondriacal complaints fade away. This spiritual confidence stays with him for forty years until, sick and despairing in a Japanese camp, he undergoes a "counterconversion" prefigured by a flare-up of his old osteomyelitis. He finds his loss of faith cathartic in an ironic way:

*I feel as if my hands and feet had been tied for a long time, and that the knots have sud-
denly been undone. This has been an eerie experience. I don't think I am going to be quite
so afraid any more. If there is a God, I must be a disappointment to him.*

At this stage of his life, Treadup stands quite alone, severed from the allegiance that
powered his efforts for four decades.

For most of his life, Treadup goes without close relationships, his need for friendship subsumed under striving in God's service and in his deep love for his wife. His
strong sexual appetite is satisfied by Emily, and she is a rock of support for him, but
they are separated for long periods and she clearly takes second place to the call in his
life. She never quite emerges distinctly, consigned in her fictional life to the role of patient, helpful missionary wife. Without Treadup, she apparently has no identity. When
he returns to New York in 1943, he finds her wan and wasted for no discernible reason
other than her separation from him. Her own call—to his service—appears finally as a
miserable duping. It is not surprising that Treadup dares not confess to her his loss of
faith, for the knowledge would show her what a cruel and pointless sacrifice her own
life has been.

Treadup's only close adult friendship comes late in his life when he shares the
stresses of Japanese internment with the British Dr. Phinneas Cunningham. Cunningham is an adamantly secular thinker, an avatar in many ways of Treadup's old teacher
Absolom Carter. His library sustains Treadup through the long gloomy spell of life
under surveillance. Cunningham operates successfully on Treadup's left arm, curing
him of his debilitating osteomyelitis. Cunningham's dedicated humanism smooths
Treadup's counterconversion and frees him finally from the powerful hold Todd has
exerted on him for years.

Todd is a strong presence in *The Call*. He is a physically imposing man, and his
rhetoric appeals to thousands. Yet despite the sincerity of his conviction, he always comes off as arrogant and vainglorious, even lacking in charity, although he
speaks in the tongues of men and of angels. His mission is clear: to save souls. He
is, then, often suspicious of the humanistic impulses of Treadup, the former pupil
of Absolom Carter. When Todd and Treadup lecture together in China, Treadup's
science demonstrations always draw larger audiences than Todd's evangelistic
preachings.

Letitia Selden and Helen Demestrie live together in their own house in the missionary compound at Paoting. Treadup is close to them both, especially to Miss Selden. In
one of the most dramatic scenes in the novel, Miss Demestrie goes mad and, naked to
the waist, runs through the compound waving a sword and screaming lines in Greek
from *Lysistrata*. She seems to have lost control of her emotions under the pressures of
isolation, work, and unexpressed sexual desire for Treadup. This mad scene appears
unexpectedly, and Hersey sketches it movingly.

The Chinese characters seldom appear in clear focus. Actual historical persons
(such as Chiang Kai-shek and Mao Tse-tung) appear in the novel briefly but remain in
the historical background. Hersey explains that several characters were suggested by

real people (he instances Y. C. James Yen) but adds that "their names, like their selves, have been changed."

Themes and Meanings

Hersey blocks out Treadup's life in ten large narrative chunks, each suggestively titled (for example, "The Test"), and then divides and subdivides so that the story is told in a great many, usually brief episodes. He interlards his conventional third-person omniscient exposition with passages from Treadup's letters and diaries to create an effective historical panorama from the mesh of viewpoints.

The story of the YMCA's Student Volunteer Movement for Foreign Missions is important in *The Call*. Hersey notes that the movement, founded in 1888, became "the most influential student movement in the country, analogous, in its feverish growth and widespread appeal, to the student radical and pacifist movements of the 1930's and to the organizations of the New Left in the 1960's." Between 1888 and 1919, more than half of the North American Protestant missionaries were SVM volunteers.

Hersey also tells well the history of Chinese workers assigned to the Allies in Europe during World War I. In February, 1917, about 140,000 Chinese coolies were working in France. Hersey's summation is blunt: "It is not surprising that the historians of the Allied cause in the First World War have played down, to the point of disappearance, the suggestion that the Allies used slave labor to relieve the manpower shortage which followed the gruesome carnage of young men in the first years of that conflict."

Hersey repeatedly notes the many times that missionary cultural advances were adapted by the Communists after the revolution. For example, putting great numbers of people to work on public projects was "one of the many innovations of the missionaries which the Communists would later take up and magnify in their transformation of China."

The most powerful theme of the novel, overshadowing all else, must be the irony to which the title is reduced by Treadup's loss of faith. Even his postwar years are frustrating, and he leaves China permanently with an admittedly broken heart. Treadup dies an atheist, virtually estranged from two of his three sons by extreme differences in temperament. What comfort that can be found in *The Call* must come from the trick of history that made the missionaries into groundbreakers and innovators for the Communists.

Critical Context

Hersey's connections to China are strong and personal. His father, Roscoe M. Hersey, Sr., was himself a missionary to China, and Hersey was born in Tientsin and lived there until he was eleven. Nothing suggests, however, that *The Call* should be read as a chronicle of his father's experience. Indeed, Hersey notes that "all characters are fictional except recognizable historical figures, who bear their own names." *The Call* is a rigorously researched novel of a man's life and an impressionistic reconstruction of an important period in modern history.

Bibliography
Fiedler, Leslie. "No! in Thunder." In *The Novel: Modern Essays in Criticism*, edited by Robert Murray Davis. Englewood Cliffs, N.J.: Prentice-Hall, 1969. In discussing authors from his point of view that "art is essentially a moral activity," the controversial Fiedler accuses Hersey of being the author of "The Sentimental Liberal Protest Novel" who fights for "slots on the lists of best sellers" with his "ersatz morality." The essay makes for lively reading at best.

Huse, Nancy L. *The Survival Tales of John Hersey.* New York: Whitston, 1983. An eminently readable and informed study on Hersey which is useful in understanding the scope and development of Hersey as a writer. Explores the relationship between art and moral or political intentions. Includes extensive notes and a bibliography.

Sanders, David. "John Hersey." In *Contemporary Novelists*, edited by James Vinson. New York: St. Martin's Press, 1982. Covers Hersey's work from wartime journalist to novelist. Cites *The Wall* as his greatest novel and considers him the "least biographical of authors." A rather dense study but helpful in quickly establishing themes in Hersey's writings. A chronology and a bibliography are provided.

_____. *John Hersey Revisited*. Boston: Twayne, 1991. A revised edition of Sanders's 1967 study. The first chapter introduces Hersey's career as reporter and novelist, and subsequent chapters discuss his major fiction and nonfiction, including his later stories. Includes chronology, notes, and bibliography.

_____. "John Hersey: War Correspondent into Novelist." In *New Voices in American Studies*, edited by Ray B. Browne, Donald M. Winkelman, and Allen Hayman. West Lafayette, Ind.: Purdue University Press, 1966. A well-known scholar on Hersey, Sanders defends him and insists that he should not be dismissed because of his popularity. Traces Hersey's origins as a war correspondent and the writings that emerged from these experiences. Finally, Sanders settles the dispute as to whether Hersey is a novelist and hails him as a "writer."

Frank Day

CANNERY ROW

Author: John Steinbeck (1902-1968)
Type of plot: Sentimental realism
Time of plot: About 1940
Locale: "The Row," a sleepy fishing village near Monterey, California
First published: 1945

Principal characters:

> DOC, a poor, sensitive marine biologist, the most respected man in
>   Cannery Row
> MACK, the leader of a ragtag crew of derelicts who wish only to be left
>   alone, to enjoy life, and to live contentedly in the Palace Flophouse
> DORA FLOOD, the local madam, a woman with a sharp business sense
>   and a heart of gold
> HAZEL,
> HUGHIE,
> JONES,
> GAY, and
> EDDIE, "the boys" of Cannery Row

The Novel

Cannery Row is a sentimental, nostalgic portrayal of the lazy, the shiftless, the good-natured lowlifes who survive at the fringes of a fishing and canning community outside Monterey, California. Working only when they must, preferring drinking, fighting, and indolence, "the boys" of Cannery Row are somewhat akin to the old picaresque heroes of the seventeenth and eighteenth century novel. The picaro of these early novels was something of a rogue who lived by his or her wits, and who, despite poverty and social ostracism, displayed a basic goodness and a sense of practical wisdom.

Like their picaro predecessors, Mack and the boys have little or no money; they live off the vagaries of chance and opportunity; they engage in low-key bargaining with tightfisted Lee Chong, owner of the Row's grocery store; some of them occasionally land in jail. They are not above working when they absolutely have to, but more often than not they borrow, barter, or somehow "find" what they need. Indeed, the essential difference between the picaro and Steinbeck's modern rascals is that the latter lack a sense of purpose or ambition. Where a Lazarillo de Tormes or a Moll Flanders proceeds from one adventure to another in a purposeful, strategic direction, from less to more, from outsider to member of the establishment, Mack and his fellows simply drift, taking one day at a time, indifferent to the possibilities of their own social reformation, of the progress from dereliction to responsibility.

The plot of *Cannery Row* reflects this drift, this flaccid indifference to significant social action. It centers on the boys' only goal—that of giving Doc a party. A marine biologist who ekes out a living collecting specimens and supplying them to commercial houses, Doc is a quiet, sensitive fellow who enjoys listening to Monteverdi arias, drinking beer in his laboratory/residence, and entertaining female guests, during which visits he pulls down the shades and turns up the music. To Mack and the boys he is something of a role model, intelligent, kind, and usually solvent, yet mysteriously one of them, a sort of virtuous bum.

After a false start, the boys begin their arrangements for a surprise birthday party. One of them even gets a job tending bar for a few weeks in order to syphon off the dregs from the patrons' glasses and eventually collects a few gallons of some alcoholic mixture. The core of the plot is their determination to give Doc a suitable present at his party: They will themselves collect all the frogs, cats, and other specimens that Doc could use, saving him time, money, and labor. Like latter-day knights-errant, they successfully carry out their expedition and execute the party, to which all the good people of Cannery Row are invited, including Dora, the good-hearted madam, and her girls. The party concludes with a drunken brawl between intruding fishermen and the locals, a fight that puts everybody into benign spirits.

The brawl is an appropriate climax to the novel, suggesting that the passive indolence of the characters is relieved only by physical violence, which, though personally cleansing, is nevertheless socially self-destructive. Thus, unlike traditional picaresque novels, *Cannery Row* ends with the characters' remaining in the relatively same social position in which they had begun. Poor but happy, they survive as outcasts, their social reclamation thwarted by their indolence, their indifference to ambition.

Such a plot is hardly sustained by tragic seriousness, but rather by comic whimsy. Whimsy, in fact, is a key ingredient in the novel's design. Using a technique that he made famous in *The Grapes of Wrath* (1939), Steinbeck broadens the main plot with interpolated chapters, virtually self-contained units which relate to the main plot largely through tone, atmosphere, and thematic consistency. Such chapters include those dealing with the Malloys, who live in an abandoned boiler, and the lyric "prose poems" describing the good life and the decent though often eccentric people of the Row. These chapters flesh out an otherwise thin, almost anemic narrative action and at their best also provide the book with a sentimental charm, a quiet, rhapsodic nostalgia amounting to an idyllic myth about a sort of California peasantry.

The Characters

The characters of *Cannery Row* are mostly stereotypes, simplifications which illustrate Steinbeck's fondness for the vagrant, the eccentric, the genial pariah. Only Doc has the complexity of a major character. Educated enough to know marine biology, sensitive enough to surround his laboratory with reproductions of works of art and to enjoy classical music, shrewd enough to know how to deal with the schemes and cons of the boys, gentle enough to befriend the simpleminded, he is at heart a loafer, a drifter, "concupiscent as a rabbit," fond of beer and company, yet a loner.

He is, too, literary kin to earlier Steinbeck heroes. Tom Joad from *The Grapes of Wrath*, for example, who was also a sensitive though politically astute individual whose natural bent seemed to be centifugal rather than centripetal: His temperament drove him away from the family unit and toward a self-imposed isolation. George Milton in *Of Mice and Men* (1937) was an even earlier antecedent of Doc, clearly the same sensitive yet isolated being, whose care and love for Lenny, the gentle but brutish misfit, keeps him apart from the mainstream of society. Doc's befriending of Hazel, the simple, slow-witted boy-man of the group, is indicative both of his role as leader and of his isolated position. Doc's compassion allows him to care for Hazel, to give him a job as laboratory assistant, but at the same time, Hazel allows Doc the opportunity to remain a private person, uncommunicative about the things that really matter, just as an adult plays with a child, keeping his real personality hidden in the game. It is this ambivalence, this need for companionship in counterpoint to his solitary nature, that gives Doc a poignancy which elevates him to the central character of the novel.

Mack is the putative leader of the boys, the angelic bums, the "beauties," the "Virtues," as Steinbeck rather sentimentally calls them. Like the boys, Mack is irresponsible, as unreliable in the conduct of social affairs as he is loyal and generous of spirit. Mack always means well, but his good intentions are often foiled by a shiftlessness and an ambition limited to the demands of the hour rather than of the future. He presides genially over the group in the Palace Flophouse, an abandoned storage shack made habitable with the discarded flotsam of the village. Yet Mack is canny when the occasion warrants. He is a born manipulator of people. For years he has been "negotiating" with Lee Chong for groceries and other staples.

In a key scene illustrating his genius, Mack and the boys are caught in a frog pond by the owner of the property. They are busily engaged in catching frogs as a present for Doc, but the irate owner, gun and shotgun poised, wants them off the grounds at once. Mack apologizes, amiably cajoles, praises the dog, and in the end heals its long-standing illness, receiving from the grateful owner a puppy, all the frogs Mack wants, and a few hours of friendly drinking at the owner's house. Crucial in appreciating the scene is the knowledge that Mack is not being hypocritical. He genuinely likes the owner and simply lets his own amiability and honesty work for him.

Dora Flood, the town madam, is of the same good-hearted nature as the others. Ironically, she is as much a success as the boys are failures. She runs "a good house," has remarkable business instincts, but treats her girls with dignity, compassion, and generosity. Her good-naturedness is proven when the town is infected with influenza and Dora and her girls nurse back to health the poor, the infirm, and the young. She is, nevertheless, not as interesting a character as Doc or Mack because she is so thoroughly stereotypical. The whore with the heart of gold was a common figure in the post-Romantic literature of the twentieth century, particularly during the Depression of the 1930's, when "good" girls sold their bodies but kept pure their souls.

Themes and Meanings

For a novel with so slight a plot, *Cannery Row* is nevertheless engaging as a social document, a record of a state of mind, of attitudes about society and behavior during the "have-not" era of the 1930's. For although the novel was published at the end of

World War II, it is suggestive both in tone and spirit of a Depression mentality. The "good" people are the unemployed, the dispossessed, or, like Doc, the marginally solvent. Some, like Dora, are successful in spite of legal sanctions and social mores. As in *The Grapes of Wrath*, Steinbeck's definitive treatment of the Depression, there are really no "bad" people, either: only those who tightly clutch the things they have and who, like Lee Chong, leer distrustfully at those who have not. Yet the socioeconomic situation is treated comically in *Cannery Row*. Already behind him, the Depression for Steinbeck was no longer a grim consequence of social pathology or a crucible of heroic despair. Instead, it had become a subject for pleasant reminiscence about a time when men survived without money, on companionship, good intentions, and kindness; a simpler time, before the postwar boom, when people were valued not for the quantity of their goods but for the quality of their hearts.

Critical Context

Many critics are quick to belittle *Cannery Row* as a silly, trivial book, suitable more as a frothy mid-century film musical than as a serious contribution from the author of *In Dubious Battle* (1936), *The Grapes of Wrath*, and the later *East of Eden* (1952). Judged by these monuments, *Cannery Row* is justifiably consigned to the second rank of Steinbeck's work, yet the novel is interesting in its own right. Discounting *The Moon Is Down* (1942), a novella with propagandistic intentions, *Cannery Row* is Steinbeck's first major work after his Depression masterpiece. It shows his renewed interest in the comic portrayal of the simple, uncomplicated lifestyles of the lovably dispossessed, a subject already treated a decade earlier in *Tortilla Flat* (1935), a picaresque novel written in mock-heroic style about the "paisanos" of Southern California, quixotic latter-day knights who are, in fact, the true literary forebears of Doc and the boys of Cannery Row. *Tortilla Flat* was Steinbeck's first major success, his first book to be bought by Hollywood, and the first in which he found his characteristic subject matter.

Ten years after *Cannery Row*, Steinbeck again returned to the treatment of the lovable bums in *Sweet Thursday* (1954), a novel far below the quality of *Cannery Row* but one which nevertheless served as the basis for a (short-lived) Broadway musical entitled *Pipe Dream*. *Cannery Row* is thus the central book in a triumvirate of novels, the first near the beginning of Steinbeck's career and the last near the end of it. *Cannery Row* balances the two. If it lacks the innocence and promise of *Tortilla Flat*, it recapitulates much of the earlier novel's spirit while evoking a more genuine nostalgia, a more tranquil whimsy. At the same time, *Cannery Row* looks ahead to the trivial entertainment of *Sweet Thursday*, a book that tries too hard at reprising an already played out tune. *Cannery Row* is thus the final effective evocation of one of Steinbeck's most enduring subjects.

Bibliography

French, Warren. *John Steinbeck's Fiction Revisited*. New York: Twayne, 1994. Thoroughly revises French's two other books in this Twayne series. Chapters on

Steinbeck's becoming a novelist, his relationship to modernism, his short fiction, his wartime fiction, and his final fiction. Includes chronology, notes, and annotated bibliography.

Hughes, R. S. *John Steinbeck: A Study of the Short Fiction.* Boston: Twayne, 1989. Divided into three sections: Steinbeck's short stories, the author's letters exploring his craft, and four critical commentaries. A good study of some of his lesser-known works which includes a chronology, a lengthy bibliography, and an index.

Lisca, Peter. *The Wide World of John Steinbeck.* New York: Gordian Press, 1958. An indispensable guide to Steinbeck's work, published in 1958 and then updated with an "Afterword" examining the writer's last novel *The Winter of Our Discontent* (1961). Admired and imitated, Lisca's work set the standard for future Steinbeck studies.

McCarthy, Paul. *John Steinbeck.* New York: Frederick Ungar, 1980. A short biographical approach to Steinbeck's work that examines each novel against the forces that shaped his life. Includes a useful chronology, notes, a bibliography, and an index.

Edward A. Fiorelli

A CANTICLE FOR LEIBOWITZ

Author: Walter M. Miller, Jr. (1923-   )
Type of plot: Science fiction
Time of plot: Around the year 2500, C.E. 3174, and C.E. 3781
Locale: The monastery of the Blessed Leibowitz, somewhere between Salt Lake City and El Paso
First published: 1959

> *Principal characters:*
> BENJAMIN ELEAZAR, perhaps the Wandering Jew
> BROTHER FRANCIS OF UTAH, the discoverer of the Leibowitzian relics
> ABBOT ARKOS, the person responsible for the sanctification of Leibowitz
> THON TADDEO, a scientific inquirer, the illegitimate son of Hannegan II of Texarkana
> ABBOT PAULO, the preserver of the monastery from Hannegan's ambitions
> MRS. GRALES/RACHEL, a two-headed mutant, perhaps the new Messiah or new Mary
> ABBOT ZERCHI, the last abbot of the monastery of Saint Leibowitz

The Novel

The Leibowitz of this novel's title was, the reader is told, a technician engaged in weapons development at the time of the nuclear war which destroyed all civilization in America and in the rest of the world. A natural reaction of the survivors of this holocaust was to turn on all scientists, on all fragments of science, and to destroy them for being in some degree responsible for the devastation that had taken place. Leibowitz, however, though repentant of his past, received permission from the pope to form a new monastic order of Albertus Magnus, whose role would be to save books and manuscripts from the "simpleton" mobs. The order's formation was successful, but Leibowitz himself was caught in the act of "booklegging" and was martyred by simultaneous strangulation and burning.

Leibowitz himself never appears in the novel, but its three separate parts follow the affairs of his order at roughly six-century intervals into the future. In "Fiat Homo," relics of the Blessed Leibowitz are discovered by chance in a fallout shelter and are skillfully used by the abbot of his monastery to have the order's founder elevated to sainthood. In "Fiat Lux," the books so carefully preserved by Leibowitz's followers are at last read by a man capable of making some sense of them, as a scientific civilization begins once more to develop and North America takes a few steps toward reunification. In "Fiat Voluntas Tua," scientific progress makes a deadly full circle, back again to rockets, satellites, and nuclear war, and the then abbot of the monastery at Sanly Bowitts finds himself dealing once more with problems of radiation, civilian casualties, and euthanasia.

The novel is distinguished, in spite of its division into three parts, by many devices working for unity. One is that in each section an abbot of the same monastery is confronted with a problem and responds to it with a similar mixture of wisdom, guile, and principle; there is a strong sense that the role is greater and more permanent than the man. In the background, meanwhile, is the tradition of the Catholic Church, presented as immutable, whatever the changes of time and circumstance; any one of the three abbots could immediately have communicated with and understood any of the others, even if they had had to talk to one another in the Church language of Latin. A further connecting feature is the one character who appears in each section, the seemingly immortal Benjamin Eleazer, known also as "the Old Jew," or "the pilgrim." Finally, there are many objects which reappear, often unrecognized by the characters in the novel, from one section to another: the glass eyeball of the poet, the skull of Brother Francis, the carving of Brother Fingo. The first two sections end with the same image of buzzards circling: The suggestion that image contains of life arising out of death, if only by the activity of the carrion eaters, is spelled out and made clear also at the end of the novel. It is a challenge for the reader to relate the three sections of this novel to one another, yet the sections are scattered thickly with clues that make such a reading both possible and enjoyable.

The Characters

The most perplexing character of the novel must certainly be the immortal Benjamin Eleazer. Since he is called different names by different people, it is perhaps conceivable that the novel contains three similar but different old Jews, but the reader is much more strongly pointed to a mythological meaning for his character. He seems in fact to be the "Wandering Jew" of popular legend, who struck and mocked Jesus Christ on His way to crucifixion and was told by Christ: "I go, but you will wait till I return." Since then, the story goes, the Wandering Jew has traveled the earth waiting for the Second Coming of the Messiah. This legend is strongly suggested in one scene in which Benjamin looks into the face of a newcomer, only to say in disappointment "It's still not Him." A second legend is equally strongly suggested in the third section, when children shout at an old tramp, "he be old Lazar, same one 'ut the Lor' Hesus raise up." Could Benjamin Eleazar be the Lazarus of John 11, raised from the dead by Jesus—and then, in legend, not permitted to die again?

The answer is not clear. Yet the role of "the Old Jew" within the novel certainly is. His function is to present a kind of detachment from the follies of humanity, as one who has literally "seen it all before," and as one who realizes that the truly significant events are not scientific, or political, or historical, but are those concerned with the salvation that he himself cannot reach. In the end, in an irony characteristic of the book, it seems that the new Messiah comes without Benjamin's awareness. Nor is the Messiah male, or even immediately recognizable as human. In a minor theme of section three, an illiterate old tomato-woman has been pestering Abbot Zerchi to baptize the rudimentary head she has growing from her shoulder (a result of the mutation-inducing radiation of the previous war). Zerchi refuses, thinking that the head has no soul. As the bombs go off a second time, however, the head comes to life and starts to take over and rejuvenate the body of old Mrs. Grales, while the Grales head dies. Zerchi, dying himself, sees this as a new Immaculate Conception and recognizes the head as needing no baptism from him. Conceivably Benjamin, who is not far off, will recognize his savior in Rachel, if both somehow survive the second nuclear holocaust.

A Canticle for Leibowitz also contains an enormous gallery of mortal characters: the three abbots, Arkos, Paulo, and Zerchi; Thon Taddeo, who in section 2 is seen reinventing basic concepts of electricity with the doubtful aid of the Leibowitzian Memorabilia; Hongan Os, or Mad Bear, chief of the blood-drinking nomads of the future Midwest; and many servants or dignitaries of the Church. Perhaps the most endearing is Brother Francis, who, in section 1, discovers the fallout shelter, guided by Benjamin, and spends most of the rest of his life working on an illuminated copy of the (ironically valueless) Leibowitz-signed blueprint he finds there.

Themes and Meanings

There can be little doubt as to the central theme of *A Canticle for Leibowitz*. The novel is an inquiry into the value of secular knowledge as opposed to spiritual knowledge, and, on the face of it, secular knowledge, or science, is given a very low rating. It leads with seeming inevitability to war, nuclear weapons, and racial suicide. While human beings seem to have an innate propensity toward collecting knowledge of this kind, as dramatized by Thon Taddeo and his eventual collaborator Brother Kornhoer, this seems only a proof of their fallen nature. Even the smallest dabbling with science carries ominous overtones, as in the scene in which the Leibowitzian monks are preparing to use their newly invented generator to light an arc lamp—for which they have, significantly, moved a Crucifix. As Brother Kornhoer touches the contacts, a spark snaps, and he lets out the mild monastic oath of "Lucifer!" Lucifer, however, means "light-bearer" (which is what Kornhoer himself is); it is furthermore a name for the devil and, in section 3, is strongly linked with new nuclear explosions. Kornhoer, then, kind and honest man that he is, is on the road from Satan to nuclear destruction; not even electric lights, seemingly, are sinless.

This apparent blanket condemnation of science and secularity is tempered, however, by a surprising feature of this novel—namely, its unwaveringly comic tone. The comedy is often, indeed usually, wry. Poor Brother Francis devotes his life to gilding and decorating a copy of a blueprint of which he knows nothing; all of his attitudes to the past are furthermore ludicrously false, as all readers immediately recognize. He thinks, for example, having little knowledge of archaic English, that a "fallout shelter" is a shelter for fallouts, a thought which frightens him almost to death, since he further thinks that a fallout is a demoniac mix of incubus and salamander. He knows very little, what he knows is mostly wrong, and no reader can avoid regarding him with a mixture of condescension, amusement—and pity, for Francis is good-hearted and is killed in the end entirely blamelessly trying to stick to the letter of a totally unjust bargain. The reader's attitude toward him, however, is only a strengthened form of the attitude which one is encouraged to take toward most of the novel's characters.

They are seen as ignorant or deluded, rather than actively wicked; the sin in which all humanity appears involved cannot accordingly be taken entirely seriously. Finally, the book is, in the end, technically and in the old sense a "comedy," even a "divine comedy." It has a happy ending of sorts, through Rachel and through the escape of a human nucleus to the stars. One is asked to believe, with Benjamin, that grace and salvation are more important than any petty turmoil, however violent, on Earth.

One further theme of importance in the novel is that of change and stability. The long perspective of the novel's three parts throws up all kinds of change in language: English evolves into separate dialects, the monastery of Saint Leibowitz becomes the city of Sanly Bowitts, the venerable monk Boedullus, who discovers an "intercontinental launching pad," turns into Bo'dollos, the giant catfish who broods in the waters of the deep crater he created. Against this, though, the Latin liturgy of Catholicism remains unaltered. Similarly, the morals of the Church remain unmoved by circumstance. There is a strong irony in the care with which successive abbots stick to seemingly trivial rules. Behind this, though, is the thought that such rules are binding on eternity, and so are not lightly to be changed. English, politics, and progress, one might say, are set against the less attractive but stronger powers of Latin, religion, and faith.

Critical Context

A Canticle for Leibowitz falls into a well-known subgenre of science fiction, the "post-disaster" story, like John Wyndham's *The Chrysalids* (1955), Algis Budrys's *Some Will Not Die* (1961), and many more. The use of nuclear weapons to end World War II naturally set many writers speculating on the possibilities of future war, mutation, and rebirth.

Walter M. Miller, Jr.'s novel is remarkable, however, for the strength of its commitment to Catholicism and the thoroughness with which it insists that all knowledge not guided by faith is potentially disastrous, however well-meaning its possessors. It could even be said that *A Canticle for Leibowitz* is an example of antiscience fiction, though if this were claimed, one would also have to say that Miller shows more understanding of and sympathy for science than most proreligious and antiscientific writers, while the fans of science fiction had no hesitation in voting him the Hugo Award for best science-fiction novel in 1961.

Miller's work contains a symbolic depth which is not easily penetrated and is informed throughout by an unusual spirit of charity. Many cruel events take place in *A Canticle for Leibowitz*. None, however, viewed close up, is entirely without excuse or sympathy for its perpetrators. That is the danger of sin, Abbot Zerchi reflects: Even Satan may have been totally sincere. *A Canticle for Leibowitz* forces its readers to reconsider the basic distinction between good and evil.

Bibliography
Aldiss, Brian. Review of *A Canticle for Leibowitz*, by Walter M. Miller. *New Statesman* 126 (September 26, 1997): 65-66. Aldiss comments on the novel's longevity

and gives a brief synopsis of the plot. Although he admires Miller's "brilliant arguments" against the violence and devastation of war, he also notes that the "tedium of religious life was too much for me."

Garvey, John. "*A Canticle for Leibowitz*: A Eulogy for Walt Miller." *Commonweal* 123 (April 5, 1996): 7-8. Garvey praises Miller's book as a "fine, compassionate, and angry novel." He traces his friendship with Miller and comments on Miller's shift in belief from Catholicism to Buddhism. He also briefly discusses Miller's grief at the death of his wife Anne and his subsequent suicide some months later.

Roberson, William H., and Robert L. Battenfeld. *Walter M. Miller, Jr.: A Bio- Bibliography*. Westport, Conn.: Greenwood Press, 1992. A comprehensive reference guide that provides a record of Miller's work as well as criticism. Included in the bibliography section are annotations and content notes. Biographical and critical essays are also presented.

Seed, David. "Recycling the Texts of the Culture: Walter M. Miller's *A Canticle for Leibowitz*." *Extrapolation* 37 (Fall, 1996): 257-271. Seed explores the way meaning in the novel is transmitted and preserved, as with fragmentary historical texts. Seed argues that Miller balances the need for retention of history with the constant process of revision and distortion of history. For example, in the book, the linear progression of history ends in the redestruction of civilization in a second atomic war.

Sponsler, Claire. "Beyond the Ruins: The Geopolitics of Urban Decay and Cybernetic Play." *Science Fiction Studies* 20 (July, 1993): 251-265. Sponsler discusses cyberpunk's influence on contemporary science fiction. She cites several classic, postholocaust examples, including *A Canticle for Liebowitz*, that reveal the ruined landscape as a symbol of alienation and danger. She concludes that although cyberpunk's acceptance of environmental decay is troubling, it is valuable for its ushering in emerging technologies and its exploration of noncorporeal modes of being.

T. A. Shippey

CAPTAIN BLACKMAN

Author: John A. Williams (1925-   )
Type of plot: Social criticism
Time of plot: 1971, alternating with dream sequences that progress over the length of the novel from 1775 to 2001
Locale: Every theater of important American military action—from the Revolutionary War to the Vietnam War
First published: 1972

> *Principal characters:*
>> ABRAHAM BLACKMAN, the black titular hero, physically and intellectually prepossessing, a career soldier in the U.S. Army with the rank of captain; often of low rank in his historical military dream sequence incarnations
>> MIMOSA ROGERS, Blackman's tall and attractive black sweetheart, a career worker in the U.S. foreign service, who appears in various incarnations in most of Blackman's historical dream sequences
>> DAVID (LITTLE DAVID) HARRISON, small in stature, a black sergeant in Blackman's Vietnam squad and a staunch best friend in the Civil War and U.S. Cavalry sequences
>> BELMONT, the black radio operator in Blackman's Vietnam squad, whose grandfather was a celebrated World War I aviator
>> WOODCOCK, the black medic in Blackman's Vietnam squad, an officer and a close friend in the World War I dream sequence; representative of "the new black"
>> ROBERT DOCTOROW, a white soldier of Jewish descent in Blackman's Vietnam squad; an ideologically committed intellectual as well as a would-be writer, appearing in both the Vietnam and Spanish Civil War sequences—in the latter, as Blackman's close friend and fellow social worker-turned-volunteer-soldier
>> ISHMAEL WHITTMAN, Blackman's implacable, flaxen-haired, blue-eyed, white antagonist, always a superior officer, whether major (Vietnam), aide to General Schuyler (Revolutionary War), Union officer (Civil War), or aide to an anonymous aging World War II general

The Novel

The novel opens tensely and excitingly with Captain Blackman pinned down, perhaps fatally, by enemy AK-47 machine-gun fire in Vietnam. When his squad blunderingly attempts a rescue, Blackman heroically "thrust[s] his six-four frame skyward" to fire his own weapon and warn his men away from ambush, a gesture that is contradictory (since he has forbidden his own troops such actions) and, ironically, futile (since, as he notes much later in the book, several of the squad die anyway in a subsequent rocket attack back at base camp).

Wounded severely, if not mortally, Blackman finds himself "as in a dream" transported to revolutionary times in America, in an authorial parallel to Mark Twain's Connecticut Yankee in King Arthur's court. Williams surpasses Twain in historical scope, however, for Blackman, who has been a diligent student of black military history (even instituting a seminar on it in his company), as he fades in and out of consciousness, proceeds through virtually every significant military action involving Americans, from the Revolutionary War to a racial military apocalypse which occurs, with fitting symbolism, at the turn of the second millennium. Interwoven with and counterpointing the historically based fantasies is the fate of the modern-day Blackman, his sweetheart, friends, and enemies in 1971 Vietnam. With additional complexity, most of these persons are incorporated and fitted into the fantasies as well.

As with the author's *The Man Who Cried I Am* (1967), the chapters in this novel have been divided into main sections, each concluding with an important climax. Expressive of the author's criticism of white society's unjust treatment of blacks throughout history is that almost every high point, achievement, or joyous moment in the action is followed and counterbalanced by some harsh disappointment or deflation. For example, in the first six chapters that compose section 1, Blackman moves through the Revolutionary War, the War of 1812, and the Civil War, encountering (or nearly encountering) many famous historical figures (Crispus Attucks, George Washington, Andrew Jackson, Ulysses S. Grant) and rejoicing in his race's splendid deeds, which culminate in the black division's bravery at Petersburg, Virginia, which shames the white soldiers for their cowardice. Yet this triumph is undermined by false face-saving reports of the action, as the sheer number of blacks now armed in the Twenty-fifth Army Corps is negated by official refusal to use the unit.

In section 2, crossing the paths of General Custer, Teddy Roosevelt, and "Blackjack" Pershing, the seasoned Civil War veteran Blackman rises to sergeant major in the U.S. Cavalry, protecting settlers and battling Indians, then fights in the Spanish-American War, finally leaving the cavalry to become a machine gunner in the infantry, where, he perceptively foresees, the military future lies. The exuberant and humorous tone of section 1 gives way to somberness in section 2, as Blackman's boon companion in both sections, Little David Harrison, is murdered in a Western saloon by white soldiers disguised as cowboys. Equally dismal is the unjust and mass dishonorable discharge of 167 black soldiers of the Twenty-fifth Infantry, with which the section concludes.

The tone swings back to optimism (though always qualified, as by the unfair thwarting of Blackman's promotion) in section 3, which deals with black American regiments' almost universally acclaimed exploits in World War I, when they were seconded to the French army, which used them to fight rather than to unload cargo, as originally planned by white American commanders. The section concludes on two jubilant notes. First, Blackman miraculously survives, unscratched, a direct hit by an artillery shell, though all are killed around him (foreshadowing his survival of his

Vietnam wounds while also symbolizing his race's indestructibility). Second, with Woodcock (his companion and superior officer through much of the section), he strides victorious into Germany.

The mood of the second half of the novel oscillates from buoyant, to bleak, and back to exuberant. In section 4, dealing with the Spanish Civil War, Blackman, in the youngest and most idealistic of his incarnations (befitting this war, the author implies), at first is optimistic about his cause and the international and racial integration of his military unit, significantly named The Abraham Lincoln Brigade; but he is quickly disillusioned by the disintegration of the soldiers' concern for their own race's and nation's wounded, his discovery of the fear and impetus to survive that override ideology, and the defeat of his side. While section 5, which deals with World War II, opens on the cheerful note of Blackman demonstrating his superiority by scoring in the top grade of the army's placement test, it quickly gives way to the gloom of his sweetheart's infidelity, the loss of his chance for becoming an officer by being caught in one of the epidemic army-base race riots, his wounds from a mortar hit in the Solomon Islands (unlike the World War I artillery shell incident, Blackman does not escape unscathed this time), his forced duty as observer of the massacre of a rebel black unit in the Italian swamps outside Tombolo, and finally the official, racial blocking of his volunteer combat in the Battle of the Bulge.

Section 6, covering the Korean and Vietnam conflicts, gradually ascends from the convalescing of Blackman's Vietnam wounds (amputation of part of one leg, loss of a lung, and consequent lifelong respiratory troubles) to Blackman's optimistic decision to survive and revenge himself on Major Whittman (who had treacherously sent him into an ambush) and all he stands for, all paralleled by the accounts of his victories over Whittman in Korea (constantly demonstrating his superior skill), Vietnam (conducting his Black military history seminar), and a final prophetic dream sequence. Set in the year 2001, when Blackman will be seventy, this last episode, which closes the book, shows the novel's only unmitigated triumph, when Blackman and his race take over the U.S. military and its nuclear forces, conclusively gaining power over their white oppressors in the United States.

The Characters

The author is capable of supplying the odd detail that provides fully rounded characters—the manner in which Johnny Griot (in Blackman's Vietnam squad) carries his M-60 like a film soldier, the priapic talk and antics of Big Dick (a soldier in Blackman's segregated World War II barracks), or the way in which Woodcock wears the biggest afro in the company, possibly to compensate for his light skin. Yet, as with his preceding novels, Williams's main purposes in characterization are didactic and doctrinal: Characters symbolize or are spokespersons for (or both) social positions or points of view in a society that is, overall, racist. Characters are sympathetic toward the black cause, hostile, or somewhere in between. This symbolic or allegorical aspect produces a flattening effect even on the most fully realized and alive character in the book, the hero. For though animating details such as his shoe size (twelve) and prefer-

ence in wine (Meursault) are provided, what is important about the hero is his embodiment of the indomitable black spirit and the hope for leaders like him who will
give blacks the opportunity to live lives of the fullest potential. His allegorical significance is markedly suggested by his name, reinforced by the World War I version of
Mimosa's speculation about it, in the middle of the book: "She thought his name:
Abraham. A man you trust. Kind. Like a father?" Besides all these and other connota-
tions of the name "Abraham" by way of Abraham Lincoln, including Lincoln's reputation as the Great Emancipator (Blackman has fought in the Civil War, as well as in
the Abraham Lincoln Brigade in the Spanish Civil War), the biblical Abraham is also
evoked as another great spiritual leader—and warrior or soldier—in an episode not
often remembered, when to liberate his nephew Lot, he takes a small band of 318 to
fight against the armies of four kings. The last name of the hero, "Blackman," combines "black" and "man," to suggest that he embodies the spirit and yearning of all his
people. The character and name of Blackman's chief antagonist in most sequences are
similarly allegorical. The surname "Whittman" is distinctly a combination of "white"
and "man," which is added to his main physical features repeatedly mentioned
throughout the novel—his blond hair (the word "flaxen" is used twice) and blue eyes.
Whittman is thus archetypally and exaggeratedly white, corresponding to the extrem-
ism of his racist attitudes and views. Ishmael, Whittman's first name, which is revealed only toward the end of the novel, helps express both the sources of Whittman's
hostility and the irony of that hostility. Just as the novel's Whittman has been constantly made aware of Blackman's superior abilities (and thus the unfairness of the
latter's inferior rank), so the biblical Ishmael was made to feel inferior and second-
class by being cast off by Abraham's family, and just as Whittman's guilt generates
hostility, so the biblical Ishmaelites were renowned for their ferocity (and often antagonism to the Israelites, Abraham's descendants). Ironically, though, the biblical
Ishmael is Abraham's son, which recalls the current theory of some anthropologists
that humanity's earliest origins were in Africa—Whittman is Blackman's "son" in
this sense.

Not all whites in the novel are malevolent, by any means. For example, Robert
Doctorow admires Captain Blackman, has attended the black military history semi-
nars (enduring the initial animosity of the black auditors), and is sympathetic to the
blacks' cause. Likewise, his Spanish Civil War incarnation is Blackman's closest
friend—about whom Blackman thinks, after learning that Doctorow has been
wounded (just as his Vietnam incarnation has): "Somehow Doctorow's life was tied to
his and now that his friend lived, Blackman knew that he would, too." Doctorow's
Jewish heritage, pointedly referred to in the novel, links him not only with the biblical
Abraham but also with another minority that has been oppressed (a motif also to be
found in Williams's *The Man Who Cried I Am*).

Finally, a complexity in the author's characterization is created by Williams's technique of the multiple versions, and thus multiple perspectives, of the characters in different eras. The seasoned, professional veteran in the U.S. Cavalry in Indian territory
is different from the Spanish Civil War Blackman, who is a young, idealistic amateur.

Nor are these versions identical to the young, urban New York-born Blackman who enlists in the army after World War II to find a better way of life for himself. Similarly, Blackman's sweetheart, Mimosa, also varies: a young, uneducated slave in the Civil War; a wholesome, somewhat parochial small-town girl during World War I; a married yet adulterously adventurous woman during World War II, who finally jilts Blackman for a sailor; a poised, sophisticated career woman in the Vietnam episode, devoted and faithful to Blackman. Human beings are not merely allegorical symbols, the author seems to be suggesting, and are importantly affected by their environment.

Themes and Meanings

As with Williams's novels *Night Song* (1961) and *The Man Who Cried I Am*, the central themes of *Captain Blackman* are the oppression, injustices, and indignities suffered by blacks in a white society, and the necessity of revolt and retribution to overcome these. The function of the numerous surrealistic sections entitled "Cadences" and set off by italics, as well as of the sections entitled "Drumtaps," is to show that such oppression is conscious and intentional, not merely unthinkingly de facto. The "Cadences" sections usually introduce chapters or parts of the novel, and the structural placement of these conspiratorial planning sessions by white power brokers, as well as their content, implies how historical events have been directed from their inception, as does the military sense of the term "cadences," denoting the underlying measure or beat which directs the marching soldiers. The "Drumtaps" sections usually conclude chapters, in harmony with the military sense of this term, and quote actual military documents that substantiate white injustice.

A number of motifs are woven through the novel, in accord with the interweaving of historical sequences. One motif that expresses the overall racial theme is the recurrent, consciousness-robbing blow to the head that Blackman receives in the Revolutionary War, Civil War, and World War II episodes, and that is always delivered by whites (and usually associated with Whittman). Blackman's revolt and retribution during the Civil War for a clubbing he receives and for the raping of Mimosa is achieved by tracking down Whittman and his white mistress, binding them after clubbing Whittman, and then raping Whittman's woman before his eyes. The simile that compares Blackman's undressing of the woman to the cleaning of a rifle suggests the dimension in such acts of war or battle that Williams sees as necessary for blacks' ultimate self-realization.

Yet salvation in the novel comes from love as well as anger. The continual circling of the plot back to versions of Mimosa helps express how important, how central, she is to Blackman, as does his very last thought—of her—just before springing up to make his sacrifice for his Vietnam squad in the novel's opening. In each historical sequence prior to Vietnam their love has been thwarted or frustrated by the climate produced by white society. Only at the conclusion of the novel, when Blackman decides to make a concerted effort at revolutionary change, are the two united; and Blackman explicitly tells Mimosa that she is the key to not only his happiness, but also his success.

Critical Context

In some respects, John A. Williams's corpus is remarkably homogeneous. Many of the obsessive themes and concerns of his previous novels *Night Song* and *The Man Who Cried I Am* recur in *Captain Blackman*. The conspiratorial view of events in society can be found in the enigmatic death of Richie Stokes (Eagle) in *Night Song* and the apocalyptic King Alfred document in *The Man Who Cried I Am*. The need to strike back is glimpsed in a remark by Eagle about getting money to buy weapons (*Night Song*) and in protagonist Max Reddick's purchase of a veritable arsenal in *The Man Who Cried I Am*. Further, the centrality of love is expressed by the relationships between the main characters Keel and Della in *Night Song* and Max Reddick and Margrit in *The Man Who Cried I Am* (indeed, Max dies saying Margrit's name, similar to Blackman's utterance of Mimosa's before firing at the Vietnamese enemy).

Also, *Captain Blackman* is in some respects adumbrated by *The Man Who Cried I Am*. The apocalyptic plan for racial genocide of blacks in the latter is answered in the former by Blackman's counterconspiracy; Max Reddick's military experience and his vow to a Kennedy aide that he could recite to him a documented history of maltreatment of blacks in the military and elsewhere are elaborated in *Captain Blackman*.

This novel is, however, an advance over the others. While as socially conscious and didactic as Williams's preceding works, it is not marred by long, repeated speeches by characters about white injustice. Characters are portrayed more deftly, with more interest shown in them, and there is a greater mustering of vivid and memorable minor characters (such as Flag Sergeant Anselmas Plancianois, Old Man Flood, black frontier scout Brit Johnson, Lieutenant Buck Himes, Richard Boston, Gummidge, Linkey, and "The Gold Dust Twins"—Flash and Tisdale). Moreover, while humor is repeatedly referred to in *Night Song* and *The Man Who Cried I Am*, this novel genuinely possesses humor, in the form of Blackman's flatulent outburst used to comment on General Schuyler's revolutionary war racism, the historical joke about Blackman and Peter Salem not clearly hearing at Breed's Hill the now enshrined remark, "Don't fire until you see the whites of their eyes" ("What did he say?" "I think he said to shoot them in the eyes"), and the ingenious way that British soldiers escape death in the hopeless charge in the Battle of New Orleans.

Perhaps his most artistically finished work, *Captain Blackman* in its scope and marvelous interweaving of different times in a single story compares favorably with John Dos Passos's *U.S.A.* (which is recalled by the "Cadences" and "Drumtaps" sections) and with Tim O'Brien's complex, more-than-Vietnam novel, *Going After Cacciato* (1978), winner of the National Book Award.

Bibliography

Cash, Earl A. *John A. Williams: The Evolution of a Black Writer.* New York: Third Press, 1975. Among the early full-length studies of Williams, this volume provides a solid foundation for further study.

Current Biography 55 (October, 1994): 55-59. Profiles Williams's life and career as a novelist whose writings chronicle the struggles of blacks in a predominantly white society. Critical reaction to Williams's work is discussed, providing a valuable framework within which to evaluate *Captain Blackman*.

Draper, James P., ed. *Black Literature Criticism*. 3 vols. Detroit: Gale Research, 1992. Includes an extensive biographical profile of Williams and excerpts from criticism on his works.

Muller, Gilbert H. *John A. Williams*. Boston: Twayne, 1984. Muller provides a critical and interpretive study of Williams, with a close reading of his major works, a solid bibliography, and complete notes and references.

Smith, Virginia W. "Sorcery, Double-consciousness, and Warring Souls: An Intertextual Reading of *Middle Passage* and *Captain Blackman*." *African American Review* 30 (Winter, 1996): 659-674. Smith asserts that Charles Johnson's *Middle Passage* was influenced by *Captain Blackman*. She points out a number of similar themes between the novels, such as war and interracial and intraracial conflict.

Norman Prinsky

CATHERINE CARMIER

Author: Ernest J. Gaines (1933-   )
Type of plot: Historical realism
Time of plot: The early 1960's
Locale: The former slave quarter on a plantation in rural Louisiana
First published: 1964

> *Principal characters:*
> JACKSON BRADLEY, a young, educated black man determined to break
>   with his Louisiana heritage
> BROTHER, Jackson's friend from his youth
> RAOUL CARMIER, a proud Creole sharecropper, father to Catherine
> CATHERINE CARMIER, Raoul's oldest daughter and main support, who
>   falls in love with Jackson
> CHARLOTTE MOSES, Jackson's aunt and patroness
> DELLA (JOHNSON) CARMIER, Raoul's estranged wife
> LILLIAN CARMIER, Raoul's youngest daughter, alienated from her
>   parents
> MARY LOUISE, Jackson's former girlfriend
> MADAME BAYONNE, Jackson's confidante and former teacher

The Novel

There is a strong autobiographical strain in *Catherine Carmier*. Like the novel's protagonist, Jackson Bradley, Gaines moved to California to get a decent education and a stronger foothold on a better life than he could find at home, in the poor rural area around New Roads, Louisiana, which, fictionalized, is the novel's setting. He also faced a similar personal dilemma, whether to return home to teach or to seek a more promising life elsewhere.

By the time he finished *Catherine Carmier*, Gaines knew that writing was his life's work, but Jackson, his fictional counterpart, has no such vision of the future. He knows only that he cannot sacrifice himself to the seemingly futile task of trying to educate children whose futures he perceives as singularly bleak.

The novel is divided into three parts, each made up of several short chapters. Throughout, Gaines uses a third-person-omniscient narrative technique, but he primarily limits forays into the thoughts of characters to those of Jackson and his romantic nemesis, Catherine. The work also develops two distinct but parallel lines of action. The first, dealing with Jackson's decision to leave Louisiana, centers on Jackson and his Aunt Charlotte; the second focuses on the intense but ultimately ill-fated love affair of Jackson and Catherine.

Part 1 starts with the imminent arrival of Jackson on a bus from New Orleans. He is to be met by his old friend Brother, who is introduced in the opening scene. Catherine Carmier also waits for the same bus, which, coincidentally, carries home Lillian, her younger sister. Thus Jackson has a brief encounter with Catherine, revealing at the outset that there is a magnetism between them; however, they do not begin their affair until midway through the novel.

It quickly becomes obvious that Jackson cannot find his bearings in the world of his childhood. His relationships with Brother, his former girlfriend, Mary Louise, and especially his Aunt Charlotte, although polite, are strained. Jackson knows that he cannot relate to Charlotte's church circle, but he dreads telling her the truth, that he must leave again. At a party thrown to celebrate his return, he feels more like an unwanted intruder than the guest of honor. Only Madame Bayonne, his former teacher, senses that Jackson cannot stay, and she quickly becomes his mother confessor.

Jackson's alienation is paralleled by Lillian's in the dysfunctional Carmier household. Taught to hate what her mother represents, she, too, longs to leave. She stays on, however, held by complex motives, including sibling jealousy mingled with a desire to free her sister from her unhealthy dependence on Raoul.

In part 2, Jackson and Catherine begin their affair, and Jackson tells Charlotte the truth about his plans, a revelation that almost kills her. It is her culminating disappointment in Jackson, foreshadowed by earlier revelations that he had quit going to church and had begun drinking and playing cards. Only after the Reverend Armstrong shows her that her possessiveness is destructively selfish does Charlotte forgive Jackson.

Meanwhile, the furtive, mercurial relationship between Jackson and Catherine is sexually consummated in a few stolen hours of love. Jackson cannot openly woo Catherine because her father tolerates no rivals, not even those of his own kind, Creoles of mixed racial heritage. Torn between her father and Jackson, Catherine goes through a ritual of self-loathing, marked by complex love-hate feelings for Jackson. For a time, she manages to break off the relationship, incurring Jackson's frustration and anger, even his accusation that her relationship with her father is incestuous.

In the last part of the novel, the love affair takes its final, implacable turn. Lillian secretively sends Jackson a note telling him that Catherine will be at a dance in Bayonne and urging him to go there. Jackson finds Catherine and takes her from the dance back to her house. They plan to run off together, but Raoul, cued by two black informants paid by Raoul's Cajun enemies, rushes to stop them. He and Jackson fight, and Raoul is beaten. Ironically, however, in defeat Raoul triumphs over Jackson, for Catherine at last realizes that she cannot leave her father. Jackson is once more left alone, to search for a meaningful identity that to the novel's end eludes him.

The Characters

Jackson is a character cut adrift from his roots, seeking to find himself. His education has put his earlier life in a sophisticated perspective that distances him from his former friends, and he resists a sympathetic engagement in their community from fears of being dragged down into a miasma of despair. He plans to leave, to continue the search for self in a world that has already scarred him with some racial bitterness. Before leaving, however, he must confront two strong adversaries.

The first is Aunt Charlotte. She has spun a moral web from which Jefferson must free himself at the cost of seeming to be a selfish ingrate. She is his patroness, and although he loves her, he knows he must disappoint her. She is a simple, strong-willed woman with a deep, abiding faith, and it is her goodness and moral rectitude that make Jefferson feel like an apostate in his darker moments. She is also the first adversary in Jackson's personal rite of passage.

The other iron-willed character is Raoul Carmier, Jackson's rival for Catherine's love and loyalty. He represents a very different sort of challenge. A proud, unyielding man, Raoul is also an imposing blocking figure. He dominates his world, made narrow by his hatred for whites and blacks alike. He treats his wife, Della, like a household servant, elevating Catherine, his favorite, to surrogate spouse. For her part, Catherine is drawn to Raoul's strength, while he, from selfish designs, has cut her off from any sort of mature relationship with other men.

In some ways Raoul is admirable. He is a hard worker who, unlike most black sharecroppers, refuses to give up the struggle against the Cajuns who have slowly displaced the blacks on the plantation's land. To survive against them, he must work long hours, plowing his fields with mules because he is too poor to afford motorized equipment. Yet there is also something ruthless and sinister about Raoul, and by the end of the novel, it is intimated that he had killed Mark, Della's son, born from a brief extramarital liaison with a black man. Strangely, it is only when he reveals his guilt that Della is once more drawn to him.

Catherine's relationship with her father hints of latent incest, but it is never expressed in overt behavior. Like her mother, she has had an amatory adventure with another man, a Creole farmer, who fathered her child, Nelson. The farmer, however, was run off by Raoul, and until her affair with Jackson, she has had no other man in her life except her father. Despite her enchanting good looks and strong passion, she is content to be her father's companion. So imbued is she with loyalty to Raoul that her love for Jackson is accompanied by feelings of guilt, betrayal, and self-hatred. At the end, Jackson is simply unable to overcome these conflicting emotions and loses the enigmatic Catherine to Raoul.

Themes and Meanings

Catherine Carmier investigates complex human relationships that in part evolve from the particular time and place in which the novel is set. Of primary importance is the racial heritage of the principal characters, for it weighs heavily on the lives of all of them, and especially on their sense of belonging and commitment.

For Aunt Charlotte, custom bound, commitment is to be found in service to the community, to the folk, accomplished principally by bringing everyone into the greater family, represented by the church. It seems a time-honored maternal mission that accepts self-sacrifice as a communal virtue, and it is strong among persecuted peoples, who, as individuals, are powerless to shape their own destinies. For the black, rural Louisiana matron living in the early 1960's, that life could offer a quiet, abiding dignity, as it does for Charlotte.

For Jackson, however, it offers only a dead end. Keenly observant, Jackson sees that Aunt Charlotte's self-sacrifice leads only to the ignominy of an obscure grave. Furthermore, he knows that what little the blacks of the quarter possess is being lost to aggressive Cajun farmers, and he wants no role in that collapsing, suffocating world. He knows that he must seek hope and personal fulfillment elsewhere.

In its subtle way, *Catherine Carmier* offers a strong indictment of racism, which has an important negative impact on the lives of all the characters and is at least the indirect cause of much misery. Although it is an oppressive cross that Jackson bitterly bears, its chief victim is Raoul Carmier. He is a man wedged between the black and white races who, because he can identify with neither, despises both. His angry, erosive intolerance weighs heavily on his family and all but destroys it. His estrangement from Della had begun because she, a mulatto who does not share his hatred for blacks, had tried to befriend the inhabitants of the quarter, and she is finally driven by the resulting desperate loneliness into the brief affair with Mark's father. After Mark's birth, she becomes a nonperson in her own house, although she does give birth to another daughter, Lillian, who is Raoul's child.

Lillian becomes the unwanted, outcast child, sent away to be reared by relatives. Deprived of parental love, she is emotionally scarred with spite, even hatred, for both her mother and father. Raoul hardly acknowledges her, caring only for Catherine and the land. Lillian's resentment leads to her attempts to promote the relationship between Catherine and Jackson, which, she knows, can destroy her father. Bigotry is thus a poison that runs deep in the Carmier family well. It is also a fundamental and insidious fact of life for all the main characters in the novel, and at least the indirect source of most of their troubles.

Critical Context

Catherine Carmier was Gaines's first novel. Although it was not a critical success, it revealed the author's unquestioned skill as raconteur and established the fictional locus that he used in succeeding works. In all of his published fiction, Gaines has dealt with poor blacks in the same locale in rural Louisiana, a former slave quarter on a plantation near the town of Bayonne, places adapted from the author's boyhood home. Typically, for Gaines's black characters, that idyllic world is slowly but relentlessly disintegrating.

In *Catherine Carmier*, he also introduces central characters who appear in one guise or another in many of his later works. One is the fatherless son, alienated from his heritage and searching for a new identity and sense of self-worth. For example, Grant Wiggins, in *A Lesson Before Dying* (1993), is in many ways Jackson's resurrected *Doppelgänger*. A second major character is the childless black matron who, like Aunt Charlotte, serves both as the young man's foster parent and benefactress and as a strong defender of the community and the Christian faith. Her counterpart in *A Lesson Before Dying* is Tante Lou, who, like Charlotte, is both the protagonist's aunt and his moral conscience. In a somewhat different guise, she also appears as the title character of *The Autobiography of Miss Jane Pittman* (1971), Gaines's most famous work.

Although Gaines would later experiment with other narrative voices and techniques, in *Catherine Carmier* he uses a plain, direct, and simple style that he has never abandoned. The folk idiom and cadences of real speech, for which he has a finely tuned ear, he exploits extremely well, making his characters both intriguing and convincing. Apparent, too, is the author's sympathetic engagement in his characters' plights, his kind, fundamental empathy, a quality that marks all of his works and attenuates the bitterness of those who suffer from poverty entrenched in racial discrimination. With his very first novel, Gaines seemed to have learned that a gentle, cajoling humanism can be a much more powerful force than a strident, divisive, and message-heavy diatribe. In *Catherine Carmier* and succeeding novels, whether his characters are black, white, or racially mixed, he asks only that readers understand, not side with, applaud, or condemn them.

Bibliography
Babb, Valerie Melissa. *Ernest Gaines*. Boston: Twayne, 1991. A major critical introduction to Gaines, with a chronology and bibliography. Chapter 3, "Et in Arcadia Ego: The Declining Pastoral of *Catherine Carmier*," discusses the novel's pastoral elements, its parallels to Ivan Turgenev's *Ottsy i deti* (1862; *Fathers and Sons*, 1867), and the racial background of its characters, especially the Creole heritage and its influence on Raoul Carmier.
Bryant, Jerry H. "Ernest J. Gaines: Change, Growth, and History." *The Southern Review* 10 (1974): 851-864. Tracks Gaines's artistic growth between *Catherine Carmier* and *The Autobiography of Miss Jane Pittman*. Argues that the first novel, although it established Gaines's storytelling skills, was stylistically flawed.
Davis, Thadious. "Headlands and Quarters." *Callaloo* 7 (Spring/Summer, 1984): 1-13. Helpful for understanding the interplay between racial heritage and Gaines's fictional locale, especially in *Catherine Carmier*. Views the old slave quarters as "a microcosm of society" under a "strain of transition." Identifies three evolving patterns—encounters, replacements, and death juxtaposed with beauty—that "provide immediate access to the action, themes and symbols" of the novel.
Estes, David C. *Critical Reflections of the Fiction of Ernest J. Gaines*. Athens: University of Georgia Press, 1994. Written by various scholars, these critical essays examine a variety of themes found in specific works by Gaines. Includes "Creole and Singaleese: Disruptive Caste in *Catherine Carmier* and *A Gathering of Old Men*," by Joseph Griffin.
Gaines, Ernest. Interview by Bob Summer. *Publisher's Weekly* 240 (May 24, 1993): 62-63. Gaines discusses his background, career, and publications. In his brief mention of *Catherine Carmier*, he acknowledges his debt to Ivan Turgenev's *Fathers and Sons*.
Hicks, Jack. "To Make These Bones Live: History and Community in Ernest Gaines' Fiction." *Black American Literature Forum* 11, no. 1 (1977): 9-19. Places *Catherine Carmier* in the perspective of Gaines's work through 1971, arguing that the author became increasingly concerned with black history and the black commu-

nity. Includes a good thumbnail explication of the novel and argues that it is "in-formed by a view of personal and racial history as a prison, a tomb, from which Jackson Bradley can never quite escape."

Rowell, Charles H. "The Quarters: Ernest Gaines and the Sense of Place." *The Southern Review* 21 (Summer, 1985): 733-750. A helpful analysis of Gaines's use of place for thematic and symbolic purposes in *Catherine Carmier* and other works.

John W. Fiero

CAT'S CRADLE

Author: Kurt Vonnegut (1922-   )
Type of plot: Science-fiction fable
Time of plot: The early 1960's
Locale: Ilium, New York, and the Caribbean republic of San Lorenzo
First published: 1963

Principal characters:

>JOHN, surname unknown, the narrator of the novel
>DR. FELIX HOENIKKER, an atomic scientist and the creator of *ice-nine*
>NEWT HOENIKKER, a midget, his son
>ANGELA HOENIKKER, later MRS. HARRISON C. CONNERS, Newt's sister
>FRANKLIN HOENIKKER, Major General and Minister of Science and
>   Progress in San Lorenzo
>"PAPA" MONZANO, the dictatorial president of San Lorenzo
>LIONEL BOYD JOHNSON, BOKONON, philosopher and opponent of
>   Monzano

The Novel

Cat's Cradle is a remarkably discursive book, full of loose ends, unexplained events, and characters who appear in focus for a moment only to vanish without apology. It does center, however, on one single object: the sliver of *ice-nine* created by Dr. Felix Hoenikker and divided after his death by his three children, only to bring about the end of the world almost simultaneously with the end of the book.

In Vonnegut's theory, ice is only one of the many possible ways in which water can crystallize. If there were other ways, ice of different kinds would be created, including a kind which would melt not at 32 degrees Fahrenheit but at as high as one hundred degrees or 130 degrees—in the case of *ice-nine*, at 114.4 degrees. Furthermore a single seed of this ice, introduced to ordinary water in crystalline form, could act as a catalyst, instantly freezing the entire body of water with which it came in contact. The purpose of such an object (a Marine Corps general suggests) would be to eliminate mud, and allow the United States Marines to fight in relatively congenial circumstances. The side effects, however, would be that anyone who touched *ice-nine* would freeze solid instantly; while, furthermore, any crystal not scrupulously isolated could, in one single chain reaction, freeze solid all the oceans of Earth and bring life almost immediately to an end. The basic plot of *Cat's Cradle* is that a journalist researching a book on Dr. Hoenikker, "the father of the atom bomb," discovers that the latter has created *ice-nine*, finds himself (as a result of a chain of improbable coincidences) on a plane bound for the island republic of San Lorenzo with two of Hoenikker's children, there to meet the third, and in the process of becoming the president of San Lorenzo releases crystalline *ice-nine* into the ocean (in the form of the frozen body of a previous president), thus precipitating, literally, the end of the world. One very minor irony is that the book on which the journalist-narrator was working was to have been called *The Day the World Ended* and was supposed to have been about events on the day that the first atomic bomb was dropped on Hiroshima. In a sense, though, *Cat's Cradle* is about the day the world ended; yet this was caused by *ice-nine*, not atomic bombs, and it would conceivably not have happened at all if the narrator had not started research on the book that he never wrote.

Such ironies, coincidences, and elements of humor are best treated by the philosophy of Bokonon, to which the narrator is converted, and which he spends much of the novel expounding.

The Characters

It is entirely characteristic of the wry tone of *Cat's Cradle* that its two most important characters should either never appear or appear only on the last page, to utter a total of twenty-three words in direct speech. The two characters are antithetical. The one who never appears is Dr. Hoenikker, though he is pervasively present all through the book in the form of memories of him recounted by his children, associates, and enemies (he has no friends), all obsessively recorded by the narrator. These recollections present Hoenikker, in brief, as a monster of scientific curiosity and human detachment: He tips his wife thirty-eight cents for giving him coffee as he leaves to collect his Nobel Prize, having forgotten who she is. Only once, the reader is told, does he ever try to play with one of his children—the game is cat's cradle—and then he terrifies the child into flight. Hoenikker is in a way a devil of the modern mythological imagination: a scientist whose curiosity has entirely devoured his conscience. People, the reader is told, were not "his speciality."

Bokonon, by contrast, is an idealized guru-figure, present almost entirely by way of his recorded sayings. His philosophy defies summary but is in essence gentle, humorous, anarchic, and skeptical. To the Bokononist, only man is sacred; there is no such thing as coincidence; the Communist Party, the General Electric Company, the notion of a "Hoosier," all rank with all nation states as examples of the *granfalloon*, in other words, something that looks like a unit but is in fact completely meaningless "in terms of the ways God gets things done." Bokonon, one learns, is not by any means a nihilist. He is, however, no admirer of organization or of convention.

The action of *Cat's Cradle* could be described as a movement from Hoenikker to Bokonon, though this would be partly misleading in that the narrator is a Bokononist by the time he starts writing. This narrator, however, is the most prominent character actually present in *Cat's Cradle*; though once more, with typical paradox, he is relatively characterless, seeming at times to be a projection of the author (both were born in Indianapolis, both went to Cornell University), at others to represent the doubts and incredulity of the reader.

Around him, finally, there orbits a gallery of grotesques: Newt, Hoenikker's midget son; Angela, Newt's gigantic sister; "Papa" Monzano, the lunatic president of San Lorenzo, given to impaling opponents on hooks; H. Lowe Crosby, a bicycle manufacturer from Illinois; and many others. Logical connection between these characters is almost always rejected: They form (according to the philosophy of Bokonon) a *karass*—in other words, the opposite of a *granfalloon*, a team designed to do God's will without ever knowing exactly what they are doing or, in many cases, so much as recognizing one another. The oddity and eccentricity of his linked characters are very much part of Vonnegut's overall design.

Themes and Meanings

It could be argued that the meaning of *Cat's Cradle* is to prove that life is completely without meaning or purpose. Though the narrator, quoting Bokonon, often speaks of "God's will," the last advice he receives from Bokonon himself is to go to the top of the highest mountain in San Lorenzo, lie on his back, thumb his nose at God, and in that position touch his lips with a crystal of *ice-nine*—at which moment the narrator will freeze into an everlasting statue of rejection and defiance. This gesture sums up a feeling always present in the book, that in reality (as in fantasy) human aspirations are continually thwarted both by a seemingly hostile fate and also by the poor qualities of humanity itself, summed up in people such as Hoenikker—or indeed Crosby the bicycle manufacturer and his "Hoosier"-obsessed wife.

The theme of meaninglessness is further reinforced by the image of the cat's cradle. This was the game that Dr. Hoenikker was playing on the day that the atom bomb was dropped. It has also become to some anthropologists (Vonnegut studied anthropology at the University of Chicago) a model in miniature of human culture: Both are complex, absorbing, and passed on from one generation to another. Both also, it could be said, lack any immediate point except to entertain the people whose time they occupy. Newt Hoenikker, whose father tried to show him the game when he was six, takes this connection further. Cat's cradle, he says, like most aspects of human culture, is a cheat. There is no cat, and no cradle; it is all merely string. Adults tell children what to look for in what they call cat's cradle, and impressionable children believe them. Exactly the same is true, he says, of religion, marriage, human relationships, and most of what people teach one another. One might sum up by saying that Newt Hoenikker believes that human culture not only is a game but also is a very dull one, and that most human institutions grossly abuse the confidence which people place in them.

There is, however, a strongly affirmative streak also present in *Cat's Cradle*, to which many readers have responded—so much so, indeed, that certain Bokononist concepts have enjoyed some slight currency even outside the world of the book. If one sees the institutions of State and Church as being so much string, Bokonon suggests, there are still useful ways for people to live. They can love one another without sexual exploitation, for example, by the Bokononist rite of *boko-maru*, a sort of foot massage. They can form relationships with people of different races, ages, sexes, and incomes, as it were, against the grain of organized society. They can tell one another stories or write calypsos. They could accomplish much, in short—if it were not for *ice-nine*.

Ice-nine is a clearly symbolic concept. It destroys the world. It is the product of Dr. Felix Hoenikker. It also sprang from the desire of a general to abolish mud. Mud, though, is a traditional image of humanity—though English Bibles prefer the more dignified word "clay." Nevertheless, when Dr. Schlicter von Koenigswald (once a physician in Auschwitz, with centuries of kind deeds to do to balance his account) offers the last rites of Bokonon to the dying dictator Monzano, he begins with the words "God made mud." In the Bokononist liturgy, the "mud" then sits up and appreciates its moment of consciousness before lying down again, content, having rehearsed a little playlet of the good life and death. The equation is absolutely clear. Humanity is only mud, but harmless mud, and mud with some potential. *Ice-nine* destroys mud, but at the cost of destroying everything else as well. *Ice-nine* becomes, then, an image of destructive science, weapons technology, contempt for humanity, and perhaps above all of the over-organization and wholly false complexity which Vonnegut sees in much of his own society. Perhaps the most telling point in *Cat's Cradle* is Vonnegut's skillful connection of such impossible figures as Dr. Hoenikker with perfectly recognizable and mildly comic ones such as H. Lowe Crosby. Both share the same intellectual errors. The spirit of *ice-nine* is real.

Critical Context

Cat's Cradle has faint connections, through places and named characters, with Vonnegut's earlier works *Player Piano* (1952) and *The Sirens of Titan* (1959). In *Cat's Cradle*, however, Vonnegut may be seen approaching the theme which obsessed him from 1945 onward, but which he was only to articulate freely in *Slaughterhouse-Five* (1969). This is his own gruesome experience as a prisoner of war caught in the firebombing of Dresden, one of the most appalling, if least intended, atrocities of this or any century. It could be said that the question which Vonnegut had to ask again and again was simply: How do people manage to do such things to one another? The answer is a complex mixture of carelessness, thoughtlessness, and a channeled curiosity—a mixture that contains surprisingly little in the way of deliberate cruelty.

Cat's Cradle is thus one of many works written in direct response to the problem of human behavior as revealed in World War II: One could compare, for example, William Golding's *Lord of the Flies* (1954) or Walter M. Miller's *A Canticle for Leibowitz* (1960). The special achievement of *Cat's Cradle*, however, lies in its style. The arch flippancy of Vonnegut's writing, with its short paragraphs, ambiguous sayings, snippets of nursery rhyme, and rejection of all intellectualizing, had a powerful effect on the youth movement of the late 1960's, in which Vonnegut had a considerable following. Vonnegut's novels have, however, withstood the test of time much better than have those of many 1960's gurus. There are two main reasons for this enduring appeal: an evident sincerity in attempting to get to the bottom of real events, both personal and historical, and a concern with intellectual issues that remains perfectly perceptible beneath a surface of fantasy, detachment, and humor.

Bibliography

Boon, Kevin, A. *Chaos Theory and the Interpretation of Literary Texts: The Case of Kurt Vonnegut*. Lewiston, N.Y.: Edwin Mellen Press, 1997. Extending the scientific theory of chaos to literary criticism, Boon uses words and phrases such as "strange attractors," "fractals," and the "micro/macro connection" to describe certain aspects of Vonnegut's prose. A somewhat offbeat but astute analysis of Vonnegut's work.

Broer, Lawrence. *Sanity Plea: Schizophrenia in the Novels of Kurt Vonnegut.* Ann Arbor, Mich.: UMI Research Press, 1989. Broer offers an in-depth analysis of individual novels by Vonnegut, including *Cat's Cradle.* His study gives the reader a unique perspective on the common themes that run throughout Vonnegut's work.

Mustazza, Leonard, ed. *The Critical Response to Kurt Vonnegut.* Westport, Conn.: Greenwood Press, 1994. Critical essays present a detailed study of Vonnegut's various works, including *Cat's Cradle.* A biographical introduction as well as a selected bibliography make this a valuable resource.

Reed, Peter J., and Mark Leeds, eds. *The Vonnegut Chronicles.* Westport, Conn.: Greenwood Press, 1996. Presenting a series of interviews and critical essays on Vonnegut's writing, this volume offers a broad variety of opinions and observations from scholars and journalists. A good source of information that helps the reader see more clearly the unique characteristics of individual novels against the wider context of Vonnegut's work.

Vonnegut, Kurt, Jr. *Fates Worse than Death: An Autobiographical Collage.* New York: G. P. Putnam's Sons, 1991. A revealing look at Vonnegut's life. This collection of Vonnegut's essays examines both the personal issues and social events that shaped his distinctive writing style as well as his view of modern culture. Vonnegut offers a rare glimpse of his heart in this intimate self-portrait.

T. A. Shippey

CAT'S EYE

Author: Margaret Atwood (1939-   )
Type of plot: Didactic
Time of plot: The 1940's to the 1980's
Locale: Toronto, Canada
First published: 1988

> *Principal characters:*
> ELAINE RISLEY, a young girl, later an artist
> CORDELIA, the leader of Elaine's childhood circle of friends
> STEPHEN, Elaine's older brother, later a brilliant physicist
> GRACE SMEATH, another of Elaine's childhood friends
> CAROL CAMPBELL, the third of Elaine's friends
> JON, Elaine's first husband
> JOSEF HRBIK, Elaine's art teacher and first lover

The Novel

    Cat's Eye is the deeply disturbing story of a young girl whose life is scarred by the cruel treatment she receives at the hands of her friends. The novel follows the girl from childhood into middle age, tracing the effects of her early experiences on her adult life.

    Atwood moves her narrative back and forth through time to tell Elaine's story, intercutting the years of the girl's troubled childhood with scenes from her later life. As a very young child, Elaine lives in relative isolation with her parents and her brother, Stephen, as their father pursues entomological research in the Canadian wilderness. When she is eight, the family settles in Toronto, and Elaine finds herself interacting for the first time with girls her own age. Her encounters with her first two friends, Grace Smeath and Carol Campbell, are marked by her confusion over social customs she has yet to learn and her desperate desire to fit in. When a third girl, Cordelia, joins the group, she quickly becomes the foursome's leader and soon begins an escalating campaign of criticism and cruelty toward Elaine, whose lack of self-assurance Cordelia has sensed from the start.

    Under the guise of "improving" their friend, Cordelia, Grace, and Carol humiliate and belittle Elaine, devising punishments and elaborate rules for her to follow. The effect of this treatment on Elaine is devastating; she begins to withdraw into deep depression and self-hatred, undergoing bouts of illness, fainting spells, and even self-mutilation before the situation at last reaches a crisis point. When Cordelia throws Elaine's hat into a frozen ravine and orders the girl to retrieve it, Elaine falls through the ice and, in a state of delirium, imagines that the Virgin Mary has descended from the bridge overhead to help her. After recovering from the episode, she returns to school and at last defies Cordelia, breaking off her relationship with all three girls.

When she encounters Cordelia again two years later, Elaine has repressed all memory of the events, and the two girls become friends throughout their years in high school. Yet while Elaine does well in school and later wins a university scholarship, Cordelia begins an emotional slide that starts with declining grades and ends in a breakdown. Elaine has developed a sharp-tongued, brittle exterior that keeps her own inner lack of self-esteem at bay, and her impatience with what she sees as Cordelia's weakness causes her to pull away from her friend.

In college, Elaine is encouraged in her work by her drawing teacher, Josef Hrbik, a Hungarian immigrant with whom she is soon having an affair. At the same time, she also meets and begins an affair with Jon, whom she eventually marries when she becomes pregnant with his child. After the birth of their daughter, Elaine joins a group of women artists whose first exhibit helps establish her reputation as a painter. Her work is dominated by images from her childhood, although she continues to repress memories of her friends' cruelty to her. She sees Cordelia twice over the years, the second time in a sanatorium to which Cordelia has been committed after a mental collapse and suicide attempt.

Elaine and Jon separate, and she moves to Vancouver, where she meets and marries Ben, with whom she has a second daughter. Her brother, Stephen, who has become an eminent physicist, is killed by terrorists during an airplane hijacking, and both her parents die several years later. In the weeks prior to her mother's death, while helping her sort through family odds and ends, Elaine comes across a blue cat's-eye marble that she had clutched in her pocket long ago during Cordelia's childhood attacks, and her past experience comes flooding back to her.

In her forties, Elaine returns to Toronto for a retrospective of her work, but it is Cordelia who dominates her thoughts. Half expecting to see her old friend, she is distracted throughout her show's opening and later decides to revisit several scenes from her childhood. While standing at the ravine that had been the turning point in their relationship, Elaine comes to terms with the knowledge that it had been Cordelia's own fears and insecurities that had led to her cruel behavior. She is left with the regret that she has been denied the ability to form close friendships and will always struggle to maintain a sense of self-worth.

The Characters

At the heart of *Cat's Eye*'s harrowing story of childhood cruelty are the contrasting personalities of Elaine and Cordelia. The initial differences between the two girls are great, with Elaine's awkwardness and lack of self-confidence making her the perfect foil for her more sophisticated friend. Having spent her earliest years largely in isolation with her family, Elaine is thrown into her first friendships with no knowledge of the traditional behavior expected of young girls, and she finds herself ill-prepared for the rigid codes and values she is expected by her peers to embrace. Elaine's natural desire for friends is intensified by her fear of not fitting in, a fear that Cordelia will seize upon and exploit.

For her own part, Cordelia is not at all the self-assured individual her new friends assume her to be. As the youngest of three daughters, she is herself excluded and frequently ridiculed by her older sisters, who subject her to a milder version of the treatment she will visit so forcibly on Elaine. It seems clear that the source of Cordelia's own insecurities and her family's damaging psychological dynamic is the girls' cold, critical father, whose love and approval Cordelia is never able to win.

As is often the case among children, Cordelia acts out among her peers a more primitive version of the treatment to which she is subjected at home, casting Elaine as the victim and herself in the role of harshly critical authority figure. For Elaine, whose family is loving and warm, this treatment is shattering, and she comes to believe that she not only must endure it but is deserving of it as well. It is an internalized lesson that will continue to haunt her throughout her adult life as she experiences periods of crippling depression and finds herself wary of friendships with other women. Cordelia, too, is permanently damaged by her status as her family's least-loved child and, unlike Elaine, is never able to achieve even a functional level of adult behavior.

Although the two girls are the book's central focus, Atwood has also created several memorable secondary characters. Through Elaine's eyes, the reader is given intriguing glimpses of her brilliant brother, Stephen, with whom she has a close relationship that fades as the two enter adulthood. Also vividly drawn is Grace Smeath's mother, a humorless religious fanatic who knows of the behavior to which Elaine is subjected and believes it is her punishment from God. As an adult, much of Elaine's rage will focus on Mrs. Smeath, who becomes her subject in a controversial series of paintings. Particularly chilling are Grace and Carol, two otherwise unremarkable girls who are quick to become Cordelia's willing allies in Elaine's torment.

Themes and Meanings

The subject Atwood has chosen to tackle in *Cat's Eye* is a difficult one: the specific nature and source of the cruelty sometimes visited upon young girls by one another. In Atwood's view, there is a distinctive type of "feminine" cruelty that arises directly from the largely powerless position of women within society. At the time in which the early part of the novel is set, a postwar return to peacetime status dictated that women restrict themselves to traditional roles centered on home and family. For Elaine, reared outside these social restrictions by a mother who is less bound by conventional thinking than other women, what begins as a socializing process quickly degenerates into a daily barrage of critical comments on her clothes, appearance, speech, posture, and general attitude. Elaine does not fit in, and under the guise of helping her, her friends come close to destroying her in their ruthless efforts to force her to conform. That she will never be able to satisfy the ever-changing standards they set for her is a crucial part of their destructive game, but strict adherence to accepted social roles is still the basis for their criticisms.

Seen in a larger context, however, it becomes clear that these messages of expected social behavior that the other girls have already internalized are coming from the adult world. Cordelia's father, in particular, has left her feeling unloved and insecure, and her response to her own unhappiness is to turn it upon someone else. Grace Smeath, too, has absorbed her mother's self-righteousness and believes Elaine to be deserving of the treatment she receives. For Elaine, the lasting result of her experience is a nearly unshakable sense of inadequacy and a deep mistrust of other women, both qualities that can only perpetuate a position of relative powerlessness.

Critical Context

Margaret Atwood is deeply concerned with examining the lives of women and how the society in which they live shapes both their experience and their self-perception. In *Surfacing* (1972), a young woman suffering from a mental breakdown retreats into the wilderness in an attempt to come to terms with herself and her place in the world. The terrifying future that Atwood imagines in *The Handmaid's Tale* (1985) finds women at the mercy of a religious dictatorship that has decreed they be either wives or childbearing servants to the wealthy. Like *Cat's Eye*, *The Robber Bride* (1993) centers on a group of female friends, one of whom uses and victimizes the others.

Cat's Eye fits easily within the context of the ongoing themes in its author's work, approaching the topics of women's relationships to themselves and to one another with particularly disturbing results. Atwood is unafraid to confront the unsettling issue of women's cruelty to one another and the existing social structure that brings this destructive dynamic into play. Although extreme in the details of Elaine's experience, the general sense of that to which she is subjected—the criticism and pressure to conform to society's standards for female behavior—is acted out in many women's lives on an almost daily basis.

Bibliography

Bouson, J. Brooks. *Brutal Choreographies: Oppositional Strategies and Narrative Design in the Novels of Margaret Atwood*. Amherst: University of Massachusetts Press, 1993. Uses feminist and psychoanalytic theories to examine Atwood's work.

Cooke, Nathalie. *Margaret Atwood: A Biography*. Toronto: ECW Press, 1998. The first full-length biography of Atwood. Examines the influences shaping her life and work.

Henger, Shannon. *Margaret Atwood's Power: Mirrors, Reflections, and Images in Select Fiction and Poetry*. Toronto: Second Story Press, 1993. Focuses on the theme of power within social structures in Atwood's work.

Howells, Coral Ann. *Margaret Atwood*. Modern Novelists Series. New York: St. Martin's Press, 1996. A critical and biographical study; includes a chapter on *Cat's Eye*.

Ingersoll, Earl G., ed. *Margaret Atwood: Conversations*. Princeton, N.J.: Ontario Review, 1990. A collection of interviews with Atwood from 1972 to 1989.

McCombs, Judith, and Carole L. Palmer. *Margaret Atwood: A Reference Guide*. Boston: G. K. Hall, 1991. Contains a bibliography and a guide to criticism and writings on Atwood's work.

Janet Lorenz

THE CENTAUR

Author: John Updike (1932-   )
Type of plot: Mythic novel
Time of plot: Monday morning to Thursday morning during the second week of
    January, 1947
Locale: Olinger, Pennsylvania, and a farm outside Olinger near Firetown
First published: 1963

> *Principal characters:*
> GEORGE CALDWELL (CHIRON), a general science teacher at Olinger
>   High School
> PETER CALDWELL (PROMETHEUS), his son and the artist who tells the
>   story
> CASSIE CALDWELL (CERES), George's wife
> POP CRAMER (KRONOS), Cassie's father
> AL HUMMEL (HEPHAESTUS), a local garageman
> LOUIS M. ZIMMERMAN (ZEUS), the Olinger High School principal
> DOC APPLETON (APOLLO), a local doctor
> VERA HUMMEL (VENUS), Al's wife and the girls' gym teacher at
>   Olinger High School

The Novel

In an interview in the *Paris Review*, John Updike confessed that *The Centaur* seemed his truest and liveliest book, a book which he was prompted to write in order to publicize the myth of Chiron, one of the few instances of self-sacrifice from the classical world. The novel contains an interesting, if at times rather disturbing, mixture of classical figures amid a realistic setting. The purpose of the actual presence of the mythological figures was to expand the significance of Peter Caldwell's nostalgia and to counterpoint an ideal with a drab level of reality.

The story is told by Peter Caldwell, who describes himself as a mediocre abstract expressionist painter. In the course of the novel, Peter, who lives in Greenwich Village with his black girlfriend, re-creates a three-day period immediately after World War II, when he was a teenager. Through his recollection, Peter is able to understand his father, George, with a clarity denied him as a younger man, and he recognizes the self-sacrifice that his father made in order to enable his son to pursue his career as an artist.

The novel opens abruptly within the mode of the mythological by introducing Chiron—disguised as a high school science teacher—who has been wounded in the ankle by an arrow in accordance with the Greek myth. He limps out of the classroom on his remaining three hooves to Al Hummel's garage to have the arrow removed. Chiron returns to his classroom by way of the school basement to avoid the principal, who hectors him throughout the novel. In keeping with the mythological setting of the first chapter, the centaur recalls meeting Al Hummel's wife, Vera, in the guise of Venus, once before in the school basement. The image of her emerging from the steam of the girls' locker room suggests both her desire for and rejection of the half-man, half-stallion. Back upstairs, Chiron finds that Louis M. Zimmerman, the principal, has taken over his class in his absence. Chiron concludes this chapter by delivering a lecture on the origins of the universe to his increasingly restive class.

The second chapter, written entirely in realistic terms, begins the action of the plot by having Peter remember a wintry morning when he was fifteen years old: He overhears a conversation between his parents in which George/Chiron confesses his fear that he has cancer. Peter wonders about disease and mortality and his psoriasis, the curse that he hides from others. Peter and his father leave for school in their converted Buick hearse, stopping along the way to pick up a hitchhiker, who makes them late when George accedes to his demands to be driven to a place that is out of their way.

The remainder of the narrative traces, for the most part, the adventures of Peter and his father as they visit the doctor's office for an examination and a set of X rays, attend a high school swimming meet, spend the night in a cheap hotel after their car fails to start, go to a high school basketball game the next evening, get stuck in the snow and spend the night with the Hummels, and finally return home, where they discover that the X rays did not reveal any disease. The next morning, Peter, sick with a fever and a cold, watches as his father once more returns to his teaching duties at the high school. The novel is brought full circle when in the final chapter the narrative returns to the mythological setting and Chiron accepts his own death, although he has been given a momentary reprieve.

The novel is one of discovery for Peter, who in recalling this brief three days of his adolescence has the opportunity to reflect on the life that he took for granted and on the people whom he also accepted without reflection. The novel is not, however, elegiac in the vein of Updike's next extended fiction, *Of the Farm* (1965), the third of the Olinger novels. In the epilogue to *The Centaur,* Zeus expresses his love for his old friend Chiron by setting him among the stars as the constellation Sagittarius, who still assists in regulating human destinies, in spite of the fact, Updike notes, that in these later days few look to the heavens and fewer still are students of the stars.

The Characters

That Updike wants his readers to make the comparisons between his characters and their mythological analogues is apparent by the presence of the mythological index which, at his wife's suggestion, he appended to the novel. Matching up various figures of the fiction with their ancient prototypes is not merely a parlor game, however, but yields a broadening significance to the fictional characters of the novel. To see George Caldwell as Chiron, Peter as Prometheus, Al Hummel as Hephaestus, and his wife, Vera, as Venus, elevates the work and ties it to the classical literary tradition of Western civilization. Such a fictional device, perhaps better called a trope, also figures in Updike's other novels, especially *The Poorhouse Fair* (1959), *Couples* (1968), and the Rabbit Angstrom books.

Updike's pantheon is fairly widespread in *The Centaur*. George Caldwell is Chiron, the centaur, who is sacrificed in order to protect the fire-bringer and legendary creator/artist, Prometheus, here associated with George's son, Peter, the painter. George's wife, Cassie, the keeper of the home fire and the one character linked to the land and fertility not only through her son, Peter, but also through her savage attachment to the farm that she coerced her husband to buy, is Ceres. Vera and Al Hummel make a good Venus and Hephaestus. The goddess of love and of the erotic, Venus seeks her fulfillment through flirtations at the basketball game and as the object of Chiron's lust and of George's wishful thinking. She is also responsible for arousing Peter's sense of manhood during their stay with the Hummels after the storm. Al is the owner of the local garage, and, through his prowess as a mechanic, he brings the mythical blacksmith up to date. Zimmerman, the principal of the high school, is Zeus, who, as an authority figure, reprimands George as Zeus did Chiron and provides a force against which George can rebel. Doc Appleton is Apollo but is also Asclepius, and Pop Kramer, Peter's maternal grandfather, becomes associated with Kronos through his connections with clocks and time.

Although most of the main characters relate to their mythological models in a number of ways, the minor figures are usually linked in only a single way. A female teacher at the high school who sticks yellow pencils in her hair recalls Medusa, and the janitor, Heller, who inhabits the Hades of the basement, at one point finds some seeds and asks the Caldwells, father and son, how the seeds came to be there, which recalls the story of Persephone. Such notations have been seen by some of Updike's critics as a bit overingenious, symptomatic of the book's tilt toward cleverness rather than profundity.

The characterizations and the links with mythology were drawn by Updike from a variety of sources, including Josephine Preston Peabody's *Old Greek Folks Stories Told Anew* (1897) and Herbert J. Rose's *A Handbook of Greek Mythology* (1928). He also made ample use of Hesiod, both *The Works and Days* (c. 700 B.C.E.) and *Theogony* (c. 700 B.C.E.), and of Pliny the Elder's *Natural History* (first century C.E.). Finally, whether or not the reader makes the various mythic connections, the presence of such background material immeasurably enriches an already complex and profound story.

Themes and Meanings

The central theme of the book is Peter's discovery of the meaning behind his father's sacrifice, especially in a world where the very idea of sacrifice holds no religious or cultural relevance. The teacher/father has relinquished his own ambitions for the good of the artist/son; the intellect has prepared the way for the integrating effects of the artist. Yet, and it is a large proviso, Peter, who now is guardian of the imagination, has not been able to profit from his inheritance. It is in the fiction which unfolds that Peter rummages back through his memories, in search of a new starting point for the creation of a meaningful future for himself.

It is at this juncture that the Chiron myth clearly becomes of value. In the original story, Chiron, accidentally wounded by a poisoned arrow, gives up his immortality for the sake of Prometheus, while Prometheus provides Chiron with an opportunity to escape from an eternity of pain. Stripped of this mythological base, *The Centaur* revolves on the ancient notion that the old order must give way to a new one—in this case, that the scientific man must succumb to the liberating imagination of the artist. Peter's dilemma is that he cannot justify his father's sacrifice merely through his works. He has already admitted to being a second-rate painter, but he can atone for his own guilt by a combination of work and faith, a faith that is present in the portrait of George Caldwell presented in the thoughts of his son. In some ways, Peter's task is to recall or recapture the real teaching of his father through nostalgia, through memory.

Perhaps it will be through the tension exerted between work and faith, between past and present, between imagination and intellect that Peter will at last be able to fashion a life without guilt over his father, a life that allows a mature growth toward personal meaning. The novel as reminiscence provides Peter with the first step toward a full maturity, however belated, in which he can truly begin the process of refashioning himself.

Critical Context

The Centaur, Updike's third novel, won for him not only the National Book Award for 1964 but also serious consideration as a writer of important fiction. Despite the quibbling of the daily reviewers over what they perceived as the book's excessive ingeniousness and its confusing interweaving of classical and realistic elements, its critical stature has risen steadily with Updike's reputation. The book has been accorded various readings: Christian, mythological, pastoral, mock-epic, antipastoral. Critics have agonized over its mixed form or praised its stylistic inventiveness. Whatever the critical view of the novel, however, it is now perceived as providing Updike with a grounding for much of his later fiction. Echoes of stylistic experimentation as well as mythic overtones have characterized his work since the early 1960's.

If Updike is correct in believing that his generation was not reared on the Bible and therefore turned to the Greek stories as the source of a more meaningful past, perhaps in *The Centaur* he not only has fashioned a novel but also has opened a fruitful new way to explore the complexity and tenuousness of modern life and discovered a unique link between past and present, providing a ground for meaning that is free from the inhibiting effects of religious and political connections.

Bibliography

McTavish, John. "John Updike and the Funny Theologian." *Theology Today* 48 (January, 1992): 413-425. McTavish argues that the influence of Karl Barth is especially apparent in *Rabbit Run, The Centaur,* and *On the Farm.* In the case of *The Centaur,* McTavish buttresses his argument by citing the epigraph from Barth that announces the novel's theme, the covenant of grace.

Schiff, James A. *John Updike Revisited.* New York: Twayne, 1998. In this readable, up-to-date overview, Schiff endeavors to understand Updike's entire body of work, putting individual works in context for the reader. Schiff provides commentary on works that have largely been ignored by the public as well as books that have received little critical attention. Includes an analysis of *The Centaur*.

Sethuraman, Ramchandran. "Updike's *The Centaur*: On Aphanisis, Gaze, Eyes, and the Death Drive." *Literature and Psychology* 39 (Fall, 1993): 38-65. Using the principles of Jacques Lacan, Sethuraman examines the Oedipal motivations of the main characters, who seem to be attracted to death wishes. The conflict between George, the father, and Peter, the son, show that both have failed to incorporate the Other into their personalities.

Updike, John, and James Plath, ed. *Conversations with John Updike*. Jackson: University Press of Mississippi, 1994. A collection of interviews given by Updike between 1959 and 1993. A revealing portrait of Updike's background and personality; his views on life, sex, politics, and religion; and his evolution as a writer.

Charles L. P. Silet

THE CHANEYSVILLE INCIDENT

Author: David Bradley (1950-   )
Type of plot: Historical neorealism
Time of plot: The late 1970's, 1930-1965, and precolonial days to the twentieth
  century
Locale: Philadelphia, the mountains of central Pennsylvania, and some areas south-
  ward, near Virginia and Maryland
First published: 1981

> *Principal characters:*
>   JOHN WASHINGTON, the narrator/protagonist, a professor of history and
>   a historical scholar
>   MOSES WASHINGTON, his father
>   JUDITH POWELL, his best friend and the woman with whom he is living
>   "UNCLE" JOSH (SNAKEBELLY) WHITE and
>   "OLD" JACK CRAWLEY, close friends of Moses Washington and
>   surrogate fathers to John Washington

The Novel

John Washington, the protagonist of Bradley's *The Chaneysville Incident*, is a successful young historian living in Philadelphia and teaching at a large urban university
in that city. Adept at his profession and comfortable in the academic world, he seems
to be almost a paragon of achievement, an exemplar of the kind of life an industrious,
intelligent black man might lead in the latter part of the twentieth century in the
United States. Still, Washington is at a critical point in his life. He is becoming increasingly aware of some compelling questions about himself and his past—questions that he knows he has been avoiding—and he realizes that he is on the threshold
of psychic chaos which can only be controlled if he stops suppressing them. The narrative thread of the novel involves Washington's efforts to discover the meaning of his
past, to understand the significance of his "home ground," and to establish a spiritual
foundation that will permit another person to share his existence. The course of the
novel takes Washington back toward his origins in the wilderness of the Pennsylvania
mountain country, west of Philadelphia, and concurrently, back through time in an examination of records, documents, personal and oral histories, and geographical relics.
His search for what he suspects in the "true" self which he has kept hidden beneath the
veneer of the competent academic leads him to a series of discoveries which enable
him to grow toward a kind of maturity of completeness. The goal of his dual journey
in space and time is to become a man who is capable of using every aspect of himself
without the need to conceal weakness, to suppress emotion, or to maintain a hard edge
of coldness to resist the harder edge of hate.

As the novel begins, Washington is summoned back into the country of his youth
by the urgent message that "Old" Jack Crawley, one of the three men who reared him,

and the only one still living, is near death in a cabin close to his old hometown. Jack Crawley and "Uncle" Josh (Snakebelly) White were his father's best friends, and Washington does not feel ready to consider all the implications of the lives of these three men. Nevertheless, he knows that he cannot deny the claim of love and kinship that Jack makes, and he begins a voyage of return which carries him into the heart of the many mysteries that he has chosen to ignore. Essentially, his journey is a quest for knowledge; an attempt to understand the power and composed madness of his extraordinary father Moses Washington; to appreciate the endurance, determination, and resignation of his mother Yvette Franklin Stanton; to look clearly at the subtly interlocked white and black communities of his childhood; and finally, to understand the ways of the natural world, which he has never had to face in his artificially secure academic urbanity. As he uses the methods of the trained historian to uncover layer upon layer of "facts," and then arrange these "facts" in a form that will reveal meaning, Washington gradually realizes the richness of his heritage. This becomes the true source of his strength as a man and enables him to cultivate qualities of character that will make it possible for him to share his life with the woman he is learning to love and to solve the mystery of his father's suicide—to understand how it is connected to the eponymous "incident" which is the key to all the other mysteries in the novel.

The events of the novel take place between March 3 and March 12, 1979, but they actually encompass a time frame that covers almost 250 years as Washington travels, mentally and physically, back and forth between the mountains and the coast. His travels are set against a background of a developing late winter storm: In this trial by elemental force, the turmoil in the natural world parallels the chaotic strife-torn state of his psychic landscape, and to deal with both "storms," he must demonstrate his ability to use not only his rational intelligence, which he has developed to the detriment of his other attributes, but also his instinctual and emotional powers, which have previously been dormant. By the end of the book, he has come to terms with those strengths of his father which he can share but never match and is reconciled to the ways of Moses Washington's severe love which he has never understood. Also, he is ready to share every part of his inner life with Judith Powell, and in a sense, his level of maturity has gone beyond that of his father, who could never fully trust anyone, particularly a woman.

The Characters

John Washington is drawn by David Bradley as a contemporary black man who has been assaulted by all the forces of a racist society at its most vicious and yet has managed to survive without being turned into a cipher or a demon. Bradley's firstperson narrative places the reader close to Washington's heart and directly in his mind. Perhaps in an attempt to reject forever the slander that black men are intellectually inferior, Washington's intellect is especially impressive, and he has taken advantage of his educational opportunities to develop an analytical power that can penetrate the most complex conundrum or confidently confront any intellectual adversary. Because he fears that he will lose his mental discipline if he yields to his emotional impulses, he fails to understand the complete meaning of anything, although he has very ably covered this up, even to himself. At first, he seems distant, self-serving, and not very likable, but his sense of fairness, morality, and ultimate decency tend to compensate for his coldness. His intense interest in all of the things of the world and his dry sense of humor make him an interesting companion for a journey, and his tremendous desire to know and understand the circumstances of his life eventually overrides his limitations and carries the reader steadily closer to him (as Judith moves closer to him) as the narration progresses. By the time that John finally decides to sacrifice all his stratagems of defense and risk his soul to make it worthy, Bradley has carefully prepared the reader to share this experience with John and to rejoice at his success.

Still, the most interesting and bizarrely heroic character in the novel is John's father, Moses Washington. "Mose," in his son's words, is an "ex-moonshiner and murderer who has taken up philosophy, eccentricity, church-cleaning, marriage and fatherhood as retirement avocations." Bradley has created this character in a conscious effort to write into American literary history a black man who is unbreakable and in most endeavors unbeatable, who is a self-taught intellectual and a veritable poet of logic, who has the physical grace of an Olympic decathlon champion and a wicked gift for ghastly humor, which he directs at every form of villainy in American life. A victim of racism, he is not a racist himself, but he feels contempt for nearly everyone who is his inferior, regardless of race. He has a very stern sense of personal justice, which he delivers, in the absence of a social justice for most black people, with Old Testament severity. He is alive with passion but bereft of love, and although his exploits seem superhuman, it is Bradley's achievement to have made them completely plausible. Moses dominates the novel and dominates his son until John finally unravels all the clues his father left—an educational legacy to make his son even stronger than he was, but in a new form for a future time. Moses' suicide at the age of seventy is finally both a defeat and a symbol of the ultimate victory of a will that must control everything.

The other characters are dwarfed by comparison, but convincing. "Old" Jack is the last survivor of previous generations, the fabled storyteller of ancient cultures who is like the storehouse of collected wisdom of his tribe. "Uncle" Josh is a kind of natural man who would thrive in a fairer world but who is not cunning or clever enough for this one. John Washington's mother is a woman who has recognized what she must do in order to accomplish her goals and has turned all her strength and intelligence to these ends. Part of Washington's real education occurs as he learns that his contempt for her is misplaced and unearned, and that she has done admirably within the limits of the society to which she was tied. The mythic "C.K." Washington, legendary leader of a band of liberated former slaves, is an example of what careful planning, calculated resistance, and an incredible sense of mission can accomplish. Judith Powell, John Washington's best (possibly only) friend, is a straightforward woman whose complexity of character could easily justify a novel itself, but who functions here as a person of love, compassion, and common sense. She cares enough about Washington to stay with him through his mean times and believes enough in him to insist on accompanying him on his quest. His reluctance to accept her as a partner is overcome by her radiant spirit and her commitment to him (sometimes undeserved), and by his eventual realization that without her, he will forever be incomplete.

Themes and Meanings

The Chaneysville Incident is David Bradley's attempt to compose an epic of black American male experience, in which the hero, as in traditional epic conception, is the epitome of a struggle to define, preserve, and extoll the values and virtues of a culture. In a bold diversion from classic epic form, however, his "hero" is twofold: twice born as father and then as son, eventually becoming unified in the hero's quest. To combat and vanquish the murderous stereotype of the ignorant black man, Bradley has composed a book whose gripping narrative is intertwined, as in Herman Melville's *Moby Dick* (1851), with a kind of lore and expertise that dazzles the mind and expands the scope of the action to cosmic proportions. To challenge the slander of the black man as a figure of violence and impulsive action, his hero is a man of contemplation, reflection, and philosophical invention. To reinvigorate the powerful black myth of "soul," his hero is akin to a figure from ballads, chants, and blues, whose humanity is universal and nonracial while his experience is specifically grounded in the customs, rituals, and patterns of the black community.

The structure of the book is controlled by language, location, and a search for knowledge which will reveal a greater or more complete self. The author's perspective is that of the trained historian, just as the mind of the epic poem is a concentration of the voices of history; his method of composition resembles the historian's painstaking sifting of evidence. His goal is a test of his training. Can he go beyond all he has been taught, employing the imagination to carry him to a conclusion unreachable by even the most careful and painstaking marshaling of the facts? Can he combine the accumulated technology of refined culture with an intuitive knowledge of the natural world? Can he combine two ways of knowing, or unite two separate societies, or reconcile two warring races? The meaning of Bradley's book is that antinomies are not necessarily always polar opposites.

Critical Context

The Chaneysville Incident was David Bradley's second novel. It was, as he notes in his acknowledgments, "ten years in the making." It received the prestigious PEN/Faulkner award as the finest novel of 1981 and, as various critics have claimed, it will take its place along with such books as Ralph Ellison's *Invisible Man* (1952) as a crucial part of American literary experience.

Bibliography

Brigham, Cathy. "Identity, Masculinity, and Desire in David Bradley's Fiction." *Contemporary Literature* 36 (Summer, 1995): 289-316. Brigham compares the way race, class, and gender mold masculine identity in Bradley's *South Street* and *The Chaneysville Incident*. She argues that although the male protagonists in both novels "create woman-free zones," the women who love them become the primary shapers in their quest for male identity.

Egan, Philip J. "Unraveling Misogyny and Forging the New Self: Mother, Lover, and Storyteller in *The Chaneysville Incident*." *Papers on Language and Literature* 33 (Summer, 1997): 265-287. Egan discusses the misogyny of John Washington, attributing his resentment toward women in part to an Oedipal conflict with his mother Yvette. However, Jack is able to transcend his misogynistic feelings with the help of his lover Judith and Old Jack, who both help him confront his past and build a new identity.

Locke, Helen. "'Building Up Fragments:' The Oral Memory Process in Some Recent African American Written Narratives." *College Literature* 22 (October, 1995): 109-120. Locke explores the memory process generated by oral cultures in her reading of works by Toni Morrison and Paule Marshall and *The Chaneysville Incident*. She asserts that the memory process is a creative reconstruction in which the reader participates by "hearing" the narrative voice within the written text.

Pavlic, Edward. "Syndetic Redemption: Above-Underground Emergence in David Bradley's *The Chaneysville Incident*." *African American Review* 30 (Summer, 1996): 165-184. Pavlic focuses on the character development of John Washington, showing how his personal encounters with his black culture and family history transform his sense of identity. As he emerges from the confines of academic life as defined by Western parameters, Jack regains a sense of traditional African American values. His encounters with ancestral spirits help him get in touch with his racial identity.

Wilson, Matthew. "The African American Historian: David Bradley's *The Chaneysville Incident*." *African American Review* 29 (Spring, 1995): 97-107. Focusing on the historian as a character in fiction, Wilson explores the different ways in which the historian is portrayed by white and black authors. In Bradley's novel, John Washington's quest to reconstruct the circumstances of his grandfather's death highlights the challenges African American historians face, since much of their literature is undocumented or forgotten.

Leon Lewis

A CHANGE OF SKIN

Author: Carlos Fuentes (1928-   )
Type of plot: Experimental
Time of plot: April 11, 1965
Locale: Mexico City, Xochicalco, and Cholula
First published: Cambio de piel, 1967 (English translation, 1968)

> *Principal characters:*
> JAVIER, a Mexican would-be writer
> ELIZABETH, his wife
> FRANZ, a Czechoslovakian emigré to Mexico
> ISABEL, his young Mexican lover
> FREDDY LAMBERT, the narrator

The Novel

Carlos Fuentes's *A Change of Skin* is a difficult novel when judged by almost any standards. At least part of its difficulty lies in the fact that it continually frustrates the reader's expectations of what a novel should be, and of how a novel should be constructed. The average reader expects the novel to "tell a story," to recount in some intelligible way events which at least could have happened in the "real world." The reader expects the novel, in a word, to be mimetic. Yet in *A Change of Skin*, Fuentes constructs a world that is absolutely and self-reflexively fictional and then deliberately destroys this world, causing it to collapse, like the Cholula pyramid of its final scene, under the weight of its own artifice.

The story of *A Change of Skin* is fairly straightforward. Javier, a frustrated Mexican writer, and his American Jewish wife, Elizabeth, are traveling from Mexico City to Veracruz to spend a holiday. They are accompanied by Franz, a Czechoslovakian who aided in the construction of the Nazi concentration camp at Theresienstadt and then fled to Mexico after the war, and his young Mexican mistress, Isabel. After leaving Mexico City, the couples stop to see the pre-Columbian ruins at Xochicalco and then continue to Cholula to see the pyramids. Their car is sabotaged and they are forced to spend the night in Cholula. There they are joined by the ubiquitous Narrator, who has been traveling to Cholula by the more direct superhighway in the company of a group of young beatniks who refer to themselves as "the Monks." At Isabel's suggestion, the two couples visit the Cholula pyramid at midnight. Here Franz, and perhaps Elizabeth, are killed in a cave-in, or, according to another contradictory version immediately following the first, Franz is murdered in the pyramid by one of the Monks to atone for his war crimes. The survivors then return to Mexico City. The story is thus in itself fairly simple. The complications and expansions that occur in the narrative presentation of this story (which include lengthy flashbacks, insertion of extraneous newspaper accounts and other real or imagined events) prolong these events, which take place in a single day, through a dizzying 462 pages and ultimately question the objective occurrence of any of the events and characters of the story by suggesting that the entire account may merely represent a demented delusion of the mad narrator who last appears incarcerated in the insane asylum in Cholula.

The Characters

The artifice characteristic of *A Change of Skin* is particularly obvious in the portrayal of its characters, who represent doubles or paired opposites in continual conflict rather than fully developed, believable personalities. Ironically, Javier is first attracted to Elizabeth because he sees her as his opposite, as a person who possesses the strength he lacks. It is only during their idyllic honeymoon in Greece that, at least in Elizabeth's later reflections, their duality is briefly transcended. Their marriage later becomes a battleground where they play out their opposition in even the most trivial of gestures. As they enter the hotel room in Cholula, Javier draws the curtains, but Elizabeth immediately opens them complaining of Javier's obsession with darkened rooms.

The fragmentation and conflict in their lives cripple Javier and Elizabeth. Javier becomes the stereotypical artist manqué, incapable of producing any work of substance. Like her husband, Elizabeth too lacks the wholeness that would enable her to create. The child she aborts stands as the tragic sign of her failure. The couple's fragmentation and alienation is further manifested in the narrative itself as it records their disjointed conversations, which often degenerate into futile monologues or impossible dialogues between people who cannot hear each other.

While Elizabeth and Javier each represent the other's opposing double, Fuentes's doubling artifice extends to the other characters as well. Isabel is clearly Elizabeth's double. Fuentes underlines this fact by duplicating their names (Isabel is the Spanish equivalent of Elizabeth). Isabel seems to represent a younger Elizabeth, a sort of alternative possibility for her life. Javier is also Franz's double, but their relationship is far more complex. On one level they are opposites since Franz represents the active strength that the passive Javier lacks. Yet on another level, the two men are almost identical. Javier himself realizes that he is another Franz; his personality is simply latent, not yet fully realized.

The doubling of characters is further complicated by the fact that the characters continually change roles within the novel, Javier becoming Isabel's lover, and Franz making love to Elizabeth. This change is only one of the innumerable "changes of skin" the characters undergo as they search for the ultimate change of skin, the rebirth that would resolve the dualities that they have come to embody.

Fuentes frequently extends his obsessive doubling of characters to include the narrator himself, who undergoes several "changes of skin" in his relationship to his protagonists. The narrator first appears as an invisible witness who observes the characters entering Cholula and describes their actions. He later appears as a character himself and participates in the lives of Elizabeth and Isabel. Indeed, much of the content of the novel consists of the retelling of incidents which the two female characters have previously related to the narrator or vice versa. The intimate nature of the information the narrator recounts and his degree of knowledge of the women's lives combine to give the narrator at least the illusion of a limited omniscience in this role. Yet by the novel's end, the narrator again shifts posture and becomes personified as Freddy Lambert, who manipulates and attempts to control the lives of the four characters who appear merely as his puppets. The narrator appears ultimately as a composite of various narrative possibilities. This shifting narrative stance underlines the artifice inherent in the act of narrating and again points self-referentially to the artificiality of the fictional construct.

Themes and Meanings

As might be expected in a novel based on the creation of deliberate fictional artifice, the themes and meanings of *A Change of Skin* are elaborately stylized and, like the novel's characters, its themes frequently split into a number of complementary doubles. Yet the most consistently developed theme equates the novel's action with a stylized re-creation of the Quetzalcoatl myth that was at the heart of pre-Columbian Mexican religion and philosophy. In pre-Columbian thought Quetzalcoatl represented the reconciliation of opposites, the union born of opposed dualities. This union was graphically represented in his chief emblem, the Plumed Serpent. In Aztec lore the serpent was associated with matter and the earthly realm while the bird denoted the opposite realm of heaven and the spirit. As God-King of the fabulous city of Tollan, Quetzalcoatl incarnated and reconciled these warring opposites. Quetzalcoatl taught his subjects the secrets of growing maize and the arts of weaving, and of working precious gold and feathers. He taught man the sacred calendar and the rites associated with its observance. He was the giver of all art and culture, and his kingdom in Tollan became idealized in later Aztec thought as a sort of indigenous Eden. Yet Quetzalcoatl was ultimately defeated by his dark double Tezcatlipoca, who caused him to succumb to the temptations of the flesh. Overcome by remorse, the God-King burned himself in sacrificial flames and was reborn as the Morning Star, the unified, pure spirit triumphant.

Many elements in the initial pages of *A Change of Skin* allude directly and indirectly to the myth of Quetzalcoatl and establish this myth as the work's central motif. The very fact that the novel's opening scene is in Cholula implicitly provides a background of Quetzalcoatl's lore, because pre-Columbian Cholula was primarily a ceremonial center dedicated to Quetzalcoatl, and the pyramid complex there terminated in a single great platform erected in his honor. The conquest of Cholula undermined the Mexicans' belief in Quetzalcoatl's power to deliver them from the conquistadores and contributed to the climate of terror and paralysis that later enabled the Spaniards to defeat Montezuma in Tenochtitlán and achieve the final conquest of Mexico. Fuentes calls up all of this historical background in the novel's opening sequence as he alternates descriptions of present day Cholula as it appears to the protagonists with passages from the chronicles which describe Cortés's entry into and destruction of the city. The juxtaposition of past and present emphasizes the contrasts between Cholula's past glory and its present squalor and poverty.

As the couples visit the church of San Francisco, a morality play is being presented to the Indians massed in the atrium. The play reenacts the Fall and loss of Eden. The parallels between the Spanish conquest and the biblical expulsion from the garden are obvious. As the chorus of the morality play sings, lamenting Adam's exile from paradise, the convertible carrying the Monks arrives, its radio blaring a pop song whose lyrics keep repeating "I'll give you back your time." This initial scene establishes the novel's basic theme: the quest for the Eden of plenitude where dualities will be reconciled and man will once more attain his original spiritual unity. In terms of the principal characters, this union would free them from their roles as opposed dualities and enable them to attain the spiritual wholeness that would allow them to live meaningful lives. The novel becomes a stylized rendering of the mythological quest genre in which Quetzalcoatl symbolizes the emblematic object of desire—the resolution of duality. The journey from Mexico to Veracruz introduces the "journey-as-quest" motif and again associates pre-Columbian culture with original plenitude, for the couples' journey retraces the route of the conquest in reverse.

Yet there is a significant departure from the traditional quest model. The union of opposites that the reader has been led to expect by the constant reference to the Quetzalcoatl myth never takes place. Precisely at midnight, the traditional time for enactment of primitive rituals of sacrificial renewal, Isabel leads her companions into the heart of the Cholula pyramid. There they face a pre-Columbian frieze decorated with locusts painted in colors symbolizing life and death. The locusts represent the expected fusion of opposites, the death which is a necessary prelude to rebirth. The desired union of opposites is acted out by Franz and Javier as they struggle in front of the frieze. At this point, however, the pyramid begins to cave in and Franz and Elizabeth are entombed. After the sacrifice of Franz and Elizabeth, the reader's attention shifts to Javier and Isabel as the source of anticipated renewal. Javier realizes, however, that there is no possibility of rebirth. He will only repeat the same destructive pattern with Isabel, converting her into a new Elizabeth. Unable to endure the repetition of the cycle of destruction, he strangles Isabel with Elizabeth's shawl.

Immediately after the narration describing the cave-in and Isabel's murder, Fuentes provides an alternative version of the pyramid sequence. In this version, Franz is ritually murdered by the Monks. After his death, Elizabeth and Javier remain alienated opposites, incapable of union. The attempt to return has failed; the rituals have lost their power and paradise remains forever lost. Javier and Elizabeth simply stuff Franz's body into the trunk of the Monks' car and return to Mexico City.

Critical Context

A Change of Skin is most noteworthy as Fuentes's best-known attempt to create an antinovel, a novel diametrically opposed to the traditional realistic novel. Everything about the novel points to its artifice, to its existence as a pure literary fiction with no relationship to the "real world." The novel's almost complete chronological disjunction is one obvious mark of artifice. Fuentes's exaggerated use of flashbacks and disjointed narrative sequences continually reminds the reader that what he is reading is a "story"—an artful, fictional construct which does not in any way attempt to imitate the normal, chronological flow of events. The narrative jumps back and forth, mixing what seem to be factual accounts of Franz's youth in Czechoslovakia with accounts of Javier's youth in Mexico, Elizabeth's childhood in New York, and events of their married life. Yet these "facts" are often impossible to distinguish from the "fictions" of the characters' imaginings or the pseudofacts of the newspaper accounts that are seemingly arbitrarily interpolated.

The shifting posture of the novel's narrator and the doubling of its characters are, as has been noted, still other ways in which Fuentes deliberately points out the total artificiality, the total fictitiousness of his tale. The two alternate endings are simply the ultimate rhetorical exaggeration and constitute the final parody of rhetorical technique and subversion of the mimetic principle. The reader is left with a sort of fictional model kit providing him with a number of possible characters, motifs, narrators and endings which he must structure in order to create his own version of the novel. It is finally this demand that the reader become creator/author that distinguishes *A Change* of Skin and makes it one of the most daring of the "new novels" of contemporary fiction.

Bibliography

Duran, Victor Manuel. *A Marxist Reading of Fuentes, Vargas Llosa, and Puig.* Lanham, Md.: University Press of America, 1994. An interesting study comparing the politics in the writings of these three important Latin American authors. Many of Fuentes's works are examined in detail.

Helmuth, Chalene. *The Postmodern Fuentes*. Lewisburg, Penn.: Bucknell University Press, 1997. A solid overview of Fuentes's work from a postmodern point of view. Several individual works are discussed, focusing on the issues of identity, national and narrative control, and reconsiderations of the past.

Ibsen, Kristine. *Author, Text, and Reader in the Novels of Carlos Fuentes*. New York: Peter Lang, 1993. Concentrating on four novels, including *A Change of Skin*, Ibsen offers valuable insight into the problem of communication, which remains one of the central preoccupations throughout the work of Fuentes. Her analysis focuses on the means of textualization by which Fuentes activates his reader and how this coincides with his notions of the role of literature in society.

Pollard, Scott. "Canonizing Revision: Literary History and the Postmodern Latin American Writer." *College Literature* 20 (October, 1993): 133-147. Scott analyzes the impact of Latin American narrative on Western literary history after World War II. Focusing on authors Alejo Carpentier, Carlos Fuentes, and Lezama Lima, Scott discusses narratives of conquest and exploration, international modernism, the fashioning of cultural identity, and the primacy of European culture. Offers valuable insight into several of Fuentes's works.

Van Delden, Maarten. *Carlos Fuentes, Mexico, and Modernity.* Nashville, Tenn.: Vanderbilt University Press, 1998. Using Fuentes's writings as a springboard for his discussion, Van Delden presents a comprehensive analysis of Fuentes's intellectual development in the context of modern Mexican political and cultural life. Includes extensive notes and a helpful bibliography.

Shirley A. Williams

CHEYENNE AUTUMN

Author: Mari Sandoz (1896-1966)
Type of plot: Historical realism
Time of plot: 1878-1879
Locale: The Great Plains, from Indian Territory to the Yellowstone Country
First published: 1953

Principal characters:

> LITTLE WOLF, one of the Old Man Chiefs of the Northern Cheyenne,
> bearer of the Sacred Chief's bundle
>
> DULL KNIFE, another Old Man Chief of the Northern Cheyenne;
> captured at Fort Robinson, Nebraska
>
> LITTLE FINGER NAIL, a young warrior and artist
>
> RED CLOUD, Chief of the Sioux
>
> LIEUTENANT WILLIAM P. CHASE, a soldier, friend of the Cheyenne
>
> CAPTAIN WESSELLS, an officer guilty of Indian atrocities
>
> BLACK COYOTE, a renegade Cheyenne

The Novel

Although based on intensive research, and supplemented by notes on sources, a map, and an index, *Cheyenne Autumn* is in fact an epic novel in which Sandoz employs dialogue and other fictional devices to re-create the historical event that is her subject. The novel recounts the fifteen-hundred-mile flight of the Northern Cheyenne in 1878-1879 from the Indian Territory back to their homeland in the Yellowstone Country. After the Cheyenne surrendered to General Miles in the spring of 1877, they were promised good treatment and an agency in their north country, but those promises were immediately broken, and they were told that they must resettle in the Indian Territory, far to the south: If they did not like it there, later they could return. The Cheyenne were refused all food and supplies until they agreed to go, so the starving tribe had no choice but to agree. The Northern Cheyenne were reunited with their Southern relatives at their new reservation near Fort Reno, in the Indian Territory, but that summer they were hungry and sick with malaria. The promised supplies never arrived, and finally Dull Knife and Little Wolf decided to lead their people north to the Yellowstone. A year earlier, they had brought two hundred warriors south, but starvation and disease had reduced their ranks to barely one hundred warriors, plus women and children.

On the night of September 9, 1878, the small troop set off on foot and horseback, slipping quietly past the army sentries under the veiled moon. They were pursued by Rendlebrock's cavalry from Fort Reno, with additional troops sent from Fort Dodge to intercept them. The Dog Soldiers, or warrior society men, defended the rear and kept the stragglers moving as the tribe wended its way through settled country.

The Cheyenne held off the first army attack at Turkey Springs on September 13 and 14, even though they were outgunned and outnumbered, by following Little

Wolf's strategy of choosing a narrow ravine in which to ambush the approaching soldiers and hold them off while the tribe slipped away. These constant skirmishes were particularly hard on the women and children, already weakened by starvation and disease. As the Cheyenne moved, they lived on buffalo and wild game or on horse carcasses left behind after the fights, but it was still hard for the hunters to find enough meat for three hundred people. Young warriors had to capture wild horses or raid ranch stock to replenish their exhausted mounts. In Kansas, they were repeatedly harassed by cowboys and troopers, who killed women and children, until in revenge the Cheyenne began attacking white settlers. With guns and ammunition in short supply, the Cheyenne searched for army supplies after each skirmish or else brought back guns from their raids. The women dried meat and prepared skins in their temporary camps, but sometimes even these scant supplies had to be abandoned in the haste to escape from the cavalry. Always the Cheyenne kept to ravines, creek bottoms, and washouts to avoid detection. The newspapers exaggerated the size of the Cheyenne band and invented atrocities, whipping up anti-Indian hysteria among the cattlemen and settlers.

The Cheyenne crossed Kansas quickly, striking for the valley of the Arkansas River, which they crossed on the night of September 23. Colonel Lewis bragged in Dodge City that he would "wipe out those murdering redskins or leave his body dead on the ground." At the battle of Punished Woman Creek, Little Wolf laid a clever ambush for Lewis's soldiers, which was spoiled when a young warrior became overexcited and fired too quickly, revealing the Cheyenne position. The Indians held their fire, however, until the soldiers approached, and they brought down Colonel Lewis in the battle, causing the rest of the soldiers to retreat in confusion.

As the band approached the site of the April 23, 1875, Cheyenne massacre at the Sappa, many in Little Wolf's band recalled the deaths of their relatives three years earlier, when soldiers and buffalo hunters had butchered almost 120 women and children, clubbing infants and throwing them on the fire. As the Cheyenne returned north, they were angered by the memory of the Sappa, and they began to raid the scattered settlements for guns and horses.

For more than a month, the ragged little band had moved more than five hundred miles north, crossed two railroads, and evaded several detachments of cavalry. Then they pushed northward to the valley of the Republican River, into the Nebraska Territory, and on to the Platte. There, soldiers of General Crook and General Miles were awaiting them, and behind them came the troops of Mauck. With the route to their Sioux relatives at Red Cloud's and Spotted Tail's agencies blocked by troops, the two old chiefs quarreled for the first time about where they should go. Dull Knife argued for the Red Cloud agency at Fort Robinson, while Little Wolf insisted that the band should continue north to the Yellowstone. The two chiefs could not agree, and the Cheyenne split that night on White Tail Creek.

Winter arrived early that year, with the fall's first blizzard coming on October 23. Major Thornburgh and his cavalry pursued Little Wolf's diminished band across the sandhills toward the Niobrara. Meanwhile, Dull Knife's band pushed west toward the

Red Cloud agency at Pine Ridge. The Cheyenne were short of meat and ammunition, and winter was upon them. Dull Knife's band tried to make a last run but was surrounded at Chadron Creek during a blizzard and forced to surrender to Colonel Carlton's and Captain Johnson's soldiers. The Cheyenne were forced to turn over their ponies and weapons and march back to Fort Robinson. There Dull Knife's band was held prisoner in the army barracks, while it was decided when to send the tribe back south to the Indian Territory.

At first the Cheyenne were treated well, but they were restless in their confinement and uncertain about their future. When Dull Knife refused to move back to the southern agency, Captain Wessells locked the Cheyenne in their barracks, without food, water, or fuel, and tried to starve them into submission. On the bright, moonlit night of January 9, 1879, the Cheyenne broke out of the barracks and fled across to the White River. The weak and poorly armed Cheyenne, numbering only 130, were pursued by five companies of cavalry and many civilians, the trigger-happy troops shooting women and children wherever they were found dug in the snow for protection. By January 22, the last of the Cheyenne had been captured, with only seventy-eight remaining, many of them severely wounded. There was widespread revulsion against the Cheyenne massacre, and Captain Wessells was investigated. Dull Knife and his family escaped to the Red Cloud agency, but the experience left him a broken man.

That winter, Little Wolf had eluded the troops and pushed north with his band of Cheyenne toward the Yellowstone. The strain of the winter created dissension among the warriors. By March, Little Wolf had reached the Yellowstone, only to be surrounded by Lieutenant White Hat Clark and his troops. Little Wolf was forced to surrender to Clark on March 25, 1879, thus ending one of the most remarkable exploits in the American West. The 114 Cheyenne remaining were brought into Fort Keogh and promised an agency of their own there. The Cheyenne found it a good, safe place, but there was nothing for them to do, and many turned to drinking and gambling. After a drunken argument, Little Wolf shot his friend Thin Elk and was afterward stripped of his chief's powers. He lived on for twenty-five years, keeping to himself and going afoot to visit relatives, often alone. He finally died in 1904, remembered by a few as the chief who had led his tribe back to the Rosebud.

The Characters

Mari Sandoz tries to be fair in her presentation of both Indian and white historical figures, though her sympathies are clearly with the Cheyenne. While not romanticizing the Cheyenne as "noble savages," she is able to view their actions from the Cheyenne cultural perspective. She manages to avoid the archetypes and clichés of Indian characterization in depicting the individual personalities of a number of the Cheyenne.

Certainly, the most admirable figures in her novel are the two Cheyenne chiefs, Little Wolf and Dull Knife, and of these two, perhaps Little Wolf is the more interesting since his fate is the more tragic. The underlying strength and integrity of his character comes through in his forbearance toward the whites and his unwillingness to engage in unnecessary violence that would risk the safety of the women and children in his tribe. He tries to keep his word and to honor his promises, even in the face of the continual failure of the army and Indian Bureau agents to honor their agreements with his tribe.

The tragic dimension of both Little Wolf and Dull Knife emerges in their depiction as the leaders of a vanishing culture and a disappearing way of life. The Cheyenne were a nomadic people whose culture and land-use patterns conflicted with the American settlement of the Great Plains. Their eventual defeat was perhaps inevitable, but they fought so bravely against such overwhelming odds that they earned the respect of many whites.

Little Wolf was a particularly shrewd and capable leader, a brilliant strategist who was able to evade a succession of cavalry attacks, even when his small band seemed hopelessly outmanned. Little Wolf's tragic fate, after his surrender, in a sense represents the tragic fate of all the Plains Indians, a once-proud, nomadic people reduced to idleness and alcoholism. Dull Knife is perhaps a less interesting figure who serves as a foil to Little Wolf, demonstrating the wisdom of Little Wolf's decision to continue pressing northward, since "the Indian never caught is the Indian never killed."

Since Sandoz' novel is narrated from the Cheyenne point of view, the white characters are not as fully developed, with the exception of several of the army officers. By far the most sympathetic of these are the young Lieutenant Chase, who gives food and clothing to the Cheyenne out of his own pockets, and Lieutenant Clark, who permits Little Wolf to surrender with dignity. Many of the other army officers are depicted as cold and ruthless men, professional "Indian haters," or the unthinking agents of a genocidal policy.

Themes and Meanings

In her historical novel, Mari Sandoz tries to present a factual and carefully documented account of the fate of the Northern Cheyenne after their escape north from the Indian Territory in 1878. Her novel was extensively researched, based on numerous interviews with Cheyenne who had actually taken part in Little Wolf's flight. Her childhood was spent near the Sioux reservation at Pine Ridge, and she heard many stories of the earlier years from both Indians and whites. Her intention in writing this novel was to tell the Cheyenne story from their own point of view, to tell how land greed and broken promises reduced "a free hunting people to sullen agency sitters" within a quarter of a century. She demonstrates that the official United States Indian policy from the 1850's onward was not accommodation but extermination of the Plains Indian peoples, with the enforced confinement of survivors on designated reservations, usually on the poorest and most unproductive land. The story of the Cheyenne's resistance in attempting to preserve their tribe and culture becomes a heroic account of a brave and determined people's struggle against overwhelming odds.

Critical Context

Cheyenne Autumn is the third in a series of six books in which Mari Sandoz tells the story of the settlement of the Great Plains, from the time of the earliest fur trappers and frontiersmen to the later Indian rebellions and immigrant settlements. Her theme is the epic pageant of the Old West, with its violence, beauty, bravery, hardship, and change. Other works in this series include *Old Jules* (1935), based on the life of her father, a Swiss pioneer in western Nebraska; *Crazy Horse: The Strange Man of the Oglalas* (1942), the story of the famous Oglala chief; and *The Buffalo Hunters: The Story of the Hide Men* (1954). *The Cattlemen of the Rio Grande Across the Far Marias* (1958) and *The Beaver Men: Spearheads of Empire* (1964) depict the history of settlement in the Old West. Of these novels, *Cheyenne Autumn* is among the most powerful, evoking an elegiac mood in its account of the heroic flight of the Northern Cheyenne back to their ancestral home. A dedicated and prolific novelist of the Nebraska frontier, Sandoz employs an honest realism to re-create the annals of Western history. Her accounts of the Indians and the white settlers attempt to present the region both as it was and as part of the enduring American myth of the Frontier West.

Bibliography

Lindell, Lisa R. "Recasting Epic Tradition: The Dispossessed as Hero in Sandoz's *Crazy Horse* and *Cheyenne Autumn*." *Great Plains Quarterly* 16 (Winter, 1996): 43-53. Lindell examines Sandoz's depiction of the treatment of the Cheyenne Indians and her portrayal of Crazy Horse.

Rippey, Barbara. "Toward a New Paradigm: Mari Sandoz's Study of Red and White Myth in *Cheyenne Autumn*." In *Women and Western American Literature*, edited by Helen W. Stauffer and Susan J. Rosowki. Troy, N.Y.: Whitson, 1982. An analysis of Sandoz's exploration of myth in the novel.

Stauffer, Helen, ed. *Letters of Mari Sandoz*. Lincoln: University of Nebraska Press, 1992. A collection of letters dating from 1928 to Sandoz's death in 1966 that focus on her career as a writer. Furnishes useful insights into Sandoz's knowledge of Great Plains history. Correspondence with readers, publishers, and other authors provides a compelling overview of Sandoz's literary career.

_____. *Mari Sandoz*. Boise, Idaho: Boise State University, 1984. A brief but solid introduction to Sandoz's works.

_____. *Mari Sandoz: Story Catcher of the Plains*. Lincoln: University of Nebraska Press, 1982. A literary biography of Sandoz, detailing her meticulous research and dedication to accuracy and her quarrels with editors and publishers. Stauffer also provides an analysis of Sandoz's writings.

Villiger, Laura R. *Mari Sandoz: A Study in Post-Colonial Discourse*. New York: Peter Lang, 1994. Villiger's study examines Sandoz's work as a series of contrasts, including regional versus universal dimensions, the indigenous world and the newcomer's world, and text and context. A useful study for further exploration of Sandoz's works.

Andrew J. Angyal

CHINA BOY

Author: Gus Lee
Type of plot: Bildungsroman
Time of plot: The early 1950's
Locale: San Francisco, California
First published: 1991

> *Principal characters:*
>> KAI TING, the only American-born member of the Ting family
>> DAI-LI TING (MAH-MEE), Kai's mother, who dies before he is seven
>> COLONEL T. K. TING, Kai's father, now a banker in civilian life
>> EDNA MCGURK TING, the Philadelphia society woman who becomes
>> Kai's stepmother
>> TONY BARRAZA, a former professional boxer and one of Kai's boxing
>> coaches
>> UNCLE SHIM, an old friend of the Ting family and Kai's calligraphy
>> teacher
>> TOUSSAINT LARUE, Kai's best friend

The Novel

China Boy is the story of Kai Ting, the American-born son of a refugee Shanghainese family. Ending an odyssey across both friendly and unfriendly terrain, the Ting family finally settles in San Francisco.

China Boy opens with Kai's retelling of how his family—including his mother, father, and three elder sisters—fled the civil war in China, and how they came to be situated in San Francisco, specifically in the Panhandle, a tough, largely poor neighborhood. It is in this "concrete crucible" that Kai does his growing up.

The almost six-year-old Kai is his mother's favorite child and only son, and she pins large hopes upon him. Kai's sisters are all considerably older than he is, and he assumes the natural position of coddled youngest child. His world revolves around his mother, whose passion, charisma, and overabiding sense of family weave for young Kai a protective cocoon. In fact, until he starts school, Kai has little sense of the world outside the Tings' home. He has even less sense of other children his age and what it will take to cross the boundary between the protection of family and the dangers of a world populated with hostile strangers.

Tragically for Kai, his mother dies. While he could previously rush home from the schoolyard and the streets of the Panhandle to the security of home, Kai is now robbed of the balance from that reality. To compound matters, his father marries Edna McGurk, who steps into her new role of stepmother with reluctance but nevertheless with draconian ideas about how to rear suddenly inherited children. From an almost idyllic existence of Chinese food, ancestral stories, the Shanghainese dialect—or "Songhai"—and the loving, doting presence of Mah-mee, Kai is propelled, within the space of months, into a subsistence that is circumscribed by a relentlessly cruel stepmother, a strictly enforced new tongue, and the still-new experience of the tough streets of the Panhandle.

As "China Boy" in his predominantly black neighborhood, Kai immediately becomes the easiest target of boyish aggression and plain meanness. His tiny frame does not help him, and neither do his nearsightedness and his inability to communicate in the language of the street. His stepmother locks him out of the house until dinnertime, and Kai has no recourse but to live his daylight hours among his street-seasoned peers. Kai is constantly beaten up, but he does manage to make two friends. One is Toussaint LaRue, and the other is Toussaint's mother. Mrs. LaRue represents for Kai the mother and all the mothering that he has lost.

After a particularly vicious attack on Kai, his father decides to enroll him at the Young Men's Christian Association (YMCA) with the hope that Kai will receive some instruction in self-defense. At the YMCA, Kai's eyes are opened to yet another new world. It is a world of aggression-driven boys, but in this environment, there are also grown men who take the time to help channel the aggression toward worthwhile ends. Puny, scared, ill-treated, and starved, Kai learns to box. He also learns to trust, especially in his coaches. Over the months, their collective instruction and their belief in their smallest student begins to show results. Kai puts on weight; Tony Barraza, the boxing coach, sees to it that the starved Kai is fed in the YMCA cafeteria. Kai is soon able to step into the ring in his beginner's class and last three rounds with an opponent. He is far from being able to beat the street bullies, but he is gaining a sense of self and what he can accomplish. He also makes friends, and his English improves.

Despite his blossoming at the YMCA, Kai is quickly brought down to earth in an encounter with the meanest neighborhood bully. Kai is once again badly beaten up. At the same time, his home situation does not improve. His father is invariably away on business, Edna is unbearably cruel, and his sisters can do little to help him. On top of that, he is stricken with the realization that his memory of his mother is fast fading.

With his YMCA mentors behind him, and with the arrival from his sister, Megan, of a photograph of his mother as extra moral support, Kai faces the street bully again in a do-or-die effort. Kai again takes brutal punishment, but this time he gives as good as he gets. His triumph gives him the much-needed first step toward a credible place in his neighborhood. He has won the first, the most important, battle of his seven years.

The Characters

Dai-li Ting, Kai's "Mah-mee," appears only in the beginning of the book. Yet her presence is an important one, for it is primarily through her that Kai has a sense of who he is, who his ancestors are. She speaks her native Songhai with Kai and his sisters and instills in them the value of family togetherness, of a cultural past that is now remote but that can nevertheless be reenacted in some semblance in their now-American lives. Dai-li Ting is vivacious, unpredictable, idiosyncratic, passionate, and she loves her only son fiercely. She is the anchor in Kai's world, and her brief appearance in the novel only serves to underscore his loss when she dies of cancer. With her death, Kai is stripped not only of love and protection but also of the most palpable reminder of his ancestral roots.

Colonel Ting is Kai's military-hero father, now a bank officer in civilian America. He abhors the degeneration in his homeland that led finally to civil war, and he is concerned primarily with becoming and being American. He is taciturn, rigid, and an iconoclast among the Chinese community in San Francisco because of his disavowal of most things Chinese. To his son, he is distant and unapproachable, and his presence does nothing to soften the blow of Mah-mee's death. Colonel Ting is the typically uncommunicative father, and it seems that the best he can do for his son is to enroll him at the YMCA, thus giving Kai over to a group of surrogate fathers.

Edna McGurk, the second Mrs. Ting, is more than Kai's tormentor. Unbearably intolerant and cruel, and unable or unwilling to reach out to her stepchildren, Edna is also Kai's constant reminder that she is not Mah-mee, that everything Mah-mee represented should be consigned to a forgettable past. Edna's cruelty to her stepchildren dramatizes Kai's bereavement and his lonely, unprotected status.

Tony Barraza is Kai's favorite coach at the YMCA. A former boxer, he now devotes his time to the molding of young bodies and minds, and as he takes Kai under his wing, he is the surrogate parent that Kai so badly craves. He offers Kai guidance, friendship, and a chance to make something of an impossibly deprived childhood.

Uncle Shim is a reminder of happier days for Kai, for this old family friend, who is Kai's calligraphy teacher, was a constant visitor when Mah-mee was alive. Together with Mah-mee, Uncle Shim represents the connectedness to Kai's cultural heritage. His visits become infrequent as a result of Edna's desire to purge all things "Asiatic" from the Ting household, but Kai manages to track him down. The meeting between Uncle Shim and Tony Barraza in the YMCA cafeteria brings together the two separate worlds represented by the two men. While Tony is the American personification of action and street smarts, Uncle Shim is the personification of Chinese tradition, passivity, and the philosophizing of life's unexplainable cruelties.

Toussaint LaRue, or "Toos," is Kai's only friend among his neighborhood peers. Toos makes the overture of befriending Kai, the "ratshitchinkface" alien; his kindness is a gritty act in the Panhandle. Toos's moral strength is grounded in the strong bond between him and his mother, and he becomes Kai's street teacher and steadfast friend.

Themes and Meanings

China Boy is a *Bildungsroman*, or rite-of-passage story. Although the novel covers only approximately one-and-a-half years of Kai's life, it depicts a pivotal point in his growing, a time of great change and uncertainty out of which he will gather strength and survive or to which he will succumb. With the death of his mother, the physical and emotional distance of his father, the cruelty of his stepmother, and the everyday violence that he faces on his neighborhood streets, Kai is plunged into a seemingly inescapable dungeon. To escape, Kai has to draw on the very last dregs of a personal integrity—the somehow unquenchable resilience of a seven-year-old—in order to salvage a childhood gone awry. Facing violence both within and without his home, Kai nevertheless soldiers along, and despite incredible odds neutralizes the neighborhood bully in the defining battle of his short life. This culminating act signals a break-through for Kai, and the novel leaves the reader with the hope that with one battle won, Kai is set to win others and, ultimately, to win the long war of his childhood.

The novel is also about displacement, about the suspension between two clearly defined, seemingly irreconcilable cultures. The culture represented by Kai's mother and Uncle Shim seems, with Mah-mee's death, to slip away with each day. Kai, speaking a five-year-old's broken "Songhai," is the flotsam from that culture. The reality of a relentlessly alien culture is all around him, but without its language, without recognizable points of reference to help him in his transition, Kai is in danger of becoming both a refugee from one culture and an unwanted stranger in another.

Ultimately, though, the novel is about the possibility of reconciliations: between past and present, between ethnicity and nationality, between passivity and action. There is time for Kai to recollect the lost pieces of his past in order to give direction and purpose to his present. Confronted by racism both at home and on the streets, Kai is befriended and aided by individuals who recognize the inherent stranger in themselves and who see in Kai only the human quality of need. Physically and emotionally brutalized by both his stepmother and the neighborhood boys, Kai is unable to retaliate. His understanding of "yuing chi," or karma, seems to feed his childish fatalism. With the bodybuilding and mind-building at the YMCA, however, Kai seems finally to be able both to assert himself and to preserve his integrity. In the novel's epilogue, Kai confronts his stepmother at their doorway. He has just survived his fight with the bully, and his clothes are drenched with blood. Edna is concerned only that he has rung the doorbell too early and that she will once again have to bleach the blood—the Asiatic blood—out of his clothes. As a recognition of his past and present, of his ethnicity, of his action, of his new self, Kai tells her, "You are not my Mah-mee! . . . I ain't fo' yo' pickin-on, no mo'!"

Critical Context

China Boy is Lee's first novel. It is at least semiautobiographical; like Kai, Lee himself is the only American-born member and only son of an immigrant Shanghai family. Also like Kai, Lee has a stepmother, whom he credits with having taught him English.

China Boy was published in 1991, in the midst of heightened literary activity among Chinese Americans and among Asian Americans in general. The book also arrived in the midst of continued debate in the Asian American literary community. Some Asian American writers, notably playwright Frank Chin, claim that much Asian American writing panders to white imagination and represents a self-orientalizing. Others, including novelists Maxine Hong Kingston and Amy Tan, insist that the integrity of Chinese American writing demands that the myths and half-truths that have been perpetuated in the name of "things oriental" still need to be addressed. In any case, *China Boy* draws as much from the "child-meets-world" American tradition of Mark Twain, Ernest Hemingway, Harper Lee, and Carson McCullers as it does from the redefining, ever-evolving American tradition represented by the continuum of Han Suyin, Jade Snow Wong, Louis Chu, and Kingston.

Bibliography

Kim, Elaine H. *Asian American Literature: An Introduction to the Writings and Their Social Context*. Philadelphia: Temple University Press, 1982. Kim's work is a seminal one, the first scholarly, full-length study of Asian American literature. The approach is chronological, providing a much-needed context for the discussion. Includes an extensive bibliography referencing both Asian American literature and Anglo-American portrayals of Asians and Asian Americans.

Lee, Joann Faung Jean. *Asian American Experiences in the United States: Oral Histories of First to Fourth Generation Americans from China, the Philippines, Japan, India, the Pacific Islands, Vietnam, and Cambodia*. Jefferson, N.C.: McFarland, 1991. Lee amasses oral histories of Asian Americans across class, age, and geographical lines. The accounts are lively and frank and together underscore the diverse nature of being Asian American. See especially "Growing Up in Mississippi," Sam Sue's account of growing up as a second-generation Chinese American marginalized by both whites and blacks.

Simpson, Janice C., and Pico Iyer. "Fresh Voices Above the Noisy Din." *Time* 137 (June 3, 1991): 66-67. Analyzes *China Boy* in the context of other works by contemporary Chinese American novelists, including Amy Tan, David Wong Louie, and Gish Jen.

_____. "From Ghetto to West Point: Gus Lee's *China Boy* Becomes a Man of Honor." *Time* 143 (March 28, 1994): 66. In this review of Lee's *Honor and Duty*, the sequel to *China Boy*, Simpson compares the two novels and concludes that *China Boy* is the more powerful and affecting. Offers insight into the main character of both books, Kai Ting.

So, Christine. "Delivering the Punch Line: Racial Combat as Comedy in Gus Lee's *China Boy.*" *MELUS* 21 (Winter, 1996): 141-155. So explores the use of ethnic humor to reinforce and question the American myth of total assimilation in Lee's *China Boy*. She examines the tensions between different minority groups, such as Chinese Americans and African Americans, and demonstrates how Lee's humor posits the possibility of an assimilated multicultural society, while also admitting that complete assimilation is probably impossible.

Stone, Judy. "Gus Lee: A China Boy's Rite of Passage." *Publishers Weekly* 243 (March 18, 1996): 47-48. Lee discusses his upbringing in a poor, mostly African American neighborhood in San Francisco as well as his success as a writer. Offers valuable insight into how Lee's background influenced his work as a novelist.

Tsai, Shih-Shan Henry. *The Chinese Experience in America*. Bloomington: Indiana University Press, 1986. A well-documented account of the history of Chinese in the United States. Includes photographs, maps, drawings, and social and historical data; also included is a bibliography that covers works pertinent to Chinese American history and sociology.

Pat M Wong

THE CHOSEN PLACE, THE TIMELESS PEOPLE

Author: Paule Marshall (1929-   )
Type of plot: Historical realism
Time of plot: Unspecified; probably the 1960's
Locale: Bournehills, a fictional West Indian island
First published: 1969

> *Principal characters:*
> MERLE KINBONA, a mulatta Bournehills native who returns to the
>   island from her studies in England
> LEESY WALKES, an old island prophetess
> VERE WALKES, Leesy's nephew, who returns to Bournehills from the
>   United States
> ALLEN FUSO, an American researcher of Irish-Italian descent
> SAUL AMRON, a Jewish American anthropologist and director of the
>   Bournehills project
> HARRIET AMRON, Saul's wife, a white Anglo-Saxon Protestant heiress
>   from Philadelphia
> LYLE HUTSON, a senator in the legislature of the island and member of
>   the power elite

The Novel

Through her experiences as an American of Barbadian heritage, Paule Marshall embodies the cultural dichotomy that provides the major tension in much of her fiction, including *The Chosen Place, the Timeless People*. This novel, exploring the means through which an individual comes to identify with a group, moves beyond the individual. It examines the problems facing many Third World countries in their struggle to establish a national identity.

The novel is divided into four books, each individual title representing one aspect of the connection between the individual and the group. The first book, "Heirs and Descendants," introduces the societal strata of Bourne Island, so determined by its colonial past, and introduces as well the newcomers who believe they have conic to change that past. The aging Jewish American anthropologist, Saul Amron, travels with his wealthy Philadelphian wife, Harriet, and a research associate, Allen Fuso, to Bournehills to study its primitive agricultural community and educate its people. They are part of the multimillion dollar development scheme of a major U.S. foundation. Saul's plan is to carry out a careful anthropological survey of the district before applying his findings to the community's development. As the researchers are quickly warned, other attempts to change the beautiful yet rugged island have failed. Particularly uncooperative have been the poor workers who have frustrated the civil servants of the island.

In book 1, the Amrons meet Merle Kinbona, a tense and eccentric middle-aged mulatta native who frightens Saul and Harriet with her seemingly disconnected chatter and boldness. Merle returns to the island from her studies in England after she receives news that her father is dying. Her purpose is to put her life in order, to make a fresh start, and the novel opens with her still consumed with her London experiences.

The second book, "Bournehills," focuses on the land itself. The community of Bournehills, a remote section of Bourne Island, is a Caribbean island clearly patterned after Barbados. The island itself, as seen from the air, is one of a group of small islands that look like stepping-stones linking North and South America. Bourne Island, however, is slightly out of line, more to the east, facing the Atlantic Ocean. It seems in its geographical position to link the New World with Africa. Despite the world's apparent abuse and then abandonment of them, the people of Bournehills hold on to their traditions as a means of sustenance and as a mark of their existence.

The third and fourth books, "Carnival" and "Whitsun," are named after ritual times of the year and hence point to both continuity and change. While the carnival is going on, Merle and Saul reveal the most intimate details of their past to each other. They also agree to become lovers. Merle reveals that her father was a wealthy white landowner who, though he did not claim her as a child, furnished her with funds to study in England. While in London, she was active in politics, led a bohemian life, and became the kept woman of a wealthy and jaded British woman. To escape the clutches of the woman and the decadence of the life she was leading, Merle married a Ugandan student and eventually gave birth to a daughter. Bitter after Merle's sudden break, the woman took revenge by informing Merle's husband about her past. Shocked and disappointed, he left Merle and took the child to East Africa with him.

Saul reveals that early in his career he deserted a Peruvian public-health nurse who had become his mistress. His first wife, a survivor of the Nazi concentration camps, died of a miscarriage while out on fieldwork with him in Honduras. His guilt for this incident had kept him out of fieldwork altogether until he met Harriet, who was recently divorced.

At the end of the novel, in the "Whitsun" section, Merle, Saul, and Allen Fuso are clearly the survivors. Merle decides to seek her daughter, though not necessarily a resolution to her marriage, in East Africa. Alone after Harriet's death, Saul continues to fight for the rights of the oppressed, though from behind a desk in the United States for an indeterminate period of time. Allen remains in Bournehills, although he is never able to participate in the life of the community completely.

The Characters

Saul and Harriet Amron are part of Marshall's purpose to provide a comment on the American role in developing countries. While much is heard about the project, very little is seen of it being worked out in practice. Saul functions as a sympathetic observer. He is a committed intellectual who has worked all of his life in underdeveloped countries and has acquired a pragmatic confidence in his ability to understand and improve them. Saul has the wisdom to learn patiently about the habits and needs of the peasants of the island and about the rhythms of the land and life there. It is his patience that earns him the respect he needs to proceed with his mission. Eventually, it becomes clear that he might not understand the island and its people as much as he had thought. As one of his last acts on the island, Saul helps to put together an organization of workers. Though he is not able to see the union fully launched, there is the strong prospect that it will continue after he has left the island.

Through his involvement with Merle, Saul Amron comes to understand the relationship between the native and the colonial government. He stands up for the islanders' rights and tries to help them overcome their economic difficulties. Saul's position in the novel is ironic; although he is a representative of the white patriarchy, he is also, as a Jew, a member of a group that historically has been victimized. This irony is broadened following the revelation that his wife, Harriet, is heir to a shipping company that was actively involved in the slave trade.

Harriet functions in the novel as the quintessential white Anglo-Saxon Protestant. Harriet, who was instrumental in getting her husband the Bournehills assignment, promises to keep out of his way on the expedition, but she subtly tries to control him. As his experience in Bournehills takes him further from her emotionally, she is threatened. Knowledge of his brief affair with Merle spurs her to have him transferred back to America. He breaks with his wife, cut off from the work that has become so vital to him, and she commits suicide.

Merle Kinbona functions as the voice of a voiceless people, the people of Bournehills. While she is the daughter of a mulatto and a black woman, she makes no attempt, unlike other islanders, to present herself as anything but black. The author draws a link between Merle's acceptance of her blackness and her refusal to deny Bournehills. She is fiercely committed to the island and its people, although she is personally rootless. Merle knits the entire cast together: the Americans, the middle-class professionals from the capital, the plantation overseers, and the ordinary people of Bournehills.

Although Merle's affair with Saul precipitates Harriet's suicide, the relationship has also begun to allow Merle to confront her past and, like Saul, to accept her flawed nature. Merle's and Saul's self-acceptance is linked with their acknowledgment of exploitation and what must be done to change society in order to end exploitation.

Leesy Walkes, the old island prophetess and native of Bournehills, is the voice of tradition. She clings to the traditional rhythms of the land and fears the coming of the technological age.

Vere Walkes, Leesy's nephew, leaves Bournehills to go to the United States in an attempt to make a success of his life, only to return a failure. Yet his mechanical talent is apparent when he rebuilds a battered old car that people had believed would never run again. Tragically, this talented young man has identified his goals in terms of technology instead of people, and it is this love for machines that destroys him: He is killed in a car race, as his aunt had known he would be. It is the capitalist world that destroys Vere; the car was built in Germany and designed in America. He is represented as a tragic victim of capitalist technology.

Allen Fuso, an American researcher, is an outsider to Bournehills. During the course of the novel, he comes to recognize his homosexual identity.

Lyle Hutson, a successful barrister, senator in the legislature of the island, and member of the power elite, has been born poor and black. He won a scholarship to the elite boys' secondary school in town and had later gone on to study in England. He had been somewhat radical in his youth, proclaiming socialism and revolution. Once he returned to the island and married into a prominent family, however, he spoke for change in more moderate terms. He had started building his future on the spoils of the past. His house is symbolic and public witness to his cultural betrayal.

Themes and Meanings

The Chosen Place, the Timeless People is a novel about neocolonialism and the reverberation of past actions in the present. Yet the novel is not a political tract; rather, it carefully explores the ways in which people's relationships are critical to the historical process. The book demonstrates that there is an ongoing interaction between the apparently faceless forces of society and the choices human beings make. The parts of the novel reflect that interaction. The novel also emphasizes the connection between character and context, while extending that connection beyond gender or racial indicators to include an entire people and their land.

The novel turns on its epigraph, a saying from the Tiv people of West Africa: "Once a great wrong has been done, it never dies. People speak the words of peace, but their hearts do not forgive. Generations perform ceremonies of reconciliation but there is no end." The theme is that of the complex series of interactions between the oppressed and their oppressors; its truth is that half measures cannot substantially change those interactions.

Finally, the novel portrays history as an active, creative, and moral process composed by human beings. According to Marshall, individuals and whole cultures decide upon the moral nature of an act, a series of acts, a history. In this novel, Marshall brings together the two themes that are most central to her work: the importance of truly confronting the past, both in personal and historical terms, and the necessity of reversing the present order.

Critical Context

In its analysis of characters who are inseparable from their particular culture, and in its insistence on the intersections of the past and present, *The Chosen Place, the Timeless People* is a culmination of Marshall's earlier work. Marshall moves from a localized setting in which she focuses primarily on one character or one family to the entire sociocultural fabric of Bournehills as a prototypical Third World country. Her scope is considerably larger than in her previous works, yet the people of this novel are psychologically related to characters in her earlier novels and stories. *The Chosen Place, the Timeless People*, in its characters, themes, and techniques, creates a coherent universe of Marshall's work. Marshall has matured as a writer in this novel, but her vision has not changed dramatically; rather, her emphasis moves from the way that the world affects an individual psyche to the way that many psyches create a world.

Marshall's presentation of a black woman as a major actor in the social, political, and cultural issues of her society can be compared to Alice Walker's depiction of the title character in her novel *Meridian* (1976). Both Merle and Meridian are new literary characters in African American women's novels, complex women struggling to understand themselves as black and female. In seeking their own identity, they find that they must pursue major social transformation. They are female literary characters of a social and political depth seldom seen in African American literature. In developing a character such as Merle Kinbona within the context of her particular society, Marshall announced the major theme of African American women's fiction of the 1970's, in which black women were being presented both as complex, developing persons and as active participants in the sociopolitical world.

The Chosen Place, the Timeless People has been praised for examining the problems facing many Third World countries in their struggle to establish a national identity. In this novel, black culture in the Western Hemisphere is linked with its African past and the promise of the future. Marshall proposes that the hope for the future lies in borrowing this past and using it as the basis for unified action and power.

Bibliography
Brock, Sabine. "Transcending, the 'Loophole of Retreat': Paule Marshall's Placing of Female Generations." *Callaloo* 10 (Winter, 1987): 79-90. Maintains that Marshall's fiction emphasizes the black woman's search for space, both physical and emotional, within the white patriarchy.
Christian, Barbara. "Sculpture and Space: The Interdependency of Character and Culture in the Novels of Paule Marshall." In *Black Women Novelists*. Westport, Conn.: Greenwood Press, 1980. Explores the author's use of culture, folklore, and environment as a means of creating character.
Marshall, Paule. Interview by Joyce Pettis. *MELUS* 17 (Winter, 1991): 117-129. Marshall discusses her concern for the need for cultural continuity in Caribbean culture. She shares her own experiences with West Indies culture and talks about her novels, including *The Chosen Place, the Timeless People*.
Meyer, Adam. "Memory and Identity for Black, White, and Jew in Paule Marshall's *The Chosen Place, the Timeless People*." *MELUS* 20 (Fall, 1995): 99-120. Meyer discusses the importance of memory and its relationship to regeneration and demonstrates that the strength of one's memory is essential not only to the wholeness of an individual but also to members of historically oppressed ethnic groups.
Pettis, Joyce. "'Talk' as Defensive Artifice: Merle Kinbona in *The Chosen Place, the Timeless People*." *African American Review*. 26 (Spring, 1992): 109-117. Pettis analyzes Merle Kinbona's use of talk to disguise her fractured psyche as she struggles to reconcile her African, European, and West Indies cultural heritages. Pettis sees Kinbona's hostile speech as a survival tactic and demonstrates that talk helps Merle accept her African American culture and identity.
Rahming, Melvin. "Towards a Caribbean Mythology: The Function of Africa in Paule Marshall's *The Chosen Place, the Timeless People*." *Studies in the Literary Imagi-*

nation 26 (Fall, 1993): 77-87. Focusing on Marshall's use of African mythology in her novel, Rahming asserts that the myths illustrate the struggle for a unified Caribbean worldview in a multicultural setting. African as well as other myths from colonial influences point to universal tendencies shared by all ethnic groups as they attempt to create a Caribbean cultural identity.

Skerrett, Joseph T., Jr. "Paule Marshall and the Crisis of Middle Years: *The Chosen Place, the Timeless People.*" *Callaloo* 6 (Spring-Summer, 1983): 68-73. Discusses *The Chosen Place, the Timeless People* as a novel about time, the crisis of old age, and generativity.

Spillers, Hortense J. "*Chosen Place, Timeless People*: Some Figurations on the New World." In *Conjuring: Black Women, Fiction, and Literary Tradition*, edited by Marjorie Pryse and Hortense J. Spillers. Bloomington: Indiana University Press, 1985. Asserts that a proper interpretation of *The Chosen Place, the Timeless People* must account for Marshall's use of history, myth, ontology, and ritual.

Stoelting, Winifred L. "Time Past and Time Present: The Search for Viable Links in *The Chosen Place, the Timeless People,* by Paule Marshall." *College Language Association Journal* 16 (September, 1972): 60-71. Maintains that healing of fragmented selves, rediscovery of lost identity, and repairing of bridges of communication between people who share a common heritage is possible only through an honest confrontation with the past.

Genevieve Slomski

CHRISTOPHER UNBORN

Author: Carlos Fuentes (1928-   )
Type of plot: Social satire
Time of plot: 1991-1992
Locale: Mexico
First published: Cristóbal nonato, 1987 (English translation, 1989)

Principal characters:

        CHRISTOPHER, a fetus in his mother's womb
        ANGEL PALOMAR Y FAGOAGA, Christopher's father
        ANGELES PALOMAR Y FAGOAGA, Christopher's mother
        DON HOMERO FAGOAGA, Christopher's uncle
        DON FERNANDO BENITEZ, Christopher' s uncle
        LADY MAMADOC, a simple girl made over as a symbol of national unity
        CONCHA TORO, a fifty-year-old sex symbol
        MATAMOROS MORENO, a would-be dictator
        D. C. BUCKLEY, an American political commentator
        WILL GINGERICH, an American professor

The Novel

Action and characterization are much less important in *Christopher Unborn* than themes and linguistic games. The basic structure of the work, comprising the gestation of the title character from conception to birth, derives directly from Laurence Sterne's eighteenth century novel *The Life and Opinions of Tristram Shandy* (1759-1767), to which Fuentes refers both directly and obliquely. Although the focus of the action is on the unborn Christopher, he participates in nothing except his uterine development, which he describes graphically and explicitly. He nevertheless frequently addresses the reader and also supplies information about other characters in flashbacks and glimpses of future events. Much of the language of the novel is deliberately obscure in the manner of James Joyce, combining humor and verbal acrobatics.

Satire, literary criticism, political denunciation, and philosophical reflection grow out of a fantasy framework. A young couple, Angel and Angeles, plan to have a male child born exactly at midnight on October 12, 1992, and to name him Christopher in order to win a government prize offered to celebrate the five hundredth anniversary of Christopher Columbus's arrival in America. Their act of conception takes place on the beach at Acapulco; overhead, the corruption of the central government is signaled by Uncle Homero's appearance in the sky in a parachute towed by a motor boat, his means of escaping from the destruction of the city then taking place—a disaster organized at Homero's own suggestion.

From an ultra-conventional home environment honoring the great physicists and writers of the past, Angel drifts into the morass of contemporary politics, where he is confused and beguiled by his two uncles. The older, Benitez, cherishes leftist and democratic ideals but has no arena in which to express them. The younger, Homero, runs for office as a candidate of the dominant Revolutionary Institutional Party, which claims to be democratic but is in its methods nationalistic and authoritarian. Although it professes to be progressive and concerned for the disadvantaged and indigenous populations, it is little different from its rival, the right-wing National Action Party. Homero comments that only the United States has had greater success in promoting a single party that pretends to be two.

As an instrument of large-scale thought control, the ruling Revolutionary Institutional Party makes over a humble secretary to resemble a mixture of Mae West and the Virgin of Guadalupe and promotes her as Lady Mamadoc, the mother of the nation. A similar national icon, a fifty-year-old bolero singer from Chile—named, like a wine from that country, Concha Toro—claims the title of Last Playboy Centerfold and becomes the idol of senior citizens.

A third figure, Matamoros Moreno, who combines literary and political idiosyncracies, displays a mixture of banality and platitude in his literary texts comparable to that in the speeches of Angel's uncles. When he asks Angel to help him find a publisher, Angel flees Mexico City. Moreno then turns to a pair of critics from the United States, D. C. Buckley and Will Gingerich, the latter a professor at Dartmouth College who is working as a tour guide while researching primitive sexual mythology. Moreno agrees to provide anthropological materials if Gingerich will guarantee to have his manuscript published by a reputable American press. Gingerich accepts the deal, while Buckley has sex with Moreno's daughter. As Angel travels with Angeles and his two uncles on a political campaign, they are attacked by a gang of highway workers instigated by Moreno. Each member of the gang rapes Angeles while Angel and the uncles are forced to watch. Up to this time, Angeles has not revealed that she is pregnant, but she is now forced to do so, because otherwise any one of the road gang could claim to be the father.

Returning to Mexico City, Angel and Angeles visit the municipal information office to find out how to enter the Columbus Day contest. Like characters in a Franz Kafka story, they are shuttled from bureau to bureau, receiving only ambiguous, irrelevant, or false answers. The government, true to form, has silently cancelled the contest. Matamoros Moreno transforms himself into an ethnic ayatollah, and with the aid of Concha Toro's melodies, he is hailed as the nation's redeemer. He strikes a deal with the government in which the entire cabinet agrees to parade through the city streets bearing religious symbols, while Moreno's men kidnap the wealthiest citizens in order to extract ransom money to shore up the government.

Angel and Angeles are eventually reunited on the shores of the Pacific, suggesting the rejection of Europe in favor of a New World common market in Pacifica, the goal of the historical Christopher. As the narrator emerges from Angeles's womb, he realizes that he is accompanied by a feminine twin. Then all is forgotten.

The Characters

The players in *Christopher Unborn* are not real people and not intended to be perceived as such. Instead, they are a miscellaneous collection of abstractions, allegories, caricatures, freaks, comic-strip personalities, and stereotypes. They have slight individuality apart from the psychological peculiarities or ideological attitudes they are intended to represent, and they lack universality because of the distinctly Mexican ambiance in which they are portrayed. Christopher himself, truculent and timorous, worries chiefly about his physical comfort in his mother's womb and seeks maximum satisfaction in sleep. As narrator, he affirms that the reader will know all there is to know about Angel at the beginning of the novel and only a little bit about Angeles at its end. True to the human condition, they engage in a constant struggle between what they are and what they would like to be. Angeles loves Angel so much that she adopts all his leftist ideology, but when he turns into a "conservative rebel," she retains her liberal outlook so that they may complement each other. Although Angel is the most prominent persona—in the sense that he takes up the greatest amount of space in the novel—he is neither hero, protagonist, nor antihero but an ordinary egoistical opportunist. He suffers the dismal effects of the Mexican government rather than initiating vigorous action of his own.

Uncle Homero represents the greed and corruption of the nation's politicians, seeking wealth and control by promoting the interests of foreign capitalists and catering to popular nationalistic, religious, and ethnic prejudices. Completely unprincipled, he is diabolical in his schemes and strategies, even trying to cheat Angel out of his father's inheritance. Uncle Benitez, superficially less invidious, occasionally protects Angel and espouses various popular causes, but he is consumed by the same drive for power.

Several episodes involve a rock band of four members, two of whom at times lose their human form, one becoming invisible and the other assuming the form of an egg. Every male character, including Angel, has sex with a teenaged girl, and every female except Angeles has some sexual aberration; even she is gang-raped. Yet Fuentes's target is not sex, which serves primarily as entertainment. His censure is directed at the social, political, and cultural deficiencies of his country.

Themes and Meanings

Like George Orwell's *Nineteen Eighty-Four* (1948), *Christopher Unborn* was published prior to the period it covers. In his dystopian vision, Fuentes finds the ills of Mexico in what he calls its dialectic, wavering between revolution and reaction, insurgency and reform, religion and positivism. The electorate has never managed to find a middle way between order and liberty, progress and tradition, justice and authority. Beset by these conflicting loyalties, Mexicans have become the pliable instruments of political parties that proclaim themselves alternately revolutionary, conservative, or liberal. Fuentes indicates as a similar problem in literary criticism the dichotomy between the universal and the national. He declares that the proper standard for judging Mexican literature should be its inherent qualities, not its national origin.

Fuentes holds the lack of a strong national identity responsible for the taking over of Mexico by foreign capital (especially from the United States), the pillaging of its natural resources, and the country's debt of $1,492 billion, a figure arbitrarily chosen to coincide with the date of Columbus's voyage. Pollution of air, earth, and water in

Mexico City, called "Makesicko City," has made the area an inferno for the poor, and Acapulco, called "Cacapulco" and "Kafkapulco," has become a fief of American tourists. The Indians are afflicted with poverty, helplessness, and injustice, and eleven thousand tons of sulphur, lead, and carbon monoxide circulate every day in the capital, which also daily produces thirty tons of garbage.

Fuentes's concern with the future also incorporates an intellectual problem, the meaning of time. He plays with its different aspects, showing it alternately as linear, circular (in the sense of eternal return), and sometimes spiraling. Chronology is frequently violated, some events are repeated, and the reality of others is established only by reports issued after the passage of days or weeks. Several recapitulations are included as an indication that history as such is unreliable. Time is a continuum, but one must choose a point and place within it to discover the face of reality. Christopher in his embryonic discourse speculates on whether a narrative, like the earth, may also be round.

Critical Context

The main political elements of this portrayal of Mexico exist also in Fuentes's first international success *Le muerte de Artemio Cruz* (1962; *The Death of Artemio Cruz*, 1964), which treats the deterioration of the ideals of the Mexican Revolution in the capitalist regimes that followed it. In *Terra Nostra* (Spanish and English editions, 1975), which is widely considered his masterpiece, Fuentes uses literary and mythical characters from three broad historical periods—the classical, the Middle Ages, and the modern—to establish an Indo-Afro-Ibero-American cultural continuum. Much of his later work, including *Christopher Unborn*, may be considered as an extension and revision of *Terra Nostra*. Fuentes himself has even described his fiction as a whole, both those works already published and those to come, as an exercise in the portrayal of time.

What distinguishes *Christopher Unborn* from his previous works is the strong element of humor it contains. These mirthful ingredients, frequently scatalogical, are conveyed primarily through satire and wordplay. Fuentes jokes, for example, about the structure of his novel in progress, even including a parody of it in miniature. He introduces a dating service called TUGUEDER, and invents a series of names ridiculing shopping malls: Mall-efic, Mall-feasance, Mall-function, and Mall-formed. Similar strokes of humor inspire ingenious puns, for example President Ronald Ranger or Donald Danger and the composer Mouzart, Mao Tsar, or Mouscart. Since Fuentes is the joint translator of the English version of the novel, its puns and slang expressions also belong to him. In this irreverent jesting, Fuentes diverges from the pattern of his own former triumphs to invoke the wit of literary predecessors such as Sterne and Quevedo.

Bibliography

Mouat, Ricardo Gutierrez. "Postmodernity and Postmodernism in Latin America: Carlos Fuentes's *Christopher Unborn*." In *Critical Theory, Cultural Politics*, edited by Steven M. Bell. Notre Dame, Ind.: University of Notre Dame Press, 1993. Concludes that the novel does not fit any paradigm of postmodernity, largely because of its eccentric carnivalesque discourse.

Ortega, Julio. "*Christopher Unborn:* Rage and Laughter." Translated by Carl Mentley. *Review of Contemporary Fiction* 8, no. 2 (Summer, 1988): 285-291. Ortega elucidates the lively comic elements of the novel while comparing it to a Latin American nightmare that portrays the miscarriage rather than the invention of the continent.

Phaf, Ineke. "Nation as the Concept of 'Democratic Otherness': *Christopher Unborn* and the Plea for Hybrid Cultures." In *Encountering the Other(s): Studies in Literature, History, and Culture*, edited by Gisela Brinker-Gabler. Albany: State University of New York Press, 1995. While minimizing the dystopian elements of the novel, Phaf interprets it as a model for a multicultural and polycultural city of the future.

Rivero-Potter, Alicia. "Columbus' Legacy in *Cristobal Nonato* by Carlos Fuentes." *Revista Canadiense de Estudios Hispanicas* 20, no. 2 (Winter, 1996): 305-325. Analyzes all references to Columbus throughout the novel, which is described as a mixture of "the sacred and profane, colloquialisms and sexual humor." Parallels are established between the hegemonies of Spain and the United States that have made Mexico to a large degree dependent upon them.

Williams, Raymond Leslie. *The Writings of Carlos Fuentes*. Austin: University of Texas Press, 1996. An articulate, sensitive, and informed summary of Fuentes's life and literary accomplishments. *Christopher Unborn* is treated in a separate section as one of the author's "lengthy, ambitious, and totalizing books" and is also referred to frequently in other sections, particularly in connection with theories of time. The appendix contains a valuable interview with Fuentes.

A. Owen Aldridge

CHRONICLE OF A DEATH FORETOLD

Author: Gabriel García Márquez (1928-   )
Type of plot: Mystery
Time of plot: Early twentieth century
Locale: An unnamed Colombian village on the coast of Caribbean
First published: Crónica de una muerte anunciada, 1981 (English translation, 1982)

> *Principal characters:*
> THE NARRATOR
> SANTIAGO NASAR, the murder victim
> CRISTO BEDOYA, his best friend and closest companion
> ANGELA VICARIO, the bride whose loss of honor is avenged upon Nasar
> PEDRO and
> PABLO VICARIO, her brothers, identical twins, who murder Nasar
> BAYARDO SAN ROMÁN, the groom who returns his bride to her parents
>   when he discovers that she is not a virgin

The Novel

The "chronicle" of the title is the attempt by the narrator to piece together events leading up to the murder of Santiago Nasar by Pedro and Pablo Vicario. He does so by drawing on his own memories as well as on the accounts of those who witnessed the murder and whom he sought out twenty-seven years after the event. Thus, the novel bears many of the trappings of a murder mystery, but it is hardly a conventional representative of that genre: The murderers had announced their intentions to everyone they met for hours before the event. What the narrator, and indeed all the characters need to learn, is how a murder so publicly announced could have occurred, with so many well-meaning people doing nothing to stop the Vicario brothers, who had little heart for carrying out the deed and who, by their open announcements, were in effect asking to be stopped.

As the novel begins, the narrator recounts Nasar's waking about an hour before his death and telling his mother his dream of walking in a drizzle through a timber forest. Although she is a renowned interpreter of dreams, she fails to recognize the ominous foreboding of death. Her failure is the first of many to come, culminating in her barring the door through which Nasar is about to escape from his attackers, when she hears the crowd approaching at the end of the novel, thinking her son already safe inside the house.

The narrator's reconstruction of the events of that morning is complicated by the varying accounts of people's whereabouts, their awareness of the brothers' intentions, and their feelings toward Nasar. They cannot even agree on the weather that morning, whether it was radiantly pleasant or oppressively funeral. The narrator objectively records all details, scarcely weighing them for consistency or import, possibly because he is attempting a purely journalistic account, and possibly because he resembles his mother in the way, as he notes, "she is accustomed to noting . . . superfluous detail when she wants to get to the heart of the matter."

Nasar is murdered by the Vicario brothers to avenge their sister Angela's dishonor. She had married Bayardo San Román the previous day, but after a day and a night of extravagant feasting by the village, the groom discovers that his bride is not a virgin and returns her to her home. Her mother beats her, and upon questioning by her brothers, Angela Vicario identifies Santiago Nasar as her "perpetrator." Their duty is clear. They take two of the knives they use in their trade of slaughtering pigs, sharpen them at another butcher's shop, then wait in Clothilda Armenta's milk shop, from which they can watch Nasar's bedroom window, until he goes out to see the bishop who is to come and bless the village. They carry out their simple plan, to butcher Nasar at his front door, and profoundly change the lives of everyone who has gathered to watch.

The Characters

There is little attempt to represent the deep psychological dimensions of the characters, as has been prevalent in the novel in English since Henry James and Virginia Woolf. The characters are rather ingredients in Gabriel García Márquez's so-called Magical Realism, a Latin American offshoot of Surrealism, in which the fantastic is ordinary. These characters are like flowers in a small garden so exotic that the observer is astonished almost beyond understanding; they are more the inhabitants of folktale, myth, and legend, than of the twentieth century.

Even the narrator remains oddly unknowable, though he is clearly García Márquez's fictive alter ego (he tells how he proposed to his wife Mercedes, for example, and mentions her sister and aunt by name). He is a sort of wide-eyed, baffled observer, a student visiting home during the period of the novel, who simply likes his fellow villagers so much that he cannot find any wickedness in them—the forgivable sins of lust and drunkenness, perhaps, but not the malice that could produce the unthinkable murder of one of their own citizens in broad daylight, with practically the whole village as witnesses.

What the characters lack in psychological shading, they make up for in abundance of color. The groom Bayardo San Román arrived in town with silver decorating his saddlebags, belt, and boots, looking for someone to marry. He had "the waist of a novice bullfighter, golden eyes, and a skin slowly roasted by saltpeter." Magdelena Oliver could not take her eyes off him and told the narrator that she "could have buttered him and eaten him alive." He could swim faster, drink longer, and fight better than any man in town, and was far richer than any of them; every woman in town would have married him, except for the girl he wanted at first sight: Angela Vicario. He bought all the raffle tickets to win a music box for her, then bought the best house in town for her, though it was not for sale. (The sight of all the money he put on the table ultimately killed the owner.)

Bayardo's character may justly be said to be flat because he is little more than a vehicle for machismo, but such a stylistic choice enables García Márquez to portray his characters as victims trapped by the prevailing codes of their lives, as outmoded as they may be judged, which leads directly to the absurd murder of Nasar because he violated Angela, although no one is ever sure that he was guilty. Indeed, the reader will not find the characters divisible into categories of major and minor, but only find those who appear more often and those who appear less, and all contribute to the unlikelihood of the central action. Magdelena Oliver, who first reacts to Bayardo's male beauty, appears but once, and her comment stands not as her own opinion but as the ultimate consensus of the village. It is as though the village itself were the main character of the novel, speaking with many voices; in this reading, the murder itself becomes a ritualistic, communal suicide in which the forty-two characters who are named in the novel (and many more of their brothers and sisters and cousins) are helpless participants.

Thus, of the murdered man and the woman he allegedly wronged, the reader learns little more than of the characters on the perimeter of the central drama: The lesser characters serve as a kind of moral reflection of the central ones. There is Maria Alejandrina Cervantes, for example, the elegant, serviceable woman who never sleeps and who, as the narrator attests, "did away with my generation's virginity," including that of Nasar, who dies for a crime that for the woman is a vocation.

Nasar is a fairly affluent young man, inclined to womanizing and drinking with friends. He dies not so much because his guilt is established, but because he is typical and therefore able to be presumed guilty. His public execution at the end of the novel is described as in slow motion and in precise detail, in more detail than any aspect of his life, because his death more profoundly affects the village than his life could. Until he dies, the characters are locked into the modes of action that will produce his death. Once that is accomplished, they are freed to pursue their individual lives again, though this time, haunted by a terrible memory.

Themes and Meanings

Where García Márquez's highly regarded novel *Cien años de soledad* (1967; *One Hundred Years of Solitude*, 1970) has the large, episodic scope of a Greek epic, *Chronicle of a Death Foretold* has the concise brevity of Greek tragedy, and it shares with tragedy the theme of guilt and its purging through recognition of the truth:

> For years we couldn't talk about anything else. Our daily conduct, dominated then by so many linear habits, had suddenly begun to spin around a common anxiety. The cocks of dawn would catch us trying to give order to the chain of many chance events that had made absurdity possible, and it was obvious that we weren't doing it from an urge to clear up mysteries but because none of us could go on living without an exact knowledge of the place and the mission assigned to us by fate.

At the political level, the book is an allegory for tyranny made possible through uncritical obedience to established codes: No one is able to step out of the accustomed modes of behavior to stop the murderers. Indeed, the attempts to purge guilt through recognition meander through the inexactitudes of memory toward self-justification offered in terms of the original misjudgments that allowed the murder to take place. It takes place over and over, in the varying accounts of witnesses, in the narrator's conclusion, in the villagers' memories, and since no one has learned what is necessary to prevent its recurrence, it will continue to be obsessively replayed as ritual and as a mystery to which no solution can be found.

Most of the characters reason that affairs of honor exclude all but those involved, a circular logic that admits no intervention. The fictional narrative, however, points to a very active involvement by supposed bystanders. For example, Nasar's maid, Victoria Guzmán, wakens him as ordered at 5:30 in the morning but fails to warn him because she pays no heed to what she considers drunken boasts. In fact, Nasar had asked her to send her daughter Divina Flor, a nubile girl whom Nasar has repeatedly manhandled, to wake him, but Guzmán herself had suffered the advances of Nasar's father, and so goes in her daughter's place. While Nasar eats breakfast, she disembowels rabbits before him and throws the entrails to the dogs; at the end of the novel, Nasar's mother orders the dogs to be killed as they howl for his intestines. Though the narrator does not draw a conclusion, evidence is strewn through the book that Guzmán would sooner see Nasar dead than have him repeat his father's conquest and that she maliciously withholds the warning that would easily save his life. Her righteous disregard of drunken boasts plays into her maternal instinct and her secret loathing of her helplessness. While she cannot act on feelings she scarcely acknowledges, her inaction in not warning Nasar is fatally effective.

García Márquez challenges the reader to look more deeply than does the narrator at the pattern of chance that produces fate. The reader is prompted to reconsider the excuses, denials, and self-justifications that blind the narrator, who seeks through his chronicle of superfluous information to understand how a death so foretold could be allowed to take place.

Critical Context

Because many characters reappear in his works, because many of the works are set in Macondo (unnamed here, but recognizable as the fictional counterpart of his birthplace, Aracataca), and because of the persistently fabulous nature of his Magical Realism, García Márquez's novels and short stories may be said to constitute one grand fiction, of which *Chronicle of a Death Foretold* is a significant part.

García Márquez's treatment of isolation and solitude in previous work extends to this novel. Macondo's search for a way inland to other villages in *One Hundred Years of Solitude* is ended here with the coming of the railroad, on which many of the characters will leave following the murder. The novel also is linked by contrast with the short story "El ahogado más hermoso del mundo" (1972; "The Handsomest Drowned Man in the World," 1972), in which a drowned man is taken in by the inhabitants of a stagnant town after he washes up on shore, becoming a source of community pride. Care for the drowned man removes the villagers from their individual and collective solitude, as contrarily the community's witnessing the death of Nasar jolts its members out of their "linear habits" and into an obsession with their guilt. Where in *El otoño del patriarca* (1975; *The Autumn of the Patriarch*, 1975) the aging dictator is isolated by his tyrannical power, here the villagers are cut off from one another by their failure to use their power to prevent Nasar's death.

In interviews, García Márquez has often equated his fiction with journalism (he began his career as a journalist in 1948) and has said that the fantastic elements in his work are merely the reality of Latin America, faithfully transcribed. In *Chronicle of a Death Foretold*, he has written an investigative report of the circumstances of a murder. Yet he turns the genre of the mystery novel inside out in order to create his own convoluted, cyclical form of storytelling. It begins when the victim rises and ends one hour later with his death, but in between the narrator retraces the impossible labyrinth of circumstances and chance and the unwinding of its terrible consequences. Thus, the artist triumphs over the journalist, as García Márquez's humanity prevails in the foolish beauty of his unfortunates, and in their resilient good nature that struggles with fate to an outcome somewhat better than a draw.

Bibliography

Bilowit, Ira J. "Graciela Daniele: Chronicle of a *Chronicle*." *Back Stage* 36 (June 16, 1995): 32-33. Profiles the efforts of director and choreographer Graciela Daniele to adapt Márquez's novel to the stage. She talks about specific scenes in the book as well as the process through which she tried to interpret Márquez's verbal metaphors into dance.

Christie, John S. "Fathers and Virgins: García Márquez's Faulknerian *Chronicle of a Death Foretold*." *Latin American Literary Review* 21 (January-June, 1993): 21-29. Christie draws parallels between Márquez's novel and Faulkner's *Light in August*. In both novels, the people in a small town manipulate facts leading to the killing of an accused criminal. It is likely that Angela's blind father is really the perpetrator, yet Santiago Nasar is the one accused and murdered.

Rendon, Mario. "The Latino and His Culture: *Chronicle of a Death Foretold* by Gabriel García Márquez." *The American Journal of Psychoanalysis* 54 (December, 1994): 345-348. Rendon discusses the mechanism of letter writing through which the protagonist achieves transcendent growth. Like psychoanalysis, it helps her to confront, and ultimately reject, the social rules that shape her identity. Rendon also makes the interesting point that the novel was published during the Cold War, when people were only too aware that they too stood at the brink of death.

Sims, Robert L. "From Fictional to Factual Narrative: Contemporary Critical Heteroglossia, Gabriel García Márquez." *Studies in the Literary Imagination* 25 (Spring, 1992): 21-60. Focusing on narratology, Sims presents a critique of Márquez's journalism and bigeneric writing. He discusses *Chronicle of a Death Foretold* in some detail.

Styron, Rose. "Gabriel García Márquez, Carlos Fuentes, and Kenzaburo Oe: From the Rose Styron Conversations." *New Perspectives Quarterly* 14 (Fall, 1997): 56-62. A revealing interview with three renowned authors. They share their views on topics such as women and power, first and lost love, journalism as literature, spirit and faith, and multiculturalism.

Robert Bensen

THE CIDER HOUSE RULES

Author: John Irving (1942-   )
Type of plot: Social realism
Time of plot: The 1880's to 1900; the 1920's to the 1950's
Locale: Maine
First published: 1985

> *Principal characters:*
> WILBUR LARCH, an obstetrician and abortionist who directs the St. Cloud's orphanage
> HOMER WELLS, an orphan, Dr. Larch's surrogate son
> CANDY WORTHINGTON (née KENDALL), Homer's closest friend, the love of his life and mother of their son, Angel Wells
> WALLY WORTHINGTON, Candy's husband, the son of a privileged couple
> MELONY (MELODY), an unadoptable, perpetually angry orphan
> OLIVE WORTHINGTON, Wally's mother, a wealthy, sensible, decent woman
> RAYMOND KENDALL, Candy's father, a master mechanic
> ANGEL WELLS, Homer and Candy's son
> ARTHUR ROSE, the chief of a crew of African American orchard workers

The Novel

Written as a tribute to the decency and dedication of the most impressive practitioners of the medical profession, *The Cider House Rules* is a multigenerational chronicle covering the life of Wilbur Larch, who as a young doctor is drawn by compassion and judgment to forge a career as an obstetrician and abortionist. Accepting an appointment as the director of St. Cloud's, an isolated, under-equipped orphanage in Maine, Larch struggles with the moral questions, medical challenges, and social difficulties involved in helping desperate, frightened, and usually penurious women whose pregnancies require, in his estimation, either termination or an expert, comfortable birth. His acceptance of the obligations involved in providing a proper home, either within or beyond the orphanage, for the children he delivers is the burden and blessing of his long life as a man who, in the spirit of the practical New Englander, wants to be of use to humanity.

Larch moves almost incidentally toward his life's work through a series of circumstances arising from accidents of timing and his upbringing. Once settled at St. Cloud's, he commits himself completely to his task as healer and symbolic father to an extended family of life's victims. His own experiences with social hypocrisy and human frailty have convinced him that social conventions are often detrimental to people's most fundamental needs, but his choices to work beyond the legalities of society are guided by a moral compass that is set firmly in accordance with a higher law.

Surrounded by faithful, adoring associates––Nurse Angela, Nurse Edna, and Mrs. Grogan—Larch struggles with the nearly impossible task of giving every orphan an opportunity to find a family built on love and respect.

The obstacles he faces are epitomized by his attempts to train Homer Wells, an orphan who can never completely settle into a life beyond the orphanage, to be his successor and the carrier of his legacy of care and encouragement. While Larch knows instinctively that Homer, like himself, will find his truest satisfaction in service at St. Cloud's, he understands that Homer must discover this for himself. The central narrative design of the novel thus follows Homer's progress into the world and his eventual return to his ultimate "home." Homer has returned to the orphanage three times between his birth in about 1920 and the time immediately before the United States enters World War II. At that time, he is invited to spend the summer at the home of Wally Worthington, who has journeyed to St. Cloud's with his girlfriend, Candy Kendall, to terminate her pregnancy. Wally and Candy live in Heart's Haven, an attractive town on the Maine coast, and as Homer enters their life of optimism, confidence, prosperity, and unreflective happiness, his somber outlook is altered by his first real opportunity to live as a member of a successful, privileged family. His friendship with Wally and Candy is immediately complicated, however, by his almost instantaneous, overwhelming romantic attraction for Candy, who is similarly attracted to him. Since both of them also "love" Wally, a complex, ongoing situation of permanent emotional turmoil is initiated.

When Wally joins the Air Force, Homer and Candy become lovers, conceiving a child they decide to keep but pretend they have adopted as an orphan. Wally's plane is shot down over Burma, and although there is no word of his fate, his family and friends continue to have intimations of his survival. Angel Wells is born with both parents uncertain how to proceed, so they choose to follow Homer's doubt-ridden strategy to "wait and see." In a parallel plot, Dr. Larch has been continuing with his work at St. Cloud's but has been forced into a defensive posture by officious trustees. In a brief idyll that concludes when Wally writes from India about his escape, Homer and Candy, with their son, live and work at St. Cloud's. Wally returns home, paralyzed and sterile but as cheerful and amiable as before. Wally's father dies from Alzheimer's disease, and Homer and Candy move to the Worthington family orchard at Heart's Haven, where Homer becomes the superintendent of the business. Angel Wells is reared by three parents after Candy and Wally are married.

There is a significant shift in narrative perspective as the novel moves forward sixteen years to the mid-1950's. From an unfolding present-tense construction, the narrative changes to a mixture of the past recollected while the present emerges as a kind of projected future already recorded (as in sentences beginning "Wally and Candy would . . ."). Homer decides that the entire truth of his relationship with Candy must be disclosed. Angel Wells falls in love with the daughter of Mr. Rose, the lethal, defensively psychotic chief of the migrant apple workers. Wally remains cheerful and accepting, and when Dr. Larch dies in his nineties, Homer finally returns to St. Cloud's in the identity of "Dr. Fuzzy Stone," a fictitious creation of Larch's designed to ease Homer into the role he was destined to fill. When the body of a woman known only as Melony arrives at the hospital, Homer recognizes an old acquaintance from his youth who has haunted his existence through the years. Their reunion in the orphanage completes the cycle of birth-search-renewal-ripeness that describes the pattern of the life of Wilbur Larch, the secular saint who is the God/Father of all the orphans.

The Characters

John Irving has said that he wanted in *The Cider House Rules* to write about a person he "absolutely" admired. Therefore, Wilbur Larch is presented in terms designed to bring the reader extremely close to the character, making his actions admirable, his moral decisions beyond the motives of personal pleasure, his personality extremely congenial, and his human complexity sufficiently realistic so that he does not become a simplistic hero. There is a comfortable quality about Larch, in spite of his rage against brutality and mendacity, that begins with his extraordinary warmth and decency—his genuine, heartfelt caring for human suffering, the vital capacity to share the pain of his patients that all doctors should possess.

The groundwork for the advancing action that covers nearly a century is the introduction of the social conditions that shape Larch as a youth and young medical student. The only other character who is treated with anything like the same thoroughness is Homer Wells, Larch's surrogate son, an orphan never officially adopted but a member of Larch's "family" at St. Cloud's. Like Larch, Homer is observed practically from birth, the social circumstances of his upbringing both within and outside St. Cloud's serving to form him. Larch's desire to see him as a worthy successor operates both as a source of strength and as an obstacle to his development as an individual. Irving illustrates the affinities and similarities of the two men as well as the single-minded intelligence that causes Homer to differ from Larch: He prefers not to use his medical skills to perform abortions, even though he agrees with Larch's philosophical and ideological arguments.

As the narrative course follows Homer away from and back to St. Cloud's in a pattern of growth and consolidation, Irving employs the primary methods available to an omniscient narrator. Dr. Larch and Homer Wells are seen in active engagement with the world, and their characters are revealed through their singular styles of expression. Most significant, they are examined in detail from a psychoanalytical perspective that permits the reader to follow the processes of their conscious (and subconscious) minds. Irving is not hesitant to explain motive and preference or to show both men in reflective moments that deepen experience. Aside from the woman known only as Melony (a corruption of Melody)—who is described as always angry, an example of the darker impulses brought out by loneliness and mistreatment—the remaining characters are presented essentially from the outside. Even Candy, who with Melony takes a crucial role in Homer's life as the polar opposites of sexual involvement, does not have an extensive separate existence away from her connection to the track of Homer's narrative. The other interesting characters are sharply sketched and convincing in their actions, but they tend to be personifications of particular human inclinations (Ray Kendall is a master machinist; Meany Hyde is always jovial) rather than fully realized depictions.

Themes and Meanings

In an interview shortly after *The Cider House Rules* was published, Irving stated, "It is a book with a polemic." In accordance with George Orwell's dictum that "All art is propaganda but not all propaganda is art," however, Irving has utilized two of the dominant modes of the novelist's art to frame his argument. The more prominent is Irving's debt (and homage) to Charles Dickens, whose conception of the novel as an arena for the exploration of dynamic social issues is apparent in the manner in which *The Cider House Rules* uses institutional rigidity, the tyranny of class consciousness, and the redemptive faculties of the extended family as focal points for its examination of the controversy surrounding abortion rights. The other, less familiar mode has its origins in the eighteenth century concern for the "Man of Feeling" featured in the work of such writers as Henry Fielding and Lawrence Sterne, whose protagonists acted out of a fusion of emotion and intellect that emphasized the heart (or passions) as important measures of moral justice. The two modes are joined throughout the narrative, as the decisions and choices Larch and Wells make are presented as the consequences of their formative contacts with American society. Neither man begins with any specific agenda other than a feeling for human suffering and a desire to alleviate it. Larch arrives at his chosen profession through his eye-opening experiences with women who are helpless and frightened. Wells, in his search for an independent identity, is always aware of the isolation of an orphan and the need to establish some kind of contact with other people. Since both men accept that the finest kind of career is "to be of use," the manner in which they can use their skills—technical and personal—is the subject of internal debate, spirited dialogue, and, at times, direct proclamations of conviction. It is in these moments that the novel fulfills Irving's description of a polemic, but it is the intensity of the genre, not its familiar form, that is applicable in this case.

While both Larch and Wells as "admirable" characters are expressions of Irving's own ideas, the novel is not simply a brief for abortion. Both the pro-choice position and the pro-life position are amply expressed, and the ultimate choice that Larch and Wells make is based on their sense of the most humane course of action in an imperfect world. Irving envisions the practitioner of the healing arts as a person who must address the fundamental needs of the human spirit by providing care, consolation, and comfort as obligatory accompaniments to the physical and technical aspects of medicine, and he is very concerned with the terrible feelings of isolation and loneliness that overcome patients ravaged by illness. In a symbolic sense, the novel suggests that everyone is ultimately an orphan in a cosmic void, and that only human love (or divine love in human form) can rescue a lost soul. The families that are organized by love are the truest means of social salvation, and for all his foibles, "St. Larch" is an exemplar of goodness in his role as the prime organizer of a community of compassion.

Critical Context

The Cider House Rules, Irving's sixth novel in seventeen years, moves away from some of his familiar themes while deepening his interest in the family (in many forms) as a source of strength in a fractured, frightening universe. Continuing to combine elements of Magical Realism with the great traditions of the Victorian novel, Irving uses the lore of apple growing and marketing and the graphic details of medical procedures as a solid ground upon which he places the terms of a debate concerning ethical practices and essential human needs.

While the power of love and the forces of eros remain as important elements for Irving, *The Cider House Rules* is a transitional work, shifting the focus of narrative consciousness from the entropic, absurdist cosmos of *The World According to Garp* (1978) toward the realm of the miraculous, which Irving's *A Prayer for Owen Meany* (1989) would bring into prominence. Wilbur Larch, who knows when to break the rules, is guided by an intuitive faith in a higher set of rules that foreshadows the spiritual quest upon which Irving would enter in the latter book.

Bibliography

Berson, Misha. "I Can't Believe I Staged the Whole Thing." *American Theater* 13 (March, 1996): 6-7. Berson evaluates Peter Parnell's theatrical adaptation of Irving's popular novel. He notes the strict adherence of the play to the novel and discusses the Dickensian themes apparent in both.

Burgess, Anthony. "A Novel of Obstetrics." *The Atlantic* 98 (July, 1985): 98-100. Review of *The Cider House Rules* by another prominent novelist. Burgess finds the novel's themes admirable but judges the book to be lacking in artistry.

Campbell, Josie. *John Irving: A Critical Companion*. Westport, Conn.: Greenwood Press, 1998. Offers a brief biography of Irving's life as well as an overview of his fiction. Devotes an entire chapter to *The Cider House Rules*, including a discussion of plot and character development, thematic issues, and a new critical approach to the novel.

Clemons, Walter. "Dr. Larch's Odd Orphanage." *Newsweek* 105 (May 27, 1985): 80. Clemons criticizes the book from a traditionalist position, citing what he claims is its lack of structure, its shallow characterizations, and its sentimentality.

DeMott, Benjamin. "Guilt and Compassion." *The New York Times Book Review* 90 (May 26, 1985): 1, 25. A balanced, subtle, probing examination of the book. Notes the novel's defects but recognizes its virtues, especially its "courage of imaginative ardor" and its straightforward storytelling.

Reilly, Edward C. *Understanding John Irving*. Columbia: University of South Carolina Press, 1991. An illuminating, clearly written study of Irving's work, with an incisive chapter on *The Cider House Rules*, which Reilly calls a "definite maturing of Irving's literary talents." Includes a brief biography and a good annotated bibliography.

Leon Lewis

THE CITY AND THE PILLAR

Author: Gore Vidal (1925-   )
Type of plot: Social criticism
Time of plot: The late 1930's to the mid-1940's
Locale: Rural Virginia, Seattle, Beverly Hills, New Orleans, the Yucatán, and New York City
First published: 1948

> *Principal characters:*
> JIM WILLARD, a homosexual youth
> BOB FORD, his first lover
> RONALD SHAW, a Hollywood screen idol
> PAUL SULLIVAN, a disillusioned young writer
> MARIA VERLAINE, a rich, lonely friend of Paul Sullivan

The Novel

The subject of *The City and the Pillar* is Jim Willard's coming of age. The novel is an *Entwicklungsroman* reminiscent in some respects of Jean-Jacques Rousseau's *Émile: Ou, De l'éducation* (1762; *Emilius and Sophia: Or, A New System of Education*, 1762-1763) or Roger Martin du Gard's *Jean Barois* (1913; English translation, 1949). The crucial difference in *The City and the Pillar*, however, is that Jim Willard is homosexual, and the novel focuses on his growing sexual awareness, on his first sexual encounter, and on his leading a homosexual existence in a heterosexual world.

The book uses a frame technique. The protagonist is first introduced as he sits in a bar where he has been drinking for several hours. The last chapter of the book takes up where the first chapter left off, and the rest of the plot is developed through flashbacks which encompass Jim's life from age seventeen until now, when he is in his mid-twenties. In the course of the book, Vidal traces Jim's progress from small-town rural Virginia to Seattle, Beverly Hills, New Orleans, the Yucatán, and New York, where he has arranged a reunion with Bob Ford, his first lover.

Jim finds expression for his budding sexuality during a weekend that he spends in an isolated cabin with Bob Ford, a year his senior. The two fall into a sexual relationship spontaneously and naturally in the course of the weekend. Vidal portrays Jim not as the kind of homosexual whom most people would have thought prototypical in the 1940's, but rather as a quite virile, athletic type much like anyone else except for his homosexuality.

Jim does not get along with his parents, and as soon as he finishes high school, he leaves home and ships out as a cabin boy. When the ship lays over in Seattle, one of Jim's more worldly crewmates takes him to a prostitute. Jim is intrigued at first but then is repulsed by the female body, and he flees in such a state of embarrassment that he is unable to return to his ship and face his friends. Instead, he goes to Beverly Hills as a tennis coach at an exclusive hotel. Jim is invited to a party at the palatial home of

Ronald Shaw, a film idol, who takes Jim in to live with him. The two have a prolonged affair.

When his affair with Shaw ends, Jim becomes the lover of Paul Sullivan, a writer who is attracted by Jim's masculine appearance and demeanor. The two have an affair, during which Jim comes more to grips with the idea of loving a man, something that he had considered unnatural in his relationship with Ronald Shaw.

When the two run into Maria Verlaine, a rich and sophisticated friend of Paul in New Orleans, she invites the two of them to go to the Yucatán with her. They accept, and Maria tries to involve Jim in an affair with her. Jim cannot respond, but the incident provides Paul, who is masochistic, with an opportunity to play the wounded one, which he enjoys. For his part, Jim is convinced, after his experience with Maria, that he is not like other men and that his homosexuality is ingrained to the point that he will never be rid of it.

With the entrance of the United States into World War II, Jim enlists in the army and Paul becomes a foreign correspondent. The two are separated. Jim, who does not like army life, becomes a physical training instructor but soon is mustered out because of arthritis.

Jim has learned still more about his sexual nature during his time in the army. Throughout his years of wandering, Jim has thought constantly about Bob Ford, his first lover. Before his discharge, while lying ill in an army hospital, Jim writes to each of the people with whom he has been involved: Bob Ford, Ronald Shaw, Paul Sullivan, and Maria Verlaine. Vidal relates the effect of Jim's letters on each person who receives one.

Significantly, Bob Ford's letter from Jim arrives on the day Bob is to be married to his childhood sweetheart. Bob is slightly discomfited by Jim's letter, which proposes that they meet in New York. He marries, however, and soon puts Jim and the letter from his mind. Bob does not answer Jim's letter, but Jim's mother tells him that Bob has married.

After a considerable time, Jim, visiting his family in Virginia, runs into Bob. They agree to meet in New York. When this happens, they sit in Bob's hotel room reminiscing and drinking. Jim has drunk so much that Bob persuades him to stay the night. After they are in bed, Jim advances on Bob, who repulses him cruelly, saying, "What are you doing, anyway? . . . You're a queer, you're nothing but a damned queer! Go on and get your ass out of here!" The two struggle, and in his drunkenness, Jim strangles Bob, leaving him dead in the room and going to the bar in which the novel opens and closes.

Recognizing that the novel was flawed by this melodramatic conclusion, Vidal published *The City and the Pillar Revised* (1965), in which he tightened up the style considerably, reduced the moralizing, and changed the sensational ending so that Jim forces Bob into a sexual encounter on the night they meet, after which they go their separate ways; Jim is thus free of the hold that Bob has had on him through the years.

The Characters

In *The City and the Pillar*, Vidal was not the master of characterization that he was to become in such later novels as *Julian* (1964), *Myra Breckinridge* (1968), or *Burr* (1973). Jim Willard, as the protagonist, is more multifaceted than are the other main characters in this novel, but even he is developed more through Vidal's omniscient presentation of him rather than by a well-constructed, consistent pattern of behavior.

In Jim, Vidal shaped a homosexual protagonist who did not fit the stereotype of the times. Handsome and athletic, Jim does not consider himself homosexual until well into the book. At first, he is able to dismiss his early affair with Bob Ford as being merely the adolescent experiment that Bob later labels it when he says, "that was awful kid stuff we did." The fact that he has lingering thoughts about Bob does not strike Jim as indicative of ingrained homosexuality.

Even during his affair with Ronald Shaw, Jim continues to regard himself as essentially heterosexual—in part because he does not fall in love with Shaw. Shaw is a less rounded character than Jim. He is proud, narcissistic, and given to self-pity and melodrama, as is evident in his parting words to Jim: "I admit I've been hurt, terribly hurt by you, but I don't hold it against you; that is probably the one quality I have that you will never find in anyone else: I could always forgive."

In Paul Sullivan, Jim finds another lover who indulges in self-pity and who manipulates situations so that they end up giving him pain. Vidal writes of Paul, "Pain, emotional suffering, finally became an end in itself . . . he opened himself wide to suffering and he was not disappointed." When the two meet Maria Verlaine in New Orleans and she suggests that they go with her to the Yucatán, Paul is quite willing, foreseeing that Maria will seduce Jim, who Paul still thinks is essentially heterosexual. Thus, Paul will experience the emotional suffering that he apparently finds necessary. Maria, portrayed quite sketchily, is necessary to the development of the novel only because she precipitates Jim's realization that he is quite thoroughly homosexual.

Jim's sexual exposure during his army experience is highlighted by Sergeant Kervinski, who wants to seduce Jim and whom Jim rejects, and by a young corporal, Ken Woodrow, whom Jim wants to seduce but who rejects Jim's one advance. Although there is a clutch of fairly obvious homosexuals on the base, Jim wants nothing to do with them. Instead, "He worked out in the gymnasium a great deal. Exercise had become a sexual release."

Bob Ford represents a fairly representative heterosexual type. There is no homosexual pattern in Bob's life, and he wants to forget his one youthful night of pleasure with Jim. His extreme reaction to Jim's advances when they meet many years later is motivated by fear: To acknowledge that he was capable of enjoying a homosexual encounter, even if that is not his primary inclination, would be to undermine his socially dictated sense of identity. In his own eyes, he would become a "queer"—a deviant, something less than a man.

Themes and Meanings

In *The City and the Pillar*, Vidal explores the inroads that experience makes upon innocence. The sexual relationship between Bob and Jim is portrayed as spontaneous and natural. As Jim's sexual sophistication increases, sexual relationships become much more complex for him. As he realizes that the encounter with Bob was, for him at least, more than merely a casual release, he is forced to face his own homosexuality.

Vidal is saying essentially that homosexuality provides a reasonable but complicated sexual option and that one need not fit the stereotype of the homosexual in order to exercise that option. When Jim rushes out of the room to which he and his crewmate, Collins, have taken the two prostitutes, he hears Collins say, just as he is leaving, "Let the queer go; don't mind him." This remark festers, and when Bob, whom Jim has idealized for seven or eight years, calls him a queer, that catapults the drunken Jim into an action that results in his killing Bob. He is also killing the idealized vision that, in his own mind if not in actuality, led him into a homosexuality that he could neither accept nor overcome.

Critical Context

The City and the Pillar was published at about the time the United States was undergoing a sexual reassessment if not an all-out sexual revolution. World War II had not been over long, and the war had brought with it a relaxation of conventional morality in the country. Alfred Kinsey had published *Sexual Behavior in the Human Male* (1948) in the same year, and in early 1949, *The City and the Pillar* headed *The New York Times'* list of fiction best-sellers while Kinsey's book was the nonfiction best-seller. Truman Capote's homosexual novel, *Other Voices, Other Rooms* (1948), was also a best-selling book of the same period.

The City and the Pillar was the precursor of a number of other homosexually oriented works of literature, most notably James Barr's *Quatrefoil* (1950), Alberto Moravia's *La disubbidienza* (1948; *Two Adolescents*, 1950), Arthur Anderson Peters's *Finistère* (1951), James Baldwin's *Giovanni's Room* (1956), Tennessee Williams's *Cat on a Hot Tin Roof* (1955), and Edward Albee's *The Zoo Story* (1960). Vidal helped to bring a taboo subject out of the closet, and, despite the book's obvious stylistic inadequacies and mawkish melodrama, it helped to open the whole genre of gay literature.

Bibliography

Baker, Susan, and Curtis S. Gibson. *Gore Vidal: A Critical Companion*. Westport, Conn.: Greenwood Press, 1997. A biographical sketch precedes a general discussion of Vidal's early writings, followed by critical discussions of individual novels. The discussions include sections on plot and character development, thematic issues, narrative style, and critical approaches.

Parini, Jay, ed. *Gore Vidal: Writer Against the Grain*. New York: Columbia University Press, 1992. A collection of essays by various critics that covers the important works of Vidal's career. An essay by Claude J. Summers offers insights into *The City and the Pillar* as gay fiction.

Vidal, Gore. "The Importance of Being Gore." Interview by Andrew Kopkind. *The Nation* 257 (July 5, 1993): 16-19. Vidal discusses the influence of his same-sex orientation on his work. He particularly notes the adverse effect of the publication of *The City and the Pillar* on his career.

_____. Interview by Jay Parini. *The New England Review* 14 (Fall, 1991): 93-101. Vidal talks about his career as a novelist and television scriptwriter. He cites writers who have influenced him, including Jonathan Swift and William Golding. He also shares his views on contemporary literary criticism. A revealing interview that offers valuable insight into Vidal's artistic motivations.

R. Baird Shuman

CITY OF NIGHT

Author: John Rechy (1934-   )
Type of plot: Bildungsroman
Time of plot: The 1950's
Locale: El Paso, Texas; New York City; Los Angeles; San Francisco; New Orleans
First published: 1963

> *Principal characters:*
> THE NARRATOR, a Mexican American male prostitute
> MR. KING, a man who craves love but pretends to be indifferent to people
> PETE, a New York street hustler
> THE PROFESSOR, one of the narrator's clients
> MISS DESTINY, a transvestite
> NEIL, a masochist
> JEREMY ADAMS, a "score," who offers love

The Novel

Based in part on John Rechy's own experiences as an itinerant male prostitute in the late 1950's, *City of Night* is a powerful evocation of a nameless narrator's journey through the underside of America's urban wastelands and a haunting description of the different people he encounters there.

City of Night is divided into four parts, roughly equivalent to the narrator's stays in New York, Los Angeles, Hollywood, and New Orleans. It is further divided into short character sketches—named after the individuals who are described—that alternate with sections entitled "City of Night," which propel the action forward. The entire novel is a first-person narrative told by the nameless narrator-protagonist, and all actions are filtered through his consciousness.

The novel begins in El Paso, Texas, the narrator's hometown, with the death of his dog, an event that shapes his consciousness and to which he returns repeatedly throughout the novel. When the child is told that dogs cannot go to heaven, he experiences a loss of faith that is exacerbated by the fact that the dog's decaying carcass has to be reburied because of its smell.

Both parents are impoverished Mexican immigrants, and the home offers the child no escape from the mother's suffocating Catholicism and fierce, protective love and the father's increasingly erratic and threatening behavior, which often manifests itself in terrifying rituals of affection. The narrator's hatred of his father leads to both acts of rebellion and withdrawal from life. This emotional withdrawal increases his isolation so that his mirror becomes the most important object in his life; for him, it narcissistically confirms the reality of his undecayed, youthful body.

Restless after a tour of duty in the Army, the narrator hurls himself into the large cities of America, where he quickly learns to earn his livelihood as a male hustler. It is in New York that the characteristic pattern of the adult narrator's life begins. He is obsessed by a need to be with and wanted by as many people as possible. Hustling seems to be the easiest way to fulfill these desires; as a hustler, the narrator maintains a heterosexual front, although in moments of intense introspection he sees through his own self-deception. His customers, called "scores," neither expect reciprocal sexual acts, nor do they wish him to appear gay. Doing so would destroy their own sexual fantasies.

Most of the narrative provides a guided tour through different sections of the 1950's gay subculture. In the hundreds of people the narrator encounters, he detects an overpowering loneliness camouflaged by various poses of defiance. Mr. King, one of the narrator's first clients, pretends not to care about any human interaction; at the same time, though, he desperately tries to impress the narrator by dressing up for him, and during their second meeting even asks the narrator to move in with him. The Professor both disguises and articulates his feelings of hurt; he talks of love and keeps a scrapbook with pictures of his "angels," but considers himself ugly and thus forced to buy sex. Even a fellow hustler, Pete, who has spent most of his life on the streets and is supposed to be tough and uncaring, drops his mask of heterosexual masculinity with the narrator; as a result, they never speak to each other again, because they both feel that they have violated the code of their trade.

Relentlessly, the narrative continues to explore the narrator's hustling in Los Angeles, San Francisco, Chicago, and New Orleans. In between, he returns to El Paso. This city becomes a refuge for him, a retreat offering sanctuary from the life of the streets and a place to contemplate life behind the protective security of his window.

From Los Angeles to New Orleans, the narrator observes some of the more bizarre aspects of gay life, from the world of transvestites (Miss Destiny) to the sadomasochistic underground (Neil). The men who offer more than money for sex, that is, the possibility of bonding and affection, are immediately rejected. It is in New Orleans, during Mardi Gras, that the narrator encounters Jeremy Adams, a man who finally—although only briefly—breaks through most of the emotional barriers the narrator has erected. Yet even Jeremy does not succeed. Nevertheless, Mardi Gras brings about an emotional crisis of such proportions that the narrator calls a number of Catholic churches, only to be rejected by all but one, in a desperate attempt to find spiritual solace. At the end of the novel, he returns to El Paso and his window to give meaning to his life and experiences, aware that his quest is not yet over.

The Characters

From the beginning of the novel, the narrator gains the reader's sympathy because of his overwhelming loneliness. As a child of poor parents and a member of an ethnic minority, he is made to feel different from an early age. This difference is used by the author to create motivation in the narrator's decision to become a hustler. Despite his attempts to display no emotion toward his clients and to kill compassion in himself, he displays an understanding of those who are different, so that people confide in him. Thus he becomes for the reader an emblem of hope for humanity in an inhumane world.

Mr. King feels guilty about his sexual orientation despite his bravado announcements to the contrary. He invites the reader's pity because, much like the narrator, he pretends that he lacks compassion. This hard exterior is quickly exposed as a veneer designed to mask his devastating loneliness. He resembles most of the narrator's clients; they are neurotic because of society's rejection and persecution of their sexual orientation.

The Professor differs from Mr. King because of his intellect and command of language, which he uses to manipulate people. His failure, as it is communicated to the reader, is his inability to recognize true love. Despite his erudition and scholarly importance, he believes that he is unattractive and therefore compelled to pay for sex. The Professor, because of his sense of captivity in an inadequate body, fails to recognize that Larry, his male nurse, loves him unconditionally. Again, the Professor is portrayed as a victim of societal expectations.

Pete is one of the male hustlers whom the narrator describes at length. He is the representative of an entire group of lost young men. Like other hustlers, he is supposed to be tough and heterosexual. When the narrator and Pete spend one night together just holding hands, even this limited show of affection and emotional need is too much for both. Their roles have been compromised, and they avoid one another from then on.

Miss Destiny, a transvestite, is the most elaborately described character in the book. Her portrait is fully developed, and her regal attitude stands in stark contrast to her seedy surroundings. She is shown as more oppressed by society than Mr. King; for example, by law she is not even allowed to wear female attire. Yet she is also described as courageous, because she defies society and its laws. Ultimately, she is as lonely as the other men in the novel, left with the sinking feeling that God played a cruel trick on her.

In many ways, Neil is the most pathetic and repulsive character in the novel. He is a masochist who sees his life's mission as initiating other men into sadomasochism. His function is to show how far a human being can stray from humaneness and still talk about love.

Jeremy is the representative of those men who want more than sexual gratification from the narrator. He has overcome the intense narcissism that enslaves the narrator and thus is able to offer affection and the possibility of love. In many ways, he is one of the most fully realized characters of the novel, and he engages the reader's sympathy. His failure to win the narrator over to his point of view is painful, because the reader wants him to succeed.

Themes and Meanings

At the most basic level, the novel is a psychological study of the narrator and his quest for meaning in life. The makeup of his family—the mother's fierce love and the father's inexplicable hatred—seem designed to push the narrator into homosexuality, thus giving expression to a view commonly held at the time of the writing of the novel. Seen in its entirety, the novel is an elaborate investigation of the narrator's fragmented identity. Since he refuses to reveal his name throughout the narrative, he deliberately frustrates a reader's normal expectations to get to know him fully. In fact, all the more elaborately described characters the narrator encounters during his wanderings are carefully chosen to create a contrast to his murky identity. At the same time, this narrative technique allows the reader to imagine the life of a hustler. Like the narrator, the reader meets a character, is drawn into his life for a short period of time, and then as abruptly withdraws. This is underscored by the fact that the narrator attempts to create complicity between the reader and himself by addressing the reader several times directly as "you"; he seems to crave the reader's approval (or, perhaps, absolution). In the same way that the narrator assumes the role of confessor for his clients, the reader becomes the narrator's confessor (or psychologist). Thus the novel can be read as a sustained cry for help, and the comfort that is wished for comes through the telling of the tale; that is, the narrative itself can be read as part of the therapy to heal the narrator's wounded self.

The novel explores the narrator's refusal to accept death and decay. His inability to face this most basic of human conditions leads him, by his own explanation, into hustling; he has lost faith in religion, so other people's desire for his youthful body becomes a substitute for salvation. This crisis of faith is not brought to a complete and satisfying resolution, but the loneliness that the novel so eloquently investigates provides a thematic and structural unity.

Apart from toying with questions of identity, the novel critiques a social system that by law discriminates against those with a different sexual orientation. While the novel tends to fixate on the pathological nature of the people the narrator encounters, the cry against social injustice, not yet fully articulated in political and social terms, cannot be ignored.

All these ideas are tightly interwoven in a circular structure. The novel begins and ends with the narrator's memory of his dog's death and the unresolved crisis of faith that this event precipitated. After all, the anarchy the narrator senses in himself throughout the novel is nothing but the fear of sharing the dog's fate: to grow old and to die. His inability to form meaningful relationships with other people must be seen in light of this. Relationships seem futile to him, because they offer what he considers false hope: the idea of permanence. Yet since the novel ends where it began, it also offers an element of hope. The narrator has come back to where his psychological crisis started, and the reader is left with the impression that when the narrator ventures forth again from his window, he will do so with a fuller understanding of himself and even greater compassion for those people he will encounter.

Critical Context

City of Night was John Rechy's first novel, and it almost overnight became a best-seller and an underground classic. Its description of parts of the gay subculture was more honest and detailed than had been attempted by writers before. In addition, the novel's narrative framework and technical experimentation show Rechy's indebtedness to other twentieth century writers such as James Joyce and John Dos Passos.

The novel demonstrates the growth of a gay awareness, although this awareness is not yet fully evolved in the book. Through the form of the *Bildungsroman*, the novel of the development of a protagonist's character, Rechy captures the tortured life of his narrator and imbues it with dignity and meaning. The novel's protagonist and structure are also indebted to the picaresque novel. Like the picaro, a hustler lives on the fringes of the law and survives by his wit and resourcefulness.

In several subsequent works, including *Numbers* (1967), *This Day's Death* (1969), and *Rushes* (1979), Rechy continued his attempt to define gay male sexuality and identity. In all these works, questions of Latino identity were almost completely pushed aside. Although Rechy has claimed that all of his main characters are Latino, the emphasis on their ethnic, rather than sexual, identities came much later. There are few indications in *City of Night*, for example, apart from the narrator's lapsed Catholicism and his recurrent feelings of guilt, that ethnic identification is central to his self-understanding. More recently, though, Rechy has investigated questions of Latino identity in his novels *Bodies and Souls* (1983) and *The Miraculous Day of Amalia Gómez* (1991). He has also written a best-selling nonfiction work, *The Sexual Outlaw* (1977), and several plays.

Bibliography
Bruce-Novoa, Juan. "In Search of the Honest Outlaw: John Rechy." *Minority Voices* 3, no. 1 (1979): 37-45. Draws connections between Nietzsche's concept of Dionysian and Appolonian consciousness and the narrator of *City of Night*. Asserts that Rechy creates opposition between lived experience and withdrawn contemplation of it.
Fry, Joan. "An Interview with John Rechy." *Poets and Writers Magazine* 20 (May/June, 1992): 25-36. Concentrates on style and narrative strategy. Rechy declares and wants readers to recognize that he is a Chicano writer. Also talks about his teaching and writers who have influenced him.
Giles, James R. "Religious Alienation and 'Homosexual Consciousness' in *City of Night* and *Go Tell It on the Mountain*." *College English* 36 (1974): 369-380. Analysis of the destructive role of religion in works by Rechy and James Baldwin. Reads both novels as gay fiction. Rechy is seen as the more important gay author because Baldwin emphasizes ethnic over sexual identity.
Ortiz, Ricardo L. "L.A. Women: Jim Morrison with John Rechy." *Literature and Psychology* 44 (Fall, 1998): 41-77. Discusses the allusion to Rechy's *City of Night* in Morrison's song "L.A. Woman," demonstrating Morrison's rejection of romanticism and presumptive stereotyping. He argues that the allusion heightens the innuendo of homosexuality and hustling in Morrison's song, highlighting potential homosexuality in male audience admiration.
_____. "Sexuality Degree Zero: Pleasure and Power in the Novels of John Rechy, Arturo Islas, and Michael Nava." *Journal of Homosexuality* 26 (August-September, 1993): 111-125. Ortiz explores common themes and formal strategies in the fiction of Chicano gay writers Rechy, Islas, and Nava. In analyses of Rechy's

use of pornography, Islas's use of cultural iconography, and Nava's use of sexual "perversions," Ortiz argues for the political efficacy of aesthetic choices characteristic to the three authors.

Zamora, Carlos. "Odysseus in John Rechy's *City of Night*: The Epistemological Journey." *Minority Voices* 3, no. 1 (1979): 53-62. Reads the novel as a *Bildungsroman* in the tradition of Johann Wolfgang von Goethe and James Joyce. Identifies the quest for identity as the book's central concept. Analyzes the protagonist's journey as providing structure and unity to the book.

Ludger Brinker

THE CLANSMAN

Author: Thomas Dixon, Jr. (1864-1946)
Type of plot: Historical
Time of plot: The 1860's
Locale: The American South
First published: 1905

> *Principal characters:*
>> AUSTIN STONEMAN, a congressional leader determined to liberate
>> southern blacks
>> ELSIE STONEMAN, Austin's daughter, in love with Ben Cameron
>> PHILIP STONEMAN, Austin's son, in love with Margaret Cameron
>> DR. RICHARD CAMERON, a southern aristocrat determined to save the
>> South
>> BEN CAMERON, the Grand Dragon of the Ku Klux Klan
>> MARGARET CAMERON, a southern belle, in love with Philip
>> MRS. CAMERON, the wife of Dr. Cameron
>> LYDIA BROWN, a mulatto, Austin Stoneman's housekeeper
>> SILAS LYNCH, a mulatto, lieutenant governor of South Carolina

The Novel

The Clansman is divided into four books covering a period from about 1865 to
1870. The first two books are centered on the activities in the nation's capital,
delineating the death of President Abraham Lincoln and the ensuing power struggle
between Capitol Hill and the White House on how the South is to be treated. Books 3
and 4 shift to South Carolina and outline the havoc that the Reconstruction-era state
governments have brought to the South, resulting in the rise of the Ku Klux Klan.

The Clansman has an omniscient narrator who relates events, allowing major characters to voice the author's philosophy. The novel opens with the celebration of the
Union army in Washington, D.C., at the close of the Civil War, while thousands of soldiers from the North and the South lie in makeshift hospitals. At the height of the celebration, President Lincoln is assassinated, and while the nation mourns, Andrew
Johnson, a southerner, becomes the next president. Lincoln's intention was to bring
the South back into the Union; Johnson, a less resolute leader, attempts to effectuate
Lincoln's design, but he is met with stiff opposition in Congress under the leadership
of Austin Stoneman. Stoneman, who controls Congress but who appears to be under
the control of Lydia Brown, his mulatto housekeeper, prevents Johnson from bringing
the South back into the Union. Instead, Stoneman persuades Congress to enact laws
that put the government of the South in the hands of blacks. This new dispensation in
the South alienates whites, causing them to retaliate against blacks. Because Johnson
balks at penalizing the South, he is impeached and tried by the members of the Senate.
He is saved from conviction by one vote. While the political battle rages on Capitol
Hill, Elsie Stoneman, who is nursing wounded soldiers, meets Ben Cameron and the

Cameron family. She introduces her brother Philip to Margaret Cameron, and soon a relationship develops between the young people. Through Elsie's intervention, Mrs. Cameron manages to see her husband, Dr. Richard Cameron, a political prisoner awaiting trial. Dr. Cameron urges his wife to return to the South to aid the poor and suffering and to manage what might be left of their own wealth. Austin Stoneman, worn out from his political struggles, falls ill and is encouraged by his physician to recuperate in the South. Stoneman's children, pursuing their love affairs, encourage their father to settle in Piedmont, South Carolina, where the Camerons live. Before leaving Congress, Austin Stoneman has been successful in getting Congress to pass several Reconstruction Acts that enable him to put the southern states under the control of blacks; therefore, he acquiesces to going South, where he can better effectuate his plan.

Returning to the South, the Camerons discover that their social status has been diminished, their wealth has been depleted, and almost all of their slaves have left. Those slaves who remain have notions of acquiring forty acres and a mule. The state government is run by rapacious, uneducated freedmen, carpetbaggers, and scalawags. Despite the adverse conditions, the relationships between Elsie and Ben and Philip and Margaret grow stronger. Ben, meanwhile, has been working with a secret organization, the Ku Klux Klan, to eliminate black domination of the South. The organization's deepest fears are realized when Marion Lenoir and her mother, neighbors of the Camerons, are found dead. It is later learned that Gus, one of the Camerons' former slaves, has ravished Marion and that mother and daughter, too ashamed to let the world know what transpired, committed suicide. The Klan searches for Gus, who has left the state, finds him, and administers its justice by lynching him.

The Klan encourages whites to take control of the government in the upcoming general election, and Austin Stoneman, fearing that the Klansmen might be successful, orders more Union troops into the South. Under these tense conditions, two black men impose themselves on Margaret Cameron while she is dining. Ben and Philip rush to her defense, killing one of the intruders. Austin Stoneman, believing that Ben Cameron shot the man, orders that he be imprisoned, tried, and executed, but Stoneman's son, Philip takes Ben's place in prison. When Stoneman discovers that it is his own son who is to be executed, he attempts to get the Union soldiers to revoke the orders, but it is too late. The Klan members, however, have been waiting to intercept the Union army and to save Philip. When Stoneman realizes that his son has not been executed, he thanks God for the Ku Klux Klan. The next day, whites win the election and take control of the government.

The Characters

Characters in *The Clansman* are basically one-dimensional types. Austin Stoneman, as his last name suggests, is a man of stone, implacable in his dealing with the Confederacy. His views of blacks contravene the prevailing opinion, which is that the physical differences between blacks and whites make it impossible for the races to coexist as political and social equals. Stoneman believes that God made all men the same and that, given the opportunity, the blacks will acquire the necessary skills and will become as morally and politically upright as whites. Because of his views, he is depicted as a fanatic who, if unchecked, will destroy both the federal government and the Confederacy. Dr. Richard Cameron, on the other hand, is depicted as the ideal southern aristocrat who, observing the deplorable conditions of state government under the black administrations, takes on the mantle of senior statesman and protector; however, he is one of the leading figures in the Ku Klux Klan. Ben, his son, is suave, courageous, and courteous, the ideal gentleman who is ever mindful of southern white ladies. At night, he becomes the Grand Dragon of the Klan, attacking blacks who refuse to acquiesce to the demands of whites. It is Ben and his father, Dr. Cameron, who are responsible for the death of Gus. Philip Stoneman, unlike his father, becomes an industrialist, starting a milling business and helping to bring economic prosperity to the South. The female characters, with the exception of Elsie, are delineated as southern belles at various stages of life. Mrs. Cameron is the virtuous matron, the epitome of grace under pressure. Margaret, even in an old, shabby dress, is stately, the ideal beauty at her peak. Marion Lenoir, the nubile southern belle, has the courage to go into a burning stable, almost naked, to save a horse, but once she has been raped by a black man, the loss of her virtue is too much for her to bear.

While whites are presented as types in *The Clansman*, blacks become caricatures. Their language, their features, and their actions all work together to highlight their primitiveness. Lydia Brown, Austin Stoneman's housekeeper, who has clouded Stoneman's life and fogged his name with "vulgar gossip," is referred to as a "leopardess" and a "she devil"; she is an animalistic individual of questionable morals. A congressman forced to acknowledge her as his equal touches her hand "as if she were a toad." The omnipotent narrator says of Lydia that "no more curious or sinister figure ever cast a shadow over the history of a great nation." Silas Lynch, the lieutenant governor of South Carolina, is also cast in a stereotypical mold. He is college educated and apparently sophisticated, but in his eyes glows "the brightness of the African jungle." Blacks are described in terms of their kinky hair, black skin, thick lips, and flat noses. Even Aleck, who protects the Camerons, and Jake, the old retainer who acknowledges Dr. Cameron as his master, are made to look like characters from a minstrel show. Dr. Cameron, who maintains that blacks are half-children, half-animals, sums up this view when he says: "[the black] race is not an infant; it is a degenerate."

Themes and Meanings

The Clansman is a polemic justifying the wresting of control of the South's state governments from the black-dominated administrations of Reconstruction. Coming as it did in 1905, when the South was still smarting from the Civil War, when southerners could still remember the pain and the poverty associated with the conflict, when blacks were still attempting to flex their political muscle for civil rights, the novel had great appeal for southerners as well as other segments of American society. Critics, though, argued that the novel opened up old wounds and deepened rifts between blacks and whites. *The Clansman*, though, is not merely about the degradation of African Americans or the glorification of whites. The novel is also concerned with healing and regeneration. Austin Stoneman and Dr. Richard Cameron, who typify strong sectional and political differences, fight to the very end of the novel. They, however, are representative of the past, of the old North and the old South; their children, the second generation, are of a different breed. They are more trusting of one another, and they refuse to be drawn into their parents' feud. The double marriage of Margaret and Philip and Elsie and Ben is not solemnized when the novel ends, but the endearing affections of these four young people suggest that there will be a union in the near future. The union of these young people from the North and the South is not merely a bonding between two feuding families but is also suggestive of the reunion of the Union.

Prior to the Civil War, the South's economy was based on agriculture; little attention was given to industry. Philip Stoneman, coming from a milling town in Pennsylvania, sees the potential the South, with its great waterfalls, has for a milling industry. With northern capital—again, the suggestion of the North and the South reuniting—Philip establishes a milling industry that brings wealth to the South and changes its economy from agrarian to industrial.

Critical Context

More so than any other novelist, Thomas Dixon helped set the tone of white supremacy that prevailed in America for the first half of the twentieth century. He might not have done so with malice, for he maintained that he did not hate blacks, but he strongly believed that the two races could not exist in America as equals. He promulgated his views in a trilogy dealing with the Reconstruction South. The first novel in the trilogy, *The Leopard's Spot* (1903), suggests that blacks are inferior; like the leopard, blacks cannot "change their spots" and therefore should be treated as inferior. *The Clansman*, the second of the trilogy, suggests how blacks might be controlled; the third installment, *The Traitor* (1907), explains how and why the controlling force, the Klan, might be abandoned when it is no longer needed. Through various mediums, Dixon managed to keep his concept of race in the public domain for the first two decades of the twentieth century. Dixon was also a professional actor, and he adapted *The Clansman* for the stage. In 1905, the play began touring the country. As drama, *The Clansman* caused as much divisiveness as the novel, but the play became so popular that two companies were touring the country simultaneously.

In 1915, Dixon's story was used as the basis for D. W. Griffith's seminal motion picture *Birth of a Nation*, which again thrilled and horrified Americans with its racial content. Together, the print, stage, and film versions of Dixon's story helped to fix a negative image of blacks in the American consciousness, an image that would persist for decades.

Bibliography

Cook, Raymond A. *Fire from the Flint: The Amazing Careers of Thomas Dixon.* Winston-Salem, N.C.: John F. Blair, 1968. A penetrating discussion of Dixon that explains how his youthful experiences might have influenced his work.

_____. *Thomas Dixon*. New York: Twayne, 1974. An insightful evaluation of Dixon's literary career.

Coulter, E. Merton. *The South During Reconstruction, 1865-1877*. Baton Rouge: Louisiana State University Press, 1947. A good discussion of the Reconstruction period; useful background for an understanding of Dixon's novel.

Osofsky, Gilbert. *The Burden of Race: A Documentary History of Negro-White Relations in America*. New York: Harper & Row, 1967. An excellent sourcebook on race relations, with a specific entry on Thomas Dixon and his attitude toward blacks.

Ralph Reckley, Sr.

CLOCKERS

Author: Richard Price (1949-　　)
Type of plot: Social realism
Time of plot: The 1990's
Locale: New Jersey
First published: 1992

Principal characters:

STRIKE (RONALD DUNHAM), a street-wise drug dealer
RODNEY LITTLE, Strike's boss
VICTOR DUNHAM, Strike's brother
ROCCO KLEIN, a homicide detective
ERROLL BARNES, one of Rodney's lieutenants
DARRYL ADAMS, another of Rodney's lieutenants
TYRONE JEETER, Strike's twelve-year-old protégé

The Novel

Hung loosely onto a mystery plot, *Clockers* immerses the reader in the drug culture of inner-city housing projects, where wealth and death are equally certain and swift. In the low-income housing projects of Dempsy, located between Newark and Jersey City, drugs, crime, and despair never sleep. Violent deaths are commonplace and excite little interest. The plainclothes police teams, dubbed "the Fury" for the dilapidated Plymouth Furys they drive, are as ubiquitous and predictable as AIDS. They follow a daily schedule of harassment, dispiritedly roughing up the "clockers" (twenty-four-hour drug dealers) and carting away the bodies that litter the streets.

Life offers two choices to residents of "the tiger pits." The first is honest hard work, a dead-end road to poverty from Strike's point of view. The second is big money with little effort, dealing crack cocaine in parks, playgrounds, and bars. For Strike, the choice is obvious. Working as Rodney's lieutenant, he supervises a team of clockers from his spot on a park bench. While they retail ten-dollar bottles hidden in pockets and socks, Strike swigs vanilla soda to soothe his bleeding ulcer. Strike follows the rules: Do not flaunt your wealth, do not get greedy, and do not sample the merchandise.

A rigid hierarchy governs the drug trade, and honesty among thieves is law. Rodney runs the neighborhood crack concession from his candy store. Rodney says he suspects Darryl Adams, another of his lieutenants who deals out of a fast-food restaurant, of buying from a second supplier who returns a higher commission. He implies that Strike must kill Darryl in order to prove his loyalty and move up in the operation. Terrified, Strike tells his brother, Victor, of what he believes to be an order to kill. Victor, a model citizen in this less than model community, has never been in trouble with the law, but he hints that "a friend" might handle things for Strike.

An unknown gunman slays Darryl outside a diner. Victor confesses to the crime. Strike thinks that Buddha Hat, the brutal enforcer of drug lord Champ, must have committed the crime. He plots to use his drug money to effect Victor's release.

White homicide detective Rocco Klein believes that Victor is lying to protect Strike. Stuck with a dead-end job, a rocky marriage, and a drinking habit, Rocco dreams of seeing his life made into a film, but the futility of his existence drags him down, turning him increasingly bitter, brutal, and despondent. Obsessed with forcing a confession from Strike, he will go to any lengths to forge a single victory from a lifetime of defeats.

Rodney closes the ranks to defend his power base, and Erroll—dying of AIDS and with nothing to lose—is his willing agent. The boy Tyrone, dreaming of emulating Strike and growing wealthy, sets out to protect his hero.

In a typical detective story, Klein would solve the mystery, and Strike's situation would be resolved, for better or worse. In Price's uncompromising plunge into the netherworld of drugs and desperation, however, things do not turn out so neatly. Both Klein and the reader walk away with more questions than answers. *Clockers* is memorable not so much for its plot as for its bold depiction of the poverty and pain that trap and mold the people of Dempsy.

The Characters

Price peoples the Dempsy scene with characters that come off as chillingly complex and authentic. Stick-thin, high-strung, and intelligent, Strike operates within a code of conscience and honor. He never considers himself a criminal, merely a man doing a job that gives him some chance for a future. In neighborhoods outside his own, Strike feels threatened and outraged. Despite the gun he carries, the streets are not safe for him. He wishes the "knockos" (narcotics cops) would "do something about it." Strike's sometime girlfriend, a decade older than he, describes him as he wishes to be seen: "clean, neat, not loud with gold . . . alert, all serious and composed." His outer composure, however, belies an inner turmoil. He finds the sight of drug use repugnant and turns away from it in disgust while chastising his clockers for open selling that could lead to arrest and loss of profits. Strike seeks the peace and security he knows will be forever denied him.

Rodney looms large—from some angles, he seems a god in heaven; from others, a devil in hell. He controls Strike and his other lieutenants with alternating compassionate nurturing and threats of violence, meted out in equal measure. Sexually promiscuous, Rodney nevertheless demands unfailing loyalty from his women, and he usually gets it. Worshipped and feared, Rodney wields the manipulative power of praise and the brute force of menace. He sits as king of the clockers. He will retain his throne at any cost.

Rocco Klein, the ruddy, heavy-set detective, cannot distinguish himself from his job; he has been at it too long. He has spent his life tracking, booking, and forgetting an "endless parade of shit-skinned losers." He is as gray as his territory, scarcely differentiating himself from what he judges "dozens of sad-sack lives reduced to shopping bags reeking of b.o. and poverty." Nevertheless, the restless spirit inside him will not let him give up. He wishes for something with "bigness in it, something that would halve his years." Without it, he settles for a drink.

Strike's brother Victor is the exception that proves the rule in Dempsy. Hardworking, soft-spoken, well respected by employers and family, he is nevertheless a tortured man. Although devoted to his wife and children, he spends too many hours alone in a bar. Is he capable of murder? Would he kill to advance Strike's career or to soothe some inner turmoil of his own? Is his confession fact or foil? Probing Victor's actions and motives sets Strike and Rocco in conflict with each other and with the unwritten laws of the streets.

Themes and Meanings

Price depicts the drug culture accurately and fully. He describes without judging, identifies without sympathizing. As narrator, he remains outside the action, but the reader sees as he sees. No novel has captured better than *Clockers* the relativity of truth. Born in a room without doors, who would think to cut one? Born in Dempsy, who would imagine security, much less seek to achieve it? When Rocco Klein invents for Tyrone Jeeter a false but plausible explanation for a crime, the reader understands immediately that truth stands not as an absolute but as a contrivance to be molded into the transient delusion called hope. Such distortions are all that allow clockers and knockos alike to endure another day, another week, another eternity.

Everyone in Dempsy—even Strike, who never touches drugs—is addicted. Strike and Rodney are as hooked on the profits and excitement of clocking as Erroll once was on heroin. Klein, bemoaning his lot one minute, delights in it the next. Sipping vodka and cranberry juice, he yearns for another fix, feeling "a thickness in his blood, anxious for something to happen, for somebody to kill somebody, for the beeper on his hip to go off."

Even the honest, hard-working citizens of the projects are addicted. Without the addicts and dealers to whom they compare themselves, they would be forced to admit they were just as "bricked up with pain" as those they condemn. They need the drug culture to confirm their superior status as much as the clockers require easy money and the addicts crave their highs.

Price finds a paradoxical dignity in the people of Dempsy, especially Strike and Rocco, despite their addictions. He lays bare their naked pettiness, villainy, and weakness, yet he allows them redemption through their sensitivity, courage, and persistence. In those who survive against all odds, Price finds hope for the human condition. Their continuing existence offers promise that the human spirit might someday triumph. The light of hope never brightens, but neither does it dim. "If God invented anything better'n drugs, he kept it for hisself," says Rodney. Strike flicks a roach off his jeans with a fistful of money and concludes that the hustler's ultimate victim is himself.

Critical Context

Richard Price, famous for his in-depth, real-life research, spent two years riding with police and living among clockers and their clients. He filled a stack of notebooks with sights, sounds, and impressions before writing *Clockers*, and his first draft exceeded a thousand pages. He needed another eighteen months to achieve the remarkable precision of the finished work. Perhaps only the clockers themselves could judge the accuracy of Price's work, but to outsiders, its tone rings true.

Price is a master of language, and *Clockers* is worth study for no other reason than to see how he captures the essence of an alien world. He writes with the lexicon of the projects. "Pipeheads" are crack smokers; drug runners are "mules." "Redi Rocks" is crack ready to smoke; "stepping on it" is the process of diluting crack with sugar, laxative, or rat poison. His descriptions, while neither lengthy nor labored, reveal his themes. For example, an indoor homicide smells, to Rocco, like "watered-down Old Spice or a sweating fat lady—not altogether unpleasant, kind of intimate, the smell of a whole life opened up to him with all its embarrassments and little drawers." The sounds of the police station's receiving unit are "disembodied shouts and barks that ricocheted off the walls like bullets fired inside a steel drum."

Price is a genius of dialogue. Each character speaks with a unique and consistent voice. Interactions are sharp, focused, lean, and rich. Pace and tension ebb and wane with an energy few writers can control. Price's description and dialect bring the street drug trade to life. Acting more as a reporter than a fiction writer, Price takes his readers into the basements and back alleys of the urban wilderness.

Bibliography

Brezinski, Steve. Reviews of *Clockers*, by Richard Price. *Antioch Review* 50, no. 4 (Fall, 1992): 769. Brezinski states that *Clockers* should be required reading for politicians who think they have solutions for "urban unrest."

Howard, Gerald. "The Bonfire This Time." *Nation* 254, no. 21 (June 1, 1992): 755-757. Howard asserts that *Clockers* will emerge as a modern classic, proving that fiction can still serve as "a vital agency of social witness and documentation."

Linville, James. "The Art of Fiction CXLIV: Richard Price." *The Paris Review* 38, no. 138 (Spring, 1996): 132. Details how *Clockers* was written and explores the cocaine addiction that plagued Price before he wrote it.

Schwartz, Gil. "Moby Book: Big Reading for the Beach." *Fortune* 126, no. 4 (August 24, 1992): 148-151. Judges *Clockers* an "intricate moral passion play . . . moving, unsentimental . . . wholly successful."

Skow, John. "An American Tragedy." *Time* 139, no. 23 (June 8, 1992): 89. Skow argues that Price has turned "no-exit reality into a superb reportorial novel."

Faith Hickman Brynie

THE COFFIN TREE

Author: Wendy Law-Yone (1947-   )
Type of plot: Psychological realism
Time of plot: The 1960's through the mid-1970's
Locale: Burma, New York City, and Chicago
First published: 1983

> *Principal characters:*
> THE NARRATOR, a young Burmese woman whose father sends her to the
>   United States
> SHAN, the narrator's elder half-brother, who accompanies her to the
>   United States
> THE NARRATOR'S FATHER, whose brief appearances in the novel only
>   underscore his tyranny over the lives of his children
> THE INHABITANTS OF 3 EAST, a psychiatric ward to which the narrator
>   is committed after she attempts suicide

The Novel

The Coffin Tree is the story of a young Burmese woman who leaves her country, where civil war is impending, to arrive in New York City in October, 1969, along with her elder brother, Shan. Their father, a revolutionary, had been in hiding in the hills of Burma for three years, but he manages to arrange for the safe departure of his two children. In exile in America, the narrator recounts the story of her childhood in "monsoon country," the traumatic early years in New York City, the death of her brother, and the time she spends in a psychiatric ward after attempting suicide.

When *The Coffin Tree* opens, the narrator's tyrannical maternal grandmother has just died, and she is left in the care of elderly maiden aunts. Her father is absent, presumably involved in the continuing Revolution of the Hilltribes, to which he has pledged his life. Readers are introduced to the family members in the narrator's home: Auntie Lily and Auntie Rosie, whose collective primary function is to run the household; the inertia-gripped Uncle, a glutton; and the narrator's adored half-brother, Shan.

There is a military coup one day, and the narrator's father has fled to the hilly north. Although the tension is almost palpable, from the narrator's matter-of-fact description of the murder of "Prince R's" son to her recounting of her aunts' efforts to procure food at the markets, there seems to be a suspension of time and space. The day-to-day has become the glue of existence. Before, such trivial details formed the invisible backdrop to life's worthier moments; now, however, the mundane takes center stage, as if by necessity, so that sense can be made from ending up, as the aunts do, with two pairs of men's undershorts instead of sugar, salt, oil, or aspirin. Uncle's inertia turns into infectious fatalism, and the household becomes entrapped in a world explained by "must be!" Suddenly, two or three years after the coup, word comes that the narrator's father has arranged for the flight of his two children, presumably to a safer place.

The narrator and her brother arrive in New York City. Fleeing the upheaval in their homeland, it would seem to the refugees that festive, year-end New York City is the perfect haven. Instead, it is the setting for their dissolution. The traumas of flight and severance from homeland are now juxtaposed against the escalating problems of being in a strange new city. When the promised funds from Burma do not materialize, the pair face unaccustomed poverty. Humiliated and penniless, they manage to reach a journalist acquaintance of their father's, Benjamin Lane. During a year spent in the journalist's basement, the narrator and Shan reach their nadir: Clinging to their pride, they decline to have their meals with the Lanes; instead, they sneak food from the Laneses' kitchen to maintain the illusion that they are fending for themselves.

Meanwhile, Shan continues a descent from sanity. While the narrator had already wondered about her brother's storytelling flights of fancy back in Burma, it is during their years in the new country that she begins to notice distinct signs that his grasp on reality is slipping day by day. Finally, in Chicago, both siblings imprisoned by Shan's illness, Shan dies one evening from a heart attack.

The second half of the novel is about the narrator's experiences among the fellow inhabitants of 3 East, a psychiatric ward, and of the events, after Shan's death, leading to her attempted suicide. After Shan's death, the narrator drifts through the numbing routines of a job and domestic chores. When she learns of her father's death, the news paradoxically shakes her from her stupor. She has found a new purpose to her days: She will systematically direct herself toward suicide. Interspersed with these accounts are flashbacks to her childhood in Burma and memories of her brother and her father.

By the end of the novel, the narrator has left 3 East behind her. She comes to a reconciliation with, if not a resolution of, the disparate strains of her life: the ones that pull her to the "monsoon country" and the unresolvable nature of familial ties, and the ones that now bind her to the new country where she has spilled her blood. The narrator points out, with neither ecstasy nor regret, that the position she writes from is that of being alive.

The Characters

The narrator is a girl of fourteen when the narrative begins, and she is in her late twenties when the novel ends. She is the cloistered younger child of an upper-middle-class family in Burma, where her father is a revolutionary hero. Though cloistered, and pampered in the material sense as a result of her family's wealth, the narrator is uncared for emotionally. To her recently deceased maternal grandmother, she was a "mother killer," blamed for her mother's death in childbirth. Her aunts seem to dote on her, yet their doting seems to derive from their own sense of function rather than from the fact that the narrator is a motherless child in need of love. With her father mostly absent, the narrator's only emotional support comes from her brother, who tells her what she never tires of hearing: "You are my sister; I'll look after you." Innocent even in the turmoil of the last years in Burma, the narrator is compelled to become self-reliant and resourceful. When her brother becomes ill, she becomes his nurse, parent, and anchor to reality.

Shan, the narrator's half-brother, is ten years older than the narrator. He is the charismatic older brother of her youth who tells her stories, shows her secret places, keeps a coterie of unsavory friends, and seems to charm everyone except his father. Best of all, he is the narrator's protector. Daring and dashing in Burma, Shan is out of his element in New York City. Here he does not have the means to play prodigal son, and he has no hangers-on with whom to play. Like his sister, he is untrained for any but the most menial jobs, but while his sister diligently seeks work, he is almost reluctant to have to think about a necessary income. Shan seems to have left much of his bravado in Burma, and the chronicle of the early years in America recounts Shan's rapid disintegration. Exhibiting such classic symptoms of manic depression as paranoia, sleeplessness, and wild mood swings, Shan becomes the narrator's millstone.

If the narrator is the emotional center of the novel, her father represents the novel's emotional void. Although he appears only sporadically, his very absence becomes a telling presence in the narrator's life. In brief appearances at his home, he is nevertheless able to send his whole household into a fearful frenzy. He is a cold, calculating man, and he seems to be defined by the violence that is a part of his revolutionary work. He is a father who tries to beat the stuttering out of his son, who is remembered by the narrator for a single manifestation of fatherly love. Even in death, he plays a pivotal role in his daughter's life, pushing her toward suicide.

Most of the inhabitants of 3 East have also attempted suicide. They are a varied group, but collectively they are a reminder of the depths to which the narrator has sunk in confrontation with life's relentless demands. In their bantering and teasing and their matter-of-fact assessments of incarceration, however, they provide the necessary respite from the narrator's lonely, guilt-ridden existence.

Themes and Meanings

The Coffin Tree is a novel about betrayal. The narrator seems to have been betrayed from birth; her mother dies giving her life, giving her over, it would seem, to no one in particular. Her grandmother reminds her constantly that she is a "mother killer." Her aunts and uncle are living in her father's house not because of her but because of their own private reasons. She is most deeply betrayed, however, by the two people who matter most to her.

The narrator's father, whom she describes as "born to wield" power, was the tyrannical god of her childhood. He is usually absent, ostensibly playing his preferred role of leader of the People's Army. Only from adult retrospection does the narrator realize the general indifference her father must have felt toward her, and she comes to realize that what she knew of her father was the "official version." Her resentment finally shows: "His business was to be a father to us, his children; why else had he given us life?" Finally, she realizes that when her father had gone into hiding after the coup, there was really no danger to her or to Shan. Even her father's enemies had known that it would not have been any use to seek his surrender by threatening his children. His feelings for his children simply did not equal his devotion to his revolutionary tasks.

Shan also betrays the narrator. The narrator has grown up believing that the elder brother and protector of her childhood would always protect her, simply because she was his sister. The brother in Burma, however, is not the same person in America. Instead of protecting her, he becomes the dependent one, dependent on her to get them through the difficult situation of their exile. As he sinks deeper into an illness for which he refuses to seek help, she begins to see through his ravings and lies. As he continues to undermine her trust and belief in him, he is also betraying her memories of him—in retrospect, perhaps the stories he had told her, which had seemed large shreds of life for her to cling to, were merely products of his selfish need to alter his own reality.

The novel also deals, unavoidably, with cultural and personal displacement, with the difficult adjustments from a familiar culture to an alien one, from wealth to poverty, from blinkered naïveté to real life, with all of its visceral betrayals. The novel also chronicles a personal odyssey. The narrator literally crosses an ocean, and the ill winds that propel her to America, a hostile new land, continue to keep her wandering from obstacle to obstacle until she is eventually able to find her own personal restoration. The novel opens with the line, "Living things prefer to go on living." It is not until the last pages of the novel, when the narrator repeats the first sentence, that the reader realizes that the novel is a testament to the commodity called "life." By then, the significance of the title is evident: At first a reference to the tree that yields wood for coffins, it becomes, by novel's end, a symbol of hope, of life itself.

Critical Context

The Coffin Tree is Law-Yone's first novel. Although Law-Yone was herself born in Burma and came to the United States when she was twenty, it is not clear to what extent the novel is autobiographical. The public events alluded to in the book roughly parallel the unrest, the uprisings by ethnic minorities, and the succession of military regimes that have ruled Burma for many of the years since its independence from British India in 1948.

The Coffin Tree was first published in 1983, several years before a pronounced escalation in the publishing of Asian American texts by mainstream publishing houses. A paperback edition appeared in 1987; however, relatively little critical attention has been paid to the novel. Law-Yone, a book reviewer for *The Washington Post*, also published a short story set entirely in Burma in 1988.

Bibliography

Aung San Suu Kyi. *Freedom from Fear: And Other Writings*. New York: Penguin, 1991. A collection of writings by the winner of the 1991 Nobel Peace Prize. Aung San charts her involvement with the Burmese National League for Democracy and the tumultuous political events of the late 1980's in Burma. Provides a helpful context for Law-Yone's fiction.

Forbes, Nancy. "*The Coffin Tree*." *The Nation* 236 (April 30, 1983): 551. Forbes notes that since *The Coffin Tree* is Law-Yone's first novel, it is "not surprising that it reads like autobiography." Forbes also states that the novel seems to be "on familiar terms with all experience, no matter how bizarre," and that Law-Yone "writes with a cool sense of incongruity."

Larson, Charles R. "Books in English From the Third World." *World Literature Today: A Literary Quarterly of the University of Oklahoma* 58 (Summer, 1984): 383-384. Larson supposes that because the "horror of the tale is simply so convincing, so dramatically total," Law-Yone's book must be autobiographical. The review makes an interesting comparison between "Americans and Europeans going crazy in exotic climes" and the converse scenario faced by the book's Asian protagonists.

Law-Yone, Wendy. "Ankle." *Grand Street* 7 (Spring, 1988): 7-24. A short story that raises a few of the themes explored in *The Coffin Tree*. The narrator is a young Burmese girl who is plunged into the company of an unsavory couple as a result of the ineffectual protection of her parents. The story has some of the pathos of *The Coffin Tree* but is much more lighthearted, almost comic, in its treatment of childhood.

Lee, Rachel, C. "The Erasure of Places and the Re-siting of Empire in Wendy Law-Yone's *The Coffin Tree*." *Cultural Critique* 35 (Winter, 1996-1997): 149-178. Explores the themes of diaspora and imperialism in Law-Yone's novel.

Pat M Wong

A CONFEDERACY OF DUNCES

Author: John Kennedy Toole (1937-1969)
Type of plot: Epic comedy
Time of plot: The early 1960's
Locale: New Orleans
First published: 1980

> *Principal characters:*
>> IGNATIUS J. REILLY, the comic protagonist, an obese, self-important, failed scholar in medieval studies and commentator on the deficiencies of the modern world
>> IRENE REILLY, his mother, a widow and closet drinker
>> MYRNA MINKOFF, his erstwhile girlfriend, who has continued to remain in touch with him through letter writing, now a radical in New York City
>> ANGELO MANCUSO, a comic policeman in search of "suspicious characters"
>> CLAUDE ROBICHAUX, Mrs. Reilly's elderly suitor, worried about Communists
>> LANA LEE, the owner of the Night of Joy bar, a part-time pornographer
>> BURMA JONES, a black porter at the Night of Joy, Lana's constant critic
>> DARLENE, a B-girl at the Night of Joy
>> GUS LEVY, president of Levy Pants, Ignatius's employer
>> MRS. LEVY, the dissatisfied wife of Mr. Levy
>> MISS TRIXIE, a senile employee at Levy Pants

The Novel

The action of *A Confederacy of Dunces* blends such disparate elements as ribald farce, sophisticated intellectual and social satire, and realistic examination of the speech and customs of ethnic New Orleans. Binding these elements together is the magnetic figure of Ignatius J. Reilly, a grossly fat, thirtyish mama's boy and failed medieval scholar who is convinced of his own genius and of the fact that "the dunces are all in confederacy against him." Ignatius is eager to condemn any product of modern culture and technology for its "offenses against taste and decency," its "lack of theology and geometry," often while he is in the act of consuming it.

As the novel begins, Ignatius, a former graduate student whose one halfhearted attempt to secure a teaching position ended in a disaster that confirmed his low opinion of the modern world, is forced to go to work by his doting, alcoholic, weak-willed, but exasperated mother, who is fed up after years of supporting his "career" as a "writer." Having caused a public disturbance in the novel's first scene because of his outlandish dress and behavior, Ignatius bellows at the investigating patrolman, Angelo Mancuso, in his pompous diction, "Is it the part of the police department to harass me when this city is a flagrant vice capital of the civilized world?" His instinct is to shift blame in every circumstance and to retreat from modernity into his ivory tower—his smelly, disordered bedroom. There he is composing, on lined Big Chief tablets at a rate of "six paragraphs monthly," what he is sure will be "a magnificent study in comparative history" exploring how, "with the breakdown of the Medieval system, the gods of Chaos, Lunacy and Bad Taste gained ascendancy." Quick to condemn disorder and bad taste in others, Ignatius never sees them in himself. He hoots at sex, marriage, a career, industrialization, the profit motive, and *American Bandstand* as gross excrescences of modern culture, but of the lot he prefers *American Bandstand*, which he watches every afternoon, chortling at its offenses in a loud voice.

Yet, as Ignatius often says, "the *rota Fortunae*, or wheel of fortune," turned against him when his mother forced him to leave his room and seek work. With his retreat cut off, he goes on the attack. He takes a job as clerk for the failing Levy Pants company. There he performs his filing duties so easily (by throwing the documents in the trash) that he has ample energy to "improve" the company in other ways, all of which glorify Ignatius. Ultimately, in one of the novel's great comic scenes, he decides to prove his talent as a revolutionary to his former girlfriend Myrna Minkoff (who is in New York advocating sexual liberation) by leading the plant's unimpressed black factory workers on a "Crusade for Moorish Dignity" against the meek office manager, Mr. Gonzalez, using a stained bedsheet as their banner. The factory workers want wage increases; Ignatius wants violence for the fun of it. His exploit results in comic failure, and, after he is fired, Fortune's wheel sinks him a notch lower; he takes a job as a hot dog vendor.

Meanwhile, two other major (and several minor) lines of action have been set in motion. His mother, Irene, has developed friendships with Patrolman Mancuso, the officer who attempted to arrest Ignatius in the novel's first scene, and Claude Robichaux, an elderly but solvent suitor who finds Communists lurking behind every chair. These new friends, to the disgust of Ignatius, who exclaims, "It's not your fate to be well treated," succeed in getting his mother out of the house for the first time in years. They take her bowling and to films and in the process gradually convince her that Ignatius is crazy and that her path to happiness is to marry Robichaux, whom her son treats with contempt, and have Ignatius put away in an insane asylum.

The other major story thread in this novel full of such traditional devices of comic plotting as parallel action, coincidence, and mistaken identity involves the Night of Joy bar, where Ignatius and his mother fled after their early brush with the law. Lana Lee, the voluptuous but mean-spirited proprietress, is running a shady operation that relies on B-girls and watered-down drinks. Business is bad, and on the side she generates cash by selling pornographic pictures of herself to schoolboys. Working in the bar are Burma Jones, a black porter whom Lana cannot fire despite his stinging diatribes because he is working for a mere twenty dollars a week to avoid a vagrancy charge, and Darlene, a pretty and good-natured but dumb blonde whose one ambition is to be an exotic dancer. Ignatius is led into the bar by a chain of circumstances on the night of Darlene's dance-act debut. The result is the novel's climax, a comic debacle that finds

Ignatius lying unconscious in the street while Patrolman Mancuso, under pressure to find "suspicious characters," makes a dramatic arrest of Lana Lee on vice charges. When the story and pictures hit the morning papers, an angry and humiliated Mrs. Reilly decides that she *must* have Ignatius put away. In the novel's final scene, however, one sees Ignatius escaping to fresh adventures with the lately returned Myrna Minkoff, while the wagon coming to take him away passes by. To the end he remains resilient, unshakably convinced of his own genius and the duncehood of others.

The Characters

Ignatius, the undefeated, stands at the center of a matrix of comic failures. These are vivid, if flat, characters who escape being mere stereotypes because of Toole's genius for telling gesture and individualized dialect. Each character has learned about defeat in his own way, yet few have submitted to it. They are almost pathetic, but not quite. Mr. Clyde, the much put-upon owner of the understaffed Paradise Vendors (and Ignatius's future employer in the hot dog business), is bitterly aware that "nobody respects a hot dog vendor," and he describes his own product containing "rubber, cereal, tripe. Who knows? I wouldn't touch one of them myself." Yet when Ignatius tries to escape without paying, after wolfing down several Paradise franks, Mr. Clyde seizes a serving fork and, pressing it against Ignatius's throat, induces him, in lieu of payment, to come to work selling weenies. Almost all of Toole's characters will seize even a mediocre opportunity if it presents itself.

When Angelo Mancuso botches his first attempt as an investigator (instead of arresting Ignatius he is egged on by accusations of being a Communist to arrest the respectable Mr. Robichaux), his disgusted sergeant sends him to search for "suspicious characters" in ludicrous costumes (for example, a T-shirt, bermuda shorts, and long red beard) and forces him to endanger health and sanity by spending whole days on stakeout in public rest rooms, but Mancuso persists and finally triumphs.

The denizens of the Night of Joy bar are equally persistent, but the efforts of its proprietress, Lana Lee, are defeated by the very dishonesty and inhumanity on which she relies in her quest for success. An object of continual satire, she complains that "business stinks," but she is rude to customers and her bar is dark, dirty, and bad smelling. She will not pay her porter, Burma Jones, enough to motivate him to clean it really properly. As the B-girl Darlene complains,

> I only work on commission for how much I get people to drink. You think that's easy? Try to get some guy to buy more than one of the kinda drinks they serve here. All water. They gotta spend ten, fifteen dollars to get any effect at all.

Darlene, the novel's purest stereotype—the dumb blonde—aspires to rise from her form of servitude by becoming an exotic dancer. She works up a clumsy strip act involving her pet parrot that contributes to the comic denouement. Jones, one of the novel's funniest and freshest characters as well as its major black voice, is as notable for his intelligent anger as for the unschooled energy of his speech. Screened behind dark glasses and clouds of cigarette smoke, Jones takes savage delight in speaking his mind against a system that exploits and cheats him. "Hey!" he says, "I'm workin in modren slavery. If I quit, I get report for being vagran. If I stay, I'm gainfully employ on a salary ain even startin to be a minimal wage." Jones's cheerful efforts at "sabotage" help to destroy the evil Lana and ultimately lead both Darlene and himself to better jobs.

Irene Reilly is another character who seems to be beaten but who refuses to submit to defeat. When Mrs. Reilly at last recognizes that the cause of her poverty and unhappiness is her own son and that her only hope for a better life is to have her "boy genius" put away and marry the dim-witted but kind Mr. Robichaux, she reluctantly but firmly decides to do so (and the novel makes clear that she has made the right choice).

The only characters who have really given up are the ones with the least reason, Gus Levy, the affluent proprietor of Levy Pants, and his wife, Mrs. Levy. Gus has given up on the pants business because his father, when he was alive, would not try any of Gus's ideas. Now that his father is dead, Gus has chosen to get revenge by running the business into the ground. Mrs. Levy has given up on her husband and turned their daughters against him because of his deliberate business failure. She is a woman of causes, but her judgment is invariably misplaced. She sees Ignatius's ill-fated "Crusade for Moorish Dignity" as the act of a "young idealist," and she condemns Gus for firing him. She also insists on attempting to rejuvenate the vividly drawn Miss Trixie, the company's senile, oldest employee. Miss Trixie, whose only wish is to retire, symbolized the present senility of Gus's company. She must be replaced if Gus is to prosper, but Mrs. Levy, congratulating herself for her insight and kindness, will not let the poor woman quit.

It takes the machinations of Ignatius, who sends a hostile letter to Levy Pants's best customer over Gus Levy's signature, a letter that occasions a potentially disastrous lawsuit, to shake Mr. Levy out of his lethargy. He ends the novel in a newly energetic frame of mind, ready to take his business in hand.

In the end, the good characters are rewarded and the evil punished through the workings of an intricate plot whose models extend back from P. G. Wodehouse to Molière and Geoffrey Chaucer to Plautus. Toole has created a very traditional comic structure. Despite its biting satire and its modern setting, the novel is in no sense a black comedy. Positive, traditional values are exemplified through the action of characters and the unfolding coincidences of the plot.

Themes and Meanings

Ignatius's "worldview," which he is convinced is very original, embraces such standard ideas of medievalism as Boethius's wheel of Fortune, which in Ignatius's mind excuses laziness (all failures are already determined). It also includes most of the canards of modernism. His highly ahistorical vision of the Middle Ages as "a period in which the western world had enjoyed order, tranquility, unity, and oneness with its True God and Trinity" is a sort of bastardization of the vision of the Middle Ages developed by John Ruskin, Henry Adams, and T. S. Elliot. He echoes with comic hyperbole the standard modernist sentiment that contemporary technological society (symbolized in the mind of Ignatius by the Scenicruiser ride he took to Baton Rouge to interview for a teaching job) is "the vortex of the whirlpool of despair," and he glibly identifies himself with Marcel Proust's imaginative seclusion and with Kurtz in Joseph Conrad's *Heart of Darkness* when, during that one departure from New Orleans to search for a teaching position, "he was faced with the ultimate horror"—work. The novel's central theme is the necessity of individual effort, and Ignatius exploits references to despair in modern literature as excuses to reject industrial society because that society demands what Ignatius calls "the perversion of having to GO TO WORK." He gives his fundamental laziness away when, in explaining his preference for New Orleans, he describes it as "a comfortable metropolis which has a certain apathy and stagnation which I find inoffensive."

The novel's comedy depends repeatedly on the way Ignatius will expend almost unlimited energy, ingenuity, and low cunning to protect his sloth. The book is a send-up of the intellectual self-congratulation and readiness to despair that is promoted by what Saul Bellow calls "the *Waste Land* mentality," and, by contrast, it is a celebration of the diversity and crude comic energy that even an "apathetic" city such as New Orleans can contain.

Ignatius is ultimately spared the imprisonment and humiliation that he appears to deserve because his sloth is less powerful than his instinct for self-preservation. His willingness to depart from his room, that travesty of a Proustian monastic cell, and to face adventure and risk in a larger world, symbolically justifies his continued life at large.

Critical Context

The story of the way Toole's novel came before the public is a strange one, involving frustration, tragedy, and posthumous triumph. Toole completed the book in 1963, but, after extended negotiations with one publisher came to nothing in 1966, he made no further attempt to publish it. In 1969, Toole committed suicide. Eventually, through the persistence of his mother, the novel was brought to the attention of novelist Walker Percy, who secured its publication in 1980. The book became a best-seller, an almost unanimous success with critics, a nominee for the PEN/Faulkner Award, and the winner of the 1981 Pulitzer Prize.

It has been praised for its comic structure, its brilliant use of dialogue, and its evocation of the setting and language of New Orleans. Most of all, critics have found it extremely amusing. They have hailed Toole as a comic genius, comparing his work favorably to that of the greatest comic and satiric writers, including Jonathan Swift, Henry Fielding, Charles Dickens, and Miguel de Cervantes. Critics have regretted that Toole's career was so tragically short. *A Confederacy of Dunces* has been recognized as a unique comic masterpiece, a book that successfully combines high and low comedy, realism and fantasy, with irresistible high spirits and sheer narrative drive.

Bibliography

Britton, Wesley A. "Two Mississippi Views on Medievalism and Determinism: Mark Twain and John Kennedy Toole's *A Confederacy of Dunces.*" *Southern Quarterly* 34 (Fall, 1995) 17-23. Britton compares Toole's Ignatius J. Reilly and Twain's Connecticut Yankee, Hank Morgan, along with some of Twain's other medieval characters. Britton demonstrates how both authors use their characters as voices for their own philosophical attitudes toward medieval determinism.

Fennell, Barbara A., and John Bennett. "Sociolinguistic Concepts and Literary Analysis." *American Speech* 66 (Winter, 1991): 371-379. A study of Toole's manipulation of sociolinguistic factors to establish the outsider status of Ignatius J. Reilly. Fennel and Bennett show how Reilly uses speech to create social distance and how he violates maxims of conversation that require speakers to be truthful, informative, relevant, clear, and polite.

MacKethan, Lucinda H. "Redeeming Blackness: Urban Allegories of O'Connor, Percy, and Toole." *Studies in the Literary Imagination* 27 (Fall, 1994): 29-39. MacKethan focuses on Catholic novelists O'Connor, Percy, and Toole and their use of religious allegory to explore modern ills. She notes that all three use the city as the nexus of modern life and the unavoidable destination of those suffering from alienation.

Rudnicki, Robert W. "Toole's Proboscis: Some Effluvial Concerns in *The Neon Bible.*" *The Mississippi Quarterly* 47 (Spring, 1994): 221-236. Compares Toole's first novel, *The Neon Bible*, with *A Confederacy of Dunces*. Rudnicki asserts that the novels share similar themes but portray them in different ways. *The Neon Bible* is tragic and deals with the growth and maturation of a boy, while *A Confederacy of Dunces* is satiric and tells of an adult's desire to regain his childhood. Both novels share the theme of decay of formally unspoiled values.

Simon, Richard K. "John Kennedy Toole and Walker Percy: Fiction and Repetition in *A Confederacy of Dunces.*" *Texas Studies in Literature and Language* 36 (Spring, 1994): 99-116. Observes that Toole's novel is a fictional reflection on Walker Percy's *The Moviegoer* (1961) and Boethius's *The Consolation of Philosophy*. Simon notes that as Percy's novel was itself a reflection on Søren Kierkegaard's notion of repetition, Toole addresses the issue as well in his novel.

Thomas Travisano

A CONFEDERATE GENERAL FROM BIG SUR

Author: Richard Brautigan (1935-1984)
Type of plot: Comic fantasy
Time of plot: The 1960's
Locale: San Francisco and Big Sur, California
First published: 1964

>   *Principal characters:*
>   JESSE, the novel's narrator and chronicler of Lee Mellon's exploits
>   LEE MELLON, the protagonist and self-styled descendant of a
>   Confederate general
>   ELIZABETH, a part-time prostitute and Lee Mellon's woman
>   ELAINE, Jesse's woman and mainstay
>   JOHNSTON WADE, a "crazy" insurance executive whom Lee Mellon
>   dubs "Roy Earle," the Humphrey Bogart character in the movie *High
>   Sierra*

The Novel

The very title of Richard Brautigan's novel emphasizes the unusual conjunction of events, characters, and places that distinguishes much of his fiction from conventional treatments of history and society. His characters are drawn to powerful figures, such as Lee Mellon, who define their own reality; fantasy, in other words, is related as fact—primarily because, in Brautigan's view, human beings make up their lives as they go along, regardless of what the history books and common sense seem to prescribe. The results of this flaunting of realism are usually comic and ironic and in the service of the novelist's perception that reality is not nearly so stable or so reliable as serious recorders of fact would have it.

Lee Mellon, for example, claims to be from the South, although he has no trace of a Southern accent. His great-grandfather was a Confederate general, he tells the narrator, Jesse, although on their trip to the library they find no General Augustus Mellon in the history books. Jesse, who admires Lee and takes on his propensity for rewriting history, begins the book by stating that Big Sur was the twelfth Confederate state. Both characters engender a sense of history that is true to their own situation—that is, as outcasts from the dominant culture, they have picked a time and a place that suits their identities; they have seceded, so to speak, from the mainstream and fashioned a counterculture.

As befits an unconventional novel, *A Confederate General from Big Sur* has no plot; rather, it follows a series of related adventures in which Lee and Jesse drop out of society. At first, however, Lee Mellon is a character (noteworthy for the great number of teeth he has lost) whom Jesse admires from afar as "a Confederate General in ruins." Lee has no army, but he does carry on a kind of assault against the status quo by illegally tunneling into and tapping the main gas line of the Pacific Gas and Electric

Company and by taking up with Susan, the daughter of the "Freezer King of Sepulveda Boulevard."

Lee Mellon's battle with society, however, does not amount to much, and he retreats to Big Sur, building his own cabin like a latter-day Henry David Thoreau (1817-1862). He is hardly a self-sufficient model, even if he does manage to live without electricity. The five-foot-one-inch ceiling of his cabin, for example, is a poor affair and reflective of his impracticality. Yet this is his charm, and he succeeds in luring Jesse to Big Sur after the latter has lost Cynthia, the woman who has kept him in San Francisco.

Much of the rest of the novel details their meager existence at Big Sur. The men are short of food, and Jesse is troubled by a melancholia relieved on occasion by Lee's energetic imagination and resourcefulness and by the appearance of two women, Elizabeth and Elaine, who (along with "Roy Earle") create a weird, momentary utopia out of a culture of scarcity.

The Characters

Although Lee Mellon is the "hero" of the novel, he is hardly an admirable character. He can be very cruel, calling the poor, demented "Roy Earle" a crazy man and keeping him in isolation from the others. When two teenagers are caught trying to siphon gas from Lee's truck, he elaborately creates a scene in which he debates with himself and Jesse over whether he should kill them. Even though his rifle has no bullets, Lee assumes an authority that is as impressive as it is frightening. In the right time, he probably would have made a vicious soldier.

Jesse is a puzzling character. He is obviously attracted to Lee and apparently is not discouraged by his partner's slimy ethics and mangy life-style. Jesse notes Lee's low-life characteristics but never editorializes—probably because he has no firm convictions himself. He is, in a manner of speaking, in Lee's tow. He is drawn to Lee's women—especially Elizabeth, who seems to be the sanest and most truly self-sufficient character in the book.

Elizabeth works part of the year as a prostitute, so that she can live the rest of the time as she likes. She is a professional and very good at pleasing men when she is on the job. If they want her to make them uncomfortable, she obliges. When she is not employed, however, she is sensitive and decent. She is obviously a woman of considerable self-confidence who copes with a corrupt society in order to get what she wants. Her sense of proportion is what makes her stand out from the other characters.

Elaine is Jesse's substitute for Elizabeth. Elaine comes from a wealthy background and surprises Jesse with her passion for him. He is unaccustomed to being able to attract and hold a woman. She makes him feel good about himself for a while, but by the end of the novel it is clear that her erotic ministrations will not be enough to pull him out of a severe depression.

"Roy Earle," whose real name is Johnston Wade, sees in Lee Mellon the reverse image of himself. Wade has been highly successful, a good provider for his family, but his dedication to business has driven him mad. Lee, on the other hand, lives as he likes with no thought of pleasing others, although he does, in fact, often make people happy—including Wade, who takes him home, much to the outrage of his family. While in some sense Lee is good for Wade, Lee does not try to hide his mixed motivations. On the one hand, he has been direct and sympathetic in a way that Wade values; on the other hand, his objective is to get Wade's truck. Furthermore, Lee romanticizes his greed by making this insurance man into "Roy Earle," although Wade, who is fat and balding, bears not the slightest resemblance to the film star Humphrey Bogart.

Themes and Meanings

In the figure of Lee Mellon, Richard Brautigan satirizes the myth of the self-made man. Lee is self-deluded in claiming ancestry from a Confederate general, although his conceit has an ironic truth to it in the sense that Lee, like Robert E. Lee, is ultimately a loser. He loses grandly, and he loses ridiculously. Like the causes of death listed for the Civil War generals in the section that prefaces the novel, "Attrition's Old Sweet Song," Lee Mellon has suffered many different kinds of defeat. His illusions do give him a kind of power, though, that eludes the more conventionally successful Johnston Wade. Like his putative Civil War namesake, Lee Mellon thrives in people's imaginations, regardless of the fact that he has been, by several different measures, a failure.

What Jesse ultimately makes of Mellon is not entirely clear, although he recognizes the appropriateness of their names—outlaws both, they try to transcend their shortcomings in legendary, tall tale exploits, in episodes such as the one in which they buy two alligators to rid themselves of the noisy frogs that disturb their peace. Near the end of the novel, italicized passages portray the none too heroic adventures of Private Augustus Mellon. Evidently, Jesse has come to imagine, if not to admit explicitly, the absurdity of Lee Mellon's megalomania. The terse, documentary style of these Civil War scenes is a stunningly effective rebuke to the characters' fantasies.

Critical Context

A Confederate General from Big Sur has had a mixed reception. It is usually not ranked as highly as Brautigan's masterpiece, *Trout Fishing in America* (1967), because the narrative point of view is somewhat clouded. Critics admire its comic inventiveness, however, and students have remarked upon its humor even when they are hard put to explain it.

Perhaps it is the unexpectedness of the connections Brautigan makes that delights some readers and dismays others. His similes and metaphors are often literally farfetched, seemingly awkward, and therefore subversive of literary conventions: "Elaine stared at the waves that were breaking like ice cube trays out of a monk's tooth or something like that. Who knows? I don't know." The inconclusiveness of the prose, the flatness of the style, can be irritating and boring. Yet the honesty inherent in forsaking smoothness and in admitting that all metaphors are only approximations, a part of the writer's search for appropriateness, is refreshing. The question in regard to this novel is whether Brautigan has balanced the opposing principles alive in all of his work: coherence and chaos.

A considerable poet as well as a novelist, Brautigan has favored writing in short units. Nearly all of his poems and short stories are quite brief, and the chapters of his novels rarely exceed five or six pages. A Brautigan novel seldom goes beyond two hundred pages. Yet there is a significant amount of monotony in his work that is the deliberate result of a casual, nearly self-negating style: "It is important before I go any further in this military narrative to talk about the teeth of Lee Mellon. They need talking about." For a different kind of writer, the second sentence would surely be superfluous, but for a Brautigan narrator there is almost a pathetic need to state the obvious. He has been called a "sweet" and a "gentle" writer because of this modest, apologetic way of imposing upon his readers.

Coupled to his assertions of the obvious is a bitterness and irony that is quite savage. Although it is masked by the cuteness of chapter titles such as "To a Pomegranate Ending, Then 186,000 Endings Per Second," Brautigan's sensibility seems at sea in a world that is disintegrating in narratives that barely hold themselves together. Thus, *A Confederate General from Big Sur* has five different endings plus a speedup of endings "until this book is having 186,000 endings per second." His world is essentially unstable, and he constantly attacks those who think life can be counted and measured. His lists of numbers and statistics are always parodies of the real thing, since the real thing, he believes, is always falling apart faster than it can be computed.

The instability of human character is what attracts Brautigan. He argues against everything that makes life static; history immobilizes human beings and novels ought to bring life back to the living and the dead, a point made by the conjunction of past and present in his title *A Confederate General from Big Sur.* Near the beginning of the novel, Brautigan demonstrates how literature is a form of renewal. Describing a Union assault on Confederate forces, Jesse remarks, "at the instant of contact, history transformed their bodies into statues. They didn't like it, and the assault began to back up along the Orange Plank Road. What a nice name for a road." On several occasions, Jesse exhibits a superb historical imagination, placing himself precisely in the past yet, as in this instance, remaining himself. As Edward Halsey Foster puts it, "the feeling that an individual should not be understood primarily as a function of time and place, as a psychological compromise between public and private needs, but rather as a self potentially and ideally independent of history underlies Brautigan's best work." That human beings are only "potentially and ideally independent of history" is what accounts for the melancholy strain and truncated achievement of much of the author's work.

Bibliography
Abbott, Keith. *Downstream from "Trout Fishing in America": A Memoir of Richard Brautigan.* Santa Barbara, Calif.: Capra Press, 1989. A personal account of Brautigan from a longtime friend. Some of the book is Abbott's own memoirs, but it also contains interesting anecdotes and insights into Brautigan's life and work.

Chapter 8, "Shadows and Marble," presents critical commentary on Brautigan's novels, in particular *Trout Fishing in America.*

Bradbury, Malcolm. *The Modern American Novel.* Oxford, England: Oxford University Press, 1983. Chapter 7, "Postmoderns and Others: The 1960s and 1970s," cites Brautigan, placing him in the genre of writers who "celebrated the hippie youth spirit." Bradbury gives succinct but insightful critical commentary on Brautigan's novels. He sees Brautigan as much more than a hippie writer, whose spirit of "imaginative discovery" has spawned a number of literary successors.

Chenetier, Marc. *Richard Brautigan.* London: Methuen, 1983. Assesses Brautigan's writing in the context of the 1960's, and traces the development of his art beyond the confines of a cult figure. An appreciative study that analyzes Brautigan in the light of his poetics.

Kaylor, Noel Harold, ed. *Creative and Critical Approaches to the Short Story.* Lewiston: The Edwin Mellen Press, 1997. See Farhat Iftekharuddin's essay, "The New Aesthetics in Brautigan's *Revenge of the Lawn: Stories 1962-1970.*" Although this essay deals primarily with Brautigan's short stories, Iftekharuddin's discussion of literary innovation and his treatment of other Brautigan critics make this an important contribution to an understanding of the longer fiction as well.

Wanless, James, and Christine Kolodziej. "Richard Brautigan: A Working Checklist." *Critique: Studies in Modern Fiction* 16, no. 1 (1974): 41-52. A compilation of secondary material on Brautigan, complete through 1973. Lists novels (including their serial form), poetry, short stories, and uncollected pieces, as well as reviews and critical commentary on individual works. A valuable resource for the Brautigan scholar.

Carl Rollyson